½

WITHDRAW

D0849686

SALADIN

SALADIN

ANNE-MARIE EDDÉ

Translated by Jane Marie Todd

THE BELKNAP PRESS OF
HARVARD UNIVERSITY PRESS
Cambridge, Massachusetts, and London, England 2011

Printed in the United States of America

This book was originally published in French as *Saladin,* copyright © Éditions Flammarion, Paris, 2008.

Library of Congress Cataloging-in-Publication Data

Eddé, Anne-Marie.
  [Saladin. English]
  Saladin / Anne-Marie Eddé ; translated by Jane Marie Todd.
    p. cm.
  Translated from French.
  Includes bibliographical references and index.
  ISBN 978-0-674-05559-9 (alk. paper)
  1. Saladin, Sultan of Egypt and Syria, 1137–1193.   2. Egypt—Kings and rulers—Biography.   3. Syria—Kings and rulers—Biography.   4. Islamic Empire—History—750–1258.   5. Crusades—Third, 1189–1192.   I. Todd, Jane Marie, 1957–   II. Title.
  DS38.4.S2E3213 2011
  956'.014092—dc22
  [B]   2011010513

To My Parents,
Henri and Roselyne

Contents

Figures

Chronology

In the chronology, the years on the Hegira calendar, a dating system specific to Islam and still in force today, appear in parentheses.

1137–1138 (532)
Birth of Saladin in Tikrīt.
Saladin's father (Ayyūb) and uncle (Shīrkūh) enter Zangī's service in Mosul.

1138–1139 (533)
October 1139: Taking of Baalbek by Zangī: Ayyūb is named its governor.

1144–1145 (539)
December 1144: Taking of Edessa by Zangī.

1145–1146 (540)
December 1145: Proclamation of the Second Crusade.

1146–1147 (541)
September 1146: Assassination of Zangī. Nūr al-Dīn succeeds him in Aleppo.

1148–1149 (543)
July 1148: Siege of Damascus by the Franks in the Second Crusade. Saladin's elder brother is killed.

1149–1150 (544)
June 1149: Nūr al-Dīn's victory over the Franks of Antioch at Inab.

1150–1151 (545)
Liquidation of the county of Edessa by Nūr al-Dīn and the Seljuk sultan of Anatolia.

1151–1152 (546)

Saladin leaves Damascus to join Shīrkūh and Nūr al-Dīn in Aleppo.

1153–1154 (548)

August 1153: Taking of Ascalon by the Franks.

1154–1155 (549)

1154: Commercial treaty between the Pisans and the Fatimids of Egypt.

April 1154: Taking of Damascus by Nūr al-Dīn; Ayyūb and his family move to Damascus.

1157–1158 (552)

Nūr al-Dīn ill in northern Syria: Shīrkūh is his representative in Damascus, where Ayyūb is military governor.

1160 (555)

November: Capture of Reginald of Châtillon (freed in 1176).

1162–1163 (558)

September 1163: The Fatimid vizier Shāwar, removed from power, takes refuge in Syria.

1163–1164 (559)

April–October 1164: First expedition of Shīrkūh and Saladin to Egypt; Shāwar is returned to power.

1164–1165 (560)

Saladin chief of police in Damascus.

1165–1166 (561)

Maimonides arrives in Egypt.

1166–1167 (562)

February–August 1167: Second expedition of Shīrkūh and Saladin to Egypt.

1168–1169 (564)

Nūr al-Dīn has a *minbar* in sculpted wood built in Aleppo, to be placed in al-Aqsā Mosque after the reconquest of Jerusalem.

November 1168: The Franks besiege Cairo; fire of al-Fustāt.

January 1169: Retreat of the Franks; Shīrkūh enters Cairo; murder of Shāwar; Shīrkūh replaces him at the vizierate.

March 1169: Death of Shīrkūh; Saladin replaces him at the vizierate.

June–August 1169: First conspiracy against Saladin; repression of the revolt of the blacks in Cairo.

1169–1170 (565)

October 1169: Damietta besieged by the Franks and the Byzantines.

April 1170: Saladin welcomes his father, Ayyūb, to Cairo.

August 1170: First measures promoting the return to Sunnism in Cairo.

1170–1171 (566)

Autumn 1170: Saladin founds two madrasas in al-Fustāt.

December 1170: Saladin's attack on Gaza and Dārūm; taking of the Île de Graye off the coast of Ayla.

February–March 1171: Saladin names a Shafite chief qādī in Cairo.

1171–1172 (567)

September 10, 1171: First Abbasid *khutba* pronounced in Cairo.

September 13, 1171: Death of Caliph al-ʿĀdid, and end of the Fatimid dynasty.

October–November 1171: Saladin's expedition against Shawbak; first tensions with Nūr al-Dīn.

About 1172: The Venetians obtain a *funduq* in Alexandria.

1172–1173 (568)

Late 1172–early 1173: Saladin's brother Tūrānshāh puts down a revolt in Upper Egypt and penetrates into Nubia.

June 1173: Saladin's campaign against Kerak.

August 9, 1173: Death of Saladin's father, Ayyūb, in Cairo.

1173: First expedition of Emir Qarāqūsh to North Africa.

1173: Commercial treaty between Saladin and the Pisans.

1173–1174 (569)

February–May 1174: Conquest of Yemen by Tūrānshāh.

March–April 1174: Conspiracy against Saladin thwarted in Cairo.

May 15, 1174: Death of Nūr al-Dīn, and beginning of the Ayyubid dynasty.

July 14, 1174: Death of King Amalric of Jerusalem.

August 1, 1174: Saladin's army repels a Sicilian fleet.

1174–1175 (570)

August–September 1174: Revolt led by Emir Kanz al-Dawla in Upper Egypt.

October 28, 1174: Saladin enters Damascus.

December 28, 1174: Saladin takes Hama.

Early January 1175: First assassination attempt on Saladin outside the walls of Aleppo.

March 17–19, 1175: Saladin takes Homs, then Baalbek.

April 13, 1175: Victory of Saladin over the Zangids at the "Horns of Hama."

May 1175: Accord signed between Saladin and al-Sālih of Aleppo; Saladin receives the investiture of the caliph of Baghdad.

Spring 1175: 'Imād al-Dīn enters Saladin's service.

1175–1176 (571)

1175: Qarāqūsh's second expedition to North Africa: taking of Awjila and al-Azrāqiya.

April 19, 1176: Arrival of Tūrānshāh in Damascus from Yemen.

April 22, 1176: Victory of Saladin in Tall al-Sultān over the Zangids of Mosul and Aleppo.

May–June 1176: Taking of Buzā'a and 'Azāz by Saladin, who escapes a second assassination attempt.

1176–1177 (572)

July 29, 1176: Peace concluded between Saladin and al-Sālih of Aleppo.

July–August 1176: Frankish raids in the region of Damascus and northern Syria.

August 1176: Saladin lays siege to Masyāf, the fortress of the Assassins.

September 6, 1176: Saladin's marriage in Damascus to Nūr al-Dīn's widow.

September 1176: Seljuk victory over the Byzantines in Myriokephalon.

Autumn 1176: Beginning of construction on the wall and citadel of Cairo.

March 1177: Start of the rebuilding of the Egyptian fleet.

1177: New revolt in Qift in Upper Egypt.

Foundation of a madrasa by Saladin near the tomb of al-Shāfi'ī in al-Fustāt.

1177–1178 (573)

1177: Saladin signs a commercial treaty with the Genoese.

November 25, 1177: Defeat of Saladin at the Battle of Ramla (or Battle of Montgisard).

1178–1179 (574)

Spring 1179: Saladin takes Baalbek away from Ibn al-Muqaddam and hands it over to his brother Tūrānshāh.

1179–1180 (575)

1179: Qarāqūsh seizes Ghadamès and Tripoli in North Africa.

June 1179: Victory of Saladin over the Franks in the region of Marj ʿUyūn.

August 29, 1179: Taking of the Castle of Bayt al-Ahzān by Saladin.

1180–1181 (576)

About June 1180: Death of Saladin's brother Tūrānshāh in Alexandria.

June 1180: Death of Sayf al-Dīn, Zangid prince of Mosul.

May–June 1180: Truce between Saladin and the Franks.

June–September 1180: Saladin conducts a campaign in Upper Mesopotamia.

November–December 1180: Caliph al-Nāsir li-Dīn Allāh reconfirms Saladin's investiture.

1181–1182 (577)

Deportation of Arab tribes from the Frankish border regions to the western Delta.

Saladin's brother Tughtegin goes to Yemen.

December 4, 1181: Death of al-Sālih in Aleppo.

Late 1181: Raid of Reginald of Châtillon directed at the holy cities of the Hejaz.

1182–1183 (578)

May–July 1182: Muslim raids against the kingdom of Jerusalem.

September–October 1182: Al-Bīra, Edessa, Rakka, the Khabur Valley, Nisibīn, Sarūj, and Hisn Kayfā surrender to Saladin.

Early January 1183: Taking of Sinjār.

Early 1183: Raid by Reginald of Châtillon in the Red Sea.

April 1183: Taking of Amida by Saladin.

1183–1184 (579)

June 1183: Aleppo surrenders to Saladin.

December 1183: Saladin hands over Aleppo to his brother al-ʿĀdil; his nephew Taqī al-Dīn is sent to Cairo.

1184–1185 (580)

September 1184: Raids by Saladin on Kerak, Nablus, and Jenin.

1185–1186 (581)

About April 1185: Death of Baldwin IV of Jerusalem; truce between Saladin and the Franks.

April–December 1185: Saladin's campaign in Upper Mesopotamia. Surrender of Mayyāfāriqīn.

January–February 1186: Saladin very ill in Harrān.

March 4, 1186: Accord with Mosul recognizing Saladin's suzerainty.

1186–1187 (582)

September 1186: Guy of Lusignan crowned king of Jerusalem.

August–November 1186: Saladin installs his son al-Afdal in Damascus, his son al-ʿAzīz in Cairo, and his son al-Zāhir in Aleppo; al-ʿĀdil named guardian of al-ʿAzīz in Cairo.

Early 1187: Reginald of Châtillon pillages a caravan between Cairo and Damascus.

1187–1188 (583)

April 1187: Saladin attacks Reginald of Châtillon's lands (Kerak and Shawbak).

July 4, 1187: Victory of Saladin in Hattīn, followed by the conquest of Acre, Haifa, Caesarea, Arsūf, Jaffa, Tibnīn, and Sidon.

August 4 and 6, 1187: Conquest of Jubayl and Beirut.

September 5, 1187: Conquest of Ascalon, followed by Gaza, Dārūm, Ramla, and Latrun.

September 20–October 2, 1187: Siege, then conquest, of Jerusalem.

November 12, 1187–January 1, 1188: Siege of Tyre.

August–December 1187: Call for the Third Crusade in the West.

Early 1188: The Almohad caliph, Abū Yūsuf Yaʿqūb al-Mansūr, retakes Gabès from Qarāqūsh.

February 1188: Murder of Ibn al-Muqaddam in Mecca, and tensions between Saladin and the caliph.

1188–1189 (584)

July–September 1188: Saladin's campaign in northern Syria and reconquest of a large number of fortresses.

November 1188–January 1189: Surrender of Kerak, Safad, and Kawkab.

1189–1190 (585)

April–May 1189: Surrender of Shawbak.

August 29, 1189: Beginning of the siege of Acre by the Franks.

1190–1191 (586)

April 1190: Surrender of the castle of Beaufort.

June 10, 1190: Death of Frederick Barbarossa in Cilicia.

Autumn 1190: Saladin's embassy to the Almohad caliph.

1191–1192 (587)

April 20, 1191: Arrival of Philip Augustus at Acre.

May 1191: Landing of Richard the Lionheart in Cyprus.

June 8, 1191: Richard's arrival at Acre.

July 12, 1191: Surrender of Acre to the Franks.

September 1191: Victory of the Franks in Arsūf: Saladin has Ascalon and the strongholds between Jaffa and Jerusalem destroyed.

October 10, 1191: Death of Saladin's nephew Taqī al-Dīn en route to Armenia.

Execution in Aleppo of the mystic al-Suhrawardī.

1192–1193 (588)

April 28, 1192: Assassination of Conrad of Montferrat. Henry of Champagne lord of the kingdom of Jerusalem.

September 1–3, 1192: Conclusion of a truce between the Franks and the Muslims.

October 9, 1192: Richard leaves the Holy Land.

Completion of Saladin's Shafite madrasa (al-Salāhiyya) in Jerusalem.

1193 (589)

March 4: Death of Saladin in Damascus, followed by the division of his states among his sons and his brother al-ʿĀdil.

1195–1196 (592)

December 15, 1195: Saladin's coffin is transferred to his mausoleum north of the Umayyad Mosque in Damascus.

SALADIN

Introduction

"Mr. Sultan, we've returned to the Orient!" These words are attributed to General Henri-Joseph-Eugène Gouraud, spoken as he stood before Saladin's tomb in July 1920, just after French troops had entered Damascus.[1] It hardly matters whether that statement was actually uttered. Its very fame attests to the strong impression that the sultan left in the collective memory of both the East and the West.

In the East, Saladin was in the first place the liberator of Jerusalem, a city that even today crystallizes the aspirations and claims of three major religions: Judaism, Christianity, and Islam. Saladin is also the man who succeeded in repelling the Westerners and in reunifying a large part of the Muslim world, from the banks of the Tigris to Cyrenaica, and from Yemen to northern Syria. His luster and popularity are therefore still keen in the Middle East, where the cult of heroes is omnipresent.[2]

If, beginning in the twentieth century, Saladin—Salāh al-Dīn in Arabic—became a true icon among Muslims (with the exception of the Shiites) in that part of the world, to the point of eclipsing other great Islamic figures of the past, it is because, precisely, the Arab world was confronted with a failure in its unification, given European colonization, then the creation of the state of Israel, the annexation of Jerusalem, and finally, the many U.S. interventions. Within that context of dependency, even powerlessness, the sultan appeared as the figure of the liberator par excellence, the model of the sovereign who knew how to restore Arab pride and dignity. And yet Saladin was not an Arab but a Kurd. Efforts have therefore been made to emphasize his linguistic and cultural "Arabness," his attachment to Islam, his respect for Arab values: hospitality, generosity, forbearance, honor, courage. These are all reasons why Arab leaders, however different they may be, have taken him as their reference point and adopted him as their hero. Both Gamal Abdel Nasser and Saddam Hussein identified with Saladin, in order to style themselves as new charismatic leaders of the Arabs.

In the West, Saladin is among the few Arab Muslim historical figures, along with Muhammad and Hārūn al-Rashīd, who strike something of a chord. His name is usually associated with the Crusades, with chivalry and courtliness, generosity and respect for one's foes. His image, portrayed since the Middle Ages in various chivalrous romances and chansons de geste, has continued to evolve in conjunction with the historical circumstances. During the Age of Enlightenment, authors such as Voltaire and Gotthold Lessing depicted him as an enlightened sovereign, tolerant and open to all religions. Even today, he is probably the only Muslim ruler in history whom Hollywood studios could imagine casting as a hero.

The first biography of Saladin composed in the West was, paradoxically, the work of a Frenchman, Louis-François Marin, in the eighteenth century—paradoxically, because French historiographers subsequently lost interest in Saladin. Many excellent studies have been published in the United Kingdom, the United States, Germany, and Israel, but very few in France. The last French biography devoted to him goes back more than fifty years and is marked by an idyllic vision of the individual and a reductive view of Islam.[3] True, there is no dearth of difficulties involved in such an undertaking. These lie in great part in the nature of the sources. Very few archival documents have been preserved, and the narrative sources available to us come in great part from Saladin's immediate circle or from the entourage of his successors. And, as they themselves admit, they describe Saladin's life and reign with a clearly panegyric intention. It is thus not always easy to make a clear distinction between Saladin's true personality and the portrait of the ideal monarch to which he is constantly compared. In many respects, these works are similar to, on one hand, hagiographical literature, known to Islamic culture from the tenth century on, which celebrates the virtues *(manāqib)* of certain venerated figures—founders of legal schools or figures known for their piety and considered "saints"—and, on the other, of "Mirrors for Princes," a literary genre heir to ancient Persian traditions and intended to highlight the qualities expected of a good ruler: piety, justice, generosity, clemency, defense of religion, a sympathetic ear and a closeness to his people. The Saladin they portray was intended to serve as a model for future generations, as Ibn al-Athīr points out in his definition of history: "When kings read the biographies of just sovereigns in history books and when they see how much they were respected by their subjects, they will truly follow their example." Other texts, conversely, originate in spheres hostile to Saladin, such as the Zangids of Mosul or the Christians of the Latin states, a fact that makes interpreting them just as difficult.

How much credence, then, can historians of today grant to our sources? What allowances are we to make for a certain form of animosity or, on the contrary, for more or less official propaganda? Is it not just as difficult to apprehend the "true" Saladin as to approach the "true" Saint Louis? To borrow the now-famous question raised by Jacques Le Goff in his excellent biography of that monarch, we might ask: Did Saladin exist?[4] Is not the Saladin that appears through the words of his immediate circle merely a model, an idealized image?

There are multiple answers to these questions, but let me make two remarks from the outset. First, the biographies written by Saladin's contemporaries do need to be read critically and with circumspection. But it would be just as regrettable to reject them en bloc as to accept them without reservation. Although the authors seek primarily to emphasize the virtues of their sovereign, to demonstrate his merit, in order to perpetuate his memory for eternity, these are men who were close to him, listened to him, counseled him, who fought and prayed beside him, who observed his actions on a daily basis, who consoled and encouraged him, and who even kept watch over him until his last breath. Their accounts, despite their embellishments and sometimes obvious exaggerations, indisputably preserve the traces of these moments of intimacy, and often attest to the profound knowledge the authors had of their sultan's personality.

It is also necessary to read these sources with eyes different from those of a historian seeking to establish "how things actually happened," to borrow the expression of the famous nineteenth-century German historian Leopold von Ranke, one of the founders of "scientific" and "objective" history. The facts have their importance, of course—no one can deny that—but the way they were presented, understood, and experienced by Saladin's contemporaries is key. What image did they retain of Saladin and of his power? How and why did they spread it? What is covered by that propaganda? Is it intended simply to glorify an individual? Through these discourses, does not a political conception of power emerge, as well as a certain vision of the world and of the religious and moral values on which the society of that time was founded? The images, metaphors, and words chosen are indicative of the idea the authors held of an ideal prince, while the description, true or false—it hardly matters in this context—of their enemies is itself the occasion to point out his good qualities. Therefore, the interest in noting the comparisons our sources make between Saladin and one biblical figure or another obviously lies not in demonstrating the validity of these comparisons but rather in attempting to understand the intentions and objectives concealed behind such an approach. In the same way, a historian would not inquire into the reality of a miracle that occurred around the sanctuary of some holy figure but would rather examine how that miracle was used by the sovereign within the framework of his religious policy.

Because the representation we have of Saladin is inseparable from the sources that speak of him, it is with these sources that I must begin.[5] Three of Saladin's close collaborators—an Egyptian originally from Ascalon, an Iranian, and an Iraqi—have provided us with the essential accounts of his life and reign. The first of these collaborators, named al-Fāḍil (1135–1200), was his adviser and friend, almost like an elder brother, two years older than he. Al-Fāḍil began his career in the Fatimid chancery before entering Saladin's service in 1171. This adviser quickly came to exert a great influence on the sovereign. In Egypt, it was al-Fāḍil who controlled the entire administration and the tax receipts needed to finance military expeditions. The journal in which he recorded his observations on a daily basis has unfortunately been lost, but a few excerpts have come down to us.[6] From the many acts he composed for the Egyptian chancery and from the vast correspondence, official or private, that he sent to rulers, emirs, ulemas, to Saladin himself, and to members of his own family—

more than eight hundred documents and letters known to date—it is possible to extract information on many aspects of Saladin's policies. Also appearing in these texts is much more personal advice from al-Fāḍil regarding the sultan's behavior and manner of governing.[7] There is no doubt that a strong friendship and mutual respect united the two men. Despite his fragile constitution and health problems, al-Fāḍil survived his master and went on to serve two of his sons. He died in Cairo in early 1200 at the age of sixty-five, leaving behind a large administrative and literary body of work as well as many charitable foundations to aid law students, educate orphans, and free Muslim prisoners detained by the Franks.[8]

'Imād al-Dīn al-Isfahānī (1125–1201), also an administrator, was a native of Isfahan and began his career in Iraq, before moving to Damascus in 1167. There he served as secretary to the chancery and as secretary of finances, while at the same time teaching law. Introduced into Saladin's circle in 1175, he was backed by al-Fāḍil, who hired him as a secretary. His extensive literary background, his experience in administration, his knowledge of Persian and of the regions east of the Euphrates were of great value to Saladin, who asked 'Imād al-Dīn to accompany him in all his travels and to compose official letters and documents along the way. 'Imād al-Dīn has provided us with a vast poetic oeuvre. Of his historical writings, let me note especially his *Book on the Conquest of Jerusalem*,[9] and a history of Saladin's reign, which is partly autobiographical.[10] He began writing the first book during Saladin's lifetime, and Saladin was therefore able to hear him read a few passages from it in 1192. 'Imād al-Dīn's account is of key importance because the information he gives about the events he directly witnessed is very precise, particularly the course of battles, the weapons used, and the negotiations conducted. The many letters he reproduces—his own but also those of al-Fāḍil—are rich in imagery and metaphors, which, beyond the obligatory rhetoric, reveal the view that the Muslims may have had of their leaders, their allies, and their enemies. The value of his information was well recognized by many later authors, who drew a large part of their accounts on Saladin's reign from his works.

The third author, equally close to Saladin, was named Bahā' al-Dīn Ibn Shaddād (1145–1234). Unlike the first two, Ibn Shaddād, born in Mosul and trained in Iraq, was not an administrator but a traditionist (expert on hadith)[11] and jurist of renown. It was only in 1188, when he returned from his pilgrimage to Mecca, that he entered Saladin's service. Clearly impressed by the sultan's victories over the Franks, Ibn Shaddād composed a treatise for him on the merits of jihad, before accompanying him on his military campaign in northern Syria. Subsequently, he was also beside Saladin during the interminable siege of Acre from 1189 to 1191. Saladin initially named him qādī of the army; that is, he was in charge of administering justice during military campaigns. Then, in 1192, Saladin appointed Ibn Shaddād to the supreme judiciary in the city of Jerusalem, which had recently been reconquered. Most of his writings consist of collections of hadith and legal works, but he owes his notoriety above all to the biography he devoted to Saladin.[12] It was written during the very last years of the twelfth century in a style close to hagiography, and its objectives are clear: first, to praise Saladin's virtues, especially his attachment to his religious obligations, his sense of justice, his generosity, his clemency, and his courage; and second, to retrace his career, emphasizing especially the events following the conquest of Jerusalem, the Third Crusade in particular. In writing his book, Ibn Shaddād likely made use of 'Imād al-Dīn's *Book on the Conquest of Jerusalem*—their accounts are very similar in places—but, from 1188 onward, the amount of original information increases substantially and gives his work all the flavor of an eyewitness account.

The importance of these three authors lies not only in the direct testimony they supply regarding Saladin, whom they knew well, but also in their roles as actors on the political and religious scene, since each in his own way influenced the sovereign's conduct and participated directly in his propaganda campaign. Conversely, the account of another great historian of that time, Ibn al-Athīr (1160–1233), sheds more light on what must have been said in the court of the princes of Iraq and Upper Mesopotamia. Born in that region, Ibn al-Athīr spent a large part of his life in Mosul, where he frequented the ruling Zangid circles keenly opposed to Saladin's power. But after a peace treaty was finally signed in 1186, by the terms of which the Zangids of Mosul recognized Saladin's suzerainty and pledged to send him troops, Ibn al-Athīr himself accompanied the emir of Mosul, when in 1188 he went to aid Saladin in his battles against the Franks of northern Syria.

Ibn al-Athīr's close proximity to the Zangids of Mosul is perceptible to varying degrees in his historical works. His *History of the Atabegs of Mosul*,[13] completed between 1211 and 1219, clearly sides with that dynasty, and its praise of Nūr al-Dīn was undoubtedly inspired by Ibn Shaddād's eulogy of Saladin. All the same, his masterwork remains his *Universal History*,[14] which ends in 1231 and was used amply by later historians. Because of his Zangid sympathies, a critical attitude toward Saladin has often been ascribed to Ibn al-Athīr. No doubt his judgment clashes with the chorus of praise characteristic of the accounts of several of his contemporaries, but his opinion is far from wholly negative. Sometimes his narrative is inspired by the work of 'Imād al-Dīn, and more rarely by that of Ibn Shaddād, two authors who cannot be suspected of evil intentions toward Saladin. Moreover, in those of his views that are apparently hostile to the sultan, his criticisms focus especially on the sultan's lack of perseverance against the cities that displayed fierce resistance to him. Ibn al-Athīr also attacks Saladin's excessive magnanimity in allowing the Frankish populations of the conquered regions to seek refuge in Tyre, which was thereby strengthened.[15] But Ibn al-Athīr was not the only one to formulate these criticisms, and he is far from insensitive to Saladin's positive qualities, particularly his victories over the Franks. He often depicts a Saladin driven by great zeal for the holy war and fighting in the front ranks beside his troops. At times he also points out the rightness of Saladin's opinions and shifts responsibility for the errors committed onto the sultan's emirs. Does he not say of Saladin in his obituary that the sultan was a generous, patient, clement, modest sovereign, respectful of religious law, cultured, very committed to leading the jihad—in short, "a rare individual in his age"?[16] One thing is sure: Ibn al-Athīr's narrative, thorough and lucid, is useful for complementing and sometimes counterbalancing the accounts of his predecessors.

Many other thirteenth- and fourteenth-century historians took an interest in Saladin's reign, and their accounts have come down to us directly and also through quotations preserved in later compilations. Of them, Ibn Abī Tayyi' has a distinctive perspective, that of a Shiite from Aleppo, an observer of the events in northern Syria. His view of Saladin is rather benevolent, no doubt because Saladin adopted a more conciliatory policy toward the Aleppine Shiites than had his predecessor Nūr al-Dīn. There are also Christian Arab sources, whose accounts are of particular interest for evaluating Saladin's attitude toward non-Muslims and for understanding the reactions of these communities, which were often held hostage by the Franks or the Muslims. Of course, the impression created by these sources differs, depending on whether their authors lived in territories subject to the authority of Saladin and his descendants. For example, Michael the Syrian, the Jacobite patriarch of Antioch living under Frankish domination, adopted a much freer tone in this respect than Bar Hebraeus, the leader of the Eastern Jacobite Church residing in Upper Mesopotamia or northern Syria. Without actually taking Saladin's side, Bar Hebraeus gives on the whole a positive image of the sultan. Significant in this respect is his laudatory obituary, recopied in full from that of Ibn al-Athīr. Not even the Muslims' capture of the relic of the True Cross and the reconquest of Jerusalem in 1187 seem to have inspired any particular regret in Bar Hebraeus.[17]

We find the same caution among the Coptic authors from Egypt, both in the massive *History of the Patriarchs of the Egyptian Church* and in Abū l-Makārim's *History of the Churches and Monasteries.*[18] When the destruction of churches and the exactions demanded from the Christians are denounced, it is rarely Saladin in person who is implicated. Saladin is even depicted as a sovereign who limited the abuses and allowed Christians to once more take their place within society and to rebuild their destroyed churches. The impression given by the Armenian manuscripts written in Christian territory, in Lesser or Greater Armenia, is very different. These manuscripts display an open hostility toward Saladin but not always a very good knowledge of the events in Syria-Palestine. Similarly, certain Nestorian authors from Mosul, though not as virulent, attest to a great sadness following the capture of Jerusalem by the Muslims. This shows that all these accounts, whether hostile or favorable to Saladin, must be analyzed with caution and circumspection, to avoid taking a polemical view of his attitude toward the non-Muslim communities.

Many other sources provide further information about Saladin's life. A few odds and ends are to be had in the biographical dictionaries devoted to various categories of individuals (ulemas, leaders, men of letters, physicians, or notables), in travel narratives by men such as Ibn Jubayr, who describe the regions they passed through, or in vast encyclopedias that contain a great deal of information on the administrative and urban organization of the states concerned. Works inciting jihad and those on the military arts provide us with a better understanding of the ideology of holy war at the time and of the course of battles in the field. In legal, administrative, economic, and scientific treatises, we find indications of the interest Saladin took in each of these areas. Finally, poetry, whether panegyric or satirical, gives us a better grasp of the way contemporaries represented Saladin and his entourage.[19]

This panorama of sources on Saladin would not be complete without the Latin texts. William of Tyre was undoubtedly the best Latin historian of the Crusades. His *Chronicle,* written between 1169 and 1184, is a valuable document

for understanding the relation between Saladin and the Franks in the first part
of his reign. William of Tyre's view of the sultan is mixed: he judges Saladin to
be ambitious and accuses him of having usurped power, but at the same time
William is in awe of Saladin and recognizes his great courage and a certain political skill that won the sultan the support of his subjects.[20]

We need to be much more cautious in our use of the other Latin and French
sources, written between William of Tyre's death and the mid-thirteenth century. Although rich in information—particularly on the Third Crusade—they
often combine historical facts with legendary aspects. The most important of
these are the French *Continuation* of William of Tyre, which has come down to
us in several recensions;[21] the *Itinerarium pereginorum et gesta regis Ricardi,* which
casts Richard the Lionheart as the hero;[22] and the *Chronicle of Ernoul and of Bernard the Treasurer.*[23] Over the course of these narratives, the image of Saladin
gradually undergoes a transformation. Having appeared as the sworn enemy of
Christendom at the time of his ascent, beginning in the 1220s he takes on the
features of the "chivalrous" sovereign, which epic and romantic literature subsequently seized on to construct the legendary history of Saladin.[24]

The reader will of course find in this book an account of the events, known or
less well known, that constituted the framework for the existence of this
unique sovereign. Above all, I wished to shed light on the aspects of the individual that have been little studied by historians until now: the influences exerted on him, his conception of power, his attachment to Syria, his methods of
governance, the application he intended to make of Islamic law, and his daily
life. Saladin was obviously a man of his time. He was immersed in a society
marked by war and violence, but also by many exchanges, an intense cultural
life, a strong religiosity, and a sense of fatality that impelled human beings to
accept all the trials of life as God's will. It was a fundamentally nonegalitarian
society where it was understood that men and women, masters and slaves, Muslims and non-Muslims, rich and poor, had neither the same rights nor the same
duties. It is within that environment that I have endeavored to place Saladin, in
order to tease out the meaning of his actions. That environment was noted for
the coexistence of diverse cultures, which are even reflected—and this is often
overlooked—in the choice of the names he and his brothers received from their

parents and that he conferred on his own children: Persian in some cases (Tūrānshāh, Shāhanshāh), Arabic (Yūsuf, Muhammad) or Turkish (Būrī, Tughtegin) in others.

Representations and images are also central to my subject: the representation of the ideal sovereign, the image of the other, the birth of a myth. All these questions will make it possible to inquire into what separates discourse from reality, literary construction from history. The heroic figure of Saladin lies not only in his intrinsic qualities, his extraordinary personality, but also, to an equal degree, in the willingness of his contemporaries and of posterity to imagine him in a certain way. On the basis of what arguments did his propaganda, and then his legend, develop? Was his defense of the Islamic religion, often evoked to advance his claims to legitimacy, the only justification for his power? In order to represent Saladin as a model sovereign and to reinforce his authority, his entourage often associated him with the mythical figures of Islamic culture, that is, with the prophets or the first caliphs. These comparisons are valuable for understanding the lineage within which Saladin wanted to situate his policy and for grasping the significance of his choices.

Behind the sovereign is the man, his aspirations, his emotions, his tastes, his shortcomings, his fears, and his suffering. This is the hidden face of Saladin, the most difficult to grasp and the least known to anyone not satisfied with the portraits drawn by his panegyrists. Years spent in the company of an individual can give the illusion of proximity. But objective history does not exist, and despite all the customary precautions, I have undoubtedly projected onto him the questions and criteria I bring to bear as a twenty-first-century historian. The Saladin I had the occasion to discover, based on all the materials collected, is therefore the man and his world, the man in his world. Indeed, to set out to find him is to go in search of a personality that exists for others before existing in itself.

Readers are thereby warned. It is now up to them to participate in the discovery of the true Saladin.

I

Ascent

I

Saladin's World

In 1188, on a plateau near Hattīn, west of Lake Tiberias, a desolate landscape appeared before the eyes of the historian Ibn al-Athīr. A year after Saladin's formidable victory, countless corpses of Franks still lay strewn on the ground, partially devoured by birds of prey. Not far from there, Jerusalem had once more become Muslim: the voices of muezzins had replaced the sound of church bells; the Frankish nobility had been beheaded; and Saladin was at the height of his glory. He had just turned fifty.

The image of the eternal jihad warrior, which it would be tempting to apply to Saladin, is nonetheless misleading, since the war against the Franks was not always at the center of his concerns. When he was young, nothing predestined him to dominate a territory so far-reaching—from Egypt to Upper Mesopotamia—and to become the symbol of the struggles against the Latin states in the East. Born in about 1137 in Tikrīt, northern Iraq, a city where his father, Ayyūb, served as governor on behalf of the Seljuks, Saladin too might have entered the service of the sultans of Iran and Iraq, if a series of unforeseen events had not determined otherwise, within an eventful political and military context.

Caliphs and Sultans: A World Marked by Violence

To understand Saladin's reign and the issues relating to it, let us briefly journey back in time. Since the middle of the tenth century, two major rival caliphates had faced off in the East: the religious authority of the Abbasid Sunni caliph of Baghdad extended from the Indus to the shores of the Mediterranean, whereas the Fatimid Shiite caliph of Cairo, at the pinnacle of his powers in the late tenth century, controlled a good part of North Africa, Egypt, the western coast of Arabia, and part of Syria-Palestine. Both men claimed to be the legitimate successor of the Prophet and to exercise political and spiritual authority over the Muslim community. The caliph of Baghdad belonged to the lineage of the Prophet's uncle 'Abbās, the caliph of Cairo to that of 'Alī, the Prophet's cousin and husband of his daughter, Fātima.

In the mid-eleventh century, the Abbasid caliph of Baghdad welcomed the arrival of a new dynasty of Turkish princes, the Seljuks, who, after establishing their power in Iran, represented themselves to the caliph as defenders of Sunnism. They delivered him from the control exerted by the Shiite Buyid emirs, who belonged to a minor dynasty of Iranian origin, and promised to help him put an end to the Fatimid dynasty. The caliph conferred the title of sultan on the Turkish princes, which meant acknowledging their military might while at the same time indicating that they drew their legitimacy from the caliph and from him alone. To the caliph, therefore, fell religious power and the privilege of granting or refusing support to the political authorities. Indeed, in order for their authority to be acknowledged by the population in the Sunni world, the Seljuks could not do without that support. Upon the sultan devolved the responsibility for defending the territory of Sunni Islam, and in particular, for expanding it at the expense of the Shiite dynasty of the Fatimids. That separation of powers was far from complete, since the caliph continued to meddle in politics and sometimes attempted to recover real authority over the territories around Baghdad, while the Seljuks for their part made every possible effort to ensure that Sunnism would prevail, by developing certain legal-religious institutions such as the madrasas, designed to train a Sunni intellectual elite.

The lands conquered by the Seljuks in the second half of the eleventh century included Syria-Palestine and Anatolia, making the Seljuks the masters of a great empire, whose center remained in Iran and Iraq. In that vast territory, populations of very diverse ethnic and religious backgrounds lived side by side.

The Arab conquerors and their descendants had imposed their political domination there in the seventh century and had gradually mixed with the local populations. Apart from the nomadic or seminomadic Arab tribes and a few prominent families, especially those that claimed to be descended from the Prophet, it was becoming difficult in many cases to distinguish the Arabs from the Arabized indigenous peoples. Arabic, the language of the Koran and of the administration, had quickly gained ground, and Islamization was also making inroads. But in the eleventh century, many regions of Mesopotamia, Armenia, Anatolia, Syria, and Egypt still had large non-Muslim populations (Jewish and especially, Christian) who, in addition to Arabic, continued to use their own languages (Syriac, Coptic, Armenian, Greek).

Although Islamized and profoundly Arabized, the Iranians too spoke and wrote in their own languages. Among these were the Kurds, numerous in the regions west and south of the Caspian Sea, and who, from the eleventh century on, began to expand into northern Syria. Finally, there were the Turks, originally from the steppes of central Asia, who had been recruited by the caliphal armies in great number beginning in the ninth century and, in the tenth, had spread into Syria-Palestine and even into Egypt. But their numbers especially grew after the Seljuk conquest of the Middle East. Their presence extended at that time to Anatolia, which came under Turkish domination for the first time in the late eleventh century. Throughout his life, Saladin would have to come to terms with these multiple traditions—Kurdo-Iranian, Arab, and Turkish—which are reflected even in the choice of the names that Saladin and his brothers bore: Persian in the case of the two eldest (Shāhanshāh and Tūrānshāh); Arabic for himself and al-'Ādil (Yusuf and Muhammad); and Turkish for the others (Tughtegin and Būrī).

On arriving in that region of the world, the Seljuks found a political system that was heir to a long Islamo-Persian tradition and was characterized by the absolute power of a single monarch. But they also imported their own Turkish traditions from central Asia, where sovereignty belonged collectively to the reigning family as a whole. The territories were therefore divided among several members of the family, and great appanages developed, theoretically under the authority of the sultan but actually independent. Such a system naturally produced rivalries not only within the ruling family but also between the family and its vassals, so that very quickly regional particularisms, succession practices, and ambitions on all sides culminated in the fragmentation of that vast empire. When the Franks arrived in the region in 1098, they found before them a multitude of rival principalities and emirates, which, in order to maintain their autonomy, did not hesitate to play on the rivalry between the Fatimids and the Seljuks. These Muslim divisions explain in great part the ease with which the Franks managed to gain a foothold in the East and to found in succession the county of Edessa, the principality of Antioch, the kingdom of Jerusalem, and the county of Tripoli.

In about 1137, the year of Saladin's birth, the Seljuk sultanate of Iraq and Iran was divided between Sanjar (r. 1118–1157), the supreme sultan, who focused his attention especially on the eastern parts of Iran, and his nephew Mas'ūd (r. 1134–1152), who, after long battling his own brother, reigned over the western part of the empire, essentially Iraq. Even within the territories under his control, Mas'ūd had to deal with many revolts by his emirs and the hostility of the caliph of Baghdad, who on several occasions was at the center of conspiracies against the Seljuks. In 1135 the caliph himself had organized an expedition against Mas'ūd, during which the caliph was taken prisoner. He was assassinated several weeks later, probably at the instigation of one of the two sultans. His successor was deposed the next year by Mas'ūd, who decided to name the caliph's more docile brother in his place. It was within that climate of violence and incessant struggle between caliphs and sultans, among the Seljuks, and between the Seljuks and their emirs, that Saladin spent the first two years of his life. He himself would be unable to escape that omnipresent violence in political relations when he took power in Egypt.

Very shortly after Saladin's birth, his father, Ayyūb, and his uncle Shīrkūh entered the service of the Turk Zangī. For some ten years that emir, a key figure in a world that was being constantly torn apart, reigned as lord and master over Mosul and Aleppo. His predecessor had been assassinated shortly before, and Zangī had thrust aside the former ruler's very young son, arguing that a strong man—a man capable of opposing the Franks—was needed in al-Jazīra (that is, Upper Mesopotamia) and northern Syria. Saladin did not neglect to use the same argument a few decades later to justify his own investiture. During a large part of his reign, Zangī was led to intervene in Iraq in the conflicts between the caliph and the sultan and in Seljuk family quarrels. In 1132, therefore, he sided with Sultan Mas'ūd against his brother. Beaten down by the opposing army, a wounded Zangī retreated to Tikrīt, where Saladin's father took care of him, then helped him escape, a gesture that Zangī never forgot and which made possible Ayyūb's and Shīrkūh's entry into Zangī's service some time later.

In Syria as well, despite the Frankish threat, struggles for power between Muslims were constant and could include both conspiracies and assassinations. For this period, we must understand by the term "Syria" (*Shām* in the medieval sources) all the territory of present-day Syria, Lebanon, Jordan, Palestine, and Israel. Each of the two major Syrian cities, Damascus and Aleppo, sought continually to extend its domination to the rest of the region at the expense of the other. Having come to power in Aleppo in 1128, Zangī tried several times to seize Damascus, taking advantage of the anarchy prevailing there at the time. The small Turkish dynasty of the Burids, who reigned in Damascus from the early twelfth century on, became the victim of numerous struggles among rival factions beginning in 1134. That year, the reigning prince escaped a first attempt on his life, then gradually descended into madness. Assassinated the next year on the order of his mother, who could no longer bear his exactions and impious behavior, he was replaced by his brother, who died five years later, murdered in his bed.

Despite that anarchical climate, Zangī was not able to take the city and only just managed to have his suzerainty recognized there. He nevertheless succeeded in nibbling away at the territory in 1138 by taking possession of Homs in central Syria, thanks to his marriage to the mother of the prince of Damascus. The following year, he obtained the capitulation of Baalbek, where, despite his promises to spare the garrison, he had thirty-seven soldiers crucified before handing over the city to its new governor, Saladin's father, Ayyūb. Seven years later, in 1146, it was Zangī who met a bloody end, assassinated by one of his Frankish slaves. Thus, within thirty-two years, between 1114 and 1146, of the nine successive governors of Aleppo, five were assassinated, two were obliged to surrender, one was killed in battle, and only one died of natural causes.

Egypt too was sinking into political violence. During the reign of Caliph al-Āmir (r. 1101–1130), the powerful vizier al-Afdal was assassinated in 1121 (perhaps at the instigation of the caliph) by members of the Shiite sect of the Nizārīs, also known by the name "Bātinīs" or "Assassins." That extremist sect, which rose up as a result of a quarrel regarding succession to the Fatimid caliphate of Egypt in 1094, first attracted notice in Iran in the last years of the eleventh century, before spreading to Syria in the early twelfth. Beyond the religious threat they represented, the Assassins were also very often the hired killers employed by rulers who wished to rid themselves of a troublesome rival. Hence the difficulty at times of knowing the real forces behind the murders that were publicly attributed to members of the sect.

Vizier al-Afdal's successor was executed in 1128, and the caliph himself fell to Nizārī extremists in 1130. The period that followed was marked by much more unrest and disturbances. In 1154, after the assassination of Caliph al-Zāfir by his vizier, power was in the hands of children, mere playthings manipulated by their all-powerful viziers. These viziers, themselves victims of that climate of anarchy, never managed to maintain power for long. The poet 'Umāra gives a vivid description of them, saying they were nothing but clouds coursing across the sky.[1] Between 1153 and 1164, the year of Saladin's first intervention in Egypt, of the five successive viziers, four were assassinated and the fifth was forced to flee to Palestine, where he was killed by the Franks.

How to explain such violence in these Middle Eastern states of the first half of the twelfth century? Was the use of assassination as a political weapon to establish one's power so common in the Muslim world? On what legitimacy could each new government base itself? The situation of the caliphs, whether Abbasid or Fatimid, was not the same as that of governors, emirs, or viziers. The caliphs had dynastic legitimacy as members of the Prophet's family, God's chosen. That legitimacy could be contested outside their own territory—the Sunni caliphate stood opposed to the Shiite caliphate—but was rarely done within their borders. No vizier, no military leader, could hope to take the caliph's place by killing him.[2] By contrast, during a period when caliphal power was weakening, the choice of a caliph within the Abbasid or Fatimid family could fall to certain powerful individuals (members of the ruling family, viziers, emirs, or sultans), and in making their choice they often favored children or other persons who could be easily controlled. The forced abdication or assassination of caliphs was not a new practice, since from the ninth century on the powerful military factions had intervened in questions of succession. But that violence was no doubt encouraged by the general weakening of the central power, which left the field open to the intrigues and yearnings of viziers, emirs, and provincial governors. In the case of Sunni Abbasid power, that weakening began in the mid-tenth century. It occurred a century later for the Shiite Fatimid caliphs, and the Seljuk sultans also fell victim to it in the first quarter of the twelfth century. During that time, the proliferation of small principalities in Iraq and Syria, governed by emirs more concerned with assuring their autonomy than with serving the sultan and the caliph, undoubtedly fostered factional struggles and conspiracies.

The organization of the Muslim armies was another factor of instability and unrest. Beginning in the ninth century, these armies were composed for the most part of slaves and mercenaries who dreamed of social ascension. All could hope to someday become emirs, that is, military chiefs, or even high dignitaries close to the caliph. They proved to be particularly bold, since they knew that political power rested on the force of their weaponry. The highest posts were not obtained through heredity—no nobility of blood existed, though the members of the Prophet's family enjoyed a particular prestige—but rather through military might and therefore most often through force. Remuneration came in the form of *iqtā's;* that is, holders of such posts were granted the tax revenues for a given territory and were required in exchange to provide a military contingent proportionate to the revenues they received. That system often had the result of granting them authority, fiscal but also administrative and political, over large parts of the empire.

The great Seljuk sultans themselves had come to power as good military leaders and had never considered themselves rulers of a monolithic empire. In conferring large appanages to members of their families and entrusting the education of their sons to powerful tutors called atabegs, these sultans contributed toward the growth of a powerful military elite. Far from reinforcing the central power, they only created new opportunities to lay claim to power themselves. Within that context of political divisions, the military leaders who managed to seize a city or province often did not have time to build dynastic legitimacy for themselves and, as a result, did not have the means to resist violent coups fomented by other emirs who, like them, dreamed of revenge and power. Because violence had become the absolute weapon for acceding to power, it spiraled out of control, ineluctably repeated.

Muslims and Franks in the First Half of the Twelfth Century

It was within that troubled and shifting political and religious environment that the Latin states in the region held their ground. In the early twelfth century, once the shock of the First Crusade had worn off, the Muslims began to react with some success to the Frankish occupation, at the instigation of Īlghāzī, a Turkish emir who had become lord of Aleppo in 1118. The unity of the military forces of Upper Mesopotamia and northern Syria, however partial, allowed him to achieve the first major Muslim victory in 1119, during a battle in northern Syria that the Franks justifiably nicknamed the *Ager sanguinis* (Field of Blood).

But there was still a long road ahead leading to Muslim reunification. To the east, caliphs and sultans were too absorbed in their struggles for power to really worry about what was happening in Syria. They confined themselves to sending an expedition from time to time, which returned empty-handed. In Egypt, the resistance of the Fatimids, greatly weakened by their internal divisions, consisted primarily of defending the cities of the Syro-Palestinian coast still in their possession: Tyre until 1124 and Ascalon until 1153. Neither Damascus nor any of the other Syrian cities had sufficient means to recover the lost territories on its own. The arrival of Zangī in Aleppo in 1128 and the threat hanging over Damascus as a result even incited the ruling powers of that city to seek an alliance with the Franks. In 1140, therefore, it was with the help of the Franks that the emir, then in power in Damascus, compelled Zangī to give up his siege of that city.

In the years that followed, Zangī abandoned Damascus and the Franks in order to consolidate his authority on the eastern and northern boundaries of his territory of Mosul. But in 1144, having conducted an expedition against the Turkish emirate of the Artukids, located in Upper Mesopotamia east of the county of Edessa and allied with the Franks for the occasion, he headed for Edessa, which in the absence of Count Joscelin was defended only by its bishops. The taking of that city by Zangī marked a very important turning point in relations between the Franks and the Muslims. The Muslims now understood that reconquest of the lost territories was possible and that Jerusalem might someday become Muslim once more. The propaganda vaunting its status as a holy city of Islam developed considerably at that time and was echoed in literature, both prose and poetry. "If the conquest of Edessa is the open sea, Jerusalem and the coast are its shores," wrote the poet Ibn al-Qaysarānī.

Upon his death, Zangī was succeeded by his son, Nūr al-Dīn (r. 1146–1174), a decisive figure, since it is likely that, without him, Saladin would never have enjoyed so much glory. It was Nūr al-Dīn who first gave the theme of the reconquest of Jerusalem its full scope. In 1168–1169, to mark his aspiration to reconquer the holy city, he had a magnificent pulpit in sculpted wood constructed in Aleppo, intended to be placed in al-Aqsā Mosque on the day Jerusalem was retaken from the Franks. The long inscription that adorned that work of art gave

Nūr al-Dīn's titulature and implored God to grant him the favor of conquering the holy city.[3] But for the time being, other more urgent tasks awaited him: the army of the Second Crusade, dispatched from the West in 1148 after the fall of Edessa, was approaching. The Crusaders had made the decision to besiege Damascus rather than attempt to retake Edessa. That choice turned out to be disastrous for them: the prince of Aleppo had not even had time to arrive before the Franks decided to beat a retreat. Nūr al-Dīn took advantage of that resounding defeat to turn against the Franks of Antioch. In June 1149, he won an important battle, during which Prince Raymond was killed and his head sent as a trophy to the caliph of Baghdad. Nūr al-Dīn immediately occupied the Frankish territories east of the Orontes, before completing his father's work by definitively dismantling the county of Edessa.

Nūr al-Dīn was lavishly praised by his contemporaries for his zeal at jihad and was presented by his panegyrists as the model of the warrior for the faith. That jihad, however, could not be completed without the political unity of the Muslim world. In 1154, upon seizing Damascus, which he made his new capital, Nūr al-Dīn succeeded where his father had failed. Subsequently, neither his continual conflicts with the Franks, nor the threat posed by the Byzantine emperor and then the Seljuk sultan of Anatolia, nor his grave illnesses, to which he almost succumbed twice between 1157 and 1159, interfered with his resolution to reunify Egypt and Syria. That project occupied him for the last ten years of his reign and was realized through the leadership of two of his officers, Shīrkūh and Saladin.

2

Training Period

Above the Aras Plain, on the present-day borders of Turkey, Armenia, and Iran, the majestic summit of Mount Ararat rises to 5,172 meters. According to biblical tradition, it is in that high volcanic country that Noah's ark ran aground after the Flood. Not far away, on the other bank of the Aras River, along one of its tributaries, was the city of Dwin, capital of Armenia at the beginning of the Arab domination and the seat of the leader (catholicos) of the Armenian church until the early tenth century. Already in the ninth century, in that region where mosques stood next to churches, a large Kurdish population lived alongside the Arabs and Armenians.

It was in Dwin or a neighboring village that Saladin's grandfather, named Shādhī, was born. The family's genealogy before him remains unknown, a situation that later allowed some to invent Umayyad forebears for the Ayyubid dynasty founded by Saladin.[1] Shādhī's two sons, Ayyūb and Shīrkūh, grew up in Dwin and, like their father, were probably in the service of the small local Kurdish dynasty of the Shaddadids. The Kurdish tribes had taken advantage of the weakening of the Abbasid caliphate of Baghdad in the tenth century, and of the Iranian renaissance movement that had accompanied it, to increase their influence in the territories they occupied, from Dwin to Mosul and from Azer-

baijan to southern Hamadān. The arrival of the Seljuk Turks in the second half
of the eleventh century in turn weakened the Kurds' power, and in the first
years of the twelfth century Dwin was endlessly fought over by Turkish emirs
and Shaddadid princes.

It was within that unsettled political context that, in 1130, Shādhī decided to
emigrate to Iraq with his entire family, encouraged no doubt by one of his former friends, Emir Mujāhid Bihrūz. The emir, it is said, had been accused of seducing the wife of an emir from Dwin. Castrated on the jealous husband's
order and forced to leave that city, Bihrūz entered the service of the Seljuk sultan Mas'ūd, who charged him with the education of the sultan's children, before naming him governor of Baghdad.[2] Mas'ūd then sent for Saladin's grandfather, to whom he entrusted the government of Tikrīt, on the Tigris River
north of Baghdad. When Shādhī died, he was buried in that locality and replaced by his elder son, Ayyūb.

Saladin's Youth

Saladin was born in 532 A.H., that is, between September 19, 1137, and September
7, 1138 C.E., on the same day that Ayyūb and Shīrkūh received Bihrūz's order to
leave Tikrīt. When Ayyūb learned that he had to abandon that city he considered his home, nothing, it seems—not even the birth of his son—could console
him. Only his secretary managed to calm him, by predicting a glorious future
for the newborn. According to some, the reason for that exile was the murder
of a Christian secretary by Saladin's uncle Shīrkūh during an altercation.[3] Was
that what attracted the wrath of Bihrūz, himself an emancipated slave, originally Christian and well disposed toward his former coreligionists? Or did he
fear the excessive influence that Ayyūb and his brother had acquired in Tikrīt?
In any event, Ayyūb left, to the great regret of the population, going to Mosul,
where, with Shīrkūh, he entered Zangī's service. At the time, Saladin had two
elder brothers: Shāhanshāh and Tūrānshāh.[4] Shāhanshāh had the same mother
as Saladin and was probably at least fifteen years older than he, since his son,
Taqī al-Dīn 'Umar, was born only two years after Saladin. Saladin's mother,
therefore, about whom nothing else is known, must have been at least thirty
when Saladin was born. The two children, Saladin and Taqī al-Dīn, grew up
side by side. Hence the very strong bond that united them until Taqī al-Dīn's
death in 1191, despite the tensions that sometimes arose between them.

Ayyūb did not remain long in Mosul. In 1139, after Zangī had conquered Baalbek, on the Bekaa Plateau northwest of Damascus, he entrusted the government to Ayyūb, who moved there with his entire family. It was in that little city, reputed for its imposing Roman ruins and the cool of its gardens, that Saladin spent the first years of his life. Unfortunately, very few things are known about his childhood and adolescence. When Zangī was assassinated in 1146, Saladin was barely nine years old. The Burid emir of Damascus took advantage of the confusion created by the event to besiege Baalbek. The city was defended by a powerful fortress installed inside the enclosing walls of the two major Roman temples of Jupiter and Bacchus. But Ayyūb could not hope to receive any help from Mosul, where Zangī's elder son had just succeeded his father, or from Aleppo, where Nūr al-Dīn was too busy establishing his power and fighting against the Franks. He preferred to surrender, and in exchange for his submission he received a military concession *(iqtā‘)* and the possession of several villages in the environs of Damascus. The family therefore moved to the former capital of the Umayyads, a city to which Saladin remained very attached throughout his life. It must be said that Damascus, surrounded by a magnificent oasis, and with powerful fortifications, many canals, houses of wood and un-baked brick, and well-stocked souks, enchanted its visitors. "By Allah, they spoke truth, who said: 'If Paradise is on the earth, then Damascus without a doubt is in it. If it is in the sky, then it vies with it and shares its glory,'" wrote the Andalusian traveler Ibn Jubayr.[5] It was in the heart of the city, in the shadow of the prestigious Umayyad Mosque, that Saladin grew up. It was also there that he and his family were besieged by the Franks of the Second Crusade in 1148, during which Saladin's elder brother, Shāhanshāh, was killed.[6]

Unlike Ayyūb, Shīrkūh, who had no territory to negotiate with the Burids, chose to remain faithful to the Zangids of Aleppo, alongside Nūr al-Dīn, whom he had already served during Zangī's lifetime. Very quickly, he attracted notice for his military skills and was entrusted by his new master with the command of the army. He received as *iqtā‘s* Palmyra and Rahba on the Euphrates, and later, after his second Egyptian expedition, the city of Homs in central Syria.[7] In 1149 he played an important role during the Battle of Inab in northern Syria, during which Raymond of Antioch was killed. From that date on, his influence continued to grow. Despite their different political choices, the two brothers remained on excellent terms, and Shīrkūh even sent his brother a part of the booty from the Battle of Inab.[8]

In about 1151–1152, Saladin, at approximately fifteen years old, left Ayyūb to join his uncle Shīrkūh, who introduced him to Nūr al-Dīn in Aleppo. Throughout his childhood and adolescence, then, Saladin was under the dual influence of his father and uncle, to whom he demonstrated affection and respect in every circumstance. The two men had very different characters. As the elder son, Ayyūb had inherited the government of Tikrīt, then of Baalbek, but he seems to have been more inclined toward administration and religious life than toward armed conflict. Several historians emphasize his kindness, uprightness, and generosity toward the ulemas and his good management of political affairs. Ayyūb, who it is said was the only emir allowed to sit down in Nūr al-Dīn's presence without having to ask permission,[9] is described as a wise man of experience, with a great influence on those close to him, including Shīrkūh.[10]

Shīrkūh was more impulsive, more violent, but no doubt also a better army leader. All the sources insist on his skill at waging war, and even William of Tyre describes him as a very courageous, energetic emir possessing a great deal of military experience.[11] When he entered Nūr al-Dīn's service in Syria, he gradually formed an army, which on the eve of his death numbered some five hundred emancipated slaves, or mamluks. That contingent of well-trained Turkish soldiers and emirs, who were called Asadiyya (from his name, Asad al-Dīn Shīrkūh), later formed one of the mainstays of Saladin's army.[12] Shīrkūh, who was able to win Nūr al-Dīn's trust and rise to the highest echelon of the military, was the chief architect of the conquest of Egypt. As a result, in 1169 he was named by the Fatimid caliph of Cairo to the post of vizier, a position no one dreamed of disputing with him. By contrast, when Saladin, who had succeeded Shīrkūh, sent for his father to come to Egypt two years later and, as a respectful son, proposed that he exercise power, Ayyūb refused, accepting only the post of comptroller.[13]

In a sense, that dual family heritage was valorized by Saladin's propagandists, who liked to point out at times his legitimacy to reign—by virtue of his military skills and victories—and at other times his virtues as a pious and just sovereign, devoid of all ambition and detached from the things of this world. From his father and his uncle, Saladin also inherited a penchant for promoting pious foundations. Ayyūb and especially Shīrkūh, following Nūr al-Dīn's example, founded many religious establishments in the cities of Syria where they resided: Ayyūb had one institution for Sufis built in Baalbek and another in Damascus, while Shīrkūh founded at least seven pious foundations in Aleppo and Damascus.[14] And finally, like his father, Saladin was an excellent horseman and was particularly fond of polo, a sport and equestrian exercise very prized by the emirs and princes of the time.

Military training, which included polo and hunting, was not the only occupation of the young Saladin, who also received a literary and religious education. He learned, probably from his earliest childhood, to read and write Arabic, as attested by some letters later written in his hand. Did he speak Kurdish? That is likely, at least at home with his family or among Kurdish officers. He seems to have had a smattering of Persian as well, as attested by 'Imād al-Dīn, who says that during a council Saladin whispered to him in that language the attitude to adopt toward a tactless imam.[15] Although it is not possible to date with exactitude the beginning of his interest in the religious sciences and in letters, we know that in his youth he took classes from a reputed Shafite jurist from Iran, who taught in Damascus and Aleppo beginning in 1145. The jurist wrote an opuscule for Saladin containing the essential principles of the Muslim faith, which Saladin later had his own children learn.[16]

The history and culture of the Arabs, particularly their genealogies and the pedigrees of their horses, interested him a great deal, and he learned by heart the poetry anthology *(Hamāsa)* compiled by Abū Tammām, a ninth-century Arab poet.[17] All the same, though Saladin showed a clear interest in the religious sciences and in letters and always displayed a great respect toward the ulemas (he enjoyed taking their courses and following their discussions), he was never himself a learned sovereign, unlike several other Ayyubid princes.[18]

When Nūr al-Dīn seized Damascus in 1154, Ayyūb, urged on by his brother, lent him aid and subsequently became part of his immediate entourage. The two brothers were generously rewarded in goods and concessions *(iqtā's)*, and Shīrkūh was named governor of Damascus and of its provinces.[19] As for Saladin, he only began to attract notice in 1164, the year of his first expedition into Egypt. At about the same time, probably in 1165, he was named chief of police of Damascus by Nūr al-Dīn, a position that led to a clash with the chief qādī, an influential figure in Nūr al-Dīn's court whose legal-religious judgments sometimes contravened Saladin's own.[20]

The Egyptian Expeditions

It was therefore in Egypt that Saladin's real career began, alongside his uncle Shīrkūh. Great difficulties confronted the Fatimid caliphate, shaken by internal crises and the fall of Ascalon into Frankish hands in 1153. In 1163, Vizier Shā-war, who had just lost his post to another emir, appealed to Nūr al-Dīn to help him reclaim power. This was an excellent opportunity for the master of Syria to move into Egypt and put an end to the Fatimid caliphate. The country, moreover, was rich. Its abundant agricultural resources and its position at the junction of the Indian Ocean, the Red Sea, and the Mediterranean assured it large commercial and fiscal revenues. The promises made by Shāwar, and later by the caliph, to share the financial wealth of the country were undoubtedly very attractive to Nūr al-Dīn. Would not getting his hands on the riches of Egypt provide him with the means to pursue jihad against the Franks? But the possession of Egypt was no less crucial for the Franks. They needed to prevent Nūr al-Dīn from establishing himself in order to keep the Latin states from being caught in a stranglehold by his territories. The Franks also found it tempting to control a country that had become the second most important commercial destination (after Constantinople) of the Venetian, Pisan, and Genoese merchants.

The events that marked the three successive Egyptian expeditions under Shīrkūh's command, between spring 1164 and early 1169, are well known and have been related many times.[21] I shall place particular emphasis on the role Saladin played. The historians Ibn Shaddād and Ibn al-Athīr mention his supposed reluctance to accompany his uncle to Egypt during all those years. He is said to have communicated his hesitations to his entourage, in order to show that his expeditions into Egypt were not motivated by any political ambition or any desire to carve out a principality for himself, as his adversaries later reproached him for doing. The words attributed to him on the eve of the third expedition in 1168—"it was as though I was being driven to death"—and his conclusion—"God Almighty gave me great dominion, for even a part of which I had never aspired"—attest to his wish to defend himself against the accusation of any political calculation on his part and to present his final taking of power as the result of God's will alone. Ibn Shaddād alludes to the following verse from the Koran (2:216): "Fighting is obligatory for you, much as you dislike it. But you may hate a thing although it is good for you."[22]

Even if Saladin felt compelled to obey Nūr al-Dīn and Shīrkūh, it would be misleading to trust in that image of a timorous individual little interested in military affairs. Would Nūr al-Dīn have sent Saladin to Egypt if he had not judged him capable of fighting in his uncle's army? It is true, however, that Saladin played only a secondary role during the first expedition. Although Ibn Shaddād says that Shīrkūh entrusted the command of his army to Saladin and made him his adviser, historians such as Ibn al-Athīr and William of Tyre do not even mention him in their accounts of the events of 1164. Ibn Abī Tayyi', himself generally favorable to Saladin, says that he was simply charged by his uncle to go to Bilbeis, a strategic site northeast of Cairo, in order to assemble the supplies necessary to support a siege. Once Shīrkūh's troops had arrived in Egypt, they made it possible for Shāwar to easily reclaim his post as vizier. Nevertheless, Shāwar went back on his pledge and appealed to the Franks for help, promising them large sums of money. When Shīrkūh learned of the Franks' imminent arrival, he retreated with his army to Bilbeis (July 1164), where the Frankish and Egyptian armies came and laid siege. But having learned of the defeat of their own forces in northern Syria against Nūr al-Dīn, the Franks quickly decided to negotiate a truce, and each side returned to its own territory.

Shīrkūh and Saladin went back to Syria, aware that Egypt, with no real authority to defend it, was now within reach. Was Shīrkūh already hoping to carve out a principality, or at least an autonomous government, as some historians suggest? That is very possible. In any event, it was at his instigation that Nūr al-Dīn decided to send out a new expedition in 1167, during which Saladin demonstrated his military skills for the first time. Shāwar, having got wind of their intentions, immediately appealed to King Amalric of Jerusalem for help, again promising an annual tribute and the large sum of four hundred thousand dinars. The confrontation between Shīrkūh's army and the Franco-Egyptian troops took place in the region of al-Ashmūnein south of Cairo, on March 19, 1167. The site, on the edge of the desert, was called Bābayn (the Two Doors), because one reached it by passing between two hills. Within Shīrkūh's army, some were of the opinion that they should turn back, believing there were too few of them and that they were surrounded by hostile populations. Others, such as Saladin, were in favor of confrontation. His view prevailed, and Saladin found himself entrusted with the command of one wing of the army. During the battle, the Franks who were allied with the Egyptians began to beat down Shīrkūh's troops, but, through a skillful counterattack in which Saladin actively participated, the situation was turned around and the Franks were obliged to retreat. It was Saladin's first important feat of arms.

Shīrkūh then decided to seize Alexandria, which was handed over without a fight by its governor and its residents, Sunnis for the most part, who were hostile to Shāwar and especially to the Franks. Amalric and Shāwar, having reassembled their forces in the region of Cairo, set off to besiege Alexandria. Rather than leave all his forces hemmed in within the city, Shīrkūh preferred to split them in two. He himself headed south to attack Qūs in Upper Egypt, while Saladin remained to defend Alexandria at the head of a garrison, which William of Tyre estimates at about a thousand men. Shīrkūh may have thought he was drawing off a portion of the opposing troops behind him, but his strategy did not bear fruit. The siege of Alexandria, lasting three months, was very difficult. According to William of T'e, the Franks had an army of about five ousand foot soldiers, not counting the considers this a low number, compared ia old enough to bear arms. But it is un-:d on such a large number of warriors: the Syrians rarely undertook actions be-r allies from Alexandria, who were more is than to military feats.[23]

d not hold out long against the Franks, d back north, taking with him Arab Bed-pt. Upon arriving in Alexandria, he dis-d a population on the brink of starvation. he siege of Qūs and by their long march re continuing to receive reinforcements negotiate a truce through the intermedi-ession. An accord was reached in early : two armies withdrew after exchanging k possession of Alexandria and, not feel-tween Shīrkūh and the Franks, engaged o had supported the Syrian army, which :d, Saladin sought out Amalric and asked)ect the amnesty. The king of Jerusalem modated his request. A guard was even ction.

lso obtained an annual tribute from the a governor and cavalrymen in Cairo to who had provided the aid of their fleet, :om the Egyptian authorities.[24] Shīrkūh, for his part, did not arrive altogether empty-handed when he returned to Syria in early September. In addition to the booty amassed in Egypt, he brought back a sum of fifty thousand dinars, which, according to Ibn al-Athīr, the Franks had paid him to get him to leave. As for Saladin, that expedition had allowed him to prove his military skills, both on the battlefield, where he had not faltered, and inside Alexandria, which he had managed to protect from an attack by the Franco-Egyptian troops. That quasi success earned him a reward from Nūr al-Dīn, who granted him two villages as *iqta's,* one in the district of Aleppo and the other in the region of Kafartāb north of Hama.[25]

The third and last Egyptian campaign took place at the end of 1168. The Franks, aware of the growing weakness of the Fatimid regime and of the danger that an alliance between Shāwar and Nūr al-Dīn might represent, seized the initiative; without even waiting for the response of the Byzantine emperor, with whom they were negotiating a joint expedition, they attacked Egypt. Was that decision precipitated by the rumor of marriage plans between Shāwar's family and Saladin's?[26] True or false, the rumor attests to the importance that Saladin had now acquired in the Muslim camp. Nūr al-Dīn immediately sent Shīrkūh and Saladin to Egypt with an army of several thousand generously equipped men. After taking Bilbeis in early November, the Franks massacred its garrison as well as a large share of its residents, Christians and Muslims alike.[27] Then, on November 13, 1168, they set off to besiege Cairo. On the eve of their arrival, Shāwar, fearing he could not defend al-Fustāt (Old Cairo), which had no enclosing wall, ordered that it be burned down. He invited its residents to take refuge farther north, in the Fatimid part of the city (al-Qāhira), previously reserved for the caliph, his entourage, his administration, and his army.

That decision was bitterly resented by the population. With heavy hearts, they had to abandon most of their possessions. Al-Fustāt, until then considered the driving force of the economy for the urban area of Cairo, was consumed by flames over the course of fifty-four days. The Fatimid caliph called on Nūr al-Dīn to help him, attaching to his message locks of hair belonging to the women of his palace, a deeply symbolic gesture that attested to his state of confusion and submission. But Nūr al-Dīn had not waited for that desperate appeal to ask Shīrkūh to make ready; he had already done so in late October. During that time, Vizier Shāwar was dragging out negotiations with the Franks, offering them large sums of money.[28] By means of an immediate payment of one hundred thousand dinars, he got them to ease up on Cairo and to move some thirty kilometers to the northeast, toward Bilbeis. He then played up the threat of Shīrkūh's arrival to obtain their definitive retreat. The Franks were not slow to heed that argument. Amalric, having attempted in vain to intercept Shīrkūh's troops, decided to return to his kingdom in the first days of January 1169, not neglecting to drag some twelve thousand Muslim prisoners with him. Shīrkūh then made his entry into Cairo, where he was received and honored by Caliph al-ʿĀdid. A few days later, on January 18, Shāwar's elimination would definitively open the doors of power to Shīrkūh.

The conditions surrounding Shāwar's assassination merit a moment's pause, since it was through that act of murder that the Ayyubid dynasty began. Contemporaries were aware of this, and the question that arose was obviously that of the legitimacy of a power acquired by violence. Most authors therefore take pains to clarify the role Saladin played in these bloody events and attempt to provide explanations, or better yet, justifications for that murder.[29] They do not all give the same version of the events, but the majority agree that on January 18, 1169, Shāwar was arrested in the streets of Cairo by Shīrkūh's emirs and under Saladin's direction. The order to execute him came from the caliphal palace, and, once it was carried out, his severed head was immediately sent to the Fatimid caliph. His two sons and his brother, who had sought refuge in the palace, were executed in turn and their heads taken to Shīrkūh. Shīrkūh was then named vizier by al-ʿĀdid, and his first gesture, to stave off the wrath of the mob, was to authorize them to pillage Shāwar's palace.

There were thus two clearly distinct phases: the arrest of Shāwar, and then his execution. Although most of the authors agree that Saladin played an important role in the arrest, almost all shift the responsibility for the murder onto the Fatimid caliph, who gave the order to have him executed. That allows Ibn Shaddād to invoke Fatimid tradition to explain the vizier's elimination, since the Egyptians had the habit, when one vizier was discharged by another, of recognizing the power of the stronger one.[30] It is true that Egypt during that period could provide multiple examples of viziers assassinated and replaced by their murderer. When presented in that way, the offense appeared neither shocking nor unusual. It was in some sense mitigated by tradition, and if there were any offense, it lay with the Shiite dynasty and not with Saladin's family. Note as well that the majority of the sources agree that Shīrkūh, the primary beneficiary of that murder, was not its direct instigator, a view that has the effect of dismissing, should any doubt remain, any evil intent on the part of the Ayyubid family.[31]

There was still a need to justify Shāwar's arrest, in which Saladin was strongly implicated. In most cases, the arrest is presented not only as a justifiable act but also as a meritorious one. Hence Ibn Shaddād, far from minimizing Saladin's role, praises his courage for having dared take on Shāwar while he was strutting about, surrounded by his guards. The primary justification for Shāwar's arrest is indisputably his failure to respect his pledges and his repeated acts of treachery. In Ibn 'Asākir's vivid account, "When Nūr al-Dīn learned of the evil that Shāwar could do and of his cunning, and when his treachery and perfidy became glaringly obvious, the Lion [al-Asad] pretended to be ill in order to catch the two foxes."[32] Some sources add that Shāwar, before being killed, had intended to eliminate Shīrkūh, a plan he ultimately abandoned on his son's advice—but his image as a traitor was thereby reinforced. His treachery was all the more grave in the eyes of his contemporaries in that it was accompanied by an open alliance with the Franks, which placed Egypt and, beyond Egypt, the Muslim Middle East as a whole in peril. How could one not conclude, therefore, that the arrest of the faithless, perfidious Shāwar, a danger to Islam, was not only excusable but licit, even salutary?

That is how the murder is presented in the sources. Although the facts are relatively clear, the intentions, as always, remain hazier. It is not difficult to imagine that many other motives lay behind Shāwar's elimination. From the start, Nūr al-Dīn and his entourage had it in mind to suppress the Fatimid caliphate, and Shāwar was a major obstacle to the establishment of Shīrkūh's power. Shīrkūh could hardly expect to win him over to his cause, since everything stood between the two men, the one Arab in the service of the Shiite Fatimids, the other Kurdish in the service of a Turkish dynasty determined to restore Sunnism. In addition, Shāwar had become very unpopular even within Egypt because of his diplomacy sympathetic toward the Franks, his cruelty, and his decision to burn down al-Fustāt. Even the Yemenite poet 'Umāra, though favorable toward the Fatimids and close to Shāwar, denounced his exactions and his penchant for executions, which Shāwar liked to witness in person.[33] It was undoubtedly that growing unpopularity that explains the caliph's decision to demand his head. Moreover, could the caliph have acted differently? By sacrificing his vizier and placing himself in the camp of the victors, he hoped to assure the survival of his dynasty. That was one way to save appearances, by letting people believe that he was the only one in charge of his auxiliaries' choices and destiny.

In any case, whatever the underlying cause of Shāwar's murder, it is apparent that taking power by means of murder was not a matter of course, since the act called for justification. Although violence was omnipresent in that society and, as in many other medieval societies, constituted the usual mode of resolving conflicts, the need felt by Saladin's propagandists to legitimate that violence served as a first limitation on its expression: murder was not considered a natural mode of conduct. Conversely, the arguments advanced to justify the elimination of Shāwar and to minimize the horror of his murder show clearly that Saladin and his contemporaries viewed any violence directed against traitors, perjurers, and those who threatened Islam as licit and even necessary.

One of Shīrkūh's first measures after Shāwar's elimination was to send the residents of al-Fustāt back to rebuild their houses, which at the same time quelled any danger of a popular uprising. But he had little time to exercise his power. Only two months after he was named vizier, on March 23, 1169, he died, probably a victim of his insatiable appetite, which had already caused him frequent bouts of indigestion and choking fits.[34] He was buried in Cairo, and his remains were later transferred to the holy city of Medina, in accordance with his wishes.

3

Vizier in Cairo

A Compromise Candidate

There have been a great many questions about why Saladin was named to replace his uncle in the post of vizier.[1] The situation was paradoxical at the very
least, since it entailed appointing a man who would be both the new leader of
the Syrian army stationed in Egypt—a decision originating in theory with Nūr
al-Dīn—and the vizier of the Fatimid caliph, a decision that could only be
made by that caliph. The events of the preceding weeks had nevertheless
shown that the caliph's margin for maneuvering was very limited. In naming
his vizier, he was obviously only saving face, since in reality the decision-
making power devolved onto the Syrian army.

Nūr al-Dīn's emirs were themselves very divided. Some, more powerful
than Saladin, would have liked to succeed Shīrkūh. In particular, there was the
Turk 'Ayn al-Dawla al-Yārūqī, the oldest and most experienced emir, as well as
several Kurdish emirs, including Saladin's own maternal uncle al-Hārimī. Saladin was in a vulnerable position in relation to them, having no troops of his
own, but he had the advantage of being Shīrkūh's nephew, which earned him
the support of his uncle's mamluks, the Asadiyya. Most of them were Turks, an
indication that the bonds uniting a master to his slaves sometimes prevailed
over ethnic solidarity. Once Shīrkūh was gone, it might seem normal that Sala-

din would succeed him. Saladin, after all, had proven his ability, first in Damascus as chief of police, later and especially in Egypt alongside his uncle, who before dying had made him his chief aide.[2]

Saladin also found significant support in the person of the jurist and Kurdish emir Diyā' al-Dīn al-Hakkārī, who belonged to Shīrkūh's close circle and who attempted to convince the emirs one by one of the advisability of the choice of Saladin. Al-Hakkārī was aided in that endeavor by a former emir of Shīrkūh's, the eunuch Qarāqūsh al-Asadī. Both played on the rivalry among the emirs, made an appeal to the Kurds for ethnic solidarity and to al-Hārimī for familial solidarity, and presented Saladin as a good compromise candidate who would allow them to avoid a battle over leaders. Although al-Hakkārī and Qarāqūsh managed to persuade most of the Kurdish emirs, the Turk al-Yārūqī refused to listen and preferred to return to Syria, accompanied by a few diehards.[3]

Did the Fatimid camp have any say in these discussions? According to Ibn al-Athīr, the caliph did not wait to have a consensus of Syrian emirs before enthroning Saladin, knowing he was the youngest and most inexperienced, and believing that he, the caliph, could therefore control Saladin most easily. It is true that Saladin could be considered less threatening than some other emirs, and it is not impossible that, faced with the divisions among the Syrians, the caliph precipitated matters somewhat, if only because that appointment ran the risk of provoking the defection of several Turkish emirs and thus weakening Nūr al-Dīn's camp. Ibn Abī Tayyi', who often expresses a point of view different from the other sources—we might wonder whether it was not dictated by his bias in favor of Saladin—rather attributes the caliph's choice to his good opinion of Saladin, whom he appreciated for his courage and intelligence. Although the relations the caliph and his vizier maintained subsequently seem to have been relatively cordial,[4] it is difficult to distinguish between propaganda and reality. The Egyptian historian al-Maqrīzī echoes the Fatimid partisans who, though defeated, nevertheless hoped to regain a little influence. Some of them would have liked to integrate the Turkish cavalrymen into the Fatimid army under the command of Qarāqūsh al-Asadī, installing them in the eastern territories of Egypt to protect the country against Frankish attacks. They suggested to the caliph that he choose an Egyptian emir who, though not the vizier, would serve as an intermediary between the caliph and the people. Other Fatimid partisans, on the contrary, defended the appointment of Saladin to the post of vizier, thinking that Qarāqūsh and his troops would as a result remain in Egypt to defend them.

Saladin was therefore a compromise vizier, proposed by the Syrian emirs and named by the caliph. His diploma of investiture, drawn up by al-Fādil, secretary to the Fatimid chancery at the time, was read out in public on March 26, 1169, in the vizierial palace, in the presence of all the important figures of the state, Syrians and Egyptians.[5] Its content gives some hints about the reasons that impelled the caliph to choose Saladin, and shows how the caliph sought to represent his power and the duties he intended to entrust to his vizier.

At the head of the text is listed, first, the titulature of the caliph al-ʿĀdid, then that of Saladin. Much more than simple ornaments, these titles, placed at the head of official documents and sometimes engraved on monuments and personal items, are indicative of a particular conception of power and of the close bonds between the political and the religious. The caliph, designated by the expressions "Servant and Friend of God, Imam who supports the religion of God *(al-Ādid li-Dīn Allāh),* and commander of believers," clearly asserts his role as a representative of God on earth, the community's guide, whose decisions are in that respect incontestable.

Saladin is called "al-Malik al-Nāsir" (the king who provides his aid), a title he would keep until his death. Then come a series of titles traditionally attributed to the viziers of the Fatimid dynasty: "Very illustrious Lord, sultan of the armies, friend of the community and glory of the dynasty, protector of the qādīs of Islam and chief propagandist of believers." Note the emphasis on the military role of the Fatimid vizier, who wielded the power of both pen and sword, and on his privileged relationship with the Fatimid dynasty. The expression "chief propagandist" is obviously rather surprising when applied to the very Sunni Saladin, since it refers to the role that the Fatimid viziers played in diffusing the Ismaili Shiite doctrine. That role is explicitly noted in the decree, which spells out that it is up to the vizier to lead the qādīs and the missionaries responsible for spreading the Fatimid doctrine. That example clarifies the theoretical aspect of this type of document, since the caliph refused in that case to acknowledge officially the consequences of the recent upheavals occurring in Egypt, and acted as if nothing had changed in the traditional duties of his viziers.

In the first part of the decree, Shīrkūh's merits—particularly his struggle against the Franks in Egypt—are recalled at length, to better underscore the weight of the family legacy behind the appointment of Saladin, who from the outset is presented in relation to his uncle's meritorious acts. If Saladin was designated to "follow in the footsteps" of Shīrkūh, it is because Saladin's family "roots" positioned him as a legitimate heir, a choice that God himself inspired in the caliph—hence its indisputable character. Referring to the famous Fatimid vizier al-Afdal, designated by the caliph in the late eleventh century to succeed his father, al-'Ādid named Saladin to succeed Shīrkūh, hoping he would be "better [afdal] than al-Afdal." That decision was consistent with Fatimid practices, according to which the son often succeeded the father.[6] All the same, the decree also clearly asserts that the right to name the vizier falls to the caliph and that the vizier's duties, though very important, remain less so than the caliph's own, since he was chosen by God. As a result, at no time does the document openly proclaim that the vizierate is hereditary, nor does it give Saladin the right to transmit it to his descendants.

The text then enumerates in detail the responsibilities and duties that Saladin must fulfill in the spirit of justice, in order to enjoin good and prohibit evil. It is noted that the vizier is the leader of the armies, Syrian and Egyptian, all united to defend the caliphate. It thus falls to Saladin, called the "sword among the swords of God Almighty," to treat his former foes, that is, the caliph's supporters, with the same kindness as his own Syrian friends, by giving them all governorships and fair remuneration. That was one way to recognize Saladin's accession to power: not as a military victory or a change in regime that would justify a redistribution of territories and posts, but merely as a decision by the caliph to replace one vizier with another. Saladin was also entrusted with the pursuit of the jihad against the infidels, he who "suckled at its breast and grew up in its bosom." But he also had to govern the people and direct the administration. To wage jihad, he would have to collect taxes moderately and mercifully, without violence or injustice, because with "a drop of justice you fill an ocean with money," and because justice, clemency, and charity would allow him to win the affection of his subjects in return.

Beyond the formulaic aspect of these recommendations, we need to recognize the scope of the powers the caliph thereby conferred on Saladin, altogether comparable to those of the viziers who had preceded him. Although the caliph constantly reaffirms that he alone is the master of the world because he is chosen and guided by God to serve as intermediary between God and men, in reality he has no other choice but to hide behind his secretary's rhetoric, so as to deny the power relations and to continue to believe that he is in possession of power.

Simultaneously with his appointment decree, the honorific gifts[7] customarily conferred on viziers were delivered to Saladin. They included a turban (white, the color of the Fatimids, as opposed to black, the color of the Abbasids); a *taylasān,* or veil, which generally covered the qādī's turban and fell to the back of the neck; and two luxurious garments. All were made of precious fabrics embroidered in gold. To these were added a necklace made of precious stones valued at ten thousand dinars, a sword adorned with gems, a thoroughbred mare (fully rigged out with precious stones) from the caliph's stables and valued at eight thousand dinars, and many other gifts and horses.[8] The sword and the mare symbolized the military power with which the Fatimid vizier was vested, while the turban and *taylasān* alluded to religious authority, in keeping with the recommendations on the diploma, which read: "[The caliph] has put his trust in you by charging you with the vizierate and making you a fortress for religion."

The First Oppositions

Once named, Saladin set about consolidating his power vis-à-vis Nūr al-Dīn, to whom he remained in principle a loyal officer, but also vis-à-vis the Egyptian troops, whose submission still remained doubtful. Nūr al-Dīn's reaction to Saladin's taking power in Egypt obviously held the attention of the authors of the time, who hastened to emphasize, depending on the camp to which they belonged, the good relationship existing between the two men or, on the contrary, their mutual mistrust. The argument that relations were good reinforced Saladin's legitimacy, while the emphasis on Nūr al-Dīn's mistrust of his lieutenant weakened Saladin's position but could also turn against Nūr al-Dīn, who was implicitly accused of having wished to thwart the future conqueror of Jerusalem.

Beyond these subjective reactions, one thing is sure: Nūr al-Dīn was not consulted when Shīrkūh was named or when Saladin was appointed. Initially, he doubtless displayed some uneasiness. So believes Ibn Abī Tayyi', later echoed by al-Maqrīzī. Both record Nūr al-Dīn's doubts immediately upon Shīrkūh's taking power. Nūr al-Dīn might even have attempted in vain to recall Shīrkūh to Syria. These historians also say that the day after Saladin was named, Nūr al-Dīn's wrath was so great that no one dared approach him. He is said to have confiscated the Syrian *iqtā's* belonging to Shīrkūh and his nephew, to have exiled their families to Egypt, and to have asked the emirs standing with Saladin to abandon him and come join Nūr al-Dīn in Syria.[9] That version of events is probably an exaggeration, as the historian Abū Shāma points out. He claims he had read a letter that Nūr al-Dīn had written in his own hand in 1168–1169, to Qāḍī Sharaf al-Dīn Ibn Abī 'Asrūn. That document ends as follows: "So come to me with your son, that I may send you both to Cairo with the agreement of my friend Salāh al-Dīn—may God afford him assistance—to whom I am *very very very* grateful—may God reward him and safeguard his life!"[10] It is clear that both Ibn Abī Tayyi' and Abū Shāma are overstating the case. It is difficult to imagine Nūr al-Dīn piling on the superlatives about Saladin; at the same time, if Nūr al-Dīn's wrath against his lieutenant had been as great as Ibn Abī Tayyi' says, he likely would not have sent Saladin's brothers Tughtegin and Tūrānshāh to him a few months later (in July) to battle the Frankish threat, demanding that they obey Saladin as they would Nūr al-Dīn himself.[11] The fact that Nūr al-Dīn took back possession of the *iqtā's* he had granted the Ayyubids in Syria should probably not in itself be taken as a sign of hostility, since there seemed to be an agreement that their territories were now in Egypt.

In any case, whatever Saladin's intentions, the decisions he made at that time did not in any way betray a desire for autonomy but rather attested to great loyalty to his master: Nūr al-Dīn's name was pronounced after the name of the Fatimid caliph at the Friday sermon *(khutba)* and henceforth appeared on Egyptian coins. As for Nūr al-Dīn, believing he alone was master of Egypt, he took care in his letters to confer no titles on Saladin other than that of *isfahsalār* emir (army leader), in order not to grant him too much importance.[12] All of which indicates that the tensions between the two men, if they existed, were still beneath the surface. They came to light publicly toward the end of 1171.

The attribution of the post of vizier to one of Nūr al-Dīn's lieutenants did not fail to raise concerns on the Egyptian side. The residents of the country were witnessing a dual and profound shift: on one hand, a Shiite power now coexisted with a Sunni power; and, on the other, a Turkish dynasty, that of Nūr al-Dīn, was being established alongside an Arab dynasty, that of the Fatimids. These two worlds had previously been in continual opposition, and many things set them apart from the start. Their perceptions of each other, consisting of many stereotypes, reflected the mutual mistrust the two ethnic groups had had in the Muslim world since the ninth century. Most of the time, the Egyptians designated Nūr al-Dīn's army by the term "Ghuzz" (Turks),[13] without always distinguishing between Turks and Kurds. They saw these "Ghuzz" as good warriors capable of defending them against the Franks, but also as often coarse and brutal soldiers. The Egyptians hated the Turks, William of Tyre tells us,[14] and the Coptic author of the *History of the Churches and Monasteries of Egypt* also denounces the many destructions of churches by the "Ghuzz."

As for the Egyptians, they were not always well regarded by the Turks or even by the Kurds. An anecdote on this matter is revealing. When Saladin's brother al-ʿĀdil wanted to accompany Shīrkūh's army into Egypt, he went to ask his father, Ayyūb, for a leather satchel. Ayyūb delivered one to him, saying: "When you get possession of Egypt, return it to me filled with gold." Ayyūb arrived in Egypt a year and a half later, and at that time he asked for the satchel from his son. Al-ʿĀdil filled it with poor-quality "black" dirhams, which he covered with a few gold dinars. Having discovered the deception, Ayyūb exclaimed: "Thou hast learned from the Egyptians how to pass off false money."[15] William of Tyre does not seem to have had a better opinion of the men in charge of defending Cairo, whom he judges "weak and effeminate." As for the author of the *Anonymous Syriac Chronicle,* he claims that the Egyptians had a reputation for being traitors and deserters.[16] No doubt these prejudices on either side must not be taken literally, but they do reflect the mistrust, not to say hostility, that often existed between the Turks and the Arabs, Syria and Egypt.

The decision Saladin made to confiscate a part of the *iqtāʿs* of the Egyptian emirs and to distribute them among his own emirs did not contribute toward calming the Egyptians' fears; in fact, it went against the recommendations made by the caliph in his diploma of investiture.[17] It is therefore not surprising that the first opposition to Saladin's power came from the Fatimid army, particularly the black and Armenian troops, and from a few members of the caliph's entourage.

It was the discovery of a conspiracy that gave Saladin the opportunity to definitively rid himself of his troublesome foes. The sources report that in August 1169, his entourage discovered a plot fomented by Egyptian notables and emirs associated with one of the caliph's black eunuchs, one of the most influential members of the palace.[18] The conspirators adopted a strategy that had proven successful several times in the preceding years: they called the Franks to their aid, hoping that Saladin and his troops would advance to meet them, while the plotters took the opportunity to seize power in Cairo. They entrusted their message to a man who concealed it in a sandal, but one of Saladin's loyalists, alerted by the difference between the man's worn-out clothes and the brand-new sandals he was transporting, exposed him, and he was arrested. It turned out that the message had been written by a Jewish secretary. Under threat of torture, he preferred to embrace Islam and denounce the instigator of the conspiracy. The head conspirator, once alerted, took refuge in the caliphal palace. After a few days, seeing that Saladin was not reacting, he ventured out and attempted to return to his residence a few kilometers north of Cairo. A detachment of the Turkish army seized him and cut off his head, which was immediately sent to Saladin. The vizier then decided to dismiss all the black eunuchs from the palace and to entrust its leadership to one of his most faithful servants, the white eunuch Qarāqūsh al-Asadī.

Such are the reported facts, the authenticity of which has been called into doubt by some modern historians. But even if all the details of these accounts cannot be verified, there is no serious argument that would allow us to claim that the conspiracy was invented after the fact to justify Saladin's struggle against the blacks and Armenians. I believe, on the contrary, that it must be seen as the predictable reaction of a certain ruling elite that had just lost a large part of its privileges, that suspected Saladin would not stop at half-measures, and that refused to accept the end of the Fatimid era. The blacks represented a powerful faction of the Fatimid army, forming the bulk of its infantry, and thought, not without reason, that they ran the risk of being ousted by the Kurds and Turks. Moreover, they could hardly count on the support of the population, which reproached them for their brutality. In 1168, they had already shamelessly looted the houses of the residents of al-Fustāt, who had fled their neighborhoods to seek refuge in Cairo. 'Imād al-Dīn considered them violent and ready to kill any vizier whose authority they did not recognize, an assessment that might be taken to have been formulated only to justify Saladin's harsh repression, were it not confirmed by a Coptic author, who also denounced their violence, their insolence, their thievery, and their assassinations.[19] Ibn al-Athīr was not to be outdone, delighting in the extermination of the blacks by Saladin's troops, and al-Maqrīzī added that they were doing a great deal of harm to the Egyptians.

The murder of the conspiracy's instigator and the dismissal of the black eunuchs from the palace caused a great commotion among the black troops in the Egyptian army. Joining with them were the Armenian contingents and all the discontented Egyptians, reportedly some fifty thousand in all. Saladin's troops confronted them on the main square of Cairo, between the two Fatimid palaces. The fighting raged for two days. The barracks of the Armenian archers in that neighborhood were burned down, and only a few men managed to escape.[20] From the caliphal palace, arrows were fired at the Syrian army, though it is not known whether the order was given by the caliph or by someone else. But facing the threat of seeing his palace burned down by a bombardment of Greek fire, the caliph immediately dispatched messengers to the Syrian troops to tell them: "Come on! Get those black dogs out of your country!"

The caliph's spectacular reversal in turning against his own troops, reminiscent of his order to execute Shāwar, gave the signal for a rout. Saladin ordered the black district of al-Mansūra, outside the Gate of Zuwayla south of Cairo, to be burned down. The black soldiers, after surrendering with the understanding that their lives would be spared, retreated to Giza on the west bank of the Nile. Saladin's brother Tūrānshāh nevertheless set off in pursuit with his troops, who massacred a great number of them. A few managed to escape and took refuge in Upper or Lower Egypt. A small number remained in the caliph's service, while others were incorporated into Saladin's army.[21] Once the revolt of the blacks was put down, on August 23, 1169, their neighborhood was razed and replaced with a park.

There is no doubt that Saladin took advantage of the discovery of that conspiracy to rid himself once and for all of his main opponents and to thereby consolidate his authority in Egypt. It is likely that he also wanted to weaken the caliph by depriving him of his most loyal troops, to avoid any reversal of the situation from that quarter, though the time had not yet come to put an end to the Fatimid dynasty. Under the circumstances, did he demonstrate a strategic caution, or pragmatism, or political calculation, or rather implacable ferocity toward the blacks? Rather than wonder in vain about his intentions, forever unfathomable, let us examine how he himself justified these bloody events that marked the beginning of his vizierate. In other words, what were the arguments invoked to legitimate such procedures and obtain the support of the population, and how do they reveal his objectives?

In the letter he sent to the caliph in 1175 to ask for his investiture, Saladin claimed he had fought the Egyptian army only because it was making deals with the infidels and was involved in conspiracies of all kinds.[22] The black foot soldiers, who were not thoroughly Arabized or Islamized, "who knew only one master, the lord of the palace [that is, the caliph] and only one *qibla*, the column of that palace, toward which they turned [to pray], docile to his orders," are compared to "beasts" or "cattle," terms that in the Koran (7:179 and 25:44) designate unbelievers. Of the black eunuchs of the palace, it is shamelessly said that they "added to the blackness of their faces the blackness of heresies." As for the Armenians, they were combatted because they were serving in the army and were exempted from the capitation, contrary to the prescriptions of Muslim law concerning non-Muslims. Finally, in Saladin's view, the elimination of the blacks and Armenians weakened the Fatimid caliph and made it possible to restore Sunni orthodoxy and the authority of the Abbasid caliphate over Egypt.

It was therefore clearly within the perspective of the defense of the Islamic religion, the struggle to reestablish Sunni orthodoxy, and efforts to promote jihad that Saladin wanted to situate his political and military action. Once again, the violence to which he had resorted to establish his power and, no doubt, to avoid being eliminated himself was presented to his contemporaries as a necessary violence legitimated by the defense of religion against anything that might threaten it: the infidels, heresy, lack of respect for the law, and disorder.

The Frankish Threat

Although Saladin found himself strengthened by that first victory, he remained aware that opposition could resurface at any moment, especially in the event of a Frankish attack on Egypt, as occurred a few weeks later. In asking Nūr al-Dīn to send reinforcements, did he not write: "If I hang back from Damietta, the Franks will take it and if I march there, the Egyptians will make trouble in my rear with Egypt's people and resources and they will rebel against me. They will follow on my tail, while the Franks are in front of me and we shall have no chance of survival."[23]

In 1168 the Franks had been defeated in Egypt, in great part because the attack by Amalric, king of Jerusalem (who had recently married Maria Comnena, great-niece of the Byzantine emperor), had been premature, occurring before the arrival of reinforcements from the Byzantine fleet, whose role was essential in blocking Egyptian supplies. A year later, Amalric, disturbed to see Nūr al-Dīn's power being established in Egypt, launched a new expedition, this time conducted with the aid of an imperial fleet of more than two hundred vessels. As in the past, economic interests combined with political interests, since even before the Frankish army's departure, Amalric promised the Pisans concessions in Cairo and al-Fustāt.

The attack unfolded on land and on sea beginning in late October 1169, taking advantage of the nautical conditions in the Mediterranean, which were favorable until the arrival of winter and the halting of all maritime traffic.[24] On October 25, a siege was mounted outside Damietta. The archers on their mobile siege towers, the sappers, and the mangonel operators set to work. Saladin dispatched his nephew Taqī al-Dīn and his maternal uncle al-Hārimī to aid the city, while he himself remained in Cairo to defend it if need be. Nūr al-Dīn, to whom Saladin appealed for help, sent reinforcements without delay, and, while a part of the troops headed for Egypt, Nūr al-Dīn undertook to open a new front in Syria against the Frankish territories. Al-Maqrīzī estimates the cost of that campaign at 550,000 dinars; he also says that Saladin obtained a million dinars in aid from the Fatimid caliph, a considerable sum and probably an exaggeration. Divisions rapidly occurred within the Christian camp between the Byzantines, who were running short of provisions, and the Franks. In the end, Amalric secretly negotiated with the occupiers of Damietta. The siege, which had lasted fifty days, was lifted on December 13, 1169, and, after burning their siege engines, the Byzantines and the Franks returned to their respective territories.

That victory temporarily put an end to the Frankish attacks, which had been occurring one after another on the Egyptian coast since the fall of Ascalon in 1153, and it was widely celebrated by Saladin's propagandists. Hence, in the letter sent to the caliph in 1175, Qādī al-Fādil clearly associates the Franks' attack on Damietta with the treachery of the Egyptian troops. It was in response to the appeal of the Egyptians that the Franks are said to have landed in Damietta, and in view of that perfidy, Saladin's zeal in service of the jihad only appeared the greater. Al-Fādil intentionally exaggerated the number of Frankish troops to increase Saladin's merit: a thousand war or transport ships on sea and two hundred thousand foot soldiers and cavalrymen on land! Even more important, Saladin's actions and his victory had made it possible to fend off infidelity and heresy and were presented as the fulfillment of divine will. Saladin's merit was twofold: a warrior for Islam on God's path, he was the only military leader able to impose his authority inside his states and to repel his enemies outside his borders.[25]

Another result of that military expedition was that it strengthened Saladin's army, since Nūr al-Dīn decided to keep in Egypt part of the troops sent there as reinforcements. In response to the Fatimid caliph, who still hoped to escape the Turkish takeover and asked Nūr al-Dīn to recall his army to Syria and leave only Saladin and his troops in Egypt, the ruler of Damascus said that he would do nothing of the kind, since no one apart from the Turks was capable of repelling the Franks. That decision shows that at the time, Nūr al-Dīn still had full confidence in Saladin, which he displayed again a few months later by authorizing Ayyūb to go join his son in Egypt.[26]

Ayyūb left for Egypt in a caravan of merchants, escorted by a few armed troops, while Nūr al-Dīn went to besiege Kerak. Having arrived in Cairo on April 16, 1170, Ayyūb was received with great pomp by Saladin and the caliph himself, who—and this was unusual—came out to meet him, giving him honorific clothing and many presents, and conferring the title of "al-Malik al-Afdal" on him. Ayyūb moved into the Pearl Palace, within the enclosure of the Fatimid palaces,[27] and Saladin handed over to him, as *iqtā's,* the cities of Alexandria and Damietta, along with the western region of the Delta, called al-Buhayra.

Saladin was now surrounded and supported by several important members of his family: his father, his brothers Tūrānshāh, al-ʿĀdil, and Tughtegin, his nephew Taqī al-Dīn, and his maternal uncle al-Hārimī. To his father he had entrusted Alexandria and Damietta, that is, the two most important commercial markets on the Mediterranean, whereas Tūrānshāh had been granted the cities of Qūs, Aswān, and the port of ʿAydhāb in Upper Egypt, which gave him complete authority over the pilgrimage route to Mecca and over commercial interchanges via the Red Sea and the Indian Ocean. Two months after his father's arrival, Saladin also had the joy of learning of the birth of his first son, born to a concubine. Saladin named him Nūr al-Dīn ʿAlī and give him the title "al-Afdal," which Ayyūb had just received from the Fatimid caliph, thus uniting in the person of his child the powers that the rulers of both Syria and Egypt had acknowledged for his family.

Toward the end of 1170, Saladin undertook new expeditions to the southern borders of the Frankish territories, into the region of Gaza south of the Palestinian coast, and toward Ayla at the entrance to the Red Sea.[28] It was important to dismantle the Frankish fortresses on the border of Egyptian territory, since they served as bases for launching and falling back from expeditions against Egypt. It was also fundamental, now that Syria and Egypt were reunified, to increase the security of communications between Damascus and Cairo. The most direct traditional route linking Egypt to Syria, namely, the coastal route passing through Farāma, al-'Arīsh, Gaza, and Ascalon, then Tiberias and Damascus, had crossed through Frankish territory since the creation of the kingdom of Jerusalem. It had therefore become largely impassable for the Muslims, who preferred to take the Sinai route farther to the south, from Suez to Ayla and then northward, east of the Frankish territories, toward Busra and Damascus. But that route itself had the disadvantage of passing through Ayla, which had been under Frankish control since 1116. It was urgent to reconquer that locality to assure the security of communications between Egypt and Syria.[29]

In early December 1170, Saladin initially decided to attack the fortresses of Dārūm and Gaza, south of the Palestinian coast.[30] He did not manage to seize them, but his expedition left a deep mark on the city of Lower Gaza. Part of its Frankish population was massacred after Miles of Plancy, who was defending the citadel, prohibited them from seeking refuge there.

The Muslim army returned to Cairo on December 22, 1170. But even before its return, another expedition was getting under way for Ayla, north of the Gulf of 'Aqaba. Disassembled boats were loaded onto camels and sent by the Suez and Sadr routes to the small fortress built by the Franks off the coast of Ayla, on the Île de Graye (present-day Jāzirat Fara'ūn). The taking of that small fort on December 31, 1170, marked an important step in Saladin's strategy. He sought, on one hand, to secure the main communication route between Egypt and Syria and, on the other, to prevent the Franks from having access to the Red Sea. That latter aspect was particularly underscored in his propaganda, which pointed out that, from Ayla, the infidels controlled the route between Mecca and Medina and thus seriously threatened the Station of Abraham and the tomb of the Prophet. With that new victory, Saladin not only reinforced his image as a valorous jihad warrior but also appeared in everyone's eyes as the savior of the holy sites of Islam.[31]

Saladin therefore returned to Cairo on February 4, 1171, bathed in glory. In less than two years, he had managed to eliminate his opponents within the Egyptian army, to avert the Frankish threat to Egypt and the Red Sea, and to make relations between Cairo and Damascus more secure. He would now be able to take on a new task: to put an end to the dynasty of the Fatimids.

4

The End of the Fatimids

Death of the Caliph

Ibn Abī Tayyi' reports that in April 1170, when Ayyūb came to join his son in Cairo, Nūr al-Dīn, himself urged on by the caliph of Baghdad, asked him to order Saladin to restore the Abbasid *khutba* in Egypt without further delay.[1] The *khutba,* a political-religious speech pronounced in the Great Mosques before the formal Friday prayer, had a very great symbolic value, since it always included the invocation of a divine blessing on the caliph and on the one who exercised power in his name. To pronounce that invocation in favor of the Abbasid caliph was thus to pay allegiance to him. There is no doubt that Saladin thought of putting an end to the Fatimid caliphate as soon as he took power in Cairo in 1169; it is also plausible that Nūr al-Dīn became impatient, suspecting that his lieutenant was letting things drag on in order to reserve for himself the Egyptian caliph's support, should relations between Saladin and Nūr al-Dīn deteriorate. In response to his father, Saladin pointed out that, to succeed, he had to proceed in stages, first consolidating his power and then eliminating his many opponents.

But as of August 1170, once the black and Armenian revolt was repressed and the Frankish threat momentarily averted, Saladin set in place several measures designed to facilitate the return to Sunnism. In mosques, the Shiite call to prayer, "Come to the best work, Muhammad and 'Alī are the blessings of mankind," was abandoned, and the names of the first three caliphs, disgraced in the Shiites' view, were reintroduced into the Friday *khutba*. In the capital, alongside the Shiite chief qāḍī, Saladin placed a member of his close circle, the Shafite jurist Diyā' al-Dīn al-Hakkārī, who was put in charge of the former Fatimid foundation of al-Qāhira. A short time later, in the old neighborhoods of al-Fustāt farther to the south, Saladin founded two madrasas for the training of Sunni religious elites, and his nephew Taqī al-Dīn established a third in the spring of 1171. Upon his return from Ayla in February or March 1171, Saladin took a further step, stripping the position of chief qāḍī from the Shiites and entrusting it to a Kurdish Shafite, who in turn named Shafite qāḍīs in the provincial cities. All these measures allowed Saladin to gradually strengthen Sunnism, while testing the reaction of the Egyptian population. In reality, they demonstrated very little opposition, since the majority of the inhabitants had remained Sunnis, despite the two-century-long Fatimid Shiite regime.

The administration itself was gradually taken in hand. The death of the head of the Fatimid chancery in early March 1171 made possible his replacement by the loyal qāḍī al-Fāḍil, a devout Sunni despite having served the Fatimid dynasty.[2] Finally, between 1170 and 1171 the army was again purged: emirs were expelled from al-Fustāt and their possessions confiscated. The caliph's protests were without effect, especially since, deprived of his troops and confined to a palace whose affairs were now managed by the eunuch Qarāqūsh al-Asadī, the caliph himself had increasingly less property and power. And though Saladin does not seem to have displayed any particular hostility toward him—some even say they were on good terms—the gradual reestablishment of Sunnism and the growing financial demands of the Turkish army ultimately weakened the caliph and destroyed his authority.

In early summer 1171, everything was in place for the final step. Nūr al-Dīn again urged his lieutenant to restore the Sunni *khutba*. Having consulted his emirs and observed that they were all aligning themselves with Nūr al-Dīn, Saladin assembled jurisconsults to obtain from them a fatwa on the subject. Not very surprisingly, they declared the dismissal of Caliph al-'Āḍid legitimate.[3] That consultation was in itself nothing but a formality, but it attests to the importance of the decision that was to follow: dismissing a caliph who claimed to descend from the family of the Prophet, putting an end to a dynasty that had ruled Egypt for more than two hundred years, were actions with much weightier consequences than the elimination of a vizier. In the eyes of the Iraqis and Syrians, the support of the Abbasid caliph and of Nūr al-Dīn was sufficient to legitimate such a decision, but in demanding a fatwa from men of law respected in Egypt, Saladin surrounded himself with all the legal guarantees possible and removed any possibility of objections from the Egyptian ulemas themselves.

The sources differ on the exact circumstances surrounding the reestablishment of the Abbasid *khutba* in the Cairo mosques and the death of the caliph, which coincided with his fall from power.[4] There is nothing surprising about these differences, since the collapse of such a prestigious dynasty could not fail to give rise to rumors and legends. From the accounts it emerges that on Friday, September 10, the name of Caliph al-ʿĀdid was omitted from the *khutba* pronounced in al-Fustāt, without being immediately replaced by that of the Abbasid caliph. When the caliph, already very ill, learned of this, his condition worsened, and he died on the morning of September 13, at the age of twenty-one. The following Friday, September 17, in al-Fustāt and Cairo, the *khutba* was officially pronounced in the name of the caliph of Baghdad, al-Mustadīʾ.[5] The sudden death of al-ʿĀdid immediately gave rise to various interpretations, more or less legendary. Some simply claimed that his fall from power had affected him so deeply that he died as a result. Others spoke of suicide: in learning of his dismissal, the caliph was said to have brought his poisoned ring to his lips. Some recounted that Saladin, having seen the caliph drinking wine and showering jewels on one of his concubines, asked the jurists for a fatwa to condemn him for having indulged in debauchery, before sending his brother to kill him.[6] Others, finally, said that he was strangled with his own turban for having refused to reveal the hiding places of his treasures.

In all these events, let us note especially the caution with which, once again, Saladin achieved his objective, preferring to make changes in stages and in consultation with religious circles. His decisions were therefore accepted without resistance by an Egyptian population that had remained fundamentally Sunni, and which was weary of seeing its leaders always at one another's throats and calling for help from the "infidels." Since he had been in power, Saladin had instead demonstrated his ability to impose order and to repel the Franks. That demonstration of force was repeated on September 11, 1171, following the abandonment of the Fatimid *khutba,* when Saladin passed all his troops in review before a large crowd of both Byzantine and Frankish ambassadors.

The order was given in all the Egyptian provinces to pray in the name of the Abbasid caliph. When Nūr al-Dīn was informed, he immediately sent his ambassador to announce the good news to the caliph of Baghdad. Along the way, the ambassador was to proclaim everywhere the end of the Fatimid dynasty in Egypt. The document that he was given to read placed the emphasis once again on the collusion between the two disgraced powers, the heretical Fatimids and the infidel Franks. The merit for that victory devolved onto Nūr al-Dīn, who had succeeded where many of his predecessors had failed. God had guided him in that conquest and had entrusted the possession of Egypt to him, in order to return it to the right path of Islam. And Nūr al-Dīn—in the words of his chancellor—added, without ever mentioning Saladin's name: "We have charged the one whom we have designated as lieutenant [that is, Saladin] to open the door of blessedness, to accomplish what we desired, to establish there the Abbasid message that guides us, and to drive the heretics to perdition."[8] He thereby declared loud and clear that all the glory to be drawn from that victory fell to him, Saladin being only his representative and the executor of his orders in Cairo.

That news caused great jubilation in Baghdad. A few months later, to reward Nūr al-Dīn, the caliph sent him, through one of his highest dignitaries, a complete wardrobe of honor. Nūr al-Dīn put on the robe, placed the heavy gold necklace around his neck, and strapped on the two swords, which were joined by their crossbelt to symbolize his domination over the reunified Syria and Egypt. Astride one of the horses the caliph had given him, Nūr al-Dīn paraded west of Damascus to the Green Hippodrome, before returning to the citadel, a black flag leading the way. He also sent Saladin the wardrobe of honor intended for him, prestigious but inferior to Nūr al-Dīn's own, the caliph having respected the power hierarchy. Along with these gifts were also honorific robes for the Egyptian ulemas and black flags to be placed in the mosques to mark the return of Abbasid authority. In December 1171, a new Egyptian coin was struck in the name of the Abbasid caliph and of Nūr al-Dīn. In the eyes of everyone at the time, the victory of Sunnism over Ismaili Shiism was Nūr al-Dīn's victory before it was Saladin's.

Takeover of the Palaces

In Cairo, the fall of the last Fatimid caliph was followed by a popular uprising against those who had supported that dynasty. Some were roughed up and

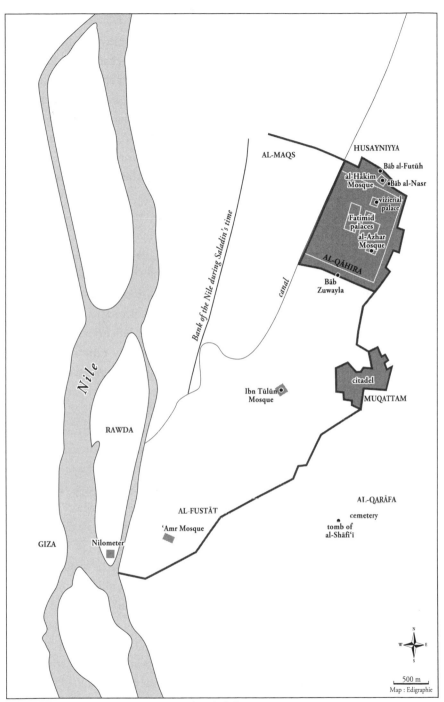

AL-MAQS

HUSAYNIYYA

Bāb al-Futūh

al-Hākim
Mosque

Bāb al-Nasr

vizierial
palace

Fatimid
palaces

al-Azhar
Mosque

AL-QĀHIRA

Bāb
Zuwayla

citadel

MUQATTAM

Ibn Tūlūn
Mosque

RAWDA

Nile

Bank of the Nile during Saladin's time

canal

AL-QARĀFA

cemetery

AL-FUSTĀT

tomb of
al-Shāfi'ī

'Amr Mosque

GIZA

Nilometer

N
W   E
S

500 m
Map : Edigraphie

Ayyubid Cairo

forced to leave the city, while their houses and possessions were pillaged. The Armenians, who had played an important social and military role under the reign of the Fatimids, were among the first to suffer from the regime change. In November 1172, their patriarch even decided to leave Egypt and move to Jerusalem, and several monasteries and churches were abandoned.[9] No doubt the Armenians remembered the fate of their brothers in the army two years earlier and feared that their situation would quickly deteriorate.

But the event that left the deepest impression was the dispersal of the treasures contained in the Fatimid palaces. The court of the caliphs had been reputed for its ostentation and sumptuousness. Several travelers left behind awed descriptions of the two palaces, which stood opposite each other in the center of al-Qāhira, each composed of a multitude of pavilions, luxury residences, gardens, and inner courtyards. Nāsir-i-Khusraw, a Persian traveler visiting Cairo, describes the marvels that were displayed before his eyes at the palace, during the feast to break the fast at the end of Ramadan in 440 (March 1049). Among other things, he admired a throne sculpted in gold, on which were depicted scenes of hunting and horsemanship, and a tree whose branches, leaves, and fruit were made of sugar and which was decorated with thousands of statuettes and figurines, also in sugar.[10]

As for William of Tyre, in his account of the Frankish embassy to Cairo in 1167, he mentions the delightful decor of the palace (despite the fact that the Fatimid dynasty was in full decline at the time) into which the messengers were ushered. Before their amazed eyes appeared the elegance of pavilions, marble columns with gold wainscoting, basins filled with water, and a multitude of rare animals and birds.[11] The few vestiges of sculpted wood that have come down to us from these palaces attest to the extreme refinement of the works of art they must have contained.[12]

Saladin seized all these palaces and their many treasures (weapons, personal items, fabrics, rock crystal, horses, tents, gems) but found very little money in the coffers, since most of the state revenues had been spent during the previous years to battle the Franks or to pay them tribute. That absence of money in the caliphal treasury fed legends of all sorts. The money was surely hidden in some secret place, and Saladin endeavored in vain to uncover it. It was even recounted that he ordered the torture of a man suspected of knowing the hiding place. The man was made to submit to the worst of torments, his head covered with beetles that were supposed to devour his brain. Against all expectations, however, the insects died and the man came out unscathed, a miracle attributed to the victim's past: years before, he had transported the head of al-Husayn, son of ʿAlī—son-in-law and cousin of the Prophet—from Ascalon back to Cairo, where the Fatimids had protected it from the Frankish threat. For a long time, the mystery of the treasure continued to trouble people. ʿImād al-Dīn alludes to it when he recounts that, in 1174, the leader of the Ismaili missionaries was crucified and died without revealing where the caliph's money was hidden. Two centuries later, the treasure still could not be found. Then, when a Mamluk vizier uncovered a large sum of money during the excavation of the foundations of his house, located at one of the gates of the eastern palace, no one doubted for a moment that the money was a part of the buried Fatimid treasure.[13]

The caliph's family, some 130 adults and 75 children according to al-Maqrīzī, were ousted from the palace and imprisoned in a residence under the surveillance of the eunuch Qarāqūsh al-Asadī. He was responsible for supporting them and for overseeing a strict separation of the sexes to prevent the birth of any descendants, who would have made it possible to revive the dynasty one day. Of the many servants in the palace, Saladin allowed those who were of free status to leave and also emancipated a large number of slaves. He distributed the rest of the slaves and many possessions to his emirs and close circle.

A large part of the caliph's treasures was sold in the streets of Cairo for several years afterward. Among the most precious items in the palace were the thousands of books carefully preserved and inventoried in the library, which was considered one of the wonders of the world, no doubt the richest library in the Muslim world.[14] It is impossible to know exactly how many works it contained: the estimates range from 120,000 to 2 million. Beyond these numbers, which are significant in any event, the importance of the library lay in the rarity of certain manuscripts, the richness of their decoration, and the quality of their writing, as well as in the large number of autograph manuscripts. All the disciplines were represented, from the Koran and the traditions of the Prophet to alchemy, grammar, lexicography, law, history, and what was called the "sciences of the ancients" (rational and natural sciences that Islam inherited from the Hellenistic and Persian world). Some authors claim the library contained nearly 2,400 richly ornamented Korans and no fewer than 1,220 copies of the famous history by al-Tabarī (d. 923). Even if these figures are exaggerated, the extraordinary quality of that library is beyond doubt.

We may therefore wonder why Saladin took no measures to preserve such a treasure. Most of the books were pillaged and sold off for a pittance by his soldiers, under the consenting eye of the eunuch Qarāqūsh al-Asadī. Many were thrown to the ground, and their bindings often torn off. 'Imād al-Dīn recounts that many buyers rushed in, identified the works that interested them, began by dismembering them, scattered their quires, and then bought them up for a very low price before reassembling them and having them bound. That practice no doubt explains in part the state of certain manuscripts that have come down to us, composed of an assemblage of assorted quires, missing sections, upside-down pages, and other anomalies of layout. Some six years later, in 1177 according to 'Imād al-Dīn, books from the caliphal library were still being sold in Cairo twice a week.

Ought that looting to be explained in terms of the desire to destroy a library that was the symbol of a disgraced dynasty and ideology? No doubt it contained a certain number of works of Shiite theology and law, and it is true that there is no dearth of historical examples of libraries being selected as the first target during a change of regime and especially of ideology. In 1076, the Fatimids had themselves burned down the library of Aleppo, which housed some ten thousand books, because they suspected that it contained works contrary to Ismaili doctrine.[15] But in the case of the Fatimid library, apart from the fact that most of the books were in no way religious propaganda, it is striking to observe that it was not burned down but squandered, sold off at very low prices, which is surely not the best way to prevent writings judged subversive from spreading. 'Imād al-Dīn proposes an explanation, saying that Qarāqūsh, "a Turk who knew nothing of books," was easily persuaded that these old, moth-eaten manuscripts had no value and could be sold for a pittance. There may be some truth in that remark, but Saladin also did not pay much attention to the books.

Qādī al-Fādil, however, did what he could to save several thousand works, which he bought up at low prices and kept in his madrasa (al-Fādiliyya) in Cairo. And in 1177, 'Imād al-Dīn brought back to Syria eight camels laden with books from that library. He said that these books were given to him by Saladin, which provided him with an opportunity to praise the vizier's generosity. But Saladin's attitude indicates above all that, in the first years of his governance in Egypt, his preoccupations were much more military and political than cultural and religious. The influence exerted on him by men of letters and of religion became more perceptible in the following years, and it is striking to compare his passivity in 1171 to his attitude in 1183, during the taking of Amida in Upper Mesopotamia. This time, according to the Christian historian Bar Hebraeus,[16] Saladin took care to preserve the very rich library of the city and delivered all its books to Qādī al-Fādil.

Following the caliph's death, the Fatimid palaces and their gardens were divided among Saladin's family and emirs, while Saladin himself continued to reside in the old vizierial palace north of the great palaces.[17] The Fatimid dynasty was definitively dead, though its followers did not immediately lay down their arms.

5

Nūr al-Dīn's Lieutenant in Egypt

Further Egyptian Resistance

In the months and years that followed, resistance to Saladin's power took the form of several revolts led by Arab tribes from Upper Egypt, supported, as of 1171, by nostalgists for the Fatimid dynasty. Historians have rightly pondered the nature of these revolts and have even wondered whether Saladin had a tendency to overstate the threats, even to provoke some of them, in order to have an excellent pretext for eliminating his opponents.[1] It is obviously very difficult to reply to such questions. None of the sources allow us to decide one way or the other, and current events continue to this day to provide examples of conflicts that may mask inadmissible interests behind an imaginary threat. Therefore, rather than venture unverifiable conjectures, I shall remain within the realm of discourse, which will inform us of the objectives Saladin sought and the means he set in motion to achieve them.

Under Islamic domination, Upper Egypt, populated by Arab tribes from northern and southern Arabia (Kaysites and Yemenites), was always a region difficult to control, because of its geographical distance from the central authority but also because of its proximity to Nubia.[2] Although bound to the Arabs by a pact concluded in 651, by the terms of which it was to pay a tribute in slaves, Nubia had never really been brought to heel. Nubian incursions regularly sowed unrest and disorder in the region. In addition, Upper Egypt had often served as a refuge for dissident contingents of the Egyptian army.[3]

The revolts of the Arab tribes of Upper Egypt in the early part of Saladin's reign were therefore not motivated solely by his taking of power, though it is indisputable that the overthrow of the Shiite caliphate gave them new momentum. The partisans of the fallen dynasty rather easily found support in that region, where Shiism was relatively well implanted and where tribal groups were not very accepting of the *iqtā'* system that the Turkish troops attempted to impose on them. In 1170, even before the overthrow of the Fatimid regime, a revolt had united Arabs and blacks, unhappy to see a property tax *(kharāj)* demanded of them. That movement was swiftly repressed by one of Saladin's emirs. Shortly thereafter, Saladin entrusted the region to his brother Tūrān-shāh as an *iqtā'*. In February 1172, Tūrānshāh put down a second revolt and made off with a large booty.[4]

But the respite was short-lived. In late 1172, the blacks and Armenians who had survived the Cairo revolt, having regrouped near the Egyptian border of Nubia, launched an expedition against Aswān and its region, more motivated by booty than by any real political aims. Tūrānshāh rushed back from Cairo to put down the rebellion but spared the peasants and lower classes who had joined the movement, perhaps out of concern not to destroy the rural economy. He cracked down in Nubia, where he seized Ibrīm and its citadel, about fifty kilometers north of Abu Simbel. According to a Coptic author, he gave no quarter: he looted the city and its church, subjected its bishop to torture, and reduced a large part of the residents to slavery.[5] Few difficulties arose in conquering the black Muslim and Christian populations of that region, whose mode of life was very primitive;[6] but remaining in Nubia was another matter, particularly given the natural barriers formed by the cataracts of the Nile. Of course, the presence of gold mines south of Aswān gave the region a certain appeal. But was it worth the effort? Not really, according to Ibn al-Athīr, who believed that Saladin and his family, in organizing that expedition, were primarily seeking somewhere to find refuge should Nūr al-Dīn take Egypt away from them. That hope of conquest was quickly dashed, and two years later Saladin's troops had to evacuate Ibrīm and abandon any idea of installing themselves in Nubia.[7]

Upper Egypt did not emerge pacified, however. In August–September 1174, a new revolt, led by a former Fatimid emir, shook the region.[8] One of the first gestures of the rebels was to attack the holders of *iqtā's* recently installed by Saladin. In addition to the political stakes, these revolts were a clear expression of the Arab reaction to the introduction of Turkish elements in Upper Egypt. But these efforts were in vain, because Saladin dispatched his brother al-'Ādil, who quickly stamped out the rebels and their leaders.

That setback did not completely discourage the Fatimid partisans in Upper Egypt. A few years later, a new revolt shook the site of Qift (the ancient Coptos), a few kilometers north of Qūs:[9] "In 1176–1177, there was a great revolt in the city of Qift. The reason behind it was that a missionary among the Banū, 'Abd al-Qawī, claimed that he was Dā'ūd, son of al-'Ādid [the last Fatimid caliph]. People rallied behind him. The sultan . . . sent his brother al-Malik al-'Ādil . . . to lead an army, which killed about three thousand residents of Qift, crucifying them on the trees outside the city using their turbans and *taylasān* [the veil that covers the turban]."[10] With that ruthless repression, whose victims were not only former soldiers but, in many cases, ulemas—as indicated by the mention of turbans—any hope of reestablishing the Fatimid dynasty collapsed. Hotbeds of Shiism continued to exist, however, in the southern part of Upper Egypt until the Mamluk period.

In Cairo as well, Saladin had to deal with attempts to restore the Fatimid caliphate. In spring 1174, a conspiracy composed of heterogeneous elements brought together emirs, religious, administrators, soldiers, blacks, residents of the palace, an Armenian Christian astrologist, and the poet 'Umāra. Some even said that the governor of Alexandria, who had supported Saladin up to that time, joined the plot. But when it came to agreeing on the choice of the new Fatimid caliph and his vizier, divisions rapidly emerged among the conspirators. Fairly early on, one of them decided to alert Saladin about what was afoot.[11] As in 1169, the organizers of the plot were accused of having solicited the help of the Franks and of having benefited from the support of a few Jewish and Christian secretaries. Ibn Abī Tayyi' even goes so far as to say that the rebels asked for the support of the Assassins of Syria, a very unlikely accusation, dictated no doubt by his hostility—expressed many times—against that extremist Shiite sect.

Saladin reacted immediately. He took no action against his own soldiers but exiled a portion of his opponents (the palace courtiers and the blacks) to Upper Egypt. He also ordered that the ringleaders of the revolt be crucified on the central square of Cairo, between the two palaces.[12] The poet 'Umāra attempted to save his own neck by asking Qāḍī al-Fāḍil to intercede on his behalf. The two men knew each other well, having served together in the Fatimid dynasty, though some sources underscore their deep-seated rivalry. Unlike al-Fāḍil, 'Umāra had never sincerely rallied behind the Ayyubid family, and his poems lauded Nūr al-Dīn's might and majesty more readily than Saladin's.[13] Believing he was poorly remunerated by Saladin, he had continually praised the generosity of Caliph al-'Āḍid (even though 'Umāra was himself a devout Shafite Sunni), lamenting his fall and attacking his adversaries: "May he who betrayed the Imam al-'Āḍid, son of 'Alī / Not see the Paradise which God has created!" he exclaimed in one of his poems, without naming Saladin.[14] That reckless attitude did not win him any indulgence from the vizier. He was therefore executed with his companions on the public square.

It is correct, as the historians Malcolm C. Lyons and David E. P. Jackson have pointed out,[15] that the discovery of that conspiracy was opportune for Saladin, who thereby found a good pretext to rid himself of all internal opposition before dealing with the Sicilian attack. These events also gave him the chance to prove to Nūr al-Dīn, whose envoy was just then in Cairo, that Saladin needed to remain in Egypt to consolidate his still-fragile power. But are we to conclude from this that Saladin played some role in triggering that affair? Although certain details differ from one source to another, there is nothing to prove that the plot was invented. Indeed, the absence of any reaction from the supporters of the Fatimid dynasty would have been much more astonishing. In any case, the attitude adopted by Saladin demonstrated to his foes that he was resolved to quash any impulse toward rebellion. The lesson seems to have been learned, since that was the last serious attempt in Cairo to reestablish the Fatimids.

In the years that followed, the timorous calls for rebellion on behalf of the Shiites were no longer taken up by the population or within the army, and were limited for the most part to a few individual initiatives. In 1188, a dozen men ran through the streets of Cairo, shouting Fatimid slogans. They were quickly arrested, and al-Fāḍil reassured Saladin in writing, telling him that no one had paid any attention to them and that Saladin could count on his people's loyalty.[16] In 1190, two members of al-'Āḍid's family, including a young man of about twenty, managed to escape house arrest.[17] This was undoubtedly the same young man who, after seeking refuge for a time in Upper Egypt, returned to Cairo two years later in an attempt to rally supporters to his cause, but to no avail. To discourage any new ideas of that kind, the decision was made to send all the members of the Fatimid family, as well as their entourage, to Syria, where they were imprisoned south of Damascus.[18]

Conquest of Yemen

The experience in Nubia of 1173–1174 had hardly been conclusive, since the region had appeared very poor and unattractive. Saladin, encouraged by his brother Tūrānshāh, therefore set his sights on Yemen, as the Fatimid caliphs had done before him.[19] Several motives seem to have impelled him in that particular direction. Yemen, by virtue of its port of Aden especially, controlled the commercial route extending from the Red Sea to the African coasts, the Persian Gulf, and the Indian Ocean, and a large share of Egypt's prosperity was founded on that commerce. From Yemen, a politically divided region where a large part of the population lived far from civilization, Saladin could thus expect major commercial revenues but also human reinforcements for his army, as attested by the urgent requests he addressed some time later to his brother.

That project also suited his religious policy. Several princes of the region, who governed more or less autonomously, had Ismaili leanings, some pro-Fatimid, others not. In 1159, one of them had even dared establish the *khutba* in his own name and had referred to his father's grave by the term "Kaaba."[20] As a result, it was easy for Saladin to justify his intervention by accusing the prince of heresy, especially since the governors of several Yemenite cities were also asking for his help. Tūrānshāh's personal ambitions also no doubt played a role in the organization of that expedition. Disappointed by Nubia and short of funds, Saladin's brother thought that Yemen, whose wealth the poet 'Umāra had highly praised and whose swords were said to be as renowned as those of India, was probably a choice governorship for him. Finally, the hypothesis advanced by Ibn al-Athīr, that Saladin and his family may have considered Yemen a place of refuge in the event of a confrontation with Nūr al-Dīn, cannot be ruled out.

Nevertheless, Saladin did not undertake anything without the prior authorization of Nūr al-Dīn, before whom he put forward the religious argument above all, that is, the abandonment of the Abbasid *khutba* by the mosques of Aden. It was with Nūr al-Dīn's agreement that, in early February 1174, Saladin sent his brother Tūrānshāh to Yemen, after generously supplying him with men, money, and provisions. In May 1174, after passing through Mecca, Tūrānshāh, without great difficulty, took control of Sanʿa, Zabīd, Taʿizz, and finally Aden, thus achieving the beginnings of political unification in the region, which in fact persisted after the domination of the Ayyubids. In each of these places, the *khutba* was now pronounced in the name of the Abbasid caliph and of Nūr al-Dīn, and an Ayyubid governor was installed. Once informed of these conquests, Saladin announced the news to Nūr al-Dīn, who immediately alerted the caliph of Baghdad. Once again, then, the power hierarchy was scrupulously respected.

Tensions with Nūr al-Dīn

Nevertheless, in the face of Saladin's successes in Egypt, then in Yemen, Nūr al-Dīn's worries continued to grow.[21] Most of the sources agree on that, the main question being at what date relations between the two men began to deteriorate. With the installation of Shīrkūh and Saladin in Egypt, Nūr al-Dīn had been anxious about the power acquired by his lieutenants, an anxiety coupled with a certain annoyance, which, however, was not expressed as real hostility. On the contrary, he had publicly demonstrated his support of Saladin by authorizing the vizier's brothers and father to join him in Egypt.

It was toward the end of 1171 that the first real friction appeared between Nūr al-Dīn and his lieutenant, on the occasion of an expedition organized against the Franks of Kerak and Shawbak, south of Transjordan. Nūr al-Dīn had asked Saladin to come aid him in his battle, and Saladin had gone to besiege Shawbak in October 1171. Nūr al-Dīn had set up his camp farther north, outside the walls of Kerak. Fewer than 150 kilometers separated the two men, and each was expecting to meet the other. It was then that Saladin's entourage warned him against Nūr al-Dīn, leading Saladin to fear that he would be dismissed and dispossessed of Egypt. We will never know whether these fears were well founded, but Saladin did not take any chances and decided to return to Egypt in mid-November 1171, on the pretext that the situation in Egypt was precarious and there was the risk of another revolt. Nūr al-Dīn was not taken in and, according to Ibn al-Athīr, resolved to expel Saladin from Egypt as soon as possible. The same historian adds that, having learned of Nūr al-Dīn's intentions, Saladin convened his council, composed of his emirs and members of his family, to decide what tack to take. The bellicose intentions of his nephew Taqī al-Dīn ʿUmar and of a few other members of his family were quickly moderated by the response of Ayyūb, who steadfastly and publicly took Nūr al-Dīn's side. This was a purely tactical move, as he told Saladin privately a few moments later: "With what sort of intelligence have you acted? Do you not realize that, if Nūr al-Dīn hears of your intention to resist him and fight, he will make us his most important consideration? Then you will be powerless against him. But now, when he hears what has happened and of our loyalty to him, he will leave us alone and occupy himself with others and fate will take its course. By God, if Nūr al-Dīn wanted as much as a piece of sugar cane I myself would fight him to stop him or be killed in the attempt."[22]

Are we to see that dialogue as merely a denunciation by Ibn al-Athīr of Ayyubid perfidy? That is difficult to say, but what especially emerges from this account is the influence that Ayyūb, portrayed as a cautious man and an astute politician, continued to exert over his son. The tension with Nūr al-Dīn eased for some time, and in March 1172 Saladin received from his master the honorific clothing sent by the caliph, which he donned to parade the streets of Cairo.

For the next two years, Nūr al-Dīn hardly had time to concern himself with Saladin, absorbed as he was by his struggle against the Franks in the region of Damascus and Tiberias, and then by his battle against the Seljuks of Anatolia, with whom he finally reached an accord in late August 1173.[23] In April or May of the same year, Saladin sent him some sixty thousand dinars, a zebra, and an elephant, as well as various gold objects and precious stones, selected from the treasures of the Fatimid palace.[24] These gifts only increased Nūr al-Dīn's irritation at his lieutenant, from whom he was expecting a much larger and more regular financial contribution: "That is not the money we needed," he exclaimed, "for it cannot fill the hole of our deficit. Saladin knows that we have not spent our gold in the conquest of Egypt [for so little], when that gold was in short supply. So what does what he has sent us represent, compared to what we have granted!"[25]

The sending of that caravan coincided, perhaps intentionally, with a new expedition by Saladin against the fortress of Kerak, which was often the home base for Frankish attacks on the caravans linking Egypt to Syria. Through that expedition, Saladin hoped less to take the fortress than to thwart the Arab Bedouins who were providing the Franks with desert guides. That is what emerges from a letter he wrote to Nūr al-Dīn to explain his actions: aware of the importance of the jihad, he felt that the best way to fight the Franks would be to expel from their territories all the Arab Bedouins who were helping them find their way. Saladin asked Nūr al-Dīn to welcome these Arab warriors and to deliver up *iqṭāʿs* in Syria to them, so that they would settle in that region. He added, not without a certain irony, that he would have rather brought them back to Egypt, but that they "preferred Syria to any other Islamic country."[26] Having laid siege to the fortress of Kerak, ravaged the region, and expelled some two hundred Arab cavalrymen to Syria, Saladin withdrew and returned to Egypt.[27] He had the unhappy surprise of learning en route of his father's death, which had occurred in Cairo on August 9, 1173, as the result of a fall from a horse. Ayyūb was buried beside his brother, Shīrkūh, and two years later their remains were transferred to Medina.

Nūr al-Dīn, however, began to grow impatient at Saladin's slowness in sending him subsidies. During the winter of 1173–1174, he therefore sent his chief accountant to Egypt to oversee the Egyptian cadastre, to take inventory of the financial resources of the country, and to set the annual fees that Saladin would have to pay him. Saladin justified himself by saying that Egypt was costing him a good deal of money. He asked his loyal friend Diyāʾ al-Dīn al-Hakkārī to deliver personally the fiscal report in the company of the chief accountant and once again entrusted to him sumptuous presents for Nūr al-Dīn. The presents, however, were never received, because Nūr al-Dīn died on May 15, 1174, the victim of acute quinsy, before the caravan had had time to arrive in Damascus.[28]

During the weeks preceding his death, Nūr al-Dīn had once more mobilized his troops. According to Ibn al-Athīr, his objective was to take Egypt away from Saladin, whom he suspected of wanting to make the Frankish state a buffer between Syria and Egypt. The account of that historian, who insists more than all the other sources on the tensions between Nūr al-Dīn and his lieutenant, would be suspect were it not confirmed by Ibn Shaddād, who reports the words that Saladin confided to him one day: "We had heard that Nūr al-Dīn would perhaps attack us in Egypt. Several of our comrades advised that he should be openly resisted and his authority rejected. . . . I alone disagreed with them, urging that it was not right to say anything of that sort. Our difference of opinion lasted until news of his death arrived."[29]

As for Saladin, he assembled troops outside Cairo, preparations he justified by saying that he was planning to meet up with Nūr al-Dīn for a joint attack on Kerak.[30] Although once again it remains difficult to fathom his intentions, it does not appear that he was planning an imminent war against Nūr al-Dīn. If that had been the case, would he have proposed in mid-May 1174 that his brother Tūrānshāh send Nūr al-Dīn reinforcements in Yemen? In reality, at no time did

Saladin wish to attack him directly. On the contrary, the vizier's interests dictated a strategy of avoiding Nūr al-Dīn and of justifying his lack of haste in aiding him on the basis of the vulnerability of Saladin's situation in Egypt. It is clear, however, that Nūr al-Dīn's uneasiness gradually increased. He was afraid he would lose hold of Saladin's power, which would have deprived him of the benefits he had anticipated from the conquest of Egypt. Ibn al-Athīr and Ibn Shaddād are not the only ones to report that. Abū Shāma implicitly acknowledges it as well, seeking to reconcile the two sovereigns after the fact: "If Nūr al-Dīn had known what magnificent conquests God in the Most High reserved for Islam after him, under Saladin's guidance, he would have been consoled, because Saladin built the jihad against the associationists [the Christians] on the foundations laid by Nūr al-Dīn, and did so in the most consummate manner."[31]

II

The Sultan

6

Usurper or Legitimate Sultan?

The difficult conditions under which Saladin acceded to power loomed large during the first ten years of his reign and determined the arguments on which his political legitimacy was founded. Nūr al-Dīn had only one son, al-Sālih Ismāʿīl, then eleven years old, and there were many candidates for the regency: the nephews of Nūr al-Dīn living in Upper Mesopotamia, the emirs of Aleppo and Damascus, and Saladin in Cairo. Egyptian-Syrian-Mesopotamian unity, patiently developed from the mid-twelfth century on, wobbled on its foundations but did not completely collapse, since, despite the divisions and the ambitions of each camp, all laid claim to the same legacy, that of Nūr al-Dīn, and each side attempted to prove that it was the best positioned to continue his work. Saladin, fresh from his successes in Egypt, Yemen, and Cyrenaica, overcame obstacles one by one and finally established himself as the one true legitimate sultan. He had supporters and detractors. Both had a tendency to remember only those aspects of his actions that confirmed their opinion, leaving the historian the task of sorting out and analyzing, through their discourses, the means Saladin set in motion to impose his authority.

Nūr al-Dīn's Difficult Succession

Great confusion reigned in the Muslim territories in the wake of Nūr al-Dīn's death. In Mosul, his nephew Sayf al-Dīn began by seizing the territories east of the Euphrates previously subject to Nūr al-Dīn's authority.[1] In Damascus, where the deceased's young son was living, Emir Ibn al-Muqaddam, designated by his peers as commander of the army and head of the administration, immediately had to fend off a raid by the Franks against Bāniyās, southwest of Damascus. All the same, in brandishing the threat of Saladin's imminent arrival and in offering to liberate twenty-some prisoners, Ibn al-Muqaddam achieved a truce. Then, shortly after July 14, 1174, when King Amalric of Jerusalem also died, Frankish pressure on the territories of Damascus eased appreciably. That was a mixed blessing for Saladin in Egypt, who of course found himself rid of his formidable adversary Amalric, but at the same time lost his main argument for an expedition into Syria, namely, the Frankish threat, which he believed he was the only one with the capacity to thwart.

In northern Syria, the city of Aleppo was an object coveted by all. Before dying, it seems, Nūr al-Dīn had had the foresight to entrust its regency to one of his emirs, the eunuch Gümüshtegin, governor of the citadel of Mosul. But by the time Gümüshtegin arrived in Aleppo, three other emirs had already seized power: two brothers from the powerful Banū l-Dāya family had divided up the administration and the police, while Shādhbakht, a eunuch and native of India, controlled the citadel. In order for their regency to be recognized, however, the Banū l-Dāya had to manage to bring the young al-Sālih to Aleppo. This they attempted to do by opening negotiations with the leaders of Damascus. Nevertheless, the many rivalries between emirs and the reawakening of struggles between Sunnis and Shiites in Aleppo culminated in the plan's failure: Shādhbakht and Gümüshtegin, with the complicity of a few emirs from Damascus who had brought them al-Sālih in Aleppo, placed the Banū l-Dāya under arrest, got rid of the most influential Shiite city leader, and installed themselves in power. Three eunuchs ruled over Aleppo at the time: Shādhbakht, governor of the citadel; Gümüshtegin, commander of the army; and al-Mujāhid Yāqūt, who was in charge of the young prince's education.[2]

In Damascus, Ibn al-Muqaddam did not immediately perceive the danger. In reply to Saladin's protests concerning the imprisonment of the Banū l-Dāya, he cautioned: "Let it not be said that you have designs on the house of the one

who elevated you, who installed you, and who made you strong. . . . That be-
fits neither your situation nor your good character."³ Very quickly, however,
Ibn al-Muqaddam's uneasiness grew. He began by making an appeal in Mosul
to Nūr al-Dīn's nephew, who thought that Ibn al-Muqaddam was trying to
draw him into a trap and preferred an alliance with Gümüshtegin of Aleppo.
Ibn al-Muqaddam's anxiety only increased, and it was then that he turned to
Saladin, who was only waiting for that appeal to intervene in Syria.

Saladin, the only ruler of Egypt for the preceding three years, was at the time
the most powerful of all Nūr al-Dīn's former emirs. The Syrian emirs were
well aware of this and feared his reactions. Yet they did not want to heed the
chief qādī of Damascus, Ibn al-Shahrazūrī, who had advised them to consult
Saladin on how to set up the regency. When Saladin learned of Nūr al-Dīn's
death, he began by insistently reasserting his allegiance to the Zangid dynasty.
Al-Sālih had written him to inform him of his father's death, of the oath the
Syrian emirs had just taken to him—a veiled appeal for Saladin to do the
same—and of the need to fight the Franks. Saladin responded by assuring him
of his devotion and of his determination to conduct the jihad. And, as further
proof, Saladin attached to his message Egyptian dinars on which the young
sovereign's name was already inscribed.

That official proclamation of loyalty to the Zangid dynasty did not prevent
Saladin from thinking from the start that he was the one best positioned to
serve as regent. In a letter to a Syrian emir, before he had confirmation of the
news of Nūr al-Dīn's death, Saladin said he had received instructions from Nūr
al-Dīn to recognize Gümüshtegin as al-Sālih's regent, but he hastened to add
that he felt ready to protect the heir should that solution not be accepted. A little while later, after being excluded from the political discussions, he asserted
in another missive that, of all the emirs, he was the one Nūr al-Dīn had trusted
the most, as attested by the fact that Nūr al-Dīn had named Saladin to rule
Egypt. Saladin claimed that, if Nūr al-Dīn had not died so suddenly, there was
no doubt that he would have designated Saladin to be al-Sālih's regent.⁴

Isolated in Egypt, far from the legitimate heir, and weakened by the tensions between him and Nūr al-Dīn in the last months of Nūr al-Dīn's reign, Saladin could hardly intervene immediately in the establishment of the regency,

especially since, in late July, he had to face down a large squadron sent to Alexandria by William II of Sicily. Despite the large number of ships and fighters, the Sicilians, having suffered heavy losses, very quickly had to beat a retreat. That victory was opportune for Saladin, since it indicated once again that he was the right man in the right place to deal with the Western threat.

In other respects as well, his assets were not insignificant. He was lord of Egypt and in control of its resources, vanquisher of the Franks and the Arab tribes of Upper Egypt, and conqueror of Yemen: none of Nūr al-Dīn's emirs could measure up to him, and the divisions among his foes could only help him. Nevertheless, military superiority was not sufficient. Saladin had to find other arguments to legitimate his power and to obtain the caliph's backing. These arguments are set out at length in the many letters he sent to al-Sālih, to the Syrian emirs, to his entourage, and to the caliph of Baghdad during the months following Nūr al-Dīn's death. Saladin tirelessly recalled his loyalty to Nūr al-Dīn and to his heir, the credit his family had enjoyed under the reign of the Zangids, his absence of designs on Syria, and his determination to unify Islam, to pursue the jihad, and to serve the Abbasid caliphate.

The takeover of Syria by the Banū l-Dāya, who had enjoyed all Nūr al-Dīn's favors, might have passed for an acceptable solution in Saladin's eyes.[5] But to abandon the reins of power to three eunuchs for whom he had only contempt was unacceptable, as he said in a letter to the caliph of Baghdad in 1175.[6] Therefore, having vanquished the Sicilian fleet on August 1, 1174, and repressed a new revolt in Upper Egypt in early September, he decided to respond to the appeals for help from Ibn al-Muqaddam and the lord of Busra, a city south of Damascus. He headed toward Syria, leading a relatively modest army, and reached Busra, then Damascus, no doubt hoping to obtain reinforcements once there. On October 28, 1174, he entered Damascus without difficulty and distributed large sums of money to win over the population. After a brief resistance, the citadel surrendered and Saladin entrusted its command to his brother Tughtegin.[7]

The Aleppine reaction was not long in coming: an embassy led by Qutb al-Dīn Īnāl, a former emir of Nūr al-Dīn's who had fought beside Shīrkūh in Egypt, went to see Saladin, who, it seems, received him most warmly. Qutb al-Dīn, however, threatened him, pointing to his sword: "These swords, which gave you Egypt, are still in our hands, the spears that emptied the Egyptian palaces are ready on our shoulders, and the men who kept the Egyptian armies away from you will repel you in the same way. Whatever action you undertake, they will divert you from it. You have stepped over the line and gone too far. You are only a servant of Nūr al-Dīn and are duty-bound to preserve [his lineage] through his son."[8]

Ibn Abī Tayyi' and 'Imād al-Dīn are in agreement that Saladin did not allow himself to be intimidated by these words but courteously reassured the emissary. The historian Sibt Ibn al-Jawzī, by contrast, reports an outburst of rage on Saladin's part: "If you had not been a messenger, I would have had your throat cut. By God, I did not come here out of greed or desire for the world here below. What I have in Egypt is sufficient for me. I came only to save that child from the clutches of those of your ilk. It is you who are the cause of the disappearance of his dynasty."[9]

From that time on, Saladin's supporters and detractors faced off. The sharpest criticisms came from the Zangid territories. In Mosul, Saladin was accused of treason and was called a "dog who bites the hand that feeds him."[10] The author of the *Anonymous Syriac Chronicle,* a Christian from Edessa, which was then under Zangid authority, also did not believe in the sincerity of his intentions and accused him of pretense and political ambition. In the Frankish camp, William of Tyre shared that view and spoke of treason against his master.[11] In response to Saladin's supporters, who pointed out his loyalty to Nūr al-Dīn's descendants and his absence of designs on Syria, his detractors accused Saladin of disloyalty, ambition, and a lust for power.

In the months that followed, Saladin undertook the conquest of the rest of Syria. His battle against the emirs of Aleppo and against the Zangids would give him the opportunity not only to prove his determination to unify Syria and Upper Mesopotamia but also to fine-tune the arguments intended to persuade the population in general, and the caliph of Baghdad in particular, of the legitimacy of his actions. The cities of Homs and Hama surrendered, but the citadels that protected them resisted. The citadel of Hama was held by a former companion of Saladin's, Jūrdīk, who was given permission to go to Aleppo to negotiate an accord between its leaders and Saladin. He was imprisoned upon his arrival by the emir of Aleppo, Gümüshtegin, who was ill-disposed toward discussions. As a result, Jūrdīk's brother, who had remained in Hama, handed over the citadel to Saladin on December 28, 1174. Two days later, Saladin set up his camp outside Aleppo, where he was met with strong resistance. The young prince al-Sālih addressed the population, which had assembled in one of the city's hippodromes: "You know well my father's kindness to you, his love for you and his good rule over you. I am his orphan. This wicked man, who repudiates my father's goodness to him, has come to take my lands. He respects neither God Almighty nor his creatures."[12]

According to some, that speech moved the Aleppines to tears, and even if this claim must be seen merely as anti-Saladin propaganda, the resistance of Aleppo is a good illustration of the problems of legitimacy Saladin must have faced. Nūr al-Dīn's family, his son in particular, enjoyed great popularity in northern Syria, and no one really believed that Saladin would be satisfied to serve as regent as he claimed. If he failed to be convincing, Saladin might have been able to impose himself by force, but at the cost of a long and costly siege, a tactic he rarely opted for during his career. While still outside the city's walls, he was the victim of a first assassination attempt by members of the Assassin sect, who acted on the order of the emirs of Aleppo. Saved by one of his emirs, who sacrificed his own life, Saladin later used that incident to show his determination to defend Sunnism, unlike his adversaries, whom he accused of depending on Shiite extremists.

The residents of Aleppo did not waste any time giving him another opportunity to strengthen his claims on the sultanate. As the siege continued, the garrison in the citadel of Homs sent word to the Franks to ask for their aid, with the agreement, no doubt, of the emirs of Aleppo. By way of payment, the resisters in Homs offered to release the Frankish hostages who had been delivered to them in exchange for the liberation of Raymond of Tripoli and of Eustache, brother of Reginald of Sidon, expecting to receive a ransom for them.

The Franks, aware that Saladin was more dangerous to them than Nūr al-Dīn's young son, and wishing to have their hostages back, responded to the appeal. But when they arrived outside the walls of Homs, the garrison, which was no doubt hoping that the approach of the Franks would be enough to make Saladin ease up on Aleppo, refused to hand over the citadel to them. Having camped for a month outside Aleppo, Saladin set off again for Homs, immediately bringing about the Franks' retreat. After a few weeks, on March 17, 1175, he seized the citadel. The garrison released the prisoners taken from Saladin's army in exchange for having their own lives spared.[13] A few days later, on March 29, Baalbek also surrendered without a fight, and it was at about that time that Saladin wrote to the caliph to ask him for the investiture of Egypt and Syria.

In the meantime, the Zangid army arrived in Syria, having been sent from Mosul at the request of the Aleppines. But the conflict between Sayf al-Dīn of Mosul and his brother 'Imād al-Dīn, lord of Sinjār, was weakening their camp. Saladin took advantage of their dissension. The Zangid army passed through Aleppo, where other troops joined it, before turning in the direction of Hama. Negotiations opened between the two camps. Saladin said he was ready to hand over Homs, Hama, and Baalbek, but insisted on keeping Rahba on the Euphrates, which was governed by his cousin (Shīrkūh's son), and especially Damascus, where he pledged to have the *khutba* pronounced in the name of Nūr al-Dīn's son. These proposals were rejected by the Zangids, who demanded all of Syria and wanted Saladin to return to Egypt. To no avail: Saladin was determined to stay in Syria. Having written to the caliph to complain about his adversaries, he sent for his nephews Farrūkhshāh and Taqī al-Dīn 'Umar, as well as his maternal uncle al-Hārimī. All three arrived in Hama with reinforcements in early April 1175. Saladin, in order to have a free hand, negotiated with the Franks and returned to them the hostages who had been held in Homs, an accord harshly condemned by William of Tyre, who believed that the Franks would have done better, while there was still time, to unite their forces and fight against Saladin.[14]

The battle between Saladin and the Zangid forces took place on April 13, 1175, north of Hama, in a place known as the "Horns of Hama." The Zangids were routed without great difficulty, but Saladin had no interest in crushing the enemy troops too decisively, since he still hoped to rally some of them to his side. In the letter he wrote on that occasion to Baghdad, he emphasized that he had spared the lives of his adversaries, allowed the fugitives to leave, and refused to keep prisoners, proof of a leniency that he hoped would earn him the caliph's gratitude and also that of the Aleppines.

He was not disappointed. Once he had returned to Aleppo, he managed to negotiate with the leaders of the city, who themselves asked for a truce. By the terms of the accord signed in early May 1175, Saladin kept his conquests and conceded to al-Sālih the entire northern part of Syria, up to but not including Hama. Kafartāb and Ma'arrat al-Nu'mān, both located between Hama and Aleppo, also fell to Saladin. Everywhere, the *khutba* was to be pronounced in the name of al-Sālih, whom Saladin pledged to support if need be, whereas the Aleppines promised to fight the Franks and to liberate the Banū l-Dāya brothers and Emir Jūrdīk, whom they were still keeping prisoner.[15]

On May 6 Saladin returned to Hama, where he received a delegation from Baghdad informing him of the caliph's decision to recognize his authority over Egypt and Syria, with the exception of al-Sālih's territories. Along with the diploma of investiture, he was given the customary black flags and honorific robes. At the same time, the caliph sent honorific robes to al-Sālih and asked Saladin to maintain good relations with him. It was a great victory for Saladin, whose power over all of central and southern Syria could no longer be contested. But in exchange for that acknowledgment, it was made clear to him that he had to abandon any idea of conquering Aleppo, at least so long as al-Sālih reigned there.

Despite the treaty he had just signed with Aleppo, Saladin completed his Syrian conquests with the taking of Bārīn (May 1175), southwest of Hama, the possession of one of Nūr al-Dīn's former emirs, whom Saladin accused of collusion with the Assassins and the Franks, accusations he had the habit of making to justify his battles against the Zangids and their supporters. The emir had joined Saladin before his attack on Homs, but, not having received what he wanted, had abandoned him to take refuge in the fortress of Bārīn. Without the means to resist, he obtained permission from Saladin to join the prince of Mosul, who delivered Edessa to him.[16] Saladin, after entrusting Hama to his uncle al-Hārimī, Homs to his cousin Nāsir al-Dīn, and Baalbek to Emir Ibn al-Muqaddam, returned to Damascus on May 23, 1175, and granted his troops a few months' leave. The Egyptian emirs returned home to collect their share of the harvest, and Saladin himself remained in Damascus until spring 1176.

The conquest of the territories formerly under Nūr al-Dīn's authority was not over, however, and would keep Saladin occupied for several more years. The accord concluded with the Aleppines stipulated that Saladin would make peace with the Zangids. But according to 'Imād al-Dīn, when the Zangid envoy arrived in Damascus, he mistakenly removed from his sleeve the text of a new treaty between Mosul and Aleppo. Saladin, furious that the Aleppines had acted without consulting him, broke off negotiations. He explained himself in a letter to the caliph, in which he again accused the Zangids of treachery.[17] That story, whether true or false—was Saladin looking for a pretext to break off negotiations and resume his conquests?—is indicative of the continuing mistrust between him and the Zangids.

Hostilities resumed in spring 1176 after an accord was concluded between Sayf al-Dīn of Mosul and al-Sālih. To obtain the Franks' support, the Aleppines agreed to release Reginald of Châtillon and Joscelin of Courtenay, who had been imprisoned, respectively, for sixteen and twelve years.[18] Saladin asked his brother al-ʿĀdil, lieutenant of Egypt at the time, to send reinforcements. His other brother Tūrānshāh, who had just left Yemen, also came to join him. Tūrānshāh arrived in Damascus a few days before the battle that, on April 22, 1176, pitted Saladin's army against the coalition army of Aleppo and Mosul, at Tall al-Sulṭān, about thirty-seven kilometers south of Aleppo. Despite overwhelming numerical superiority, the Zangid army—far from its bases, divided, and poorly commanded—was defeated. Once again, Saladin did not attempt to destroy the vanquished forces and liberated many prisoners. Sayf al-Dīn returned to Mosul, while his brother ʿIzz al-Dīn Masʿūd remained in Syria to come to al-Ṣāliḥ's aid.[19]

Aleppo feared being besieged in turn, but Saladin preferred to seize the surrounding territories first: to the northeast, Buzāʿa surrendered on May 4, and Manbij on the 11th. The governor of Manbij, Quṭb al-Dīn Īnāl, liberated by Saladin, went to see Sayf al-Dīn in Mosul, who gave him Rakka on the Euphrates as an *iqṭāʿ*. In the second half of May, Saladin set up his camp outside ʿAzāz, a day and a half on foot northwest of Aleppo. During the siege of May 22, he was again attacked by four Assassins and was wounded in the cheek. All the attackers were carved to pieces by his companions. ʿAzāz surrendered on June 21 and was given as an *iqṭāʿ* to Saladin's nephew Taqī al-Dīn ʿUmar.

Gümüshtegin, thinking that the next target would be Hārim, a stronghold on the road between Aleppo and Antioch, rushed off to defend it, but Saladin made the decision to attack Aleppo. Among the ambassadors he sent to negotiate with the Aleppines was ʿImād al-Dīn, who complained that he was treated harshly, lodged all night long in a hovel without a bed, water, or food. The content of the accord delivered to him the next morning without negotiation could not, we suspect, have satisfied Saladin, who had the impression that it was all merely a masquerade designed to gain some time and to allow Gümüshtegin to return to Aleppo. In the letter he wrote to the caliph on July 2, 1176, Saladin again lamented the failure of his attempts at reconciliation, which according to him were attributable to his adversaries' complete refusal to compromise. In spite of that, aware that a siege of Aleppo would be long and the outcome uncertain, and that his troops were tired, he decided on July 29 to sign a peace agreement, by the terms of which he gave up the guardianship of al-Ṣāliḥ, whose power in northern Syria was confirmed. Buzāʿa and

Manbij remained in Saladin's hands, but he agreed to hand over 'Azāz to al-Sālih's sister, who was still only a little girl. The Banū l-Dāya and Emir Jūrdīk were finally released, and whereas Jūrdīk decided to remain in al-Sālih's service, the Banū l-Dāya went to Cairo, where they were very well received.[20]

As soon as that matter was concluded, in early August Saladin headed for the fortress of Masyāf, the Assassins' seat of power, wishing to stamp out that sect, which had twice tried to eliminate him. But very quickly, for reasons that remain unclear, the siege was lifted and Saladin returned to Damascus on August 25, 1176, where he allowed himself a few days of rest. On September 6, he married 'Ismat al-Dīn, Nūr al-Dīn's widow and the daughter of the former Burid emir of Damascus. 'Ismat al-Dīn, it should be noted, was not the mother of al-Sālih, Nūr al-Dīn's son and successor.[21] That marriage not only reinforced Saladin's claims to Nūr al-Dīn's legacy but also assured him of the support of his wife's family, which had joined the Zangid camp in 1154. Saladin consolidated the unity of that family by giving his own sister Rabī'a Khātūn in marriage to his new brother-in-law Sa'd al-Dīn Mas'ūd ibn Unur, thereby following a policy of matrimonial alliances commonly applied in his time.[22]

A few days later, having designated his brother Tūrānshāh lieutenant in Syria, and having sent an ambassador to Mosul to ratify the treaty signed with the Aleppines, Saladin decided to return to Egypt to organize his government and allow his troops some time to rest. He made his entry into Cairo on October 2, 1176.[23] Within two years, he had succeeded in conquering a great part of Syria and in having his power recognized by the caliph and by his adversaries, though the northern part of the country, in the hands of Nūr al-Dīn's son, was still beyond his grasp. He seems to have accepted that situation, since in the five years that followed he made no further attacks against Aleppo. It was Sayf al-Dīn's death in Mosul in 1180, then al-Sālih's in Aleppo in 1181, that reawakened Saladin's aspiration to claim all these regions and allowed him to complete his work of unifying the Muslim territories.

Unifier of the Muslims

Saladin spent the next three years first in Egypt, where he remained until autumn 1177, and then in Syria-Palestine, where he launched several raids against the Franks. But he had not given up—far from it—imposing his authority in the region of the Euphrates. In 1179 he sent his nephew to repel a raid by the

Seljuk sultan of Anatolia on a stronghold in the Upper Euphrates Valley,[24] and the next year, having concluded a truce with Jerusalem and Tripoli, he set off for Upper Mesopotamia. His first action was to settle a matrimonial dispute between the Seljuk sultan of Anatolia and the Artukid emir of Hisn Kayfā, a strategic site in the Upper Tigris Valley.[25] The role of arbitrator that he was asked to take on did not displease him, since it only increased his influence over the region. In addition, the circumstances played out in his favor. He had barely reached the Upper Euphrates Valley when he learned of the death of Sayf al-Dīn of Mosul. Sayf al-Dīn's brother 'Izz al-Dīn immediately asked Saladin to recognize him as the heir. An agreement was concluded, and though Saladin did not manage to take over the Mesopotamian territories recaptured by the Zangids upon Nūr al-Dīn's death, he did manage to curb the Seljuk's ambitions, to make the Artukid beholden to him, and to impose himself as a political authority among the Zangids.[26]

Saladin spent the following year in Cairo, and it was there that he learned of al-Sālih's death, which had occurred on December 4, 1181, in Aleppo, after an illness lasting seventeen days.[27] Before dying, the young prince had asked that his possessions be handed over to his cousin 'Izz al-Dīn, the only person, according to him, able to resist Saladin. As soon as he learned of the illness of Nūr al-Dīn's son, Saladin readied himself to intervene in Syria. He justified his actions by saying that he had made no attempt against al-Sālih "out of respect for his father," but that Aleppo was certainly part of the Syrian territories for which the caliph had given him the investiture. In reality, the caliph's diploma had recognized Saladin's authority over Syria with the exception of the territories controlled by al-Sālih, a clause that Saladin had respected until then but that he now judged null and void because of the young heir's death.[28]

The measures he had taken to make sure that he would be alerted of al-Sālih's death as quickly as possible leave no remaining doubt about his impatience: in Aleppo, Hama, and Homs, carrier pigeons were waiting at the ready, and in Busra, messengers on dromedaries were positioned to make a run for Egypt. Saladin's plan was to send troops to the Euphrates to cut off Aleppo from any reinforcements arriving from the east. Nevertheless, a confrontation with Reginald of Châtillon in Transjordan thwarted that brilliant plan, and Saladin could not keep 'Izz al-Dīn of Mosul from arriving in Aleppo on December 29, 1181, where he quickly married al-Sālih's mother, to strengthen his right to the legacy. He was not reckoning on his brother 'Imād al-Dīn, lord of Sinjār, who, having married Nūr al-Dīn's daughter, was laying claim to the same legacy. Since 'Imād al-Dīn threatened to deliver his city to Saladin if Aleppo were not handed over to him, his brother yielded, giving up Aleppo in exchange for Sinjār on February 27, 1182.[29] Note the role played by the women in that series of matrimonial alliances. Muslim society, without going so far as to recognize a daughter's right to inherit the throne—as in the Latin states at that time—did grant a certain importance to familial or dynastic inheritance, which women transmitted to their spouses and children. That inheritance, more symbolic than real, was also transmitted by the widows of deceased sovereigns: hence the eagerness of princes in quest of legitimacy to marry them.

Saladin set off again for Syria in May 1182. After a few raids launched against the Franks, he headed for Aleppo, arriving on September 19, 1182. There he attempted in vain to negotiate for the city with the new Zangid lord. The support he received from the emir of Harrān encouraged him to go to Upper Mesopotamia, to isolate Aleppo from Mosul. He first passed through al-Bīra, on the Euphrates northeast of Aleppo, where the Artukid emir, threatened some time earlier by his cousin from Mardin, was requesting his aid. Saladin received the keys to the city before going to take Edessa, Sarūj, and Rakka.[30] He then seized the Khabur Valley and went back up to Nisībīn, which he took without any real resistance. The Artukid Nūr al-Dīn Muhammad of Hisn Kayfā also joined him, in exchange for the promise that he would receive Amida once it was conquered.

In early November 1182, Saladin set out for Mosul, the largest city of Upper Mesopotamia. Nevertheless, believing it was too well defended, he did not linger long and went to seize Sinjār (late December–early January 1183). Then he headed for Harrān, where he arrived in late February 1183.

Faced with the unified forces of his Zangid enemies, reinforced by troops from the lord of Akhlāt, a major city in Armenia, and by those of the Artukid emir of Mardin, Saladin led a new offensive to the east, which forced his adversaries to retreat and allowed him to bring Mardin to heel. But Saladin's most spectacular conquest of that campaign was Amida, about eighty kilometers north of Mardin. With the caliph's agreement, Saladin seized it on April 16. There as elsewhere, he displayed great leniency, allowing its governor to leave with his family and belongings. The city and its many treasures were preserved. Notably, the library, which according to Ibn Abī Tayyi' contained more than a million books—an estimate that is surely exaggerated but indicative of

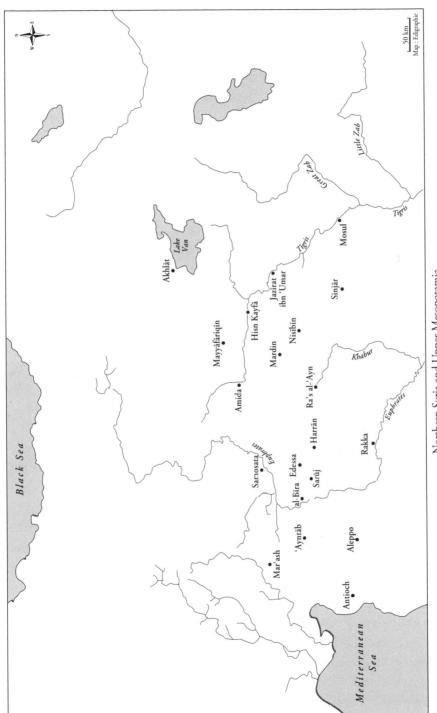

Northern Syria and Upper Mesopotamia

its richness—was entrusted to Qāḍī al-Fāḍil. As had been agreed upon, Amida was handed over to the emir of Hisn Kayfā, who swore his allegiance to Saladin, promised his military aid for the jihad, and committed himself to repairing the damage caused to the city and to eliminating the illegal taxes, as had been done in all the other cities conquered.[31] Some criticized Saladin for that generosity, but he justified it in the name of his political interests: "When the sultan had received Amida, he offered it, with everything it contained, to Nūr al-Dīn Muhammad Ibn Qarā Arslān. To ratify his possession of Amida and its region, he drew up a diploma for him, thereby respecting his pledge. The sultan was then told: 'You promised him Amida but not all the goods and treasures it contains. These amount to three million dinars!' He replied: 'I will not be miserly toward him on that account, since he is now one of our companions and friends.'"[32]

After that impressive series of victories, Saladin crossed back over the Euphrates, still with the same objective: to surround Aleppo with a network of fortresses and to isolate it from Mosul by seizing all the major cities between them. Having easily assured himself control of the fortresses north of Aleppo, he finally set up camp outside the city's walls on May 21, 1183.

A few days later, while the Aleppines were tenaciously defending themselves, negotiations opened with 'Imād al-Dīn—cornered and short on money—through the intermediary of the governor of the citadel. As the residents of Aleppo were stunned to discover when Saladin's troops entered the city, an accord was secretly signed on June 11. 'Imād al-Dīn was jeered as he left the citadel, but he received from Saladin some of the recent conquests in Upper Mesopotamia: Sinjār, the Khabur Valley, Nisībīn, Rakka, and Sarūj. "We have exchanged a silver currency (dirhams) for a gold currency (dinars)," it was said in the entourage of Saladin, who had just realized the dream he had been nurturing for nearly ten years. Rakka was delivered to the former governor of the citadel by 'Imād al-Dīn, who pledged to respond in person to Saladin's appeal in the event of a military expedition. Saladin displayed his customary generosity, showering 'Imād al-Dīn with gifts of all sorts (precious fabrics, clothing, horses, camels), before allowing him to leave.[33]

It is clear that, at the time, Saladin viewed his conquests in Upper Mesopotamia as currency to be used in exchange for the taking of Aleppo and as a means to obtain the military aid he needed. That, in any case, is what was proclaimed everywhere on his orders: "Those who submit will keep possession of their territory, on the condition that they join the sultan's army and follow him, to aid him in his war against the infidels."[34] After the taking of Aleppo, Saladin would also seize Hārim, whose governor was accused by his own troops of having called in the Franks to rescue them. On a day when the governor had left the citadel, the garrison of Hārim therefore delivered it to Saladin.

In less than a year, then, Saladin had seized a large part of Upper Mesopotamia and all of northern Syria, without encountering any resistance. The reasons for that success were related, first and foremost, to favorable historical circumstances, with the almost simultaneous deaths of the two Zangid princes, Sayf al-Dīn of Mosul and al-Sālih of Aleppo. But Saladin also succeeded by applying a clever strategy, consisting, on one hand, of separating Aleppo from Mosul, and, on the other, of winning over a large number of emirs through his conciliatory attitude toward them. In addition, the incontestable political stature he had acquired since his last pass through the region in 1176, and the credit he had enjoyed until then from the caliph, designated him, among all the princes and governors of the region, as the only one capable of restoring the cohesion of the territories once controlled by Nūr al-Dīn. The taking of Aleppo was in fact strongly resented by the Franks, who were not fooled: "From the beginning, it was clear to the Christians that if Saladin managed to annex Aleppo to his domains, our country would be surrounded by his forces and his might, as in a state of siege,"[35] wrote William of Tyre.

Nevertheless, the control exerted by Saladin over the territories east of the Euphrates remained fragile, as the events that followed would show. Having handed Aleppo over to his young son al-Zāhir, eleven years old at the time, and having entrusted the regency to one of his emirs, Saladin returned to Damascus in early 1184. An embassy from the emirs of Jazīrat Ibn 'Umar and Irbil—cities located, respectively, to the north and east of Mosul—came to ask for his support against the Zangid prince of Mosul, who, for his part, sent Saladin a messenger as well. Saladin was probably not unhappy with the role of arbitrator he was again being asked to play. He promised his support to the emirs, even while treating the envoys from Mosul with consideration. His secretary 'Imād al-Dīn suggested that Saladin make a proposal to the Mosul delegation: the delegation would allow the two emirs to choose freely whose authority they wished to be under. But the emirs persisted in claiming full and complete authority over the two cities. The ambassadors ultimately left Damascus on March 22, 1184, without finding a solution, and the city of Mosul then turned eastward, asking for the help of Pahlawān Muhammad, a powerful atabeg and the true lord of the eastern Seljuk empire, and his brother Qizil Arslān. This brother sent a contingent of three thousand undisciplined cavalrymen, who pillaged everything in their path and whom the emir of Irbil had no trouble eliminating.[36] Saladin understood the advantage he could draw from these divisions and from the weakness of Mosul. Having led a raid against the Franks of Kerak (summer 1184) and thereby shown his desire not to abandon the jihad, he prepared for a new expedition to the east and asked his brother al-ʿĀdil, to whom he had just given the governorship of Aleppo, to join him with his troops.

Saladin crossed the Euphrates in April 1185, heading for Mosul. It was at that moment no doubt that ʿIzz al-Dīn sent him an embassy, headed by Nūr al-Dīn's daughter, to assuage him, but without great effect. Saladin was already beginning to distribute the territories of Mosul to his emirs when he learned on July 21 of the death of the lord of Akhlāt, a city on the west bank of Lake Van. The notables of that city, apparently tempted to play up the rivalry between Saladin and Pahlawān in order to keep their autonomy, requested Saladin's protection.[37] He decided it was more urgent to intervene in the north than to besiege Mosul. He therefore sent troops to Lake Van, writing at the same time to the caliph to ask him for the investiture over these new territories. He himself went to Mayyāfāriqīn, where in late August he concluded an agreement with the widow of the Artukid emir Qutb al-Dīn (he had died in autumn 1184), and with the emir responsible for defending the city. But that detour through Mayyāfāriqīn gave Pahlawān time to reach Akhlāt, which dissuaded Saladin from intervening and impelled him to return to Mosul, where he arrived in November 1185. Although Saladin appeared to be in a position of strength, the nine-month campaigns had worn down his army, and he himself fell ill during the month of December. He therefore resolved to accept the offer to negotiate from the lord of Mosul. Having been assured that coins would be minted and the *khutba* pronounced in his name, in late December he left the region for Harrān.

That long expedition on Saladin's part shows the complexity of the situation in Upper Mesopotamia, where each party was trying to play on the divisions of his adversaries in order to remain in power. The submission of the Artukid and Zangid emirs to Saladin was never definitively achieved. They often used that relationship as a weapon against an adversary. It could also be abandoned from one day to the next if the threat disappeared or if, upon an emir's death, his successor decided to adopt a less docile attitude. These events attest as well to the considerable energy expended by Saladin to control Upper

Mesopotamia. Of course, as he himself said, domination of that region would allow him to obtain reinforcements for his jihad against the Franks. But to achieve that, was it necessary to extend his power into such distant places? There is reason to doubt it and to believe that Saladin, heady from his many successes, allowed himself to be dragged much further into that quest for power than he had initially intended.

In Harrān, his illness worsened to such a degree that rumors of his death were already beginning to circulate, and doctors from Syria were urgently sent for. In his letters, al-Fādil, who had remained in Damascus, asked that Saladin be transported as quickly as possible to Aleppo, so that he could receive better care than he would in a tent. Al-Fādil also stressed the danger of leaving Saladin in Harrān after his troops had dispersed, particularly given the Turkoman threat.[38] The news reaching al-Fādil about Saladin was mixed. In February 1186, a letter from 'Imād al-Dīn announced that Saladin's health had improved, but it was soon followed by another informing him of the sultan's relapse. While al-Fādil was fretting in Damascus, kept there by his government responsibilities and by an increase in Turkoman attacks that made the roads very dangerous, al-'Ādil arrived at his brother's bedside from Aleppo. One of Saladin's elder sons, al-'Azīz, thirteen years old at the time, was already there and was soon joined by his half-brothers Tūrānshāh and Malikshāh, four and three years old, respectively, accompanied by their mother, the favorite of the moment no doubt. Saladin's state of health seemed so desperate that he decided to divide his territories between his sons and named al-'Ādil as regent.

The sultan gradually recovered, however, and on March 4 was even able to receive an embassy from Mosul that had come to negotiate a peace treaty.[39] Both parties had an interest in putting a definitive end to the hostilities: the Zangids had not obtained the support they were hoping for from the caliph, and Saladin, very weakened, was no longer in a position to mount a siege on Mosul. The terms of that accord were reported in several letters sent by Saladin's entourage to members of his family: 'Izz al-Dīn confirmed his pledge to acknowledge Saladin's suzerainty in the *khutba* and on the coinage and promised, if necessary, to send him troops, whom he would personally command. Each recognized the other's sovereignty over different territories;[40] then, following his habit, Saladin made numerous gifts to the family of the prince of Mosul.

Saladin returned to Damascus in April 1186. The accord he had just concluded with the Zangids, the death of Pahlawān in March 1186, and the difficulties in succession faced by the Seljuks left him untroubled about the eastern front. That was his last campaign east of the Euphrates: he would now devote all his efforts to jihad. Since taking power in 1174, he had spent twice as much time fighting the Muslims as he had battling the Franks. He justified his policy many times, saying that a victorious jihad was not possible without the unification of the Muslim world, which he was the only one capable of leading. His true motivations were undoubtedly more complex, but it behooves us to note the coherence of his arguments. And though that war cost him dear—the resources of Egypt were no longer sufficient—the events that followed would show his real need for the armies from the east in order to fight effectively against the Franks.

Ruler of Yemen and Conqueror of North Africa

The political, economic, and religious motives that impelled Saladin to conquer Yemen in 1174 were diverse: the desire to control the commercial route and wealth of Aden; the personal ambitions of Tūrānshāh; the need to secure a base to retreat to in the event of problems with Nūr al-Dīn; the desire to eliminate the last Ismaili hotbeds of the region and to impose the Sunni *khutba*. Yemen, however, continued to be an unstable and poorly controlled region under Saladin's reign, particularly when a governor who had become powerful sought to emancipate himself from the central power.

Once the conquest was achieved, Saladin expected revenues from Yemen, but they never lived up to his hopes. When Tūrānshāh left Yemen in 1176 to join his brother in Syria, he was accompanied by Majd al-Dīn Ibn Munqidh, who had served as governor of Zabīd. Some years later, Majd al-Dīn was accused of misappropriating the city's revenues. Arrested in Cairo in 1181, he was released in exchange for a payment of more than eighty thousand dinars, an indication of the size of revenues expected for that single region.

Upon leaving the country, Tūrānshāh had appointed governors, but their financial contributions remained very modest. Saladin once complained to his brother al-'Ādil that he had conquered Yemen at great expense without receiving anything in return. In a letter to the governor of Aden, al-Fādil as well asked for an accounting. But the subsidies had trouble arriving, especially since the new governor of Zabīd, Hittān Ibn Munqidh, brother of Majd al-Dīn, had entered into conflict with Emir 'Uthmān al-Zinjārī. The emir, who was ordered by Saladin to arrest Hittān, proved to be a bloodthirsty tyrant, and his

troops were defeated as he was attempting to seize Zabīd. Hittān offered to
bow to Saladin and promised to send ten thousand dinars and supplies for the
Egyptian army.[41] But Saladin preferred to send a former governor of Cairo,
commanding five hundred men, to Zabīd to restore order to its military and financial affairs. In April 1183, Saladin, who was then outside Amida, wrote the
governor to ask for money: "Yemen is a treasury, and we have no trustier guardian of it than you."[42] But a few weeks later, the governor died and was replaced by
Saladin's own brother Tughtegin. In Zabīd, Tughtegin got hold of possessions
whose value, it is said, was more than a million dinars.[43] Hittān and al-Zinjārī
tried to flee with all their belongings, but they were caught and their wealth confiscated. Hittān's riches were also estimated at a million dinars. These two totals,
even if exaggerated, attest to the commercial prosperity of that region and of the
revenues that could be expected from it, despite a political and military situation
that was tumultuous at the very least.[44]

Tughtegin succeeded in becoming a powerful monarch in Yemen while
still remaining loyal to Saladin, as indicated by the coins he had minted in the
name of his brother and Caliph al-Nāsir.[45] He survived Saladin by several years,
and upon his death in 1197, his son al-Muʿizz Ismāʿīl succeeded him. That son
was driven by boundless ambition and even went so far as to lay claim to the
caliphate and to adopt the reign name "al-Hādī" (the Guide),[46] claiming that
the Ayyubids were descended from the Umayyads.[47] Nevertheless, his plan was
rapidly aborted and he was assassinated in the spring of 1202. The Ayyubid expansion into Yemen and, more broadly, into the Arabian Peninsula did not give
Saladin the means—men and money—he had hoped for, though economic relations between the two banks of the Red Sea continued to develop, to the
greater benefit of a few localities in Upper Egypt.[48] That victorious policy in
Yemen made it possible for Saladin's propaganda to burnish his image as a conquering sultan, protector of holy sites, fighter of Shiism, and servant of the Abbasid caliphate. His expansion into Cyrenaica and Tripolitana would also contribute toward reinforcing that image.

In the twelfth century, the region between Alexandria and Tripoli, called
the Barka region by medieval authors, was a buffer zone between Egypt and
the empire of the Almohads, controlled by the Arab and Berber tribes who
lived on its soil.[49] Its conquest by Saladin was part of a policy of general expansion, the first in a series of expeditions, which would be followed the next year
by one to Nubia and some time later by one to Yemen. Saladin made the decision

to send troops west of Egypt in the spring of 1172, and the undertaking was entrusted to his nephew Taqī al-Dīn, who himself assigned one of his Armenian mamluks, Qarāqūsh al-Armanī, to lead the expedition. Like Yemen, North Africa may have represented a potential refuge for the Ayyubid family within the context of the time, namely, the tensions between Nūr al-Dīn and Saladin. That function as a territory of refuge reemerged somewhat later, in 1186, when Qarāqūsh proposed that Taqī al-Dīn, recently dismissed from his post as governor of Egypt, should come take possession of the Barka region. In addition, though Qarāqūsh did not himself take the initiative for the conquest and seems to have remained loyal to the Ayyubid family until 1190, his personal ambitions no doubt played an important role, since he quickly acquired great autonomy in that region.

Some sources also mention economic motives. Saladin was at the time in quest of money to reconstitute the Egyptian army, to fortify the cities, to build madrasas, and to make up for his elimination of illegal taxes in Egypt. It was pointed out to him that the Barka region could provide him with the wealth he needed and that, moreover, it would be easy to conquer. Recent research has shown that North Africa had not been as devastated as previously thought by the invasion of the Arab tribes—the Banū Hilāl—in the mid-eleventh century.[50] Although cities such as Kairouan, whose decline had begun even before the arrival of the Hilalians, took a long time to rise from their ruins, other regions such as Tripolitana were much less affected. In the mid-twelfth century, in any case, the geographer al-Idrīsī attested to the prosperity of Tripoli, mentioning its very popular markets and its territory rich in cereals. The city of Awjila, south of Barka, was very commercial, and the oases of Waddān and Zuwayla were surrounded by date palms and cultivated fields. Zuwayla was an important commercial crossroads, where copper and iron from the north encountered gold and precious stones from Sudan, while on the coast west of Tripoli, many Western merchants came to trade their goods in Gabès.[51] What emerges from the descriptions that have come down to us, therefore, is the image of a region with fertile oases and prosperous markets, traversed by roads linking the Mediterranean to the heart of Africa, and it is easy to understand why Saladin allowed himself to be tempted. Qarāqūsh's campaign against the tribes was justified by the need to establish security on the roads, which was imperiled by the many robberies, and to collect the tithe (zakāt) on the tribal herds.[52]

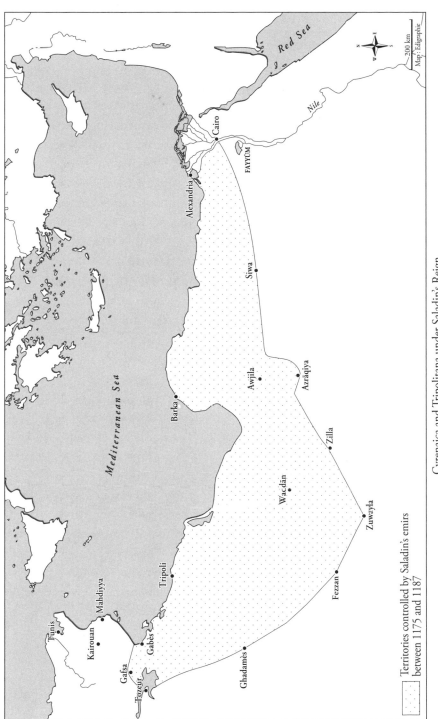

Cyrenaica and Tripolitana under Saladin's Reign

Territories controlled by Saladin's emirs
between 1175 and 1187

Qarāqūsh conducted a first reconnaissance expedition in 1173, during which he reached Tripoli and even made an incursion into the territory of Tunis before returning to Egypt. He left again two years later, this time seizing Awjila and al-Azrāqiya. He left a lieutenant in the region before returning to Cairo with his companions, who, it is said, were homesick. In the letter he wrote to the caliph in 1175, Saladin claimed to control not only the city of Barka but also the Tunisian cities of Gafsa and Tozeur, taken from the Almohads, where according to him the *khutba* was already being said in the name of the Abbasid caliph.[53]

The new expedition that Qarāqūsh organized in 1176 began inauspiciously, since he was arrested in Fayyūm even before he set out, for reasons that remain unclear, and was imprisoned in Cairo on the order of al-ʿĀdil, governor of Egypt at the time. But in 1179 Qarāqūsh returned to Awjila without difficulty and used it as a base to conduct new conquests to the west. With the aid of another of Taqī al-Dīn's emirs, who had arrived in the region some time before with the hope of also making conquests there, he seized Ghadamès, took Tripoli, and then, in the early 1180s, extended his domination to the southern part of present-day Tunisia, making Gabès his capital.[54] In 1185 the arrival of the Banū Ghāniya, a family of Berbers related to the Almoravids, whose power they attempted to restore, only strengthened Qarāqūsh's hold over the region. The Banū Ghāniya solicited the aid of the Abbasid caliph of Baghdad in exchange for recognition of his authority, and the caliph asked Saladin to provide them with the support they needed to impose Abbasid suzerainty in North Africa. The combination of their forces with those of Qarāqūsh led in 1185–1186 to the domination of the greater part of the region, with only Tunis and Mahdiyya still resisting.

Saladin did not draw any direct advantage from these conquests. The tributes paid by the many places conquered and the wealth seized never reached his coffers. They were spent on site or seized by Taqī al-Dīn's successive emirs in the region.[55] The profits to be drawn from these conquests must have been large, since in 1179 serious dissensions arose among the emirs, and each attempted to rally the others' troops to expand his territory. The Arab tribes of the region, themselves divided, lent their aid sometimes to one, sometimes to another. From that fratricidal struggle, which lasted several years and weakened the troops Saladin had sent into North Africa, no emir really came out the winner, since the Almohad reaction was not long in coming. In 1187 the Almohad sovereign Abū Yūsuf Yaʿqūb al-Mansūr himself took over operations, reestablishing control over Gabès and Gafsa in early 1188.

Was Saladin still interested in conquering North Africa, as he had boasted in his letter to the caliph of 1175? By 1189 the context had changed a great deal, and his priorities lay elsewhere: Syria-Palestine in particular, where, to confront the threat of the Third Crusade, he called on the aid of the Almohad sovereign. Qarāqūsh, defeated by the Almohads and deprived of Egyptian support, no longer had any choice but to abandon the alliance with the Banū Ghāniya and submit to the Almohad, which he did in Tunis. In the letter Saladin sent to Abū Yūsuf Ya'qūb al-Mansūr in 1190, Qarāqūsh and his companions were strongly disavowed for their looting and violence: "If the ambassador is questioned about the mamluks Yūzābā and Qarāqūsh, and if he is reminded of what they did within the borders of the Maghreb accompanied by that rabble, whom the combat forces had not wanted, let him explain that these mamluks and their companions were neither mamluks of importance nor emirs nor ranking members of the prince's guards (tawāshiya) nor his officers. Both of them, having failed at their careers, persuaded good-for-nothings like themselves to follow them. Straggling behind great armies are always large mobs, loose elements that constantly drift away as others come in, without anyone realizing whether their numbers are increasing or diminishing."[56]

But ought we to impute cynicism to Saladin, who supposedly sacrificed a loyal lieutenant to obtain the armed support of the Almohads? We will likely never know his real motivations. He had every interest, of course, in condemning the looting by the Turkish armies in order to obtain the aid he required; but it is also clear that, once in North Africa, the emirs acting in his name did as they liked, driven only by their own self-interest, with methods that were not his own and with results from which he drew no benefit. Saladin was aware of this in 1186 when, learning that Taqī al-Dīn was preparing a new expedition into North Africa, he exclaimed: "Although the conquest of the Maghreb is important, that of Jerusalem is even more important. . . . If Taqī al-Dīn takes our veterans with him, I shall have to spend my life assembling men anew, whereas if we conquer Jerusalem and the coast first, we will then be able to attack those provinces."[57]

Qarāqūsh and the other mamluks were therefore abandoned to their fate, and North Africa definitively slipped from Saladin's grasp.

7

The Caliph's Backing

Once Nūr al-Dīn was dead, Saladin strove by every means to obtain the recognition of the Abbasid caliph of Baghdad. The caliph's backing was indispensable to Saladin because, though he held power de facto, he still lacked "authority" (*auctoritas* in medieval Latin texts), that is, the right to lead and command, which only the caliph, the representative of divine authority on earth, could confer on him. Throughout his reign, Saladin regularly wrote the caliph to inform him of his actions, his needs, and his victories. In all his letters he attempted to justify himself and to prove that he was the only one capable of fulfilling the caliph's expectations. Whether he was sincere is a secondary question. In any event, he had little choice: he needed to be invested by the caliph to be recognized as Nūr al-Dīn's legitimate successor, to silence his detractors, and to unify the Muslim Middle East under his authority. The important matter is to determine on what arguments he based his claims and by what paths he achieved his objectives.

Over the course of his reign, Saladin had dealings with two caliphs with very different personalities. Whereas al-Mustadī' (r. 1170–1180) played only an insignificant role in Iraq, al-Nāsir li-Dīn Allāh (r. 1180–1225) would restore a power and luster to the caliphate of Baghdad that it had long lost. Even the political landscape of the Middle East evolved a great deal from one reign to the next. Until about 1180, Saladin, busy imposing his authority in Egypt and Syria, did not have the means to intervene directly in Iraq, and the caliph had no reason to feel threatened. The expedition of 1182, during which Saladin annexed most of the cities of Upper Mesopotamia, obviously changed the rules of the game. Under such conditions, there is nothing surprising in the fact that the two caliphs' attitudes toward him were very different. Al-Mustadī' tended to be accommodating toward Saladin, but al-Nāsir li-Dīn Allāh often displayed mistrust of him and never provided him with the support he was expecting.

The Foundations of Legitimacy

In 1175, the very first arguments Saladin advanced before the caliph to justify his right to succeed Nūr al-Dīn were religious: his defense of Sunni orthodoxy, his struggle against Shiism, and his actions on behalf of the Abbasid caliphate of Baghdad. He began by recalling that it was he who had put an end to the Ismaili dynasty of Egypt and who had "returned to Islam its fugitive children," even though others had sought to attribute the merit to themselves:

We lit the fire with our hands, and others benefited from the brightness.
We made water flow through our hands, and others drank of it.
We exposed our chests to the arrows, and others appropriated the image of it.
We faced the sabers, and others aspired to the highest honors.
There is no doubt that we are claiming our due in the name of justice, which
    restores what has been taken by force.[1]

Was Saladin thinking of Nūr al-Dīn and his posterity in writing those lines? In any event, he appealed to the caliph's sense of justice, demanding fair compensation for his efforts, since he had needed many men and a great deal of money and energy to defeat the enemies of Islam, a coalition of heretics, infidels, *dhimmīs* (non-Muslims living in Islamic territories) with no respect for Muslim law, and African slaves. Saladin thus presented the conquest of Egypt as an undertaking that had allowed the reestablishment of righteous religious law. That religion had been threatened by the Franks in even the most holy sites, Mecca and Medina, but Saladin had known how to protect it by retaking Ayla and barring the Franks access to the Red Sea. Similarly, the conquest of

Yemen was a war against "the lost sheep, the heretic, the rebellious innovator who has left his marks there and has taken his revenge on Islam . . . he who professed innovation, called the people to his father's tomb, to which he gave the name Kaaba, who extorted and squandered the subjects' secured goods, and made intimacy with forbidden bodies licit." Saladin underscored that desire to work on behalf of orthodoxy even in his efforts to conquer Syria, where, he said, "we have corrected false beliefs, irregularities in business matters, corrupt opinions, the jealousy of emirs, the encroachments of the ambitious, and misguided thinking." As for the recent expeditions into North Africa, they had no other aim, according to him, than to curb the Almohad expansion and impose the *khutba* in the name of the Abbasid caliph:

> The rumor had spread that the Banū ʻAbd al-Muʼmin [Almohads] were all-powerful, their kingdom prosperous, their army always victorious, and their authority completely beyond reach. Thanks be to God, we have taken possession of the territories bordering our respective states and extending over a distance of more than a month on foot. We have sent one army after another there and have achieved victory after victory. . . . In all these regions, the *khutba* is said in the name of our master Imam al-Mustadīʼ bi-Amr Allāh, emir of believers—may God's peace be upon him—a situation that Islam had never known, and it is under his insignia and his victorious flag that judgments are made there.

All past and future victories were presented as conquests granted by God to the Abbasid dynasty, through the intermediary of Saladin's armies. But in most of his other letters to the caliph, Saladin also stressed the need for Muslim unification, indispensable for the jihad against the infidels, which, he claimed, he was the only one capable of leading. At a time when he still dominated only part of Syria, he emphasized that it would be impossible to send for Egyptian troops to fight the Franks in Syria-Palestine without at the same time depriving Egypt of defenses and placing it in danger. He also used that argument to demonstrate that only Syrian unity would allow for the enemy's defeat.[2] Between 1180 and 1186, all his undertakings in al-Jazīra were thus justified by the need to strengthen his army in order to fight the Franks. On the ground, meanwhile, he was making the governors of the conquered cities promise to send him troops in the service of jihad. From the caliph he constantly demanded recognition of his power over the region, and though he was pleased to have obtained it for Amida, he regretted not having also received "the key to Mosul."[3] Any argument would do to achieve his ends, including the most unrealistic, such as a pledge to the caliph to fight not only for the conquest of Jerusalem but also for that of Constantinople, the Christian kingdom of Georgia, and the Almohad territories in North Africa:

> Your servant hopes that Mosul will be the access route to Jerusalem and its coast, to Constantinople, the seat of infidelity—despite the distance that separates us from it—and to the land of the Georgians, since, if they all had [true] Islam as their neighbor, their territories would become accessible; and likewise for the lands of the descendants of 'Abd al-Mu'min [Almohads], since a sword bringing water would allow us to put out the fire consuming them. Then the lofty word of God would rise up, Abbasid authority would fill the world, churches would once more become mosques, servile altars would once more become places of devotion, the raised crosses would be nothing but wood in blazing fires, and the whinnying rattles [*nāqūs*] would henceforth be mute in the sanctuaries.[4]

It would be futile, however, to seek behind that bombastic rhetoric any real ambition to extend the empire from the Caspian Sea to the Atlantic, or any desire to obliterate all trace of Christianity. Saladin's actions on the ground, his clearly displayed priorities—to reunify the Muslim Middle East and drive out the Franks—and the measures he took to allow non-Muslims from his territories to live in peace are proof of that. In fact, the words of his secretary al-Fādil must be read simply as the expression of a desire to obtain the caliph's backing whatever the cost, by placing the emphasis on Saladin's desire to unify the Muslim world in order to better fight the Christian states and defend the Abbasid caliphate. The idea of Muslim unification as a condition for the success of the jihad was in itself realistic and surely did not lie within the sphere of mere propaganda. Regardless, it allowed Saladin to justify his expeditions into Iraq with exclusively religious arguments, which can be summed up by this sentence: "To conduct jihad on the path of God, to eliminate the wrongs done to the devotion to God, and to obey the caliph of God."[5]

The portrait Saladin drew of his adversaries allowed him to point out his own positive qualities by way of contrast. When he proclaimed himself a jihad warrior, defender of the righteous religion and of the caliph of Baghdad, he was accusing the Zangids of supporting the heretics, compromising with the infidels and the enemies of the Abbasids. Al-Sālih, Nūr al-Dīn's heir, was the only one to be spared by Saladin, who still wanted to present himself as a faithful servant of his master. It was therefore al-Sālih's youth and inexperience that were emphasized, traits that left him vulnerable to the risk of becoming only a plaything in the hands of unscrupulous emirs. Everywhere in Syria discord and anarchy reigned and the Franks threatened. In addition, Nūr al-Dīn's grand emirs had been thrust aside in favor of incompetent mamluks: "In a word, Syria's order cannot be restored with its present government, and Jerusalem has no leader capable of governing and protecting it." That leader was Saladin himself, of course, whose military successes against the Fatimids and against the Franks had earned him the fear and respect of all, including the "lord of Constantinople, the greatest tyrant and most faithless of the Goliaths, ruler of an empire that has lasted for centuries, leader of a Christendom that recognizes his power and has bowed down to him."[6]

Between the time he took power and the early 1180s, Saladin's criticisms against the Zangids of Mosul became increasingly pointed. In 1182, in the letter he sent to the caliph while in the region of the Euphrates, Saladin accused the Zangids of having concluded an eleven-year truce with the Franks, and of having promised an annual tribute of ten thousand dinars, the surrender of several strongholds along the border of the kingdom of Jerusalem, and the release of all Frankish prisoners, all so that they could attack Saladin on several fronts and prevent him from seizing Mosul. Was not the best proof of their perfidy the fact that their emirs and subjects were soliciting his protection against these greedy governors with no respect for religious law, who were, moreover, traitors to the caliphal cause? For these men, he claimed, "kingship is an inheritance they claim to hold from their ancestors and not from the investiture given by the caliph." In addition, they were corresponding with the enemies of the Abbasid court. Elsewhere, Saladin very clearly accused the Zangids of seeking to restore the Seljuk influence, which was itself being weakened by the efforts al-Nāsir was making to burnish the caliphate's image and authority. That accusation was not groundless, and the caliph could not remain impervious to it. Mosul had in fact asked for Pahlawān's aid in 1184, though it had done so more to put down the emirs' revolt than to oppose the caliph.[7]

Dashed Hopes

Initially, al-Mustadī' responded rather favorably to Saladin's request that the caliph acknowledge him as Nūr al-Dīn's legitimate successor. In 1175 he sent Saladin a diploma of investiture for the territories the sultan was already occupying and for his future conquests, with the exception of al-Sālih's territories. The text of that diploma has come down to us and deserves more attention than it has been given thus far, since it is of great importance for the rest of Saladin's career. It also sums up very well the conception the caliph had of Saladin's power and the qualities he recognized in him.[8]

From the first lines, the titulature granted Saladin stresses the elevated rank at which the caliph wishes to place him: "the very illustrious al-Malik al-Nāsir, the great lord, the learned man, the righteous man, the jihad warrior, and the warrior of the borders." The title "al-Malik al-Nāsir" (the victorious king) was already one Saladin had received from the Fatimid caliph al-'Ādid when he had acceded to the vizierate. Its confirmation by al-Mustadī' was thus an acknowledgment of his power over Egypt. "Very illustrious" and "great lord" (al-ajall al-sayyid al-kabīr) were titles that grand emirs and certain princes, such as Nūr al-Dīn, bore in Syria in the twelfth century. Nūr al-Dīn was also often called a "learned man" and a "righteous man" (al-'ālim, al-'ādil), with reference to his actions on behalf of Sunni law. The epithets al-mujāhid and al-murābit ("jihad warrior" and "warrior of the borders") were intended to place the emphasis on his battle against the Franks; they too held an important place in Nūr al-Dīn's protocol. In attributing all these titles to Saladin, the caliph thus officially acknowledged Saladin's right to a large share of Nūr al-Dīn's moral and political legacy.

Also emerging from that diploma is the essential reason why the caliph granted the investiture to Saladin, namely, his victories in Egypt and Yemen, which allowed for the restoration of Sunni "orthodoxy" in that part of the world. It was to thank Saladin for having strengthened the Abbasid dynasty, and thereby for having served God, that the caliph gave him the investiture over Egypt, Yemen, and all the neighboring territories to be conquered, as well as over Syria, with the exception of the territories controlled by al-Sālih. Al-Sālih's authority was legitimate, since he was the son of Nūr al-Dīn, who had also worked hard on behalf of Islam. Even as the caliph firmly recalled that dynastic legitimacy, he invited Saladin to aid al-Sālih and to remain modest concerning his own victories. In the afterlife, Saladin's true reward would come from God, while in the world below the caliph was already rewarding him with his diploma of investiture and with the honorific trappings that accompanied them, such as the necklace that Saladin would wear around his neck as a sign of their alliance. That privilege clearly placed him above other mortals; Saladin could glory in it and celebrate the anniversary of that recognition every year.

The caliph also sent Saladin a series of injunctions on good governance, as was the custom with that type of diploma. He exhorted him to respect justice, to eliminate the illegal taxes, and to surround himself with qāḍīs and governors of irreproachable honesty. A good sovereign is one who knows how to govern without violence, to control his anger, and to offer the best part of himself. Generous toward the poor, he must perform legal alms. He must pursue the greater jihad, that is, the one waged against oneself for the purpose of fighting one's own evil propensities.[9] But he must also conduct jihad against the infidels and reconquer their territories, especially Jerusalem. For that, he must fortify the border areas—particularly the most vulnerable ones, namely, those on the coast—must equip them with garrisons and with a fleet capable of defending them. Thus, in conferring that diploma on Saladin, the caliph placed him far above his rivals: "The noble *dīwān* confers on you this letter to thank you. In mentioning your name, it places you above its friends, saying: 'You are the one in whom limitless trust is placed, and for the dynasty you are an arrow that goes straight to its target, like a shining flame, an imperishable treasure when the others disappear. What do the absent ones matter, if you are present to defend it?'"

The power hierarchy (God, his Prophet, and the caliph) is underscored, and Saladin's authority exists only because the caliph, lord on earth, delegates it to him. Note as well in the caliph's recommendations the importance granted to justice, which "is equal to sixty years of devotion,"[10] to the need to surround oneself with aides of integrity, and to the ruler's generosity toward the poorest people. All these themes recur constantly in the literature on the good government of princes, and are also central to the praise given Saladin by his panegyrists. As for jihad, the caliph now asked Saladin to engage not only in occasional operations against the Franks but in a vast, adequately funded expedition of reconquest, even though the caliph promised nothing more than his moral support. That diploma nevertheless strengthened Saladin's position a great deal, and he continued to lay claim to it, especially in 1181, after al-Ṣāliḥ's death, when Saladin judged that the restriction imposed by the caliph regarding Nūr al-Dīn's son no longer had any justification, and that Aleppo now ought to devolve onto him.

During the last years of the reign of al-Mustadī', Saladin continued to maintain fairly good relations with the caliph. He informed him regularly of his activities and pointed out the difficulties he faced, given the treachery of the Zangids and the threat of the "infidels"—Armenians, Sicilians, or Franks. At the same time, Saladin assured the caliph of the efforts he was making to satisfy his demands in the matter of justice, the security of the roads and borders, fortifications, and the restoration of the fleet and the army. In a letter of 1179 to the caliph's vizier, Saladin justified his expedition against his rebellious emir, Ibn al-Muqaddam of Baalbek, by accusing al-Muqaddam of seeking the Franks' aid. And, as if in response to the injunctions of the caliph, who had exhorted him a few years earlier to reign without violence, he added that he had abandoned the idea of seizing the city by force, in order to cast into relief his clemency by contrast to his emir's "folly." During the same period, to prove his determination to fight the Franks, Saladin asked the caliph's ambassador to accompany him on an expedition against them and regularly kept al-Mustadī' informed of all victories, particularly the one Saladin had that year in Bayt al-Ahzān. In 1178 al-Mustadī' made a goodwill gesture toward Saladin, agreeing to accept Saladin's intercession in favor of his brother-in-law 'Izz al-Dīn Aq-Burī, who was involved in a revolt against the caliph and had taken refuge in Syria in 1176. He even offered Saladin aid in the form of men and money, in the event that Saladin undertook an offensive against the Franks.[11]

The death of al-Mustadī' and the accession to power of his son al-Nāsir li-Dīn Allāh, at the age of twenty-two, would mark an important turning point in caliphal relations with Saladin: first, because of the new caliph's personality; and second, because of Saladin's new expansion policy in al-Jazīra.[12] The tensions were not immediately perceptible, however, as attested by the arrival of a caliphal embassy in Damascus in November–December 1180, which bestowed on Saladin a new diploma, a set of jewels, and honorific presents, including a black satin robe with wide sleeves embroidered in gold, a black and gold turban and *taylasān*, a necklace adorned with precious stones, a throne, a black flag, horses, gold thread, and many fabrics. Saladin was delighted and jubilantly paraded on horseback in Damascus, dressed in his brand-new finery.[13]

In 1182 the caliph's fears began to become apparent, when Saladin annexed most of the cities of al-Jazīra. Had he seized Mosul, about 350 kilometers from Baghdad, he would have come within close proximity to the lands belonging to the caliph, who did not look kindly on his expansionist aims. That is certainly the reason why al-Nāsir li-Dīn Allāh persisted in refusing to grant Saladin the investiture of Mosul and made an attempt at mediation on several occasions between 1182 and 1184. That mediation was thwarted, however, by the efforts of Mosul to form an alliance with its enemies, the Seljuks of Iran. In 1186, the recognition of Saladin's power by the emir of Mosul, who also renounced the territories south of the Little Zab, only increased the uneasiness of the caliph, who nevertheless managed to retake control of Tikrīt in 1189 and of al-Hadītha in 1190. In reality, during that time Saladin had to face major difficulties resulting from the Third Crusade, and there is nothing to prove that the caliph's fears were founded. From 1186 on, Saladin's priorities were in Syria-Palestine, where he already had his hands full with the Franks. It is difficult to imagine how, at that time, he could also have threatened the caliph's lands.

That is undoubtedly why Saladin did not really understand al-Nāsir li-Dīn Allāh's uneasiness and seems to have attributed the caliph's reluctance to doubts about Saladin's intention to wage jihad. Hence the many passages in his letters evoking his past exploits and asserting his desire to battle the Franks with the aid of the troops from al-Jazīra. Despite the tensions that marked Saladin's relations with the caliph in the following years, the sultan's missives suggest that Saladin continued to hope, at least until 1191, that the caliph would help him.

A first crisis pitted the two men against each other in late 1187. Saladin, as was his habit, had taken care to inform the caliph of his victories against the Franks, which, he said, were intended to strengthen the Abbasid caliph's authority and to fulfill the duty imposed by God. But he made the error of sending a young Iraqi soldier to Baghdad to announce the taking of Jerusalem, instead of dispatching a well-known and respected figure. The caliph took great umbrage. That news, which ought to have delighted all Muslims, also arrived at a time when anti-Saladin propaganda was becoming widespread in the court of Baghdad. In recent years, several dissident notables had left Baghdad to take refuge in Syria, which had encouraged rumors about the ambition of the Ayyubid sovereign. Echoes of that propaganda against Saladin can be heard in the account of the Christian Bar Hebraeus, who explains that relations with the caliph deteriorated because Saladin stopped sending him the Syrian tribute and especially because, under the effect of drink, he said to anyone willing to hear it that he was ready to eliminate the Abbasid *khutba* to reestablish that of the Fatimids. That caricature is devoid of all foundation, but it is probably indicative of the rumors circulating at the time in Iraq to discredit Saladin.[14]

The caliph's response, which Saladin received in December 1187 while he was besieging Tyre, was thus much less enthusiastic than expected. Saladin found he was being criticized for usurping the title "al-Nāsir," for welcoming the Iraqi exiles, and for intervening on the very edge of caliphal territory by corresponding with the Turkomans and Kurds. Meanwhile, his brother Tughtegin of Yemen was accused of creating unrest at the holy sites of the Hejaz. 'Imād al-Dīn closely followed that affair because the caliph's ambassador was none other than 'Imād al-Dīn's brother. And the sultan's secretary was himself given the task of responding to the caliph. 'Imād al-Dīn attests to the emotion Saladin felt upon reading that message. To his secretary and the caliph's ambassador, Saladin protested his good faith and recalled all his past actions, from the conquest of Egypt and Yemen to that of the Syrian coast and Jerusalem, not omitting to mention his absolute submission to the caliph. He added that if the caliph preferred to call him "Salāh al-Dīn" rather than "al-Nāsir," the sultan would be very honored. Other witnesses, less concerned with sparing Saladin's image, record much franker remarks, in which his bitterness and anger clearly come through. The sultan is said to have remarked that the title "al-Nāsir" had been ratified by the Abbasid caliph al-Mustadī' during Nūr al-Dīn's time, as a way of thanking Saladin for putting an end to the Fatimid dynasty. Saladin himself had in his army ten thousand Turkoman and Kurdish soldiers, many of whom bore the title "Salāh al-Dīn," but he took no offense. Finally, concerning Jerusalem, which the caliph claimed had been conquered "under his standards and with his army," Saladin supposedly exclaimed: "Where, then, are his standards and his army? By God, I conquered it only with my own standards and my own army!"[15]

'Imād al-Dīn attempted to smooth things over by imputing the harshness of the caliph's words to the tactlessness of the messenger sent by Saladin, a man of arms unworthy of that mission; to that of the secretary, who had not known how to articulate the caliph's thoughts "in a more delicate, softer, more correct, and more seemly expression"; and to the scheming of Saladin's foes in Baghdad. It was 'Imād al-Dīn who composed the response to the caliph, in which Saladin, even while refuting the accusations made against him, assured the caliph of his greatest respect and complete obedience.[16]

Shortly thereafter, in February 1188, a new crisis nearly caused another misunderstanding between the two men. During the pilgrimage to Mecca, a conflict erupted between the Iraqi leader of the pilgrimage and Saladin's emir Ibn al-Muqaddam, head of the Syro-Palestinian pilgrimage. During the scuffle that ensued, Ibn al-Muqaddam lost his life. The caliph's apologies were not sufficient to erase the uneasiness and the climate of suspicion that arose from the incident. Four years later, when Saladin was planning to make his pilgrimage to Mecca, several of his advisers dissuaded him from doing so, arguing that some might suspect him of wanting to avenge Ibn al-Muqaddam's death.[17]

The correspondence between Saladin and the caliph nonetheless continued. In late March 1189, an ambassador arrived in Damascus to ask that the name of the caliph's heir presumptive henceforth be pronounced in the *khutba* and inscribed on coins. To inform the caliph of his recent victories over the Franks, Saladin sent his own ambassador in return, who arrived in Baghdad with, in addition to the traditional gifts, Frankish knights as prisoners.[18]

Nevertheless, on August 29, 1189, the Franks' siege of Acre began. It would last nearly two years. Muslim optimism in the first weeks quickly gave way to anxiety. A new embassy was sent to the caliph to propose that the province of Shahrazūr be exchanged for a few armed troops.[19] Since the embassy did not return quickly enough, in October Saladin dispatched one of his closest friends, Qādī Ibn Shaddād, to ask the emirs of the region and the caliph for immediate aid. But that initiative did more to spread confusion than to bring about a solution. Ibn Shaddād returned empty-handed. After Saladin's ambassador had gone back to Baghdad once again, in late 1189, to inform the caliph of the unprecedented mobilization of the Western Christian armies, the response that reached Saladin outside Acre in spring 1190 was again disappointing. Two loads of naphtha, a few good-quality spear shafts, five experts in Greek fire (*naft*), and a letter of credit authorizing Saladin to borrow twenty thousand dinars from merchants on the caliph's behalf: that was the sum total of the caliph's participation in the battles against the Franks. Saladin confided his disappointment to his close circle, remarking ironically that such a sum would only just cover expenses for one day, pointing up the contrast to the million dinars the Fatimid caliph had sent him during the siege of Damietta. It was al-Fādil who best summed up Saladin's resentment and that of his entourage: "The letter from Baghdad is an insipid, cold, and dry letter, there is nothing to be drawn from it, it is neither here nor there. We were asking for molten gold, but we were hit with cold iron."[20]

Saladin made several more attempts. In early summer 1190, he informed the caliph of the ominous rumors that had reached him regarding the German Crusade. And, throughout the winter of 1190–1191, as he faced increasing difficulties, Saladin turned to al-Nāsir li-Dīn Allāh several times. "Islam is asking for your aid the way a drowning man would cry for help!" he wrote in one of his letters. And he recalled that the Franks were arriving by the thousands from all regions of the West. In his letters, Saladin also complained about the length of the siege of Acre and of his men's weariness, and asked that fresh troops be sent to him. His arguments were religious but also political. In the West, he said, the pope was sparing no effort to mobilize the forces of Christendom to liberate Christ's tomb. Was not the caliph the worthy successor of the Prophet Muhammad? Saladin reminded him that the Muslim community had been entrusted to the caliph, which also meant that the caliph was obliged to defend it. The sultan asserted that, for his part, he would stand fast to prevent anyone from destroying the Prophet's posterity—that is, the caliph—and Ayyūb's posterity, namely, himself, a comparison that may not have been to the caliph's liking.[21]

Saladin continued to write after the fall of Acre on July 12, 1191, to explain his tactics against the Franks and to communicate the losses he was inflicting on them, but also his own difficulties in procuring horses and weapons, his army's poor morale, and the inadequacy of the reinforcements he was receiving from Iraq.[22] The caliph's preoccupations lay elsewhere, however. The letters he sent to Saladin in the autumn of that same year show that he was primarily concerned with strengthening his power in the East in the face of the decline of the last Seljuks. For the most part, he expressed his discontent to Saladin at seeing the sultan's nephew Taqī al-Dīn, who had just received a large part of Upper Mesopotamia, leading an offensive against Akhlāt, to the north of his territories. The caliph also demanded the release of the Seljuk sultan Toghril's brother-in-law. Finally, al-Nāsir li-Dīn Allāh asked that al-Fādil be sent to him to settle the matter.

Saladin responded with his usual arguments: Taqī al-Dīn had crossed the Euphrates only to assemble troops for the jihad; Saladin had not given the order to attack Akhlāt and had asked Taqī al-Dīn to retreat; the Seljuk had been neutralized only because he was conducting raids and pillaging caravans, but in Syria he would receive *iqtāʿs* to induce him to join the jihad. As for al-Fāḍil, Saladin expressed his regret at not being able to send him on the journey to Baghdad because of his secretary's poor state of health.[23]

That dialogue of the deaf continued throughout 1192. In July the caliph had one of his grand emirs incarcerated, accusing him of having secretly turned to Saladin to incite him to send troops to Iraq. In early October, the lieutenant of the vizierate sent an embassy to al-ʿĀdil to invite him to play the role of intermediary, in order to open new negotiations between Saladin and the caliph. Nevertheless, though Saladin once again sent his loyal ambassador Diyāʾ al-Dīn to Baghdad,[24] nothing more transpired before Saladin's death on March 4, 1193. A few months later, al-Afdal, who had succeeded his father in Damascus, sent Diyāʾ al-Dīn on an embassy to the caliph with his father's military equipment (saber, helmet, coat of mail, and horse) and various valuable gifts, including the relic of the True Cross taken from the Franks, a number of precious fabrics, and four young slave girls, among them Balian's daughter and the daughter of the lord of Jabala. The letter sent to the caliph effusively praised Saladin's past actions and asserted al-Afdal's desire to pursue his work, with the caliph's recognition and support.[25]

In the history of his relations with the caliphate, the results Saladin achieved were therefore very limited. The recognition of his power in 1175, renewed in 1180, initially allowed him to establish his authority over Egypt and Syria. By contrast, his claims on Upper Mesopotamia were much less well received by the caliph, who remained deaf to all his demands of military and financial aid on behalf of the jihad. That attitude can be explained primarily by the fact that the caliph suspected Saladin of having designs on Iraq and that the caliph himself needed all his forces and means to rebuild his authority and his territory against the last Seljuks. That lack of communication and dialogue was certainly one of the failures Saladin had the most difficulty facing and accepting.

8

Conception of Power

In his advance toward power, Saladin was aided primarily by his military successes and by the divisions among his adversaries. In addition, his family heritage, his determination to apply religious law and to lead the jihad, and above all the caliph's backing provided him with the necessary authority, without which his reign would have appeared to be a tyranny. In contemporary societies, a political authority finds its legitimacy in elections. In Islamic countries of the Middle Ages, that legitimacy rested on respect for a hierarchical system for delegating powers. The caliph held his power from God. He delegated a part of it to the sovereign (sultan, prince, grand emir), who himself named representatives or aides to exercise justice in his name, to manage the administration, to keep order, and to defend the territory, all theoretically in the service of God and for the good of the subjects.

Although Saladin strove to conform to that general pattern, he also introduced more-personal touches dictated by the circumstances, the influences upon him, or quite simply by his character. For example, to each of the regions subject to his authority—Egypt, Syria, and Upper Mesopotamia—he ascribed a determinate place and role, as a function of his two principal objectives: Muslim reunification and the battle against the Franks. In his method of government, he privileged caution and negotiation, which did not prevent him from some-times resorting to violence to eliminate his adversaries. His main source of sup-port was his family, and from the beginning his brothers, nephews, and later his sons were appointed to very important positions. Under his authority, they ruled territories that soon constituted a vast family confederation.

Geopolitics, or "Love of Country"?

Would Egypt, the first territory to come under Saladin's control, be the seat of his power? From the foundation of the new city of Cairo in 969, the Fatimids had made it their capital, from which they had attempted to control—not al-ways successfully—Ifriqiya (present-day Tunisia), the cradle of their dynasty, as well as Syria and the holy sites. At the time, Egypt was considered a rich coun-try, and the notion of its self-sufficiency was fairly widespread among its inhab-itants, who readily said that the world needed Egypt but that Egypt could very well dispense with the world. From a political point of view, that maxim could have encouraged the establishment of an Egyptian power that was turned in on itself, and whose only objective in terms of foreign relations would have been to serve its own interests.[1] In reality, the aim of that popular tradition, evoked by the sources in descriptions of what their authors call a city's or re-gion's "merits" (fadā'il), was primarily to praise Egypt and show its preemi-nence. Every leader, Saladin first and foremost, knew that the country drew its wealth not only from its soil and its artisanal products but also from trade, open to both the Indian Ocean and the Mediterranean. The question that arises is therefore less whether Egypt would draw back behind its borders than whether Saladin would choose it as the seat of government for his states.

The importance of Egypt in Saladin's military plan of action was indisput-able. That country, which had witnessed the birth of his power, had, by the end of Nūr al-Dīn's reign, become the point of departure for his domination of Nu-bia, Yemen, Cyrenaica, and Tripolitana, and throughout his reign it remained his main supplier of men and money. In autumn 1174 Saladin left to conquer Syria at the head of an Egyptian force of some seven hundred cavalrymen, and was joined in April 1175 by new reinforcements, who helped him defeat the Zangid army. A few weeks later, Saladin authorized his men to return to Egypt, since it was difficult to keep such an army mobilized for long. After a few months, the soldiers yearned to return to their families, and the emirs, remunerated through a system of tax levies on the lands of Egypt, were eager to be there at harvest time. In that respect, the distance that separated Egypt from Syria did not simplify matters.

From 1176 to 1183, Saladin regularly asked his brother al-'Ādil, his representative in Egypt, to send him armed reinforcements. The Egyptian troops sometimes paid a heavy tribute to the war, as in the case of the Battle of Ramla in November 1177. In 1187, the Egyptian army participated in the Battle of Hattīn alongside the Syrian and Mesopotamian contingents, and, on various occasions, Saladin sent to Egypt for emirs in whom he had every confidence. In 1188, for example, he appealed to Qarāqūsh al-Asadī—who had already demonstrated his abilities by overseeing fortification projects in Cairo—to rebuild the fortifications of Acre. In addition, Egypt was the only Muslim country in the region to possess a fleet, and Saladin made use of it many times to attack the Frankish cities on the coast.[2] In 1187, the Egyptian fleet participated in the defense of all the coastal cities retaken by Saladin, just as it took an active role in the blockade of Tyre and the resistance to the Franks' siege of Acre in 1190–1191.

The considerable efforts that Egypt agreed to expend in the conquest of Syria and the pursuit of jihad were not lost on the Franks, who understood the extent to which the Muslim defense of Syria now depended on the arrival of Egyptian aid. That is why the Frankish attacks in the thirteenth century, as a matter of priority, were directed against Egypt. That financial and military participation also had very severe consequences for the Egyptian public treasury. Al-Fādil, to whom the burdensome task of managing the Egyptian budget fell, complained many times about the country's state of impoverishment. In 1184 he warned Saladin about the exorbitant Egyptian military expenses: five million dinars were needed that year to pay for raising an army in just one province of the country.[3] In 1189–1190, he again counseled moderation, reminding Saladin of the many difficulties facing Egypt, though al-Fādil remained aware of the need for these expenses:

> Our master spent Egypt's money to conquer Syria, Syria's money to conquer al-Jazīra, and the money of all to conquer the coast. God willing, the money of Constantinople will be spent for the conquest of Rome, and all the rulers will then be only his bursars, watching over their treasuries while waiting to hand them over to him. God thanks him for everything he has [already] taken from

them and despises them for all the gold and silver they have hoarded.
Let there be no distress in our master's heart, for God will not reduce the supplies the master generously distributes, especially since
it is thanks to that generosity that people earn their livelihood.[4]

The Egyptian influence on the political and administrative system set in
place by Saladin was also apparent in his assimilation of a number of former
Fatimid institutions. Saladin began his career as vizier to the Fatimid caliph
and was surrounded by former Fatimid administrators, foremost among them
al-Fāḍil, his chief adviser. Several of them composed treatises for him describing in detail the religious, civil, and military administrative institutions of
Egypt during the Fatimid era. This ought to be seen as a desire not to destroy
the work of his predecessors—even if they were his Shiite foes—but rather to
preserve the memory of it. Hence the Ayyubid institutions and posts retained
visible traces of that Fatimid legacy, which was assimilated in the same way as
the Abbasid and Seljuk legacies.[5]

All the same, despite Egypt's crucial role in the military and financial
realm, Saladin only rarely governed from Cairo. In his nineteen years of reign,
from 1174 to 1193, he resided in Egypt for a total of only two and a half years,[6]
and when he left that country in March 1182, he never went back. The governorship of Egypt was then entrusted to his brother al-ʿĀdil until 1183, to his
nephew Taqī al-Dīn ʿUmar from 1184 to 1186, then again to al-ʿĀdil until 1192.
During that entire period the administration was headed by Qāḍī al-Fāḍil. Saladin for his part ruled from Syria, especially Damascus, but usually in an itin-
erant manner, as his military campaigns allowed. In addition, despite the decisive influence exerted on him by the Fatimid institutions, Egypt's highly
centralized system never took root in the rest of his territories and remained
an Egyptian particularism, a legacy of its history, also attributable, no doubt,
to its particular geographical situation.[7]

As for Syria, it held a central place in Saladin's plan of action, primarily for
geostrategic reasons. He needed to move closer to the battlefield, that is, to the
Franks, and in 1175 Saladin wrote to the caliph: "From Egypt, we could not
undertake that conquest [of the Frankish territories] because of the great distance, the deserts to be crossed, and the fatigue of the mounts on which the
strength of the jihad rests. When we moved closer, the matter was simplified,
we drew great advantages from that move and a greater efficacy."[8]

From Syria, Saladin could extend his domination over Upper Mesopotamia, between the Tigris and the Euphrates, in order to draw the reinforcements necessary for the jihad even while remaining close to Egypt, from which a large part of the money and men came. But Saladin's interest in the region also had more personal roots. Syria was the country of his childhood and youth. Baalbek, Aleppo, and Damascus were cities where he had lived for several years alongside his father and uncle and to which he was very attached. That was especially true of Damascus, of which Ibn Shaddād said: "[Saladin] loved this city and preferred residence there over all other places."⁹ One day in 1186, Saladin confided to ʿImād al-Dīn, upon returning to Damascus after his campaign in Upper Mesopotamia: "Praise be to God, who has brought us back and who, in repelling adversity, has returned our homeland to us."¹⁰ The Damascenes reciprocated that love, if we are to judge by the enthusiastic welcome they showed him that day.

The correspondence he exchanged in about 1184–1185 with Ibn Najā, an Egyptian sermonist, illustrates his deep fondness for Damascus. Disappointed that Saladin was no longer living in Egypt, Ibn Najā attempted to entice him back by praising the delight of the Nile and its gardens, the beauty of the Cairo Nilometer, the majesty of the pyramids, palaces, and mosques, all qualities that according to him made that country, mentioned in the Koran and in the narratives of the first Islamic conquests, a land superior to all others.¹¹ Saladin replied, in the words of ʿImād al-Dīn—who was himself very attached to Damascus—in terms that left little doubt about his preferences. Nothing in his eyes equaled the climate, the landscapes, the souks, and the fruits of Damascus, whose canals were at least as beautiful as the Nilometer of Cairo. Saladin's arguments and those of his secretary reiterated all the qualities traditionally attributed to Syria in the literature of the *fadāʾil*, that is, works vaunting the merits of a city or region. Like Egypt, is not Syria, which the Prophet had called the "best of countries, where God will lead his best worshippers," mentioned in revelation?¹² Was it not chosen as a residence by several Companions of the Prophet? The conquest of Damascus marked the beginnings of Islam, and even Egypt occupied its prominent place in the Koran only because the prophet Joseph was brought there from Syria. That country, where the jihad was conducted against the infidels, was superior to all others. Even the pyramids can hardly compare to the sacred esplanade of Jerusalem,¹³ the majesty of Mount Lebanon. And Saladin went on to cite an apocryphal hadith: "Love of country is a sign of faith."¹⁴

Finally, though it is true that Egypt is remarkable for the abundance of its products, the excellence of its water, and the great number of its kings, did not al-Fādil himself affirm that Damascus is the garden of Egypt, hence the most beautiful garden in the world?

These epistolary exchanges were a kind of literary sparring match, often engaged in during that period, which repeated a number of topoi. But they also reflect the real attachment Saladin felt for Syria. In all these texts, the merits of a city or region are assessed with reference to religious texts (the Koran and the Sunna), to what God and his Prophet said, and to the specific role of the place in the early days of Islam. The importance of the religious is also perceptible in the evocation of the jihad and in the allusion to "love of country [watan]," in accordance with the words of the Prophet. At that time, the term watan had no political connotations but rather the general sense of a birthplace or residence. Fidelity to the native land, that longing for one's native country—which is also echoed in the West[15]—was fairly widespread in Arabic literature. "If the bird is homesick for its nest, how much more may a man pine for his country!"[16] wrote the famous prose writer al-Jāhiz in the eleventh century.

Saladin had several opportunities to display his affection for Syria. One day, in a letter to al-Fādil, he compared the Egyptian phase of his career to an affair with "a whore [Egypt] who in vain had tried to part me from my faithful wife [Syria]."[17] Outraged by that provocative metaphor, al-Fādil replied in the same tone: How dare the sultan insult a country that had come to his aid when the Franks were threatening to destroy him? The sufferings of Damascus, when compared to those of Egypt, were only "a drop of water in the sea," and if, by some unhappy chance, it occurred to Saladin to launch a single arrow against that country, al-Fādil said he himself would raise his hand high enough to stop it.

Saladin was not the only one in his family to attest to such love for Syria. He learned one day that his brother Tūrānshāh wished to leave Yemen and return to live in Syria. Saladin sent him a messenger to dissuade him and to remind him that Yemen was a great, rich country. Tūrānshāh then sent for the majordomo, handed him a thousand gold pieces and "ordered him to send to the market and buy a lump of ice with that sum." The majordomo replied: "My lord, this is Yemen, and how can ice be found in it?" Tūrānshāh said: "Tell them then . . . to buy with it a tray of [lawzī] apricots."[18] The majordomo replied: "How could such a fruit be found here?" And the dialogue went on, with the enumeration of all sorts of fruits found in Damascus and unavailable in Yemen. Tūranshāh concluded by turning to Saladin's messenger: "I should like to know what is to be done with these riches, since they cannot procure me the pleasures of life, nor furnish me with what I desire?"[19] Saladin finally gave him permission to return to the country of their childhood, to which both were so deeply attached.

Saladin's perception of Iraq was completely different. His first expeditions into Upper Mesopotamia had no other aim than to secure possession of northern Syria, first by preventing reinforcements from arriving from Mosul, and then by exchanging the cities he had seized in al-Jazīra for Aleppo. After 1183, by contrast, his expeditions east of the Euphrates were justified primarily by the need to recruit troops for his jihad against the Franks and to strengthen the defense of the Syrian cities, which Egypt, itself threatened from within and without, was no longer up to protecting.[20] Although Saladin was briefly tempted to extend his power well beyond the border regions of his states, the illness to which he almost succumbed in 1186 brought him back to more realistic objectives, closer to those he was officially proclaiming. Once the accord with Mosul and the principal cities of al-Jazīra was signed, his actions on the ground show that he had given up his expeditions into that region, though he continued to complain about not receiving as much aid as he had wished. In 1191, two years before his death, he agreed to entrust the western part of al-Jazīra to his nephew Taqī al-Dīn, but made him promise to respect the accord previously concluded with the other emirs. The consolidation of the Ayyubid presence in that region corresponded less to Saladin's immediate interests than to Taqī al-Dīn's ambitions. Saladin could hardly refuse to hand over the territories of al-Jazīra that his nephew was demanding, but if he expected any more military aid, the events that followed—namely, Taqī al-Dīn's death that same year and the onset of the revolt by Taqī al-Dīn's son al-Mansūr—would show Saladin that family solidarity could not always be taken for granted. In the end, it was al-ʿĀdil who inherited these ill-assorted and fragmented territories of Upper Mesopotamia, and it was he, much more than Saladin, who laid the foundations of Ayyubid power in that region.

The system set in place by Saladin, which made Syria a strategic region, thus resulted both from geopolitical considerations and from a strong personal attachment to the country. Saladin's homeland was Syria, Damascus in particular, and when he was gravely ill in 1185, he expressed the wish to be buried there. It was in fact in that city that he died a few years later and that he was interred. Hence, though Egypt indisputably retained a central political and economic role throughout his reign, expressed especially in its monopoly on minting gold coins, Syria prevailed in the sultan's heart. That is undoubtedly the reason why he seems to have hesitated to divide up the territories among his sons. Saladin at first left his eldest son, al-Afdal, in Egypt, under the guardianship of Taqī al-Dīn, but later, in 1186, sent for al-Afdal to come to Damascus. And before his death, Saladin bequeathed that city to his eldest son. Egypt devolved on his younger son al-'Azīz. In the thirteenth century, however, al-Afdal's rather weak personality and the much greater resources of Egypt would reinforce the central role of that country in the Ayyubid balance of power, a role Saladin had not so clearly attributed to it.

Caution and Coordination

Is it possible to speak of Saladin's methods of government while at the same time avoiding the eternal debate about how much faith ought to be granted to the praise bestowed on him? Perhaps not completely. But solely in terms of his actions on the ground, it is easy to observe that his internal and external policy, toward the Muslims and toward the Franks, was most often characterized by an attitude of caution, coordination, and negotiation.

From the beginning of his political career in Egypt, Saladin displayed great prudence. Like his troops of Kurdish and Turkish soldiers, Saladin was considered a stranger in Egypt, a devout Sunni in a country where Shiism played an important role—though the majority of the population remained Sunni—and he had to advance one small step at a time to be accepted. For more than two years, therefore, he took time to eliminate his political foes, to quash the revolts in Upper Egypt, to repel the Franks, to secure connections with Syria, and to begin the redistribution of the major religious posts before he definitively considered eliminating the Fatimid caliphate. That slowness and caution were criticized by Nūr al-Dīn and led some—the historian Ibn al-Athīr in particular—to suspect him of evil intentions, but after the fact they proved to have been effective, since the change of regime in Egypt gave rise to very little backlash and few revolts.

Saladin employed the same political caution in the wake of Nūr al-Dīn's death. Rather than lay claim to his succession directly, he at first presented himself as the servant of the Zangid dynasty and claimed that he wanted nothing more than to serve the young heir, al-Sālih. In the face of resistance from al-Sālih and his entourage, Saladin gradually came to declare that Nūr al-Dīn's succession ought to devolve on him because of his own family legacy—Shīrkūh was one of Nūr al-Dīn's closest collaborators—but also because he was the only one capable of continuing the battle for Muslim unity and the jihad against the Franks.

He also displayed caution in his attitude toward Aleppo, preferring to accept the caliph's arbitration, leaving the region to al-Sālih rather than pursuing a struggle that risked being long and exhausting. The same was true in Mosul in 1182, when he preferred to withdraw, head held high, in order not to suffer a setback or to expend all his strength in a siege with an uncertain outcome. In his letters, however, he insisted that he had struck camp only in obedience to the caliph.[21] And finally, he was cautious in his strategy toward the Franks, which led him at first to conduct defensive raids for the most part, or raids intended to assure security of communications between Egypt and Syria, before considering expeditions of greater scope once Muslim unity had been realized. There again, his detractors sometimes said that the struggle against the infidels interested him less than the acquisition of new territories, but it should be noted that without the unification of the Egyptian, Syrian, and Mesopotamian armies, the victory of Hattīn and the conquests that followed from it could hardly have come about.

In his conduct of political affairs, Saladin also strove to follow the advice of Sheikh al-Harawī, who wrote in the late twelfth century: "If an affair is tormenting the sultan, if an enemy attacks him, if a misfortune befalls him, if some unpleasantness affects him, or if a calamity tests him, he must consult among his friends and family, his courtiers, and the dignitaries of his kingdom, people of good counsel and experience."[22]

At the time, the term "council" (majlis) covered the rather vague notion of a political and religious entourage. Saladin's council took various forms, depending on the circumstances and where he happened to be. It did not always include the same people, and it met when the sultan needed it. Saladin rarely governed alone. Before any important appointment or strategic decision, he liked to surround himself with emirs, men of religion, and administrators to ask for their opinion on the path to take. The discussions seem to have been fairly free, with opposing opinions often expressed, and Saladin did not always impose his own point of view. He frequently came to adopt the view of his emirs or advisers, out of conviction or simply pragmatism. The council he assembled around him in autumn 1189 during the Franks' siege of Acre illustrates fairly well the climate in which the debates occurred:

> On Thursday, the 29th day of Sha'ban, 585 [October 12, 1189], the greatest among the emirs presented themselves to the sultan. He told them: "Know that those people [the Franks], enemies of Allah—and of us—have brought their cavalry and their infantry. They are pressing down on us with all their might, have come out with all their impiety against Islam as a whole, have assembled and concentrated their troops, have been lavish with their resources. If we do not march in haste against their militias while the sea is cutting off their retreat, tomorrow the evil they do will be impossible to remedy, and it will be difficult to thwart them. In fact, when the sea is calm and the traveler finds navigation easy, the number of enemies will double. . . . None of the Muslims will aid us, none in the land of Islam will support us. Our soldiers are present, our resolutions are impervious to delay, the eyes of our swords look toward the enemy to attack. . . . As a result, we are entirely of the opinion that we should prepare ourselves for combat before they are informed of the debates that keep us from them." And he added: "Let each of you give your opinion, and do not hazard a word that would exceed your good judgment!" They therefore tugged back and forth and differed in their opinions based on the diversity of their inclinations. . . . Some said: "For fifty days, we have not dismounted and, during those nights, we have not tasted sleep, we have not closed our eyes for nocturnal dreams. . . . Our emaciated mounts are exhausted, our sabers are chipped, our soldiers weary. And now winter is come. . . . The right choice is to temporize over the winter, to rebuild our strength and that of our horses, to withdraw from those positions and so gain the advantage we are hoping for, to name those who will serve as replacements to prevent them from leaving. When the cold ends we shall come back to tame those savages. . . . Without a doubt, the Muslims will aid us. . . . Then we will reach the end of temporization: we will prove our

tenacity in combat and in victory. . . . We will break them, be they mountains! We will wear them down, be they seas!" . . .

We did not cease to deliberate, to confer, to discuss, to respond, to contest, and to fight, until the views had been sifted through and what seemed to be the fairest way of proceeding came to light. In the end, we were inclined toward repose, we wanted an end to our troubles and to be at peace, to abandon the siege for a peaceful sojourn, the dusty battlefield for the camp toward which one hastens.[23]

That decision displeased 'Imād al-Dīn, who attributed Saladin's retreat to his great physical fatigue. Nevertheless, this was not the only time that Saladin adopted the viewpoint of his emirs. In late 1187, the decision to lift the siege of Tyre was made at their instigation, and in September 1192, it was under pressure from them that Saladin resigned himself to signing a truce with the Franks. Other times, the decision was made unanimously, as in September 1191, when Ascalon had to be destroyed.[24]

With his adversaries as well, Saladin privileged diplomacy. All the sources underscore his natural predisposition toward negotiation and clemency. It might be thought this was merely panegyrics, but the facts confirm that character trait, which Saladin seems to have erected into a political and military strategy. Negotiation with the Franks raised special problems, but with his Muslim foes Saladin usually managed through discussion to avoid depleting his forces in long, pointless sieges. It was rare that he took a Muslim stronghold by force. Most of the cities of Syria and Upper Mesopotamia offered their submission immediately or after a relatively short siege. There were several reasons for that. Upon arriving in Syria, Saladin had only a few hundred soldiers. Even if he could count on the troops from Damascus to arrive fairly quickly, he could not hope to conquer the entire region and confront the Zangids solely with his own military forces. He had to negotiate, to persuade his adversaries that they would have everything to gain by accepting his authority. When an army was defeated, such as the Zangid army in 1175 and 1176, he seized the weapons and matériel but let the prisoners go and did not seek to wipe out the defeated. When the governor of a citadel or a city agreed to come over to his side, Saladin let him keep his post or gave him another stronghold in exchange for his own. And, to obtain the surrender of a city, Saladin sometimes even allowed its governor to leave his territory and go enter the service of the sultan's adversaries.

Among the significant cases, that of Ibn al-Zaʿfarānī, one of Nūr al-Dīn's former emirs, is particularly enlightening. Ibn al-Zaʿfarānī, having rallied behind Saladin upon the sultan's arrival in Syria, had retreated to his citadel in Bārīn, southwest of Hama. In exchange for his surrender in May 1175, he was allowed to leave Syria, and he took that opportunity to go join the Zangid prince of Mosul, who entrusted Edessa to him. When Saladin mounted a siege outside that city a few years later, in 1182, the emir agreed to surrender and Saladin took him back in his service, despite his former betrayal. He treated his bitter rival, Emir Qubt al-Dīn Īnāl, lord of Manbij, with the same indulgence. This was the same man who had insulted and threatened him after Nūr al-Dīn's death. The citadel of Manbij was one of the few that Saladin took by force, in 1176, and his enmity toward its governor no doubt played a role. All the same, even in that case, Saladin spared Qutb al-Dīn's life. ʿImād al-Dīn even claims that Saladin attempted to make good use of Qutb al-Dīn's services and keep him nearby, an offer that Qutb al-Dīn is said to have rejected. Although ʿImād al-Dīn may have exaggerated the generosity Saladin displayed, the emir, once liberated, went to join the prince of Mosul, who entrusted Rakka on the Euphrates to him. It was outside the walls of that city that Saladin found him in 1182. This time, the emir surrendered without resistance and was allowed to keep his own possessions. A few weeks later, the Artukid emir of Hisn Kayfā also agreed to hand over his fortress in exchange for Saladin's promise to give him Amida.

Many other examples could be cited to illustrate that policy both generous and pragmatic. In late 1182, Saladin showed the same clemency toward the governor of Sinjār, then in 1183 toward the governor of Hārim, to whom he promised, in exchange for his fortress, the governorship of Busra, a house in Damascus with an adjoining bath, a village in the area, and thirty thousand dinars for him, along with ten thousand dinars for his brother. The governor had the foolhardiness to refuse that offer and to seek an alliance with the Franks. Then the garrison appealed to Saladin, offering to hand over the citadel in exchange for its freedom. In reply to an emir who attempted to warn him against these soldiers, whom the emir judged unreliable, Saladin said: "We still wish to seize a certain number of places. If we refuse what we have promised and are not generous with the benefits, no one will ever trust us again."[25]

Saladin's concern to spare his enemies and to avoid humiliating them, to leave those who submitted to him with their possessions, to avoid pillaging, and to respect his pledges thus stemmed less from a "chivalrous generosity" or from some idealistic view of the world than from a carefully considered policy, though it is not always easy to establish a clear distinction between his personal convictions and his political self-interest. It is because he knew how to combine military pressure and skillful diplomacy that Saladin achieved his ends. The discipline he imposed on his armies could only increase his popularity with the people and hence facilitate his conquests. In preventing looting, he also preserved the prosperity of the regions that now belonged to him. Once victory was achieved, Saladin took a series of measures designed both to reassure and to satisfy the populations. He received the notables with honor, eliminated the illegal taxes, and repaired the damage caused by his army or by the siege. It is clear that such a wise and prudent policy was in great part the source of his successes.

9

Founding a Dynasty

To legitimate power taken by force, a sovereign could use a number of arguments: religious (suppression of heresy, restoration of orthodoxy), military (his unique ability to repel the enemy), or dynastic (a prestigious ancestry). Saladin could not lay claim to any well-known family. For the most part, therefore, he used a religious and military line of argument. His nephew al-Mu'izz ibn Tughtegin in Yemen went much further than he, not hesitating to invent an Umayyad ancestry for himself, in an attempt to be recognized not only as a prince but also as a caliph. That claim was destined to fail, but it is still indicative of the role played by such fictive genealogies, designed to assert, in the East and in the West, nobility or political legitimacy. For the West, we need only recall the importance assumed by the myth of the Franks' Trojan origins, which surfaced in the seventh century. For the East, there were many Persian, Turkish, or Berber dynasties that converted to Islam and that strove to link their families to the great Arab tribes of the Arabian Peninsula. For example, in fifteenth-century Samarkand, at the heart of the Turkish-Mongol empire, the Arabic inscriptions on Tamerlane's mausoleum presented him as a descendant of 'Alī, cousin and son-in-law of the Prophet, to reinforce his image as an ideal Muslim ruler.[1] Although no one gave any credence to the claims of al-Muʿizz—he was, moreover, harshly condemned by the other Ayyubid princes, who had no interest in antagonizing the caliph of Baghdad—it was still possible to read a text in the second half of the thirteenth century diffusing a fictive genealogy for Ayyūb that had him descend from Adam through the Arab tribes from the northern Arabian Peninsula.[2]

Saladin laid claim to his family legacy in a completely different manner. He used it to succeed his uncle Shīrkūh to the Fatimid vizierate and then to assert his rights to act as regent to the young al-Sālih. He was not unaware that this legacy gave him no right to reign. He acquired his legitimacy as a sovereign much more through his religious, political, and military actions. But to assure its solidity and continuity, in the early days he opted for a political system founded on family solidarity and on group spirit, or the spirit of kinship, which the great historian Ibn Khaldūn defined in the fourteenth century as the principal driving force of history: "When a person sharing in the spirit of kinship [ʿasabiyya] has reached the rank of chieftain and commands obedience, and when he then finds the way open toward superiority and [the use of] force, he follows that way, because it is something desirable. He cannot completely achieve his [goal] except with the help of the spirit of kinship, which causes [the others] to obey him. Thus, royal superiority is a goal to which the spirit of kinship leads."[3]

In distributing power among the members of his family, Saladin situated himself in the tradition not only of the Seljuk Turks but also of the Armenian and Kurdish dynasties of northwestern Iran. The territories of the small Kurdish dynasty of the Shaddadids (r. ca. 950–1170), whom Saladin's grandfather Shādhī had served, were already divided between two main branches of the family, and when Shādhī left Dwin with his two sons, Ayyūb and Shīrkūh, to settle in Iraq, they found the same system of family sovereignty there, organized on a much vaster scale by the Seljuk Turks. The influence of these Turks on Saladin is obvious, even though it was exerted indirectly through the Zangid dynasty of Syria, which was itself an offshoot of the Seljuk system.

That omnipresent familial conception of power did not cancel out the head of the family's authority or suzerainty. But in that realm, two traditions sometimes stood opposed: the one inherited from the Islamic Persian tradition privileged father-to-son succession, while that of the Turks of central Asia preferred to award power to the eldest member of the family, whether or not he was the previous ruler's son. That dual influence explains no doubt the very

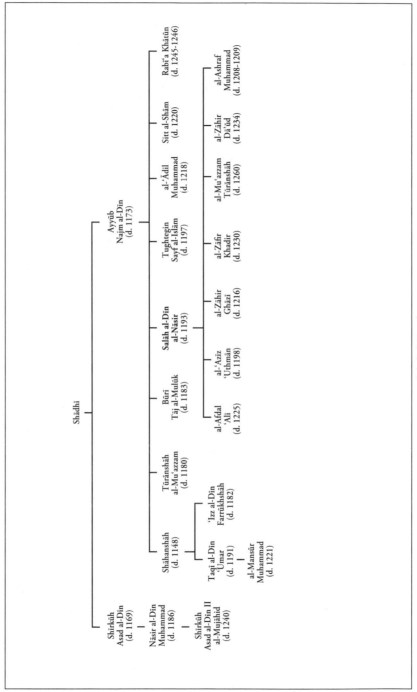

Saladin's Family

important place Saladin initially granted to his brothers and nephews, and then his decision in 1186 to redistribute his territories among his sons.[4]

1169–1186: A Familial Conception of Power

Once he had settled in Egypt, Saladin turned his attention to gathering his family around him. His maternal uncle al-Hārimī and his brother al-ʿĀdil had been part of Shīrkūh's expedition in late 1168 and had supported Saladin when he was named to the post of vizier. In July 1169, Saladin was joined by his other brothers, Tūrānshāh and Tughtegin. As the eldest, Tūrānshāh could have refused to obey Saladin, but Nūr al-Dīn had warned him: "If you are going to Egypt to maintain that your brother is only Yūsuf, who was once in your service, then do not go, since you would do harm to the country, I would make you come back here, and you would have the punishment you deserve. Conversely, if you consider him the lord of Egypt and my representative there, if you serve him as you would serve me, then go, strengthen him and aid him in what he is doing."[5]

Their father, Ayyūb, arrived the following year, in April 1170, accompanied by his family, and in particular his son Būrī, barely nine years old at the time, and his daughter Rabīʿa Khātūn.[6] Saladin's second sister, Sitt al-Shām, was already married to one of Nūr al-Dīn's former emirs. Like the rest of the family, she and her husband moved to Egypt with their son.[7] In 1187 that son played an important role in Saladin's army and received as compensation Nablus and its dependencies, but in 1191 he met an early death in Damascus, where he was buried in the mausoleum his mother had built outside the city.[8]

Ayyūb's eldest son, called Shāhanshāh, had died during the Franks' siege of Damascus in 1148, but Shāhanshāh's two sons, Taqī al-Dīn ʿUmar and Farrūkhshāh, entered their uncle's service very early on. Taqī al-Dīn was already fighting beside him in late 1169 during the Franks' attack on Damietta. The date of Farrūkhshāh's arrival in Egypt is not known, but it must have occurred around the same time.[9] Within a few months, the whole family was thus gathered around Saladin. His father died in 1173; but without the military support of his brothers and nephews, Saladin would no doubt never have reached the height of power.[10]

Tūrānshāh, al-ʿĀdil, and Taqī al-Dīn ʿUmar are three personalities on whom we need to focus our attention here, since they were Saladin's base of support and received significant remuneration for their efforts. In 1169 Tūrān-shāh was given the responsibility of quashing the revolt of the black contin-gents from the former Fatimid army, and it was also to him that were entrusted the expeditions in Upper Egypt and Nubia between 1171 and 1173, which culmi-nated in the taking of Ibrīm. His military support earned him large *iqtāʿs* in Upper Egypt, where the sites of Qūs, Aswān, Būsh, and ʿAydhāb alone yielded him some 266,000 dinars a year. Saladin also awarded him the Giza district of Cairo, where the pyramids stood on the west bank of the Nile, and Samannud in the region of Damietta. Tūrānshāh's successes encouraged Saladin to en-trust the conquest of Yemen to him in 1174. But that country, despite its wealth, seemed very backward to Tūrānshāh. In spring 1176, after a grave illness, and deeply affected by his son's death, he decided to return to Saladin in Syria, to support him in his battle against the Zangid army. That year, before returning to Cairo, Saladin designated him as his lieutenant in Damascus and charged him with repelling the Frankish attacks in the region, a sign of the total confi-dence Saladin had in his brother. And in 1178, when Tūrānshāh asked Saladin to have Baalbek added to the former's territory, Saladin, who was very fond of his brother, was unable to refuse him, incurring the risk of a major crisis with its governor, the powerful emir Ibn al-Muqaddam, who had invited him a few years earlier to come and seize Syria. In spring 1179, after several months of re-sistance, Ibn al-Muqaddam finally gave in and exchanged Baalbek for several small localities in central Syria.[11]

Tūrānshāh proved to be a poor administrator, however. ʿImād al-Dīn criti-cized him for thinking only of amusements in Damascus and for selling large quantities of cereals to the Franks to avoid their attacks, even though famine was raging in Syria. That transaction, let it be said in passing, was approved by Saladin, who simply reproached his brother for not having made a better profit from it. Was it to brush Tūrānshāh aside that Saladin persuaded him to accept Alexandria in exchange for Damascus and Baalbek? In a letter to his brother al-ʿĀdil, the sultan said he had made that decision to strengthen the Egyptian coast, to discourage an eventual attack on the Sicilian fleet, to allow al-ʿĀdil to be freer in his movements, and to lighten the burden on Syria that year, a pos-sible allusion to his brother's excessive spending. Tūrānshāh left Damascus for Egypt on May 3, 1179. But the climate of Alexandria did not suit him. Subject to chronic intestinal troubles, he eventually succumbed to such an attack in about June 1180, leaving behind the memory of someone whose great generosity and love of life had drained the coffers. The satirical poet al-Wahrānī said that, once Tūrānshāh had arrived in Alexandria, he thought only of his own amusements and distributed some 170,000 dinars to "buffoons and panders." That violent satire, perhaps dictated by the poet's resentment that he himself had not received anything, was nonetheless confirmed by Ibn al-Athīr, who said that after Tūrānshāh's death, Saladin had to absorb his debts, which amounted to nearly 200,000 dinars.[12]

Al-ʿĀdil, to whom Saladin also entrusted major responsibilities early on, was very different from Tūrānshāh. On two occasions, in 1174 and again in 1176–1177, al-ʿĀdil was charged with quashing the pro-Fatimid rebellions in Upper Egypt. In 1174, when Saladin undertook the conquest of Syria, it was al-ʿĀdil who assumed the heavy burden of representing him in Egypt. Officially, he was even considered Saladin's heir presumptive, as attested by the foundation inscription on the citadel of Cairo, whose construction al-ʿĀdil was given the responsibility of overseeing. His name was also pronounced at the Friday sermon (khutba) in Cairo, immediately after those of the caliph and of Saladin—a symbol of his great authority—and ʿImād al-Dīn said of al-ʿĀdil that he was "the true sultan of Egypt."[13] The bond between al-ʿĀdil and Saladin was so close at the time that in the spring of 1182, four of Saladin's young sons, born between 1173 and 1176—who were therefore between six and nine years old— were promised in marriage to four of al-ʿĀdil's daughters, with a dowry of twenty thousand dinars for each of them, while Saladin's daughter was married off to al-ʿĀdil's eldest son, an adolescent at the time. That matrimonial policy could not show more clearly Saladin's desire to keep unified the two branches of the family on which all his hopes to found a dynasty rested.[14]

It was apparently at al-ʿĀdil's request that, in December 1183, Saladin agreed to award him Aleppo in exchange for Cairo. Did al-ʿĀdil hope thereby to carve out a principality for himself in northern Syria and Upper Mesopotamia? It is difficult to make that claim, but one thing is sure: at that time, Saladin could not do without his brother, who was exerting a great influence on him. No decision of importance was made without Saladin asking for al-ʿĀdil's opinion. A better administrator than his brother, al-ʿĀdil was called on several times to resolve Saladin's financial difficulties. He undoubtedly drew the money from the revenues of the Egyptian public treasury but also from his personal fortune, as attested by the loan of 150,000 dinars he awarded to Saladin in 1184 in exchange for Aleppo.

From the start, Taqī al-Dīn 'Umar also played the role of a true brother to Saladin, who loved him a great deal, not only because they were near the same age but also because Taqī al-Dīn's father, Shāhanshāh, and Saladin had the same mother, a situation that, in a polygamous family system, strengthened the bond among brothers. Taqī al-Dīn participated in most of Saladin's battles and even lost a son at the Battle of Ramla in 1177. Another of his sons remained a prisoner of the Franks for seven years, having allowed himself to be deceived by empty promises, before being liberated by Saladin in exchange for a ransom and the emancipation of all the Knights Templar held prisoner by him.[15]

It was under Taqī al-Dīn's control that the conquest of Cyrenaica and Ifriqiya was launched in 1173, and it was also to his nephew that Saladin entrusted the important 1179 mission of repelling the Seljuk sultan of Anatolia, Qilij Arslān, who was attempting to regain ground north of Syria. In 1178, Taqī al-Dīn received the large territory of Hama in central Syria, a region that remained in the hands of his descendants almost without interruption until the mid-fourteenth century. In 1182, he stood at the gates of Mosul with Saladin, who delivered the city of Sinjār to him, which seems to indicate that from that time on Taqī al-Dīn had some hope of expanding into Upper Mesopotamia. All the same, he abandoned that stronghold to al-'Ādil when the latter took possession of Aleppo; Taquī al-Dīn replaced al-'Ādil in Cairo, where Saladin entrusted him with the guardianship of the sultan's son al-Afdal and handed over to him al-'Ādil's former Egyptian possessions, which covered a considerable amount of territory.[16] In all, the revenues exceeded 700,000 dinars—that is, about 15 percent of the total budget of Egypt—if we are to believe al-Maqrīzī, and even more according to al-Mansūr, Taqī al-Dīn's son. In his chronicle, al-Mansūr kept the text of the diploma that Saladin had given to Taqī al-Dīn on that occasion, and in which Saladin called his nephew "our son," praised him for the efforts he was making against the infidels, and asked him to stand ready to send troops as soon as Saladin expressed the need for them.[17]

Other members of Saladin's family aided him, though they did not play as important a role as the three already mentioned. His brother Tughtegin was granted Yemen a few years after Tūrānshāh's departure, in about 1183, with the understanding that he would restore order and see that subsidies were sent to Syria; but his geographical distance allowed him fairly quickly to remove himself from Saladin's power. The sultan received no response to his many requests for reinforcements. Būrī, the youngest of Ayyūb's sons, a man of letters and poet when the mood struck him, held the province of Fayyūm in Egypt as an *iqtāʿ*, from which he drew more than 100,000 dinars a year in revenues, and did battle beside his brother outside Mosul in 1182. The next year, his early death at the age of twenty-two, during the siege of Aleppo, affected Saladin very deeply.[18]

As of 1175, Taqī al-Dīn's brother Farrūkhshāh also distinguished himself in his uncle's battles, particularly against the Franks, and it was he who was designated to succeed Tūrānshāh in Damascus and Baalbek in 1180. Saladin was able to count on him to continue the expeditions against the Franks, but in 1182 Farrūkhshāh fell ill during one of them and returned to die in Damascus, leaving behind a reputation as a courageous, just, and generous prince who loved letters and poetry.

The only one to have marked some distance from Saladin at the start was his cousin Nāsir al-Dīn Muhammad, Shīrkūh's son. Nāsir al-Dīn had shown no haste in coming to join Saladin in Egypt, as the other members of his family had done, even though Nūr al-Dīn had taken Homs from Nāsir al-Dīn after the death of the latter's father in 1169. All the same, when Saladin came to seize Syria in 1175, Nāsir al-Dīn joined his troops and subsequently fought loyally at his side in Syria and Upper Mesopotamia. He was even one of the men who saved Saladin's life when the Assassins attempted to kill Saladin while he was besieging ʿAzāz in 1176. Saladin gave his cousin the city of Homs as soon as it was retaken and granted him all the former possessions of Nāsir al-Dīn's father farther to the east, namely, the oasis of Palmyra and the city of Rahba on the Euphrates, both important stops on the route connecting Upper Mesopotamia to central and southern Syria.[19] Nasir al-Dīn's designs on the eastern territories extended even farther, and in 1183 he offered Saladin a large sum of money in exchange for Mosul, which Saladin was then endeavoring to conquer.[20] But Nāsir al-Dīn died suddenly in early March 1186. The rumor spread that he had been poisoned by Saladin, who had supposedly suspected him of wanting to seize Damascus in the event that Saladin did not recover from his illness in Harrān. Some chroniclers add that Saladin distrusted him because Nāsir al-Dīn believed that, as Shīrkūh's heir, power ought to have devolved on him. Although there may be some truth to these allegations, the facts attest to Nāsir al-Dīn's unfailing loyalty to Saladin, who, after Nāsir al-Dīn's death, granted all his cousin's possessions to the deceased's young son, twelve years old at the time.[21]

The Turning Point of 1186

Saladin's illness in Harrān, in making him more aware of the problem of succession, would introduce major changes into the organization of his states. His loyal adviser al-Fāḍil was among those who encouraged him to entrust more power to his eldest sons, who were now at an age where they could govern alone or under guardianship. As al-Fāḍil wrote in a letter to Saladin, the sultan could of course count on his brother al-ʿĀdil and his nephew Taqī al-Dīn, who were as devoted to Saladin as sons would be, but "each of them also possesses a nest with many chicks," all of whom dreamed of possessing their own territory one day. Cautiously and diplomatically, al-Fāḍil attempted to convince Saladin, who had had a brush with death shortly before, that there was reason to consider assuring his own sons' futures.

In reality, upon taking power in Egypt, Saladin had appeared anxious to assure himself a large number of descendants. When he arrived in Egypt, he was nearly thirty-two years old and, as far as we know, still had no children; but in the following years, his concubines collectively gave birth to more than one son a year. Within twelve years, from 1170 to 1182, he had fourteen sons. In all, he would have seventeen sons and one daughter, not counting the children who died in infancy. Thanks to that large male lineage, he was assured of a long-lasting dynasty. In 1174, he said of Nūr al-Dīn's succession that "rulers build their kingdom only for their descendants." In the letters he sent a few months later to the Abbasid caliph and his vizier to ask for the investiture of Egypt, Yemen, the Maghreb, and Syria, his viewpoint is equally clear: "We desire that investiture with all the insignia of power, for us and for our brother or son, to whom we shall bequeath power after us, as the guarantee of a lasting favor and a renewal of the [Abbasid] message."

At the time, since Saladin was not yet assured of having a male lineage that would survive him, it was natural for him to imagine investing one of his brothers after his death. His entire policy in the early years tended in that direction. But in 1183, he turned his attention to establishing a system that would not go against his sons' interests. That year, he entrusted the city of Aleppo for a few months to his son al-Zāhir Ghāzī. This son, being only eleven years old, was placed under an emir's regency, and though he had to yield his place rather quickly to his uncle al-ʿĀdil, that brief interlude was a first step toward a distribution of the territories in favor of Saladin's descendants.

True to his manner of governing, Saladin carried out that distribution cautiously and in stages. If we are to believe al-Maqrīzī, in 1184, when Saladin's eldest son, al-Afdal, was still in Cairo under Taqī al-Dīn's guardianship, Saladin considered a total reorganization of his territories. Al-Afdal would govern Damascus under the guardianship of his uncle al-ʿĀdil, lord of Aleppo, while Saladin's second son, al-ʿAzīz, would rule Egypt under Taqī al-Dīn's guardianship. If one of the young men were to die, he would be replaced by another of his brothers, and if one of the guardians should pass away, the other would replace him until the young princes came of age.[22] That organization, though it was never applied, shows that Saladin was now concerned about the future of his lineage and indicates the importance he granted to Syria, since he wished to entrust it to his eldest son, al-Afdal.

Saladin's illness in 1186 precipitated things somewhat. When he seemed on the brink of death, his brother al-ʿĀdil rushed to his bedside. He appeared to be one of those who might campaign to succeed Saladin. But in Egypt, the impetuous Taqī al-Dīn also gave free rein to his ambitions, and in Homs, Shīrkūh's son Nāsir al-Dīn did not conceal his designs on Syria. All this is encapsulated in an anecdote depicting a convalescent Saladin in dialogue with one of his close emirs, ʿAlam al-Dīn Ibn Jandar, who tells the sultan:

> "When the bird wants to build a nest for its young, it heads to the top of a tree, to better protect them. But you have delivered the fortresses to members of your family and have left your children on the ground. Aleppo is in the hands of your brother, Hama in those of Taqī al-Dīn, Homs in those of Shīrkūh's son. Your son al-Afdal is in Egypt with Taqī al-Dīn, who will drive him out when he likes, and your other son here is in the same tent as your brother [al-ʿĀdil], who can do with him what he likes." "You have spoken the truth," replied the sultan, "but keep it to yourself."[23]

Whether this conversation actually took place or whether Ibn al-Athīr embellished things somewhat is of little import, since it accurately reflects how contemporaries understood the new measures taken by Saladin. It must be said that the situation in Egypt also led Saladin to reconsider the distribution of the territories. Frictions had arisen between al-Afdal and Taqī al-Dīn, who complained that the young prince had interfered with his decisions and had supported Taqī al-Dīn's foes. Saladin thus began by recalling his eldest son to Damascus, which rather too obviously delighted Taqī al-Dīn, causing his uncle to worry. As for al-'Ādil, he undoubtedly regretted having exchanged Egypt for northern Syria and proposed to Saladin that Aleppo be given to al-Zāhir, so that al-'Ādil could return to Cairo to serve as al-'Azīz's guardian. That solution suited Saladin, because al-'Azīz, at age fifteen, was himself insisting that his uncle accompany him.[24]

In late 1186, al-'Azīz, who had lived in Syria since his father had conquered it, therefore moved to Egypt, with al-'Ādil as his guardian and al-Fādil as his adviser and administrator. Full ownership of the entire province of Qūs in Upper Egypt was granted to him. Al-Afdal, sixteen years old at the time, was recalled to Damascus by his father in August 1186, where he received what Saladin saw as a triumphant welcome. He and his mother, along with their entire retinue, were installed in a palace of the citadel, and by the end of the year al-Afdal married one of his cousins, the daughter of Nāsir al-Dīn of Homs and the granddaughter of Shīrkūh. That matrimonial alliance strengthened the bonds with the descendants of Shīrkūh, whose heir Saladin aspired to be, and at the same time neutralized the claims that might have emerged from within that branch of the Ayyubid family.

Saladin also ratified the marriage of his son al-Zāhir (fourteen years old), now lord of Aleppo, to one of al-'Ādil's daughters. That union was perfectly consistent with practices in the Arab Muslim world, according to which marriage between first cousins was not only possible but preferred. In that, Saladin was respecting a well-established kinship and alliance system, but he was also affirming his desire to see his sons succeed him and to maintain around them the family solidarity that had brought him to power. All the same, Saladin left unanswered the difficult question of who would be the head of state, judging no doubt that suzerainty would be exercised by his eldest son, al-Afdal, in Damascus.

Such arrangements were obviously not to the taste of Taqī al-Dīn in Cairo, who almost succumbed to the temptation to take refuge in Cyrenaica. His emir Qarāqūsh al-Armanī had invited Taqī al-Dīn to join him there and to pursue the conquest of North Africa. That idea did not please Saladin, whose priorities at the time were directed more toward the conquest of Jerusalem than toward that of the Maghreb. Taqī al-Dīn was thus "invited" to come join Saladin without delay in Damascus in early November 1186; and to erase his nephew's bitterness, Saladin generously granted him all his former Syrian possessions,[25] and added Mayyāfāriqīn, north of the Tigris, between Upper Mesopotamia and Armenia.

Extended Family or Direct Descendants?

None of the members of Saladin's family defected from the fight against the Franks in 1187 and 1188. His sons participated in their first battles, the two eldest in 1187 and al-Zāhir in 1188. But his chief auxiliaries were still his brother al-ʿĀdil and his nephew Taqī al-Dīn, because of their great military experience. Both, encouraged by the conquests of the Frankish territories and by the fact that the young princes were now of an age to govern on their own, demanded new lands from Saladin. Al-ʿĀdil thus obtained most of Transjordan in 1187,[26] while in 1188 Taqī al-Dīn added to his Syrian possessions the ports of Latakia, Jabala, and Bāniyās, between Tripoli and Antioch, as well as an inland fortress.[27]

In October 1190, the death of the emir of Irbil during the siege of Acre had major repercussions on the distribution of the Ayyubid territories. The emir's brother Muzaffar al-Dīn Gökbörī obtained the city of Irbil, which he had long coveted, in exchange for his possessions in Upper Mesopotamia, which Saladin granted to his nephew Taqī al-Dīn.[28] Henceforth Taqī al-Dīn found himself in charge of a vast dual principality that included, on one hand, central Syria around Hama, with a foothold in the Mediterranean and, on the other hand, a large part of Upper Mesopotamia. In heading east in early March 1191, Taqī al-Dīn's first objective was to consolidate his power in his new territories, but also, against Saladin's instructions, to extend his domination in the direction of Armenia. It was in attempting to seize Akhlāt and Malazgirt, two cities in the region of Lake Van, that he fell ill and died on October 10, 1191. His body was brought back to Mayyāfāriqīn and was later moved to its burial site in a Hama madrasa. His ambitions had therefore taken him far from Saladin's battle against the Franks, and there is little doubt that he intended to carve out a principality in the east for himself and his descendants. Saladin took offense and imputed to him part of the responsibility for Acre's falling into the Franks' hands. Not only had Taqī al-Dīn deprived Saladin of his support in Palestine by waging war within the borders of Armenia, but he had also caused a delay in the sending of reinforcements by the princes of the region, who were upset to see Taqī al-Dīn attacking their territories. Saladin did not have words harsh enough for his nephew, judging that it was the wrong time to be arousing such hostility. And he evoked a Koranic verse to refer to Taqī al-Dīn's expansionist designs: "Here is a work of Satan" (Koran 28:15).

His rage quickly gave way to grief when he learned of his nephew's death. Taqī al-Dīn was described by his contemporaries as an experienced prince, courageous and generous. 'Imād al-Dīn personally attested to that generosity, having himself received from Taqī al-Dīn two hundred dinars to rebuild his house after it was devastated by a fire. The Christian sources are more divided. Bar Hebraeus denounces his massacres of Armenian peasants, whereas in Egypt, the author of the *History of the Patriarchs* praises his righteousness and authority. What is certain is that, with his death, one of the best supporters and most valiant commanders of Saladin's army disappeared.[29]

After Taqī al-Dīn's death, his son al-Mansūr, who was about twenty, could have inherited his possessions, but he was ill-served by his tactlessness and inexperience. Fearing that his father's legacy would not be conferred on him, he thought it wise to demand a solemn oath from Saladin. The sultan, angered by what he considered an affront, exclaimed that no member of his family had ever displayed such mistrust. Suspecting his great-nephew of rebellion, Saladin asked his son al-Afdal to march on al-Mansūr's lands east of the Euphrates. Al-Mansūr immediately requested the intercession of his uncle al-'Ādil. Al-'Ādil once again used his talents as a negotiator, which allowed him to avoid family strife and above all to obtain new possessions. Al-Mansūr was allowed to keep part of his father's Syrian territories but had to give over to al-'Ādil all his lands east of the Euphrates and to al-Afdal the ports and fortresses west of Hama.[30]

Whereas al-Afdal emerged with a consolation prize, in spring 1192 al-'Ādil, as the most influential person in the family after Saladin, was truly in charge of Transjordan and a large part of Upper Mesopotamia. The major centers of Cairo, Damascus, and Aleppo, along with the territories that depended on them, were of course ruled by Saladin's sons, now old enough to govern, but al-'Ādil held in his own name a principality at the margins of the empire, east of the Euphrates in fact, where it was still possible to expand at the expense of the Zangid and Artukid dynasties. He added to all his possessions the citadel of Qal'at Ja'bar, overlooking the Euphrates southeast of Aleppo, which had been annexed shortly before to his nephew al-Zāhir's territory. After a few hesitations, Saladin once more agreed to take a territory from his son in response to his brother's demands, thus showing that it was still not possible for him to count on his sons' strength alone and to totally abandon the conception of a power shared among brothers.

The history of family relations within the Ayyubid family and the distribution of Saladin's territories on the eve of his death clearly show his desire to found a dynasty and to consolidate his power by relying on the principal members of his family. Of course, within their borders, the Ayyubid princes had to accommodate the emirs, to whom portions of the territory were redistributed as *iqtā's*, but overall this system allowed Saladin to control quite closely the governance of his states. By contrast, in the wake of his death, the difficulties of succession that this family policy brought with it would expose its weakness and contradictions.

10

The Support of the Elites

If family support was truly at the heart of the political system developed by Saladin, it by itself could not assure his success. When he took power in Egypt, Saladin had only a handful of emirs behind him. But to unify Islam, to get the populations to follow him, to lead the jihad, and to have a powerful army at his disposal, it was imperative that he have the support of the religious and military elites, who for the most part had previously served the Fatimid or Zangid dynasties.

The support of the ulemas was essential for Saladin in more than one respect. It was they who had the power to persuade the population of a ruler's legitimacy and of his fitness to govern. The most preeminent jurists could also affect the prince's actions by promulgating fatwas that acknowledged, or refused to acknowledge, that his decisions conformed to religious law. Several times Saladin made use of such legal consultations, the surest means he had to assure that decisions that might prove unpopular would nevertheless be accepted. That is what he did, for example, before dismissing the Fatimid caliph in 1171, and before ordering the execution of the poet 'Umara in 1174 and of the mystic al-Suhrawardī in 1191.[1]

The religious elites also played an important role in the conduct of the jihad. Saladin appealed to them to negotiate truces, draw up treaties, galvanize the troops on the battlefield—they themselves sometimes fought—legalize special tax levies, pronounce *khutbas* from the *minbars* vaunting his actions, or call soldiers to battle. Ibn Shaddād was exemplary in that respect, dedicating a treatise on jihad to Saladin, accompanying him on the battlefield, exhorting the troops to fight, raising his lord's morale, and praising his actions. In 1182 the negotiations conducted outside Mosul highlighted the role the ulemas could play on the political scene: the caliph sent the leader of the Sufis to Saladin as part of an embassy. Saladin then appointed al-Fāḍil, 'Imād al-Dīn, and the jurisconsult Dīyā' al-Dīn al-Hakkārī to conduct negotiations with the envoys from Mosul. Among these envoys was an Alid sharīf, that is, one who claimed to descend from the family of the Prophet, who, for that reason, was greatly respected in religious circles.[2]

As for the ulemas, they had every interest in supporting Saladin's policy. The measures he took to foster the strict application of religious law and the suppression of illegal taxes, and his crackdown on non-Muslims and increased monitoring of morals were all of a nature to please them. In addition, Saladin continually attested to having the greatest respect for the ulemas, both privately and publicly. He personally attended the funeral of Ibn 'Asākir, a renowned Damascene traditionist. On many occasions, he granted the ulemas considerable material benefits, giving them honorific robes and sums of money, and redistributing to them, in the form of *waqfs*, or donations, goods confiscated from his enemies and the proceeds from certain taxes. In 1177, for example, he made the decision to give the jurisconsults of Alexandria a portion of the duties imposed on Frankish merchants.[3]

Whereas the ulemas held the key to legitimating the sovereign's power and to seeing that his decisions conformed to religious law, the emirs were crucial in achieving military victories. Saladin chose his military leaders carefully, as Ibn al-Athīr suggests in his account of the events of 1188, following the defeat inflicted on the caliph of Baghdad by the Seljuk sultan:

> At that time, I was in Syria in Saladin's army with the intention of participating in the jihad. He received news of the departure of the Baghdad army from his couriers and said, "I can foresee your bringing the news of their defeat." Someone present asked him, "How is that?" "There is no doubt," he replied, "that my men and my family know more about war than the vizier and have a more

obedient following among the army than he does. Nevertheless, I do not send one of them in a squadron to war without fearing for him. This vizier is not knowledgeable about war and is new to wielding authority. The emirs do not consider him fit to be obeyed and he has personally undertaken to make war on a valiant sultan. Who with him will obey him?" This was how the matter turned out. News came to him of their defeat and he said to his followers, "I told you such and such and reports of that have now arrived."[4]

Experience in war and the ability to command obedience from his troops were the foremost qualities Saladin expected from an army leader. In the choice of his emirs, therefore, he granted more importance to the qualities of authority, courage, and endurance than to ethnic, dynastic, or familial factors. That explains his pragmatic "outstretched hand" policy toward the most valorous and most experienced emirs who had served the previous dynasties. Even more than the ulemas, the emirs were generously remunerated by Saladin, who distributed to them, in the form of *iqtā's,* a large portion of the lands confiscated from his adversaries or retaken from the Franks. That is how very powerful families came into being. On the whole, they remained loyal to their ruler, though they went on to pose serious problems for his successors.

The Immediate Entourage

In addition to his family, Saladin's immediate entourage included men of letters and of religion, foremost among them al-Fādil, 'Imād al-Dīn, and Ibn Shaddād, whose names have become familiar over the course of this book, not only because of the firsthand information they provide about Saladin's life but also because they were major players in the legal and administrative life of his time. I have already spoken of their writings in my introduction. Here I will discuss only their personal relationships with Saladin.

Al-Fādil was undoubtedly the one closest to Saladin, and the trust the sultan displayed toward him was never betrayed. He bore the title of qādī, not because he exercised the duties of a judge, but as an honorific distinction, as had been the custom in the Fatimid administration. Having become Saladin's right-hand man in 1171, he accompanied the sultan several times on his military campaigns. Very quickly, however, al-Fāḍil's presence in Egypt proved indispensable for managing the budget and the administration. In the vast correspondence he maintained with his lord, his respectful devotion and real affection always come through. On several occasions, for example, he was anxious about the sultan's state of health. The moral authority al-Fāḍil was able to hold over Saladin sometimes led the qāḍī to contradict or even fondly reprimand him, with all the usual oratorical precautions. Toward Saladin's sons and nephews, al-Fāḍil similarly adopted a paternal tone, not hesitating to admonish them on occasion if need be. In return, Saladin often attested to his respect and friendship for al-Fāḍil. At his encampments, he liked to have the qāḍī at his side and had an opening made between al-Fāḍil's tent and his own so that they could more easily communicate with each other. Saladin did not much care to see al-Fāḍil leave for distant lands and risk his life on the roads, even to complete the pilgrimage. In 1179, for example, when al-Fāḍil wanted to go to Mecca, Saladin allowed him to leave only under the escort of a few armed troops and not before making him swear that he would not stay there permanently but would soon return.[5]

In addition to his intellectual and literary talents—a collection of his poems has come down to us[6]—and his skills as an administrator, al-Fāḍil was very pious and scrupulous in the application of religious law. It was probably under his influence that Saladin ordered that the discrimination measures against non-Muslims be once again enforced.[7] Al-Fāḍil was married and had several sons, but his true passion was books, which he collected in great number in his library. Physically, he was a small man, stunted and hunchbacked. He was in fragile health, and his letters record his fatigue. At age fifty, he already felt himself growing old and complained of no longer being able to travel long distances, probably because of his gout, which caused him a great deal of suffering toward the end of his life. His hump gave satirical poets the opportunity to mock him mercilessly. Ibn 'Unayn did not hesitate to accuse him, in very crude language, of every sort of vice.[8] In response, al-Fāḍil was content to display publicly a detachment tinged with contempt: "I am not afraid to hear the camel roar, so how could I fear the bleating of baby goats?" he asserted in one of his poems.[9] But it was he who urged Saladin to banish the poet.

'Imād al-Dīn's personality was completely different. It was in the spring of 1175 that this talented Iranian administrator was introduced to Saladin, thanks to a poem ʿImād al-Dīn had composed in the sultan's honor. A protégé of al-Fādil, ʿImād al-Dīn was eternally grateful to him: "If I had not been supported by him, I would have had no strength; if he had not granted me his favors, I would have acquired neither fame nor power. Therefore, throughout my life I will thank him for his kindness and will give thanks to him for his generosity."[10] By an odd coincidence, ʿImād al-Dīn found himself in the service of a man whose father was governor of Tikrīt when the Seljuk vizier had ʿImād al-Dīn's uncle executed there. Of that execution, ʿImād al-Dīn, who did not want to appear critical of his new master's family, took care to say that Ayyūb had disapproved of it.[11]

ʿImād al-Dīn accompanied Saladin on almost all his military campaigns. He kept track of the prisoners and drew up the texts of truces and the many missives sent to the caliph, to emirs, and to the sultan's entourage to inform them of his victories, his intentions, or his needs. On certain occasions, ʿImād al-Dīn was even given the task of conducting negotiations with the Aleppines or with the emirs of al-Jazīra, a region with which he was very familiar. All these missions gave him trouble, as he himself said with a certain frankness. Once Saladin had dictated the content of his letters to him, ʿImād al-Dīn had complete freedom of expression in composing them. He was in fact known for his verbal and stylistic virtuosity. He followed the tradition of using rhymed and rhythmic prose, a literary genre highly valued in the Arab chanceries. Beyond the preciosity of his style, the information he provided is of enormous interest, though he projects an image of himself as a man full of self-importance, sure of his talents: "Every historical event related by someone other than myself will disappear with him; the rumor of that exploit will cease as soon as his voice falls silent. But what I report is like the gardens that thrive when the sky is covered with rain clouds, like the heavenly body that shows itself when daybreak pours gold over the silver of the stars."[12]

It is true that Saladin had found a choice propagandist in him, a secretary whose literary talents contributed greatly toward disseminating the sultan's exploits throughout the Muslim world. More than once, Saladin had occasion to show his gratitude by offering ʿImād al-Dīn sumptuous gifts: a house, slaves, birds of prey. ʿImād al-Dīn was certainly less detached from the things of this world than al-Fādil. During an expedition, for example, he sold his kit at the military marketplace to take advantage of the inflation raging at the time. On several occasions, he complained of financial problems or the loss of his possessions and even considered leaving Saladin's service in his final years, a plan from which al-Fāḍil finally dissuaded him.[13]

As for Bahā' al-Dīn Ibn Shaddād, a native Iraqi, he met Saladin for the first time in 1184, as part of an embassy sent to Syria by the Zangid prince of Mosul. At that time, Saladin attempted in vain to keep the eminent Shafite traditionist and jurist by his side, offering him a teaching position at a madrasa in Cairo. The two men met again in al-Jazīra in 1186, but it was not until 1188, when Ibn Shaddād was returning from his pilgrimage to Mecca, that he finally agreed to enter the sultan's service. Ibn Shaddād never left Saladin again, accompanying him on the military campaign into northern Syria and remaining at his side during the long siege of Acre from 1189 to 1191. Saladin named him qāḍī of the army and gave him the task of exhorting men to pursue jihad. Saladin himself enjoyed listening to Ibn Shaddād relate the traditions of the Prophet concerning holy war and very much liked to pray beside him.

Ibn Shaddād's talents as a negotiator played a role in settling more than one conflict, both with the emirs of Iraq, whom he knew well, and within the Ayyubid family itself. In 1192, it was he who served as a liaison between Saladin and his rebellious great-nephew al-Manṣūr, then between Saladin and his brother al-'Ādil regarding the redistribution of the territories in al-Jazīra. In late 1192, Saladin left Ibn Shaddād in Jerusalem, after appointing him to the post of qāḍī of that city and giving him oversight of the construction of the hospital and madrasa that the sultan had just founded. But a few weeks later, perhaps feeling the end of his life approaching, Saladin asked Ibn Shaddād to come join him in Damascus. With al-Fāḍil, Ibn Shaddād was beside Saladin during his final moments. After the sultan's death, Ibn Shaddād continued to play an influential role with Saladin's sons, especially al-Ẓāhir in Aleppo, where Ibn Shaddād chose to reside until the end of his life in 1234.

The great Iraqi scholar 'Abd al-Laṭīf al-Baghdādī met all three men in 1192, in the Muslim camp set up outside the walls of Acre. His account illuminates quite well the role they played beside Saladin, even on the battlefield:

> I introduced myself to Bahā' al-Dīn Ibn Shaddād, who was then qāḍī of the army. Since he had heard of the reputation I enjoyed in Mosul, he affably received me, set aside what he was doing to tend to me, and told me: "Let us go see the secretary 'Imād al-Dīn." 'Imād al-Dīn's tent was next to that of Bahā' al-Dīn. We went to it, and I

found him busy writing a dispatch in *thulūth* script to the august Dīwān [the court of the caliph of Baghdad], without even making a draft copy. "This letter, he told me, is for your city." He proposed several questions of speculative theology to me, then said: "Come with me to Qādī al-Fādil." We went to the qādī and I saw a frail sheikh, all head and heart. He was writing and dictating to two people at the same time. His face and lips were making all kinds of movements, trying as he was to find the words. It was as if he were writing with his whole body. He questioned me about a verse from the Koran . . . and asked me many other questions, but without stopping his writing and dictating.[14]

Their presence on the battlefield was not always easy for secretaries, however, men more used to manipulating rhetoric and the stylus than the spear and the sword. 'Imād al-Dīn made no secret of that fact in 1177, while en route to Ramla beside Saladin: "The return [to Syria] seemed dangerous to me. I am only a man of the pen, not a man of the sword, and I was afraid they might regret the result of that raid; the end was far off and the matter difficult. The road was nothing but sand, my camels and mules could not carry [what was necessary]; that battle was of sabers and not of pens. Each of us must complete his work and not overstep his duties."

That was the only battle during which he did not accompany Saladin. The sultan allowed him to return to Egypt and pray for victory, which led 'Imād al-Dīn to write: "I was told to go to jihad, but what will that effort bring me? / My courage will not strengthen the army, and my bow has no string for its arrow."[15]

Within Saladin's entourage, but on somewhat less intimate terms with him no doubt, were a few other scholars, his loyalists from the earliest days, who supported him from the time he was first named vizier to the Fatimid caliph. Safī al-Dīn Ibn al-Qābid was one of them. That Syrian administrator, described as honest and capable, having stood beside Ayyūb and Shīrkūh, entered Saladin's service when Saladin was still only the chief of police in Damascus under Nūr al-Dīn's reign. Later, Saladin named him treasurer and made him responsible for the administration of Damascus. Although the luxury in which Safī al-Dīn lived in the citadel did not please the sultan very much, the treasurer remained wealthy and influential until his death in 1191. Since he had no heir, he distributed a portion of his possessions during his lifetime to his mamluks and, on the eve of his death, bequeathed the rest to Saladin.[16]

Also very close to Saladin were the emirs who took his side from the start and who offered their support out of loyalty to his family. Qarāqūsh al-Asadī, a eunuch, freedman, and originally a Christian, formerly in Shīrkūh's service, occupied a special place.[17] First named majordomo in Cairo, he later performed important political and administrative duties. Saladin assigned him to guard the family of the deceased Fatimid caliph, which was assigned to house arrest, and then, as of 1176, to supervise the implementation of the new cadastre. It was to Qarāqūsh al-Asadī as well that was entrusted the construction of the Cairo citadel, of the city's ramparts, and of the bridge spanning the Nile opposite Giza, en route to the pyramids. His talents as a prime contractor quite naturally led to his being named in 1188 to supervise the rebuilding of the fortifications of Acre. Saladin is reported to have said on that occasion: "I see only one man who is up to that important undertaking, to the resolution of that grave question, a dynamic man of penetrating insight, a man of enlightened understanding, a warring hero, an experienced engineer, an upright and sagacious man, respectable and quick-witted, one whose opinion prevails, who applies himself and succeeds, who is capable, who assumes the task of overcoming resistance and resolving difficulties. That steadfast man who does not tremble, that immovable mountain, is Bahā' al-Dīn Qarāqush."[18]

Qarāqūsh remained in Acre during the long siege of that city by the Franks, keeping watch over the wall, always quick to fill the breaches and rebuild the sections that had collapsed. When the city surrendered to the Franks in 1191, he was one of the prisoners taken and was liberated only in October 1192, in exchange for a large ransom,[19] which he personally went to gather in Damascus. It is said that his entire fortune went toward it. He then returned to Egypt, where he remained after Saladin's death in the service of the sultan's son al-ʿAzīz. When al-ʿAzīz died in 1198, Bahā al-Dīn Qarāqūsh was named regent of the young heir al-Mansūr, but it appears that his decisions were no longer unanimously accepted, and he was quickly replaced as regent by al-Afdal, Saladin's eldest son. In addition to his courage and determination, Qarāqūsh had

the reputation of being a kind man, and he established several pious or charitable foundations. He had an establishment for Sufis built north of Cairo, in the
district of al-Maqs, and a free caravansary for travelers in a northern suburb of
Cairo, outside the Gate of Conquests (Bāb al-Futūh); he also had a well and
cistern dug at the foot of al-Muqattam Plateau. His contemporaries Ibn Shaddād and 'Imād al-Dīn were not sparing in their praise of him, and he has remained a celebrated figure in the popular tradition of Egypt.

As a result, it is surprising to read the accounts of those who contested his
judgments and who placed his intelligence in doubt. Ibn Mammātī, the author
of a work titled *Book on the Foolishness of Qarāqūsh's Judgments*, was one of the
most virulent. As the historian Ibn Khallikān rightly remarks, if these stories
of stupidity had had some foundation, would Saladin have granted Qarāqūsh
all his trust? Was this the same Qarāqūsh, and if so, how are we to explain that
contradictory view of him? Paul Casanova suggests that we seek the reason in
the political struggles surrounding the young al-Mansūr when a regent had to
be chosen for him. The historian al-Maqrīzī says that the side hostile to Qarāqūsh's being regent, when he was already of a very advanced age, took to slur-
ring him, giving him a reputation for being miserly and wishy-washy.[20] Within
that context, it is possible to imagine that Ibn Mammātī, author of the first
satire against the emir—which inspired a series of others—belonged to the
clan of Qarāqūsh's adversaries. If such were the case, his success was total, for
not only did Qarāqūsh have to step down in favor of al-Afdal, but he became
the very symbol of stupidity in the popular imagination.[21]

Emir 'Izz al-Dīn Jawālī was also one of Shīrkūh's former emirs.[22] It was in
his tent outside 'Azāz that Saladin was sitting in 1176 when he was attacked by
a member of the Assassin sect. Considered one of Saladin's best officers, Jawālī
fought beside the sultan until his death in 1192, after a fall from a horse.[23] The
Kurdish Sayf al-Dīn al-Mashtūb (the Scarred) was also typical of these emirs,
former companions of Shīrkūh who immediately rallied behind Saladin. His
loyalty was unfailing, and Saladin rewarded him by handing over Sidon after
the conquests of 1187, making Sayf al-Dīn al-Mashtūb one of Saladin's most
powerful officers. Named leader of the relief garrison that arrived in Acre during the winter of 1190–1191, al-Mashtūb was captured by the Franks in July 1191
and freed in April 1192, in exchange for fifty thousand dinars, a ransom he had
difficulty raising. Upon his return to Jerusalem, the sultan received him with
joy and gave him Nablus and Sebaste. The importance of his role beside Sala-

din is accentuated by the fact that he was among those who took an oath with the sultan on September 3, 1192, to seal the accord concluded with Richard the Lionheart. Two months later, however, he died in Nablus and was buried in Jerusalem.[24]

At the juncture between religious and military circles, Diyā' al-Dīn 'Īsā al-Hakkārī was an unusual figure. A Kurd, he had started out as a Shafite juris-consult before pursuing his career in the army. He therefore wore a military uniform but kept his ulema's turban. Having served in Nūr al-Dīn's army, he took Saladin's side from the start and became his close adviser.[25] In 1177 the Franks took him prisoner, and he remained in their jails for three years. After falling ill, he was cared for by a Christian Arab doctor, who had him freed from his chains and transported home, standing as guarantor for him. In 1180 Sala-din got him released in exchange for a large ransom (sixty to seventy thousand dinars). The sultan subsequently made good use of al-Hakkārī's diplomatic talents, sending him to negotiate with Pahlawān, lord of Azerbaijan, in 1185. Similarly, the ties al-Hakkārī had established with the Eastern Christians of Je-rusalem during his captivity led Saladin to entrust him with negotiations with those same Christians in 1187.[26]

Winning and Losing Support

It was one thing for Saladin to count on the support of his family and friends, quite another to win over the servants of the fallen Fatimid dynasty and of Nūr al-Dīn's legitimate heir. In Syria, one of the most spectacular cases of someone rallying behind Saladin was undoubtedly Kamāl al-Dīn Ibn al-Shahrazūrī, a renowned jurist from a mountainous region east of the Tigris, between Mosul and Hamadān. Named chief qāḍī of Damascus in 1160, he had clashed with Saladin when the latter was chief of police, but after Nūr al-Dīn's death, Ibn al-Shahrazūrī had indicated that he favored reaching an understanding with the new lord of Egypt. As soon as Saladin entered Damascus in 1174, he went to pay Ibn al-Shahrazūrī a visit and allowed him to keep his post, an adroit political gesture that won over the Sunni population of Damascus. From that time on, Ibn al-Shahrazūrī was showered with honors by Saladin, who made him one of his close advisers. Before his death in 1176, Ibn al-Shahrazūrī expressed the wish to see his nephew Diyā' al-Dīn succeed him. The sultan had other plans, however. Saladin did not alienate Diyā' al-Dīn, a respected figure and a very good orator, but appointed him official ambassador to the caliph of Baghdad. Nevertheless, the sultan gave the post of chief qādī to Sharaf al-Dīn Ibn Abī 'Asrūn (also from Mosul), one of the best-known personalities during Nūr al-Dīn's reign. Saladin thereby killed two birds with one stone: he showed his gratitude to Sharaf al-Dīn, who had taken his side from the start, while clearly situating himself in Nūr al-Dīn's wake, at a time when his predecessor's memory was still very much alive in Syria.[27]

Even when Sharaf al-Dīn lost his sight a short time later, Saladin decided to let him exercise his duties, with the aid of his son Muhyī al-Dīn and another surrogate.[28] Sharaf al-Dīn remained chief qādī of Damascus until his death in 1191. His son succeeded him, but in 1192 the post was passed on to a third important Syrian family, the Banū l-Zakī, who, from the early twelfth to the late thirteenth century, provided Damascus with no fewer than seven Shafite chief qādīs.[29] In thus naming personalities from influential Syrian families to the most prestigious religious post, Saladin assured himself of their support and won the adherence of the majority of the population.

In Aleppo, Saladin likewise attempted to reconcile himself with the local ulemas, who were a priori more hostile than those in Damascus because of their special attachment to Nūr al-Dīn's dynasty. His first measures upon entering the city in 1183 were intended to reassure religious circles, the Shafites and Hanafites in particular. The Shafites were satisfied with recovering the positions of chief qādī and preacher in the Great Mosque.[30] Would the Hanafites, especially the Banū l-'Adīm, resent Saladin for removing them from control of the supreme judiciary, despite the pledges made during negotiations prior to his entering the city? It does not seem so. In any event, no hostility comes through in the account by the historian Kamāl al-Dīn Ibn al-'Adīm—on the contrary. Saladin proved to be very respectful as well of the best-known Hanafite personality of the moment, 'Alā' al-Dīn al-Kāsānī, to whom he entrusted control of the Hanafite madrasas of the city, that is, the management of their *waqfs* and the appointment of their teachers. Al-Kāsānī, from Fergana in central Asia, was a jurist of very great renown and had moved to northern Syria in about 1169–1170, where he taught in one of the most prestigious madrasas of Aleppo.[31]

Religious life in Syria was deeply marked by personalities from the east, under Nūr al-Dīn's reign and that of his immediate predecessors. In Egypt, it was under Saladin's reign that immigration from the east became significant. In fact, though the functionaries in the Egyptian administration were generally men who had already served the Fatimid dynasty, the ulemas who surrounded Saladin were often Syrians, Iraqis, or Iranians. There is nothing surprising about that, since, however necessary continuity may have been for the proper functioning of the administration, the new legal-religious orientation in favor of Shafism required recruitment from outside Egypt, which was emerging from two centuries of Shiite domination.[32]

A certain number of Egyptian emirs also chose to rally behind Saladin. Despite the purges in the Fatimid army in the early 1170s, of which the blacks and Armenians were the primary victims, Saladin did not hesitate to keep the most valorous officers in his service. That was the case, for example, for Shams al-Khilāfa, a man close to the late vizier Shāwar. Al-Khilāfa was named lieutenant to Saladin's brother Tūrānshāh in Upper Egypt in 1170.[33] Ibn Māsal, the former governor of Alexandria, who had delivered the city to Shīrkūh and Saladin, was also undoubtedly among those who, in 1174, contributed toward foiling the plot by Fatimid partisans. Saladin seems to have remained very grateful to him, since, upon Ibn Masāl's death in 1178, the sultan supposedly exclaimed: "I shall never have another friend like him," before granting all Ibn Māsal's possessions to the latter's son.[34]

But the most important case of winning over an adversary was no doubt that of Admiral Husām al-Dīn Lu'lu', an Armenian freedman. It was to him that Saladin entrusted the command of the fleet. The admiral's victory over the Franks in the Red Sea made him famous, and later it was he as well who commanded the fleet sent from Egypt to aid the besieged city of Acre. After the fall of Acre in 1191, Husām retired from military life and devoted himself to charitable works. In particular, he had food distributed in al-Qarāfa cemetery south of Cairo, where a host of poor people were living: every day, twelve thousand loaves were thus divided up, twice that many in periods of rising prices.[35]

Toward Nūr al-Dīn's former emirs in Syria and in al-Jazīra, Saladin adopted the same policy of openness. Every time he had the opportunity, he offered to take them into his service, forgiving them for initially having opposed him, and he often displayed a great deal of patience toward the most reluctant. The career of Emir 'Izz al-Dīn Jūrdīk provides a good example of that conciliatory attitude. Jūrdīk was first sent to Egypt by Nūr al-Dīn, along with Shīrkūh and Saladin. He participated in the murder of Shāwar alongside Saladin but decided to return to Syria when Saladin was named vizier, probably because he disapproved of that choice. Governor of the citadel of Hama, he refused to hand it over to Saladin in 1175. The sultan nevertheless allowed Jūrdīk to go to Aleppo to negotiate an accord between Saladin and the Aleppines. Immediately imprisoned by Gümüshtegin, regent of Aleppo at the time, Jūrdīk was freed in 1176 after the accord concluded between Saladin and the Aleppines. Jūrdīk decided, in spite of everything, to remain loyal to his former master's family and remained in the service of al-Sālih, Nūr al-Dīn's young son. When Aleppo was taken in 1183, he was one of the negotiators, and once the accord was concluded, he finally entered Saladin's service and never left it. He continued to battle valiantly beside the sultan and in 1187 was named governor of Acre. Jūrdīk likely did not remain there long: during the Franks' siege of the city, he was in the Muslim army outside the city. After the accord signed with Richard the Lionheart in 1192, Saladin named him governor of Jerusalem, and Jūrdīk was enthroned after the Friday prayer, at the Dome of the Rock.[36]

Other emirs from Aleppo joined Saladin's ranks after the death of al-Sālih Ismāʿīl in 1181. The Banū l-Dāya belonged to a family that had played a very important role under Nūr al-Dīn. Majd al-Dīn in particular, Nūr al-Dīn's foster brother and adviser, had been named lieutenant in Aleppo and commander of the northern Syrian army. He died in 1170, but his three brothers, Shams al-Dīn, Badr al-Dīn, and Sābiq al-Dīn, still controlled a large number of fortresses in northern Syria at the time of Nūr al-Dīn's death. They were, however, dispossessed of all their property by the new regent of Aleppo. Thrown into prison, they were not freed until two years later, in 1176, thanks to Saladin's intervention. A short time later, Sābiq al-Dīn received several major fortresses[37] from Saladin, and his role in the sultan's service grew continually, to such a point that he actively participated in the negotiations with Richard the Lionheart.[38] Among the other grand emirs of Aleppo who joined Saladin in the early 1180s was ʿAlam al-Dīn Ibn Jandar, whom Saladin generously thanked by awarding him the citadel of ʿAzāz in 1183, then the citadels of Darbsāk and Baghrās bordering the principality of Antioch.[39] Similarly, Badr al-Dīn Dildirim, who received three powerful fortresses north of Aleppo, was one of the chief negotiators of the accord concluded with the Franks and even seems to have been on excellent terms with Richard the Lionheart.[40]

Emirs from eastern provinces also abandoned the Zangid camp to follow Saladin once he had demonstrated his might. The most important was no doubt Muzaffar al-Dīn Gökbörī—son of a former administrator of Mosul—who had fought in 1176 at Tall al-Sultān. Lord of Harrān in Upper Mesopota-

mia, he sought out Saladin in 1182 to encourage him to seize the territories east
of the Euphrates. Saladin thanked him by handing over Edessa, which he had
captured that same year, as well as Samosata.[41] In the spring of 1185, Gökböri
momentarily fell into disgrace. Saladin, not having received the financial aid
from him as promised, seems to have suspected him of sympathies toward the
leaders of Mosul. En route to Mosul, Saladin therefore stopped at Harrān,
where he had the emir imprisoned. Al-Fādil suggests that, at that time, Gökböri demanded the territories belonging to his brother, lord of Irbil, which
Saladin refused to give him. Saladin's faithful chancellor remained convinced,
however, that it was only a misunderstanding attributable to the emir's excessive temerity, and he appealed to the sultan to forgive Gökböri in a letter sent
to one of his trusted men: "I have no doubt that Saladin's kindly feelings will
soon appear. . . . The cause of offense is only over-boldness. . . . My absence at
a time like this, by God, is hard for me to bear and the choice was not mine. . . .
But if—and may God forbid it—you see something that requires my presence,
I will come even if I have to travel by mule and endure the heat even without
[the shelter of] a tent."[42]

The matter was quickly settled, and the misunderstanding dissipated,
since Saladin had no interest in alienating one of the most powerful emirs in
the region. That not only would have deprived him of important support but
also would have upset the other emirs of al-Jazīra. Gökböri therefore spent
only a few days in prison. Along with his freedom, Saladin returned his territories to him, and some time later even granted him the hand of the sultan's
sister Rabī'a Khātūn, whose first husband had just died. Once trust was restored, Gökböri was considered one of Saladin's best emirs. It was to him that
the command of the left wing of the army in the Battle of Hattīn was entrusted, and, the next year, 'Imād al-Dīn was unsparing in his praise, describing him as the man who "made fire burst forth from the tinder box of victory,
when he hid his celebrated saber in the enemy's blood." Gökböri had never
forgiven his brother for having inherited Irbil in his place. His brother's death
in 1190 finally allowed Gökböri to receive from Saladin an exchange of territories (Edessa, Harrān, and Samosata) for those of the brother. In November
1190, Gökböri left Saladin to go take possession of Irbil and never saw the sultan again.[43]

It is therefore difficult to speak of a real opposition to Saladin on Gökböri's part. As for the rare cases of resistance, they were rapidly resolved or

skillfully negotiated. In Egypt in 1174, the former Fatimid emir Kanz al-Dawla, whom Saladin had named governor of Aswān, led a revolt but was quickly arrested and executed. The revolt in Baalbek of Emir Shams al-Dīn Ibn al-Muqaddam almost took a more serious turn. He was a former emir of Nūr al-Dīn who, upon the latter's death, had been named administrator in al-Sālih's name. It was Ibn al-Muqaddam, however, who appealed to Saladin in autumn 1174 to thwart the ambitions of the Aleppine emirs. For joining Saladin's ranks, he was awarded the governorship of Baalbek. But in 1178 Tūrānshāh demanded that city from his brother, and Saladin could not refuse him. Ibn al-Muqaddam firmly opposed him and attempted to resist from within his fortifications. Saladin would once more display a great deal of patience and political skill. He began by mounting a siege on Baalbek in 1178, but without attacking it. His attempts to persuade the emir having proved fruitless, he returned to Damascus, leaving one of his emirs to continue the siege. The matter dragged on for a few months more. Negotiations finally allowed the emir to surrender in spring 1179. Baalbek was taken from him, in exchange for other possessions in central Syria,[44] to which Saladin added the governorship of Damascus in 1183.

That generous solution allowed the sultan to regain the trust of the emir, whose loyalty never faltered subsequently. After the taking of Jerusalem, the emir asked to go on pilgrimage. Saladin tried to make him delay his plan, but in vain. Al-Muqaddam felt himself growing old and did not want to put off his trip. As the pilgrimage rites in Mecca unfolded, he exhibited Saladin's banner and ordered the beating of drums, a way to publicly demonstrate the sultan's suzerainty over the holy sites. This greatly displeased the representative of the Abbasid caliph, who was leading the Iraqi pilgrimage. A squabble broke out between the two camps, and Ibn al-Muqaddam was mortally wounded. He died in Minā, a few kilometers from Mecca. It was a grievous loss for Saladin's army.[45]

Finally, Saladin had the unpleasant surprise at the end of his reign of clashing with al-Mansūr, the son of Taqī al-Dīn, Saladin's nephew and beloved brother-in-arms. No doubt this was less a rebellion than a blunder attributable to the inexperience of a young man of twenty who had the temerity—not to say the impudence—to ask Saladin for an official oath acknowledging the young man's legacy from his father. Saladin took it as a mark of defiance, which he found especially intolerable from a member of his own family. Ibn Shaddād, who intervened directly in the negotiations, recounts:

> The sultan [was] . . . very angry against al-Manṣūr for having caused this trouble in the family. No-one in the family had ever feared him before or demanded an oath from him. . . . When al-Manṣūr heard of the sultan's anger against him, he sent an emissary to al-'Ādil, asking him to intercede to reconcile the sultan with him and asking for one of two lots of territory, either Harrān, Edessa and Sumaysāt [Samosata] or Hama, Manbij, Salamiyya and Ma'arrat [al-Nu'mān], with guarantees from his brothers. Al-'Ādil approached the sultan several times, but he would not accept this and agreed to nothing suggested. All the emirs interceded vigorously with him, which stirred the well-spring of his generous spirit. . . . Later, al-'Ādil asked for a signed document from the sultan, which he refused. After he had been importuned, he tore up the text of the oath on 29 Rabī' II [14 May]. The arrangement was over and discussion broken off. I had been acting as go-between for them both. The sultan was overcome with rage that he could be addressed in such a way on the part of one of his grandchildren. . . .
>
> After al-Afdal had set out, al-'Ādil softened the sultan's heart towards the son of Taqī al-Dīn, whose situation was much discussed. The sultan sent me to consult the emirs in the service of al-'Ādil about the case. I gathered them before him and explained the matter concerning which the sultan had sent me to them. The Emir Abū'l-Hayjā' was deputed to make a reply. "We are his slaves and his mamlukes," he said, "while that person is a boy. Perhaps his fear has led him to ally himself with another party. We are unable to combine fighting Muslims with fighting infidels. If the sultan wants us to fight Muslims, he will make peace with the infidels, march to those parts and we will fight under his leadership. If, however, he wishes to persevere in the Holy War, he will make peace with the Muslims and be lenient." This was the answer of them all.

The sultan relented and, when I had written a fresh copy of the oath for the son of Taqī al-Dīn, the sultan duly swore it and gave him his signed warrant for what had been agreed upon.[46]

That account makes clear the combination of diplomacy, prudence, and political realism with which Saladin confronted resistance. Although he was sometimes overcome by anger, he was also capable, when the interests of his states required it, of listening to the advice of his entourage, of negotiating, and if necessary of taking back his decisions. That attitude allowed him to defuse fairly quickly the few internal crises that arose in his path.

II

The Elaboration of an Image

Saladin's greatest success was no doubt the image of himself that he managed to project and which remains alive to this day. It is true that, given our sources, nothing is more difficult than to establish a clear distinction between representation and reality. The comparison of the accounts—Christian and Muslim, Eastern and Western—and of the few archival documents that have come down to us through literary sources allows us to extract the main lines of his politics and reign, but it is obvious that the discourse of his secretaries and panegyrists must be constantly analyzed and decoded, not only as a function of the events they relate but also in terms of their intentions and influences. Indeed, they consisted not simply of praise addressed to a victorious sovereign but of actual propaganda, whose aim was to transmit a message to the caliph of Baghdad, to the rulers of the neighboring states, to the population itself, and later to posterity. That propaganda was relayed by the texts and by royal inscriptions on building foundations, coins, and some personal items.

Why was Saladin the object of such idealization? Did he himself participate in the elaboration of his image, or was it constructed independent of his will? By what paths, with what arguments, and according to what models did that image come into being? Other great Muslim men, beginning with the Prophet himself, initiated a process of image construction, which served as the basis for a certain concept of exemplarity. The Sunna of the Prophet—that is, the complete record of his conduct, acts, and sayings (the hadith)—have thus come to constitute the second source of Muslim law, after the Koran. Some of his successors, such as ʿUmar ibn al-Khattāb (r. 634–644), or the eighth Umayyad caliph, ʿUmar ibn ʿAbd al-ʿAzīz (r. 717–720), were also presented as models to be followed.[1]

Often the objective of the historians was to provide the sovereigns of their time with edifying examples:

> If princes and those who hold the power to enjoin and to prohibit
> familiarize themselves with the biographies of tyrants and oppres-
> sors and see that they are written down in books that people have
> circulated, and that they are transmitted from generation to gen-
> eration, they can observe the consequences of such behavior. . . . If
> they see the admirable biographies of righteous rulers and the good
> reputation that follows them after their death, as well as the pros-
> perity of their country and kingdom and the abundance of their
> goods, they shall approve of that conduct, shall want constantly to
> imitate it and to leave aside what would be contrary to it.[2]

That search for exemplarity and for models, whether ancient and prestigious such as the prophets of Islam, or much closer in space and time, was an
essential characteristic of the elaboration of Saladin's image.

The Holy Man and the Ideal Sovereign

The message to be transmitted was political as well as religious. Above all, there was a need to legitimate the authority of Saladin—considered by some to be a usurper—by emphasizing his personal virtues and his qualities as a sover-eign, one who had concern for the good of his subjects and especially for the interests of Islam, a defender of orthodoxy, an architect of Muslim unity. Only that unity had given him the means to conduct jihad against the Franks. Just as Ibn Shaddād devotes the entire first part of his biography of Saladin to the de-scription of his many virtues, ʿImād al-Dīn, in his various writings in prose or verse, never fails to enumerate the qualities that would provide posterity with an ideal image of his master:[3] a just, pious, generous sultan, keeper of the peace, one who is kind toward the disinherited, solicitous of the widow and orphan, who knows how to surround himself with good ulemas and officials, who has a vested interest in Muslim law, who grants his protection to those who deserve it, who loves austerity, a valiant jihad warrior, vanquisher of the infidels, destroyer of heresies, defender of Islam, one who is victorious by the grace of God, the conqueror of Jerusalem, beloved of his subjects, but one who knows how to command fear and respect. "Brightness," "the dew," and "hope" are a few of the terms applied to him, which give way to "darkness," "drought," and "weeping" at the time of his death.

It is likely that these portraits were not merely flattery or rhetoric, and Saladin probably deserved some of the praise. But beyond what might have been based in reality, the way his actions are presented, the qualifiers applied to them, the virtues attributed to him, the praise heaped on him, and the bonds that link him to illustrious figures in the biblical and Islamic tradition stem from a dual legacy: that of the holy man and that of the ideal sovereign. In Islamic hagiographical literature, the *Manāqib,* or Saints' Lives, were often composed by a disciple of a saint or someone else close to him, and were intended to perpetuate his memory. The saint's virtues and miracles were described in a series of narratives that retraced his path, from his conception to after his death. The biographies of Saladin bear a strong resemblance to that type of narrative. For example, the prediction made to his pregnant mother that she was carrying in her womb "the sword of God" is reminiscent of the signs that announce the holiness of an individual even before his birth.[4] And just as the saint, by virtue of his exemplary conduct, is often associated with a scriptural model (Moses, Jesus, Muhammad), Saladin is compared to Joseph or Solomon.[5] His piety is frequently emphasized in his titulature. Saladin is "the just, the learned, he who unites the word of faith with the uprightness of the state and of religion [salāh al-dunya wa l-dīn]." In the inscription he had engraved in al-Aqsā Mosque in Jerusalem, to commemorate the construction projects he had ordered there, Saladin even adopts the expression "friend [walī] of God," which, in Islam, is generally reserved for holy men.[6]

In addition to the influence of hagiographical literature, there is that of the Mirrors for Princes, a literary genre that enjoyed great success in the East and in the West. That genre, which originated in Islam in the late Umayyad period but was heir to a long classical tradition—Persian, Greek, Hellenistic, and to a lesser extent, Indian—offered sovereigns a great deal of advice on good government and drew the portrait of the ideal monarch: God-fearing, righteous, just toward his subjects, one who surrounded himself with good advisers and honest administrators, one who knew how to conduct diplomacy and war.[7] In an anecdotal and moralistic style, the authors of these works combined ancient legends and historical information and gave advice to rulers both on the ethics of power and on the practical conduct of affairs. Gradually, the material inherited from the Hellenistic and Sassanid civilizations was supplemented by elements proper to Arab Muslim culture, such as quotations from biblical figures drawn from the Islamic tradition and words pronounced by the Prophet, his Companions, and the first caliphs. That literary genre, which spread widely throughout the Arab Muslim world, was still developing in Saladin's time, several works of this type having been composed in Syria toward the late twelfth and early thirteenth century.[8]

The influence of that tradition on Saladin's biographers is obvious. If proof is required, we need only examine one of these Mirrors for Princes, composed by an anonymous Persian author in Syria in about the mid-twelfth century.[9] The themes evoked are very diverse and, as often in this type of work, extend beyond advice on governance in the strict sense. In it are also found general rules for good conduct and civility as well as more literary aspects, illustrated with anecdotes on the interpretation of dreams, strange and wondrous phenomena, the education of children, and many other subjects relating to family and social life. All these themes are indicative of the close kinship existing between the Mirror for Princes genre and what was called the *adab*—a literary form widespread in Islamic countries during the Middle Ages—which combined, in a didactic and entertaining way, everything a gentleman ought to know or possess to be considered a good Muslim and to be appreciated for his good manners.

The ideal sovereign's virtues and duties are nearly the same as those set out in the *Book of Counsel for Kings,* the first part of which was compiled by the great thinker al-Ghazālī (d. 1111): absolute submission to God; the protection of orthodoxy; the observance of religious duties; the defense of Islam; modesty; detachment from the things of this world; consideration for the pious and for the ulemas, whose advice must be sought out; generosity; kindness and magnanimity toward one's subjects; fairness and justice; a sympathetic ear for complainants; and the repression of exactions perpetrated by one's delegates or lieutenants.[10] All these principles had their roots in very ancient traditions and seem to have directly inspired Saladin's biographers, as can be seen particularly in the portrait Ibn Shaddād draws at the beginning of his book.[11] I do not mean to say that all was just embellishment and propaganda in the writings of Saladin's close circle. It is simply that these writers found in such works all the criteria for good governance, which then allowed them, by emphasizing and sometimes exaggerating one character trait or another, to make Saladin's image correspond to that presented in the Islamic tradition as exemplifying the ideal sovereign.

Justice in particular, closely associated with respect for religious law in the Islamic religion, was always presented as the essential virtue of the ideal sovereign, and Saladin's image was no exception to that rule. It is clear that he himself administered justice, as those in his close circle attest, but there is no question that they exaggerated his actions in that realm. We are told that he himself held court sessions twice a week when he was in Damascus, surrounded by jurists, and that he heard the grievances of his subjects.[12] Anyone could approach him, and no complaint was rejected, including those lodged against the rich and powerful. The comparison that can be made to the praise showered on other sovereigns, before or after him, invites us to remain cautious about the interpretation to be given to these statements. The image transmitted of his predecessor Nūr al-Dīn, the "Just Ruler" *(al-Malik al-ʿĀdil)* even surpassed Saladin's in that respect. Even in our own time, the Nūr al-Dīn madrasa in Damascus continues to attract visitors, who appeal to him for justice and, especially, for the release of political prisoners. When their wish is granted, they light candles beside his tomb. In the footsteps of the historian Ibn al-Athīr, some go so far as to place Nūr al-Dīn on a par with the first four caliphs who succeeded the Prophet, and with the very popular Umayyad caliph ʿUmar ibn ʿAbd al-ʿAzīz.[13]

Everything indicates, moreover, that Saladin, in that realm as in others, strove to imitate his predecessor. That, in any case, is how his biographers depict him, and the anecdotes reported concerning the two sovereigns have many points in common. Let me cite as an example the very similar accounts in which they are shown dealing with a complaint lodged against them by a private individual: they bow to the religious judgment rendered by the qāḍī, have their names cleared, and display the same magnanimity by showering with kindnesses the very person who had unjustly accused them.[14] Everyone, even rulers and the powerful, must submit to justice. "No fault is more serious in the eyes of God than that of kings," we read in the treatise of al-Ghazālī.

Whence the custom on the part of the kings of Persia of opening their audiences with the population's grievances against the sovereign.[15] Ibn Jubayr recounts that a mamluk who was enjoying the sultan's favor came one day to demand justice against a dishonest camel driver. Saladin replied: "What can I do for you? The Muslims have a qadi who decides between them; over both the chief men and the people the justice of our law extends, and its injunctions and its interdicts we must alike obey. I am but the servant of the [divine] law. . . . Justice will decide for you or against you."

Saladin is not only described as a just ruler but is also praised for his clemency. Ibn Jubayr also reports: "He had just forgiven the crime of someone who had offended against him and said, 'For my part, I would rather miss the mark in being merciful than inflict undeserved punishment.'"[16] In the twelfth to thirteenth centuries, there was nothing original about that topos of the just and merciful sovereign. Similar anecdotes were circulating, for example, about Sultan Baybars (r. 1260–1277), whom his chancellor and biographer Ibn 'Abd al-Zāhir also presented as a merciful, generous ruler respectful of religious law.

Saladin too was depicted as a generous and magnanimous sovereign. Generosity, like justice, is one of the stereotypes of the ideal ruler. Plutarch had said of Alexander that he "was naturally most munificent, and grew more so, as his fortune increased."[17] In the Islamic tradition, the importance granted to generosity rests as well on many hadith, authentic or apocryphal, such as this: "When a generous man stumbles, God takes him by the hand."[18]

Saladin's generosity, however, was far from mere legend. All the Arab authors, Muslim and Christian, and even his Latin adversaries, point to it. William of Tyre says it was one of his most formidable weapons, since it allowed him to win the hearts of his subjects.[19] Ibn Shaddād adds that his generosity was so famous that there was no point in even dwelling on it. Upon Saladin's death, he says, his treasury contained only one gold coin and a few dirhams.[20] That generosity satisfied the emirs and his close circle but also served Saladin's strategic and military objectives. Hence 'Imād al-Dīn estimates that, within three years (1189–1192), Saladin had offered his troops twelve thousand horses as the Third Crusade was unfolding, not counting the money he gave soldiers to care for their wounded horses.[21] The Christian Bar Hebraeus reports this very significant anecdote: when Saladin took Amida, he had the city's treasure brought in and asked his commander in chief to share it by the handful with the emirs and troops. He complied by giving a few coins to each one, but Saladin encouraged him to give more. The commander then began to laugh and recounted that, one day, Nūr al-Dīn had made a similar request regarding grapes and, as the commander was beginning to distribute them, Nūr al-Dīn had told him: "Gently. If thou distributest them in this manner, grapes cannot come to them all." Saladin, laughing in turn, replied: "Avarice belongeth to merchants and not to kings. Do not therefore distribute them with thy one hand, but with both."[22] That story, whether true or invented, illustrates well the difference in the image the two rulers enjoyed: Nūr al-Dīn was perceived by his contemporaries as a virtuous man, a good administrator, but rather austere, whereas his successor's boundless generosity was judged excessive by some.

The works relating Saladin's great deeds were not the only vehicles for conveying that image of the ideal ruler. His titulature, composed of a series of honorific titles and laudatory qualifiers, which duly appeared at the top of official documents, on his coins, on the foundations of his monuments, and on certain personal objects, contributed to that image as well.[23] Saladin was not an innovator in that respect, since such was the habit of sovereigns of his time, but the series of epithets and titles appended to his name was intended to underscore quite particularly his role as unifier of Islam chosen by God, his gallantry, and his victories over the Franks. The first title he bore, from the start of his career in Syria, was "Salāh al-Dīn" (uprightness of religion), which the Latins translated as "Salahadinus" or "Saladinus," the name by which he was henceforth known. Many other qualifiers were bestowed on him once his power was established: "sultan of Islam and of the Muslims, assisted and aided [by God], jihad warrior, warrior on the borders, the one who unites the word of faith, subjugator of the worshippers of the cross, devoted friend of the emir of believers, reviver of the dynasty of the emir of believers, sultan of Islam and of Muslims, lord of glory, power, and resounding victory, liberator of Jerusalem from the hands of the polytheists, servant of the two noble Sanctuaries."[24]

There was nothing original about that emphasis on a ruler's victories: it was a centuries-old practice. But whereas, in the classical period, a king's brilliant successes allowed him to be considered a man above men, an intercessor between men and God, and sometimes led to his being actually worshipped, in Islamic culture the emphasis was rather placed on the humility of the victorious sovereign, "God's shadow on earth."[25] 'Imād al-Dīn expresses that idea in an excerpt written in 1188, after the taking of the castle of Burzayh: "These castles we have taken, the fortified places we have seized, if Allah had simply trusted in our personal effort to take a single one of them, it would certainly have been impossible, even supposing that all the world's armies had come to our aid. But Allah made the undertaking easy and simple, gave victory and success, and rained down triumph."[26]

The ruler, and the caliph in particular, always drew his power from God and was deserving of his position only to the extent that he respected religious law. As a result, he was obliged to remain modest before that divine omnipotence, as the caliph of Baghdad also said, when he bestowed the investiture over Syria and Egypt on Saladin in 1175: "Beware of looking upon your efforts with admiration, saying: 'I have conquered all these territories, after many others had given up on them.' But know that the land falls to God and to His Prophet, and after him to the caliph. Merit does not devolve on the slave who becomes Muslim but on God, who gives the gift of Islam to his slave."[27]

The power hierarchy, here very clearly invoked by the caliph, was also reflected in Saladin's titulature. Expressions such as "devoted friend (or associate) of the emir of believers" and "reviver of the dynasty of the emir of believers" alluded to Saladin's role as the caliph's aide and subordinate, while on coins, the name of the caliph always appeared on the obverse and Saladin's name on the reverse.[28]

The exercise of power in the Abbasid world was thus necessarily conceived as a delegation of caliphal power. But there were several levels of delegation, and the holders of political and military power could be sultans, kings (malik), emirs, or atabegs. The title "sultan," which appeared as a supreme title in the mid-eleventh century and was bestowed for the first time by the Abbasid caliph on the Seljuk Toghril Beg, was indisputably the highest title that a Muslim prince could receive. It was reserved for the main branch of the Seljuks of Iran and Iraq until the mid-twelfth century, when the Seljuks of Anatolia and the Khwarezmians of central Asia appropriated it as well. In Saladin's case, the use of that title was more complicated. When he was vizier in Cairo, he received from the Fatimid caliph the title "al-Malik al-Nāsir" (the king who brings his aid) and was called "al-sultān," as the viziers of that dynasty traditionally were,[29] though that title did not have the same importance as in the Abbasid world. Perhaps that is the reason Saladin is often called "sultan" in the literature of his time, though some Syrian and Iraqi authors apply that term to him only with a certain caution. The Aleppine historian Ibn al-'Adīm, for example, designates him thus only after the conquest of Aleppo in 1183, calling him before then only by his title "al-Malik al-Nāsir," to mark clearly the beginning of his reign over northern Syria. Ibn al-Athīr calls him simply "Salāh al-Dīn" and reserves the title "sultan" for the Seljuk rulers of Iran and Iraq.

Although many historians adopted the habit of calling him "sultan" from the late twelfth century on, that title was never officially bestowed on him by the caliph of Baghdad, and Saladin never had it inscribed on his official documents, his monuments, or his coins. The title "sultan of Islam and of the Muslims," frequently mentioned in his titulature after the early 1180s, and the rarer title "sultan of the Muslim armies," do not have the same political significance, as Nikita Elisséeff has shown in his study of Nūr al-Dīn's titulature. To function as a supreme title, the term "sultan" had to appear alone at the beginning of the protocol, preceded by "our master" *(mawlāna al-sultān)* or followed by al-Malik *(al-sultān al-Malik al-Nāsir).*

For Saladin, such was not the case,[30] with the possible exception of nine magic copper cups fabricated in Mecca and now housed in various museums and private collections. These cups, almost all identical in style and dating to 1184, are covered with inscriptions that indicate their many healing powers: for scorpion bites and snakebites, fevers, migraines, labor pains, rabies, dysentery, epilepsy, bewitchment, unruliness in children, and so on. They also contain an inscription that begins, "our master the sultan."[31] The title of sultan was thus cast in relief at the head of the protocol. The date and place of manufacture of these objects suggest that they may have been offered to Saladin by his brother Tughtegin, who had been sent to Yemen shortly beforehand, or by the emir of Mecca, or by some rich Muslim pilgrim. But Gaston Wiet has called that attribution into question, rightly pointing out that neither the title "al-Nāsir" nor that of "Salāh al-Dīn" is given. The very expression "our master the sultan," which appears on no other inscription referring to Saladin, does not encourage us to recognize these inscriptions as an allusion to him.[32] These cups were quite probably manufactured posterior to Saladin by an artisan who wanted to attribute them to him but who nevertheless reproduced a titulature closer to those in use during his own time than to those used in Saladin's era. That hypothesis is confirmed by Eva Baer's observation that the practice of decorating metal objects with long inscriptions mentioning the name and titles of their owner did not spread to Syria and Egypt until the early thirteenth century, reaching its apogee in the Mamluk period.[33] Many indications therefore lead us to believe that these cups were not intended for Saladin. In any case, they cannot be used as a basis for attesting that he officially bore the title of sultan.

The situation began to change in the last years of the twelfth century, with the disappearance of the Seljuk dynasty of Iran and Iraq. The title "sultan" lost a great deal of its value at the time and was borne by many Muslim rulers, who no longer waited for the caliph to grant his official acknowledgment of it. So it was that a number of Ayyubid princes—and not only the major figures of the dynasty—had it included in their titulatures.[34] In the fourteenth century, when the Abbasid caliphate of Baghdad had disappeared and there was only a puppet caliph in Cairo, the Egyptian author al-Subkī established a hierarchy between the sultan, the king (malik), and the emir, on the basis of the size of the territory each controlled. That is why, in his view, Nūr al-Dīn, unlike Saladin, had never been a sultan.[35] But at the time, this view was far from the political conception of the Seljuk sultanate.

All in all, though Saladin's titulature tended to grow more impressive over the years, it remained relatively modest compared to that of his successors and some of his contemporaries whose power was inferior to his own.[36] Before him, Nūr al-Dīn had used many more epithets, especially those that highlighted his qualities as a pious and ascetic ruler. Saladin primarily chose the honorific titles that underscored his role as unifier of the Muslims, jihad warrior, and aide to the caliph, thereby indicating his priorities where his actions were concerned.

Saladin, Joseph, and Solomon

"His forces of jinn and men and birds were called to Solomon's presence, and ranged in battle array. When they came to the Valley of the Ants, an ant said: 'Go into your dwellings, ants, lest Solomon and his warriors should unwittingly crush you'" (Koran 27:17–18).

Saladin is often compared by his panegyrists to Joseph and to Solomon, two biblical figures with a significant presence in the Koran and in religious literature, but also in several edifying tales popular during the Middle Ages that recount the life of the pre-Islamic prophets. The respect surrounding Solomon in the Koran and the great success the different versions of these tales met with explain why Muslims often used them to defend a cause, a venerated individual, or a charismatic leader. The story of Moses and the pharaoh, for example, served as a point of reference for the first Shiites, who, within the context of their anti-Umayyad propaganda, identified with the small number who did not apostatize while Moses was on Mount Sinai.[37] Imam al-Shāfiʿī, founder of the legal school that bears his name, was compared in Saladin's time, or shortly thereafter, to the prophet Noah, to justify the program for restoring Sunnism set in place in Egypt after the fall of the Fatimids. Just as Noah knew how to lead and preserve a minority of elect who remained faithful to God, so too those who would follow al-Shāfiʿī would remain faithful to Sunni orthodoxy and would put an end to the Shiite heresy. That comparison is reflected even in the architectural design of his mausoleum, built in Cairo in 1211, where one of the pendentives of the cupola still contains a verse from the Koran evoking Noah, and a bark similar to Noah's ark appears at the crown.[38]

In Saladin's case, there are many reasons for the comparison to Joseph and Solomon. Although homonymy and the similarity of situations certainly played an important role, it is obvious that this choice also reflected a political and religious ideology. Solomon, alongside Abraham no doubt, has been one of the most popular biblical figures in the Muslim world, from the Iberian Peninsula to central Asia and from the Middle Ages to our own time. Countless pilgrimage sites are associated with his memory. In Syria-Palestine, his memory is venerated in the city of Jerusalem, but also in Gaza, where he is believed to have been born; in Hebron, whose first structure he built; in Tiberias, near where he is said to have constructed a hydropathic establishment; and in Baalbek and Palmyra, which were supposedly built by him. The geographer Yāqūt said, with a certain lucidity, that every time the residents of a place did not know the origin of an astonishing piece of architecture, they attributed it to Solomon aided by jinn.[39] He is designated in the Koran as a true apostle of Allah, a divine messenger, and a prototype of Muhammad, and his image has always been that of a sovereign ruling over a vast kingdom: just, cautious, perspicacious, chosen and aided by God, from whom he received many powers over nature and demons.[40] "To Solomon We subjected the raging wind," says the Koran (21:81), which the caliph quotes in his 1175 letter of investiture to Saladin to evoke the fleet he would have to equip.

In the Islamic tradition, Solomon is also associated with the founding of Jerusalem and the construction of the Temple, at the very site where the Dome of the Rock and al-Aqsā Mosque were erected in the Umayyad period. Of the many legends about him, one even claimed that he was buried in the Dome of the Rock. It is therefore not surprising that Saladin's entourage chose that emblematic figure to highlight his actions as a just ruler, conqueror of Jerusalem and vanquisher of the Franks.

Despite what we could be led to think, however, that identification predates the taking of Jerusalem. After the capture of Aleppo by Saladin in 1183, it already found expression in the adoption of Solomon's principal attribute, his famous seal, or ring-talisman, composed of a six-pointed star. The silver coins Saladin struck in that city were all decorated with that motif, with inside it an inscription in the name of the caliph and in Saladin's own name. That motif was used only for Aleppine coinage, with the exception of a few silver coins struck in Upper Mesopotamia.[41] Saladin's choice certainly had symbolic value. The importance Aleppo assumed in his eyes, the resistance the city mounted against his expansion, and its surrender after negotiations were somewhat reminiscent of the account in the Koran of the confrontation between the queen of Sheba and Solomon and also of the negotiations that finally allowed the king to take over the kingdom he so coveted.[42] In displaying the seal of Solomon on coinage, a quintessential symbolic object of the ruler's power and legitimacy, Saladin identified with a figure whose authority and power were respected by all Muslims. In about the same period, the six-pointed star, along with other symbols of power, such as the lion and the sword covered with a shield, also adorned the monumental entry to the fortress of Sadr that Saladin built west of the Sinai Peninsula. That motif is even found in the shape of the oculi in the fortress's bath.[43]

Other allusions to Solomon come through in accounts of Saladin's exploits. Al-Fādil wrote in December 1172 that the Nubians resembled the "ants crushed by Solomon,"[44] a clear allusion to the Koranic verse previously cited. And according to 'Imād al-Dīn, the reconquered Jerusalem was the object of Saladin's solicitude because it was the third holy city of Islam, but also because it held "the throne of Solomon and the oratory of David."[45] The image that emerges from these statements is of Saladin as a new Solomon protected by God, a powerful and just ruler whom no one resists, the new founder of Jerusalem.[46]

The comparison between Saladin and Joseph, by contrast, was dictated more by homonymy—Yūsuf, Saladin's given name, is the Arabic translation of "Joseph"—and by a resemblance between certain episodes in their lives.[47] In Egypt, many places preserved the memory of Joseph and became pilgrimage destinations for the Jews, Christians, and Muslims. His grave, by tradition located in a village near Nablus, attracted many visitors.[48] Joseph is an important figure in the Koran, where he appears as a precursor to the Prophet Muhammad, embodying knowledge, clemency, and uprightness, and preaching faith in a single God. Sura 12 bears his name and recounts his story in a narrative strongly influenced by the Jewish and Christian traditions but also marked by ancient Egyptian and Greek legends. As a result, Joseph enjoyed great success in later Arab Muslim literature, both religious and profane.

Authors liked to make Saladin a new Joseph, linking not only their names but also those of their fathers, Yaʿqūb (Jacob) and Ayyūb, which sound similar and which poets rhymed with each other in their verse. Like Joseph, Saladin left Syria-Palestine more or less against his will to settle in Egypt; like him, he sent for his father and brothers.[49] One of Saladin's letters to his brother Tūrānshāh begins with this verse from the Koran (12:90): "I am Joseph, . . . and this is my brother. God has been gracious to us. Those that keep from evil and endure with fortitude, God will not deny them their reward." Like Joseph, who came from nothing, Saladin rose to be the ruler's right-hand man and governed Egypt. He overthrew the Fatimids and seized power: "The kingdom of Pharaoh hath come to an end, and that of Joseph hath begun," wrote Bar Hebraeus.[50] Joseph's uprightness and moral qualities were compared to Saladin's actions on behalf of law and justice. The poet al-ʿArqala evokes Saladin's appointment to the position of chief of police in Damascus by alluding to the well-known story of the wife of Potiphar trying to seduce Joseph: "Be careful, thieves of Syria, that's the advice I can give you. Watch out, for behold the namesake of the prophet Joseph, lord of intelligence and beauty. Friends, if one cut women's hands, the other cuts off men's hands."[51] The very title that Ibn Shaddād gave to his biography of Saladin, *The Book of the Sultan's Rare Deeds and the Blessings of Joseph,* is revealing. Al-Fādil as well, on the occasion of the birth of Saladin's twelfth child, rejoiced that God had granted Saladin one more star than Joseph, who, as the Koran reveals (12:4), saw eleven stars bow down before him. Upon his master's death, al-Fādil also wrote: "The night the sultan died, someone heard a voice in a dream saying: 'Last night, Joseph left his prison,' which is in keeping with the saying of the Prophet: 'This world is a prison for the true believer and paradise for the infidel.' In fact, our Joseph—may God have mercy on him—was in prison here below, compared to the place he occupies in the next world. May God have mercy on his soul and open paradise to him: that is the supreme victory on which the sultan had his heart set!"[52]

Of course, the comparison had its limits. Joseph's pacifism was a long way from Saladin's jihad, and Saladin impoverished Egypt much more than he filled its coffers. But that was not the view of his panegyrists, who, to glorify their master's actions, selected only the aspects that linked the two men, both of whom were chosen and rewarded by God. Both were his faithful servants endowed with wisdom and knowledge, and both were defenders of the "true" religion of Abraham.[53]

The identification of a ruler with a pre-Islamic prophet venerated by Islam has several objectives. First, it links him to a model of sainthood, since saints often appear as the heirs to one or several prophets. Second, it gives the ruler a model to follow and may influence his behavior. Finally, it is an excellent propaganda tool for affirming his legitimacy and authority in the eyes of a population steeped in these images of prophets, not only through a vast legendary literature but also, and perhaps above all, thanks to the popularity of the many pilgrimage sites in Syria-Palestine and Egypt linked to the memory of these great religious figures.

A Flawless Sultan?

It appears at first sight that Saladin's good qualities and virtues were given more prominence than his flaws. Yet there is in the sources no dearth of allusions, more or less veiled, to some of his weaknesses, often presented as the reverse side of his positive qualities. Moreover, Saladin's errors are sometimes emphasized to show his inclination to recognize and right his wrongs, and therefore further highlight his merit.

His generosity, for example, is sometimes judged excessive, and he is criticized when it leads to lack of foresight and poor administration. In 1187, for example, his loyal secretary 'Imād al-Dīn laments the dispersal of the wealth of the city of Acre, which had recently been reconquered: "If someone had taken the care to store up all that booty, to collect all those supplies, to centralize in the public treasury those goods of every sort and of such high value, we might have had a reserve for the days of trial, a basis for the success of future undertakings."[54]

Saladin had the opportunity to respond to that accusation, since the passage was read out in his presence in 1192. He shifted responsibility for the waste onto his son al-Afdal, his nephew Taqī al-Dīn, and the Kurdish emir Diyā' al-

Dīn al Hakkārī. That response, however, only half persuaded the historian Ibn al-Athīr, who believed that Saladin and his son distributed the great wealth of Acre much too generously to their entourage.[55] 'Imād al-Dīn implicitly made the same reproach during the reconquest of Jerusalem. He estimates the ransoms paid by the Latin patriarch and the widows of Amalric and Reginald of Châtillon at two hundred thousand dinars, a considerable sum that Saladin allowed to slip through his fingers.[56] He also reports the words of al-'Ādil, who said that he had seventy thousand dinars delivered to Saladin one evening, but that in the morning his treasurer came back to ask for money, because everything had been distributed during the night.[57] He adds that, after the taking of Jerusalem, Saladin continued to distribute gifts and largesses: "His generosity was censured a great deal, what he distributed far and wide was found to be excessive, but he replied: 'How could I refuse those who deserve it as their due? What I spend, ultimately I keep. When someone deserving accepts something from me, he does me a favor, since he delivers me from what was entrusted to me and releases me from that obligation: what I have at my disposal I hold in trust for those worthy of it.' "[58] Beyond Saladin's excessive generosity, it was his lack of organization and foresight that was being denounced. Even Ibn Shaddād remarks that the employees at the public treasury were sometimes obliged to conceal money to cover the most urgent expenses, knowing that otherwise Saladin would immediately spend it.[59]

Saladin's image as a sovereign who always lent a sympathetic ear to his people sometimes also suffered. In late 1188, when he was besieging the fortress of Safad, a delegation of Egyptian notables arrived to see him. Saladin complained at the time that he was constantly being pestered by complaints and even considered sending the men away: "Before my time, subjects used to fear rulers, flee them, and were afraid of meeting some misfortune because of them. Today, they crowd around us and come to see us so much that they annoy and tire us. As soon as we set off on horseback or on foot, they vie with one another in the stories they have to tell and make us dizzy with their distress."

Al-Fādil gently lectured him and reminded him of his duties, saying: "You ought to be the first to thank God for that blessing. . . . Today, it is you who are the sultan of all, and God has directed toward you and your good actions the hopes of seeing them carried out. All these various people have assembled outside your door and have come to you because, after God, they find no one but you and your liberality. Therefore, be generous toward your visitors!"[60]

Saladin, we are told, hastened to heed that appeal, swearing he would never again close his door to anyone making a request of him.

Saladin was also not always the just, kind, and magnanimous sultan whose image has come down to us. Ibn al-Athīr accuses him, at the beginning of the sultan's reign, of having closed his eyes to the exactions by his emirs and soldiers in Damascus, a departure from Nūr al-Dīn's irreproachable administration of justice. Saladin, alerted by his close circle, corrected himself, we are told, and righted his wrongs. The same historian adds that the councils held by the two rulers were very different in nature. In Nūr al-Dīn's, only religion and jihad were discussed. In Saladin's, by contrast, the racket made during disputes was so deafening that the great traditionist Ibn ʿAsākir, when he attended one in Damascus for the first time in 1174, could not make himself heard. When Saladin later asked him the reasons for his absence from the council, he replied: "'I observed that your council resembled a souk council, where no one hears anyone else. In those of Nūr al-Dīn, everyone was serious and respectful, and when someone spoke the others were quiet and listened to him.' Then Saladin asked his companions to conduct themselves better in Ibn ʿAsākir's presence."[61]

Some doubts might arise about Ibn al-Athīr's objectivity, given his bias in favor of the Zangids, but it should be noted that the aim of his remarks is not solely to denigrate Saladin, since each time he adds that Saladin made amends. It is rather the sultan's lack of governmental experience that is pointed out, at a time—the very beginning of his reign—when he must have appeared to the population to be more soldier than sovereign. In any case, the speed with which Saladin endeavored to respond to these criticisms shows how concerned he was to polish his image and to model it as much as possible on that of Nūr al-Dīn.

Saladin also knew how to be ruthless in the punishments he meted out to his enemy prisoners, and on certain occasions he did not recoil from the use of violence. Violence was an inherent part of the world in which he lived. But at the state level, violence, to be justified, had to obey certain rules and was on principle limited by religious law, which the ruler more than anyone else was obliged to respect. In this case, however, it is necessary to distinguish between two types of violence. That practiced in war, particularly in the fight against the infidels, was not only legitimate but recommended, to assure the victory and security of Islam. The violence that a sovereign committed within his own territory against prisoners, rebels, or heretics was more questionable and often gave rise to legal precautions and ideological justifications. In that case, it was better to take the advice of competent jurists, whom the sovereign would ask to issue a fatwa to legitimate the violent act he was preparing to commit. Several times, Saladin asked the ulemas for fatwas that would allow him to execute prisoners, such as the pro-Fatimid poet al-'Umāra, accused of rebellion in 1174, or the Iranian mystic al-Suhrawardī, charged with heresy in 1191.[62] Other times, the violence against prisoners was justified simply because they had breached the rules of honor on which the society of that time was founded, in both the East and the West. So it was that the execution of Vizier Shāwar, which marked the beginning of the Ayyubid dynasty in Egypt, was justified by his treason and treachery. Similarly, the decision to have Reginald of Châtillon beheaded after the Battle of Hattīn was legitimated by his continual violation of the truces he had signed. Finally, Saladin's violence against the Frankish prisoners who fell into his hands after the Franks retook Acre in 1191 was motivated primarily by the massacre of Muslim prisoners carried out despite the promises that had been made.

But beyond that "legitimate" violence, Saladin also allowed himself to be tempted by more ordinary violence and was sometime called to account by his close circle. It was 'Imād al-Dīn who boasted of setting him back on the right path in 1176 during the siege of 'Azāz, when troops seized one of the Aleppine cavalrymen who were harassing Saladin's army. The sultan wanted to have the cavalryman's hand cut off like a common thief, but 'Imād al-Dīn remarked that such behavior was contrary to religious law. Saladin accepted the reproach and changed his attitude. His cousin, having arrived as this was happening, was outraged at what he called an act of cowardice, but the sultan lectured him and calmed his anger.[63]

'Imād al-Dīn's account was likely intended as much to present himself in an advantageous light as to point out the virtues of a sovereign who, having regained his self-control, recovered his calm and uprightness. 'Imād al-Dīn nevertheless gives a glimpse—in spite of himself as it were—of a reality on the ground that was very different from the ideal image of Saladin diffused elsewhere. That reality is illustrated by another anecdote reported by the same author. In 1178, when Saladin was in Syria, Frankish prisoners were brought to him. He ordered all of them executed by ulemas. The prisoner whom 'Imād al-Dīn was supposed to kill with his own hands was a young boy, whom he asked to keep as a slave and who was finally exchanged for a Muslim prisoner.

That practice of having prisoners executed by religious notables was not peculiar to Saladin, but al-Fādil condemns it in the name of Islamic law, which prohibits the execution of defenseless captives.[64]

Saladin was also reproached at times for his intransigence. When he refused to respond to the demands of the embassy from Mosul headed by Nūr al-Dīn's daughter in 1185, he attracted the disapproval not only of the residents of Mosul and the followers of the Zangids but also that of al-Fādil, to such a degree that Saladin regretted having lost "both his good reputation and his chance to take the city" at that time.[65] Some even suspected him of having been behind the death of his cousin Nāsir al-Dīn Muhammad of Homs in 1186. That accusation is difficult to verify and is contradicted by Saladin's attitude toward his cousin's son and heir; it should probably be ascribed to Zangid propaganda.

A few accounts also give a glimpse of a less courageous Saladin than the one usually depicted. 'Imād al-Dīn and Ibn al-Athīr relate the fear that took hold of him after the assault on his person by the Assassins during the siege of 'Azāz. At the time, he had a wooden tower constructed outside his tent and slept in it, no longer allowing strangers to approach him.[66]

At the military level, tactical errors were several times imputed to Saladin. In 1187 Ibn al-Athīr attributed to him full responsibility for the failure of the siege of Tyre, saying Saladin was wrong not to take the city, given that it was so defenseless, and to have allowed such a large number of Franks to take refuge there, which allowed the city to await the arrival of reinforcements from the West.[67] Sibt Ibn al-Jawzī was of the same opinion, judging that Saladin's decision to let the Franks of Jerusalem leave for Tyre was an error with serious consequences: it allowed the fall of Acre during the Third Crusade and the massacre of Muslim prisoners. It would have been better, according to Sibt Ibn al-Jawzī, to propose that the Franks convert to Islam and to kill them if they refused.[68]

Even 'Imād al-Dīn, usually so laudatory of his master, implicitly reproaches Saladin for his tactical errors, such as the one he committed in late August 1191, when he did not respond to his son's appeals for his help in wiping out the Franks marching southward, between Acre and Haifa.[69] Other veiled criticisms can be discerned in 'Imād al-Dīn's lamentations when Saladin ordered the fortifications of Ascalon destroyed in 1191: "If care had been taken to restore [the city] from the day it was taken and held, its strength would not have been impaired, its hand would not have withered away, its tip would not have been blunted, and we should not have tired of loving it."[70]

Similarly, when Saladin retook Jaffa in 1192, he spared the citadel, giving Richard the Lionheart time to return and seize the city. "Regret is pointless when the opportunity is lost. If the sultan had refrained from trusting them, if he had continued to weaken them, we would certainly have demolished that citadel to its foundations and would have swept that piece of terrain clean."[71]

On other occasions, it was Saladin's lack of authority over the troops that was implicitly criticized, as in Burzayh and Latakia in 1188, where the looting was deplored,[72] or in 1191, when his weary troops outside Acre balked at providing him with the aid he needed to take the enemy by surprise and save the city's Muslim garrison.[73] Similarly, in September 1191, Saladin was met with his emirs' refusal to defend Ascalon as he would have liked. Their reply: "If you wish to hold the place, then come in with us yourself and one of your older sons. Otherwise none of us will enter lest we suffer what the men at Acre suffered." Saladin had to resign himself to having the city destroyed.[74]

The situation was hardly better in Jaffa in July 1192, when Saladin did not succeed in mobilizing his troops—they were too busy looting the city—to seize the citadel before Richard the Lionheart came to its aid. The undisciplined conduct of the soldiers slowed the evacuation of the citadel by the Franks, who had agreed to surrender, and ultimately allowed the English ruler to regain the upper hand. Ibn Shaddād does not neglect to point out that Saladin should have demonstrated more intransigence toward the garrison of Jaffa and that the sultan was of his opinion, but that the army was little inclined to obey him. Ibn al-Athīr is even more explicit when he describes the squabbles within the Muslim army itself between Saladin's emirs and his own mamluks, all fighting over the booty.[75]

An attentive reading of the sources, then, allows us to discern, though at times not without difficulty, what Saladin's likely weaknesses were. But it is clear that the image that emerges from these sources is much more positive than negative, even in the works of authors who prove most critical of him. Our attempt to portray that image without losing sight of the propaganda of which it was part does not signify that Saladin possessed none of the virtues attributed to him. In comparing the historical witnesses, especially the sources that are a priori less favorable to him, it is possible to conclude that some of these qualities must be attributed to him. But the emphasis placed by his close circle on glorifying his virtues and actions means that, to govern, Saladin had to attend to his image and make it correspond as much as possible to the widely diffused one of

the ideal ruler, defender of Islam and protector of his subjects. That was especially important in Saladin's case because he had before him many adversaries
and had to erase from the collective memory his absence of dynastic legitimacy. Yet we cannot lose sight of the fact that, if his image as ideal sultan took
hold with such force, it was not only because he had good propagandists but
also and above all because his victories on the ground were real. And, because
of his reconquest of Jerusalem, they assumed great symbolic importance in the
eyes of Islam as a whole.

III

Jihad

12

Image and Propaganda

"The Franks know that, in us, they have an adversary that no calamity can take down before that day when they become discouraged, a leader who will not lay down his sword until they disarm. If our view gains the [caliph's] high approval, we will fight with a sword formidable even in its sheath, by the will of God we will achieve all our desires. Believers will not even need to take their hands out of their mantles, and we will liberate the mosque where God transported his servant during the night."[1]

Saladin wrote these words to the caliph in early 1175. Nearly thirteen years stood between his letter and the retaking of Jerusalem from the Franks, since, in the first part of his reign, Saladin expended most of his energy fighting his Muslim adversaries and achieving recognition as the uncontested ruler of Egypt, Syria-Palestine, and part of Upper Mesopotamia. Nevertheless, though it was not until 1186 that he finally made the struggle against the Franks his sole objective, early on he understood the advantage to be drawn—in terms of establishing his power and obtaining acknowledgment from the caliph—from an active propaganda campaign in favor of jihad. In perfect continuity with Nūr al-Dīn's work, his entourage therefore elaborated a discourse tending to represent him as the only ruler capable of defeating the Franks and of inciting the Muslim community as a whole to follow him into battle. His adversaries, by contrast, were accused of inaction, or worse, of collusion with the enemies of Islam.

Various means were used to diffuse the themes of that propaganda, and they targeted every audience. These included: monumental inscriptions on which Saladin's titulature pointed out his actions against the infidels, "slaves of the cross";[2] sermons and Friday *khutbas* inciting the population to jihad and giving thanks to God for the successes achieved; books vaunting the merits of holy war and praising Jerusalem; treatises in the art of war; letters to the caliph of Baghdad and to the ruling elites announcing Saladin's victories; poems glorifying his battles; biographies and chronicles listing his virtues as a jihad warrior. The aim of all these discourses was at once to unite the Muslims, to develop the spirit of jihad, and to glorify Saladin.

The Unity of Islam, Condition for Jihad

One of the very first themes of that propaganda was Islam unity, a condition sine qua non for the jihad's success. Saladin often used that rationale to justify his battles against the Zangids and, more broadly, against all his Muslim foes. Was he sincere in his assertions, or was this just a pretext in the service of his ambitions? It is hardly possible to give a definitive answer to that question: indeed, though it is difficult to refute the need for Muslim unification to ensure the success of jihad, it is also clear that that unity was realized under Saladin's command and to his own advantage. Hence, rather than wonder pointlessly about the nature of his intentions, I shall focus once again on the discourse and arguments of his propaganda, which underscored the urgency of such a reunification and affirmed that Saladin was the only one capable of bringing it about.

Saladin, of course, was not the first to speak of uniting against the Franks. From the days following the First Crusade, there were poets and jurists, such as the Damascene al-Sulamī, who called on their contemporaries to be cognizant of the devastating effect of their divisions, which had allowed the Franks' searing success. But the religious and political cleavages were so deep, and individual ambitions so great, that it took several decades for that idea truly to take root and to be implemented by the rulers. Nūr al-Dīn played a decisive role in that realm, managing to reunify under his authority all of Syria and Egypt and part of Upper Mesopotamia.

Upon his death, that auspicious unity was shattered, and Saladin had to reconstitute it patiently on the foundations laid by his predecessor. The arguments developed under Nūr al-Dīn's reign were taken up and amplified: Islamic unity had to be defended to avoid wearing down the Muslims in fratricidal battles and to allow them to devote all their strength to the jihad. Saladin claimed to be the person best placed to spearhead that unity because, from the start of his reign in Egypt, he had demonstrated his ability to overthrow Shiism, to instill respect for the authority of the Sunni caliph of Baghdad, and to defend the holy sites against the incursions of the Franks on the Red Sea. By contrast, his Zangid enemies were merely traitors, ready at any instant to ally themselves with the Franks and with the heretical Assassin sect, whom they promised anything and everything. Each of Saladin's expeditions against them between 1175 and 1186 was justified by these accusations, and all his attempts to subdue northern Syria and Upper Mesopotamia were legitimated by his desire to unite the Muslim Middle East so as to have more troops at his disposal to conduct the jihad.

According to that same discourse, the Zangid prince ʿIzz al-Dīn had succeeded in seizing Aleppo only because Saladin's army was mobilized on the Red Sea combating the Franks. Hence, while ʿIzz al-Dīn was unfairly claiming for himself a city that the caliph had promised to Saladin, the sultan was defending access to the Prophet's tomb.[3] Several of his letters accused the Muslim rulers of turning away from jihad to concern themselves only with money and pleasure, whereas he, Saladin, was striving to rally the Muslims to battle the infidels and was planning to take Mosul only in order to conquer Jerusalem.[4] In showing it was useless to trust impious and perfidious foes who were not competent to govern, he was in some sense justifying, by way of contrast, his own right to reign, a method often used by rulers whose power had been acquired by force.[5]

In 1183, the taking of Aleppo allowed Saladin to control the whole of Syria-Palestine and Egypt. This restored unity could have marked a turning point in his preparations for jihad, as he himself wrote in this letter to one of his emirs in Yemen: "Now that all the Muslim regions are placed under our jurisdiction or under that of our subordinates, we must, in return for that favor from heaven, direct our resolve, use all our power, against the accursed Franks. We must fight them for the cause of God. With their blood, we will efface the stain with which they have covered the Holy Land."[6]

In reality, for another three years Saladin's ambition to expand into Upper Mesopotamia prevailed over his aspiration for jihad. But after the accord concluded with Mosul in December 1185, and especially, in reaction to the illness that almost took his life a few weeks later in Harrān, he swore that, should he recover, he would devote himself exclusively to the struggle against the Franks and the reconquest of Jerusalem. Al-Fāḍil encouraged him to renew that oath during his convalescence in Damascus. Saladin, approaching his fiftieth birthday, was no doubt becoming aware that his days were numbered. His close circle encouraged him on that path, as attested by the statement of one of his emirs at his council: "The people of the East curse us and say, 'He has given up fighting the infidels and has turned his attention to fighting Muslims.' In my opinion our best plan is to take a course of action that will vindicate us and stop people's wagging tongues."[7] Muslim unity was only imperfectly realized, but Saladin would now focus all his efforts on jihad. He nonetheless continued regularly to remind the rulers of neighboring territories of the need to support him militarily and financially in his struggle against the Franks.

The Sultan, Champion of Jihad

The image of the sultan as living symbol of the sacred struggle against the infidels, sparing no effort in the holy war, was already a widespread theme in propaganda under Nūr al-Dīn's reign. It was adopted and elaborated around the person of Saladin, particularly by his biographer Ibn Shaddād: "The Jihad, his love and passion for it, had taken a mighty hold on his heart and all his being, so much so that he talked of nothing else, thought of nothing but the means to pursue it, was concerned only with its manpower and had a fondness only for those who spoke of it and encouraged it."[8]

Al-Fāḍil, citing a verse from al-Mutanabbī, a tenth-century poet in the court of Sayf al-Dawla of Aleppo, addressed Saladin as follows: "You are not a king routing his fellow, you are Islam putting infidelity to flight."[9]

Saladin was thus presented as a man who was performing without fail his duty to wage jihad "on the path of God," and especially, as a providential leader guided by God. Jihad is a collective duty of the Muslim community, which must fight to advance the spread of Islam. That duty, collective under the guidance of the community's leader, becomes individual when Islamic territories are attacked or threatened. In both cases, the ruler's role is essential, and Saladin's entourage wanted to diffuse that image of a charismatic leader fully assuming his place at the head of the jihad. Such a ruler does not hesitate to leave his family, his children, his homeland, and his comfort to devote himself fully to it; to read assiduously the jihad treatises composed for him by the ulemas in his court; to proclaim continually that, in waging that battle he is only carrying out the will of God.[10] When the Sicilian admiral attempted to negotiate with Saladin after the taking of Latakia in 1188, the sultan replied: "It is God who ordered us to have dominion over the earth: it is our duty to obey him and to devote ourselves to jihad; it is he who will make us master of these lands. Should all the nations of the world conspire against us, we shall invoke the support of God and shall fight, without taking heed of the number of our enemies."[11] In 1189, when he asked for reinforcements from his brother Tughtegin, in Yemen at the time, Saladin told him that, in responding to the sultan's appeal, it was God whom Tughtegin was obeying, the Prophet he was defending, and Islam he was saving.[12]

In the eyes of Muslims, jihad is, by its very nature, in the service not of men but of God, who alone grants the power to prevail or to die. Victory is a gift from God, just as defeat is divinely sent to test men's patience.[13] According to his entourage, then, Saladin was chosen by God to lead the Muslims to victory, to succeed where all his predecessors had failed. After the taking of Jerusalem, 'Imād al-Dīn wrote: "The good news has arrived concerning the grace Allah has bestowed on us through that important conquest, that complete victory, that significant blessing, that signal favor, on a bright, glorious, and illustrious day, and concerning the greatness that Allah reserved for this century, to make it superior to the others. . . . Thus he made other rulers incapable of garnering his assistance and winning his favors. For the one he has made to advance under his auspices, he reserved the effects of his sublime decree and his ever-growing might."[14]

Saladin was the one everyone had been waiting for, the one whom God finally brought to life. The continuity of Saladin's work with that of Nūr al-Dīn, often emphasized in the first years of his reign, had a tendency, over the course of his victories, to give way to the idea of a rebirth after a long period of darkness and degradation. Indeed, it was truly victory that conferred on Saladin that status as "unique being."[15] To be victorious was to be cherished by the deity, as the Greeks also believed during the Hellenistic period. That was the reason why Saladin, according to his biographers, relied fully on God and never lost hope in him, even in the darkest times—in Acre in July 1191, for example, when, though overcome by sadness at the announcement of the garrison's surrender, he did not cease "his calling upon God and his recourse to Him, patiently, trustingly, determinedly and zealously."[16] Similarly, in 1179, when he was told that the famine ravaging Syria was not propitious for fighting, he responded that God would be responsible for feeding the Muslims.

To properly emphasize the religious dimension of jihad, the authors insisted as well on Saladin's strict observance of his religious duties during his fight against the Franks and on the signs of assistance sent to him by God. Jihad itself could exempt a person from performing the ritual obligations stipulated by Muslim law, such as prayer, fasting, legal alms, or pilgrimage. Saladin used it to justify his never having gone to Mecca. Nonetheless, his battles never led him to forget his other duties, prayer in particular, and Ibn Shaddād tells us that, during the last year of his life, Saladin set out to make up for all the fasting days he had missed because of illness or the battle against the Franks.[17]

Various phenomena could be interpreted as signs of God's favor, including victories over the Franks achieved on a Friday, the day of the great weekly prayer.[18] Saladin liked to choose that day for launching a battle, especially at the hour of the mid-day collective prayer, to benefit from the prayers of the entire Muslim community. Jerusalem and a great number of strongholds in northern Syria fell into his hands on a Friday, "a sign of the acceptance of the Muslim preachers' prayers and of the blessed good-fortune of the sultan, in that God enabled him to achieve these victories on the day during which the reward of good deeds is multiplied. These are rare victories on successive Fridays, unparalleled in history," wrote Ibn Shaddād. The taking of Jerusalem occurred not only on a Friday but also on a date very close to the anniversary of the Prophet's ascent *(mi'rāj)* from Jerusalem into heaven, and that proximity was interpreted as a further sign of God's grace.[19] Conversely, the loss of a city on a Friday, such as the fall of Acre into the Franks' hands on Friday, July 12, 1191, was felt with great intensity. The Muslims' defeat was made all the more painful when they saw the Franks' banner waving on the minaret of the Great Mosque on the day of great prayer.[20]

Premonitory dreams reinforced the idea that Saladin was guided by God, since in the Islamic tradition, the "true dream" is perceived as a "path to the knowledge of the secret dimensions of life"[21] and usually comes from God. "If there be a prophet among you, *I* the Lord will make myself known unto him in a vision, *and* will speak unto him in a dream," it is written in the Old Testament (Numbers 12:6; KJV). The Prophet Muhammad also saw dreams as divine intervention. Hence the importance, in the centuries following the birth of Islam, of Arab oneiromancy, which was classified as one of the legal sciences with religious import, midway between the religious sciences and the so-called exact sciences.[22] Premonitory dreams also play an important role in Muslim hagiography, with the line between a saint's dreams and his visions sometimes being difficult to draw.[23] To link Saladin's major victories to premonitory dreams was thus to affirm that he was God's chosen. In the wake of the Battle of Hattīn or the taking of Jerusalem, for example, attestations of premonitory dreams multiplied. Among the most edifying accounts was a dream that Ibn Abī Tayyi' had about his father. One day in 1160, when the father was at the home of the sheikh of Mosul, a man appeared, saying: "'Sheikh, last night I dreamed I was in a strange, unknown country filled with pigs. A man brandishing a saber was killing them all before the eyes of the crowd. I then asked someone: "Is that Jesus, son of Mary, or the Mahdi?"[24] "No," he replied. "Who is it then?" "It is Yūsuf," he told me, without another word.' The assembly was moved by the account of that dream; it was concluded that the Christians would be killed by a figure named Yūsuf, and predictions focused on Yūsuf, son of 'Abd al-Mu'min, ruler of Maghreb. Since Caliph al-Mustanjid bi-llāh had just ascended to the throne that year, some believed it was about him."[25]

Ibn Abī Tayyi' adds that he had forgotten that story until the defeat of the Franks at Hattīn reminded him of it, and he then understood that it was about al-Malik al-Nāsir Yūsuf, that is, Saladin. Others also cited a poet who, in sibylline lines, had predicted Saladin's conquests some ten years earlier: "The protector of religion took possession of the well-defended fortresses, when religion had lost hope of being protected. / He will take Jerusalem after rolling up [conquering] the edge to his advantage and killing the Caesar."[26]

By "edge," the historian Abū Shāma comments, one must understand "coast," and by "Caesar," Reginald of Châtillon, whom Saladin killed with his own hands. The doctor and biographer Ibn Abī Usaybi'a reports the prediction of an Arab Christian doctor, who, while living in Latin territory (Jerusalem) in 1184, predicted through astrological signs that Saladin would take the city. One of the doctor's sons announced that good news to Saladin, who showered him with gifts and gave him a yellow flag—yellow was the color of Saladin's dynasty   and an arrow bearing his coat of arms *(rank)*, recommending that he hoist them over his father's house in Jerusalem at the proper moment. So it was, the author recounts, that the house escaped destruction as well as the tribute imposed on all Christians of Jerusalem, when the city fell into Saladin's hands. The doctor's family, moreover, was exempted from the capitation, a special privilege they kept at least until 1270.[27]

Then there was the story that the Andalusian theologian Ibn Barrajān (d. ca. 1141), in his commentary on the Koranic verse "The Romans have been defeated" (30:2),[28] had predicted the month and year of the retaking of Jerusalem, a prediction that two jurists in Saladin's entourage reported to the sultan. Saladin generously demonstrated his gratitude to them following the auspicious event.[29]

Not all these predictions were invented by Saladin's propagandists for the needs of his cause. Some were sufficiently vague as to be applicable to any situation desired. Others were eschatological prophecies of the time, based on astronomical calculations that instilled fear that the world was about to end as a result of a conjunction of the planets. Saladin remained unimpressed by these prophecies when they did not concern any auspicious event of his own reign. In 1186–1187, therefore, he displayed hostility toward the astrologists who were terrorizing the population by announcing the approach of the end of time.[30] Nevertheless, omens, premonitions, dreams, astrological predictions, and interpretation of unexplained phenomena were part of the daily life of the people and allowed them to explore the world of the invisible and of the future, one way among others to find reassurance in face of the unpredictable, to comfort themselves in the face of uncertainty.[31] Both Christians and Muslims granted them the same importance. The *Itinerarium,* for example, notes that the taking of Ascalon by Saladin in September 1187 was accompanied by a solar eclipse: "'As if in sympathy, the sun took from the city and the globe' the benefit of light."[32] In September 1189, while the Franks and Muslims were facing off outside the walls of Acre, a magnificent stallion escaped a Frankish ship and swam to the harbor of Acre, before being delivered to Saladin: "The enemy found that incident to be a bad omen; we saw it as a sign of victory and favor," exclaimed 'Imād al-Dīn in triumph.[33]

According to some, the vast divine favor that Saladin seemed to enjoy linked him to the Prophet himself and to the first Muslim conquerors. His battles against the Franks were compared to those that the Prophet, having taken refuge in Medina, waged against the unbelievers of Mecca. In 1175, in response to

Saladin's request for investiture over Syria and Egypt, the caliph encouraged him to retake Jerusalem, alluding to Hudaybiyya, an expedition by the Prophet against Mecca.[34] As for 'Imād al-Dīn, he was convinced that the conquest of Jerusalem was nothing less than a new Hegira for Islam. And, in the letter of 1187 that he wrote in Saladin's name to the caliph of Baghdad, announcing the good news, he commented on a verse from the Koran, "We had already shown you favour" (20:37), with these words: "The first time was in the century of the Prophet—may God bless and hail him—and of his Companions. The second is the present time, which has seen Islam freed from the slavery of misfortune."[35]

Saladin was also compared to the first caliphs, under whose reign Islam had expanded triumphantly. In particular, he was compared to the "two 'Umars," that is, 'Umar ibn al-Khattāb (r. 634–644), the first conqueror of the city of Jerusalem, and 'Umar II ibn 'Abd al-'Azīz (r. 717–720), the eighth Umayyad caliph, who for later generations was the incarnation of the just, virtuous, and pious sovereign.[36] Ibn Shaddād wrote that Saladin's perspicacity made him think of this saying of the Prophet: "In my community there are those who are perspicacious and who express their views, and 'Umar is one of them." Another historian pointed to Saladin's desire to follow 'Umar's example in his decision not to destroy the reconquered Jerusalem.[37] Saladin himself is supposed to have said, during his illness in Upper Mesopotamia: "If I die, I have designated Abū Bakr, 'Umar, 'Uthmān, and 'Alī to succeed me," alluding to the first four caliphs. He meant thereby his brother al-'Ādil Abū Bakr, his nephew Taqī al-Dīn 'Umar, and his two sons al-'Azīz 'Uthmān and al-Afdal 'Alī.[38]

The Importance of Jerusalem

Jerusalem, taken by the Franks in 1099, was at the heart of jihad propaganda about Saladin, though the arguments developed in favor of its reconquest only repeated those that his predecessor had already put forward. More than Nūr al-Dīn, however, Saladin used Jerusalem to justify taking power and conducting expeditions against his Muslim adversaries.[39] In 1175, he insisted on the importance that Syria was acquiring as his base for the conquest of Jerusalem, and attacked the Zangids of Aleppo and Mosul, who had completely lost interest in the holy city. "March to Jerusalem, conquer it, and spill rivers of blood, which will purify it," 'Imād al-Dīn told him in 1177 with his usual grandiloquence.[40] Ten years later, on the eve of taking the city, Saladin invited Egyptian and Syrian men of religion to come witness the conquest, to better mark its sacred character.

Nevertheless, it is the letters, poems, and sermons written after the taking of the city in 1187 that best allow us to assess the place held by Jerusalem in the popular imagination and in the politico-religious discourse of that time.[41] The reader will forgive me, therefore, for anticipating somewhat and analyzing them here. Beyond the rhetorical and lyrical aspects, several themes repeatedly recur. The victory is at first seen as coming in the wake of Nūr al-Dīn's accomplishments. Was not one of Saladin's first actions in Jerusalem to install, in al-Aqsā Mosque, the sculpted wood pulpit (minbar) that his predecessor had ordered to be made in Aleppo in expectation of that great day? 'Imād al-Dīn, in any case, saw that symbolic gesture as an opportunity to associate the two sovereigns in the Muslim prayers.[42]

The same author was also pleased to point out the importance of Jerusalem, closely linking it to Mecca, the first holy city of Islam:

> I therefore announced the deliverance of the Jerusalem mosque to the Mecca mosque. I chanted the verse: "He has ordained for you the faith which He enjoined" (42:11); I gladdened the Black Stone [of Mecca] with the White Stone [of Jerusalem], the site of Revelation with the place of the nocturnal journey [of Muhammad], the dwelling of the leader of Allah's envoys—seal of the prophets—with the residence of the envoys and of the prophets, the Station of Abraham with the imprint of the Chosen's foot. The Muslims celebrated at length the honor of holding the two holy cities; the people communicated with one another the tale of that noble victory, that important conquest; from every remote mountain pass they came on pilgrimage, following every road leading there; from Jerusalem, they clothed themselves in ihrām to visit the temple of Mecca, enjoying the bloom of divine favors in these glad gardens.[43]

Connections between the Temple of Jerusalem and the Kaaba of Mecca had existed since the early days of Islam.[44] A common Semitic heritage, Judeo-Christian traditions reinterpreted by Islam, and Koranic exegesis were the source of many associations between the two sanctuaries. The water from the pool of Siloe ('Ayn Sulwān), a pilgrimage destination for both Muslims and

Christians, was thus compared to that of the Zamzam Well in Mecca.[45] In his letter to Saladin in 1175, the caliph of Baghdad urged him to conquer Jerusalem, "sister of Mecca," on behalf of the veneration of which it was the object.[46] More broadly, in the eyes of Saladin's contemporaries (as in those of Muslims today), Jerusalem had a profound connection to the very origins of Islam. Is not Abraham, "forefather" of the Arabs and founder of pure monotheism—which Muslims believed they had restored—associated both with the Kaaba, which he is said to have built (Koran 2:127), and with Jerusalem, where he lived?

The Muslims also linked Jerusalem to the memory of David, Solomon, and Jesus, and it was there that God "cast [his Word] to Mary: a spirit [that is, Jesus] from him" (Koran 4:171). Muhammad belonged to that long line of pre-Islamic prophets venerated by Islam. Very early on, the "farther temple [al-Aqsā]" mentioned in the Koran (17:1) was identified by exegetes as Jerusalem. It was to that city that God sent his Prophet to undertake his nocturnal journey toward the heavens, and it was also in the direction of Jerusalem that Muhammad asked the first Muslims to pray. Over time, then, Jerusalem became "the first of the two *kiblas* [directions of prayer], the second of the two sacred Mosques, the third after the two holy cities."[47]

All these traditions, which made Jerusalem a holy city and an important pilgrimage site within the Muslim world, had been well established in Syria-Palestine since at least the tenth century,[48] though it is true that the Franks' settlement of the region resulted in increased interest in the holy city. Under Nūr al-Dīn's and then Saladin's reigns, men of religion, in elaborating the discourse on Jerusalem's holiness, mobilized the energies of Muslims around their sovereign. That same discourse then allowed them to glorify the man who had reconquered it. Many preachers of the time recalled the several hadith that incited Muslims to come live in Jerusalem: "He who lives in Jerusalem is considered a warrior for the cause of Allah," "Dying in Jerusalem is nearly the same as dying in heaven," and, "He who visits Jerusalem, impelled by devotion to that place, will enter paradise." Pilgrimages to Jerusalem by Muslims increased after 1187, and many pilgrims stopped in Jerusalem while on their way to or from Mecca.[49]

Saladin's taking of Jerusalem also provided Muslims with the opportunity to delight in the humiliation of the Franks. This was a religious humiliation resulting from Christianity's submission to Islam, the victory of the oneness of Islam over the Christian Trinity, the elimination of religious symbols such as crosses and church bells; but it was also a military humiliation linked to defeat, with its share of deaths, prisoners, violated women, and looted treasures. ʿImād al-Dīn expresses that satisfaction in his unique style:

> By the tears of those who fear Allah, the sacred Rock has been puri-
> fied of the polytheists' stain. Those who are idle on Sunday have
> been removed far from it by the approach of those who proclaim
> divine unity. . . . May the temple of Mecca be strengthened by the
> deliverance of its brother, the temple of Jerusalem, by the dawn of
> Islam after the long nocturnal darkness of impiety, by the purifica-
> tion of the places where the prophets lived. May Allah preserve
> them from filth and turpitude. . . . The bonds that held impiety
> have been loosed, and it has fallen from its heights; its cables have
> been worn through; its knots undone; its dwellings have become
> sepulchres . . . what was precious was given away for nothing by
> the force of spears. . . .
>
> How many women whose veils were torn off! . . . How many
> domestic women were subjugated! How many beautiful ones sub-
> jected to harsh ordeals! How many virgins deflowered! How many
> noble ladies married by force![50]

Emphasis was placed not only on humiliation but on the purification of Islam, since wresting Jerusalem from the "polytheists"[51] meant taking it from
"impurity" to "purity." The notion of purity is omnipresent in Islam, as it is in
Judaism. It is an integral part of the faith, accompanying not only religious rituals but also all acts of everyday life. "Purity is half of faith," proclaims a hadith
of the Prophet,[52] and without purity there is no valid religious act. It is therefore not surprising to find purity associated with the reconquest of Jerusalem.
The sources denounce the filth introduced by the Franks in the Noble Sanctuary (Haram al-Sharīf), no doubt because al-Aqsā Mosque had been turned into
a residence for the Knights Templar with all the related consequences, namely,
the installation of latrines, storehouses, and shelters for animals. But that filth
did not have only a material aspect. It was also spiritual and religious, as we
find in the description of ʿImād al-Dīn, who goes so far as to see the sculpted
sheep adorning the Dome of the Rock, which the Franks had turned into a
church, as "effigies resembl[ing] those of pigs."[53] Once the monument was rid
of all its Christian attributes, an inscription was placed on it: "Salāh al-Dīn has

purified this holy place [*Bayt al-Maqdis*] of the polytheists."[54] Since the seventh century, the Muslims had had the habit of designating, with a play on words, the Church of the Resurrection (*Qiyāma*), or Church of the Holy Sepulchre, as the Church "of Filth [*Qumāma*]."[55] The same idea of impurity, linked to the mere presence of the Franks in the region, is apparent in the account of the Andalusian Ibn Jubayr, who calls Baldwin IV, king of Jerusalem, "the Pig," and his mother, "the Sow." His description of the streets of Acre is indicative of the close link he establishes between infidelity and impurity: "Its roads and streets are choked by the press of men, so that it is hard to put foot to ground. Unbelief and unpiousness there burn fiercely, and pigs [Christians] and crosses abound. It stinks and is filthy, being full of refuse and excrement. The Franks ravished it from Muslim hands in the first . . . decade of the sixth [twelfth] century, and the eyes of Islam were swollen with weeping for it."[56]

Nothing about that connection was peculiar to Islam. The same association between infidels and impurity, reconquest and purification, is also found in Western Christian literature. In *De rebus Hispaniae*, Rodrigo Jiménez de Rada describes the taking of Cordova from the Muslims in 1236 and the conversion of the mosque into a church: "The Arabs of the city departed safe and sound and, on the day of the Feast of the Apostles Peter and Paul, the patrician city was purged of the muck of Muhammad." In the Cordova mosque, "the filth of Muhammad was eliminated and holy water sprinkled about."[57]

We are told that Saladin, who had made Jerusalem his principal objective, displayed toward it "a great concern that would move mountains."[58] In any event, no negotiation could have persuaded him to yield that city to the Franks, as he told Richard the Lionheart in October 1191, saying it was pointless even to discuss it.[59] That is also what the poets boasted after the signing of the treaty in September 1192, when they advised the "English dog" to abandon Jerusalem forever and thanked Saladin for having defended it and prevented it from "weeping tears of blood a second time."[60]

The reestablishment of Muslim authority in the holy city caused such a stir that Saladin remained for posterity "the conqueror of Jerusalem [*fātih Bayt al-Maqdis*]."[61] The sacredness of the city also spread to the region as a whole, as attested by the expressions "dwelling of the prophets," "land of the Resurrection," and "holy land," which were henceforth paired with the names of Syria-Palestine (*Shām*) and of the coast (*sāhil*).[62]

Martyrdom at All Cost?

In Islamic doctrine, the warrior who dies during a jihad acquires the status of martyr *(shahīd)* and thus enters paradise, where he is assured a favored place near God. Did Saladin encourage his fighters to die as martyrs in order to obtain that ultimate reward? Is he himself depicted as seeking out martyrdom, eager to die on "the path of God"? To respond to these questions, we have statements from men in his entourage but also a treatise enjoining jihad, written for him by a certain al-Tarsūsī. The work consists of two parts unequal in length: the first and longer part describes in detail the weapons that ought to be used against the enemy; the second deals with military tactics, including a section devoted to inciting jihad. In addition to the many Koranic verses and hadith relating to jihad, there is a model *khutba,* intended to be pronounced by a preacher in the ranks of the soldiers on the battlefield, to give them courage. Although that *khutba* has only theoretical value and develops themes that were relatively widespread in Islam, it merits a moment's consideration, if only for the conservative and normative character of the discourse on jihad in Saladin's time to which it attests.

On reading this text, we are immediately struck by the omnipresence of the theme of death. But what is more natural, since the matter at hand was to convince Muslims to go fight, at the risk of paying with their lives? Many arguments are therefore advanced to make such a death appealing. The warrior's death is first presented as the will of God. To die in battle is to submit to divine will. Is not man destined to die in any event? Better to die in jihad, therefore, and to obtain the rewards attached to it. In addition, that death, decided by God, is simply the beginning of a new life in the next world, which is far superior to the world here below. And, just as there is truly life in death by jihad, there is also a death in ignorance, that is, in the opposition to Islam: "And I testify that Muhammad—may God bless and hail him—is His servant, sent to wage jihad against anyone who opposes his lord's order and follows only his own views, so that ignorance has killed and buried him."

If death by jihad is the source of life, it is also the source of forgiveness. The martyrdom achieved in battle against the infidels purifies anyone who attains it. His body does not need to be washed, because it is pure. Nor is there reason to pray for him, since he has been cleansed of his sins. But his act has value only if it is performed with the sincere intention of serving God. Purity and sincerity are associated with martyrdom; so too is light. In the model *khutba,* the martyr basks in light, he is illuminated by God, his nights gleam, and his wounds will shine bright on the Day of Resurrection. In fact, that brilliance, and the scent of musk that will emanate from him, "will testify" that he has waged jihad. Hence he is called *shahīd* (witness). The martyr, then, in Islam as in Christianity, is linked to the notion of bearing witness. Of course, in Christianity, "bearing witness" is expressed more through resistance to persecution than through a battle with weapons, but the idea that one can achieve martyrdom by dying in battle against the Saracens was far from absent from the Western medieval mentality.[63]

Death by jihad should not sadden, therefore, but delight, according to the prescriptions in the Koran repeated by preachers: "[They are] pleased with His gifts and rejoicing that those they left behind, who have not yet joined them, have nothing to fear or to regret" (Koran 3:170).

There are many cases in the medieval Arab sources—so many that they may be considered topoi—of mothers who delight in the death of a son who died a martyr and who forbid others to grieve, they who ought to be the first to weep over the death of their child. That idea is also evoked by Saladin's entourage. When one of the emirs was killed in battle against the Franks in 1189, Ibn Shaddād saw the deceased's brother, a smile on his face, tell those who had come to give their condolences: "This is a day for congratulation, not a day for condolence."[64]

Are we to conclude that there was a real desire in the ranks of Saladin's army to die a martyr? In certain cases, it appears so. The example of a man who, aged or ill, is approaching the end of his life and seeks to die a martyr is relatively common in descriptions of battles. In 1189 Emir Tumān, lord of Rakka, was in Saladin's army, fighting the Franks, when he fell gravely ill. 'Imād al-Dīn describes his final moments as follows: "When the end arrived, when hope left him and his death was not to be put off, he was sorry for his life and troubled by his fate, grew sad at not having succumbed in the holy war and at not having died a blessed martyr. 'Bring me my horse,' he said, 'so that I may take part in the battle, that I may be killed for Allah, and that I may fight until I fall in exhaustion; I see it as a swindle to die in my bed, when you have known me to be valiant and not a coward.' "[65]

Whether topos or reality, such cases were not described only in Saladin's time, and the matter was often debated in religious circles. There are many

Koranic verses and several hadith that expressly counsel against seeking martyr-dom.[66] It is up to God and not man to determine the moment of death. The atti-tude of the Kharijites, who throw themselves into combat to achieve martyrdom, is therefore disapproved of by most Muslims.[67] Some, such as the Mu'tazilites, followers of a rationalistic religious current, assert that martyrdom can be achieved only through the warrior's death. But the killing of a Muslim is an act of impiety, and therefore the Muslim must not wish for that act to occur.[68]

Such is the theory. But the biographical traditions and hagiographical works are filled with accounts depicting early Muslims rushing into battle, bare-chested and with smiles on their faces, to die as martyrs. 'Imād al-Dīn also seems—in theory at least—to take the side of those who sought out danger during a battle outside Acre in 1189: "And several nobles who sold their souls to attain paradise and who held out their chests to the enemy's sword fell there as martyrs."[69] Saladin himself is reported to have told Ibn Shaddād one day that he wished to die "the noblest of deaths," that is, death "on the path of God," death by jihad.[70]

Was that deep conviction or merely rhetoric? It behooves us to observe that martyrdom was not always sought out, even by the most pious. In 1189 al-Fādil congratulated 'Imād al-Dīn in an unofficial letter for having fled in the face of the Franks' offensive, "because congratulations on safety are better than felici-tations on martyrdom."[71] Such a declaration could always find support in cer-tain hadith, which placed the emphasis on the "greater jihad," that is, the "ef-fort" or "battle" against one's own flaws, but also the safeguarding of one's faith through the study and teaching of religious law. "The scholar's ink is more pre-cious than the blood of martyrs," says one of these hadith.[72]

The question of the limits to Saladin's jihad also arises in relation to its spa-tial expanse and objectives. Would Saladin confine himself to a defensive jihad, retaking possession only of the territories lost during the First Crusade, or did he wish to do battle with the Christians even on their own lands, in the Medi-terranean and the West? After Jerusalem, would he launch a conquest of Con-stantinople and Rome? The question may appear naïve, but it was raised by his own advisers and has been considered anew by some modern historians. In one of his letters, al-Fādil says that Saladin spent the money of Egypt to con-quer Syria, the money of Syria to conquer al-Jazīra, and the money of all of them to conquer the coast. If it be God's will, he adds, he will spend the money of Constantinople to conquer Rome, and all rulers will place themselves in his service.[73] In a letter to the caliph of 1183, Saladin said that, if he were given Mosul, he would conquer Jerusalem, Constantinople, Georgia, and the Almohad territories of North Africa, and would turn all the churches into mosques.[74] That same idea of overseas conquest is expressed in the letter from Saladin to Frederick Barbarossa in 1188.[75] Ibn Shaddād also recounts that in early 1189, while in the company of Saladin, he was contemplating the dangers of the sea rippling before his eyes, along the shoreline between Ascalon and Acre. The sultan confided: "I have it in mind that, when God Almighty has enabled me to conquer the rest of the coast, I shall divide up the lands, make my testament, take my leave and set sail on this sea to [the Franks'] islands to pursue them there until there no longer remain on the face of the earth any who deny God—or die [in the attempt]."[76]

Are we to understand these texts literally and believe that Saladin really intended to take the jihad to Constantinople and to the Mediterranean, so as to rule the world? Hannes Möhring has advanced the hypothesis that these ideas, despite their unrealistic character, were something more than mere propaganda, since Saladin was persuaded that he was accomplishing a mission entrusted by God. Möhring does not rule out the possibility that Saladin's ambitions may have extended even beyond the confines of the Latin states.[77] In my view, that hypothesis is very unlikely. Malcolm C. Lyons and David E. P. Jackson have rightly linked Saladin's words to those pronounced by Napoleon in spring 1799, as he was walking along the shore in that same region during the unsuccessful siege of Acre, in the company of his private secretary Louis-Antoine Fauvelet de Bourrienne: "If I succeed, as I expect, I shall find in the town the pacha's treasure and arms for 300,000 men. . . . I shall then march upon Damascus and Aleppo. . . . I will announce to the people the abolition of servitude and of the tyrannical government of the pachas. I shall arrive at Constantinople with large masses of soldiery. I shall overturn the Turkish empire and found in the east a new and grand empire that will take its place in posterity."[78]

Do not these discourses contain topoi, recurrent literary motifs, associated with all the great conquerors? The idea of world domination existed in all the great ancient civilizations, from pharaonic Egypt to Greece and Rome. Was it not said of Alexander the Great that, after conquering the East, he would capture the West?[79] In uttering these words, Napoleon undoubtedly had the example of his illustrious predecessor, whom he so liked to take as his model. In April 1798, before setting out for Egypt, he had even confided to Bourrienne:

"We are only twenty-nine, the same age as Alexander." And Bourrienne commented: "Just as Alexander departed from Macedonia for the Temple of Ammon, he will depart from Paris for the cataracts of the Nile."[80]

Nevertheless, though the memory of Alexander lived on in the East as in the West, it seems to me that the discourse on Saladin's imperial designs stems much more from the Muslim tradition and the ideology of jihad. From the start of Muslim expansion, the conquest of Constantinople was one of the themes of jihad propaganda. Several attempts were actually made during the Umayyad period, between the mid-seventh century and 717, but none succeeded.[81] Yet the boldness of these expeditions against the prestigious Byzantine metropolis gave birth to a series of legends, and this motif was often adopted in Muslim apocalyptic literature.[82] In addition, apocryphal hadith predicting the conquest of Constantinople surfaced to legitimate those distant wars, but also no doubt to reinforce the glory of the Umayyad dynasty, one of whose members, it was predicted, would accomplish that exploit.

A hadith therefore circulated claiming that a caliph, bearing the name of a prophet, would take Constantinople. The Umayyad caliph Sulaymān ibn 'Abd al-Malik (r. 715–717), who bore Solomon's name (i.e., Sulaymān), thought the prophecy applied to him. It is only one more step to believe that Saladin, named Yūsuf (Joseph), dreamed the same thing; but that step is not easy to take. His entourage was likely familiar with that hadith, and with the one claiming that the fall of Constantinople would anticipate the fall of Rome, as well as with the traditions that linked the conquest of Constantinople to the splendor of Jerusalem.[83] In proclaiming such totally unrealizable objectives, Saladin was not elaborating any precise plan. How could he have envisioned, even for an instant, the conquest of Constantinople, when Tyre and Acre were still resisting him, and when he was complaining that he had not received enough reinforcements from the caliph and his Muslim neighbors? How are we to believe, moreover, in his desire to conquer the territory of the Almohad ruler, when he was writing to him during that same time to ask for his help against the Franks? In reality, Saladin—or his entourage—had only to articulate such objectives for his actions to be linked to the jihad of the early Muslims, a comparison from which he could hope to draw some prestige. But realizing these conquests was certainly never at issue.

13

Strategic Interests

The Muslims and the Franks faced off on many different fronts, not all of which assumed the same strategic importance. For Saladin, the absolute priorities were to defend Egypt; to bar the Franks access to the Red Sea, that is, to the holy sites of Islam and to trade in the Indian Ocean; and to assure security of communications between Egypt and Syria. It was only later that he dedicated himself to liberating Syria-Palestine—Jerusalem in particular—from Frankish control.

The Defense of Egypt

In 1168, King Amalric of Jerusalem's defeat in Egypt did not keep the Franks from hoping to take over that region. Control of it seemed to be of the utmost importance to them, both to prevent the sending of reinforcements to the Muslims of Syria and to capitalize on its economic importance. In autumn 1169, Saladin had to face a new Franco-Byzantine attack against Damietta, and the next year his expeditions on the southern border of the Frankish territories, near Gaza and Dārūm, were aimed chiefly at laying waste those localities, which served as a base of support for the Franks in their expeditions against Egypt.

In July 1174, at a time when Nūr al-Dīn's succession was not yet settled, a fleet sent by the Norman king of Sicily, William II (r. 1166–1189), appeared off the coast of Alexandria. That well-funded expedition was responding not only to the commercial interests of the Sicilians but also to William II's desire to style himself the "protector of Christians overseas." In a letter to an emir of Syria, Saladin claimed there were two hundred ships, each transporting one hundred and fifty foot soldiers, which is to say, thirty thousand men. Some thirty-six other ships were transporting fifteen hundred cavalrymen (a thousand lancers and five hundred more lightly armed turcopoles) and their horses, while forty-six ships were loaded with servants, craftsmen, and all the food rations and war matériel, including wood for the construction of siege engines and the stone blocks needed to operate the mangonels. It is always difficult to discern how exaggerated the numbers put forward were, but there is no doubt that this was a very large expedition. On July 28, 1174, when the Sicilian ships appeared on the horizon, Saladin was still in Fāqūs, nearly two hundred kilometers from Alexandria. He immediately had the fortifications of Damietta reinforced and sent aid to Alexandria. The Sicilians attempted to take Alexandria but, facing Muslim resistance, had to retreat rather quickly. They set off again on August 1, leaving behind many dead and many captives, and "only the knights who tore off their clothes and leapt into the sea could escape" back to their ships.[1]

Nevertheless, the Westerners did not give up on their expeditions against Egypt. Twice, in 1175–1176 and then in 1177–1178, the Sicilians waged new attacks on the port of Tinnis, east of the Delta. The second time, they captured and burned down the city.[2] In 1177, the arrival in the Holy Land of Philip, count of Flanders, allowed Baldwin IV (the young leper king of Jerusalem) and the Byzantine envoys at his court to hope that a new expedition could be organized. That hope was quickly dashed by Philip of Flanders's refusal to participate.

In 1181, the Franks launched further raids against al-'Arīsh on the Egyptian border and against Tinnis, where they seized merchant ships.[3] Three years later, the Franks took advantage of the absence of Egyptian troops, which had been called to Syria by Saladin, to attack Fāqūs, east of the Delta, and took many prisoners. The residents of Bilbeis, somewhat farther to the south, fearing they would be attacked in turn, fled en masse, taking refuge in Cairo. The soldiers in the Egyptian army took the opportunity to pillage the abandoned city.[4]

The danger of Egypt being occupied by the Sicilians or the Franks was therefore real, and though these enemies did not manage to coordinate their offensives to seize the country in a lasting manner, the raids they launched disrupted economic life and impoverished the region of the Delta. Saladin quickly became aware of this, and in the first years of his reign he had large fortification projects undertaken in Cairo and in the cities located on the Mediterranean periphery. In 1171, soon after being named vizier, he went in person to inspect the walls of Alexandria and had the destroyed parts of the rampart and towers restored. That same year, he assigned one of his trusted men, the eunuch Qarāqūsh al-Asadī, to oversee the restoration of the rampart in the Fatimid part of Cairo, known as al-Qāhira.[5]

Since its founding in 969, al-Qāhira had been protected by a wall, which was restored and modified several times. Farther to the south, the ancient city of al-Fustāt, founded by seventh-century Arab conquerors, had continued to accommodate the majority of the population (al-Qāhira was reserved for the Fatimids, their entourage, army, and administration) but had never benefited from the protection of a wall. The last Fatimid vizier, Shāwar, had considered such a project and had even begun construction of a rampart with eight gates cut into it, but he did not have time to complete it before his death.

It was probably Shāwar's project that Saladin took over in 1176, giving it a greater scope, this time with the intention of joining al-Qāhira and al-Fustāt within the same wall, which would measure nearly twenty kilometers north to south.[6] The two cities were separated at the time by vast zones devoid of construction, but rather than surround each with a rampart, Saladin preferred to join them together, in order, he said, to locate a single garrison there. The memory of the fire of al-Fustāt ordered by Shāwar in 1168 to keep the city from falling into the Franks' hands was still fresh in everyone's minds, and Saladin was prepared to launch large-scale construction projects to prevent such a thing from happening again. No doubt he was also encouraged in his undertaking by the example of Nūr al-Dīn, who had restored many fortifications in Syria.[7] The construction of the rampart, begun in autumn 1176, was still going on sixty years later. The vestiges preserved to this day north and east of the city, as well as excavations undertaken in al-Fustāt, show that the rampart was in fact built northward and eastward under Saladin's reign, before continuing to the south under his successors' rule. The digging of a moat was even begun outside the northeast wall in 1192. By contrast, the part of the west wall that was to run along the Nile was never built, since the river already assured effective protection of the city on that side.[8]

Saladin's other major project was the construction of a large citadel built into the east part of the wall, between al-Qāhira and al-Fustāt, on a projecting escarpment of al-Muqattam Plateau.[9] There is no doubt that, through these major construction projects, Saladin wished to protect the urban area as a whole, but it is likely that, in distinguishing himself from his Fatimid predecessors and moving the seat of power closer to the citadel, he also wanted to mark the birth of a new dynasty and establish a royal residence comparable to those familiar to him in Syria. In Damascus and Aleppo, in fact, rulers had lived since the eleventh century in citadels built into the walls of cities. In addition to its defensive role against attacks from outside and inside the city, the citadel functioned as the royal residence and decision center. The sovereign had everything there necessary for his daily life and his government: palaces, baths, mosque, lodgings for his guards, administrative offices, cisterns and wells, and even at times (in Aleppo, for example), a hippodrome for military training and polo.

As often in such cases, explanations have been sought for the choice of the citadel's location. According to legend, Saladin placed pieces of meat in various places in Cairo, then observed that the one hanging over al-Muqattam stayed fresh the longest, attesting to the most salubrious air.[10] In actuality, the choice of al-Muqattam can be explained much better by its strategic position overlooking the city, since the presence of a large quantity of debris ruled out the choice of a site farther north.

The fortification project in Cairo continued throughout Saladin's reign, under the energetic leadership of Emir Qarāqūsh al-Asadī. That gigantic project was certainly very expensive, though a large part of the labor was provided by the thousands of Franks then held prisoner by the Egyptians.[11] The many stones needed for the project were in great part cut from the soft limestone of al-Muqattam, but in certain cases some were transported from farther away, the pyramids of Giza or a region farther south.[12] Visitors to Cairo never failed to be impressed by the scope of the work site. Different witnesses describe the road that Qarāqūsh had constructed to bring the stones from the pyramid region to the port of Giza on the west bank of the Nile, and mention the obligation imposed on every boat passing through the ancient city of Abūsīr, twenty-five kilometers south of present-day Cairo, to transport at least one block of stone to the capital.[13]

When Saladin left Egypt in 1182, never to return, the walls of the citadel were just rising up from the ground. The task of completing the project fell to his brother al-ʿĀdil (r. 1200–1218), then to al-ʿĀdil's son al-Kāmil (r. 1218–1238). It is not easy to determine the exact dimensions of the citadel under Saladin's reign. It is clear that it extended over the entire northeastern part of the present-day citadel—a large complex some thirteen hectares in area—and perhaps even farther to the south.[14] In any case, it is certain that no citadel in the Middle East had previously reached such a great size. The famous Crusader fortress called the "Krac des Chevaliers" (Castle of the Knights), for example, measured only 200 by 140 meters over an area of about two and a half hectares.

A moat was dug all around the citadel's wall, which was itself furnished with round or square towers that could accommodate a large number of soldiers. Several gates allowed access to the inside of the fortress, the principal one being the Gate of the Staircase (Bāb al-Mudarraj), which opened toward the city and whose foundation inscription, dating to 1183–1184, has been discovered. The bent-axis entry gates made it possible to slow the march of potential attackers and to prevent the use of rams. That technique, which is also found in the construction of the gates of al-Qāhira rampart rebuilt in Saladin's time, would be commonly used in thirteenth-century Syria.[15] To assure the supply of water, Saladin ordered the digging of a well impressive in size: almost square (5 by 7.8 meters for the top part, 3.4 by 4.4 meters for the lower part) and nearly 90 meters deep, it included a three-hundred step staircase allowing access to the bottom. It was therefore called the "Spiral Well" but was later renamed "Joseph's Well." A system of overshot wheels driven by oxen made it possible to raise the water from the well into a reservoir located halfway up, and from there to bring it up to the surface. An aqueduct was then built to circulate the water inside the citadel. Although construction of the citadel began in 1176, the fortress was not equipped with royal residences until 1207–1208, and the southern end was not added until the second half of the thirteenth century.

Although Saladin was primarily concerned with fortifying Cairo, he did not neglect the ports of the Delta, which were particularly vulnerable to attacks from the west. In a letter to his brother Tūrānshāh in 1177, he said he had fortified Damietta, built a citadel in Tinnis, and in one year spent forty thousand dinars for the restoration of the ramparts of Alexandria. He was personally involved in inspecting the walls of these three cities and made sure their garrisons were well equipped.[16] In all, then, these large-scale construction projects were the beneficiaries of the experience Saladin had acquired in Syria and Upper Mesopotamia, and they underscore the importance the sultan granted to the defense of Egypt.

On the Sinai Peninsula and the Red Sea

The control of the Sinai Peninsula and of the Red Sea was closely linked to Egyptian policies and the struggle against the Franks of Syria-Palestine. The taking of Ayla in December 1170, well before Nūr al-Dīn's death, had already allowed Saladin to open communication routes between Egypt and Syria, while preventing the Franks from having access to the Red Sea. A dual challenge therefore presented itself: to retake control of the Sinai route, abandoned during the Fatimid period to the Arab tribes, who did not hesitate to hire out their services to the Franks; and to preserve the monopoly on navigation on the Red Sea, the main pilgrimage route to Mecca and the principal trade route to the Indian Ocean and the Far East.

Until 1187, the only practicable route between Egypt and Syria for the Muslims was the one that crossed through the central desert of Sinai, from Suez to Ayla, then went back up toward Busra and Damascus, circumventing the Frankish territories. The main challenges of that journey were to find water in the desert and avoid attacks by the Bedouins and Franks. The reconquest of Ayla was the first phase in a policy of fortification intended to increase the security of the communication routes. In 1181–1182, a tower was built in Suez, and a small garrison of about twenty cavalrymen was installed inside it, to protect the Sinai route but also the alum trade from Upper Egypt.[17] Twenty-eight stopover points marked the Sinai route connecting Egypt to Syria, and depending on whether the army was advancing alone or was accompanied by a caravan, it took between nineteen and thirty days to travel from Cairo to Damascus. Some 260 kilometers separated Suez from Ayla, and about a week was required to cover them. The road was rough and strewn with obstacles, as attested in the thirteenth century by Thietmar, a Western pilgrim: "You must know that there are many dangers in this desert: frequently lions, whose fresh prints I have seen, dangerous worms and snakes, and rain as well, since, when it rains, the waters coming from the mountains collect and cause such flooding across the desert that no one can escape that peril. There is also the excessive heat, from which men perish, and the scarcity of water, which is found only once every five or six days. Finally there are the bandits, savage Arabs [Bedouins], whose thefts and assaults are feared. No one can cross that desert in summer, and even birds are rare there."[18]

To assure protection of that strategic route, Saladin had two fortresses built, one in Sadr, west of the peninsula, where there was probably already a small older fort, and the other near Ayla, on the Île de Graye.[19] Construction of the two sites began in the 1170s and intensified in the following decade. The site of Sadr, which took its name from a Bedouin tribe established in the region, had a dual advantage: the rocky butte on which the fortress was built made it possible to keep watch over the region within a radius of about thirty kilometers in clear weather; and above all, a spring located four kilometers south of the fortress assured the supply of water. A reservoir dam designed to collect the waters from two streams was also built north of the fortress, while inside the wall two cisterns made it possible to keep a reserve available.

On the Île de Graye (Jazīrat Fara'ūn), located at the north end of the Gulf of 'Aqaba, two rocky islets linked by a lagoon inlet sheltered a small fort (Qal'at Ayla) built by the Franks, which Saladin turned into a true fortress after 1170. That structure not only protected the route linking Cairo to Damascus but also barred access to the Red Sea, that is, to the holy sites and the Indian Ocean. It could also be used by Saladin as a base for launching attacks against the Frankish territories of Transjordan and for retreat in the event of failure.

These two sites, in addition to their defensive role, also had a religious function linked to the jihad. Sadr in particular had a mosque and three oratories, one of them open-air, all built between 1183 and 1187. That fortified construction is somewhat reminiscent of the ancient *ribāts* located on the borders of the Muslim world, where jihad warriors divided their time between battles and prayers. In addition to soldiers, Sadr also sheltered men of religion who chose to reside there for greater or lesser periods of time. Moreover, in the inscriptions that adorned the monumental entrance, the towers, and the prayer sites, the titles attributed to Saladin—"revitalizer of the state and of religion," "the sultan of Islam and of the Muslims," "the devoted friend of the emir of believers"—forcefully pointed to his aura as a jihad warrior and defender of Islam.

It took time, however, for the Frankish incursions into the Sinai to stop completely. In 1178 and especially in 1183, new raids were conducted by the Franks with the aid of the local Arab tribes. The route between Cairo and

Kerak thus remained a harsh ordeal, because of the insecurity and the lack of water.[20] The fortress of Graye also did not prevent the Franks from undertaking expeditions in the early 1180s, to the south and in the direction of the Red Sea. Saladin's chief adversary in that region was Reginald of Châtillon, lord of Kerak and Transjordan, whose fiery bellicosity provoked the Muslims more than once. In 1181, despite the truce concluded between the king of Jerusalem and Saladin, Reginald set out for Ayla and attempted to reach Taymā', a locality on the road to Medina, by the overland route. Did he really intend to proceed farther, or was this simply a reconnaissance expedition? In any case, that march, interpreted by the Muslims as an attempted expedition against the holy cities of Arabia, immediately elicited a reaction from Farrūkhshāh, Saladin's nephew and the governor of Damascus, who set out to pillage the territories around Kerak, in order to make Reginald reverse direction.[21]

But it took more than that to discourage Reginald, who in early 1183 organized another expedition, ordering the construction of boats that could be disassembled. These were transported, with the help of Arab Bedouins, to the Gulf of 'Aqaba on the backs of camels, a technique that Saladin had used back in 1170 to travel from Cairo to the Red Sea. The entire fleet seems to have consisted of no more than five ships, two of which were sent against the Muslim garrison on the Île de Graye. It is unlikely that Reginald, who did not take part personally in the expedition, sought to seize Mecca and Medina, any more than he could have hoped to take control of trade in the Red Sea with such a small fleet. In actuality, that attack was one of the many Frankish raids whose principal aim was to disrupt relations between Syria and Egypt. No doubt as well Reginald hoped to obtain a rich booty from that region, which was heavily traveled by merchants. Finally, as Carole Hillenbrand has suggested, it is not impossible that the sixteen long years Reginald had just spent in an Aleppine jail had fed a deep desire for revenge, which would explain his hatred of Islam and his zeal for war.[22] In all cases, that raid must be seen as an isolated operation of destruction and plunder rather than a large-scale expedition aimed at acquiring new territories.

These events were nevertheless judged alarming by the Muslims, unaccustomed to seeing Westerners navigating on the Red Sea. The Franks, we are told, set fire to sixteen ships before arriving at the port of 'Aydhāb, across from Mecca, where they attacked a caravan and a shipload of pilgrims, leaving death in their wake. They then set upon localities on the coast of the Hejaz and took by force several Muslim merchant ships coming from Yemen. The most startling rumors circulated: it was even believed that the Franks' objective was to seize the coffin of the Prophet in Medina and transfer it to their own territory, where the Muslims would be obliged to go on pilgrimage.[23] The stakes were not only military but also and primarily religious, especially since, from the ninth century on, apocalyptic Islamic and Christian traditions had predicted that Byzantine and Ethiopian attacks would someday target the holy cities of Islam.[24]

As might be expected, the Muslim reaction was swift and violent. Saladin's brother al-'Ādil, then in charge of Egypt, sent a fleet under the command of Admiral Husām al-Dīn Lu'lu', whose exploits would leave a deep impression on the population. He began by breaking the blockade around Ayla. The Frankish ships were destroyed and the survivors pursued overland by the Bedouins, who now sided with the Muslims. Other Frankish vessels were chased down and boarded on the Red Sea; Muslim merchant prisoners were released and their belongings returned to them. The Franks were driven into the desert with the aid of horses taken from the Bedouins northwest of Medina. A number of Franks—170, according to a letter from Saladin—were taken prisoner.[25] The Andalusian traveler Ibn Jubayr, in the region at the time, saw some of them, mounted backwards on camels, being led to Alexandria, where they were triumphantly paraded through the streets of the city to the beat of drums and the sounding of trumpets. Others were executed in Cairo, and two of them were even sent to be slaughtered in Minā, near Mecca, where the traditional immolation of animals at the end of the pilgrimage took place. That human sacrifice was ponderous in its significance, but no Muslim author was shocked by it. The fear, justified or not, of seeing the Franks seize the holy sites had been so great that, in the eyes of the Muslims, it justified any punishment, even the most cruel.[26]

All the Frankish incursions into Sinai or the Red Sea at the turn of the 1180s remained without effect. Even in the absence of Saladin, who had gone to fight in Upper Mesopotamia in 1182, that region was constantly and effectively defended by Farrūkhshāh from Damascus and by al-'Ādil from Cairo. After 1187 Saladin's victories over the Franks of Jerusalem, and the reconquest of Ascalon and the principality of Transjordan, neutralized the Frankish threat to the Red Sea and Egypt and also made it possible to reopen the Mediterranean coastal route between Egypt and Syria-Palestine. The route passing through Sadr and

Ayla fell into disuse, and the two citadels, having lost their strategic defense function, were turned into prisons by Saladin's Ayyubid successors. Incarcerated in the fortress of the Île de Graye were Frankish prisoners, whom the Western pilgrim Thietmar described in 1217: "The Christians were captives, French, English, Latin; but all, Christians and Saracens, were fishermen in the service of the sultan of Babylon [Cairo]. Neither farmers nor warriors, they performed no service other than fishing, with no other means of subsistence. They rarely eat bread and are located more than five days on foot from any habitation."[27]

The Holy Land

For Saladin, the reconquest of Syria-Palestine—Jerusalem in particular—was of great strategic interest, and early on, his propaganda made reference to that conquest, though it took him a number of years to realize his dream. From 1174 to 1185, the Holy Land was the object of a series of raids and skirmishes, but neither of the two adversaries truly gained the upper hand. Initially, the Franks, encouraged by the problems of succession the Muslims were having after Nūr al-Dīn's death and by the arrival of reinforcements from the West, resumed their offensives in Syria and Palestine. In addition to their attempts to expand southward and in the direction of Egypt, they conducted many incursions south of Damascus, on the Bekaa Plain and in northern Syria. Most often, however, they encountered the resistance of Saladin's troops. Saladin, though absorbed in his battles against the Zangids, never completely let up on the Frankish front. It must be said that he was also very well served by his faithful lieutenants, Tūrānshāh and then Farrūkhshāh in Damascus and Ibn al-Muqaddam in Baalbek. As of 1179, the Muslims in turn took the offensive and had a few isolated successes, but without managing to regain ground in a lasting manner. Each camp then attempted to take advantage of its adversary's difficulties: the death of Farrūkhshāh in 1182 gave the Franks the opportunity to launch raids on the region of Damascus; then the difficulties of succession within the kingdom of Jerusalem beginning in 1183 allowed Saladin to conduct several incursions into Latin territory, until a truce was signed in 1185. All these events are well known, and I shall recall only their main lines here.[28]

The year 1176 was marked primarily by Frankish raids against the region of Damascus and northern Syria. But neither of the two camps truly prevailed. In

1177, the arrival in the Holy Land of Philip, count of Flanders, raised many hopes on the Frankish side, which were quickly dashed when it became obvious that he would not do battle in Egypt. By contrast, his decision to spend the winter in Antioch led Saladin to fear a large-scale attack on northern Syria. Saladin therefore decided to go on ahead to Ascalon, arriving on November 23, 1177. His battle against the Franks two days later took place at a site that is difficult to determine exactly, a half-day on foot from Ascalon.[29] It proved a disaster for Saladin, who suffered one of his greatest defeats there. Yet the Muslims had the numerical advantage and initially sowed terror among the Frankish population: only three hundred and seventy-five Frankish cavalrymen against twenty-six thousand Muslim cavalrymen, reports William of Tyre, who doubtless exaggerated the disparity. Ramla was burned down, Lydda was besieged, and the residents of Jerusalem prepared to flee.

But Saladin committed a dual tactical error when he allowed his troops, weary and short on supplies, to disperse and engage in looting, while leaving no army outside Ascalon. The Frankish counteroffensive came from that direction. Taken by surprise, the Muslims were quickly routed. Those who were able to do so set out for al-'Arīsh through the desert sands but had difficulty surviving, given the absence of guides and the lack of water. Saladin himself was saved at the last minute by al-Fādil, who had set out to find him, accompanied by guides and provisions. So it was that they managed to return, exhausted, to Egypt in the second half of December.[30]

As Saladin was struggling to reconstitute his forces in Egypt, the situation was hardly brighter in northern Syria. His uncle, governor of Hama, was very ill, while in Aleppo new divisions were tearing apart the entourage of Nūr al-Dīn's son al-Sālih.[31] On November 14, 1177, the Franks of Tripoli, backed by the count of Flanders, took the opportunity to attack Hama. The arrival of reinforcements kept the city from falling into their hands. They then went off to lay siege to Hārim, a strategic position thirty-six kilometers east of Antioch, whose garrison was in revolt against al-Sālih. Their attack met with no greater success, and William of Tyre, very critical of the count of Flanders and his troops, attributed to them a large part of the responsibility for that defeat:

> For they were given over to frivolity and paid more attention to games of chance and other evil pleasures than military discipline or the rules of siege operations permitted. They were continually

going back and forth to Antioch, where they spent their time at the baths and at banquets and indulged in drunken debauches and other pleasures of the flesh, thereby forsaking the work of the siege for the delights of idleness. . . . The count himself daily remarked that he must return home and intimated that he was detained at Harim against his will. This attitude not only hindered those who were honorably endeavoring to carry on the siege outside, but it furnished an incentive to a bolder resistance on the part of the townspeople.[32]

An accord was ultimately reached between the Franks and the Aleppines in March 1178, as Saladin was preparing to leave Egypt for Syria, since neither of the two parties wanted him to intervene in northern Syria. Before he even had time to arrive in Damascus, the Franks withdrew, in exchange for the payment of a sum of money.[33]

Throughout 1178, the Franks pursued their policy of building fortifications in Palestine. Within a few months, from October 1178 to March 1179, they built the castle of Bayt al-Ahzān on Jacob's Ford,[34] to better control the crossing of the Jordan north of Lake Tiberias, about a day on foot from Damascus.[35] The fortress was given to the Knights Templar, and the Franks resumed their raids on the grazing lands south of Syria. For several months, Franks and Muslims faced off. From his camp set up near Bānīyās, Saladin sent Bedouins to pillage Galilee and Frankish territory as far as the region around Sidon and Beirut. The Franks attempted to respond but were defeated in the area of Marj ʿUyūn and Beaufort, south of present-day Lebanon, in early summer 1179. Count Raymond III of Tripoli and King Baldwin IV managed to flee, but Eudes de Saint-Amand, Grand Master of the Knights Templar, "a wicked man, haughty and arrogant, in whose nostrils dwelt the spirit of fury, one who neither feared God nor revered man," was among the many taken prisoner. "It is said that within the year he died a captive in a squalid prison, mourned by no one," adds William of Tyre.[36]

Saladin did not let up and, in August of that year, attempted to destroy the new castle of Bayt al-Ahzān. The tunnel the Muslims dug under the walls of the castle resulted in the collapse of the main tower, and of the fifteen hundred men constituting the garrison, seven hundred were taken prisoner.[37] Inside the castle Saladin's troops also found about a thousand suits of armor, many crafts-

N
W · E
S

Tripoli
Batrūn
Jubayl
Baalbek
Beirut
Sidon
Damascus
Mediterranean Sea
Beaufort
Bānīyās
Tyre
Tībnīn
Safad
GOLAN   HAURAN
Acre
Lake Tiberias
Rā's al-Mā'
Haifa
Hattīn
Kafr Sabt
Tiberias
Nazareth · al-Fūla
GALILEE
Habīs Jaldak
Kawkab
'Ayn Jālūt
Caesarea
Baysān
Jordan
SAMARIA
Sebaste
Nablus
TRANSJORDAN
Jerash
Arsūf
Jaffa
Lydda
Ramla · Bayt-Nūbā
Jericho
Jerusalem
Bethlehem
Ascalon
Hebron
Dead Sea
Gaza
Dārūm
al-'Arīsh
Kerak

10 km
Map : Edigraphie

Palestine in the Twelfth Century

men and servants, and about a hundred Muslim prisoners, who had been used as labor for the construction of the fortress. These prisoners were all freed, the Muslim apostates were executed, and the fortress was razed. It is said that the well in the fortress was so deep that the human and animal corpses thrown into it were not enough to fill it. Saladin wrote the caliph to announce his victory, then returned to Damascus on September 13, 1179, not without first pillaging the territories around Tiberias, Tyre, and Beirut. About ten of his emirs, and undoubtedly an even greater number of his soldiers, died in the following days of an illness, which some attributed to the heat and the decomposition of the corpses in Bayt al-Ahzān.

Saladin spent the winter in the region and conducted a few more raids, but in early summer 1180 all the conditions seemed aligned for concluding a new truce. On the Frankish side, discussions on the successor to the leper king Baldwin IV, who was increasingly debilitated by illness, were proceeding. Divisions arose about the possibility of a regency and the marriage of his sister Sibylla, heir to the throne should Baldwin die. Under such conditions, a truce with Saladin could only be welcome. On the Muslim side, the troops were faced with difficulties receiving supplies, because of a prolonged drought in the Damascus region. But above all, Saladin was more preoccupied with Upper Mesopotamia than with Palestine. The accord was therefore concluded, and Saladin set out for the Upper Euphrates Valley.

He returned from the east some six months later and arrived in Cairo on January 1, 1181. He remained there the entire year and did not go back to Syria until May 1182. At that time, the truce with the Franks was coming to an end. The Muslims believed that it had already been broken the previous year by Reginald of Châtillon's expedition against the holy cities of Islam. Farrūkh-shāh and Saladin therefore launched several raids from Damascus against Lake Tiberias and the Jordan Valley. Then, in early August, when an Egyptian fleet of thirty to forty ships was sent as reinforcements, the sultan attacked Beirut, while his brother al-ʿĀdil conducted an expedition against the southern coast of Palestine, thus gaining the advantage of an attack on two fronts. The Frankish fleet left the ports of Tyre and Acre to come to the aid of Beirut, but Saladin, judging it was not yet time to put all his forces into battle, lifted the siege and set out for Upper Mesopotamia. It is clear that he did not wish to make the jihad his priority so long as his work unifying the Muslims was not complete.[38]

His successes troubled the Franks, however. Rumors, sometimes contradictory, circulated in the kingdom of Jerusalem about his fate in Upper Mesopotamia: "Some reports indicated that he was meeting with much success in Mesopotamia in the vicinity of Mosul, where he had subjugated the entire region to his power; others, on the contrary, were to the effect that all the princes of the East had united in an effort to drive him from the land by force of arms and thus recover the territory which he had won from them by intrigue and bribes. His progress caused the Christians much uneasiness; they viewed the increase of his power with great alarm, lest with large reinforcements he should return against them."[39]

Nevertheless, Saladin's absence from Syria and Farrūkhshāh's death in 1182 gave the Franks the opportunity to retake the offensive in October of that year and to launch raids as far as the environs of Damascus.[40] Upon learning of them, Saladin was not overly concerned and said: "While they are destroying villages, we are taking possession of cities. We will rebuild them later and will be stronger to attack their territories."[41]

In February 1183, the Franks, to assure the defense of the kingdom, decided to levy a specific tax on property and revenue, payable by everyone—great and small, laypeople and religious. But the taking of Aleppo by Saladin in June 1183 was another hard blow for them. "From the beginning, it was clear to the Christians that if Saladin managed to add Aleppo to his domains, our country would be surrounded by his forces and his might, as in a state of siege," wrote William of Tyre.[42] New attacks were conducted, in fact, in September 1183, and in late October Saladin went to rejoin al-ʿĀdil's Egyptian troops outside the walls of Kerak. The city was taken by the Muslims, but the overcrowded citadel—the wedding of Humphrey IV of Toron to the king's sister Isabella was about to take place there—resisted.[43] The advancing Frankish reinforcements, led by Baldwin IV and Raymond III of Tripoli, impelled Saladin to lift the siege and to return to Damascus on December 12, 1183. The Ramadan fast was approaching, his army was tired and undoubtedly did not have all the siege engines needed to take such a fortress.[44] Winter passed, and the Franks were more than ever embroiled in their problems of succession, as King Baldwin IV was gradually overcome by paralysis and blindness.

In late August 1184, Saladin led another large-scale expedition against Kerak. Reginald of Châtillon was still his principal target: Kerak, wrote Ibn Shaddād, "caused great trouble to the Muslims, for it cut communications with Egypt, so that caravans were only able to move with sizeable military escorts. The sultan was very concerned about it, to make the route to Egypt passable."[45]

This time, nine mangonels were set up outside the walls of the fortress, but the arrival of Frankish reinforcements ended the siege after only a few days. Saladin retreated to the north and went to pillage Nablus, Jenin, and surrounding areas. These events, which occurred between September 8 and 10, 1184, seem to indicate that the tactic adopted by Saladin at that time was still to conduct raids rather than a true war of reconquest.[46] He probably also wanted to complete his work of unification in Upper Mesopotamia, while showing the caliph and "public opinion" that he was waging jihad and therefore needed the aid of all the Muslim forces.

In spring 1185, after the death of King Baldwin IV, and before Saladin again departed for a long expedition to the east, the sultan concluded another four-year truce with Raymond III of Tripoli, regent of the young Baldwin V.[47] That truce gave him a free hand in Upper Mesopotamia, until his illness in Harrān impelled him to change course and to devote all his efforts to the reconquest of the Frankish territories.

During that period of about a decade, neither the Franks nor the Muslims had the means to achieve a decisive victory. The Franks were prevented by their internal divisions and the problems of succession to the throne. The Muslims, with Saladin in the lead, were still too caught up in eastern affairs. Both therefore confined themselves to successive raids and looting, which, roughly speaking, resulted in a maintenance of the status quo. Whenever their forces were depleted, a truce was negotiated until the next round of confrontations.

14

The Victorious Campaigns

The Battle of Hattīn and Its Consequences

Both 1187 and 1188 were years of glory for Saladin: they would form the basis
for his legend, trigger a new Crusade, and change the course of history for the
Latin states. Would the Battle of Hattīn, the first in a series of Muslim victories,
have had the same outcome if the kingdom of Jerusalem had not been so divided? It is impossible to rewrite history, but it is indisputable that the situation
of the kingdom of Jerusalem had become increasingly critical since Amalric's
death in 1174. Baldwin IV (r. 1174–1185) was only thirteen years old when he succeeded his father; he was, moreover, afflicted with leprosy, which took his life
eleven years later. Throughout his reign, he fought heroically to maintain
royal authority, but he could not prevent the division of his kingdom into two
opposing factions and was frequently obliged to designate a regent, first because of his youth and then because of his illness. Initially, the regent was
Count Raymond III of Tripoli, his closest relative, who, after marrying the
widow of the lord of Tiberias, had also become lord of Galilee and thus the
most powerful of the king's vassals. He remained regent until Baldwin came of
age in 1176. Having had a great deal of experience with the Muslims—he had
been their prisoner for about a decade—Raymond usually opted for negotiation. He was head of the faction that could be called the party of old families,

which included Humphrey II of Toron, the Ibelins, Reginald of Sidon, and William of Tyre.

The other party was dominated by men who had arrived more recently in the Holy Land and who were preoccupied with carving out territories for themselves.[1] They included Reginald of Châtillon, freed by the Muslims in 1176, who, thanks to his marriage, became lord of Kerak and of the principality of Transjordan. With him were the brothers Aimery and Guy of Lusignan, driven from their native Poitou by Richard the Lionheart; Joscelin III of Courtenay, a count without a county ever since Edessa had been retaken by the Muslims in 1144; and his sister Agnes of Courtenay, who had a great deal of influence over her son King Baldwin IV. Agnes's party, the "party of the court," became more important beginning in 1176, when Raymond stepped down from the regency, and was particularly strengthened after 1186, thanks to the support of the Knights Templar and Hospitaller.

It was within that context of deep rivalries that the problem of finding a successor for Baldwin IV arose, since he could neither marry nor have children. Attention focused on his sister Sibylla: in the Eastern Latin states, the crown could be transmitted through women to their husbands or sons. Sibylla's first husband (with whom she had a son, the future Baldwin V) had died in 1177, and her remarriage in 1180 to Guy of Lusignan was a victory for the party of the court. In addition, Sibylla's half-sister Isabella was married to Humphrey IV of Toron, who was Reginald of Châtillon's stepson. Tensions with the opposition party only increased, to such a point that in 1182 the king forbade Raymond from entering his kingdom.

In 1183 Baldwin IV, very debilitated by illness, was once again obliged to name a regent. He chose Guy of Lusignan, considered to be his successor or, at least, the one who would be named the regent of Baldwin V. But a few months later, the king took the regency from him and had Baldwin V crowned as heir to the throne, which had never before been done in the kingdom of Jerusalem. The disgruntled Guy of Lusignan revolted, and in 1184 Raymond III was called back to be regent.

Upon the leper king's death in 1185, it was therefore Baldwin V who succeeded him, with Raymond as his regent. But the new king died young, in late summer 1186, and Sibylla, with the support of the patriarch of Jerusalem and Reginald of Châtillon, succeeded in having herself crowned queen of Jerusalem and in herself crowning her husband, Guy of Lusignan, as king. A furious

Raymond III retreated to Tiberias and decided to establish relations with Saladin. According to 'Imād al-Dīn, Raymond placed himself under the sultan's protection and asked him for aid to oppose his adversaries. He was even followed by several men from his party. On that occasion, Saladin, only too happy with the divisions tearing apart the Franks, released several of Raymond's knights whom he was holding in his jails.[2] The Christian author of *History of the Patriarchs* also notes that alliance and calls Raymond III a Judas, traitor to his lord.[3]

The casus belli that would allow Saladin to again take up arms against the Franks was provided him in early 1187 by Reginald of Châtillon, who broke the truce established two years earlier, by attacking a caravan—though it was protected by a military escort—that was transporting merchandise between Cairo and Damascus. It is difficult to fathom Reginald's true motivations: Revenge for the attacks against him? Mere bravado? Or the hope of laying his hands on a large booty? In any case, he rejected the intercession of Guy of Lusignan and stubbornly refused to return to Saladin the people and goods seized. It is likely that Saladin, urged on by his entourage and anxious to respect his dual oath of the previous year, would have launched a major offensive against the Franks in any event, but the pillaging of that caravan gave him an excellent pretext.[4]

On March 13, Saladin left Damascus, without even waiting for all his armies to assemble. He sent his nephew Taqī al-Dīn north to keep watch on the border with Antioch and on the Armenian principality of Cilicia, while he himself set out for Busra, south of Damascus, his priority being to assure the security of the caravan of pilgrims returning from Mecca, which included his sister and nephew. Armed troops and a caravan carrying Taqī al-Dīn's family and possessions were arriving from Egypt at the same time.

The fighting began on April 26, when Saladin, leading his troops, rushed onto Reginald's lands (Kerak and Shawbak), ravaging villages and harvests over a month's time as he passed. Behind him, the troops under the leadership of his son al-Afdal, seventeen years old at the time, had been cautiously left at Rā's al-Mā', on the border between Damascus and Frankish territory. Their presence prevented the Franks from sending forces to aid Reginald. On the instructions of his father, al-Afdal, from the other side of the Jordan River, sent the troops of Damascus, Aleppo, and Harrān to pillage Frankish territory, while he himself remained slightly in the rear. A first confrontation between the Muslims and the Christian military orders took place on the road to Sepphoris, during which many Knights Templar and Hospitaller lost their lives, including the Grand Master of the Hospitallers.

In that perilous situation, the Franks closed ranks. Raymond III abandoned the Muslim camp to reconcile with Guy of Lusignan. Shortly before, the Byzantine emperor Isaac II, having got wind of the alliance between Saladin and Raymond, had written to Saladin to ask him to intercede in favor of his brother, who was being detained by Raymond. Saladin replied that, before the intervening breach, he had extracted a promise from Raymond that the latter would release his prisoner in exchange for a ransom; then Saladin proposed an alliance with the emperor in the event that Isaac wished once more to turn against the Franks. Hence, though in discourse the battle against the Franks was always presented as that of Islam against Christendom, in actuality Saladin did not hesitate to seek an alliance with those who could be most helpful to him, whatever their religion. Although there was little chance that Isaac would agree to support him in his jihad, Saladin's appeal was no less indicative of what would today be called "realpolitik."[5]

In northern Syria during that time, Taqī al-Dīn was launching raids on the territory of Antioch. But having learned of Raymond III's defection, he concluded a truce with Bohemond III of Antioch in early June and hastened to join Saladin north of Busra, where the whole Muslim army regrouped: not only the troops of Egypt and Syria but also those that had been sent by the eastern cities. Contemporaries remarked on the size of that army, which they generally estimated at twelve thousand professional cavalrymen, not counting a large number of volunteers[6]—probably more than thirty thousand men in all, both cavalry and foot soldiers. Saladin organized them into several units. He himself took command of the center, entrusting the right wing to Taqī al-Dīn and the left wing to Gökbörī. This time Saladin, no longer content with raids, seemed determined to face down the Franks in a decisive manner. He needed the battle so as to shore up his image as a jihad warrior in the Muslim world and, more prosaically, to make the most of a large-scale Muslim mobilization that would likely not be repeated for a long time.

The Franks regrouped in Sepphoris, the usual place for assembling their forces, at the crossroads of the Galilee route, between the coast and the southern part of Lake Tiberias. The kingdom's army was joined by small contingents from Antioch and Tripoli. In all, their numbers were far smaller than those of the Muslims. Historians' estimates vary somewhat but hover

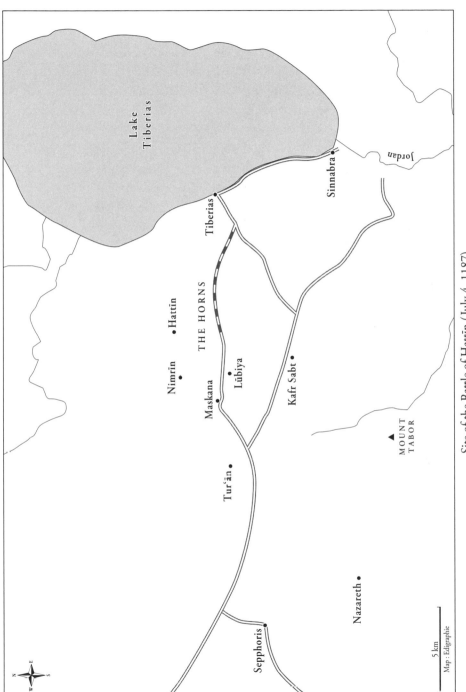

Lake
Tiberias

Jordan

Sinnabra

Tiberias

THE HORNS

Hattin

Nimrīn

Maskana

Lūbiya

Kafr Sabt

MOUNT
TABOR

Tur'ān

Nazareth

Sepphoris

5 km

Map : Edigraphic

Site of the Battle of Hattīn (July 4, 1187)
(based on B. Z. Kedar, "The Battle of Hattīn Revisited")

around twenty thousand men, approximately twelve hundred in the heavy cavalry.[7]

In the last days of June, Saladin reached the southwestern part of Lake Tiberias and camped with the bulk of his army in the region of Kafr Sabt (Cafarsset), about ten kilometers west of Tiberias. There he had several sources of water available and controlled one of the two east-west routes leading to Tiberias. He also sent a detachment to the more northern route, which passed above the village of Lūbiya. He thereby managed to threaten both Tiberias and Sepphoris, where the Franks were massed. He chose first to attack Tiberias, pillaging the lower part of town, while Raymond III's wife and the garrison locked themselves inside the citadel. In attacking that stronghold, Saladin hoped to make the Franks of Sepphoris come to its aid and so lead them onto the terrain of his choosing. Raymond, though his wife was under siege in the fortress, did not want to fall into that trap. Favoring a retrenchment of the Frankish troops in Sepphoris around a waterhole, he thought that the Muslim army would disperse once Tiberias was taken, contrary to the views of Gerard of Ridefort, Grand Master of the Knights Templar, and of Reginald of Châtillon. Even the Arab authors reported these new Frankish divisions:

> The count said, "Tiberias is mine and my wife's. Saladin has already done to the city what he has done. The citadel remains and my wife is in it. I would be happy if he took the citadel, my wife and our possessions there and retired. By God, I have seen the armies of Islam both in the past and recently but I have never seen such a numerous and powerful army as Saladin has. If he takes Tiberias, he will not be able to stay there. When he leaves and retires, we shall recover it. If he does stay there, he will only be able to do so with all his forces and they will be unable to endure the long time away from their homes and families, so he will be compelled to leave and we will ransom our people who have been taken prisoner."
>
> The lord of Kerak, Prince Reynald, said to him, "That is enough making us frightened of the Muslims! There is no doubt that you are on their side and favour them, otherwise you would not have spoken so."[8]

Several versions of the *Continuation* of William of Tyre confirm Raymond's reluctance to attack Saladin immediately, but 'Imād al-Dīn says rather that he was one of the first to urge the king to take the offensive: "When the count learned of the taking of Tiberias and the occupation of the country, he was staggered by it, lost all resolve, handed over everything he possessed to the Franks, and told them: 'Remaining calm is now out of the question: we must treat those people harshly. With Tiberias taken, the whole country is conquered; our hereditary property and our acquisitions are lost; I cannot bear that; I shall not recover [from] that wound.'"[9]

That attitude tallies with the contents of a letter sent to Pope Urban, in which it is said that Raymond and his stepsons urged Guy, "with tears in their eyes," to go save their wife and mother in Tiberias. In reality, it is difficult to have an exact idea of Raymond's attitude, since the Arab sources are often based on rumors, and the Latin sources were influenced by the struggles of the different parties.[10]

The king finally opted to fight. No doubt he was remembering that in 1183, his decision to remain inactive near a spring in 'Ayn Jālūt, after Saladin's attack on Baysān, had been criticized by many. In addition, Gerard of Ridefort, in order to recruit mercenaries, had just spent part of the money given him by Henry II, king of England, to expiate the murder of Thomas Becket. He had done so without consulting Henry II, as he ought to have done; he and Guy of Lusignan were therefore admonished to obtain tangible results to justify that decision or face being disavowed.[11] The Frankish army, then, set out for Tiberias at dawn on July 3.[12]

Saladin abandoned the siege of the fortress to go out to meet the Frankish army, sending other troops to harass its flanks with arrows and to cut off any possibility of retreat from the rear. That tactic was made possible by the large number of Muslim troops. The Franks, weakened by thirst, decided to leave the main road passing north of Lūbiya in an attempt to reach the nearby springs of the village of Hattīn, about eight kilometers north. That decision turned out to have weighty consequences: when the Franks, in an extreme state of fatigue, arrived on July 4 at the basalt peak of the Horns of Hattīn overlooking the plain, they found that they were barred access to the springs by the Muslim troops. The lack of water, the stifling heat, and the brushfires lit by the Muslims managed to wear them down, while Saladin's opposing troops had access to the water from Lake Tiberias, which was brought to them in wine-skins on the backs of camels.

The whole battle, therefore, hinged on the access to water. The knights attempted a first charge, and the Muslim ranks allowed them to pass before closing in on them. It was a total rout: only one detachment, led by Raymond III and including, notably, Joscelin III, Reginald of Sidon, and Balian of Ibelin, managed, by charging through the Muslim ranks, to reach the lake, and from there, Tyre. The infantry, cut off from the cavalry, took refuge on the north summit of the Horns of Hattīn. The remaining cavalrymen were powerless, exposed to arrows without the protection of the foot soldiers. They retreated to the south peak of the Horns, surrounding the king's tent. Twice more they tried to attack the Muslims from the top of their hill, but in vain. On the evening of July 4, the Muslims succeeded in climbing the hill and reached the king's red tent. Saladin's eldest son, al-Afdal, who was witnessing his first battle, later recounted the scene to Ibn al-Athīr:

> I was alongside my father during this battle, the first I had witnessed. When the king of the Franks was on the hill with that band, they made a formidable charge against the Muslims facing them, so that they drove them back to my father. I looked towards him and he was overcome by grief and his complexion pale. He took hold of his beard and advanced, crying out "Give the lie to the Devil." The Muslims rallied, returned to the fight and climbed the hill. When I saw that the Franks withdrew, pursued by the Muslims, I shouted for joy, "We have beaten them!" But the Franks rallied and charged again like the first time and drove the Muslims back to my father. He acted as he had on the first occasion and the Muslims turned upon the Franks and drove them back to the hill. I again shouted, "We have beaten them!" but my father rounded on me and said, "Be quiet! We have not beaten them until their tent falls." As he was speaking to me, the tent fell. The sultan dismounted, prostrated himself in thanks to God Almighty and wept for joy.[13]

Those Franks who had not perished in the battle were taken prisoner: King Guy of Lusignan, Reginald of Châtillon, Marquess William III of Montferrat, Humphrey IV of Toron, and a large number of cavalrymen.

Saladin treated the king with a great deal of courtesy, speaking to him through an interpreter. He offered him a cool drink, but when Guy of Lusignan held the cup out to Reginald, Saladin hastened to say that the gift was not his, meaning by that that he did not feel bound by the duty of hospitality. He offered Reginald the chance to convert to Islam, and upon his refusal, by his own hand beheaded him.

How are we to explain that gesture? Most Muslim historians invoke the oath Saladin had twice taken to kill Reginald himself, the first time when Reginald was threatening the holy cities and the second when he led the surprise attack on the Egyptian caravan. In giving him the opportunity to convert, Saladin was seeking neither to evade his oath nor to appease his conscience. He was applying Muslim law, which authorizes the beheading of a prisoner who refuses to convert to Islam and who represents a threat to the Muslim community.[14] In Reginald's case, the exasperation he provoked among the Muslims is summed up in these few words that Saladin spoke to Guy: "It has not been customary for princes to kill princes, but this man transgressed his limits."[15]

Saladin also ordered the execution of the turcopoles and of the Knights Templar and Hospitaller. The Franks used the turcopoles, an indigenous population, in their light cavalry, and the Muslims considered them traitors or apostates. The Knights Templar and Hospitaller were perceived to be the sworn enemies of Islam, and Saladin did not think he could get a ransom for them.[16] He purchased them for fifty Egyptian dinars a head from the Muslim fighters who had taken them prisoner, and had them all executed, first giving them the chance to convert to Islam, as he had done with Reginald. Very few agreed, but those who converted subsequently proved to be good Muslims, according to 'Imād al-Dīn. Only Gerard of Ridefort, Grand Master of the Knights Templar, was spared, because he was considered good currency.

There were so many Frankish slaves thrown onto the markets of Syria that the price of them collapsed. In Damascus, they were sold en masse at auction for three dinars a head. Some even cite the case of a prisoner exchanged for a pair of sandals.[17] The Frankish leaders, for whom a large ransom could be expected, were sent to Damascus. Sent with them was a priceless relic that had fallen into Muslim hands during the Battle of Hattīn, a fragment of the True Cross that had accompanied the Franks in their battles. That loss was deeply felt by the Franks, and inauspicious consequences were continually attributed to it in both the East and West: "It is to be noted as well that, beginning that

same year of our Lord when the Cross of the Lord was taken by Saladin overseas, the children born since that time have only twenty-two teeth, or only
twenty, whereas before they normally had thirty or thirty-two."[18]

The Muslims knew very well the value the Christians ascribed to the relic
of the Cross, and 'Imād al-Dīn describes it at length: "The Christians claim it
is made of the wood on which, they say, the one they worship was crucified;
that is why they venerate it and have covered it in pure gold, crowned with
pearls and gems. . . . In their eyes, the taking of it was a graver matter than
the taking of the king; for them, it was the most terrible misfortune on the
battlefield."[19]

Affixed upside down to a spear, the relic was carried in procession through
the streets of Damascus by the chief qādī. Subsequently, the Franks often demanded it but never recovered it. Saladin's son al-Afdal sent it to the caliph of
Baghdad after Saladin's death,[20] and that was the last anyone heard of it.

Although it is difficult to assess the number of those killed and taken captive, it can be said that that battle decimated the army of the kingdom of Jerusalem, which was subsequently unable to defend the holy city. For a long time,
the region of Hattīn was strewn with desiccated corpses and human bones;[21]
Saladin, meanwhile, had a commemorative monument built at the summit,
calling it the Dome of Victory (Qubbat al-Nasr). Despite the renown of that
success, the edifice was poorly maintained and by 1217 had fallen into ruin.[22]
Does that mean that the Battle of Hattīn quickly sank into oblivion? No, because in reality a monument erected in the nonurban zone, away from the
population, had no chance of survival unless it became a site welcoming visitors and pilgrims. But in Islamic countries in the Middle Ages, pilgrimages developed almost exclusively around the holy cities (Mecca, Medina, Jerusalem)
or the graves of prophets and venerated figures. Commemorative monuments
usually celebrated events with religious or sacred connotations, and, until the
thirteenth century at least, monuments commemorating military feats were
rare. The one Sultan Baybars ordered to be built on the site of 'Ayn Jālūt in
1260, after the Mamluks' victory over the Mongols, may have been inspired by
Saladin's monument. It bore a similar name, "Sanctuary of Victory," and seems
to have survived somewhat longer than the monument in Hattīn, since it could
still be seen in the early fourteenth century.[23] It must be said that the victory of
'Ayn Jālūt was much more renowned than the Battle of Hattīn, because it allowed the Mongol invasion to be repelled, and that invasion was far more dan-

gerous than the Frankish conquest. In the eyes of some, the young Mamluk dynasty thereby saved Islam as a whole from annihilation.

The causes of Saladin's victory at Hattīn were diverse. They include the indisputable numerical superiority of the Muslims, the galvanizing presence of the sultan among his troops, and a good strategic choice that allowed them to cut off access to the springs of Hattīn and any possibility of a Frankish retreat. For the opposing camp, the divisions that weakened Guy of Lusignan within his own party played an important role. Often mentioned is Guy's tactical error in abandoning a defensive position that was well protected and well supplied with water to venture out onto the terrain chosen by Saladin. Malcolm C. Lyons and David E. P. Jackson have tempered that judgment by showing that Guy's hope of reaching the springs of Hattīn before Saladin's army was not all that unrealistic, and Benjamin Kedar has observed that the flow of the spring of Tu'rān, where the Frankish forces were posted, was in any case insufficient to supply an entire army, which would explain Guy's decision not to linger there too long.[24]

One of the first consequences of the Battle of Hattīn was that, the very next day, Raymond III's wife handed over the Tiberias fortress to Saladin, who displayed magnanimity in allowing her to leave with her possessions. To make the most of his advantage, Saladin was now obliged to act quickly, before a new army arrived from the West. Two possibilities presented themselves: conquer Jerusalem, his principal objective, or first take the cities of the coast to prevent Frankish aid from landing. In choosing the second option, Saladin calculated well. Deprived of defenses, the cities of the coast fell into his hands one after another at bewildering speed.[25]

By July 9, 1187, Acre was surrounded and the burghers were obliged to hand over the keys to their city to Saladin. Although Jerusalem was the main pilgrimage site and the capital of the kingdom, Acre was its richest and most populous city. Built on a sandstone promontory at the north end of a sandy cove, it owed its prosperity to its port, protected by large stone breakwaters, and to its favorable position between Egypt, Palestine, and Syria, which had made it the hub for commerce between East and West. Genoese, Venetian, and Pisan merchants had obtained significant privileges there in the early twelfth century and possessed entire neighborhoods, where they had residences, churches, warehouses, and shops. In the port, their boats unloaded their heavy cargos of merchandise: wheat, wine, dried fruit, salt pork, and above all, cloth from Flanders and Champagne, hemp, copper, iron, and horse saddles. Many products sold at the markets of Acre also came from the Far East, Arabia, Iraq, Syria, or Egypt. They arrived by caravan or by boat despite the war and the battles, and the Italian merchants who brought them from the West made their fortunes on them. Spices, incense, medicinal drugs, fragrances, silk and textiles of all sorts, products for use in dyeing, cotton, ivory, and sugar also reaped large profits.

Acre was therefore a rich city teeming with activity. "Its roads and streets are choked by the press of men, so that it is hard to put foot to ground," notes Ibn Jubayr, who lived there for only three years before it fell into Saladin's hands. The same traveler notes that Christians and Muslims sometimes shared prayer sites in Acre: "God kept undefiled one part of the principal mosque, which remained in the hands of the Muslims as a small mosque where strangers could congregate to offer the obligatory prayers. Near its mihrab is the tomb of the prophet Sālih—God bless and preserve him and all the prophets. God protected this part (of the mosque) from desecration for the benign influence of this holy tomb."[26]

Once taken by Saladin, the city was pillaged by his troops, to the great regret of 'Imād al-Dīn, who lamented that so many riches were not used more wisely. It must be said that the house 'Imād al-Dīn received as a gift from Saladin was completely looted, even before he had time to take possession of it. Saladin entrusted the governance of Acre to his son al-Afdal, known for his generosity—not to say prodigality—who also displayed great largesse. All the possessions of the Knights Templar inside the city and in the surrounding area were given to Emir Diyā' al-Dīn al-Hakkārī. As a result, therefore, of his lack of vigilance and no doubt his lack of foresight, Saladin did not gain all the profit he might have expected from his conquest. The cathedral returned to its original function as a Great Mosque, and al-Fādil, having reestablished a *minbar* and a *mihrāb*,[27] had the Friday prayer recited there. About four thousand Muslim prisoners were freed and, with Saladin's help, were able to return to their native regions.[28]

Part of Saladin's army, traveling south across Galilee and Samaria, then took without difficulty Nazareth, Sepphoris, the castle of la Fève (al-Fūla), Dabūriyya, Mount Tabor, Jenin, Zar'īn above 'Ayn Jālūt, and Sebaste. In Sebaste, the Saint John the Baptist Cathedral, a pilgrimage site venerated by Christians and Muslims, was turned into a mosque. The treasure accumulated by the canons in charge of the place, thanks to the gifts required of pilgrims, was seized. In Nablus and the surrounding villages, the majority of the population was still Muslim. Therefore, when the residents learned of the Franks' retreat, they wasted no time revolting against the Frankish garrison of Nablus, which rapidly surrendered.[29]

On the coast during that time, other emirs led their troops south of Acre and seized the ports of Haifa, Caesarea, and Arsūf. Al-'Ādil, having arrived from Egypt by the al-'Arīsh route, had no difficulty taking Majdal Yābā, twenty-one kilometers east of Jaffa, before attacking the port of Jaffa, which was completely pillaged, its residents sold in great number as slaves. The historian Ibn al-Athīr was struck by the misfortune of these people. He himself acquired a young female slave from the city; her six brothers had been killed and her husband and two sisters had disappeared. He recounted: "In Aleppo I saw a Frankish woman who had come to a door with her master. He knocked at the door and the owner of the house came out and spoke with them. Then he brought out another Frankish woman. When the first one caught sight of this other, they both cried out and embraced one another, screaming and weeping. They fell to the ground and sat talking. It transpired that they were two sisters. They had a number of family members but knew nothing about any one of them."[30]

While his emirs were advancing southward, Saladin, who had remained outside Acre, turned his attention to the north and sent his nephew Taqī al-Dīn to attack the fortress of Tībnīn, the forward bastion of Tyre, some forty-five kilometers directly northeast of Acre. Things were less easy there, and the resistance stronger than expected. Called to the rescue by his nephew, Saladin left Acre on July 17 and arrived at the fortress walls two days later. The garrison ultimately surrendered on July 26, in exchange for their lives being spared. The fighters had to leave their weapons, horses, and supplies behind but were allowed to take their personal belongings and were transported under escort to Tyre. The Muslims would soon come to regret that generosity, since Tyre quickly became the place to reassemble the Frankish forces.

Rather than lay siege to Tyre, Saladin preferred to circumvent the city and head north, via the Sarafand orchards, to Sidon, which was handed over without a fight on July 29. By that evening, he was outside the walls of Beirut, and while he was besieging the city, he sent to Damascus for one of the prisoners of Hattīn, the Genoese Hugues Embriaco, lord of Jubayl (Byblos). He wanted the prisoner to ransom himself in exchange for the surrender of the city, which he did. The taking of Jubayl on August 4 marked the farthest point of Saladin's march northward. Two days later, Beirut surrendered as well. Although very ill, 'Imād al-Dīn, who was accompanying the sultan at the time, drew up the act of surrender: "The sultan called in all the secretaries of his *dīwān,* all the eminent men of the state who could hold a stylus, but what they wrote did not satisfy him, what they set down was not adequate. Under these circumstances, someone came and asked me to dictate it to him: the minds of the healthy men were sick, but mine was not. So it was thanks to what I wrote that we took possession of Beirut."[31]

Saladin immediately departed again, going south to Ascalon. Along the way, he made only a brief attempt to seize Tyre, which he judged too difficult to take because of the size of its fortifications and the dispersal of his troops. He therefore preferred to join his brother al-'Ādil, who was urging him to attack Jerusalem.[32] The words attributed much later to al-'Ādil in 1225, which is to say, seven years after his death, may explain the strategy adopted by Saladin and, in any case, reveal the arguments used in the thirteenth century to justify the decision to momentarily give up the siege of Tyre and to focus on taking Jerusalem: "One of the arguments that I advanced when I was speaking to Saladin and urging him to take the opportunity of capturing Jerusalem was this: I pointed out that he was liable to attacks of colic and I said: 'If you die of an attack tonight, Jerusalem will stay in the hands of the Franks. Strive therefore to take it, and carry out what God has the right to expect of you, in gratitude for the favors He has showered on you.' He said: 'I shall do what you order and advise.'"[33]

The importance of Jerusalem is clearly emphasized, and the political context of the 1220s is likely part of the reason. During that period, in fact, the Ayyubid princes no longer recoiled at the possibility of giving Jerusalem over to the Franks, to the great displeasure of some men of religion, who attempted to make its status as a holy city a major selling point. But it is also true that, in 1187, Saladin's health was still fragile, and he was eager to see his name attached to a reconquest of Jerusalem after he was gone. In addition, Tyre was a well-fortified city, where a siege had no chance of succeeding unless the Muslim forces were reassembled. For the moment, they were dispersed in the various Frankish territories. Finally, the Latin and Arab sources all insist that, at the last minute, Conrad of Montferrat's arrival in Tyre prevented the city from sur-rendering. Unaware of the recent events, Conrad had first appeared off the coast in his ship. But alerted by various unusual signs—the silence of the bell that ordinarily announced a ship's arrival, the absence of Franks coming to meet him—he passed his vessel off as a merchant ship, gained some time, and set off again before Saladin's son had had time to react. Having learned that Tyre was still in the Franks' hands, he set sail for that city: "When they arrived before Tyre, the Christians in the city were overjoyed because God had sent them a ship at such a moment of crisis. They sent to find out who was on board and were delighted to discover that it was the marquis of Montferrat. A large section of the people of the city went and begged him to land and come to their aid, for unless the city was succoured by God and by him, it would be surren-dered to the Saracens as soon as he was gone, for Saladin's banners were al-ready in the city."[34]

While pointing out that Saladin justified his strategy on the basis of the priority he granted to the taking of Jerusalem, 'Imād al-Dīn has no trouble writing in hindsight that it would have been better to seize Tyre immediately, rather than allow it to be reinforced.[35] Saladin decided otherwise, and with the conquest of Jerusalem in view, he privileged the taking of Ascalon, Gaza, and Dārūm, in order to eliminate any threat to his rear guard and to facilitate com-munications between Egypt and Syria. On August 23, having rejoined al-ʿĀdil and his troops, Saladin arrived outside the walls of Ascalon, where he applied the same strategy he had used in Jubayl. From Damascus he brought in Guy of Lusignan and Gerard of Ridefort, Grand Master of the Knights Templar, and promised their release in exchange for the surrender of Ascalon (some say of all the remaining strongholds). When the garrison refused, the city was besieged and the mangonels set in operation. Despite their will to resist, the Franks quickly had to face the facts: the walls were beginning to crack, and no rescue operation could reach them now. Negotiations therefore began, and on Sep-tember 5, 1187, Saladin once more allowed the residents to leave the city with their families and belongings.

South of Ascalon, and on the road between Jaffa and Jerusalem, strong-holds fell one after another: Gaza, Dārūm, Ramla, Yubnā. In exchange for the release of their Grand Master Gerard of Ridefort, the Templars also surren-dered Latrun. In the meantime, the Egyptian fleet arrived to keep watch on the coast. Now in control of the entire coast from the Egyptian border to the city of Jubayl—with the exception of Tyre—Saladin turned to Jerusalem. On September 20, 1187, he installed his siege engines outside the holy city.[36]

The Taking of Jerusalem

A large number of people had taken refuge in Jerusalem, counting on the sacredness of the city to protect them. The city was overcrowded, with probably sixty to a hundred thousand souls, or more than three times its usual population. In preparation for the siege, the Franks had reinforced the fortifications, deepened the moat, and readied mangonels. The major problem was the near total absence of Frankish knights. Balian of Ibelin, a survivor of Hattīn, had come to Jerusalem to find his wife. He agreed to assure its defense and made the defenders of the city swear an oath to him. He dubbed the sons of knights aged fifteen and over and even—and this was unusual—some sons of burghers.

The Muslims, having camped for five days west of the city, time enough to observe that its powerful fortifications would not allow them to take it from that side, set up their camp and their ballistae to the north and northeast of Jerusalem, the same place where the Crusaders had taken it by force in 1099.

Despite strong resistance, Saladin's troops, by means of intensive bombardment and skillful undermining, managed to make a large breach in the wall. The Franks, facing that desperate situation and certain that no help would arrive, asked to negotiate. But Saladin, no doubt aware that the city was about to capitulate, at first proved reluctant. "I want to take Jerusalem," he said, "the way the Christians took it from the Muslims ninety-one years ago. They inundated it in blood, leaving it not a moment's peace. The men I will slaughter, and the women I will make slaves."[37]

Balian threatened to kill all the Muslim prisoners, between three and five thousand of them, and to destroy the holy sites of Islam, al-Aqsā Mosque, and the Dome of the Rock. Saladin, encouraged by his emirs, finally agreed to conclude an accord on October 2, 1187. A ransom of ten dinars for every man, five for every woman, and two for every child was demanded, with payment due in forty days. The Franks were allowed to take their personal belongings, with the exception of weapons and horses. Those who could not pay were to be kept as slaves.

The Muslims thus took possession of the city without bloodshed, but they did loot the church treasuries. The Christian author of the *Anonymous Syriac*

Chronicle, who was in Jerusalem at the time, describes how, before his horrified eyes, the sacred vessels of the churches were sold at the marketplace, and churches were turned into animal sheds, bars, and various places of debauchery.[38] Balian spent thirty thousand dinars to pay the ransom for the most destitute, but it was not enough, and fifteen to sixteen thousand people were reduced to slavery. Saladin and his brother, a Latin source affirms, themselves redeemed a great number of the poor and set them free.[39] Michael the Syrian seems to indicate something similar, saying that Saladin restored the freedom of "four thousand old men and women."[40] But he immediately adds that sixteen thousand others were reduced to slavery and put to work building the fortifications of Jerusalem and Egypt, among other tasks, suggesting that only the aged were freed, from whom no profit could be extracted.

The Arab authors mention no redemption of prisoners by Saladin but rather complain about the disastrous way the ransom was collected. The gates of the city had been locked, and on principle no one could leave without a receipt. But the overall disorder allowed a great number of officials and emirs to turn to their own profit the money paid by the Franks, taking in one hundred to two hundred thousand dinars (the figures vary a great deal, depending on the source). 'Imād al-Dīn's report on the matter is enlightening: "If the revenues from the tax had been kept as they ought to have been, they would have considerably enriched the public treasury. But in this respect, there was complete negligence and a general disorder: anyone who could make a gift under the table was released, and the officials left the straight path for that of misappropriation. Some of the residents slipped over the walls with the aid of ropes, others left by concealing themselves among the baggage. Some fled clandestinely, disguised in the uniform of the [Muslim] army; others were the object of an imperious intercession that no one could disobey."[41]

The Eastern Christians—Melkites, Jacobites, and Armenians—several thousand of them according to 'Imād al-Dīn, also had to ransom themselves but were allowed to remain in the city with their former status as "protected persons" *(dhimmīs).* The ransom of the Armenians from the former county of Edessa, which had been broken up by Muslims between 1144 and 1150, was claimed by the emirs of Edessa and al-Bīra, on the pretext that the Armenians had once lived on their territories. The emir of Edessa thus pocketed the ransom of a thousand people, the emir of al-Bīra that of about five hundred.

To find the money required, the Franks and their allies tried to sell their belongings as quickly as possible, often for a pittance, to Eastern Christians or merchants. In the opinion of all, Saladin proved to be magnanimous toward the knights' wives and the princesses. He allowed Balian's wife, who was none other than Maria Comnena, King Amalric I's former wife, to leave with all her possessions, and did the same for Queen Sibylla, who went to join her husband, Guy of Lusignan, held prisoner in Nablus. Similarly, he authorized Reginald of Châtillon's widow to go to Kerak and promised her the release of her son if she obtained the surrender of the garrison, which she was unable to do. Nevertheless, Saladin let her leave with all her belongings and assured her that he would free her son once Kerak and Shawbak gave in. The Latin patriarch of Jerusalem was also allowed to leave the city, laden with the treasures of the Holy Sepulchre, under 'Imād al-Dīn's disapproving eye: "So I told the sultan: 'These are great riches; they are clearly worth two hundred thousand dinars. Permission to take one's own possessions does not apply to those of the churches and convents; do not therefore leave them in the hands of those infidels.' He replied: 'If we interpret it to their detriment, they will accuse us of perfidy, for they do not know the heart of the matter. We will therefore deal with them by applying the safeguard agreement to the letter, and will not let them accuse the Believers of having violated the sworn faith. On the contrary, they will speak of the blessings we have showered on them.'"[42]

The Frankish exiles set off for Tyre or Tripoli in convoys under escort, which did not prevent them from being pillaged by Muslims, or, in the case of those who attempted to take refuge in the county of Tripoli, even by Franks. Some found refuge in Alexandria, where they were put onto Italian boats, against the will of the merchants. These merchants were no doubt unhappy to have to take charge of them without provisions or money. That incident gave a Latin author the opportunity to remark indignantly on the contrast between the Muslims' generosity and the Franks' selfishness.[43] The Muslim prisoners incarcerated in Jerusalem were all granted their freedom. Saladin gave them clothing and helped them return to their native countries. The money, the goods seized, and the enslaved Franks were then generously distributed by Saladin to his troops and close entourage. Finally, the Jews, who had been driven from Jerusalem at the time of the First Crusade, were allowed to return and settle there.

Saladin enjoyed a great deal of glory as a result of the taking of Jerusalem, both in the eyes of his contemporaries and in those of posterity. His generosity and magnanimity, so often vaunted, were practiced toward the Muslims to thank them for their support and to assure their loyalty, but also toward high-ranking Franks, to spread the image of the sovereign respectful of his enemies, to shore up his good reputation among his adversaries, and to facilitate future conquests. During these events, Saladin, true to his usual line of conduct, proved to be steadfast and determined, respecting his promises and Muslim law, attending to the image he might be presenting of himself, and striving to consolidate his support and obtain the surrender of his adversaries through negotiation rather than by force. Let us refrain, however, from projecting onto him our modern conceptions of openness and tolerance. For Saladin, delivering Jerusalem, the third holy city of Islam, from the authority of the "infidels" was a religious obligation. He had to defeat, subjugate the enemy, enslave those from whom he could draw no profit, tear down the crosses, and "assure the triumph of truth over error," in order to prove the superiority of one religion over another, consistent with the ideals of his time. Political and religious interests were thus intimately linked and were served by his generosity, natural no doubt, but not devoid of calculation.

For several days, Saladin received in his tent outside the city the emirs and ulemas of Syria and Egypt who had come to congratulate him. ʿImād al-Dīn, having only just arrived from Damascus, where he had gone for medical treatment, was given the task of writing letters to spread the news of that victory as widely as possible. He boasted of having composed seventy in a single day. Many poets also wrote verses to celebrate the memorable event.

Very quickly, the face of Jerusalem changed. The churches and monasteries were converted back to Muslim buildings, beginning with those on the old Temple Esplanade east of the city, where the two main Muslim pilgrimage sites in Jerusalem were located, al-Aqsā Mosque and the Dome of the Rock. Built at the turn of the eighth century by the Umayyad caliphs, these two monuments had left the stamp of Islam on the city of Jerusalem and evoked its privileged link to revelation and to the Prophet. Al-Aqsā (the Farther One) bore the name of the mosque mentioned in the Koran, to which God had led Muhammad, on a fantastic white horse, from Mecca to Jerusalem, having him ascend at night to the heavens, before taking him back to Mecca. The Dome of the Rock, an octagonal building surmounted by an enormous cupola, was erected on the rock from which, according to that same tradition, the Prophet had taken flight toward heaven. In constructing these two monuments, both greatly inspired by

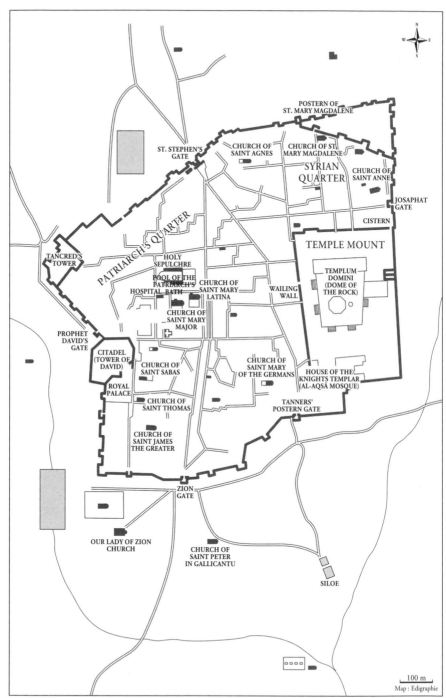

POSTERN OF
ST. MARY MAGDALENE

ST. STEPHEN'S
GATE

CHURCH OF
SAINT AGNES

CHURCH OF ST.
MARY MAGDALENE

SYRIAN
QUARTER

CHURCH OF
SAINT ANNE

JOSAPHAT
GATE

CISTERN

PATRIARCH'S QUARTER

TANCRED'S
TOWER

HOLY
SEPULCHRE

POOL OF THE
PATRIARCH'S
HOSPITAL BATH

CHURCH OF
SAINT MARY
LATINA

WAILING
WALL

TEMPLE MOUNT

TEMPLUM
DOMINI
(DOME OF
THE ROCK)

CHURCH OF
SAINT MARY
MAJOR

PROPHET
DAVID'S
GATE

CITADEL
(TOWER OF
DAVID)

CHURCH OF
SAINT SABAS

CHURCH OF
SAINT MARY
OF THE GERMANS

HOUSE OF THE
KNIGHTS TEMPLAR
(AL-AQSĀ MOSQUE)

ROYAL
PALACE

CHURCH OF
SAINT THOMAS

TANNERS'
POSTERN GATE

CHURCH OF
SAINT JAMES
THE GREATER

ZION
GATE

OUR LADY OF ZION
CHURCH

CHURCH OF
SAINT PETER
IN GALLICANTU

SILOE

100 m

Map : Edigraphie

Jerusalem on the Eve of Its Reconquest by Saladin

Byzantine architecture, the Umayyads had forcefully asserted that, alongside Judaism and Christianity—for which Jerusalem was a holy city—there was now a new religion, Islam. Their aim was nonetheless political: without disputing the preeminence of Mecca and Medina within Islam, the affirmation of the sacredness of Jerusalem extended to all of Syria-Palestine and thereby allowed the Umayyads to justify the choice of Damascus as the capital and seat of their power.

Initially, the Franks had turned al-Aqsā Mosque into a royal residence, and then, as of 1120, into a residence for the Knights Templar. They had preserved a number of inscriptions containing Koranic verses or evoking the restorations done by the caliphs, as attested by al-Harawī, author of the *Guide to Pilgrimage*, who visited Jerusalem in 1173.[44] Saladin had al-Aqsā Mosque completely restored. Its marble *mihrāb,* which according to the sources had been used as a grain storeroom or as a latrine, was renovated; later Ayyubid rulers, al-'Ādil in particular, continued to improve it. Saladin also sent to Aleppo for the carved wood pulpit *(minbar)* that Nūr al-Dīn had ordered constructed with the intention of installing it in the Jerusalem mosque once the city was reconquered. The entire mosque was cleaned from floor to ceiling, then purified with rosewater and incense. Important figures such as Saladin's nephew Taqī al-Dīn were eager to participate personally in these operations and, for that occasion, distributed generous sums of money for the maintenance of the building and the support of devout worshippers.

As for the Dome of the Rock, the Franks had turned it into a church (Templum Domini), adorning its walls with paintings and statues and building a cupola supported by marble columns inside the edifice, above the rock. The imprint of Muhammad's foot preserved on the rock had become for the Christians the footprint of Jesus, and according to 'Imād al-Dīn, pieces of it had been broken off and sold as relics in Constantinople and Sicily.[45] With the reconquest of Jerusalem, the Dome of the Rock returned to its bygone splendor and function. The paintings, statues, and small internal cupolas concealing the rock were removed; the imposing cross that stood above the large dome was torn down. In that building, Saladin installed one of the best specialists on the Koran and, to see to his needs, granted him as mortmain property *(waqf)* a house, a plot of land, and a garden. He also appointed all the religious in charge of these two prestigious edifices and ordered the destruction of the cemeteries established by the Franks within proximity of the Dome and the Gate of Mercy.

The northwest quadrant of the city was filled with many Christian monuments, often predating the Frankish conquest. There was in the first place the Holy Sepulchre, in a vast architectural complex built beginning in the fourth century at the site of Christ's crucifixion and resurrection. It was there that all Christian pilgrims from East and West converged. In Saladin's entourage, opinions were divided about the fate that ought to be reserved for it. Some proposed that it be destroyed, to remove all temptation for Western Christians to return. Others thought that, even reduced to a mere esplanade, the place would continue to attract pilgrims wishing to gather at the site where Christ had died and risen again. Caliph 'Umar ibn al-Khaṭṭāb himself, they said, had not judged it wise to destroy the Holy Sepulchre when he had seized Jerusalem in 638, an argument to which Saladin, concerned about his image and the comparison that would unfailingly be made between him and that prestigious figure, could not remain insensitive. The Holy Sepulchre therefore escaped destruction and was entrusted, as in the past, to the Christians of the Melkite rite.[46] As the author of the *Anonymous Syriac Chronicle* says—though the Arab sources do not speak of it—it is likely that the Muslims, in sparing the Holy Sepulchre, also sought to preserve an important source of revenue, since every pilgrim had to pay a relatively high fee to enter.[47]

South of the Holy Sepulchre was the House of the Hospitallers. The Knights Hospitaller took their name from a hospital founded at that site by a resident of Amalfi in the mid-eleventh century, to care for Western pilgrims who came to Jerusalem. With the arrival of the Franks, the monks responsible for its operation had gradually become militarized and, like the Knights Templar, had adopted a special Rule that made them soldier-monks; but in Jerusalem their institution continued to be a place for medical treatment. Saladin allowed about ten of the Hospitallers to remain for a year to care for the patients still there.[48] In 1192, Saladin's son al-Zāhir was living in what must have been part of the building; later, in about 1216, Saladin's nephew al-Mu'azzam founded an establishment in one corner of the edifice, no doubt intended to accommodate Sufis.[49]

Between 1187 and 1192, many other Christian buildings in Jerusalem were gradually converted into Muslim charitable institutions and were granted the religious overseers and mortmain properties necessary for their support. A church located near the Holy Sepulchre was turned into a hospital, the Patriarchate became a Sufi institution, and a Shafite madrasa was established in the

Saint Anne Church northeast of Jerusalem. On the west part of the rampart, at the summit of the Tower of David, which the Franks had made their fortress, there had once been an oratory that the Muslims called Mihrāb Dā'ūd (Mihrāb of David), where pilgrims came to meditate. It was renovated, and Saladin appointed an imam and muezzins for it. He also restored the tombs of holy figures and repaired several cisterns whose water was intended for passersby.[50]

The local Christians who remained in Jerusalem—several thousand, according to 'Imād al-Dīn—no doubt kept several of the many churches in Jerusalem, though our information on the subject is rather vague.[51] The Our Lady of Zion Church south of the ramparts of Jerusalem seems to have been used for a time as al-'Ādil's residence,[52] while the Church of Saint Mary Magdalene, at the northeast corner of the city, was turned into a madrasa by one of Saladin's emirs.[53]

On October 9, 1187, the Friday great prayer, which brought Muslims together in al-Aqṣā Mosque, took on special importance. Everyone was waiting impatiently for Saladin to designate the one who would have the honor of pronouncing the first *khutba* in the holy city in eighty-eight years. There were many candidates, and "all, without exception, were preparing themselves, observing . . . insinuating themselves. Some proved enterprising, while others abased themselves, stood at the ready, or sought an intercession."[54] Saladin maintained the suspense until the last minute, before opting for the chief qādī of Aleppo, Muhyī al-Dīn Ibn al-Zakī, who had predicted that Saladin would seize Jerusalem.

The chief qādī mounted the *minbar* wearing a black robe that 'Imād al-Dīn had received from the caliph and had lent him for the occasion. The Friday sermon was, in the first place, an opportunity to reaffirm the authority of the legitimate sovereign, in whose name it was pronounced. The qādī uttered the *khutba*, linking the name of the Abbasid caliph of Baghdad to that of Saladin. He began by praising God, quoting a few verses from the Koran: "Thus were the evildoers annihilated. Praise be to God, Lord of the Universe" (6:45).[55] He then evoked the Muslim victory, the expulsion of the Franks, the "purification" after the "filth," and recalled all the qualities that made Jerusalem a holy city for Islam: it was the land of Abraham and dwelling place of the prophets, the holy land promised to Moses by God (Koran 5:21), the place where Mary and Joseph had heard the word of God, the site of the Prophet's nocturnal journey and his ascent to heaven, and the first *qibla* (direction of prayer) for Muslims. The qādī also recalled the conquests of the first caliphs and rejoiced that the

Muslims had resumed these exploits and received God's reward. He exhorted his audience to pursue the jihad and reconquer the territories of the infidels: "Do not [be] like the woman who unravels the thread she has firmly spun" (Koran 16:92). He also called on Muslims to remain humble and modest and not to attribute that victory to their strength alone, for "victory comes only from God; God is mighty and wise" (Koran 8:10). He expressed his best wishes for the caliph and the sultan, and ended with this passage from the Koran: "God enjoins justice, kindness and charity" (Koran 16:90), a very symbolic verse since in the Koran it is preceded by a condemnation of the polytheists and unbelievers. Having finished his sermon, the chief qādī descended the steps of the *minbar* and took up his position in front of the *miḥrāb* to lead the prayer.

After that official *khutba*, Saladin allowed the sermonist Ibn Nāja to give a more populist sermon in al-Aqsā Mosque, one that repeated the same themes and deeply moved the listeners: "Some noisily wept; other shouted, exchanging their complaints: hearts softened; sadness was alleviated; howls rose up; tears flowed; sinners repented; the afflicted returned to God; the penitent moaned; the repentant lamented."[56]

Saladin thus granted a great deal of attention to the re-Islamization of Jerusalem, adding an indisputable religious dimension to his political and military success. He would no doubt have liked to remain there longer, but his campaigns were not finished, and on October 30, four weeks after entering the city, he departed again in response to the appeal of the governor of Sidon and Beirut, who was urging him to attack Tyre. On November 4, he arrived in Acre.

In slightly more than two months, the greater part of the kingdom of Jerusalem had fallen into the Muslims' hands. The causes of that lightning victory—*Al-Barq al-Shāmī* (The Syrian thunderbolt) was the title that ʿImād al-Dīn gave to his account of Saladin's conquests—were obviously multiple. The difficulties surrounding the succession to the throne and the political divisions inside the kingdom of Jerusalem account for the Franks' weakness. The Muslims' numerical superiority and the elimination of nearly all the Frankish knights in the Battle of Hattīn allowed Saladin quickly to acquire the advantage. Only the fortresses that had their own garrisons, such as Kerak, Safad, Belvoir, and Montreal (Shawbak), resisted somewhat longer, but they too ultimately fell, between November 1188 and April 1189.

Saladin's military and political strategy turned out to be very effective. In establishing security of communications between Egypt and Syria, and in deciding to take control of the coastal cities to prevent any Frankish aid from reaching Jerusalem, Saladin perfectly controlled the progress of his conquests. His only mistake was to allow a pocket of resistance to survive in Tyre, where the Frankish forces reconstituted themselves while awaiting the arrival of the Third Crusade. By contrast, in granting favorable conditions to the defeated if they agreed to surrender and in keeping his promises, Saladin applied the policy he had successfully tested on his Muslim adversaries and very quickly obtained the surrender of numerous localities that no longer had the means to resist. Balian's remarks on the eve of the surrender of Jerusalem show the extent to which the negotiation card could be a major asset in the political game: "If we despair of having our lives spared, if, unable to count on your kindness, we have everything to fear from your might, if we remain convinced that there is neither salvation nor happiness nor peace nor settlement remaining for us, no longer truces or security, no longer benevolence or generosity, we shall set out to meet our deaths; it will be a bloody struggle of despair; we shall exchange life for the void; we shall throw ourselves into the flames rather than accept destitution and shame. For every wound, each of us will respond with ten."[57]

Finally, some cities, such as Sidon, Beirut, and Jubayl, still had a relatively large Muslim population, the Franks having understood at the time of their conquest that it was not in their interest to drive away all their inhabitants. That Muslim presence no doubt impelled the Franks to negotiate more quickly with Saladin.[58]

The Siege of Tyre

Saladin remained in Acre for only four days. He then set out for Tyre, about forty kilometers north, where, in no haste, he arrived on November 12, 1187. Conrad of Montferrat had had time to reinforce the city, which had originally been built on an island and linked to the land by a narrow causeway under the reign of Alexander the Great in 332 B.C.E. Over the centuries, an actual isthmus had formed, bordered on the east by three walls behind a moat, which barred access to the city and the port.

Saladin was not in the best situation to conduct a siege.[59] His troops were partly dispersed: al-'Ādil had remained in Jerusalem, al-Afdal was in Acre, al-'Azīz had returned to Egypt, and a number of his emirs were busy guarding the conquered cities. All the same, his son al-Zāhir, who had just turned fifteen, came to join him with his army from Aleppo and participated in his first major battle. The Frankish ships posted on both sides of the isthmus bombarded the Muslims with arrows as they tried to approach the city. Saladin then brought in about ten Egyptian galleys posted in Acre, as well as ships from Beirut and Jubayl. The sea blockade thereby set in place was supposed to prevent the Frankish fleet from leaving the port. Crossbows and mangonels were set in operation; palisades were erected to protect the fighters; and mobile towers, covered with hides and loaded with crossbowmen, took their positions.

In early December, al-ʿĀdil, al-Afdal, and Taqī al-Dīn came to join Saladin, but the troubles began. The cold wet weather did not facilitate matters, and the Muslim troops, accustomed to the easy conquests of the previous months, met with strong resistance. The motivation of the Franks, who were fighting for their survival, was without a doubt very strong, whereas the Muslims were tired and somewhat unmotivated after the taking of Jerusalem. The arrival of an embassy from Baghdad during that month of December, bearing an at-best ambivalent missive from the caliph in response to the announcement that Jerusalem had been taken, completely demoralized Saladin and his entourage.

It was at that moment that the Franks began their counteroffensive. At dawn on December 30, seventeen galleys and ten smaller boats, previously blockaded in the port, attacked five Muslim boats and surprised the crews during their sleep. Many were taken prisoner, and the remaining fleet, now insufficient to stamp out the Franks, was redirected toward Beirut. Moreover, the inexperienced crews, attacked en route by the Franks, abandoned the fight and leapt into the water. Their boats had to be hauled in and dismantled on the beach to keep the Franks from seizing them. Only one ship, commanded by the governor of Jubayl, managed to return safely to port.[60] It was the first major setback for Saladin since Hattīn, and his camp took it hard. It was essential that he succeed in Tyre, the last Frankish bastion in the kingdom of Jerusalem, to cut off the interior of the country from supplies or reinforcements from the sea; but his emirs and their men were worn down, discouraged, and running low on provisions. In the last days of December, Saladin attempted to recruit new troops by sending a thousand dinars to Acre, but the sum was insufficient, and the emirs were afraid they would have to lend him money again[61] (recall that Saladin's major weakness was financial management). A new Muslim offensive was attempted on the last two days of the year, but in vain. In the end, facing the discouragement of his emirs, Saladin reluctantly struck camp. To acquit him in the eyes of posterity, his entourage insisted on his desire to continue the siege: "If we give up on Tyre, we shall have no excuse before Allah and the Muslims" are the words that 'Imād al-Dīn attributes to him. This suggests that, by the end of the twelfth century, the Muslims were aware that on January 1, 1188, they had allowed the opportunity to eliminate the Franks to slip away from them. "This was his practice," wrote Ibn al-Athīr, who is much more critical of Saladin than 'Imād al-Dīn. "Whenever a city held firm against him he tired of it and its siege and therefore left it." The historian concedes that the army wanted to strike camp but adds: "No-one was to blame for this but Saladin, for he was the person who sent the Frankish troops there and supplied it with manpower and resources from the populations of Acre, Ascalon, Jerusalem and elsewhere."[62]

It is obvious that Saladin's leniency had allowed him speedily to take cities while limiting human and financial losses, but it had also favored the reinforcement of Tyre, and it was probably a strategic error to have waited so long to attack it. Once the decision was made to withdraw, the army dispersed, and the only consolation for the Muslims was the surrender, during the siege, of the fortress of Hūnīn, north of Galilee and east of Tyre.

Saladin then returned to the encampment outside Acre. Having for a moment considered ordering the destruction of the city to prevent the Franks from regaining a foothold there, he instead decided to strengthen its fortifications. To that end, he sent for Emir Qarāqūsh, already in charge of the fortifications of Cairo, who brought with him from Egypt the men and matériel necessary. Saladin also took advantage of his stay in Acre to receive embassies from Iran, Azerbaijan, Anatolia, and Upper Mesopotamia. The news of his recent victories had spread widely in the Muslim world, and these embassies attested to the desire of rulers in the neighboring states to consolidate their ties with him and perhaps as well to sound him out regarding his intentions. The Artukid lord of Amida and of Hisn Kayfā even asked for the hand of al-'Ādil's daughter in marriage, no doubt to make sure that no one would take his possessions from him. 'Imād al-Dīn was given the task of drawing up the marriage contract.[63] Saladin ultimately settled matters in Acre and named Emir 'Izz al-Dīn Jūrdīk its governor.

The Campaign in Northern Syria

Saladin left Acre in March 1188 for Damascus, where he stayed only five days. His objective was to pursue his conquests in northern Syria as quickly as possible, so as not to give the Franks time to reconstitute their forces.[64] In mid-May, he rejoined 'Imād al-Dīn Zangī and his army south of Lake Homs, where they had come from Upper Mesopotamia to meet him. Three historians were also part of the group: Ibn Shaddād, who had just joined Saladin's service; Ibn al-Athīr, who had arrived with Zangī; and 'Imād al-Dīn. Saladin's nephew Taqī al-Dīn and son al-Zāhir were given the task of keeping watch on the border of Antioch, while the sultan's brother al-'Ādil was still in Egypt and his other son al-Afdal in Acre. Several emirs had also remained behind to watch those fortresses of the kingdom of Jerusalem that were still in the hands of the Franks (Kawkab, Safad, Kerak, and Shawbak).

The Muslim army set off for the Homs Gap, bypassing the Krac des Chevaliers, a mighty fortress in the hands of the Knights Hospitaller which for the moment appeared impregnable. Saladin launched several raids against the territory of Sāfīthā (Chastel Blanc) and several other fortresses in the region.[65] From there, two possibilities presented themselves: he could either focus his efforts on the coast and the capitals (Tripoli and Antioch), to prevent the Franks from receiving reinforcements—but that undertaking looked to be long and uncertain—or he could attack the weak spots in order to rapidly extend his conquests and give satisfaction to his emirs, on whom all the strength of his army rested. The appeal sent him by the qādī of Jabala—a small port south of Latakia occupied by the Franks—who warned him of Tripoli's might and said he was ready to turn Jabala over to him, as well as an encounter with the Muslim leaders of Jabal Bahrā', who had come to assure him of their support, ultimately persuaded Saladin to avoid a frontal attack on Tripoli and Antioch and attempt rather to seize less well-defended places such as the port of Tartūs, which happened to be nearby.

Tartūs was taken by force in early July, and only one tower, defended by the recently liberated Gerard of Ridefort, Grand Master of the Knights Templar, continued to resist. But its church, dedicated to the Virgin, was destroyed;[66] its fortifications were razed, to prevent the Franks from retreating to them; and the city was burned to the ground. Saladin continued northward. He passed alongside the powerful fortress of Marqab, defended by the Hospitallers, through a narrow coastal passage. There he was assaulted by arrows shot by Sicilians, who had arrived as reinforcements on several dozen vessels.[67] That fleet, under the command of Admiral Margarit, had been sent by William II, king of Sicily, to reinforce Tyre. After disembarking, a detachment had gone

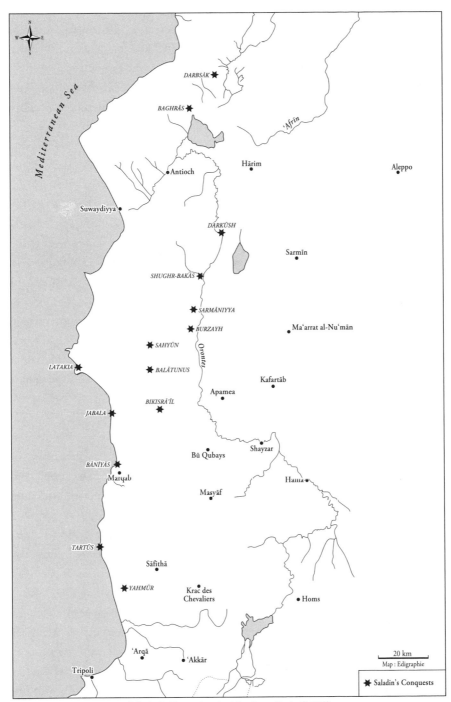

Saladin's Campaign in Northern Syria (1188)

to Tripoli and from there had followed Saladin's troops northward. To allow his troops to advance, Saladin had palisades erected, and from behind them his archers and crossbowmen showered arrows down on their enemies. The small localities of the coast that the Franks could not defend were evacuated, with residents seeking refuge in the surrounding fortified cities.[68] Upon arriving at a point south of Jabala, Saladin was joined by his son al-Zāhir from Aleppo.

Jabala was taken with the help of the Muslim population and its qādī on Friday, July 15, 1188. A few kilometers to the east, the fortress of Bikisrā'īl, already more or less under the control of the mountain dwellers, also surrendered. Latakia fell on July 21, and the twin fortified castle that protected it on the northeast side surrendered on the evening of Friday, July 22. The qādī of Jabala served as an intermediary between the garrison and the sultan. The lives of the Franks were spared, but all their possessions were plundered. Latakia was a large and rich city surrounded by orchards, with beautiful residences, streets lined with porticos, and lively markets, and 'Imād al-Dīn could not refrain from lamenting its ruin: "I saw with sadness its prosperity disappear and everything that adorned it vanish, but my joy grew to see it come back to support Islam and to shine with new brilliance. Had it been able to preserve its beauty and its condition once truth had been substituted for error, how desirable and admirable it would have been, and what superiority its return to life [conversion] would have given it!"[69]

The Eastern Christians and even a few Franks were allowed to remain in the city with the status of *dhimmīs*. Saladin then received Margarit, admiral of the Sicilian fleet posted opposite the port of Latakia. Margarit attempted to persuade him to leave the city to the Franks in exchange for their submission. He dangled the threat of a new Crusade should Saladin refuse, but to no avail.

In the following days, most of the fortresses located inland of Latakia, which had assured protection of the coastal cities and more or less directly controlled the roads linking central and northern Syria to the coast, fell one after another.[70] On August 23, Saladin himself took command of the assault on Burzayh, a high-perched castle reputed to be impregnable, located northwest of Apamea. The lady of that fortress was none other than the sister-in-law of Bohemond of Antioch, whose wife, Sibylla, occasionally fed information to Saladin.[71] The sultan had therefore pledged to Sibylla not to do her sister any harm. After his army outstripped him and seized her and her family, Saladin, to honor his promise, had to ransom her from her ravishers and have her escorted safe and sound to Antioch. In returning north, rather than directly attack Antioch, Saladin chose to seize the two strongholds protecting the area near the city: Darbsāk and Baghrās fell, respectively, on September 16 and 26, 1188. These fortresses had a strategic position of foremost importance, since they controlled all the roads linking Aleppo to Cilicia, and the Knights Templar who held them had made them their base for the raids they were launching against the territory of Aleppo.[72]

Within three months, then, Saladin had carried out an impressive number of conquests. His strategy, which consisted of wagering on the support of the Muslim populations, the swiftness of the attacks, and the takeover of inland areas to assure connections between the interior of Syria and the coast, had paid off. But so long as Tripoli and Antioch had not fallen, a counteroffensive with the aid of reinforcements from the West still remained possible. To definitively expel the Franks from northern Syria, it would no doubt have been more effective to take control of these two capitals before seizing the fortresses of the interior. Saladin was not unaware of this, but he also knew that such an operation was much more difficult and ran the risk of depleting his forces without any real result, as the experience of Tyre had recently demonstrated. And he needed to gain territory rapidly to satisfy his family members and emirs. The most astonishing thing is undoubtedly the lack of reaction from the county of Tripoli and the principality of Antioch. In fact, several fortresses fell not because the Muslims took them by force but because their occupiers, despairing of seeing reinforcements arrive from Antioch, ultimately delivered them in exchange for the promise that their lives would be spared. During the siege of Shughr, 'Imād al-Dīn himself noted that the Muslims were becoming discouraged, when suddenly the besieged agreed to surrender. Similarly, the weak resistance of the Knights Templar—known, moreover, for their bravery and bellicosity—did not fail to surprise: "The submission of those obdurate men astonished us: they handed over [their castles] to us, though they were jealous even of the sun penetrating through."[73]

No doubt the Franks of Antioch and Tripoli feared that, in taking the offensive, they would use up their forces, which were already severely compromised by the lost battles, the lack of deliveries of supplies, and the high cost of provisions. Bohemond III hoped primarily that his many attempts to obtain reinforcements from the West would ultimately bear fruit. He knew, moreover, that his principal advantage against Saladin was control of the sea and that, for that reason, Saladin would have as much if not more difficulty seizing Tripoli and Antioch as he had had in Tyre.

It may have been because he was aware of these difficulties that Saladin abandoned taking the road to Antioch, which was nevertheless open before him, and preferred to conclude an eight-month truce with Bohemond III, which was to begin on October 1, 1188. All the Muslim prisoners were to be released, and it seems that Bohemond also promised to hand over Antioch to the Muslims if no help reached him before the truce expired.[74] Saladin's close circle justified the truce by insisting on the army's state of exhaustion and the eagerness of the eastern troops to return home, while minimizing the concessions made to the Franks:

> The sultan had chosen well, since the truce was set to expire before the ripening of the grains and harvest time; the Franks could not gather them in, or transport them, or dispose of them. The sultan had no great desire to conclude that peace, because of our overall good fortune in the war and the abundance of our gains; but the foreign troops, tired of remaining there, displayed their weariness, and demanded peace and calm. And it was said: "During that truce, the might of Antioch will not increase, it will not recover its vigor; it will not be able to count on the aid of a certain number, whereas we will keep our promise by returning against it upon the expiration of the truce. As for its fortifications, we have seized their honey and killed their bees."[75]

All that remained was to distribute the conquered fortresses. Saladin wanted first to thank the Aleppine emirs who had rallied behind him in 1183.[76] He also rewarded his most faithful emirs, particularly Mangüverish Ibn Khumartegin, son of the Turkish emir who had given his life to defend him against the Assassins in 1174, and 'Izz al-Dīn Ibn al-Muqaddam, whose father, killed in Mecca shortly before, had delivered Damascus to him in 1174. Ghars al-Dīn Qilij, a former emir of Shīrkūh's who had played a major role the previous year in the taking of Caesarea, and Saladin's nephew Taqī al-Dīn were also generously thanked.[77] That victorious campaign in northern Syria had not only weakened the Franks but had also allowed Saladin to establish closer ties with a number of his emirs.

On October 5, 1188, the sultan arrived in Aleppo, where he received a royal welcome from his son al-Zāhir. He did not linger, however, but set out for Damascus three days later. Autumn had already arrived, the Ramadan fast was to begin in ten days, and the troops were hoping for some rest. But Saladin did not seem to want to observe any sort of truce, either religious or hibernal. His principal objective remained to take the fortresses in the kingdom of Jerusalem that were still resisting him.[78] For more than a year Kerak had been besieged by Muslim troops. The garrison, worn down and with no hope of receiving aid, finally surrendered to al-ʿĀdil in November 1188. Saladin, for his part, established his camp northwest of Lake Tiberias, outside Safad, which the Knights Templar handed over to him fairly quickly in the first days of December. He had no great difficulty defeating two hundred Frankish troops who had come from Tyre to aid Kawkab (Belvoir), held by the Hospitallers, four kilometers southwest of Lake Tiberias. Saladin went in person to the foot of that mighty fortress, which had been besieged by the Muslims for more than nine months. Despite the resistance of the garrison and the deplorable weather conditions, the Muslim sappers, in rain, cold, and mud, undermined the wall. The Hospitallers finally surrendered in early January 1189. Saladin offered the fortress to several emirs, but none wanted it. He finally gave it to the leader of the siege, who already had Tiberias in his possession. He accepted it—reluctantly, though no one really knows the reason for the emirs' lack of enthusiasm about possessing Kawkab.[79]

That conquest marked the end of Saladin's campaign. The troops returned to rest, and Saladin, accompanied by al-ʿĀdil, set off for Jerusalem in late January 1189, "making that pilgrimage to win favor and blessings."[80] Unable to go to Mecca in that month of Muslim pilgrimage[81] for fear of leaving the field wide open to the Franks, Saladin, in visiting Jerusalem, symbolically linked the two cities and once again styled himself the defender of the Muslim religion. To properly mark that symbolic connection, he arrived in the holy city on the very day the pilgrimage to Mecca was beginning. At the Dome of the Rock, he performed the same prayer rituals, the distribution of alms to the poor, and the immolation of an animal on the tenth day of the month, the day of the Feast of Sacrifice (ʿĪd al-Adhā).[82] The day after the feast, he went to inspect all his recent conquests between Ascalon (there he took leave of al-ʿĀdil, who returned to Egypt) and Acre. Before departing from Acre in March 1189, he named Qarāqūsh al-Asadī as its governor.

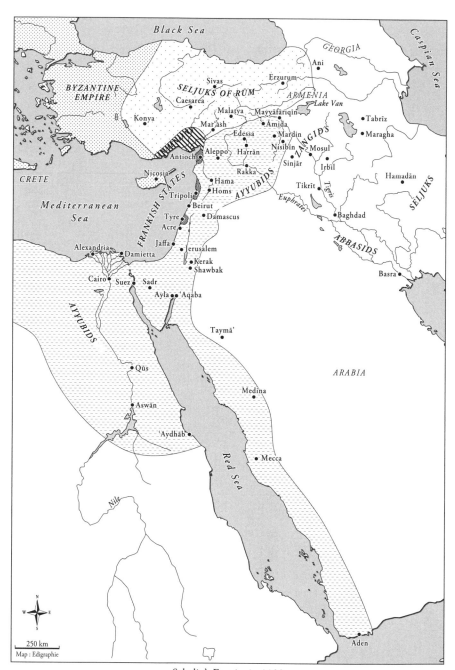

Saladin's Empire in 1190

The balance sheet for the campaigns of 1187 and 1188 was indisputably positive for Saladin. Of the kingdom of Jerusalem, only Tyre remained; the fortress of Shawbak finally fell in its turn in spring 1189, and Beaufort in April 1190. Of the principality of Antioch, there was still the city of Antioch and, a little farther to the south, the fortress of Qusayr. Only the county of Tripoli had come out relatively well, since, though Jubayl had fallen, the capital and the main fortresses had resisted.[83] Nevertheless, Saladin knew his task was not complete and that the most difficult thing would be to hold on to his recent conquests. His anxiety is perceptible in a letter he sent to his brother Tughtegin in Yemen. In it he shares his plan to conquer Antioch and Tripoli but does not conceal the fact that alarming news—that Western military preparations were being made against Egypt and Syria—had reached him from Alexandria. Saladin therefore asked Tughtegin to come join him as soon as possible with reinforcements of men and money.

15

The Third Crusade

By the early 1160s, a growing number of appeals for aid had reached the West, but the political situation was hardly favorable to a new Crusade. Emperor Frederick I Barbarossa (r. 1152–1190), the most powerful Western ruler, was engaged in a long struggle against the papacy and the Lombard cities. Even within Germany, he had to face the opposition of the Guelfs. It was only after 1184 that he could finally think about a Crusade. As for the kings of England and France, though they were closely linked—Henry II (r. 1154–1189) held the entire western part of France as the vassal of Philip Augustus (r. 1180–1223)—relations between them were tense. Each looked to the other, neither wanting to go on a Crusade by himself. Henry II sent money to the Holy Land and in 1166 established the first Western property tax on both the clergy and laymen, to be used as aid for the Latin states. But the Third Crusade still remained in the planning stage. In 1184–1185, an embassy from Jerusalem headed by Patriarch Heraclius came to ask for help. Frederick Barbarossa promised a Crusade for 1186, but in November 1185 the election of Pope Urban III reactivated the conflict between the papacy and the empire and called everything into doubt once again. The embassy also went to France and England, without significant results, except that a new tax for the Crusade was established.

The defeat of Hattīn would change everything. The ailing Pope Urban III died upon learning the news. An appeal for a Crusade was launched in late October 1187 by the new pope, Gregory VIII. He died a few weeks later, but his call was taken up by his successor, Clement III. The first to respond was William II of Sicily, who sent a fleet of some fifty galleys to aid Tripoli. Richard the Lionheart took up the cross in November 1187 when he was still only count of Poitou. On January 21, 1188, an accord was reached between Henry II and Philip Augustus, in Gisors, Normandy, but their quarrel did not really end before Henry II's death on July 6, 1189.

To finance the Crusade, a 10 percent tax, the so-called Saladin tithe, was instituted in France and England on all revenue and movable property. Those who took up the cross were exempt and could keep the tithe paid by their vassals and tenants, a measure that displeased the clergy, for whom on principle that tithe was intended. In England, the Jewish communities were compelled to deliver 25 percent of their revenues, but that was not enough to protect them from exactions and massacres. Once more, the population held them responsible for every evil. In Germany there was no specific tax, but every Crusader had to take enough money to subsist for two years, so a large number of undesirables were eliminated.[1]

Saladin's Diplomatic Efforts

In the face of that new threat, Saladin used diplomatic means with all the Franks' potential adversaries, beginning with the Byzantines. In the early 1170s, the Franks still had hopes of receiving help from the Byzantines in their attempt to disembark in Egypt. In 1171 Amalric had been very well received in Constantinople by Emperor Manuel I Comnenus (r. 1143–1180), who even had reparations made to the Church of the Holy Sepulchre in Jerusalem; and in 1173 a community of Orthodox priests had been allowed to reestablish themselves there. All the same, the Byzantine policy in the Mediterranean remained ambiguous at the very least, their principal concern being to oppose the hegemonic ambitions of the Normans of Sicily. Therefore, when the Normans organized an expedition against Egypt in 1174, it was Emperor Manuel in person who warned Saladin about it. In 1176, the rout of the emperor's troops in Myriokephalon by the Seljuks of Anatolia finally dashed the Franks' hopes of finding protectors in Syria-Palestine among the Byzantines and allies in the conquest of Egypt. The

Byzantines, very weakened and threatened by the Normans of Sicily, then turned to Saladin.

In 1181 Saladin received an ambassador of Maria of Antioch, widow of Emperor Manuel and regent for her son Alexis II. An accord was reached between the two parties, and by autumn 1181, some 180 Muslim prisoners were freed.[2] The following year, the uprising of the Byzantine population and the massacre of the Latin community of Constantinople did not improve relations between Eastern and Western Christians and no doubt impelled the new emperor, Andronicus I Comnenus (r. 1183–1185), to turn to the Muslims. At the time, the Byzantines were seeking to regain Cyprus, which had passed into the hands of a rebel duke, Isaac Comnenus; in the meantime, they had increasing anxiety about the Normans, who had established closer ties with the Germanic empire through the marriage of the heiress Constance of Sicily to Frederick Barbarossa's son, the future Henry VI. In 1185, talks took place between Andronicus and Saladin, and then between Andronicus's successor, Isaac II Angelus (r. 1185–1195), and the sultan. The unrealistic nature of the proposals the emperor reportedly made to Saladin has led some to doubt the very existence of these negotiations: he stipulated that Antioch and the surrounding region, plus Jerusalem and the entire coast (except Ascalon), were to revert to the Byzantines, while the Seljuk territories of Anatolia were to be divided up between the emperor and Saladin. Nevertheless, most historians today concede that a rapprochement between the Byzantine emperors and Saladin did indeed take place during that time.[3]

Isaac II Angelus agreed all the easier to negotiations with Saladin because he had earlier spent some time with him. The arrest of Isaac's brother Alexis in Acre, made by Raymond of Tripoli and Bohemond III of Antioch, only brought Isaac closer to the sultan. The emperor asked for Saladin's intercession in an effort to have his brother Alexis released. Saladin was obliged to inform him of his falling-out with Raymond but offered him an alliance in the event of an attack on the Franks. This was on the eve of the Battle of Ḥaṭṭīn in 1187. A few months later, when Saladin reconquered Palestine, a Greek fleet appeared in the waters of Cyprus to reduce the rebel duke, Isaac Comnenus, and perhaps even to lend a hand to the Muslims. The plan failed, but that did not prevent Saladin, after his first victories and the taking of Acre, from offering to release Alexis or from giving Isaac II Angelus very rich presents, including an elephant, more than a thousand horses, saddles, bows and arrows, about a hundred Byzantine prisoners, and a quantity of spices. The Byzantine emperor

replied with an even more sumptuous embassy, which arrived in Acre in early
1188, to thank Saladin for the release of his brother, to congratulate him for the
conquest of Jerusalem, and to inform him of the preparations being made in
the West for a new Crusade. Saladin sent his own ambassador, laden with gifts,
back to the basileus in an attempt to negotiate an alliance against the Franks.[4]

Embassies sent back and forth between the sultan or his brother al-'Ādil and
Isaac II Angelus continued until 1190. Political interests mingled with religious
concerns. The emperor sought to strengthen the authority of the Greek church
over the Holy Sepulchre and to obtain the return of a Greek patriarch to Jerusalem, and he demanded the restitution of the relic of the True Cross; Saladin
wanted the Constantinople mosque reopened. On that last point, the Muslims
obtained satisfaction in about 1189. Saladin sent a *minbar* by boat to be placed in the
restored mosque, along with a preacher assigned to pronounce the *khutba* for the
Muslim community there, composed primarily of merchants.[5] In August–
September 1189, another Byzantine embassy came to inform Saladin of the progress of the German Crusade. In his letter, the basileus apologized for having allowed it to pass through Anatolia, but reassured him: the Crusaders had escaped
the Byzantine troops, but in such a state of weakness that they no longer represented a threat to Saladin, with whom, Isaac II said, he was ready to resume negotiations. Ibn Shaddād indicates that Saladin gave the embassy a very good welcome, but says not a word about his response.[6] One thing is sure, however: the
more or less passive resistance mounted by the Byzantines against the Crusaders
was real, and it was harshly condemned by the Westerners, whose resentment
against their Eastern coreligionists only increased. Some Latin sources attest to it:

> Whereas the Latins are equally proficient in knowledge and arms,
> the Greeks know that they themselves are completely ignorant and
> unwarlike. . . . Perfidious people, wicked and altogether degener-
> ate generation! Their decline is the more extraordinary because
> they used to be so illustrious. It is as if gold were transformed into
> slag, grain into chaff, purity into dung or glory into confusion. . . .
> Although those people could not prevent our army's passing in the
> abovementioned places, they did what they could. All the local in-
> habitants went up into the mountains, taking away all the comforts
> which can be bought. Those approaching found empty houses with
> everything removed.[7]

Nevertheless, though the basileus regularly assured Saladin of his desire to oppose the Crusade and sent him the information to which he was privy, apart from a few services rendered on either side, their alliance remained in large part theoretical. No precise mutual defense agreement was signed, since the basileus was not powerful enough to oppose the Germanic emperor openly and was no doubt realistic enough to know that Saladin could not do a great deal to help him. As for Saladin, he was ready to make the most of his opportunities and to negotiate with anyone willing to slow the arrival of the Crusaders. That was why, despite his negotiations in progress with the basileus, he did not hesitate to come to terms with the rebel of Cyprus, Isaac Comnenus. Somewhat later, the rebel duke in fact mounted a certain resistance to the passing Crusaders, capturing one of their ships, but that action turned against him with the taking of the island by Richard the Lionheart in May 1191. Some time later, when Isaac Comnenus, nicknamed *Malik al-'atīq* (the emancipated king) by the Muslims, wanted to rebel against the king of England, he sent word to Saladin that he was ready to establish relations with him. Al-Fādil encouraged Saladin to accept that alliance, which according to him would have sown discord in the Christian camp and would have been more effective than the negotiations under way with an emperor whose every undertaking was doomed to fail.[8] Al-Fādil seems not to have been heeded.

Just as relations between the Franks and the Byzantines were turbulent, those that Saladin maintained with the Seljuks of Anatolia also had their highs and lows. Strengthened by his victory in Myriokephalon over the Byzantines in 1176, Qilij Arslān had attempted, in early summer 1179, to recuperate the stronghold of Ra'bān in the Upper Euphrates Valley, which Nūr al-Dīn had taken from him in 1173. Saladin, busy at the time fighting the Franks, sent his nephew Taqī al-Dīn to Ra'bān in his place. Taqī al-Dīn's subsequent victory dissuaded Qilij Arslān from setting foot in the region again. After the taking of Jerusalem, he could do nothing more than send an embassy to Saladin to congratulate him. It even appears that marriage plans were made between Saladin's only daughter and one of the Seljuk sovereign's sons, but they met with the opposition of his other sons. In reality, however, Qilij Arslān's support of Saladin always remained very patchy.[9] He did not provide Saladin with any military aid during the Third Crusade and, even worse, agreed to sign an accord with Frederick Barbarossa allowing the Crusaders to pass through his territories. The judgment of Saladin's entourage was as harsh toward him as the Franks' view of the Byzantine emperor: "Qilij Arslān openly displayed his fear of the [Holy Roman] emperor, but secretly he was concealing an alliance with him. Once the emperor had entered his states, Qilij Arslān publicly revealed the perverse designs he had until then dissimulated and concluded an accord with him. He gave him hostages as a guarantee for the guides he would send with him, to lead him to the land of the son of Leon [the ruler of Lesser Armenia]."[10]

Saladin could not fail to take an interest in the political situation in Anatolia. "If these lands fall into the hands of the unbelievers, then there will be no more Islam," he wrote to the caliph in early 1191. Hence his growing anxiety about the quarrels between Qilij Arslān and his sons.[11] An alliance with Saladin interested the Seljuks only within the context of the fierce struggle for power among the members of the ruling family. So it was that in late September 1191 Saladin received one of Qilij Arslān's ten sons, who had come to ask for aid against his father and brothers.[12] Saladin treated him honorably and gave him the hand of one of his nieces, with a tidy dowry of one hundred thousand dinars. That alliance no doubt protected Qilij Arslān's son against his own family, but above all, it assumed great symbolic importance, since for the first time a prince of blood from the prestigious Seljuk dynasty had entered the service of an Ayyubid.[13] In July 1192, Saladin received a new Seljuk embassy in Jerusalem, sent by another of Qilij Arslān's sons, who asked that troops be dispatched to occupy his lands, sensing that he was unable to defend them himself. Saladin, detained in Palestine by other concerns, did not respond to this request.[14]

A deep distrust alienated Saladin from his potential Byzantine and Seljuk allies. Both saw the sultan only as potential support against their rivals, whereas Saladin tried to drag them into his fight against the Franks. Under such conditions, there was little chance that a real alliance would come about, and the primary objective of the exchanges of embassies was to maintain contact, to assure Saladin's interlocutors of his good intentions, and thus to prevent a new military front from opening up. It follows that, in the East at least, the battles in preparation in no way constituted a religious war, despite what the discourse would have us believe. It was not Islam and Christianity facing off, but rather sovereigns confronting internal and external difficulties, who attempted to find allies—whatever their religion—against those threatening them. Hence the Byzantine Christians sought Saladin's alliance against other Christians, Sicilian or German; Saladin was ready to support the Byzantines or the Christian rebel of Cyprus if they supported him in a battle against the Franks; and the Seljuks did not hesitate to offer their services to the Germans to combat the same man they had just congratulated for taking Jerusalem from the Franks.

The negotiations conducted during the same period between Saladin and Frederick Barbarossa were of a different nature.[15] The two rulers had not waited until the Battle of Hattīn to establish relations. In the early years of Saladin's reign, some embassies were exchanged, though it is not always possible to know their substance or to date them with accuracy. The Latin sources record an embassy from Frederick to Saladin in 1175 in the person of Burchard of Strasbourg, who left behind an account of his journey.[16] Burchard went by ship to Genoa, skirting Corsica and Sardinia, before heading for Sicily and then Cyrenaica. From there he arrived in Alexandria, where he disembarked after forty-seven days at sea. He went to Cairo, but since Saladin was in Damascus at the time, Burchard set off for that city, where he arrived some three weeks later. Unfortunately, his narrative says nothing about the reasons for his mission or the results obtained. Did he meet Saladin? Is his silence the result of secrecy or of the failure of his mission? Nothing is known about it. Having visited Damascus and the surrounding region, Burchard headed for Palestine, visited the holy sites, and continued his journey to Egypt, whence he embarked for the West.

Was it in response to that embassy or to another, earlier one that Saladin himself dispatched an ambassador to Frederick to assure him that he had received his message of friendship?[17] The ambassador, conducted by the Genoese to the emperor's court, handed Frederick a letter informing him of the reestablishment of Sunni orthodoxy in Muslim territories—an allusion to the fall of the Fatimid caliphate of Egypt—and of the failure in Damietta of the Franco-Byzantine expedition.[18] With that embassy, Saladin was obviously seeking to maintain good relations with the emperor, perhaps to test his reactions, while at the same time urging him to undertake no action against the Muslims, whose recent victories in Egypt attested to their determination and strength.[19]

After the fall of Jerusalem, relations between the two rulers could not remain as they had been. In March 1188, the emperor sent a new embassy to Saladin under the leadership of Heinrich von Dietz, attested in the Western but not the Arab sources. Was it an ultimatum, which Saladin rejected, or even a declaration of war, as the author of the *Itinerarium* asserts, reproducing both the letter from the emperor and Saladin's reply?[20] As Hans E. Mayer and Hannes Möhring have shown,[21] the letter from Frederick to Saladin preserved in the Latin source is an obvious forgery, but it is more difficult to reach a verdict on the one Saladin sent Frederick, which is fairly consistent with that type of correspondence and only repeats arguments often advanced elsewhere: the Muslim forces would always outnumber the Christians, and the Bedouins and the rulers of the neighboring states would offer their aid if necessary. Saladin says he is even ready to take the battle to the emperor's territories, and recalls that twice already the allied forces of Christianity had been defeated, in Damietta and Alexandria.[22] In addition, the conquest of Tyre, Tripoli, and Antioch was imminent. In exchange for a truce, Saladin offered to return the relic of the True Cross, to release his prisoners, allow pilgrimages, let a priest remain in the Holy Sepulchre, and restore the Christian monasteries that preexisted the Frankish conquest. The titulature bestowed on Saladin at the end of the letter reproduces, with a few awkward translations, the titles generally attributed to him by Arabic texts and epigraphy.[23] Möhring, who has analyzed at length the terms of that letter, considers it a forgery and doubts the very existence of that embassy. The arguments he advances, however, do not seem either conclusive or totally persuasive to me, and in my view it remains as difficult to conclude that the letter is a forgery as to assert its authenticity.[24]

For Mayer, the counterfeit letter from Frederick to Saladin appearing in the *Itinerarium* does not rule out the existence of an embassy. It is not very surprising, in fact, that such an embassy should have occurred, since during the same period Frederick, in preparation for his expedition, sent other embassies to Serbia, Hungary, Constantinople, and Konya, capital of the Seljuk sultan of Anatolia.[25] It was a German lord named Gottfried von Wiesenbach who was sent to Sultan Qilij Arslān. The sultan responded by dispatching in turn an ambassador, laden with gifts, to assure Frederick that the sultan would support him when the German armies crossed through Qilij Arslān's territories. Because of the great tension at the time between Frederick and the Byzantines, the embassy was detained for several weeks in Constantinople, stripped of its gifts, and finally freed after the accord concluded between Frederick and Isaac Angelus. But the embassy did not reach the German emperor until February

14, 1190, at a time when he had been traveling to the Holy Land for over nine months.

The Beginning of the Siege of Acre

This was not the first time that Frederick Barbarossa, now sixty-seven years old, had taken up the cross. In the company of his uncle King Conrad III, he had also participated in the Second Crusade. Accompanied this time by his son Frederick of Swabia and by many bishops and German nobles, he left Regensburg on May 11, 1189, at the head of a very large army, and opted for the overland route through the Byzantine Empire and the Seljuk sultanate. Having passed with some difficulty through Byzantine territories, the army crossed the Bosphorus Strait, arriving in Seljuk territory on April 25, 1190. Although Frederick had taken the precaution of negotiating the passing of his troops with Qilij Arslān, he had not foreseen the hostile reaction of the latter's eldest son, who inflicted heavy losses on the German army before being himself badly beaten on May 18, 1190. Even less had Frederick foreseen that his life would end on June 10, 1190. He drowned in the Selef, a waterway in Asia Minor not far from Seleucia. His son set off for the Crusade in his place, but the troops were no longer so motivated, and many returned home or died on the way, victims of the Muslim attacks in northern Syria and epidemics in Antioch. The survivors reached the region of Acre on October 7, where they reunited with those who had preferred to take the sea route. Little remained of the original army, however, and the Germans played only an insignificant role in the subsequent Crusade. Their most enduring action was to found a German hospital east of Acre, the beginning of the Order of the Teutonic Knights.[26]

The Third Crusade played out for the most part around the city of Acre. Saladin was in Damascus in late March 1189. From there he went first to Marj 'Uyūn, now in southern Lebanon, where he launched a few reconnaissance missions targeting the castle of Beaufort, still controlled by Reginald of Sidon. Reginald, who spoke fluent Arabic and had an interest in Muslim culture, managed to gain a little time by promising to hand over his fortress if he obtained a three-month delay to send for his family in Tyre. When Saladin realized in early August that Reginald had used that delay to reinforce the fortifications of his fortress, he had Reginald taken prisoner and sent to rot in a Damascus jail. Several months had elapsed, however, during which Saladin had not attacked

Tripoli as he had planned, while the Franks were continuing to grow in strength in Tyre. Guy of Lusignan, freed the previous summer in exchange for his promise to no longer fight the Muslims, had been released from his vow and, after assembling a few troops in Tripoli, had arrived in Tyre, where Conrad of Montferrat refused him access to the city. After securing the aid of a Pisan fleet, he decided to besiege Acre, arriving there in late August 1189. It was the start of a siege that would last two years.

Since the course of the siege of Acre is well known and has often been described, I shall summarize only its principal phases here.[27] First, the Franks set up their camp on a tell east of the city, from which they could control the Acre plain. Saladin left Beaufort to return to Acre through the interior of the country, somewhat belatedly in the eyes of some, who would have preferred that he attack the Franks while they were still en route. The two camps began by keeping watch on each other while awaiting reinforcements. Saladin was joined by his nephew Taqī al-Dīn and Emir Gökbörī, and by the armies of Mosul, Sinjār, and Diyār Bakr. Two of his sons, al-Afdal and al-Zāfir Khadir, were at his side. He established his troops on hills in three different places, a few kilometers east of the city, and throughout the siege moved his troops, depending on the needs of strategy, from one hill to another, with attempts to surround the Franks, sometimes to the north, sometimes to the south of Acre.

As for the Franks, they were quickly reinforced by Conrad of Montferrat's troops from Tyre, and, for the entire duration of the siege, Frankish ships continually disembarked reinforcements in the little bay north of Acre. Sometimes the ships were dismantled to build barricades, fortifications, or machines. Men of every background arrived: Friesian, Scandinavian, Flemish, French, English, Italian, German. Their number and diversity attest to the great trauma the West had experienced upon the loss of Jerusalem. In September, they managed to surround Acre, while the Muslims were hesitating on the tactic to adopt: should they conduct a joint attack with the besieged; withdraw in order to draw the Franks into pursuing them; or attempt to break the blockade? Some hoped the Egyptian fleet would arrive, others said that winter was approaching. On October 4, a confrontation initially turned to the Franks' advantage. 'Imād al-Dīn, who was observing the battle with a few men of religion from the hilltop camp, retreated with some others to Lake Tiberias, which did not prevent him from subsequently castigating the Muslims who had fled: "The soul of the coward was frightened by his idle imagination and worries; he began to flee with no other resolve than his aspirations. . . . It was then that the steadfast men were recognized and the true believers held firm."[28]

Some fled as far as Damascus. Then it was the Franks' turn to be defeated by the Muslims. Gerard of Ridefort, among others, was captured and executed. Many corpses of Franks were thrown into the river south of Acre: more than 4,100 for the left wing alone, writes Ibn Shaddād, based on the statement of a man who made a knot in a string every time he threw a body into the river.[29]

In October 1189, Saladin held a council: he favored an immediate offensive before the arrival of Frankish reinforcements. The Muslims had no hope of receiving further help, except that of al-'Ādil, who was on his way from Egypt. But others thought that the army's morale was at a low point after fifty days of fighting, that the rainy season was beginning, that the Acre plain was gradually turning into a mire, that Saladin's health was fragile, and that it was therefore better to withdraw, leaving behind a small force that would be relieved on a regular basis. New troops could then be recruited and reinforcements might come from the caliph. During that time—and while the rumor was spreading of Frederick Barbarossa's imminent arrival at the command of an army of two hundred thousand men—the Franks entrenched themselves in their camp, digging moats and building walls to protect themselves from both the garrison of Acre and Saladin's camp. All that greatly displeased 'Imād al-Dīn, who would have liked the Muslims to take the offensive without delay.

In late October 1189, Saladin sent his faithful adviser Ibn Shaddād to the east to obtain new reinforcements from the cities of Upper Mesopotamia, and especially from Baghdad, but to no avail. Since the eastern armies had been given permission to return home, Saladin could no longer count on anyone but his own forces and those of al-'Ādil, who arrived in Acre toward late November 1189. Even though it was no longer the season for sailing, fifty galleys were also sent from Egypt under the command of Admiral Husām al-Dīn Lu'lu', who enjoyed great prestige because he had pushed the Franks back into the Red Sea. He arrived in late December with a number of emirs, who reinforced the garrison of Acre. During the winter, the conflict became entrenched, with a succession of offensives and counteroffensives but no conclusive results. The Franks' maritime blockade eased somewhat, allowing Saladin to send supplies to Acre. When it resumed with the return of fair weather, communications between Saladin and the garrison continued via homing pigeon. In addition, a few oarsmen were paid to spread the news and to transport in their belts money for the troops, usually at the risk of their lives.[30]

In the early months of 1190, Saladin launched new appeals for help from his brother Tughtegin in Yemen, who continued to turn a deaf ear, and from Qizil Arslān, lord of Hamadān in Iran. But Qizil Arslān was in a conflict with his nephew, the young sultan Toghril, who for his part sent a messenger to Saladin to ask for aid against his uncle.[31] Saladin therefore could not hope to obtain reinforcements from that side. Fearing that Egypt would also be attacked, he had Alexandria and Damietta reinforced and gave the order to build new boats to come to the aid of Acre.[32]

In the spring, some good news finally reached him. On April 22, he learned that the castle of Beaufort had surrendered in exchange for the garrison's lives and the release of Reginald of Sidon. Then the long-awaited reinforcements began to arrive from Syria and Upper Mesopotamia.[33] Saladin reaped the fruit of the efforts he had made during the first part of his reign to impose his authority east of the Euphrates. On June 14, another piece of good news raised the Muslims' morale: the arrival of the Egyptian fleet—which the sultan had ordered built up—laden with supplies. Although one or two boats sank in the battle against the Franks, the others managed to reach the port with their cargo.

But Saladin could not really take advantage of that assembling of forces, since he quickly had to send troops to northern Syria to stop the German Crusade. It was Gregory IV, the Armenian catholicos, who had warned Saladin in early summer of the arrival of the German troops. Gregory was worried about his own lands and also wished to spare the Muslims, among whom he was living in harmony.[34] In his letter, the catholicos recognized Saladin's sovereignty and conferred on him the title of unifier of Islam and defender of justice. He described Frederick Barbarossa's ravaging armies, which had forced the king of Hungary to submit, pillaged the Byzantine emperor's lands, taken hostages (including the emperor's son and brother), vanquished the Seljuk Qutb al-Dīn, and obtained a truce from the latter's father, Qilij Arslān. The catholicos concluded by announcing the emperor's death, on June 10, 1190, and the succession of his son. Saladin viewed that missive warily, wondering how much credence to grant it. He therefore dispatched spies to Anatolia, proof of his lack of confidence in the information Qilij Arslān was sending. All that attests, once again, to the complexity of political relations in the region, composed of a mix of distrust and pragmatism and not merely of religious cleavages.

While awaiting new information, Saladin asked the emirs most affected to go defend their territories in northern Syria. Al-Zāhir of Aleppo and the emirs of Manbij, Shayzar, and Baalbek returned home, accompanied by their troops.[35] Saladin's nephew Taqī al-Dīn followed them in July, and the sultan's ailing son al-Afdal also withdrew, along with the military governor of Damascus. That meant all the fewer forces for Saladin. In July, however, he was happy to learn, through another letter from the catholicos, of the state of weakness suffered by the Germans, who had lost their horses and weapons. The princes of Lesser Armenia and Antioch attempted to take advantage of that situation, seizing those possessions the Germans still held.[36] But with the return of warmer weather, new reinforcements reached the Franks outside Acre. Henry of Champagne, the count and future lord of Jerusalem, disembarked in late July and took the command of the army away from Guy of Lusignan, whose influence and authority were in sharp decline.[37]

During the summer of 1190, Saladin, having inadequate forces to defend all the cities of the coast, and fearing that the Franks would seize them and entrench themselves, made the decision to destroy Jaffa, Arsūf, and Caesarea south of Acre, and, farther north, to dismantle the fortifications of Sidon and Jubayl, whose populations were moved to Beirut. Tiberias met the same fate. Protests arose even among Saladin's close circle. Al-Fādil, in Egypt at the time, did not hesitate to write: "We have refused to battle [the enemy], we have beaten a retreat, and even more extraordinary, while an army in flight takes along only men, we are fleeing with our cities on our backs."[38]

Despite that reproach, al-Fādil continued to support Saladin and, in his many letters, encouraged him to display patience and endurance throughout the ordeal. God had chosen Saladin from among many others for his strength and determination. The only one able to dominate the enemy, Saladin had to pray that Jerusalem—God willing—would not become Christian again and that victory would finally come about.[39] The tone of these letters, like the decision Saladin made to dismantle the coastal cities, is indicative of the pessimism reigning at the time in the Muslim camp.

During that same period, Saladin asked al-Fādil for further reinforcements: the Egyptian supply boats, delayed by the lack of wind, ultimately arrived laden with provisions and munitions on September 16, 1190. They were a great relief to the besieged, who were beginning to suffer cruelly from the lack of food. In October–November, once the threat of the German Crusade had been eliminated, Saladin had the pleasure of witnessing the return of his son al-Zāhir,[40] his nephew Taqī al-Dīn, and the emirs of Shayzar and Baalbek. But on October 14, judging his forces still insufficient, and in view of the caliph of Baghdad's passivity, he made the decision to send an embassy to the Almohad caliph to appeal for his help.

Saladin's Appeal to the Almohad Caliph

The appeal to the Almohad caliph marked an important shift in Saladin's policy. Until that time, the North African Sunni Almohads, who had proclaimed themselves caliphs in 1130, were considered foes of the Abbasid caliphate, and on several occasions Saladin had announced to the caliph of Baghdad his desire to fight them in the caliph's name. In his letters, al-Fādil himself does not conceal his hostility toward the Almohads: "Whereas darkness is spreading over the Maghreb, it is only al-Nāsir's [Saladin's] justice and enlightenment that is spreading to the east. God blesses only those who follow His way."[41]

In line with certain apocalyptic traditions that affirmed that the danger to Egypt would come from the west,[42] some even feared that the Almohads would one day seize that country. The Andalusian traveler Ibn Jubayr reports a telling anecdote on the subject:[43] There was in Cairo, between the Ibn Tūlūn Mosque and the Fatimid city, two statues mounted on ancient columns. One looked toward the east and the other toward the west. When the one that looked toward the east fell, the Turks overthrew the Fatimids. People thought that the fall of the statue turned toward the west would usher in the Almohads' rule over Egypt. According to Ibn Jubayr, a renowned scholar from Egypt had even already prepared a sermon for the arrival of the Almohads. That sort of legend was in no way unusual. In another context, and for a much more ancient period, many Arab historians recounted that when the Muslims crossed the Pyrenees in the early eighth century, they came across a statue on a vast plain, on which could be read: "Sons of Ismail, turn around. You can go no farther. I will give the explanation if you ask me, but if you do not turn back, you will be killing one another until Resurrection Day."[44]

Apart from the role that some wanted to attribute to statues and omens, the Ayyubid expansion into North Africa represented a real threat for the Almohad dynasty. For example, in 1187 the ruler Abū Yūsuf Yaʿqūb had personally taken command of an expedition to drive off Emir Qarāqūsh al-Armanī of Gabès, and he recaptured Gafsa in early 1188. But in the following months, the political context in the East changed quickly. Saladin needed the Almohad fleet: it was the only Muslim fleet capable, if not of rivaling the Italian fleets, then at least of mounting a certain resistance to them. The Almohads had in fact developed the fleet to fight the Christians of Spain and Portugal and to conquer the central and eastern Maghreb.[45] The Maghrebis therefore had a reputation for being the best Muslim sailors.

In autumn 1190, Saladin sent a letter to the Almohad sovereign, Abū Yūsuf Yaʿqūb. Its precise context has been an object of a great deal of debate. ʿImād al-Dīn and Ibn Shaddād, ordinarily very well informed, give no details about it. The Damascene historian Abū Shāma, however, reproduces the ambassador's mission letter, a document he says he was able to see thanks to a trustworthy sheikh.[46] In that letter, the ambassador was assigned the task of learning about the practices and customs of the peoples he would meet along his way. He was supposed to inform the Almohad sovereign, called *Jināb*—a term that could be translated as "Majesty" or "Highness"—of all Saladin's exploits since his arrival in Egypt: the suppression of the Fatimids, his expeditions against the infidels, the conquest of Jerusalem. He would also inform him of the countless Crusader reinforcements who continued to arrive from the West, of the siege of Acre, the Muslim resistance, and of the need to send Saladin, optimally, the Almohad fleet, or at least money and men. The ambassador would point out to the Almohad caliph that he could not deny Islam his help when the Franks were receiving so much aid, especially since the caliph himself had to face the same enemies in the West. The ambassador was also asked to break ranks with the Egyptian emirs Qarāqūsh and Yūzbāh, who were accused of having cut off ties with Saladin. If the Almohad sovereign asked for explanations about the fall of the Fatimids and the fate of their army, the ambassador ought to remind him that they had asked for aid from the infidels and were about to hand over the country to them. He should tell the Almohad as well that it was not the army but only its corrupt leaders that had been attacked. Time was of the essence. It was necessary to act before winter prevented the boats from arriving.

The letter to the Almohad caliph, written by al-Fādil, has come down to us in two different versions: one, undated, refers to events that would situate its drafting in autumn 1189; the other version may have been composed a year later.[47] One of the most hotly debated differences between these letters has to do with the title attributed by Saladin to the Almohad caliph, a detail that is not without importance, since the recognition of Sunni sovereignty within Islam followed from that title. In the first letter, probably written in autumn 1189, Saladin granted the Almohad the title of Emir (or Prince) of Believers, generally attributed only to the caliph: "May Allah, by the hand of the Majesty of our Sire, Prince of Believers, lord of worlds, partner in the governance of the temporal and spiritual, open the doors of blessed fortune and the sources of prosperity."[48]

The second, sent a year later, grants flattering and laudatory titles to the Almohad sovereign, but the supreme title "Emir of Believers," which would have made him the leader of the entire Sunni community in the East and in the West, is not conferred on him. Some members of Saladin's entourage seem to have urged him to use the title "Emir of Believers" to earn the Almohad's goodwill. Others, such as al-Fādil, were resolutely opposed, probably so as not to displease the caliph of Baghdad, who had given Saladin the task of repelling these same Almohads and from whom help was still anticipated.

In a letter that al-Fādil sent to Saladin from Cairo, he asserts that his disagreement has to do not with the content of the missive to the Almohad ruler but with its form. He says that, in composing it, he introduced all the marks of homage and respect possible and that it was difficult to go any further. Since Saladin's ambassador, with whom al-Fādil had spoken, told him that he would not take responsibility for that letter to the Almohad unless the expression "Emir of Believers" appeared in it—a necessary condition for the success of the enterprise, demanded by Saladin himself and his brother al-ʿĀdil—al-Fādil replied that that formula could be implied but not clearly expressed. Such, he affirmed, were the practices of the Egyptian administration. For example, some thirty years before, when the Fatimid vizier of Egypt had addressed the heir to the Almohad throne, he had called him "Emir of noble extraction and very illustrious one." That had been sufficient, and the vizier, though in a position of weakness at the time, had received the response he was expecting. Saladin ought not to position himself beneath that vizier, who was much less important than he, when dealing with a ruler who was having trouble ridding himself of two outlaw mamluks and who took six months to go from Marrakesh to Kairouan.

Since the ambassador was still reluctant and feared disobeying Saladin, al-Fādil told him it would be enough to acknowledge orally the Almohad sovereign's title of Emir of Believers, making him all the promises he wanted, since spoken words could always be denied. Such was not the case for a letter: once it was read on the *minbars* of the Maghreb, it would be equivalent to a public acknowledgment of the caliphate, for a sovereign who had no legitimacy to it. It would mean humiliating oneself and placing the unity of Islam in peril, opening a door that would then be impossible to close. The ambassador, still hesitant, declared that he would remain in Alexandria to complete his preparations for the sea voyage while awaiting the sultan's response.

Al-Fādil therefore sent Saladin the draft of the letter for the Almohad sovereign, asking him to complete the formula—by which the sender usually designated himself—at the head of the letter, before handing it over to his ambassador. That formula, he added, ought to repeat the terms used to invoke Saladin's name during the Friday great prayer: "Yūsuf son of Ayyūb, avid for [the mercy] of God Almighty,"[49] and should not include the expression "servant" *(khādim)* of the Almohad sovereign. Moreover, al-Fādil left to his master the task of deciding about the title "Emir of Believers." If Saladin absolutely insisted on it, he could ask his secretaries to recopy the text and add the title, but the sultan ought not to forget to add his closing formulas *('alāma)* himself. Otherwise, it might be thought that the letter had been written in Egypt in his absence, which would give rise to all sorts of rumors.[50]

The letter is interesting for many reasons. In the first place, it underscores the opposition between the two Sunni caliphates and the delicate situation in which Saladin found himself. We have seen that he had always styled himself the defender of the caliphate of Baghdad, and there is no reason to call into doubt his sincerity on that score, nor the sincerity of al-Fādil, who, though he had served the Fatimid dynasty, always remained fundamentally Sunni, devoted to the Abbasid caliphate. Al-Fādil's stubborn refusal to call the Almohad sovereign "Emir of Believers" only confirms his hostility toward and mistrust of the Almohads.[51] Saladin's position seems to have been more nuanced, dictated more by his difficulties with the Franks. Obtaining the aid of the Almohad fleet to drive the Franks out of Syria-Palestine was well worth a few politico-religious concessions, and that no doubt explains his initial attitude.

Conversely, if we are to believe the final version of the letter, Saladin seems to have yielded to the arguments of al-Fādil, whose influence over him, by virtue of his long political and administrative experience, was very great. Note as well that the reference point of the Fatimid dynasty was still very present in

Egypt even twenty years after its fall. Saladin's prestige and power were measured by the yardstick of those of the Fatimid viziers, and the protocols of the Fatimid chancery were still taken as a guideline. Finally, it is interesting to note that a document was always authenticated by apposing the motto or closing formulas of the sultan, who had to inscribe them in his own hand. That sometimes presented a problem, as in the present case when he was far from his chancery.

As for the content, in that letter to the Almohad caliph dating to September 1190, Saladin recalls the conquest of Jerusalem and of other strongholds and indicates that Tripoli, Tyre, and Antioch were still in the infidels' hands. He mentions the German Crusade and the Crusade of another king who had put to sea. Franks from all the Western regions had responded to that appeal and were constantly arriving by ship, with reinforcements of weapons, machines, provisions, iron, gold, and silver. Saladin claims that the number of Franks outside Acre surpassed a hundred thousand, a figure that was obviously exaggerated to rouse the Almohad sovereign. Saladin also says that he had had a fleet built up and that it was fighting the best it could against the many Frankish ships. He informs the Almohad ruler of the fate of the German army—Frederick Barbarossa had drowned en route and his son was attacked by troops from northern Syria—and in conclusion sends him a few flattering words to persuade him to come to Saladin's aid. As sultan of Islam, commander of the holy warriors on the way to paradise, the Almohad caliph more than anyone else deserved to be implored for aid, since his own exploits on behalf of jihad, and also those of his ancestors, were well known. The Almohad caliph, whose renown had spread to every region, would undoubtedly agree to lead his armies on the sea to battle the infidels. The list of presents that Saladin sent him included a valuable Koran, musk, amber necklaces, aloe, balm of Judea, about a hundred bows, some twenty horse saddles, the same number of Indian sword blades, and finally, some seven hundred arrows of the best quality.[52]

If we are to believe Abū Shāma—and his version is very credible—the ambassador departed from Alexandria on October 14 on a galley with a crew of 120. He arrived in Tripoli on November 25 and met the Almohad sovereign in January 1191, at a place that has not been determined.[53] He returned to Alexandria on July 11, 1191, on the eve of the surrender of Acre. In the following days, Saladin asked al-Fādil to write to the ambassador and urge him to arrive with Maghrebi reinforcements, not knowing that the ambassador had just disembarked in

Alexandria.[54] That letter mentions fifty thousand dead among the Franks, but also the reinforcements they were continually receiving, the fall of Acre, Saladin's determination to continue the fight, and the need, more urgent than ever, for the Almohad fleet. But Saladin would never receive any help from either the Almohad caliph or the Abbasid caliph.

Stalemate and Resolution

During the autumn of 1190, troubles accumulated in the Muslim camp. Emir Gökbörī, upon the death of his brother, received the city of Irbil and its region from Saladin, in exchange for his other Mesopotamian territories, and obtained permission to go take possession of his new lands.[55] Other departures also weakened the army, such as that of Sanjarshāh of Jazīrat Ibn 'Umar, who surreptitiously left the Muslim camp on November 1. Having reached Tiberias, he received a letter from Saladin enjoining him to return immediately or risk breaking the alliance. He seems to have given little thought to the matter until he met Saladin's nephew Taqī al-Dīn coming from Hama, who returned him, with or without his consent, to his uncle's camp. Saladin did not like that emir very much and said of him: "I never heard ill of anyone without finding it less than had been reported, except in the case of Sanjarshāh."[56]

Saladin himself fell ill again, demoralizing his entourage. With the arrival of winter, the fighting let up, and the troops of Upper Mesopotamia were allowed to go home, provided they return in the spring. But more than eight hundred kilometers as the crow flies separated Acre from Mosul, and it took six months for the troops to come back. As might be expected, Sanjarshāh, who was in such a rush to leave, never reappeared. It must be said that, on his own lands, he encountered the prince of Mosul, who laid siege to him in Jazīrat Ibn 'Umar between May and September 1191, encouraged by Saladin, according to some.[57]

In the meantime, the Franks also ran into difficulties. The conflicts between Conrad of Montferrat and Guy of Lusignan resumed after the death of Sibylla and her two daughters in October 1190. Since Guy no longer had the right to rule, Conrad had the marriage of Sybilla's sister Isabella annulled, so that he could marry her. This he did in November 1190, even though he was himself already married.[58] 'Imād al-Dīn takes offense at the fact that Isabella, pregnant at the time by her former husband, Humphrey IV of Toron, was allowed to remarry so quickly, a situation that, he remarks, could not have occurred under

Islam. He probably did not verify what seems to have been only a rumor, since no child of Isabella and Humphrey is known to have existed, and in Christendom, as in Islam, strict rules regarding remarriage had to be respected. Under other circumstances, William of Tyre did not neglect to remind the count of Flanders that the law of the kingdom forbade a widow from remarrying until a year after her husband's death, particularly if she was pregnant.[59]

The winter of 1190–1191 was harsh, and reinforcements by sea had a great deal of trouble reaching Muslims and Christians alike. In December, nearly the entire fleet sent by Egypt, with men and goods aboard, was shipwrecked just outside Acre. It was a hard blow for the Muslims, who saw it as the first sign of defeat, especially when, a few days later, part of the wall of Acre collapsed and had to undergo emergency repairs.[60] Saladin again appealed for aid from the Abbasid caliph. The Franks too were suffering greatly from hunger and epidemics, which in early 1191 killed as many as two hundred a day; nor were their boats safe from shipwrecks. On both sides, soldiers deserted and joined the enemy camp.[61]

During these few winter months, the Franks temporarily suspended their marine blockade. Their ships, unable to remain in the open sea, were dragged to the bank or given safe harbor in the port of Tyre. Saladin took the opportunity to relieve some of his troops in Acre and to send fresh supplies to the city. But he seems to have had difficulty finding volunteers to replace the sixty or so emirs stationed there, and only about twenty relieved them, to protect a population that 'Imād al-Dīn estimates at some twenty thousand. Emir Sayf al-Dīn al-Mashtūb assumed leadership of the garrison in February 1191, and Qarāqūsh al-Asadī was retained in his post.[62] For a time, al-Zāhir returned to his territory in northern Syria, while Taqī al-Dīn, to whom the sultan had just given Samosata, Harrān, and Edessa—all abandoned by Gökbörī in exchange for Irbil—asked to go take possession of them. Saladin allowed him to leave but asked him to come back as soon as he had distributed the *iqtā's* to his emirs. Taqī al-Dīn left in early March 1191 and never returned.

In April, the siege of Acre took a new turn, given the resumption of sailing, the fresh supplies that reached the Franks, and especially, the gradual arrival of the French and English armies.[63] The landing of Philip Augustus on April 20, 1191, did not initially impress the Muslims: "He arrived with six vessels transporting the Franks, all ominous and hateful men. The Franks had wanted to frighten us by speaking of his coming and his violence, and had reported his terrifying threats to us: 'Upon his arrival, he will command, consolidate, break, or solidify, will distribute the money he has brought, will forge ahead'; . . . so when he arrived, followed by a small number of men and looking about feebly, his mediocrity gave us pleasure. In him greatness and abasement were one in our eyes, and we said: 'His attack is not close to transpiring, nor his might close to enduring.' "[64]

The French troops, however, were followed seven weeks later by the much more numerous troops of Richard the Lionheart. The Crusade by the two kings had been delayed by the Franco-English conflict and by Richard's revolt against his father. Peace between France and England was restored only shortly before Henry II's death in July 1189. His son Richard, known for his military prowess, succeeded him at age thirty-nine. By contrast, Philip Augustus, at twenty-five, did not have the same political weight or, especially, the same financial means as Richard.

The two rulers left Vézelay on July 4, 1190, and arrived in Messina, Sicily, where they spent the winter. Richard the Lionheart wasted no time entering into conflict with the occupier of the throne, Tancred of Lecce, and Messina was left to the mercy of the Crusaders' plunder. In spring 1191, the sovereigns set off again for the Holy Land, and while Philip Augustus arrived in Acre, Richard the Lionheart stayed over in Cyprus through May, taking it from the local Byzantine despot, Isaac Comnenus, who was in revolt against the emperor. It was there that Richard met Guy of Lusignan and took his side,[65] whereas Philip Augustus supported Conrad of Montferrat, yet another occasion for a confrontation between the English and the French.

Despite these problems, the Franks were considerably reinforced with the arrival of the western troops, while Saladin still had only part of his forces available. Of course, al-'Ādil was beside him, and in April contingents from Baalbek, Aleppo, and Damascus joined him as well. But Taqī al-Dīn and Gökbörī, who were among his best generals, were absent, and the eastern armies had not yet returned. The Muslims' attempts to stop the English ships failed, and the twenty-five galleys, "each of which resembled a hillock and was equal to a citadel,"[66] managed without mishap to join the Franks outside Acre. Throughout June, the two armies engaged in a number of skirmishes. At the end of the month, Saladin received more Egyptian reinforcements as well as troops from Sinjār and Mosul. In the Frankish camp, Conrad returned to Tyre. He feared losing that city, in fact, since the problems of succession to the throne were still unresolved.[67] Negotiations then opened between the king of England and the sultan, the former attempting to test the reactions of the Muslims, the latter seeking primarily to gain some time.

Inside the city of Acre, the situation was becoming untenable. Further desertions occurred in the ranks of the emirs; the walls were beginning to crack; and the residents, short on provisions, were on the brink of collapse, encircled within a city without the slightest source of water. On several occasions, Sayf al-Dīn al-Mashtūb attempted to negotiate the surrender of the city, but to no avail. Finally, despite the arrival of new reinforcements for Saladin's army,[68] the garrison surrendered on July 12, 1191, after a heroic resistance of almost two years. The conditions for the surrender of Acre were negotiated not by Saladin but directly between the besieged and the besiegers: Acre was handed over with everything it contained, including the ships in the harbor, and the entire booty was divided up between the French and the English. The lives of the residents of Acre were spared, and they were allowed to leave the city with their belongings, on the condition that Saladin hand over the relic of the True Cross, pay a ransom of two hundred thousand dinars, and release fifteen hundred anonymous Christian prisoners, plus a hundred or so Frankish ones whose names appeared on a list composed by the Franks. Ten thousand dinars were also supposed to be paid to Conrad, and four thousand total to his companions.[69]

The loss of Acre was felt very keenly by Saladin, who received a messenger from Qarāqūsh after the surrender of the city, imploring the sultan to accept the conditions imposed by the Franks in order to save the prisoners. Saladin's close circle urged him likewise, while 'Imad al-Dīn and Ibn Shaddād encouraged him to undertake the defense of the coast and of Jerusalem. 'Imād al-Dīn wrote several letters announcing the fall of Acre, explaining the defeat of the Muslims by the incessant arrival of Frankish reinforcements and the might of their fleet and war machines. He praised the courage of the Muslim soldiers, while at the same time accusing certain emirs of desertion, and added that the surrender had come about only in the most dire of straits. But after darkness, daylight was breaking, he said, and the time of revenge would come, because God was with the Muslims and "though the city is lost, the faith is not; though the city has perished, Islam has not died."[70]

A few weeks after the fall of Acre, the Franks inflicted on their prisoners a fate that came as a very hard blow to the Muslims. The accord stipulated that all the Muslims of Acre would be released if Saladin kept his pledges. Saladin was granted a period of two months to gather together the ransom and to release the prisoners and return the relic of the True Cross. But, short of money, he had to wait for financial resources trickling in from his territories to pay off his debt. There were further discussions with the Franks. 'Imād al-Dīn said that, after a month, the Franks demanded half the amount, the relic of the Cross, and all the prisoners. Saladin proposed to pay half the amount on the condition that the Franks free his companions and loved ones without delay. Hostages would be left behind until the entire ransom was paid. The Franks replied that they would release only the prisoners they chose, which reinforced Saladin's conviction that they would not keep their promises and would hold those prisoners from whom they could expect a high ransom. The Franks, for their part, accused Saladin of equivocating and suspected him of not wanting to return either the prisoners or the relic.[71]

Richard the Lionheart put an end to the discussion by deciding, on August 20, 1191, to order the execution of all those prisoners from whom he did not think he could make a profit. Between twenty-six hundred and three thousand were thus massacred on the plain outside Acre, a decision that the Latin author of the *Itinerarium,* favorable to the king of England, justified by saying that the deadline given to Saladin had long since expired and the death of these Muslims would avenge the many Christians killed by the Turks. Other Western sources adopted the same view, but some condemned the act and ascribed it to Richard's quick temper.[72] At any rate, the Muslims considered that massacre a grave violation of the rules of war. Ibn Shaddād notes in passing that, in the event that the pledges were not respected, the Franks ought to have kept the prisoners as slaves and not massacred them. The first consequence of that barbarous act was that Saladin decided not to pay the ransom and to send the Frankish prisoners and the relic of the True Cross to Damascus.

The human losses during the siege of Acre had been heavy on both sides. Among the Franks, "Queen Sibylla, Patriarch Heraclius, five archbishops, six bishops, four abbots, a prior, an archdeacon, two dukes, a landgrave, ten counts, three viscounts, and thirty other nobles" were among the victims, not to mention the countless soldiers and servants who had died in battle.[73] 'Imād al-Dīn estimates them at fifty thousand, "a figure that this chronicler does not allow himself to exaggerate rhetorically, but that he has observed with his own eyes to this year."[74] On the Muslim side, it is not possible to advance a figure, but the dead were also surely very numerous.

What were the reasons for that Frankish victory, which allowed the kingdom of Jerusalem to live on for nearly another century? In strictly military terms, it is clear that the reinforcements of men, ships, and provisions from which the Franks benefited almost continually, as well as the very clear superiority of their fleet, were decisive factors. Saladin had the greatest difficulty keeping the Muslim troops permanently mobilized against them and never obtained the help he had hoped for, either from the Seljuk sultan of Anatolia or from the caliphs of Baghdad and the Maghreb. Of course, the armies of Mesopotamia represented a large reserve of men, but emirs who were absent too long from their territories risked losing them, and their troops balked at being mobilized far from home for such a long period of time. The distances were great, and it often took the armies from the east a great deal of time to come back. With the departure of his nephew Taqī al-Dīn and his emir Gökbörī, Saladin was deprived of his two best generals, just as the armies of Philip Augustus and Richard the Lionheart were meeting up with the Franks. Saladin himself begrudged his nephew for having sought to extend his power in the east, and for threatening the emirs of those regions—they no longer dared leave their lands—instead of coming back to lend a hand. As for Gökörī's absence, it can no doubt be explained in terms of the crumbling power of the Seljuks of Iran, one of whose consequences was an attempt by Caliph al-Nāsir to expand into northern Mesopotamia. Directly and indirectly, the caliphate of Baghdad was involved in Saladin's failure outside the walls of Acre. On many occasions, Saladin felt very alone in his jihad, as he wrote to the caliph: "It is surprising and distressing news for all the devout defenders of religion. . . . Jihad is the personal duty of all Muslims . . . yet your servant is left to bear that oppressive burden all alone."[75]

Lack of money as well certainly played a role in that defeat. Egypt had already been heavily taxed, and in his letters al-Fādil complains of finding the roads cut off, economic activity suspended, and gold coins nowhere to be found.[76] Al-ʿĀdil proposed that an additional 1 percent tax be levied on Egyptian revenues, but Saladin replied that the measure would be far from adequate.[77] Finally, psychological factors may have played a role in the Franks' victory. They were much more motivated than the Muslims, since their future in the region was at stake in that battle. On the Muslim side, though the garrison of Acre fought with exemplary courage, as all the Muslim and Christian authors attest, Saladin's army gave the impression that they no longer had much motivation. Jerusalem had been reconquered, the emirs were eager to return home, and the troops were weary from having fought so long. As a result, Saladin did not appear to be completely in charge of his troops. The siege of Acre and its epilogue remained engraved in Muslim memories for a long time.

The End of the Crusade

Although Philip Augustus had headed back to France in late July 1191, the Third Crusade was not over. The French army remained in the Holy Land under the command of the duke of Burgundy, alongside Richard the Lionheart. The English king, having repaired the fortifications of Acre, continued to fight Saladin for another year, and Saladin's armies gradually fell apart. South of Acre, the Franks won the Battle of Arsuf on September 7 and subsequently seized Jaffa. From there they could have set out either for Jerusalem or for Ascalon. Saladin, sick at heart and without enough men to defend both cities, decided to sacrifice Ascalon. On September 11, 1191, he ordered its fortifications dismantled, its population evacuated, and its houses destroyed. The destruction of that small seaside city, pleasant and verdant and surrounded by beautiful fortifications, was intended to prevent the Franks from entrenching themselves there. Had they been allowed to establish themselves in a lasting manner, they would have been able to attack Egypt and to cut off relations between that country and Syria. Saladin could not take that risk. The destruction of Ascalon was a hard blow to the Muslims, and according to Ibn Shaddād, Saladin himself said: "By God, I would prefer to lose all my sons rather than demolish a single stone of [Ascalon]. Yet, if God decrees it and prescribes it as a way of preserving the best interests of the Muslims, what else can I do?"[78]

They saved what they could. For example, the very beautiful sculpted wood *mihrāb,* which the Fatimid vizier Badr al-Jamālī had installed in the sanctuary where the head of Husayn was kept, was sent to Hebron to be placed in the Tomb of the Patriarchs.[79] But the residents were obliged to sell off their belongings for next to nothing, even as the price of renting beasts of burdens was soaring. It took about two weeks to destroy the fortifications, and the whole city was burned to the ground. To consider just the ancient tower of the Hospitallers, overlooking the sea and magnificently fortified, it reportedly burned for two days and two nights. Ascalon never completely recovered from that catastrophe. Rebuilt by the Franks in the thirteenth century, it was again destroyed by the Muslims in 1247. In 1270, Sultan Baybars completed the razing of its fortifications, and in 1355, the Maghrebi traveler Ibn Battūta wrote, while visiting the region: "Then I left the noble Jerusalem with the plan to visit the fortress of Ascalon, which is ruined. It is now nothing but effaced vestiges and obliterated traces. Very few cities have united so many beauties as those Ascalon used to possess. Here the beauty of the place was combined with the force of its location, and it joined the advantages of the continent with those of the sea."[80]

As Richard the Lionheart was having Jaffa fortified, Saladin decided to pursue his policy of dismantling the strongholds on the road between Jaffa and Jerusalem. The fortifications of Ramla and Lydda were destroyed, and their stores of grain distributed to the army.[81] In Jerusalem, conversely, Saladin inspected the city's defenses and supply system; then, in the early days of October, he had the castle of Latrun, on the road to Jaffa, demolished. These measures give a good indication of the sultan's state of mind. After his defeat at Acre, he no longer believed he had the means to keep all his conquests and was most intent on holding on to Jerusalem. In destroying the fortresses to the west and engaging in a scorched-earth policy, he obliged the Franks to undertake long and costly restorations, thereby preventing them, for the time being, from using the fortresses as bases from which to conquer the holy city.

In October, negotiations opened between the Franks and the Muslims. On both sides, the land had been laid waste and the population was in a state of collapse from all those years of war. Saladin was represented by his brother al-'Ādil, a skillful negotiator, who took advantage of the divisions between Richard the Lionheart and Conrad of Montferrat, sometimes talking with Richard's envoys, at other times with Conrad's.[82] Richard demanded Jerusalem, the territories west of the Jordan, and the relic of the True Cross. Saladin replied that Jerusalem, as holy to the Muslims as it was to the Christians, was not negotiable, and that the territories demanded were Muslim possessions. The Franks had succeeded in seizing them only because the Muslims were too weak to defend themselves at the time.[83]

The oddest subject of negotiation was no doubt that of a marriage between al-'Ādil and Joan, sister of Richard the Lionheart and the widow of William II of Sicily. The accord that the Franks proposed to the Muslims stipulated that the newlyweds would live in Jerusalem, where no Frankish garrison would be allowed but where Latin religious could reside. The Frankish lords, the Knights Templar, and the Hospitallers would be allowed to possess villages but not fortresses in the surrounding area. The relic of the True Cross would be returned to the Franks, and the prisoners on both sides released. The new kingdom thus created would be governed by al-ʿĀdil but would be among Saladin's possessions. Al-ʿĀdil seemed favorable to these proposals, which Saladin also accepted, thinking that Richard the Lionheart was setting a trap for him and that he would take no action. According to ʿImād al-Dīn, the affair was almost concluded when it was learned that Joan, who had not been consulted, would not hear of the matter, and that the other Frankish lords similarly rejected that marriage between a Christian princess and a Muslim.[84] Richard the Lionheart attempted to persuade al-ʿĀdil to become a Christian, a proposal he certainly knew had no chance of being accepted.

In early November, Conrad and Richard the Lionheart each sent messengers to Saladin to continue the discussions. They were very well received by the sultan, who was aware of the advantage he could draw from the Frankish divisions. His council, meeting on November 11, was of the opinion that it would be better to negotiate with Richard the Lionheart, the more powerful sovereign but also the one farther from his own lands. Richard had not given up on the marriage plan and proposed to ask the pope for permission for Joan to marry. Otherwise, Richard offered the hand of his niece in marriage. Saladin agreed to ask for the pope's authorization but flat-out refused to consider the niece. It is likely that, in reality, neither sovereign was ready to sign an accord. Ibn Shaddād himself says that Saladin did not really want peace, which he feared would strengthen the Franks. Ailing, deeply affected by the news that had just reached him of his nephew Taqī al-Dīn ʿUmar's death, and uncertain about his own future, Saladin wanted to take advantage of what remained of the mustering of Muslim forces to fight on. As for ʿImād al-Dīn, he scarcely believed in the king of England's sincerity. And the author of the *Itinerarium* accuses Saladin outright of having sought to distract the king's attention so that the sultan would have time to destroy other fortresses.[85]

In the following weeks, Richard the Lionheart's army advanced toward Jerusalem, reaching Latrun. Saladin immediately ordered the fortification projects for the holy city accelerated. Egyptian reinforcements, placed under the command of Emir Ḥusām al-Dīn Abū l-Hayjāʾ, joined him, and a few raids were launched in the region of Ramla. Richard, aware that Saladin would resist to the end in Jerusalem, and likely also hindered by difficult weather conditions, decided to turn back and to set off instead for Ascalon. He arrived there on January 21, 1192, and undertook to have the city rebuilt. Saladin allowed his troops to disperse, but he remained in Jerusalem to defend it. Since he also feared a Frankish attack on Egypt, he gave the order to evacuate the women and children of Tinnis and Damietta, and to cut down all the trees around Damietta so that the enemy could not use them to build siege engines. The moat protecting the city was also deepened.[86]

The months that followed were marked by a resumption of negotiations, but the question of Jerusalem continued to be the stumbling block. Richard the Lionheart, having returned to Acre, reopened discussions in February 1192. Saladin once again assigned al-'Ādil to negotiate an accord or, in any event, to make the discussions drag on until the return of the Muslim troops in the spring. Saladin provided him with a list of possible concessions: The Franks could—if they insisted—recover Beirut, on the condition that it remain without fortifications. The relic of the True Cross could be returned, a Latin priest allowed to dwell in the Holy Sepulchre, and the Franks' freedom to take the pilgrimage to Jerusalem could be granted, provided they enter unarmed. The marriage to Joan was no longer on the table. Al-'Ādil left Jerusalem on March 20, and having met with the Frankish negotiators, he informed Saladin of their demands: an equitable division of the coast and possession of Jerusalem, with the exception of the Dome of the Rock, which they were quite willing to leave to the Muslims. Further discussions concerning Jerusalem allowed al-'Ādil to obtain as well control of the citadel and an equitable division of the city and surrounding villages, with the assurance that no Frankish great lord would live there.[87]

These negotiations were interrupted by new quarrels within each camp. On the Muslim side, al-Mansūr Nāsir al-Dīn, who had just succeeded his father, Taqī al-Dīn 'Umar, in Upper Mesopotamia, was suspected of treason and accused of seeking an alliance with Bektimur, lord of Akhlāt, against his uncle. That situation risked undermining Saladin's authority east of the Euphrates and bringing about a new coalition among his Muslim enemies. Saladin was obliged to send al-'Ādil to settle the matter in May 1192, which somewhat weakened his position in relation to the Franks. Ibn Shaddād even suggests that Richard the Lionheart broke off negotiations when he got wind of that affair.[88] The Franks, for their part, were still not managing to speak with a single voice. Parallel to the negotiations conducted by Richard the Lionheart, Conrad conducted his own. Saladin, aware of the advantages that the situation might procure him, agreed to discuss with Conrad a division of the territories and the possible release of prisoners.

In the meantime, new events were about to upend the political life of the Latin kingdom and to change the rules of the game. Richard the Lionheart knew he could not stay in the Holy Land forever, and the most urgent thing for him was to settle the problem of the succession to the throne of Jerusalem before he left. After acknowledging Guy of Lusignan as king, with Conrad as heir, he came under pressure from the barons. He therefore authorized the choice of Conrad, who, in marrying Isabella, had acquired the most legitimacy to rule. In compensation, Guy was recognized as lord of Cyprus.

But Conrad did not have time to be crowned or to conclude the accord with Saladin that was about to occur. On April 28, 1192, he was stabbed by two members of the Assassin sect, who, disguised as monks, had infiltrated his entourage.[89] A rumor in both camps accused Richard the Lionheart. Some, however, thought the crime had been ordered by Sinān, leader of the sect, while others said it was Saladin who had arranged it. An Ismaili hagiographical source, anxious to present its hero, Sinān, as the sultan's loyal collaborator, even claims that the murder was ordered by Sinān to aid Saladin, who was having trouble with the Franks.[90] In reality, Saladin seems to have had scant motivation to kill Conrad, with whom he was preparing to sign an accord. 'Imād al-Dīn quite rightly points out that the murder was not in the interest of the Muslims, since Conrad was corresponding with Saladin and opposed Richard the Lionheart. Every time Conrad indicated he was ready to negotiate, Richard became more conciliatory. Whether the desire was to keep Conrad from the throne or to prevent him from signing an accord with Saladin, it will likely remain difficult to know who exactly was behind that assassination. As for the succession to the throne, it was settled by the marriage of Conrad's widow to Count Henry of Champagne, who was thereby recognized as lord of Jerusalem, having refused the title of king.[91]

Negotiations between Richard and Saladin resumed. Richard was still demanding an equal division of the territories, while Saladin was laying claim to Ascalon and Jaffa, so as to control the road to Egypt and to secure for Jerusalem access to the sea. But the slow pace of the negotiations gave rise to renewed attacks by the Franks. On May 23, Richard the Lionheart seized Dārūm, south of Ascalon, somewhat weakening communications between Syria and Egypt. In early June, Saladin, after receiving a few reinforcements from northern Syria, learned that the Franks intended to march on Jerusalem and were regrouping in Latrun. Negotiations had not totally broken off, but raids were launched on both sides against the caravans supplying the opposing camp. On June 24, the Franks' attack, between Ascalon and Hebron, on a caravan coming from Egypt was of particular import. The Muslims were advancing on their positions but were betrayed by Arab Bedouins. A thousand cavalrymen and the same number of Frankish foot soldiers carried off a large booty, including various commodities, pack animals, and prisoners.[92]

During that time, Saladin was preparing to withstand a siege of Jerusalem. Each section of the rampart was assigned to an emir responsible for overseeing its restoration, while outside the city, the sources of water were poisoned, the wells and cisterns destroyed. Within the army, some would have preferred to confront the Franks on the battlefield, even at the risk of losing Jerusalem, rather than have to withstand a siege. They feared they would meet the same fate as their coreligionists in Acre. Tensions between the Kurds and the Turks were palpable. To avoid any protests, the sultan, on the advice of one of his emirs, designated a member of his family, Bahrāmshāh, son of Farrūkhshāh of Baalbek, to represent Saladin in Jerusalem should he have to absent himself.[93]

The Franks, though they had reached Bayt Nūbā, turned back toward Ramla on July 5, 1192. The attack on Jerusalem no doubt seemed too risky to them. Richard the Lionheart was afraid of running out of water and of not being able to conduct a sufficiently long siege. The Muslims were on their own terrain and were expecting reinforcements from the east as well as al-ʿĀdil's return. The Muslims' determination to hold on to Jerusalem was strong, and their position much more difficult to assault than the port of Acre, where the Franks had had control of the sea.

As soon as the Franks had gone, Saladin received another messenger from Henry of Champagne, who had come to negotiate peace in exchange for the territories conquered by Saladin on the coast. Saladin's testy refusal did not prevent discussions from continuing. The Franks, Richard the Lionheart in the first place, insisted that they were all bankrupt and that it was better to make peace. Saladin's emirs seemed to be in agreement to leave the coast to the Franks. The Muslims would keep the hinterland, and the territories in between would be divided up. Ascalon, however, would be destroyed and so would belong to no one. Richard the Lionheart asked to install some twenty Franks in the citadel of Jerusalem and pleaded for the right of Franks and Eastern Christians to live freely in the city. But Saladin wanted to recognize only the Franks' right of pilgrimage. Richard was very reluctant to destroy Ascalon, which he had just restored at great cost. By way of compensation, Saladin offered to let him have the surrounding villages. Some emirs also suggested giving him Lydda, inland of Jaffa. But Richard asked to control the entire coast, from Dārūm to Antioch.

While negotiations were continuing, throughout the month of July reinforcements were arriving for Saladin: his sons al-Afdal (July 2), then al-Zāhir (July 17), his brother al-'Ādil (July 23), and finally the troops from the east (Mosul, Amida, and Sinjār). That allowed him to retake Jaffa temporarily on July 30. But Richard the Lionheart, who had gone off toward Acre with the idea of attacking Beirut, set sail to the south without delay and, with the help of a fleet of some fifty ships, retook possession of Jaffa.[94]

Both men were running out of steam, however. Richard the Lionheart was ill and in a hurry to return home; Saladin was suffering physically and morally. The country was devastated, economic trade cut off, prices very high. It was becoming obvious to everyone that no decisive military victory was in the offing. Negotiations resumed, this time with the desire to bring them to a conclusion. The stumbling block was still Jerusalem, which neither of the two parties wanted to let go of, and Ascalon, more important to the Muslims than to the Franks, despite the sums Richard the Lionheart had spent for its reconstruction. The king of England, who held his French territories as a vassal of the king of France, offered to hold Jaffa and Ascalon as Saladin's vassal. Saladin replied that he was quite willing to give up Jaffa, but not Ascalon.

The continuing negotiations did not prevent skirmishes or shows of force, which were intended to compel the parties to find an agreement. In August, Saladin again received reinforcements from Mosul, Egypt, and Hama. Finally, on September 1, 1192, an accord was reached, the text of which was drawn up by 'Imād al-Dīn.[95] A truce of three years and eight months was set in place on land and sea; the coast, from Tyre to Jaffa, remained Christian; and Ascalon, which had been at the heart of the negotiations, was returned to Saladin, but only after its fortifications were destroyed. Those of Gaza and Dārūm were likewise to be demolished. Jerusalem remained Muslim, but Christian pilgrims were allowed to go there. It was decided that the revenues from Ramla and Lydda would now be divided up. Saladin kept Nazareth and Sepphoris, southeast of Acre. No exchange of prisoners seems to have been stipulated, as generally occurred in such cases. On September 2, an ailing Richard the Lionheart sent Henry of Champagne and a few other Franks, including Balian of Ibelin, to take the oath. As Ibn Shaddād rightly notes, in the case of a treaty, Western rulers rarely took oaths in person.[96] They sent their vassals to do so in their name, which prevented any risk of perjury on their part. The next day, it was Saladin's turn, and that of several members of his entourage: al-ʿĀdil, al-Afdal, al-Zāhir, al-Mansūr, and Emirs Sayf al-Dīn al-Mashtūb, Badr al-Dīn Dildirim, and Ibn al-Muqaddam, which is to say, all those whose territories were adjacent to those of the Franks. A herald went through Saladin's camp announcing the truce and freedom of movement for everyone throughout Christian and Muslim territories.

In terms of the immediate power relations and the demoralization of his troops, Saladin came out relatively well: although he did not recover Jaffa, he had yielded neither on Ascalon nor on Jerusalem. It must be said that his position over the long term appeared stronger than that of the Franks. The Muslims were defending their own territories and could hope to receive new reinforcements. Saladin was less pressed for time than Richard the Lionheart, who was ill and far from his kingdom, and did not want to leave without concluding an accord. In any case, the peace was welcomed with great relief on both sides, though Saladin remained anxious about the future. Since the Franks had kept a foothold in the region, he thought they would soon be reinforced and would regain ground. Ibn Shaddād, to excuse him in the eyes of posterity, describes him as clear-sighted and reluctant to conclude an accord. At the same time, however, he says that Saladin was right to have signed since, according to him, such was the will of God, who knew that Saladin's end was near. If his death had occurred before the conclusion of the peace, the consequences would have been catastrophic for Islam.[97] An emir was sent to destroy the fortifications of Ascalon, accompanied by a Frankish detachment. The Frankish garrison demanded to be paid, but Richard the Lionheart sent orders to vacate. The demolition began on September 7, and, as the Muslim armies were returning home, Saladin went back to Jerusalem. As for Richard, he left the Holy Land on October 9, 1192.

Tripoli and Antioch were included in the accord, even though they had remained neutral throughout the recent events. In late October 1192, Saladin warmly received Bohemond III of Antioch in Beirut, accompanied by fourteen barons. The sultan handed over the lands of al-'Amq and Azarghān in northern Syria, whose revenues amounted to fifteen thousand dinars a year, and offered Bohemond a pension of twenty thousand dinars on the joint territories of Antioch, as well as generous gifts for his companions.[98]

16

The Rules of War

The Necessity of Negotiation

In the early part of his reign, Saladin often denounced the agreements between Zangids and Franks, in order to attack his foes and to burnish his own image as a jihad warrior. That discourse did not prevent him from negotiating with the Franks himself in 1175, as many times as necessary: because he wanted to have his hands free elsewhere; because Egyptian affairs required his return to Egypt; because he sought to rebuild his forces; or quite simply because a military conflict was at an impasse.

The objective of the negotiation was sometimes to conclude an alliance or nonaggression pact, or to recover a city or a fortress, or to end the fighting for a determinate period of time, or to divide up territories, or to exchange prisoners. Truces with the Christian enemy were always a delicate matter for Saladin. Although his entourage continued to spread the image of the perfect jihad warrior, he, like any ruler of that era, also had to adapt to the reality on the ground and to the power relations. His panegyrists therefore expended a great deal of effort explaining and justifying the truces he concluded with the Franks.

For all Muslims, a truce with the infidel was authorized first and foremost by the Koran (8:63): "If they incline to peace, make peace with them." That verse was used several times by Saladin's close circle to persuade him to end the fighting or to justify his action. Often the suspension of hostilities was portrayed as a temporary phase to impel the enemy to disperse, or to give his own troops time to rest and, during that time, to regain strength so as to better attack again.[1] Unlike a peace *(sulh)*, a truce *(muhādana)* was always concluded for a determinate length of time, generally between two and four years. Saladin was thereby conforming to Muslim law, which prohibits signing a definitive peace with the Christian enemy and authorizes truces for a maximum duration of ten years.[2] The Muslims were well aware that any end to the fighting also gave the other camp the opportunity to rearm. But, given the distances involved, they could legitimately hope that the Franks' rearmament would be long and laborious. They knew that the Crusade, especially the Third, once dispersed, would require many years to reconstitute itself and to mobilize armies comparable in might.

Saladin and his entourage always presented the truce between him and the Franks as a political, economic, or tactical necessity. For example, in early summer 1180, al-Fādil encouraged Saladin to sign a truce ending hostilities in Palestine, in order to return as quickly as possible to Egypt to resolve financial problems. According to William of Tyre, Saladin was compelled to conclude that truce because of the serious problems with supply deliveries that Syria was encountering at the time, after five long years of scarcity. Saladin justified himself in a letter to the caliph, evoking the obligation he had to thwart the ambitions of Qilij Arslān, the Seljuk sultan of Anatolia.[3] Similarly, in 1185 Saladin accepted the request for a truce by Raymond of Tripoli, regent of the kingdom of Jerusalem at the time, because, Saladin said, he wanted to be free to attack Mosul.[4] His biographers refrained from mentioning that point, since it was too much in conflict with his propaganda against the Zangids.

In other circumstances, by contrast, Saladin is represented as a sovereign determined to continue the fight, trusting in Allah's assistance, and yet willing to listen to his emirs' advice. That combination of steadfastness and flexibility is accurately reproduced in the letter he sent to the caliph in September 1192:

> Your servant, balking at peace, did not judge it wise to grow soft
> away from the hostilities—a characteristic trait of the princes of
> this time. But the emirs and the judicious men who are beside him
> unanimously thought that our advantage commanded us to con-
> clude the peace, that it would be a bad bargain for the infidels,

whereas Islam would gain thereby. . . . In fact, it is a peace that harms them more than the war: it removes them—what am I saying? It drives them off—from these regions. When, therefore, will the formidable strength of these enemies be reassembled? When, therefore, will the reinforcements of those damned, who arrive by water in wave upon wave, meet up, when such a concentration will not overcome their dispersal for another five years, when, of thousands of men, only a few hundred have arrived as reinforcements?[5]

The temporary cessation of fighting was also sometimes presented as a victory over the Franks, who, driven back by the sword, were forced to negotiate. "That truce was established in such a way that Islam lifted its head and idolatry bowed its neck," Saladin wrote to the caliph. Here as elsewhere, the account intentionally minimizes the concessions and emphasizes the gains. The truce constituted a victory for the Muslims, submission and humiliation for the Franks. The truce of 1180, for example, was presented as a positive outcome thanks to which Saladin managed to free Islam from the tribute his predecessors had paid to the Franks.[6]

On principle, the messengers responsible for conducting negotiations enjoyed immunity *(amān)*. It is known, for example, that in 1179 the envoy of Tripoli stood by powerless as the Franks were massacred after the taking of the castle of Bayt al-Ahzān, but he himself emerged safe and sound.[7] When exchanges with distant regions occurred, the ambassador's first mission was to make sure the messages previously received were genuine. That precaution was less necessary in the case of missives from the Byzantine emperor, which were sealed with a gold seal bearing the emperor's effigy;[8] it was obligatory, however, for a letter sent by a Western ruler. Consider the precautions Saladin took in his replies to Frederick Barbarossa. During his first embassy to the emperor, he charged his envoy with verifying beforehand, in Genoa, that the letter he had received from the emperor was authentic. That same doubt surfaces in 1188 in the wording of his letter to Frederick—if that letter is in fact authentic: "A certain man named Henry (count of Dietz) came to see us, saying that he was your messenger. He brought us a certain document, which he said was from you." The end of the letter notes: "If the document which came to us by the hand of the said Henry was the king's document, we have written this document in reply."[9]

The lengthy negotiations between the Franks and the Muslims on the eve of the fall of Acre and in its wake, described many times in the sources, are a good illustration of how such negotiations were generally conducted. Several times, Richard the Lionheart expressed the desire to meet Saladin, but the sultan never consented and preferred to entrust the task of negotiating to his brother al-ʿĀdil. At the request of the king of England, Saladin sent the following reply: "Kings do not meet unless an agreement has been reached. It is not good for them to fight after meeting and eating together. If he wants this, an agreement must be settled before it can happen. We must have an interpreter we can trust to act between us, who can make each of us understand what the other says."[10]

Richard the Lionheart and al-ʿĀdil, by contrast, met several times in both Frankish and Muslim territory. Their relations were excellent, and they were united in friendship to such a degree that Richard considered giving his sister in marriage to al-ʿĀdil. But no decision was considered without the agreement of Saladin, to whom al-ʿĀdil regularly referred the matter. The interpreters' role in these discussions was very important, and each side was generally accompanied by his own translator. Certain Frankish lords, born in the East, spoke good Arabic. Humphrey IV of Toron, "a handsome youth, although he was clean-shaven as is their fashion,"[11] served as interpreter to Richard the Lionheart, and Reginald of Sidon was Conrad's messenger to Saladin.[12] During the siege of Acre, the Crusaders had flocked to that city from every region of Europe and were therefore very difficult to understand. To communicate with their prisoners, the Muslims were obliged to appeal to a succession of interpreters: "When we take a prisoner, or when one of them places himself under our protection, we need several interpreters to understand them. They translate one another in succession: the words of the first are translated by a second, and the words of the second by a third."[13]

The Franks, in their negotiations, also made use of the indigenous peoples. These were usually Christians who knew Arabic and who, having had contact with the Franks, had learned Latin. Conrad, for instance, sent a certain Yūsuf at least twice to Saladin in spring 1192.[14] On the Muslim side, one of Saladin's trusted men, by the name of Najīb al-Dīn al-ʿAdl, was sent several times to Richard the Lionheart, who, it is said, had a great appreciation for him.[15] The Byzantine messengers often spoke several languages: one old diplomat, impressive in appearance, whom Saladin received in 1190, knew Arabic, Greek, and Latin.[16]

Any negotiation entailed exerting pressure both military and psychological. We have seen that raids and skirmishes increased in number during the negotiations between Saladin and Richard the Lionheart. Each side had at all cost to show the adversary it was not bargaining from a position of weakness. To mark their superiority, leaders, in their role as hosts, outdid one another displaying their might and pomp. Saladin took care to receive the Franks' messengers surrounded by all his troops. When summoned to appear before him, they did so standing on their feet.[17] Messengers often arrived with presents of a value designed to impress the adversary. A few weeks after his arrival in the East, Richard the Lionheart, having tried to send gifts to Saladin, drew the following retort: "Al-Malik al-'Ādil responded: 'We will accept these presents only on the condition that we reciprocate with something equivalent.' The envoy continued: 'We have falcons and other hunting birds; the crossing has sorely tested and weakened them. They are worn out and exhausted, and we desire fowl suitable for feeding them. When they have recovered, we will bring them to you as a present, as is proper and in accordance with custom.' Al-'Ādil replied: 'No doubt your king, being ill, needs hens and chickens. We will send him everything he needs, so don't use the falcons' requirement for food as a pretext to ask for them. Try another tactic!'"[18]

The next time, the envoys arrived with a Maghrebi prisoner as a gift, whom Saladin accepted and then freed. A few days later they returned, this time to ask for fruit and ices on behalf of the ailing king of England. The ices came from packed snow exported from the summits of Mount Hermon overlooking Bāniyās; it is called "Snowy Mountain" by the Arab authors, because snow covered its mountaintops winter and summer.[19] Saladin granted them what they asked for and allowed them to visit the army's market, with its thousands of shops and many baths, to prove to them that the Muslims did not want for anything.[20] In 1192 other goods were exchanged. Richard the Lionheart, still ill, sent two falcons to Saladin, who in return sent fruit and ices to him, taking advantage of that opportunity to try to obtain some information about his foes.[21]

Embassies and espionage readily went hand in hand. Men were sent to reconnoiter the terrain and to inform the sultan about it, so that he would "know, once en route, where to stop, without hesitating or making a halt at random, which could lead him to a place with scarce water and fodder, where the enemy might surround him and have the victory."[22] Others were given the task of sounding out the enemy's intentions and of secretly negotiating with the opposing forces. Shortly before Nūr al-Dīn's death in 1174, Saladin received an ambassador named Georges from the Franks, whom he suspected of conspiring with the supporters of the deposed Fatimid dynasty. Saladin in turn decided to have a Frank spy on Georges.[23] Sibylla, Bohemond of Antioch's third wife, secretly provided information to Saladin, who, by way of thanking her, freed her sister, the lady of Burzayh, after the fall of her fortress in 1188.[24] In 1191, during the siege of Acre, the Christian sources report that from inside the city spies were sending the Franks messages, written in Hebrew, Latin, or Greek and attached to arrows.[25]

The Franks also made use of the services of Bedouins, who, provided they were well compensated, had no scruples about betraying the Muslims.[26] Other spies, conversely, informed Saladin about the movements of the Franks and about the dissension among them.[27] But it was often difficult to distinguish true information from false. Rumors spread among the Muslims that the king of France had died in Antioch, that Richard the Lionheart had died as he was leaving the Holy Land, and, in 1192, that the pope had arrived in Constantinople leading an enormous army.[28]

The negotiated accords were usually put in writing and a copy preserved by both sides. They were rarely signed but were generally read aloud, with each party then pledging an oath to respect them. 'Imād al-Dīn drew up the accord of 1192, which was likely translated into Latin. Representatives from each camp then swore to respect it. Richard the Lionheart, too ill to read it, simply said: "I herewith make peace and here is my hand."[29] Anyone who broke a truce was thus considered a perjurer. Reginald of Châtillon, who perjured himself on several occasions, had for that reason a very bad reputation among the Muslims. In 1182 the Franks in turn accused Saladin of having broken the truce concluded two years earlier, when he set conditions impossible to meet regarding the return of people who had been shipwrecked.[30] But the Muslims believed that the truce had previously been broken by Reginald of Châtillon's expedition in 1181 against the Hejaz region.

After the truce, it was time to divide up the lands and allow the population freedom of movement. In addition to the territories conceded to each camp, accords sometimes stipulated a division of the revenues on certain borderlands administered jointly. In Habīs Jaldak (Cave de Sueth), east of Lake Tiberias, for example, revenues were divided up, and the Franks offered the protection of their fortress to the Muslims cultivating the surrounding lands, fertile in cereals, grapes, and olives.[31] Similarly, in 1192, the accord concluded between Richard the Lionheart and Saladin stipulated a division of revenues from Ramla and Lydda. The timing of the harvest played as important a role in wars as in negotiations. The aim of the spring raids was to destroy the greatest number of crops, starve the population, and push up prices. In 1188 'Imād al-Dīn was pleased that the truce granted to Bohemond III would expire before the harvest season, which would keep the Franks from having access to the crops during peacetime.[32]

Once the fighting was over, the different populations did not hesitate to mingle. In 1167, after the lifting of the siege of Alexandria, residents came out to talk things over with the Franks, who themselves went in to admire the city.[33] A witness named Sharīf al-Idrīsī, who had served as a messenger between the city's governor and Shīrkūh, reports that Saladin obtained a promise from the Franks to transport boatloads of the sick and wounded to Syria. Al-Idrīsī was among these passengers, who disembarked in Acre, where they were imprisoned until King Amalric's return. Once released, they were then able to go back to Damascus in complete safety.[34]

After the truce of September 1192 was concluded, the Muslims went to Jaffa, which was under Frankish occupation, to take care of their personal business, while a crowd of Franks went on pilgrimage to Jerusalem. Saladin even had them escorted on the way to assure their safety. He hoped that, once their pilgrimage was completed, they would quickly depart again for the West. Paradoxically, Richard the Lionheart sought to limit their number and asked Saladin to accept only those who were in possession of a written authorization from the king. Saladin did nothing of the kind and courteously received the Frankish nobles who decided to go.[35] 'Imād al-Dīn observes, not without reason, that Richard the Lionheart was afraid, if he allowed the Franks to fulfill their wish to complete the pilgrimage, that they would lose their ardor to go back and liberate Jerusalem. He decided not to go himself, since to visit Jerusalem without being able to liberate it would have meant tacitly accepting Muslim authority over the city. Later, when Louis IX landed in the Holy Land, his entourage told him the same thing, to dissuade him from going to Jerusalem: "If he, who was the greatest king of the Christians, made his pilgrimage without delivering the city from the enemies of God, all other kings and pilgrims who came after him would be content to make their pilgrimage as the king of France had done, and would not concern themselves with the deliverance of Jerusalem."[36]

Much rarer no doubt, but no less interesting, were the rapprochements and exchanges between Franks and Muslims during the siege itself, a fraternization somewhat reminiscent of certain episodes in more recent history, particularly the fraternization between French and German soldiers on Christmas Eve during World War I. ʿImād al-Dīn recounts:

> Here is one of the rare and surprising events, one of the tantalizing and strange deeds. For a few days, both sides had had enough of being continually at war. "How long will this battle go on?" said one of the Franks. "Men have perished: therefore, have your young men come out to meet our own, and let both be under your protection and ours." Then two of their young men advanced, and two others from the city: they fought for a long time and found the heat of war blazing-hot. Then one of the two Muslims leapt on one of the two young infidels, threw him to the ground, jumped him, held him, clutched him in exhaustion, then dragged him off as a prisoner. A few Franks redeemed him for two dinars.[37]

Confrontations

All types of confrontations occurred in Saladin's time: skirmishes, raids, major battles on open terrain, and sieges of cities and fortresses. Both sides frequently used raids accompanied by looting with no real aim of conquering, but simply to punish the adversary, exert pressure on him, demoralize him, or obtain booty. In those cases, speed and the element of surprise counted for a great deal. The troops involved were hardly numerous: two to three hundred men, sometimes only a few dozen. Caravans, herds, and crops were particular targets. In 1182, for example, in the region of Damascus, villagers concealed their crops in cavities covered with earth to protect them from pillagers. In 1191, the raid by the prince of Homs on herds in the county of Tripoli yielded several hundred animals for the Muslims. The prince himself kept nearly four hundred and on that occasion offered ʿImād al-Dīn a mule "of the Frankish race." In spring 1192, a Frankish raid on a Bedouin encampment near Dārūm yielded about a thousand head of cattle.[38] Raids also targeted caravans of merchants, travelers, and pilgrims, especially between Egypt and Syria, before Saladin retook the fortresses of Kerak and Shawbak, southeast of the Dead Sea. Until

1189, therefore, Saladin often had caravans escorted by military guard. It was one of these raids, conducted by Reginald of Châtillon, that triggered the major conflict between Saladin and the Franks in 1187.

In the major battles on open terrain, as in Hattīn for example, the number of soldiers and especially of cavalrymen—the real strike force of the armies—was of course important, but far from conclusive in every case. Saladin won victories with an undermanned army and lost others with troops more numerous than those of his enemies.[39] To leave nothing to chance, he had to take into account a number of other factors. He had to plan a possible route of retreat; choose good terrain in a dominant position, with the sun at his back; secure access to water; anticipate a tactic of encirclement or false retreat; maintain the cohesion of his troops; prevent the arrival of enemy reinforcements; and choose the right moment to attack by exploiting a weakness in the other camp (a power vacuum, difficulties of succession, battles engaged on other fronts, fatigue of the troops, and so on). In this respect, Saladin was a good strategist. On several occasions, he drew the Franks onto terrain that was favorable to him, as in 'Ayn Jālūt in 1183 and especially Hattīn in 1187. In 1176, he won the battle against the Zangid Sayf al-Dīn because the latter did not manage to capitalize on his advance position on the terrain or the fatigue of the opposing troops to attack immediately. In addition, his commander committed the grave error of setting up the Zangid banners in a deeply embanked and almost invisible site, so that the army, thinking its leader was routed, rapidly scattered.[40]

On the battlefield, the army was theoretically divided into three branches: the center—the most powerful troops—the right wing, and the left wing, to which two additional wings were sometimes added. In each of these branches, men were organized into battalions under the banner and command of an emir or prince. In the front ranks were usually the foot soldiers, protected by shields or sections of palisade planted in the ground to form a protective rampart of sorts. Archers, crossbowmen, and javelin throwers were responsible for initially repelling the enemy army's assault. Then they moved off, so that the main military strike force, the cavalrymen armed with spears and arrows, could pass through. After charging once, the cavalrymen sometimes returned to their starting point, and the foot soldiers returned to position to protect them.

These first attacks, which had a strong psychological impact, usually occurred with the sounding of drums and trumpets, and to cries of "God is great!" "There is no god but God!" or "Huzzah for Islam!"[41] war cries amplified by the musical instruments, which urged the fighters on, allowed them to regroup under the same banner, and which also frightened the adversary.[42] Men in lesser number were sometimes posted in the rear guard, to observe the situation and intervene in case of emergency. In the course of the battle, Saladin was generally in the front ranks, or instead at the head of the rear guard, to act in desperate situations and prevent the troops from dispersing. Ibn Shaddād's description of the battle of Arsūf on September 7, 1191, gives a fairly clear image of the way battles unfolded:

> I saw [their cavalry] grouped together in the middle of the foot-soldiers. They took their lances and gave a shout as one man. The infantry opened gaps for them and they charged in unison along their whole line. One group charged our right wing, another our left and the third our centre. Our men gave way before them. It happened that I was in the centre, which took to wholesale flight. My intention was to join the left wing, since it was nearer to me. I reached it after it had been broken utterly, so I thought to join the right wing, but then I saw that it had fled more calamitously than all the rest. I determined to join the sultan's guard, which was in reserve to support all the others as was customary. I came to him but the sultan had kept no more than seventeen fighting men there and had taken the rest into battle, but the standards were still there and the drum was beating without interruption. When the sultan saw this reverse that had befallen the Muslims, he returned to his guard and found there this scanty number.
>
> He stood amongst them while men were fleeing on all sides, but he was commanding the drummers to beat their drums without stopping. . . . The Muslims were, in fact, in a complete rout. . . . All who saw the sultan's troop holding its position with drums beating were ashamed to pass beyond it and feared the disaster that might follow, so they rallied to his troop and a large number assembled there.[43]

The Frankish cavalrymen's armor protected them from head to foot, and their horses were similarly covered with caparisons down to their hooves. But that heavy gear constricted them considerably in extreme heat, and slowed them down when their horses collapsed and they had to flee.[44] Saladin's cavalrymen were protected by much lighter coats of mail and breastplates, which, on one hand, allowed them to maintain greater mobility and, on the other, put less weight on their Arabian horses. Saladin himself never parted with his brigandine (kazāghand), a kind of coat of mail covered with leather or padded cloth.[45] Helmets made of metal or treated leather protected their heads. According to Abū Shāma, Saladin's helmet was gilt.[46]

Spears and swords were the essential weapons for Muslim and Christian cavalrymen. Usāma Ibn Munqidh, admiring how the Franks used their spears, gave some advice in this area to the Muslim cavalrymen: "My comment is that he who is on the point of striking with his lance should hold his lance as tightly as possible with his hand and under his arm, close to his side, and should let his horse run and effect the required thrust; for if he should move his hand while holding the lance or stretch out his arm with the lance, then his thrust would have no effect whatsoever and would result in no harm."[47]

Contrary to most illustrations of battles between Franks and Muslims in Western manuscripts of the thirteenth to fifteenth centuries, Saladin's warriors were armed with straight-edged, not curved swords. Sabers with curved blades appeared only later in the Middle East, between the mid-thirteenth and the early fourteenth century, and probably originated in central Asia.[48] Tempered steel was known in the West as Damascene steel, but it is likely that the term "damask" was associated more with delicate blade decorations inlaid with gold and silver, for which Damascus was renowned, than with the procedure for manufacturing these blades. In great part, iron was imported from the West by Italian merchants, despite repeated bans by the papacy, and from Anatolia, Spain, the Maghreb, India, and China; already-manufactured blades also came from these places.

On both sides, warriors were also armed with bows and arrows. In the treatise on the armies that he dedicated to Saladin, al-Tarsūsi describes at length all the types of bows existing in his time, from the simplest to the most sophisticated. Use of the crossbow was common, especially in wars of siege. A large arbalète à tour of sorts, comprising three to four crossbows mounted on a frame, constituted a particularly powerful weapon:

> Among the varieties of bow is the ziyār. This is the one with the greatest range, the greatest capacity, and the most deadly arrow. It

takes many men to pull back the bow string. It is made of various sorts of wood. It is fired at towers and similar obstacles, and no one dares face it. . . . Sheikh Abū l-Hasan ibn al-Abraqī al-Iskandarānī, with his superior talent, his extreme intelligence, his shooting skill, and the quality of his experience, described to me a ziyār bow of his invention, whose firing capacity is said to be the equivalent of twenty men shooting with his expertise, but which can be maneuvered by a single man, with one of the greatest ranges and the most deadly force.[49]

Shields were made of very diverse materials: wood, metal, gut, animal hides. In Saladin's time, Muslims primarily used round shields, whereas the Franks used elongated targes pointed at the tip. Al-Tarsūsi's remarks in that regard are of interest as well, since he suggests that the practice of depicting coats of arms on Frankish shields was spreading at the time: "Next comes the *tārīqa* [targe]: that is the shield used by the Franks and Byzantines who [prepare?] it by gilding it and rubbing it with oil, by painting it with all sorts of colors, designs, and artistic arrangements. It is a long shield shaped to conceal the cavalryman and the soldier on foot; it starts out round, then gradually tapers, and the tip has a sharp point like the tip of a pike."[50]

During battles, the Franks liked to keep at hand their liturgical objects and religious symbols, which were the first targets of Muslim attacks. As early as 1149, Saladin's uncle Shīrkūh, during the Battle of Inab, had killed the Frank who was carrying the cross.[51] And we know the key role that the relic of the True Cross, captured during the Battle of Hattīn, would play in the negotiations between Franks and Muslims. Outside Acre in October 1189, during a battle between the Franks and the Muslims, the king of Jerusalem, in the center of the army, advanced behind Gospels carried by four people and covered with satin fabric.[52]

The standards under which the warriors were organized also had very strong symbolic significance. On the battlefield, these standards indicated the location of the troops of the emirs or sultan who commanded them. Nevertheless, to deceive the enemy and dodge his attacks, the sultan sometimes stood far from his banners. Saladin's were yellow in color, like the silk tunics that covered his breastplate and those of the cavalrymen in his guard.[53] Ibn Khallikān, a biographer of Saladin from the second half of the thirteenth century, said that, during a visit to Saladin's tomb, he had seen a yellow tunic belonging to the sultan, its sleeves ending in black cuffs.[54] Yellow was therefore Saladin's color, sometimes combined with red: these were the colors of the standards, which 'Imād al-Dīn compares to anemones, and of the tent that Saladin set up during his military campaigns. One day, noticing that the tent of one of his physicians, Ibn al-Mutrān, was also red, and fearing it would be confused with his own, Saladin immediately had it taken down.[55]

Why that choice of yellow and red, two colors close in their luminosity, their intensity, and even their semantic value?[56] The symbolism of yellow is ambiguous in the Arab world as elsewhere: the color of gold and of the sun, of butter and honey, it is also that of sulfur and consuming flames. Yellow can symbolize royal power and glory as well as cowardice and betrayal. Red, the color of fire and blood, is often linked to the vital force, to power, and to bellicosity, but it can also be a symbol of infernal power. Was it merely by a process of elimination that Saladin chose these two colors? Because black was the color of the Abbasid caliphate of Baghdad, the standards and honorific robes sent by the caliph were black, and Saladin could not have adopted that color without gravely offending him.[57] White was the color of the Fatimid caliphs, the Shiite dynasty that Saladin overthrew. Blue had always been a troubling color for the Arabs, who considered it a magical, inauspicious color, and a source of bad luck.[58] Green, the symbol of nature and vegetation, was considered the color of paradise[59] and that of the martyrs of the jihad: "Allah places their souls in the bodies of green birds, who come to drink from the rivers of Eden, and to eat its fruit," says a famous hadith.[60] That left yellow and red, which, along with green, are the colors most often cited in books written in Arabic prior to the twelfth century.[61]

But we must undoubtedly look elsewhere for the true reasons for that choice. Note, in the first place, that many other examples of yellow banners have existed throughout the history of Islam. Although the Prophet was usually attributed a black banner, some traditions ascribed a white or even a yellow one to him.[62] Some also claimed that the Prophet gave yellow banners to the residents of Medina who joined his side *(Ansār)*. During the famous Battle of Siffīn in 657, the predominant colors seem to have been black, white, and red but also, to a lesser degree, green and yellow.[63] It is difficult to draw conclusions from these indications, which are not always coherent, but we may note that yellow is often associated with Shiite or eschatological traditions. Hence the Shiite rebel Abū l-Sārāya al-Shaybānī, executed in al-Kufa in 815, displayed yellow banners, as did ʿAlī's descendant Ibrāhīm ibn ʿAbd Allāh, who revolted against Caliph al-Manṣūr in 762–763.[64] It is also noteworthy that even in our time the flag of the Lebanese Shiite party, the Hezbollah, is yellow.

At the eschatological level, according to a belief widespread among Sunni and Shiite Muslims, the Mahdi (the Guided One) will come to rule over earth before the end of the world, to restore the true religion and justice.[65] His reign will be preceded by the arrival of Jesus, who, in certain versions, will come down to earth in Damascus and will then go to Jerusalem, where he will pray in accordance with the ritual of Muhammad. He will kill the Antichrist (al-Dajjāl), and there will be only a single community, that of Islam. Jesus will live forty years and will be followed by the Mahdi.[66] Regarding the Sufi traditions about the Mahdi, the great historian Ibn Khaldūn writes: "It has been stated in the tradition that Jesus will descend at the white minaret east of Damascus. He will descend between two yellowish colored ones, that is, two light saffron-yellow colored garments."[67]

In certain traditions, the Maghrebis, who, it was feared, would invade Egypt and Syria, were called the "bearers of yellow flags." Their arrival, associated with the end of time, would announce the coming of the Mahdi. These traditions likely stemmed from the fear among Syrians and Egyptians during the great Berber revolt of 740, during which two Umayyad armies were defeated and Kairouan fell into rebel hands.[68] Saladin's entourage probably knew these traditions, but to conclude from that fact that Saladin, in brandishing his yellow banners, wanted to announce the arrival of the Mahdi is, in my view, a step impossible to take.

Let us note above all that the association between red and yellow already existed in the Fatimid court of Egypt. Although they were not the colors of the dynasty, red and yellow did decorate the shafts of the soldiers' swords during processions and also appeared on certain banners.[69] Was Saladin inspired by them in choosing the colors of his dynasty? The political, military, and institutional system of the Fatimids influenced his government in more areas than one. His closest adviser, Qāḍī al-Fāḍil, had long served that dynasty, and it is not impossible that Saladin allowed himself to be influenced by what he had seen in the court of the Fatimid caliph when he was his vizier.

No source informs us about the motifs or inscriptions with which the yellow banners flying over the battlefields were adorned. It was only at the end of the Ayyubid period, and especially in the Mamluk era during the second half of the thirteenth century, that emblems and coats of arms spread to the Muslim world.[70] In 1250 Joinville had noted, during his Crusade in Egypt with Louis IX, that the sultan bore gold coats of arms, and that his mamluks added roses, vermillion (that is, red) bands, birds, and other "ensigns" as well.[71] The thirteenth-century doctor and biographer Ibn Abī Usaybiʿa speaks of an arrow supposedly bearing Saladin's coat of arms.[72]

If Saladin had a coat of arms, we know nothing about it. The eagle—originally double-headed—carved on a stone in the west wall of the Cairo citadel has sometimes been attributed to Saladin, but nothing allows us to make that claim. Leo Ary Mayer noted—and more recently, Nasser Rabbat has confirmed—that in the absence of epigraphic or textual data, it is at present impossible to know if the eagle dates from the Ayyubid or Mamluk period, or even from the early Ottoman period.[73] Elsewhere, a lion or the seal of Solomon are represented, as, for example, on the gate of the fortress of Sadr in Sinai.[74] One thing is sure: all the representations of Muslim coats of arms that can be admired in the Latin illuminated manuscripts of the thirteenth, fourteenth, and fifteenth centuries are part of an imaginary heraldry, well described by Michel Pastoureau, which in Saladin's case was inspired by his incipient legend in the West.[75] In some of these manuscripts, Saladin is seen displaying the coats of arms of important Western families, that of the Anglures, for example.[76] Other times, Muslim coats of arms depict a crescent, considered by Westerners from the thirteenth century on to be the emblem of Islam,[77] or various animals, usually with negative connotations (scorpion, toad, snake or dragon, leopard, or boar), whereas the coats of arms attributed to the Crusaders primarily represented the fleur-de-lis, the cross, the lion, and sometimes the eagle.[78] The fifteenth-century romance *Saladin* describes, hoisted on the mast of a Muslim ship, "an enormous standard, on which were depicted the four Saracen gods with swords in their hands, as if using them to threaten the Christians."[79]

But all that was only legend. In the absence of any contemporary iconographic or textual information, it is impossible to know what Muslim emblems and coats of arms were on the battlefield in Saladin's time. Those of the Crusaders, which were beginning to spread, are not much better known. Ibn Shaddād notes simply that in 1190, outside the walls of Acre, the Franks waged battle around their white flag adorned with a red cross, hoisted above a mule-drawn wagon and standing "very high like a minaret."[80] The white banner with red cross was of course the emblem of the Knights Templar, but in the early twelfth century, in his *History of Jerusalem,* Fulcher of Chartres also says several times that the king of Jerusalem's banner was white, and it would not be surprising if it also bore a cross.[81]

On both sides, the number of dead during these battles was ponderous. The figures provided are often exaggerated to give a greater impression of victory, which was considered proportionate to the number of dead in the opposing camp. In the field, however, Muslims made an effort to estimate their losses. At the end of the fighting, secretaries were charged with counting up the dead.[82] The battlefield often remained strewn with cadavers, which the victors stripped of their weapons and breastplates. A year after the Battle of Hattīn, for example, Ibn al-Athīr could still see many bones at the site of the conflict. "How lovely it was, the cadavers of the damned lying about!" exclaimed ʿImād al-Dīn in 1190 after a battle won by the Muslims outside Acre. Intoxicated by words as much as by victory, he continued as follows: "How many headless bodies, unsupported carcasses, slit throats, spilt blood, severed hands, gaping bellies, chopped necks, mutilated noses, opened jugular veins, gashed backs, wounded gullets, rent chests, Knights Templar wiped out and swimming in their own blood, Crusaders whose spines were broken, whose hearts were torn from their chests, men of arms to whom death had come, and whose gushing spring had run dry!"[83]

However spectacular, ʿImād al-Dīn's lyricism and choice of vocabulary were related more to a form of literary extravagance familiar to the author than to the expression of a particular violence or cruelty. Let us not forget, however, that hand-to-hand conflict with the enemy at that time was intended in the first place to break him down, that is, to kill the largest number of fighters possible. Violence was an integral part of the act of war and was not at all shocking. It is also found in the iconographical representations of war during the Middle Ages.[84] No one imagined a "clean war" or a war without deaths. Usāma Ibn Munqidh, so often cited to evoke the peaceful relations sometimes established between Franks and Muslims, nevertheless describes, as naturally as can be, how he and his companions personally beheaded the bodies of some twenty Franks who had drowned in the river during a raid into Muslim territory, in order to exhibit the heads in the fortress of Shayzar.[85] In the Middle

Ages, just as violence in political life was not reprehensible when it respected a certain number of rules, so too safeguarding human life in a conflict was not at all a priority.[86] The scope of a victory was assessed in terms of the number of enemies killed. As a result, authors were able to embroider at length on that theme without fear of shocking their contemporaries.

Since fortified cities and buildings were numerous in Syria-Palestine, wars of siege were much more common than major battles on open terrain. To resist the attacks of the Franks effectively, Saladin conducted a very active policy of restoring urban fortifications and fortresses. I have already mentioned the scope of the construction projects undertaken in Cairo, Alexandria, Tinnis, and Damietta. Under his reign, the fortifications of Damascus were also reinforced: one of the towers of the citadel was rebuilt, the rampart girdling the city was consolidated, and a former gate south of the citadel that had been sealed was broken open and renamed the Gate of Victory (Bāb al-Nasr).[87] In 1187–1188, the fortifications of Acre were entirely restored, which did not prevent the city from falling into the Franks' hands in 1191, but allowed it to withstand a two-year siege. Sometimes, as in July 1191, Saladin was compelled to make the choice to sacrifice the fortifications in certain places (Ascalon, Ramla, Lydda, Latrun)—for fear they would fall into the Franks' hands—in order to restore others, those of Jerusalem in particular. During the winter of 1191–1192, two thousand Frankish prisoners, it is said, were put to work restoring the fortifications of the holy city, but all Muslims, great and small, also got involved. Fifty stonecutters were sent expressly by the emir of Mosul to deepen the moat and cut the stone; and Saladin, to break up the hard rock, had new, especially sharp steel picks manufactured. He himself actively participated in the construction projects so that his men would put their hearts into their work:

> He divided up the construction of the various parts of the wall among his sons, his brother al-Malik al-ʿĀdil, and his emirs. Every day on horseback, he pressed on with the construction. In keeping with his wishes, people came out to transport the stones to the places where building was under way. The sultan saw to it in person, surrounded by all his courtiers and emirs: the undertaking brought together scholars, qādīs, Sufis, the army's varlets, servants, subjects, and merchants. Arriving on horseback, followed by my pages and servants, I kept the sultan's courage up and demonstrated

my solicitude to him by transporting stones. That construction, which required several years, was thus completed in the shortest time frame possible.[88]

All the rampart's towers, from the northern Gate of Damascus to the western Gate of Jaffa, were restored. The new wall enclosed the Church of Zion to the south, which had previously been some two hundred meters outside the city.[89] Nevertheless, it took time for Jerusalem to recover its prosperity. On the eve of Saladin's death, al-Fādil, in one of his letters, once again lamented the city's state of disrepair and worried that the Franks might exploit it by organizing a new Crusade.[90]

In northern Syria, when Saladin handed over the conquered strongholds to his emirs in 1188, he assigned them the task of restoring their fortifications. That was the case for Sahyūn, for the twin fortress of Shughr-Bakās, for Burzayh, and for Balātunus.[91] Depending on where they were located, the primary objective of these fortifications was to defend a city, protect a crossroads or path of communication, or serve as a home base for occasional raids or larger-scale attacks against Frankish territory. They also provided shelter for the emirs' residences in their garrison and offered great protection to the villagers in the surrounding area, who were then able to cultivate the nearby land.

The siege of a stronghold was meticulously prepared on both sides. Inside, people stored up weapons and provisions: nonperishable goods such as cereals, lentils, peas, oil, fat, dried fruit, salt, and salted and dried meats.[92] Straw was needed for the animals and wood as fuel, especially in winter. It was also recommended that all the wood in the surrounding area be cut down, to keep the enemy from using it to build towers and siege engines. Above all, residents could not neglect to pile up large blocks of stone to feed the mangonels, which, from inside the city or atop the walls, would bombard the enemy's ranks. Other, much more unusual projectiles sometimes made an appearance. As Saladin was beginning to besiege Mosul in 1183, one of his generals came looking for him and threw at his feet a shoe stuffed with nails, a projectile that had just hit him full in the chest. Furious, the general announced that he refused to continue fighting against people engaging in such pranks. These same residents of Mosul had no lack of imagination in their war stratagems: at night, by a secret door, men left the citadel equipped with torches, which they then extinguished before returning, only to set out again, thus giving the impression that a major nocturnal attack was in the offing.[93]

As for the besiegers, they had to study well their plan of attack. In his treatise, al-Harawī emphasizes, for example, that it is pointless to attack a too powerfully fortified citadel and risk depleting one's forces. Several times, Saladin preferred to bypass cities or fortresses reputed to be impregnable (Mosul in 1183; the Krac des Chevaliers, Tripoli, and Antioch in 1188) in order to take less well-defended strongholds. A siege was always a costly undertaking in terms of both men and money. It was therefore important from the start to set everything in place to obtain surrender through negotiation. The policy Saladin followed, to always offer to spare the lives of the besieged and to let them take their belongings with them in exchange for surrender, as well as his practice of respecting his pledges, was therefore based on military as well as humanitarian principles. In any case, it allowed him to accelerate considerably his conquests.

The siege of Acre between 1189 and 1192 was extraordinarily long and had the peculiarity of positioning the two opposing armies face to face outside the city. The Frankish camp was primarily resupplied by sea, while in the Muslim camp actual markets were set up. The great scholar 'Abd al-Latīf al-Baghdādī has left us a lively description of them: some 140 blacksmiths were at work there; cooks busied themselves around giant kettles; and several thousand shops sold provisions and miscellaneous items.[94] Maghrebis installed makeshift baths by digging pools in the ground, which they lined with clay and filled with hot water. Surrounded by walls and covered with roofs of tree branches or matting, these improvised baths allowed soldiers to wash themselves for the price of one dirham. These markets were a strong temptation for the Franks, who did not always resist the desire to pillage them, at the risk of being taken by surprise.[95] Conversely, during that same siege, the Muslims witnessed—some indignantly, others enviously—the disembarkment in the enemy camp of some three hundred Frankish prostitutes:

> They were remarkable, adorned with their youth and bedecked in
> their beauty. . . . They had left their home countries to assist the
> exiles . . . [and] they were burning to indulge in debauchery and
> fornication. Each of these fallen women was impulsive, superb,
> shameless. . . . Upon their arrival, they had given themselves, had

sacrificed their modesty, the most precious thing they possessed. They said they had resolved to go in order to give the gift of their charms on the path of God. . . . They separated themselves off in the tents and pavilions they had set up. Young men of the same age joined them there; then they opened the doors of voluptuous pleasures, engaged in and permitted all liberties. . . . They gave free rein to the market in vice . . . shut themselves up in their rooms under the males' amorous raptures, offered the enjoyment of their merchandise, invited the lewd to embrace them, had bare chests mount upon their backs, gave their goods to the indigent, drew their earrings close to their ankle bracelets, stretched out on the rug for games of love. . . . The men of our army heard tales about the excesses of these shameless women, and wondered how they could be claiming to act devoutly while abandoning all restraint, all modesty. Nevertheless, a certain number of mamluks, poor, foolish ignoramuses, felt the sting of passion and followed the people of error.[96]

At other times, the zeal of the besiegers suffered because of the proximity of an alluring city, as, for example, in 1178, when the Franks besieging Harīm, if we are to believe William of Tyre, preferred the diversions offered them in Antioch to the rigors of war.[97]

The descriptions of sieges under Saladin's reign provide many indications about the weapons used. The most formidable were without a doubt the ballistae and trebuchets, called mangonels in the East. These war machines, equipped with a large mobile arm fixed to a vertical axis, made it possible—by human strength or the use of a counterweight—to send huge blocks of stone, possibly surpassing a hundred kilograms, over a distance of one to three hundred meters. Both the besieged and the besiegers used them, one to bombard the troops, the other to pelt the city's residents, crack the walls, or fill in moats. These impressive machines were often mounted on wheels so that they could be moved, and were covered with hides soaked in vinegar to withstand fire. The Muslims and Franks used them in most of the major battles. Those that were set up outside the walls of Jerusalem in 1187 are described by 'Imād al-Dīn as follows: "The foundations of the walls and the merlons of their battlements were destroyed and knocked down by the stones of the war machines. The mangonels being maneuvered seemed to have gone mad, they were like bold men who cannot be equaled. They seemed to be mountains drawn by ropes; they were like flights of locusts activated by men, mothers of misfortune and death, pregnant women who gave birth to calamities. No protection against their stones! . . . How many stars fell from on high! How many rocks shot up from their emplacement! How many firebrands spread from their sparks!"[98]

To succeed in getting a foothold on the ramparts, the Franks, more often than the Muslims, used high mobile towers, built of wood (sometimes with metal parts) and mounted on wheels, and into which a large number of archers and crossbowmen crowded. The height of these towers varied with the elevation of the city's walls, but they could be as many as five or seven stories tall, or twenty to thirty meters. Those that were erected outside the walls of Acre in 1190 made a strong impression on the Muslims: "These towers seemed like mountains. We could see them from our positions, dominating the city walls. They were mounted on wheels and each one could accommodate more than 500 men, as it was claimed. Their flat tops were large enough for a trebuchet to be set up there."[99]

Similar techniques were used on the sea. During the siege of Acre, for example, the Franks attempted to seize a tower protecting the entrance to the harbor, the Tower of Flies, by approaching it with a fortified vessel with a tower so high "that a mountain could not rival it." The tower, packed full of naphtha and wood, was designed to set fire to the Tower of Flies. "But when they moved the ship to the well-stocked turret, when the mast touched the wall, things went counter to their calculations, and their schemes were ruined by bad luck. In fact, the wind was coming from the east, and the fire could not rise up against the tower; on the contrary, the mast caught fire, the flames turned back against the crew, acting blindly against those ignoramuses, and burned up the vessel loaded with wood that was following behind."[100]

To take a stronghold by force, it was necessary to move close to the wall. To avoid the besieged's arrows, the besiegers usually took shelter behind wooden palisades or stone parapets. In 1191, outside the walls of Acre, the Franks even built a large talus of earth, which they gradually moved toward the rampart.[101] Often the fortifications were protected by a moat, which the attackers labored to fill. In 1184, outside the walls of Kerak, Saladin ordered the construction of a gallery with brick walls and a wooden roof to protect his soldiers from enemy projectiles as they were attempting to fill the moat.[102] In 1191, to fill the moat of Acre, the Franks threw in everything within reach, including animal carcasses and human cadavers, while the city's garrison strove to prevent them:

> The enemy's pressure on the city and their extreme efforts to fill
> in the moat went so far that they were throwing in all their dead
> horses and, finally, they were even throwing in their own dead.
> People said that whenever one of their number was wounded mor-
> tally and beyond hope, they would throw him in. Reports of all this
> came in constant letters from our men in the city. The garrison [of
> Acre] itself was divided into different parties, one going down into
> the moat and cutting up the corpses and horses that were thrown
> in to make them easy to carry, one carrying away what the former
> had cut up and throwing it into the sea, another giving protection
> and defending them so that they could manage their task, and yet
> another at the trebuchets and guarding the walls.[103]

Once the moat was filled, the rams could go to work knocking down the
gates or making breaches in the wall. Some rams were impressive: single- or
double-headed, they were built of long ship's masts and mounted on wheels.
The most spectacular of them was perfected by the Franks in October 1190 during the siege of Acre. Before the terrorized Muslims destroyed it by setting it
ablaze, they compared that infernal machine, inside which warriors had taken
position, to the Beast of the Apocalypse evoked in the Koran (27:82):

> The Franks began construction on a fearsome rolling tower, a
> menacing machine ending at the top with a figure called a ram.
> That machine bore two horns long as spears and big as two thick
> columns. . . . That gallery looked like the arch of a hump bridge,
> covered with iron by means of stays, like its ram. . . . The ram's
> head was faced with iron, then with copper; it was covered with
> strong sheets to protect it from fire. . . . That machine was stocked
> with bellicose warriors, vigorous defenders. . . . When that rolling
> tower was properly set up, when its mass of iron was moving in
> waves, when those raging goats, moving around that ram with no
> fear of their engine catching fire, calmly set it in motion, flattened
> the ground ahead of it, leveled it this way and that, accompanied it

while hauling it, seeing with fresh eyes—what am I saying? with fresh souls—thanks to it, and moved it toward us, then it appeared before us, fearsome to behold, like a pasture closed to grazing, startling in appearance, like a mechanism inspiring terror.[104]

The iron salvaged by the Muslims after the destruction of the engine was estimated at about a hundred Syrian quintals, or twenty metric tons.[105]

Whereas the Franks were masters in the art of building mobile towers and giant rams, the Muslims excelled at undermining the ramparts. The Aleppines in particular were reputed for their expertise, which consisted of digging a subterranean gallery in the direction of the fortification. Under the wall to be destroyed, they widened the mine, shored it up with wooden piles, added undergrowth or straw if necessary, then set it on fire, which, when the soil was light enough, caused the wall to collapse.[106]

Fires thus played a major role in these battles, and the Muslims were certainly more skillful than the Franks in making use of Greek fire, a technique inherited from the Byzantines, Romans, and Greeks. A flammable mixture with a petroleum base, mixed with either sulfur, pitch, quicklime, or resin, was shut up in a clay pot. Naphtha launchers then launched the pot by hand or with the aid of light mangonels. Naphtha was relatively rare and expensive. Saladin received some from Mosul in 1189 and from Baghdad during the siege of Acre.[107] The Franks sought to take precautions against Greek fire by covering their towers and ballistae with metal sheets or hides soaked in vinegar. Things were then in the hands of whoever could display the greatest ingenuity, as attested by the story of the Damascene ironmaster's son. In May 1190 he had asked Saladin for permission to enter the besieged city of Acre to participate in the holy war. Once inside, he offered to compose the proper mixture for the Greek fire. The defenders of the city initially mocked his youth and inexperience, but, given the inability of the pyrotechnists to destroy the Franks' three powerful mobile towers, they ultimately allowed him to proceed. The young man began by launching onto the tower, with the aid of a mangonel, pots he had prepared, but without setting them on fire first. Their contents therefore spread across the top of the tower, catching fire all at once when other flaming pots struck the tower in different places, from the base to the summit. Trapped Frankish soldiers died by the dozens, as the other two towers burned in the same way.[108]

Whatever the type of battle and whatever the tactic used, the major problem in that region of the world was always the supply of water. Before abandoning their houses to take refuge in a fortress, the villagers emptied the water from the reservoirs and polluted the springs and wells, to prevent their enemies from using them. In 1185, outside Mosul, some even advised Saladin to divert the course of the Tigris so that the city's residents would suffer from thirst. The problem was especially acute in the height of summer, when the heat became suffocating for the soldiers in their coats of mail. William of Tyre reports cases of soldiers who died of sunstroke, and we have seen that even the Battle of Hattīn turned in great part on access to water.[109]

The Fate of Prisoners

With respect to Islamic law, the fate of prisoners varied as a function of whether they were men who could fight, or rather women, children, the elderly, or the infirm, who in principle did not participate in the war against the Muslims. In theory, the fate of the men was supposed to be decided by an imam, who could either have them executed—as punishment or because they represented a danger for Islam—reduce them to slavery, exchange them, or liberate them. A non-Muslim prisoner who was released without compensation had to be granted the status of tributary, so that he could not return to the land of the "infidels." As for the other prisoners, women and children in particular, if they did not participate in the war against Islam, they could not be executed. They were merely reduced to slavery, exchanged, or freed.[110] The conversion of a captive to Islam did not automatically give him or her the right to emancipation but considerably increased the chances of obtaining it.

In the case of Muslim prisoners, since fratricidal war was banned on principle by Islam, they could only be released. The clemency vis-à-vis the caliph that Saladin displayed in 1175, letting all his own prisoners go after his victory over the Zangids at the "Horns of Hama," was therefore in reality only the strict application of Muslim law. The Franks for their part chose not to massacre systematically their prisoners and the residents of the conquered localities, as they had done in Ma'arrat al-Nu'mān in 1098 and in Jerusalem in 1099, having understood that local populations were indispensable for cultivating the lands and keeping the economy functioning, and that prisoners of war could be put to work or used as a currency of exchange.

The two camps did not have the same attitude toward their captive coreligionists, at least during the first century of the Crusades. Islamic law encouraged the release of captives by imposing on every believer the payment of legal alms *(zakāt),* some of which were set aside for the liberation of Muslims who had fallen into the hands of enemies: "Alms shall be only for the poor and the destitute, for those that are engaged in the management of alms and those whose hearts are sympathetic to the Faith, for the freeing of slaves and debtors, for the advancement of God's cause, and for the traveller in need. That is a duty enjoined by God. God is all-knowing and wise" (Koran 9:60).

A good Muslim ruler was thus obliged to free his coreligionists held captive in non-Muslim territory, an obligation that contributed in part to the many exchanges of prisoners that occurred between Byzantines and Muslims until the mid-eleventh century.[111] Similarly, biographers do not neglect to praise the leaders and notables who established mortmain properties *(waqfs)* for redeeming captives. Saladin's brother-in-law Gökbörī, lord of Irbil, was lauded for having devoted one hundred thousand dinars every year for the redemption of Muslims who had fallen into the Franks' hands, this in addition to his other charitable works.[112] Saladin and his entourage were not to be outdone. The sultan decided that a large part of the revenues of Bilbeis, Egypt, would be earmarked for the redemption of the residents of that city taken prisoner by the Franks in 1168, and al-Fādil devoted part of his fortune to a foundation of the same kind.[113] During his visit to Damascus in 1184, Ibn Jubayr admired the efforts by the Syrians in that area:

> One of the beneficent works of God Most High towards the Maghribi [and Muslim Andalusian] prisoners in these lands of Frankish Syria is that every Muslim of these parts of Syria or elsewhere who makes a will in respect of his property devotes it to the liberation of the Maghribis in particular because of their remoteness from their native land and because, after Great and Glorious God, they have no other to deliver them. They are strangers, cut off from their native land, and the Muslims kings of these parts, the royal ladies, and the persons of ease and wealth, spend their money only in this cause. Nur al-Din—God have mercy on him—during an illness which had struck him, swore to distribute twelve thousand dinars for the ransoming of Maghribi prisoners. When he was

cured of his sickness, he sent their ransom, but with them were despatched a group who were not Maghribis, but who were from Hamah, one of his provinces. He ordered their return and the release of Maghribis in their place, saying, "These men can be ransomed by their kindred and their neighbours; but the Maghribis are strangers and have no kindred here."[114]

Merchants whose caravans connected the interior of Syria to the Frankish ports on the coast also participated in such acts, which were judged very meritorious. Ibn Jubayr speaks of two rich merchants from Damascus, including an emancipated slave, who served as intermediaries and had captives freed on their own behalf or on that of other Muslims.

In Judaism as well, alms are considered a religious duty. The Mediterranean Jewish communities developed large-scale charitable activities for the most needy and allocated a great deal of money for the redemption of prisoners.[115] It is no doubt for that reason that a twelfth-century rabbi wrote that a Jew, unlike a Christian, never abandons a captive coreligionist to his fate but strives to redeem him.[116] The Jewish communities of Egypt redeemed a great number of their fellows taken prisoner in Jerusalem in 1099, and clubbed together again to deliver the prisoners of Bilbeis in 1169.

The mobilization of the Franks in that area was slower. That is no doubt because, in the West, as Christianity expanded from the Carolingian era on, the practice of reducing prisoners of war to slavery was gradually lost, and only those prisoners from whom a ransom could be expected were kept. The collective redemption of captives—a mission that many saints in the Merovingian period had performed—became pointless outside the borders of Christendom, where Christians were still fighting pagans or Muslims.[117] In Eastern societies, conversely, slaveholding was deeply ingrained, and alongside acts of sea piracy, battles between armies of different religions remained the chief providers of slaves. That undoubtedly explains the need felt by the Jews, Muslims, and Byzantine Christians to develop the means necessary to redeem captives. Jean Richard writes: "The Latin East only slowly arrived at an awareness that the redemption of captives was a duty incumbent on all Christians. That awareness began to come about in the late twelfth century, and the large round-up of prisoners occasioned by Saladin accelerated it."[118] It was therefore as a result of the Crusades that, at the very end of the twelfth century, religious orders such as the Trinitarians came into being, with as their principal aim the redemption of captives. They were the sign of a new awareness, within the context of a general expansion in charitable foundations and works in the West at that time.[119]

In the treatment of his prisoners, as in many other areas, Saladin quite faithfully applied Islamic law. The main difference between him and his predecessors was the appreciable growth in the number of Frankish prisoners who fell into his hands on land and sea. A single battle often allowed for the capture of several hundred prisoners. After the victory, when it came time to tally things up, Saladin's secretaries estimated the number of Muslim losses and made a list of the most important Frankish prisoners. In 1179, for example, after the Battle of Marj 'Uyūn, 'Imād al-Dīn sat beside Saladin to note in a registry the names of the 270 knights taken prisoner, "not counting the other captives."[120] That same year, the taking of the castle of Bayt al-Ahzān yielded the capture of some seven hundred Frankish prisoners. Conversely, about a hundred Muslim prisoners used by the Franks on construction sites were liberated.[121] In 1187, thanks to Saladin's victories, more than twenty thousand Muslim prisoners were released, according to 'Imād al-Dīn, who also says there were five times as many Frankish prisoners, figures that, even if exaggerated, do reflect the considerable number of prisoners on either side.[122]

Theoretically, Islamic law stipulated that the booty—once the "fifth" for the sovereign and the public treasury was taken—would be shared equitably among all the combatants. But in the field, warriors often appropriated the prisoners they had taken. Saladin was therefore sometimes obliged to redeem them from his soldiers or emirs so that he could dispose of them as he liked. After the Battle of Hattīn, those who were sold at the Damascus markets were so numerous that their price fell to three dinars a head.[123] By contrast, when Saladin promised to spare the lives of the residents of a city in exchange for their surrender, they kept their freedom and sometimes even obtained the right to take with them some personal belongings. In Jerusalem, residents had to pay a ransom of ten, five, or two dinars to buy their freedom, and the some fifteen thousand people who could not come up with the sum necessary were reduced to slavery.

Many others were taken prisoner on the seas, by piracy or in battle. The ships that linked the West to the East in the Mediterranean at that time were almost exclusively Frankish, most of them Italian. They transported warriors in both directions, but also merchants with their goods, and many pilgrims. They therefore sailed packed full of men, women, children, horses, weapons, and merchandise of all sort, and constituted a target of choice for the Egyptian fleet. In 1179 an attack against several Frankish ships allowed the Egyptians to bring back about a thousand prisoners.[124] In 1182 a vessel with Frankish pilgrims aboard was shipwrecked off the coast of Damietta. The survivors, some 1,676 of the 2,500 travelers, we are told, fell into the hands of the Muslims. Those figures are no doubt overstated, though several reports of ships able to transport 1,500 passengers are attested to in the twelfth and thirteenth centuries.[125] In 1180 the two-year truce reached between the Muslims and the Franks required on principle that the prisoners be freed, but a few weeks before the date of payment, Saladin could not make up his mind to lose such a large booty and set such stringent conditions on Baldwin IV, king of Jerusalem, that the king was compelled to reject them. The truce was broken, and Saladin resumed battle against the Franks.

At the end of that same year, while he was preparing to cross the Euphrates, Saladin learned that a ship transporting Frankish refugees fleeing the massacres of Constantinople had been boarded and searched by Egyptians. The Muslims brought back more than four hundred prisoners, some of them distinguished, and great riches.[126] On several occasions between 1182 and 1183, Frankish vessels transporting weapons or wood to be used in the construction of ships were intercepted and their men and goods seized.[127] During the siege of Acre, Frankish vessels arrived in even greater number, and every time one of them fell into the Muslims' hands, more prisoners were taken. Particularly important was the taking of six ships off the coast of Beirut in late May 1191. In addition to the prisoners sold as slaves, the Muslims seized munitions, wood, money, precious objects, fabric, and about forty thoroughbred horses. That booty allowed the governor of Beirut to make very fine gifts to Saladin during his visit in 1192: garments in European cloth and clothing from Venice, mantles and blankets, gold and silver coins, saddles, bridles, spurs, and belts.[128]

Thanks to his conquests, Saladin took a greater number of prisoners than the Franks. But the Franks possessed several thousand Muslims, whom they, like their enemies, used as a means to exert pressure or as currency of exchange. In 1184 the bishop of Sebaste freed eighty Muslim prisoners in exchange for the promise that his city would be spared.[129] During Saladin's siege of Jerusalem, the four to five thousand prisoners detained by the Franks in the city were an important factor in the negotiations, since Balian of Ibelin threatened to execute them all if Saladin persisted in making no concessions. Once the city was conquered, Saladin restored their freedom and helped them return home.

In 1191, by contrast, the fate that Richard the Lionheart reserved for his three thousand prisoners in Acre deeply shocked Saladin and his people. The Latin sources attribute responsibility for that massacre to the sultan, who supposedly did not respect his pledges, while the Arab sources assert that Saladin mistrusted the Franks, who were demanding that he fulfill his promises before they would free the prisoners.[130] No doubt the massacre resulting from that dialogue of the deaf was ascribable more to the difficulties the Franks would have had keeping and, especially, controlling the prisoners any longer than to a mere craving for revenge. Ibn Shaddād remarks that the Franks spared the lives only of Muslims of a certain rank or those who could be used on the construction sites, but he also notes that among the explanations given for that massacre was that the king of England was afraid of leaving too large a number of prisoners behind him as he was preparing to march against Ascalon.[131] It is true that, to dispose of his prisoners in the Muslim world, Saladin possessed a much vaster market than the Latin states, which were reduced to a few coastal cities at the time. Although there were a few protests, the massacre was not generally perceived in the West as barbarous, since the slaughter of prisoner combatants from whom there was no hope of drawing a profit was not especially unusual. Did not Jacques de Vitry, bishop of Acre from 1216 to 1228, himself write that Richard the Lionheart had contributed a great deal toward weakening the enemy by massacring several thousand Muslims who, had they survived, would have done harm to the Christians?[132]

On both sides, the use of the prisoners who were allowed to live varied as a function of their status. Women were sold as domestic slaves and, in the Muslim world, as concubines. The most robust men, such as those whom Ibn Jubayr saw working in Cairo in 1183, were used as labor on construction sites:

> The forced labourers on this construction, and those executing all
> the skilled services and vast preparations such as sawing the mar-
> ble, cutting the huge stones, and digging the fosse that girdles the
> wall noted above—a fosse hollowed out with pick-axes from the
> rock to be a wonder amongst wonders of which trace may remain—
> were the foreign Rumi prisoners whose numbers were beyond
> computation. There was no cause for any but them to labour on

this construction. The sultan has constructions in progress in other places and on these too the foreigners are engaged so that those of the Muslims who might have been used in this public work are relieved of it all, no work of that nature falling on any of them.[133]

The distinguished prisoners, emirs or knights, members of the ruling family or of a sovereign's close circle, were usually redeemed with large ransoms, exchanged for other prisoners, or freed in exchange for the surrender of a fortress or city.[134] Thus Jubayl surrendered to Saladin in 1187 in exchange for the release of its lord, the Genoese Hugues Embriaco, who had been taken prisoner in Hattīn. In Ascalon, by contrast, the garrison refused to surrender in exchange for the release of King Guy of Lusignan and Gerard of Ridefort, Grand Master of the Knights Templar. The Grand Master was nevertheless freed a few days later, in exchange for the fortress of Latrun held by the Knights Templar. Several Latin sources also give an account whose authenticity is difficult to verify, since it is not confirmed by the Arab sources. During the siege of Tyre in 1186, Saladin is reported to have sent to Damascus for another of his prisoners from Hattīn, William III of Montferrat, father of Marquess Conrad of Montferrat, and offered to release him in exchange for the surrender of Tyre: "Conrad replied that he would not give him even so much as the smallest stone of Tyre in return for his father. 'But tie him to a stake and I shall be the first to shoot at him. For he is too old and is hardly worth anything.' They brought him before the city. The marquis cried out and said, 'Conrad, dear son, guard well the city.' And he took a crossbow in his hand and shot at his father. When Saladin heard that he had shot at his father, he said, 'This man is an unbeliever and very cruel.'"[135]

That tale seems to echo another concerning the taking of the castle of Beaufort. In August 1189, after trying for several months to gain some time by negotiating with Saladin, Reginald of Sidon, lord of Beaufort, was finally arrested and brought to the foot of its citadel to obtain its surrender. 'Imād al-Dīn, who gives a detailed description of that episode, says that Reginald encouraged the garrison to resist. Saladin's threats were without effect; Reginald was locked up in Damascus and freed the next year when the citadel finally gave up.[136] The Latin sources have a different view of that episode. According to the author of the *Continuation*—who is mistaken about the chronology of events—Reginald was subjected to every sort of torture, until he asked his garrison to hand over the fortress. In another version of the same work, however, the garrison reacted like Conrad in Tyre, refusing to hand over the fortress and aiming their arrows at Reginald.[137]

There is reason to wonder about the matter. Does not the insistence by several Latin sources on the intransigence of the garrisons of Tyre and Beaufort belong to legend, intended to show the Franks' courage and will to resist, the heroism of one or another of their leaders or, on the contrary, the humanity of Saladin (who freed William of Montferrat shortly thereafter in exchange for an emir), in contrast to the cruelty of the Latins, who did not hesitate to shoot their own lord? There is undoubtedly nothing unlikely about Saladin's proposal to exchange William of Montferrat for Tyre, since that was how he proceeded in other places; but it is strange that the Arab sources, which go on at length about the siege of that city and never fail to mention such negotiations when they occurred, say not a word about it. Note, moreover, that the theme of the Crusader as prisoner of the Muslims, forced by them, in exchange for having his life spared, to appeal to his coreligionists to yield to their demands, is also found in other Latin sources strongly tinged with hagiography. Upon his return from the First Crusade, for example, Peter Tudebode composed a narrative in which he presents the Crusaders who died in battle as true martyrs. He recounts, in particular, how the Muslims attempted to force a certain Reynald Porchet to appeal, from atop the walls of Antioch, to the Crusaders, camped outside the city. Instead of asking that a high ransom be paid for him, Reynald exhorted the Crusaders to be unyielding and to take no mind of saving his life.[138] It is therefore not impossible that, a few decades later, in Christian accounts of the resistance of Tyre and Beaufort, legend and reality somewhat mingled together.

Prisoners could be redeemed for a sum of money or could recover their freedom following an accord. The ransom could range from about a thousand gold coins for an ordinary knight to eighty thousand for Raymond of Tripoli, one hundred and twenty thousand for Reginald of Châtillon—who spent sixteen years of his life as a prisoner in Aleppo—or even one hundred and fifty thousand for Baldwin of Ibelin, lord of Ramla and a potential candidate for the throne of Jerusalem.[139] These are considerable sums when compared to the two hundred thousand dinars spent for several tens of thousands of residents of Jerusalem in 1187. Nevertheless, though financially solvent individuals, which is to say, those of a certain social rank, could hope to be exchanged for a ransom, not all prisoners of distinction escaped captivity. If we are to believe an Arab source, for example, the daughter of Balian of Ibelin and that of Hugues of Jubayl were among the presents offered to the caliph of Baghdad by Saladin's eldest son following his father's death.[140] In 1177, two emirs close to Saladin were captured by the Franks. They were redeemed two years later at a cost of sixty or seventy thousand dinars, plus the release of several Frankish prisoners. Taqī al-Dīn 'Umar's son, known as Shāhanshāh, had also fallen into the Franks' hands some time earlier. Sold to the Knights Templar, he was ultimately freed after seven years of captivity in exchange for a large ransom (the amount is unknown) and the liberation of all the Knights Templar then in Saladin's hands.[141]

Prisoner exchanges were often at the heart of negotiations between Saladin and Latin Christendom. For example, letters were exchanged on that subject between Saladin and his brother al-'Ādil on one hand, the papacy on the other.[142] In a letter to a pope—probably Alexander III (r. 1159–1181)—Saladin approved the proposals made by the pope's ambassador, one Olivier Vitalis, but asked for a reassessment of the value of the prisoners, his own being of noble extraction, whereas the Muslim prisoners were only peasants and members of the lower classes. In another letter, probably dating from March 31, 1183 (preserved in Latin translation), al-'Ādil wrote to Pope Lucius III (r. 1181–1185) in response to a letter delivered to Saladin by the legate some months before. Al-'Ādil said he was ready to grant the pope's wishes and confirm the agreement reached between Saladin and Alexander III regarding the liberation of prisoners, but set as a condition that the Franks of the kingdom of Jerusalem respect that accord. In 1188 Saladin also obtained from Bohemond the release of the prisoners held in Antioch, and the same issue remained at the center of discussions throughout the difficult negotiation between Franks and Muslims in 1192. Oddly, however, no clause concerning prisoner exchanges is mentioned in the final accord between Richard the Lionheart and Saladin.

Prisoners also sometimes served the sovereign's propaganda. They were exhibited in triumphal parades upon the return from battle. Rulers saw that practice, inherited from antiquity and widespread in the Middle Ages, as a means to display their might and to justify their power in the eyes of their own population. Saladin did not abuse the practice but also did not refrain from it in certain circumstances. After the taking of Jerusalem, in 1189 he sent to the caliph both knight prisoners and the large gilded cross that had been torn down from atop the Dome of the Rock. The prisoners were exhibited in Baghdad, wearing their weapons and mounted on their horses, but with their standards pointing toward the ground. The caliph had the cross buried under the threshold of one of the gates of Baghdad, so that it would be trampled by his subjects. In an irony of fate, the name given to that gate, the Nubian Gate (Bāb al-Nūbī), evoked the solemn entry in 836 of George, son of the king of Nubia, accompanied by bishops and a retinue bearing gold crosses.[143]

What was Saladin's attitude toward his prisoners? Was he simply the merciful sovereign, as the image spread by his legend suggests, or did he demonstrate severity, even intransigence?[144] His close circle criticized him for his excessive generosity toward the Franks. He often restored their freedom, thereby allowing them, for example, to return to Tyre, where they grew in strength. Reports of that liberality are many and do not come only from the Muslim sources. For example, after the taking of Tiberias, Saladin let Raymond's wife leave, along with her family, servants, and belongings. Once Jerusalem was conquered, he freed without ransom Reginald of Châtillon's widow; Balian's wife, Maria Comnena; and Sibylla, the wife of Guy of Lusignan, who was allowed to rejoin her husband, a prisoner in Nablus.[145] Such a chivalrous spirit is somewhat reminiscent of that of Alexander the Great toward the women in the family of his defeated enemy Darius. Alexander, mentioned in the Koran under the name Dhū-l-Qarnayn, was a historical figure, and both historians and the authors of Mirrors for Princes readily evoked him as a model sovereign: wise, just, generous, and courteous toward his friends and enemies.[146] It is difficult to say whether that image, conveyed especially through the Iranian versions of the Romance of Alexander, had a direct influence on Saladin. He, in any case, was rarely associated with Alexander, unlike some Mamluk and Ottoman sultans.[147] His concern to appear in everyone's eyes as the example of a magnanimous sovereign, respectful of his pledges, was nonetheless great. Witness this dialogue, which he had with ʿImād al-Dīn regarding the Latin patriarch of Jerusalem, who was preparing to leave the city with the treasures of the Holy Sepulchre: "So I told the sultan: 'These are great riches; they are clearly worth two hundred thousand dinars. Permission to take one's own possessions does not apply to those of the churches and convents; do not therefore leave them in the hands of those infidels.' He replied: 'If we interpret it to their detriment, they will accuse us of perfidy, for they do not know the heart of the matter. We will therefore deal with them by applying the safeguard agreement to the letter, and will not let them accuse the

Believers of having violated the sworn faith. On the contrary, they will speak of the blessings we have showered on them.' "[148]

In that, Saladin was not wrong, since his courtesy and magnanimity were the principal themes of the legend that developed around his image in the West. In terms of the reality, it is of course more difficult to weigh his oft-expressed generosity toward the Franks against his desire to repel and punish the enemy, and sometimes to avenge the atrocities committed. Saladin's clemency in certain circumstances has also been contrasted to his "ferocity" in others. Attesting to his clemency are the many accounts that mention his sense of honor, his compassion toward the weak, and his desire to avoid, as much as possible, pillaging, gratuitous violence, and bloodbaths. After the Battle of Hattīn, Saladin treated with great courtesy the king of Jerusalem and all the barons taken prisoner, and most were freed in the following months in exchange for a fortress, a prisoner, a ransom, or—in the case of Guy of Lusignan—simply a promise to no longer fight against the Muslims. His attitude contrasts with that of his predecessor, Nūr al-Dīn, under whose reign Reginald of Châtillon spent sixteen years in prison (1160–1176), Raymond III of Tripoli and Joscelin III of Courtenay about ten years each (1164–1174 or 1175). The words Saladin addressed to Guy of Lusignan before slaying Reginald of Châtillon—"It has not been customary for princes to kill princes, but this man transgressed his limits"[149]—are indicative of the importance he granted to the political and social rank of individuals and to the tacit code of honor that, in principle, followed from it. In 1190, for example, while he was encamped outside Acre, several Frankish prisoners of distinction were brought to the sultan. 'Imād al-Dīn, who was at his side, describes the scene: "He had arranged these captives around him, and it was only at that time that Allah showed his favor toward those unfortunate souls. The sultan extended his interview with them and gave them fruit to eat once he had put them at ease; then he had the table prepared to sate them and quench their thirst. Finally, he brought in garments, with which he dressed them. He placed his own pelisse on their principal leader, since the weather had grown colder and winter was coming on. He allowed them to send out their pages to bring them what they desired and to inform their friends, to whom they were eager to give word. Then he sent them to Damascus, where they would be kept captive and laden with heavy shackles."[150]

During the siege of Ascalon in 1187, when the garrison had refused to surrender in exchange for Guy of Lusignan's release but was no longer in a position to resist, Saladin decided in spite of everything to spare the lives of the residents, "out of pity, to spare the wives and children of the Muslims in the town from the violence of the army, as well as to protect the town itself from being ravaged by pillagers."[151] It is clear here that his conciliatory attitude toward the Franks could also be dictated by the interests of the Muslims. In 1191, when Frankish prisoners from Beirut were ushered into his presence, several of his very young sons asked for permission to execute one of them with their own hands. Saladin refused, so that, he said, they would not become accustomed to spilling blood and drawing glory from it at an age when they were not yet able to distinguish a Muslim from an infidel. Among these prisoners was an old man: "The sultan said to the interpreter, 'Ask him, "What brought you to come here when you are this old? How far is it from here to your land?" He replied, 'Between me and my land is a journey of months. As for why I came, it was just to go on pilgrimage to the Sepulchre.' The sultan had pity on him, gave him gifts, freed him and sent him back to the enemy camp on horseback."[152]

Similarly, Ibn Shaddād and 'Imād al-Dīn report the story of a three-month-old baby girl abducted from her Frankish mother by Muslim thieves during the siege of Acre in 1191. Frankish lords advised the weeping mother to go see the sultan. "He has a merciful heart. We give you permission to go to him. Go and ask him for the child and he will restore it to you." Saladin received her while he was riding horseback in the company of Ibn Shaddād. He allowed himself to be moved by her distress and tears and immediately commanded someone to go in search of the child. The little girl, who had just been sold at the market, was redeemed from her owner by Saladin, who returned her to her mother, then had both of them accompanied back home.[153] 'Imād al-Dīn's final condemnation of these baby thieves ("in pursuance of holy war, they found this iniquitous crime committed in the dark of night to be licit") illustrates that holy war in no way justified all the acts of violence committed against the enemy, and highlights by contrast Saladin's merit. Moreover, the words attributed to the Franks in that story indicate that, with the advent of Saladin's reign, the Muslims knew the reputation acquired by their sovereign among his enemies.

The panegyric intent of all these narratives is obvious. But must they be rejected en bloc? I do not think so, since the facts—the liberation of many prisoners without compensation—are confirmed by the Latin sources. Nevertheless, a more violent image is sometimes provided, of a Saladin driven by the desire for revenge. We must no doubt be wary, here as elsewhere, of the legendary character of certain episodes related in only a few Latin sources. Consider, for example, the prisoners seized on Christian ships arriving in Acre, who did not know the city had just fallen into the Muslims' hands, and whom Saladin supposedly "allowed to leave, poor and naked," after they had been mocked and abused. He wanted to make an example of them, so that those wishing to come to the Holy Land would be dissuaded from doing so.[154] Consider also the tortures that Saladin inflicted on Reginald of Sidon at the foot of the castle of Beaufort,[155] or the torments imposed on Baldwin of Ibelin, whose teeth were supposedly pulled out, to compel him to gather together his ransom.[156] It is nevertheless true that most of the Arab and Latin authors mention Saladin's initial desire to seize Jerusalem by force and by blood, in order to avenge the Muslims who had died in 1099 during the taking of that city by the Franks. Later, however, Saladin came to understand that such an attitude risked bringing on the destruction of the holy places and the death of Muslim prisoners. It is also known that Saladin showed no pity toward the Knights Templar and the Knights Hospitaller—except when he could extract a high ransom from them—and had almost all of them executed after the Battle of Hattīn, believing they were the worst enemies of Islam. Two days after the victory, he sent for them and ordered them beheaded before his eyes. The ulemas actively participated in the massacre: "Each of them asked to be granted the favor of executing a prisoner, unsheathed his saber, and bared his forearm. The sultan was seated; he had a smile on his face, while those of the miscreants were somber. The troops having lined up, the emirs were standing in two rows. Some of these religious sliced and cut well, and were thanked; the sabers of others hesitated and leapt back up, and they were forgiven; still others were mocked and replaced. And there I was, watching the sultan smile at the massacre; I saw him as a man of his word and of action."[157]

Saladin proved similarly inflexible toward Reginald of Châtillon. He was accused of being a faithless and lawless warrior, having violated his word many times, and the sultan wanted to behead him with his own hand. This strong symbolic gesture impressed the Latin authors to such a point that some did not hesitate to write that "Saladin took some of [Reginald's] blood and sprinkled it on his own head in recognition that he had taken vengeance."[158]

Other episodes are sometimes evoked to show that Saladin was not always the "valiant knight" of legend. In 1178, he ordered the execution of all the Frankish prisoners brought to him, with the exception of a single one, whom

'Imād al-Dīn had asked to be pardoned.[159] During the taking of the castle of Bayt al-Ahzān in 1179, Saladin had all the prisoners who were apostates or crossbowmen executed; the crossbowmen were no doubt the most tenacious defenders of the fortress. By contrast, the massacre of the other prisoners occurred outside his control, carried out by volunteer jihad warriors who were not part of the regular army.[160]

The treatment he reserved for the some 170 Frankish prisoners after Reginald of Châtillon's 1183 raid in the Red Sea also involved great violence. The Franks had no doubt been promised that their lives would be spared, but Saladin proved intractable and asked his brother al-'Ādil to make an example of them. The interests of Islam, he said, and the extraordinary nature of Reginald's attack required that no account be taken of the promise. There was not even any need to consult the ulemas on the legality of the executions. Saladin was also letting his enemies know that they had performed a blasphemous act. And by his steadfastness and intransigence, he wanted to dissuade them from repeating the act and to affirm, in the eyes of Muslims, that he was the one and true defender of the holy places. The prisoners, mounted backwards on camels, were triumphantly exhibited in the streets of Alexandria. Most were executed, and two of them were even slaughtered in Minā near Mecca, where the traditional immolation of animals always takes place at the end of the pilgrimage.[161]

Until August 1191, then, Saladin's line of conduct remained the same: spare the high-ranking prisoners to obtain ransoms, or simply in the spirit of "chivalry"; avoid bloodbaths; and come to the aid of the most destitute non-combatant prisoners. He had no pity, by contrast, for those he judged dangerous to Islam, particularly the military orders, Reginald of Châtillon, and apostates. For him as for his entourage, ordering the execution of all these prisoners—even with a certain pageantry—was not a display of cruelty. On the contrary, it was a duty and a mark of virtue. Is it not for that reason that Ibn Shaddād introduced, in his first chapter on Saladin's virtues, the execution of the man he called a "monstrous infidel and terrible oppressor," namely, Reginald of Châtillon? He seems in that way to vindicate Saladin for having kept his vow to kill the man. After all, Reginald had insulted Islam, having replied to those he had taken prisoner during a period of truce, and while they were making their way peacefully in a caravan: "Tell your Muhammad to release you!"[162]

In the summer of 1191 and thereafter, following the massacre of several thousand Muslim prisoners by the Franks, Saladin hardened his position. "He had taken an oath to kill all the Franks he seized, because of their massacre of the residents of Acre." In three days' time, therefore, between August 29 and 31, 1191, twenty-eight prisoners were executed in cold blood.[163] This was not the first time that atrocities had given rise to further atrocities, in a spirit of revenge: "On Sunday 29 Jumādā I {23 June [1191]}, many enemy foot-soldiers came out on the bank of the freshwater stream. A detachment of our advance guard met them and a serious battle ensued. . . . The enemy seized a Muslim and, having killed him, burned his body. The Muslims then seized one of them, and killed and burned him. I saw the two fires blazing at the same time."[164]

Vengeance has always fostered the escalation of wars, but let us recall that in the Middle Ages it did not have the pejorative connotations it has in our own time. Not only was vengeance not always condemned, it was often a duty. Claude Gauvard has shown that in the West, far from being the fruit of vindictive impulses or social disorder, vengeance was a mode of conflict resolution, closely linked to violence, which itself contributed toward the founding of the public order.[165] In cases of homicide, the law of retribution (qisās) and blood revenge (tha'r) were very widespread in the Arab tribal system. They were considerably attenuated in Islamic law, which in particular encouraged the payment of blood money (diya). The ancient practices, however, remained not only a matter of custom but also a matter of law.[166] In theory, every intentional murder of a Muslim could be punished by the death of the murderer. Unlike ancient pre-Islamic tribal customs, Muslim law on principle prohibited taking revenge on the members of the family or tribal group, but it is well known that the rule was not always respected in practice (nor is it even today). In the context of war against the infidel, Saladin could therefore easily have allowed the practice of vengeance, albeit collective.

The large number of prisoners taken by the Muslims inevitably raises the question of how many changed sides by defecting or converting to Islam. It remains very difficult to say. The Muslims designated Franks who placed themselves under their protection by the term musta'min ("he who asks for protection"), and such cases were not rare. Late twelfth-century law in the kingdom of Jerusalem stipulated the case of returning knights who had taken the Muslims' side, distinguishing between those who had denied their faith and those who had not.[167] It was also fairly common to find Frankish mercenaries in the Muslim armies, since they were not asked to renounce their faith.[168] Mentions of them are even found in romances from the early thirteenth century, such as the character of Reginald of Brittany in the *Estoires d'Outremer*. He is Saladin's prisoner and gonfalon-bearer, and defends Damascus against the Crusaders. There were various reasons for the conversions and defections. Some prisoners may have accepted conversion to save their lives. But others entered the service of the Muslims to escape punishment after a grave injustice or quite simply to pursue a career. Some converted, while others did not.[169]

One of the best-known cases is that of a certain John Gale. According to the Latin sources, that knight, born in Tyre, sought refuge with Saladin after killing his lord, whom John Gale had caught in his wife's arms. Such a murder was considered very grave under feudal law. Saladin welcomed him warmly and even entrusted him with the military education of his nephew, whom John Gale was also supposed to teach "courtesy and good manners."[170] One day, when he was with the young man in Aleppo, that knight, whose faithlessness is denounced even in the Latin sources, entered into contact with the Knights Templar at the fortress of Baghrās, near Antioch, and offered to sell them Saladin's nephew in exchange for a ransom and permission to return to the kingdom of Jerusalem. The deal was concluded, and, on the pretext of going hunting, John Gale brought the nephew to the territory of the Knights Templar. There the knights took the young man prisoner. The same Latin sources claim that in September 1188, when Saladin laid siege to the castle of Roche-Guillaume north of Antioch,[171] not far from Baghrās, he was seeking to wreak revenge on the treacherous knight, whom he suspected of being in the fortress. But events obliged him to lift the siege. 'Imād al-Dīn gives a slightly different version of that story:[172] a "protected" Frank who lived in Damascus deceived Saladin's nephew, making him believe that the king of the Franks would give him power if he went to join him. The young man fell into the trap, was sold to the Knights Templar, and remained a prisoner for seven years before being redeemed by Saladin.

Sometimes these "protected" Franks were sent by Saladin on true "commando" operations:

Franks who had asked for our protection [*musta'mins*] had obtained barks, on which they made incursions and war raids, using masts and pulleys, stinging with their boats like scorpions and vipers. They landed in a district of the island of Cyprus on a feast day. The priest had gathered the population from near and far together in a church; our Frankish allies prayed there with them, then locked the doors of the church, to make sure they would not escape, and took them all prisoner. . . . They collected all the precious objects that were in the church, were merciless toward the priest, took people and objects onto the barks, and sought refuge in Latakia, where they sold everything they had taken from the church—in particular, twenty-seven women, boys, and girls, whom they disposed of for a low price—and divided up the proceeds of that sale.[173]

On at least one occasion, during Saladin's conquest of Latakia in 1188, Franks asked to remain on Muslim soil with the status of *dhimmīs*. According to 'Imād al-Dīn, they were compelled to do so because of the attitude of Sicilian sailors, who had arrived off the coast of Latakia and taken control of a boat of refugees, accusing them of having handed over the city to the sultan.[174]

Between 1190 and 1192, the weariness of the troops during the siege of Acre and subsequent campaigns was such that desertions occurred on both sides. In the last weeks of 1190, some Franks, impelled by the terrible famine wreaking havoc in their camp, joined the Muslims' ranks. Some converted to Islam, others kept their own religion, still others had regrets and returned home.[175] During the following year, many cases of desertion were also recorded: starving Franks offered their services to Saladin and brought him, in addition to prisoners, the rich cargo of a Frankish merchant ship that was preparing to unload its ingots and silver goods.[176] Two servants—probably Sicilians—of Joan, Richard's sister and the widow of the former king of Sicily, also took refuge in Saladin's camp, claiming they had secretly remained Muslim. They received an excellent welcome from the sultan.[177]

Conversely, the Franks used Muslim converts to Christianity, called turcopoles, in their army.[178] Saladin was merciless toward these renegades. When he took them prisoner at the castle of Bayt al-Ahzān, he had every last one of them executed. It is also known that renegade Aleppine sappers provided their aid to Richard the Lionheart during the assault of the fortress of Dārūm in 1192.[179]

Some ultimately had regrets—for example a Muslim at the Krac des Chevaliers who had fought alongside the Franks and had even gone to Rome to collect money.[180] In addition to the renegades, the Franks could also count on the aid of many Bedouins, who served them as guides, spies, and sometimes military aides.[181] Without entering the service of the Franks, other Muslims, including some important ones, did not hesitate to sell them provisions during times of famine. The lord of 'Azāz in northern Syria, for example, made a fortune selling cereals to Antioch at exorbitant prices, at a time when Saladin was about to conquer the castle of Baghrās a few kilometers away.[182]

According to the *Itinerarium,* on the eve of the fall of Acre, some Muslims, besieged for nearly two years and at the end of their strength, deserted and asked the Franks to baptize them: "There is justification for doubting the extent of their merits, since they asked for this more as a means of escape from the danger which threatened them than from the inspiration of divine grace; but there are many routes to salvation."[183]

But all the armies were faced with that problem, whether of deserters or of runaways, when battles went on and on, and that is why al-Fādil implored Saladin's indulgence toward them: "The army is not tired but anxious, human strength certainly has its limits, God's fortunes have an objective. . . . I remind our master of all that, only so that he will have no animosity toward those who recant or retreat, as the verse says: 'Therefore pardon them and implore God to forgive them' (Koran 3:159)."[184]

17

The Gaze of the Other

By Saladin's time, Middle Eastern Muslims had already lived in proximity to the Franks for nearly a century. Even before the Crusades, many Western pilgrims were coming to the Holy Land, and Italian merchants regularly visited the Egyptian ports. Nevertheless, those two worlds, Eastern and Western, though not unacquainted, remained profoundly alien to each other, separated by language, religion, history, and culture. Each watched the other with a mix of fear and admiration, attraction and repulsion. In daily life, of course, the Franks sometimes took to frequenting the baths and adopted some local vestimentary or culinary practices.[1] There were a few mixed marriages between Franks and Eastern Christians, Armenians especially, but there was no real mingling of populations or cultures. The ancient legacy that the Arabs had transmitted to the West in the realms of science and philosophy passed through Sicily and Spain much more than through the Latin states of the East.

Only rarely do the sources inform us about the daily contacts between Franks and Muslims. Fortunately, the autobiographical writings of the Arab emir Usāma Ibn Munqidh (1095–1188), well known to historians, are the exception. Usāma was a Syrian Arab emir and a poet, whose family owned the castle of Shayzar in central Syria, on the banks of the Orontes. His extraordinary longevity, the many contacts he had with the Franks, and his literary talent played a large role in his notoriety. He met Saladin for the first time in Damascus in 1154, and, when the sultan took power in the Syrian capital in 1174, Usāma was summoned to his court. The two men had a great appreciation for each other. Saladin liked Usāma's poetry and often asked his advice on literary matters and also on military affairs, since the elderly man had waged war against the Franks throughout his life. His son Murhaf also became one of Saladin's close emirs.

Usāma's vivid and colorful testimony is a gold mine of information, even though, as Carole Hillenbrand has rightly pointed out, he sometimes exaggerated, voicing a few clichés about Westerners that date back to a period well before the Crusades.[2] Since the tenth century, all sorts of popular stories had contributed toward the spread of a stereotypical image of the West and its inhabitants: travel literature, prison narratives, and the accounts of pilgrims, merchants, and ambassadors. The legacy of Ptolemy, who divided the world into seven zones or "climates," defined by their latitude, figured prominently in the work of the Arab geographers, who attributed to the sixth climate a direct influence on the Franks' physical appearance and character. The Franks, good and courageous warriors, were noted for their coarse manners, their lack of hygiene, and their slow-wittedness. Some Muslim authors go so far as to associate them with the animal kingdom. For Ibn Abī l-Ashʿath, a tenth-century doctor living in Mosul, the Franks, like animals, had only generic characteristics and completely lacked individuality. Two centuries later, Usāma Ibn Munqidh wrote: "Mysterious are the works of the Creator, the author of all things! When one comes to recount causes regarding the Franks he cannot but glorify Allah (exalted is he!) and sanctify him, for he sees them as animals possessing the virtues of courage and fighting, but nothing else; just as animals have only the virtues of strength and carrying loads."[3]

Despite these clichés, the Muslims—unlike the Crusaders, most of whom disembarked in the East without having the slightest idea about the religion of Islam—were very familiar with Judaism and Christianity, which had a great many points in common with Islam. In the seventh century, an entire literature of religious polemics had developed in the East. The two most difficult Christian doctrines for the Muslims to understand were that of the Trinity—a single God in three persons, which earned the Christians the name "associationists" and even "polytheists"—and the dual nature (human and divine) of

Christ. The author of a Mirror for Princes composed in Syria in about the mid-twelfth century effectively sums up that incomprehension: "The most amazing thing in the world is that the Christians say that Jesus is divine, that he is God, and then say that the Jews seized him and crucified him. How then can a God who cannot protect himself protect others? . . . They believe in this utter iniquity, that their God came forth from the privates of a woman and was created in a woman's womb, and that a woman was made pregnant by their God and gave birth to him. . . . Anyone who believes that his God came out of a woman's privates is quite mad; he should not be spoken to, and he has neither intelligence nor faith."[4]

Whether clichés, prejudices, ignorance, or incomprehension, many obstacles stood in the way of exchanges between Westerners and Easterners. Nevertheless, several decades after the First Crusade, the Muslims were beginning to have a better understanding of the Franks' motivations and objectives. More than ever, the Franks were considered enemies, but behind the fear and hostility, admiration and respect for one individual or another in the opposing camp sometimes shine through.

Better Understood Objectives?

In the aftermath of the First Crusade, few Muslims understood the Crusaders' true motivations; or, at any rate, the reports that have come down to us are rare. The treatise on jihad (Kitāb al-jihād) by the Damascene jurist al-Sulamī is a felicitous exception. He displayed a great deal of perspicacity, placing the First Crusade in the context of Christian expansion into Spain and Sicily, and asserting in 1105, regarding the Crusaders, that "Jerusalem was the ultimate fulfillment of their desires" and the new Frankish war was a "jihad against the Muslims." Unfortunately, it is not known whether his point of view was unusual or broadly shared. The rarity of the accounts during this era has led historians to think that the Muslims did not immediately understand what was at stake in the Crusade. It is very possible that al-Sulamī had disciples in religious circles, but it does not appear that his writings were widely diffused. One thing is sure: the recommendation that he gave Muslim rulers, to unite in order to confront the Crusade, had no immediate results, and it was not until the mid-twelfth century that Muslim unity really took shape. The other reports on the Franks that have come down to us date from that later era. Most attest to a

No one knows what Saladin really looked like. Representations of him in Western art of the fifteenth and sixteenth centuries primarily reflect the artistic and cultural context of the Italian Renaissance. Such is the case for the portrait attributed to Cristofano dell'Altissimo (about 1530–1605), who recopied many portraits of illustrious men at the request of the grand duke of Tuscany, Cosimo I de' Medici. Florence, Uffizi Gallery. © Dagli Orti Collection, Uffizi Gallery, Florence / Alfredo Dagli Orti.

A few decades earlier, in fifteenth-century Italy, the Saladin painted on a parchment scroll, alongside other famous personalities from antiquity and the Middle Ages, was distinguishable from Westerners only by his turban and saber. *The Six Ages of the World.* London, British Library, add. 30359, no. 86. © Heritage Images / Leemage.

(*Opposite*) During the age of the Crusades, representations of Jerusalem multiplied in the West, often inscribed in a circle, symbol of the perfection of heavenly Jerusalem and of the central place of earthly Jerusalem, "navel of the world." On the map from the mid-twelfth century, taken from a heterogeneous collection, note the orientation (east appears at the top) and the presence of strong walls with gates cut into them. Recognizable inside the city are, among other things, the Holy Sepulchre and the Tower of David to the west, the Church of Saint Anne, the Temple of the Lord (Dome of the Rock), and Solomon's Temple (al-Aqsā) to the east. Outside, sites far from Jerusalem are depicted: Bethlehem, the Jordan Valley, and Mount Sinai. The presence of small groups of pilgrims advancing, staffs in hand and bundles on their shoulders, gives this representation of the holy city a picturesque quality. Brussels, Bibliothèque Royale de Belgique, ms. 9823–24, fol. 157 recto. © Bibliothèque Royale de Belgique.

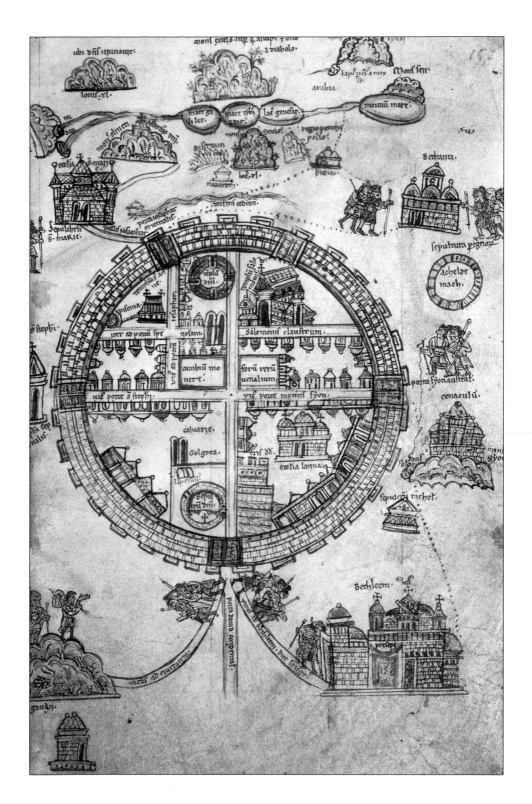

The Battle of Hattin (July 4, 1187), which cost a large part of the Frankish cavalry their lives or their freedom, and during which the relic of the True Cross was lost, elicited strong emotions in the West. Here it is represented in a fifteenth-century illumination by Loyset Liédet illustrating William of Nangis's *Chronique abrégée des rois de France (Abridged Chronicle of the Kings of France;* late thirteenth century). The numerical superiority of the Muslims (to the right) is accentuated by the artist. In the center, the figure of the bishop carrying the relic inserted into a T-shaped cross, or "Cross of Tau," underscores the importance granted to its capture. Paris, Bibliothèque Nationale de France, Fr. ms., 6463, fol. 46 verso. © BNF.

Following the victory at Hattin, Saladin treated Guy of Lusignan, king of Jerusalem, with respect but was merciless toward Reginald of Châtillon, whom the Muslims criticized for conducting many attacks and for not respecting the oaths he had taken. Saladin had sworn he would execute Reginald with his own hand, and he kept his word. In the West, Reginald is portrayed very differently, in particular, as a martyr defending his faith, as in this illumination from the early fifteenth century illustrating a universal chronicle titled *Trésor des histoires (Treasury of Stories)*. Reginald is kneeling in a humble and pious attitude, which, by way of contrast, highlights Saladin's gesture of anger. Paris, Bibliothèque de l'Arsenal, ms. 5077, fol. 351 verso. © Bibliothèque de l'Arsenal / BNF.

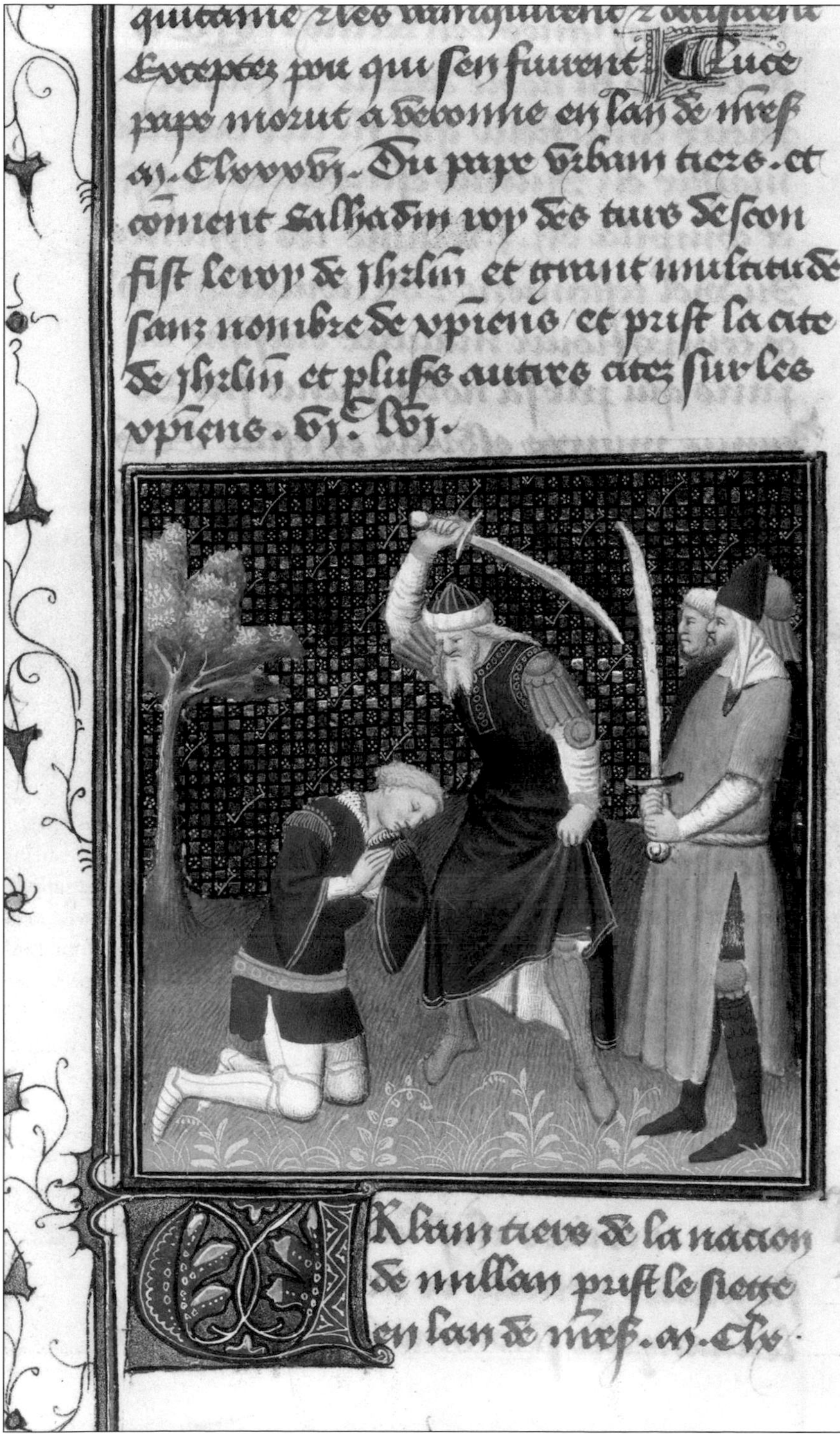

quitaine et les vangnitene 2 auge en
excepte pou qui sen surent. Luce
pape morut a veronne en lan de nreff
ai. Cloxvbi. Du pape brbam tiere. et
coment salhadin roy des turs descon
fift le roy de jhelm et grant multitude
sanz nombre de vpiens/ et prift la ate
de jhelm et plufre autres atez sur les
vpiens. bi. lbi.

Rbain tiers de la nacion
de millan prift le piege
en lan de nreff. ai. clx

Le Pas Saladin, a French poem composed at the turn of the fourteenth century, recounts Saladin's progress through a narrow mountain pass defended by Richard the Lionheart and twelve Christian knights, a story inspired no doubt by Richard's victory near Jaffa. In the late fourteenth century, Marquess Thomas III of Saluzzo inserted *Le Pas Saladin* into his romance *Le chevalier errant.* This illumination (early fifteenth century) is taken from a manuscript of that work and is particularly interesting for the coats of arms that appear on it. Saladin is represented here as a Christian ruler and bears the legendary coat of arms "of gules fretted with silver bells," inspired, with a few variants, by those of the Anglure family. Paris, Bibliothèque Nationale de France, Fr. ms. 12559, fol. 127 recto. © BNF.

The domed building that holds Saladin's tomb, north of the Ummayad Mosque of Damascus, remains a pilgrimage site in our time. The cenotaph in sculpted wood, right, dates in great part from the Ayyubid era; the white marble one was built in homage to Saladin in the late nineteenth century by the Ottoman sultan Abdülhamid II and was later restored by the German emperor William II. Postcard, private collection of the author.

The representation of Saladin as a victorious sultan on a Syrian banknote, or as a liberator of Jerusalem on a Jordanian postage stamp, illustrates the political use still being made of his image. Private collection of the author. Studio de Création, Flammarion. © photo12.com-Fıonline.

The statue of Saladin erected in 1192 in front of the citadel of Damascus is no doubt the most spectacular expression of the interest that Arab political leaders have taken in him. It expresses both the humiliation inflicted on the Franks (slumped down behind the horse) and the union brought about under Saladin's banner between the warriors and the Sufi surrounding him.

fairly good knowledge of the nature and objectives of the Crusades, a perception that would be a major advantage for Muslims in defining their strategy and negotiating with the Franks.

The importance that Westerners granted to Jerusalem was one of the first of the Muslims' discoveries. Ibn al-Athīr recounts the story of a Frankish prisoner whose mother had gone so far as to sell everything she owned, namely, her house, to send her son to liberate Jerusalem.[5] At about the same time, al-Harawī was also aware of the importance for Christians of the Holy Sepulchre, the site of the crucifixion and resurrection of Christ;[6] and 'Imād al-Dīn, in a speech attributed to the Franks during the siege of the holy city in 1187, outlines the view that the Muslims may have had of Christian doctrine and the place occupied in it by Jerusalem. It reveals an astonishing mix of truth and error, allusions to the Koran, and clichés about Christian practices:

> It is here where our Church of the Resurrection is found, and from here that we will be resurrected. . . . It is our honor to pay tribute to that holy place, our salvation depends on its own, its stability assures our own, its longevity is the gauge of our longevity. If we abandon it, shame will cling to us, and we will deserve dishonor. . . . Here the images of the apostles in their conversations are to be found, here that of the Fathers in their teachings, of the monks in their monasteries, of the priests in their assemblies, of the sorcerers with their ropes;[7] of the priests and their illusions; the image of the Lady [the Virgin] and of the Lord, the Temple and the nativity, the Table and the fish, what is sculpted and carved, the disciple and the master, the cradle and the speaking child; the image of the goat and the donkey, of paradise and hell, of the bells and the laws. They also said: it is in these places that the Messiah was crucified and the victim immolated as a sacrifice; here was divinity incarnated, God became man and humanity became God.[8]

Saladin was perfectly aware of the importance the Franks ascribed to Jerusalem, even though, in his reply to Richard the Lionheart in 1191, he did not want to make any concessions in that area: "Jerusalem is ours just as much as it is yours. Indeed, for us it is greater than it is for you, for it is where our Prophet came on his Night Journey and the gathering place of the angels. Let not the king imagine that we shall give it up, for we are unable to breathe a word of that amongst the Muslims."⁹

He also seems to have had a good understanding of the religious motive behind the Crusade and of the connection between the Crusaders' pilgrimage and their battle against the Muslims. That is why he facilitated access to Jerusalem for the Franks of the Third Crusade, following the truce concluded with Richard the Lionheart. In allowing them to realize their wish, Saladin probably hoped they would be less inclined in the future to set off again for the Holy Land.¹⁰ Nor were the Muslims unaware of the importance of the relic of the True Cross for Christians: they had an inkling of the advantages they could draw from its capture. In a letter Saladin asked Qādī al-Fādil to draft announcing to the Abbasid caliph the victory of Hattīn and the taking of Jerusalem, he wrote: "The king was taken prisoner, holding in his hand the most solid of his supports, the strongest of his connections to his religion, the cross of the crucifixion, which guides the arrogant people. They never allow themselves to be caught without its two arms stretching out to them. It rouses them, but this time, with its arms extended it bid them farewell. . . . Under that cross, they conduct the keenest of battles."¹¹

Along with Jerusalem, that relic was at the heart of negotiations between Richard the Lionheart and Saladin throughout 1191–1192. The Eastern Christians—Greeks and Georgians—demanded it as well and offered to purchase it for large sums of money, but to no avail.¹² Even more significant, the Muslims were well informed about the spiritual advantages accruing to the Crusaders. The pope's role as leader of the Crusade, though distorted, was also known: "The Pope [bābā], who lives in Rome," wrote al-Fādil, "has prescribed to his people abstinence in food and drink. He told them: 'He who will not march for the deliverance of Jerusalem shall be excommunicated; marriage and meals [in common] will be prohibited him.' "¹³

'Imād al-Dīn also grasped the role of the clergy in the Crusade, of the indulgences granted to the Crusaders, and of the propaganda that encouraged them to go rescue their Christian brothers persecuted by the Muslims: "All those who depart to fight Islam will obtain forgiveness for their sins and will be purified of all stain; those who are unable to go will provide equipment and wealth to those who go."¹⁴

For al-Fādil, as for his predecessor, al-Sulamī, the Christian Crusade was comparable to the Muslim jihad: "If the jihad that the Franks are proposing to

make had been made with the pure intention to sacrifice themselves for a heavenly reward, no one could have preceded them to paradise."[15]

Knowing the enemy's motivations allowed Saladin not only to better
combat the Franks but also to incite the Muslims to jihad by contrasting their
spinelessness to their adversary's religious zeal:

> Where, therefore, is the Muslims' ardor, the pride of the people of
> the true religion, the zeal of the people of certainty? We are infi-
> nitely surprised to see the idolaters helping one another on behalf
> of polytheism, lending support to one another to broaden its way
> and set its course, to see Muslims stand apart from Muslims and
> not rush [to holy war], to abstain from rescuing them, to let the
> bonds of their cohesion come undone. . . . Just look at the
> Franks: . . . to preserve their faith, they have deemed the gift of
> their soul and of their life a modest price; they have aided their im-
> pure race with every sort of armament and with warriors capable
> of fighting; they have acted and given only out of religious fervor
> and enthusiasm for their faith.[16]

That Christian fervor was fanned by a full-scale propaganda campaign,
oral and written but also iconographic. The influence exerted by images in the
Frankish camp did not escape the attention of Saladin's entourage. Ibn al-Athīr
recounts that, in 1189, the Franks had a picture painted in Tyre depicting the
Messiah, his face bloody, being struck by an Arab, with the following inscription: "This is the Messiah with Muhammad, the prophet of the Muslims, beating him. He has wounded and slain him!"[17] Ibn Shaddād gives a rather similar
account of this propaganda of images:

> The marquis [Conrad of Montferrat] produced a picture of Jerusalem
> on a large sheet of paper, depicting the Sepulchre to which they come
> on pilgrimage and which they revere. The tomb of the Messiah is
> there, where he was buried after his crucifixion, as they assert. . . .
> He pictured the tomb and added a Muslim cavalryman on horseback
> trampling on the Messiah's tomb, upon which the horse had staled.
> This picture he publicised overseas in the markets and assemblies, as
> the priests, bareheaded and dressed in sackcloth, paraded it, crying

doom and destruction. Images affect their hearts, for they are essential to their religion. Therefore multitudes of people, whom God alone could number, were roused up.[18]

Was that improved perception of the enemy's motivations and propaganda mutual? Did the Franks similarly understand the religious nature of the jihad and what Jerusalem represented for the Muslims? The historian Benjamin Z. Kedar thinks not, pointing out that nowhere does William of Tyre consider the role of religion in the enemy's motivations. Significantly, Kedar also compares the account of the negotiations between Richard the Lionheart and Saladin as presented by Ibn Shaddād to that in the *Itinerarium*. Whereas Ibn Shaddād demonstrates that he is able to present both parties' attachment to Jerusalem and to understand the value of the True Cross for the Christians, the *Itinerarium* has Saladin say that he cannot accept the proposals from the English king because they are an outrage to "l'honor paganismi" (pagan honor).[19]

By Saladin's time, however, the image of the idolatrous pagan Muslim, still very widespread at the time of the First Crusade, had gradually been toned down in the West, at least in educated circles. Major efforts had been made to learn more about Islam, especially under the influence of Peter the Venerable, abbot of Cluny, to whom we are indebted for the first Latin translation of the Koran in 1142. Of course, until the end of the Middle Ages, literary and hagiographical works sometimes continued to assimilate the Saracen and the pagan, but these representations were perpetuating a tradition that no longer had any relationship to what was happening on the ground.[20] In Saladin's time, most Franks knew that Muslims were not idol worshippers, though a few zealous propagandists still sought to disseminate that idea. In addition, the ruling elite could not have been unaware of the importance the Muslims granted to Jerusalem, which was reaffirmed many times during negotiations. It is also unlikely that the Franks never inquired about their adversaries' reasons for fighting, though it is true that neither William of Tyre nor his successors, for reasons that escape us, ever found it useful to speak of them.

Designating the Enemy

The generic term most often used to designate the enemy was *Franj* (Franks), applied indiscriminately to all Westerners, whatever their place of origin. *Rūm*

(Romans) was reserved for the Byzantines. The Muslims knew, however, that the Franks comprised men of different backgrounds. Richard the Lionheart was called "the king of England" (malik Inkiltār), and Ibn al-Athīr, speaking of Frederick Barbarossa, referred to him as "king of the Germans" (malik al-Almān), "a race of Franks among the most numerous and the most valiant."[21] Similarly, Saladin's contemporaries knew fairly well the political situation of the Latin states, as attested by 'Imād al-Dīn's relatively faithful description of the crisis of succession to the throne of Jerusalem after the death of Baldwin IV.[22]

But beyond the objective perception of the adversary and his aims, the many qualifiers, epithets, and metaphors used to designate their foe reveal the image the Muslims wanted to spread of the Franks. These were most often animal metaphors. The Franks, intoxicated by fear and thirst, staggering like drunks, were contrasted to Saladin, "like the lion who moves through the desert, like the rising moon."[23] The Muslim is usually compared to the lion, king of beasts, while the Frank is by turns assimilated to the wolf, fox, hare, dragon, jackal, vulture, dog, ape, snake, pig, hyena, fly, and wasp. These are animals that cannot be trusted, that attack from behind—in the sura of Joseph, the wolf is the beast that supposedly devoured him (Koran 12:13, 14, and 17)—and which are held in contempt as venomous, scavenging, predatory, repellent, cunning, or quick to flee.[24]

Sometimes, however, the fervor of the Franks and their zeal for battle linked them to rams, eagles, lions or other big cats, which, when assaulted by the Muslims' arrows, rather quickly became hedgehogs, butterflies, fledglings, or sheep.[25] Similarly, descriptions of battles on sea depict the Muslim boats as thoroughbred horses, eagles "soaring over idolatry, as high as the Aquila constellation," or crows "cawing against the enemies of Allah," while enemy ships are called dragons, snakes, and scorpions.[26] The pinnacle of these animal metaphors is no doubt reached when 'Imād al-Dīn, to mark his contempt, compares the head of Reginald of Châtillon, awash in his own blood, to a frog leaping into a pond.[27]

The Franks are also often associated with darkness, night, garbage, and filth, in opposition to the light of dawn, daybreak, and purity of Islam.[28] An entire vocabulary with polemical religious connotations was used to spread that negative image of the Franks. 'Imād al-Dīn has no dearth of qualifiers in that register: seditious, polytheistic, impious, idolatrous, people of depravity, Sunday idlers, faithless demons or demons of error, infernal beings, maleficent counts, corrupt barons, bands gone astray, champions of deception, worshippers of human and divine nature who, upon death, will populate hell, in opposition to the martyred believers who populate paradise.[29] In a less lyrical style, al-Fāḍil calls the Franks associationists, infidels, the arrogant, companions of the left (as opposed to the Muslims, companions of the right), and people of the cross (as opposed to the people of the Koran). Balian of Ibelin is even called the "tyrant of their infidelity."[30]

It is an astonishing paradox: in the West, Islam was long accused of being merely idolatry—traces of this view can be found in chansons de geste, liturgical dramas, and Saint's Lives until the early Renaissance[31]—whereas in the East, the Muslims, deeply attached to God's oneness,[32] understood nothing of the doctrine of the Trinity (a single God in three persons) and accused the Christians of being "associationists," or worse, "polytheists." These accusations, disseminated from the seventh century on in the literature of the Muslim-Christian controversy, were still very widespread under Saladin's reign.

Mixed Feelings

Muslims had various reactions to the differences in culture, religion, and traditions. Astonishment often went hand in hand with incomprehension: "As for the infidels, . . . they left their country, . . . they fought army and subjects, believing it permissible to massacre human beings out of religious scruple: nothing is more peculiar than a massacre out of religious scruple! . . . They were rust-brown, as if fire had burned their austere faces, their blue eyes seemed to be made of the same metal as their sabers."[33]

Physically, the faces of the Franks, light-complected, blue-eyed, clean- or poorly shaven, never failed to surprise the Muslims and could even frighten small children. Once, when Saladin was in the company of his loved ones, one of his very young sons burst into tears at the mere sight of the Frankish messengers, with "their shaven chins and their cropped heads and the unusual clothes they were wearing."[34] It is amusing to observe that these differences in the treatment of facial and body hair elicited astonishment on both sides. Usāma Ibn Munqidh's well-known anecdote is a good illustration:

> We had with us a bath-keeper named Sālim, originally an inhabitant
> of al-Ma'arrah, who had charge of the bath of my father (may Allah's
> mercy rest upon his soul!). This man related the following story:

I once opened a bath in al-Ma'arrah in order to earn my living. To this bath there came a Frankish knight. The Franks disapprove of girding a cover around one's waist while in the bath. So this Frank stretched out his arm and pulled off my cover from my waist and threw it away. He looked and saw that I had recently shaved off my pubes. So he shouted, "Sālim!" As I drew near him he stretched his hand over my pubes and said, "Sālim, good! By the truth of my religion, do the same for me." Saying this, he lay on his back and I found that in that place the hair was like his beard. So I shaved it off. Then he passed his hand over the place and, finding it smooth, he said, "Sālim, by the truth of my religion, do the same to madame [al-dāma] (al-dāma in their language means the lady), referring to his wife. He then said to a servant of his, "Tell madame to come here." Accordingly the servant went and brought her and made her enter the bath. She also lay on her back. The knight repeated, "Do what thou hast done to me!" So I shaved all that hair while her husband was sitting looking at me. At last he thanked me and handed me the pay for my service.

Consider now this great contradiction! They have neither jealousy nor zeal but they have great courage, although courage is nothing but the product of zeal and of ambition to be above ill repute.[35]

A century later, the geographer and cosmographer al-Qazwīnī, on the basis of prior accounts, wrote: "[The Franks] shave their beards, and after shaving they sprout only a revolting stubble. One of them was asked as to the shaving of the beard, and he said, 'Hair is a superfluity. You remove it from your private parts, so why should we leave it on our faces?' "[36]

Among the reproaches made to the Franks, in addition to the lack of modesty already mentioned, was dirtiness. It is true that Easterners, like all the populations of the Mediterranean periphery, frequented the baths more than the residents of northern Europe, for reasons of climate as well as history. The use of baths, very widespread from the Roman era on, was even more necessary for Muslims, since ablutions before each of their five daily prayers were among their religious obligations. The major cities of Syria and Egypt were equipped with very elaborate water supply systems and included many public baths, which were important as a place to meet and talk. Upon Saladin's accession, Damascus and its outlying area had at least fifty-seven public baths, not to mention the private baths.[37] It is therefore not surprising that the Muslims were shocked by the Franks' lack of hygiene. But behind the observed reality, we must also seek an allegorical interpretation for Frankish "dirtiness." When Ibn Jubayr describes it in Acre, for example, he means to castigate the Franks' religious and moral "impurity," in opposition to the purity of Islam and of true believers. Pious Muslims considered the Franks' very presence in the region to be a source of filth, particularly since many mosques had been turned into churches. It was the violation of that sacred Muslim space that unavoidably made the Franks "polluters." That image of "impurity" linked to non-Muslim religious buildings, though certainly amplified by the Crusades, had existed for a long time: even in the tenth century, it had been the habit to designate, with a play on words, the Church of the Resurrection *(Qiyāma),* or of the Holy Sepulchre, by the name "Church of Garbage" *(Qumāma).*[38]

In terms of mores, the Muslims noted the special place of women in the Frankish world, even in the system of dynastic succession. Shocked by the quick remarriage of Princess Isabella to Henry of Champagne after Conrad's assassination—despite the fact that she was pregnant by Conrad—'Imād al-Dīn wondered: "Who then will claim the child? . . . Behold therefore the licentiousness of that band of miscreants!"[39] The Muslims' astonishment at the relative independence enjoyed by Western women, their freedom to appear in public, to move about, and to speak to men, was not new. That feeling, founded no doubt on a real difference in the condition of women in the East compared to the West, was nonetheless fostered by a few legends. In the tenth century, for example, Ibrāhīm ibn Ya'qūb mentions the existence of an island in the Western sea called the City of Women. Men had no power over the women who lived there, who rode horseback, fought in wars, possessed harems of male slaves, and killed their male children, keeping only the girls. The ancient myth of the Amazon women is of course recognizable here. Like the clichés of the Franks' bravery, coarseness, and dirtiness, the freedom of Western women corresponded in part to firmly rooted prejudices. Under such conditions, it is not so surprising to read Usāma's account denouncing the absence of jealousy on the part of Frankish husbands:

When I used to visit Nāblus, I always took lodging with a man named Mu'izz, whose home was a lodging house for the Moslems. The house had windows which opened to the road, and there stood opposite to it on the other side of the road a house belonging to a Frank who sold wine for the merchants. . . . One day this Frank went home and found a man with his wife in the same bed. He asked him, "What could have made thee enter into my wife's room?" The man replied, "I was tired, so I went in to rest." "But how," asked he, "didst thou get into my bed?" The other replied, "I found a bed that was spread, so I slept in it." But," said he, "my wife was sleeping together with thee!" The other replied, "Well, the bed is hers. How could I therefore have prevented her from using her own bed?" "By the truth of my religion," said the husband, "if thou shouldst do it again, thou and I would have a quarrel." Such was for the Frank the entire expression of his disapproval and the limit of his jealousy.[40]

Nor should we misunderstand 'Imād al-Dīn's notorious passage regarding the three hundred Frankish prostitutes who disembarked in the Frankish camp during the siege of Acre and deduce from it that fundamental differences existed between the East and the West.[41] The author pretends to believe that this is a Western custom encouraged by the church, but he was not unaware that prostitution was also widespread in Muslim countries. Whereas the Muslims took offense at the freedom granted Latin women, Jacques de Vitry, who had recently arrived in the East in 1217, was indignant to see that "Poulain" women (Eastern Franks were called "Poulains"), under the influence of Oriental mores, were kept cloistered at home.[42] Both sides undoubtedly had a tendency to generalize a few extreme cases. On one hand, the bishop of Acre's well-known hostility toward the Poulains likely impelled him to exaggerate now and again. On the other, the Muslims' discourse must be placed within the context of propaganda aiming to denigrate the Franks on every front: military, political, but also religious and moral.

The Muslims' view of the Frankish woman, however, cannot be reduced to that of hussy. The women who participated in battles, at the risk of being taken prisoner or killed on the battlefield, elicited not only astonishment but a hint of admiration: "Among the Franks there are lady knights who wear breastplates and helmets. In that male clothing, they leap into the fray, and these mistresses of the gynoecium conduct themselves like the stronger sex. In their eyes, that is an act of devotion, by virtue of which they believe they are assuring their salvation, and that is why they dedicate themselves to that life. . . . On battle days, these women can be seen advancing with the knights, whom they take as their example. They are as ruthless as the men despite the weakness of their sex. These women have no costume other than a coat of mail and are recognizable only when undressed and stripped bare; several of them were taken and sold as slaves."[43]

In the Muslim camp, examples of women warriors defending their fortresses, their families, or their honor were not unusual.[44] Some even came up with stratagems to entice the Franks and kill them. Usāma Ibn Munqidh speaks of a women living in Shayzar who had managed to bring home three Franks, whom she asked her neighbors to kill. The story does not say what means she used to attract them, but it is clear that the participation of Muslim women in battle was generally limited to a few ruses of that sort and to defensive actions during the siege of a city or fortress. As a general rule, they were not seen fighting alongside the men on the battlefield, and that is certainly why the presence of women in enemy ranks so surprised the Muslims.

In the tenth century, as I said, the Muslims saw the Franks as valorous warriors. That image was reinforced in the era of the Crusades. The Arab authors report on many occasions their endurance, their courage, and their capacity for resistance. Their assaults are compared to moving mountains, and their bravery is sometimes used by poets as a literary motif to accentuate Saladin's merit:

> They claim to be rich in bravery, but you are richer and more amply provided
>   with victories,
> That weapon betrayed them; they did not know how to use their spears or to
>   make their sabers ring out,
> And their impious gibberish gave way to silence when that bravery had
>   turned to cowardice.[45]

The Knights Templar and the Knights Hospitaller were particularly feared by their adversaries. "I will purify the earth of those two impure races," Saladin is reported to have said following the victory of Hattīn, before having all the prisoners belonging to those military orders executed, with the exception of the Grand Master of the Knights Templar, whom he hoped to exchange for a high ransom or a fortress.[46] That hatred was sometimes combined with a clear admiration for their bellicosity. Witness this exclamation by a thirteenth-century historian regarding the mamluk warriors who, in 1249, inflicted a bitter defeat on the Franks and took Louis IX prisoner: "It is they who were the Knights Templar of Islam!"[47] The Muslims also had respect for the sense of honor of the Knights Templar and for their steadfastness in keeping their word. During discussions about the exchange of prisoners after the fall of Acre in August 1191, for example, Saladin asked that the Knights Templar act as guarantors for the Franks' oath, "because they are sincere religious who respect their pledges." But the Knights Templar replied: "We will not take an oath or give any guarantee, for we fear the betrayal of our own people."[48] Those two sentences sum up fairly well the Muslims' mixed feelings about the Franks.

A few Frankish individuals similarly elicited varied reactions. We must of course read with a certain caution the reports that have come down to us, placing them within their original context. In 1174, for example, upon the death of King Amalric, "whose like for bravery and subtle cunning the Franks had not had since they appeared in Syria,"[49] Saladin sent a letter to his nephew Farrūkhshāh, in which he played on the king's name ("Murrī" in Arabic; *murr* means "bitter" in that language): "May God curse him, may he condemn him to torments like unto his name, may he cast him into the blazing fire reserved for wretched sinners."[50]

At the same time, he wrote a much more diplomatic letter of condolence to Baldwin IV, Amalric's son and successor:

> This news has afflicted the hearts of true friends, the announcement of his death, which we wish were false, that of the just, the most powerful king, to whom God dispensed the same blessings as to his fellows. . . . Our ambassador al-Ra'īs al-'Amīd Mukhtār al-Dīn . . . represents us, to present condolences and to describe the sadness that has seized us after our separation from that friend, and his death. . . .
>
> May [the king] know that we have the same dispositions toward him as toward his father: a sincere friendship, complete trust, an affection that has been established for life and for death, personal thoughts that fulfill all the obligations incumbent on them, despite religious differences.[51]

The Muslims often complained of what they called the disloyalty of the Franks, who did not respect their treaties. This comes through in certain letters sent to the caliph to obtain military aid.[52] And that is also what Saladin thought of Count Raymond III of Tripoli in 1183: "His insincere nature is known; he says what he does not do and promises what he does not perform."[53] The shift in political alliances changed the rules of the game, however. In 1187, at the time of his alliance with Saladin, Raymond was depicted by Ibn al-Athīr as a courageous individual of good counsel, and ʿImād al-Dīn even went so far as to say that Raymond would have converted to Islam had he not feared his coreligionists.[54] Even Raymond's return to the Franks' camp did not manage to efface completely that positive image.[55]

Raymond was a Frankish lord born in the East, one of those with whom the Muslims could interact more easily than they did with his coreligionists fresh off the boat from the West. Recall the well-known reflection of the Frankish chronicler Fulcher of Chartres (d. 1127) regarding the Eastern Franks called Poulains: "Westerners we were, and are become Easterners. The Roman and Frank of yesteryear, transplanted, has become a Galilean or a Palestinian. The man who lived in Rheims or Chartres finds himself a citizen of Tyre or Antioch."[56] And Usāma attests that the Franks who "have become acclimatized and have associated long with the Moslems" were much more pleasant to deal with than those who had just arrived, but he hastened to add that they were merely the exceptions.[57] Of these Eastern Franks, Saladin had a particular regard for Reginald of Sidon, who belonged to the Garnier family, one of the great houses of the kingdom of Jerusalem. Reginald spoke Arabic and took a keen interest in Muslim culture: "He was one of the Frankish nobles and one of their wise heads who knew Arabic and had some familiarity with histories and Ḥadīth collections. I heard that he kept a Muslim who read to him and explained things. He was a man of cautious deliberation. He came before the sultan and ate a meal with him. . . . [Once] agreement was given . . . he continued to frequent the sultan's presence, disputing with us about his religion while we argued for its falsity. He was an excellent conversationalist and cultured in his talk."[58]

Saladin was taken in by that climate of congeniality, which in reality concealed a stratagem: Reginald was seeking to gain some time to prevent his castle of Beaufort from falling into Muslim hands. According to ʿImād al-Dīn, Saladin's friendship kept him from heeding those who warned against Reginald, and it was only unwillingly that Saladin was obliged to face the facts. Confronted with what he considered a betrayal, the only thing he could do was to imprison Reginald in Damascus. But Saladin freed him a few months later in exchange for the surrender of the fortress. The information given by a Latin source, which says that Saladin returned half the seigneury of Sidon[59] to Reginald, is not confirmed by any Arab source and is probably legend. 'Imād al-Dīn remarks simply that Reginald, at the time of his release, was well treated by Saladin, an obvious sign of his warm feelings.[60] That no doubt explains why, in 1191, Reginald was chosen by Conrad of Montferrat as an emissary to conduct negotiations with Saladin.[61] During the same period, another Poulain, Humphrey IV of Toron, also a member of an important family of Frankish lords, served as messenger and interpreter to Richard the Lionheart in his negotiations with al-'Ādil.[62] Saladin had very different feelings about another Reginald, this one from the West, the sire of Châtillon-sur-Loing,[63] who in 1153 married Constance, princess of Antioch. He was held prisoner by the Muslims in Aleppo from 1160 to 1176. Then, thanks to his second marriage, he found himself in charge of the large principality of Transjordan. Few Franks elicited as much animosity and hatred among the Muslims as he did: "The prince of Kerak, Reginald, was the most treacherous and the most wicked of the Franks, the most greedy, the most bent on destroying and on doing evil, on breaking firm pledges and serious oaths, on going against his word and perjuring himself."[64]

The Arab authors point out that he was already in command of the army of the kingdom of Jerusalem in 1177, when a humiliating defeat was inflicted on Saladin near Ramla.[65] But above all, the Muslims blamed Reginald for the threat that, in 1182, he had brought to bear in the Red Sea on the holy cities of Mecca and Medina, and for his many broken pledges, the most grave of them being the attack on the caravan in 1187. Hence Saladin's oath to kill him with his own hands: "The sultan had vowed to spill his blood and had said: 'To be sure, I will see that he perishes as soon as I encounter him.' When Reginald was in his presence, Saladin had him sit next to the king [Guy], who was himself seated near the sultan. Saladin reproached Reginald for his treachery, reminded him of his misdeeds, and said to him: 'How many times have you sworn and violated your oaths, made pledges that you contravened, concluded a pact that you broke, accepted an accord that you rejected?' Reginald responded through the interpreter: 'Such is the custom of kings; I merely followed the beaten path.'"[66]

Other Frankish lords also provoked the Muslims' wrath. 'Imād al-Dīn's judgment of Conrad of Montferrat was unqualified: "Among the infidels, that man was one of the worst demons, a pernicious devil, one of the most cunning foxes, one of the most cruel wolves, an abject dog, a scourge, a calamity. It is for him and his ilk that hell was created."[67]

By contrast, Henry of Champagne was looked on kindly by Ibn al-Athīr, who describes him as a good, wise, and tolerant man, a friend to the Muslims: "After the king of England had departed, Count Henry sent to Saladin to win his sympathy and his regard and to ask him for a robe of honour. He said, 'You know that wearing a robe (qabā') and a tall bonnet (sharbūsh) we hold to be shameful, but I shall wear them from you out of love for you.' Saladin sent him a sumptuous honorific robe, with in particular a qabā' and a sharbūsh, and Henry wore them in Acre."[68]

Richard the Lionheart also enjoyed a certain esteem among the Muslims. Admired for his high rank, his courage, his political acumen, and his bellicosity, he was "wise and experienced in warfare," writes Ibn Shaddād. "An outstanding man of his time for bravery, cunning, steadfastness and endurance," adds Ibn al-Athīr.[69] We have already mentioned the good relations established between Richard and Saladin's brother al-'Ādil during the negotiations of 1191–1192.[70] The meetings often took place in a relaxed atmosphere and were accompanied by exchanges of gifts. In their messages, the two men called each other "my brother" or "my friend." During a discussion, the king of England even asked to hear a Muslim singer. The singer, who was brought in with her harp, delighted Richard.[71] Ibn Shaddād also says that the king maintained the best of relations with Saladin's emirs: "He had made friends with several of the elite mamlukes and had knighted some of them. He was on very good terms with them as they met with him on numerous occasions. He had also made friends with several of the emirs, such as Badr al-Dīn Dildirim."[72]

Others were harsher, however. Qādī al-Fādil never forgave Richard for the massacre of the Muslim prisoners of Acre, denounced his "perfidy," and did not believe that peace with him would be possible: "Those people make peace when they are weak, and denounce it when they become strong," he wrote.[73] Richard's reputation as a great warrior, it seems, won him a place in the popular tradition as the "villain" who incites fear: "King Richard's renown terrified the Saracens so much that when their children cried their mothers would scare them with the king of England and say, 'Be quiet for the king of England!' When a Saracen was riding and his mount stumbled at a shadow, he would say to him, 'Do you think the king of England is in that bush?' and if he brought his horse to water and it would not drink, he would say to it, 'Do you reckon the king of England is in the water?' "[74]

Over the years, then, the Muslims had gotten to know the Franks better. Those Muslims who remained in the Frankish territories encountered Franks on a daily basis. The peasants worked for them—as Ibn Jubayr points out (not without some bitterness), these peasants were somewhat better treated than those who lived in Muslim territory—and Christian and Muslim leaders often met for negotiations. The two groups were united by social relationships and sometimes even in friendship. There is nothing unusual about that within the context of prolonged occupation or colonization. The exchanges remained superficial, however: the language barrier was only rarely abolished, and the religious gulf especially seemed insurmountable. Since the political and the religious were intimately linked, to defend one's land was above all to defend one's religion and to affirm its supremacy over that of the adversary. Each side was convinced it possessed the truth and that the other could only be in error. At best the other could be tolerated, sometimes converted, but in no case could he be assimilated. Nor could one submit to his laws. That is what emerges from this story told by Usāma:

> In the army of King Fulk, son of Fulk, was a Frankish reverend knight who had just arrived from their land in order to make the holy pilgrimage and then return home. He was of my intimate fellowship and kept such constant company with me that he began to call me "my brother." Between us were mutual bonds of amity and friendship. When he resolved to return by sea to his homeland, he said to me:
>
>> My brother, I am leaving for my country and I want thee to send with me thy son (my son, who was then fourteen years old, was at that time in my company) to our country, where he can see the knights and learn wisdom and chivalry. When he returns, he will be like a wise man.
>
> Thus there fell upon my ears words which would never come out of the head of a sensible man; for even if my son were to be taken captive, his captivity could not bring him a worse misfortune than carrying him into the lands of the Franks. However, I said to the man:

By thy life, this has exactly been my idea. But the only thing that prevented me from carrying it out was the fact that his grandmother, my mother, is so fond of him and did not this time let him come out with me until she exacted an oath from me to the effect that I would return him to her.

Thereupon he asked, "Is thy mother still alive?" "Yes." I replied. "Well," said he, "disobey her not."[75]

IV

In Everyday Life

18

Between Image and Reality

Barring any unexpected discovery, Saladin will remain for us a "faceless king."[1] Thus far, no known source provides us with a physical description of the man, and all the representations we have of him were done long after he died. It must be said that his contemporaries took little interest in the art of the portrait, in literature or in visual art. Illuminations were rare in Arabic manuscripts prior to the thirteenth century, and they did not claim to be a faithful reflection of reality. As for the historical texts, authors generally recorded in them only an individual's unusual characteristics: light-colored hair, blue eyes, an unusual skin color, the nakedness of a clean-shaven face (it was uncommon for a man not to wear a beard), a height below or above average, a notable defect. We know, for example, that Nūr al-Dīn had very dark skin and that al-Fāḍil was short, sickly, and hunchbacked. But Saladin was not distinguished by any particular physical feature. The absence of description that attests to that fact leaves us in ignorance about what made him unique. His destiny leads us to suppose that he had a presence, a vivacity, charisma. Any other hypothesis is a product of the imagination.

His daily life is also very shrouded. The many sources that have come down to us are rich in military and political information. They also give us a great deal of information about institutions, cities, monuments, and cultural and religious life, but speak more often of the elites than of the lower classes, of urban more than rural activities, of men more than women and children, of major events more than everyday life. Saladin's biographers dwell on descriptions of him performing his religious and military duties. They tell us very little about his family life, his leisure activities, his emotions. It is nevertheless possible to collect here and there information that, when assembled, ultimately plumbs part of the mystery of the man Saladin.

Prayers and Devotion

What value are we to grant to Saladin's religious gestures? Do they attest to a profound conviction, or were they intended only to construct an image? It is once again difficult to reply to these questions because of the very nature of our sources (panegyric) but also because of the inextricable connections prevailing between religion and politics. Even today, when a head of state takes an oath on the Bible or the Koran, who could distinguish personal conviction from political opportunism intended to reassure the population and to persuade them that he is protecting the values he says he is ready to defend?

Over the course of his reign, Saladin performed many acts of piety, accompanied by all the publicity needed to win the trust of religious circles. He seems to have had a real interest in religious science, which he studied from his youth. He could read and write, and in Egypt took courses in language and religious science from several great teachers. Most of his letters were composed by his secretaries, but he readily took up the pen to correspond with his family and loved ones.[2] He knew the Koran by heart and liked to hear it recited, requiring that it always be done by the best imams. And when his busy days left him the time, he summoned the major specialists on hadith to listen to them report the traditions of the Prophet. His sons and his most faithful mamluks were invited to these sessions. His entourage said of him that he had an honest and pure faith, based on "proof by means of study with the leading men of religious learning and eminent jurisconsults. He understood of that what one needs to understand, such that, when disputation occurred in his presence, he could contribute excellent comments, even if they were not in the language of learned specialists."[3]

Saladin, like his father, displayed the greatest respect for the ulemas. He never failed to engage in discussions with scholars of renown, whatever their legal school, when they crossed his path. In Jerusalem in 1189, he met the great Hanbalite jurist al-Nāsih Ibn al-Hanbalī al-Shīrāzī al-Dimashqī, who had traveled the Islamic countries in quest of knowledge. Saladin asked him, among other things, what he thought about people dyeing their hair black. Did the question have personal ramifications? That is difficult to ascertain. What we do know, however, is that the jurist replied that such a practice was reprehensible.[4]

When a sheikh did not wish to travel or was unable to do so, Saladin visited him to benefit from his teachings, sometimes taking one or several of his sons. In Alexandria in 1177, for example, he dedicated himself for three full days to listening to the hadith from the mouth of the famous traditionist Abū l-Tāhir al-Silafī. Saladin himself then transmitted these hadith, referring to the sheikh's teaching.[5] In 1182, also in Alexandria, he studied, under the jurist Abū Tāhir Ibn 'Awf, the chief legal work (Kitāb al-Muwatta') by Mālik ibn Anas, founder of the Malekite school.[6] In 1188, returning from his campaign in northern Syria, he insisted on paying a visit to an ascetic living as a recluse in a village; then, at the invitation of his nephew Taqī al-Dīn, he went to attend a religious recital by Sufis in Hama.[7]

At home, he enjoyed reading the collections of hadith that Ibn Shaddād brought to him. He also liked to participate in the lively discussions of jurists and, according to 'Imād al-Dīn, sometimes proved to be more learned than the jurisconsults present.[8] During his serious illness in 1186 and throughout his convalescence in Damascus, he took pleasure in following the debates of the ulemas, though he complained of the incessant quarrels among them.[9] Even in wartime, he habitually consulted works of religious science. In the midst of his campaign against the Franks, for example, he found time to read a work by the Shafite jurist Sulaym al-Rāzi on the sources of Muslim law, with his friend Ibn Shaddād. Another time, he asked that a collection of hadith be recited in his presence for the cavalrymen, mounted and ready to fight.

Ibn Shaddād also reports that Saladin scrupulously observed his duties as a believer. In the first place, he prayed five times a day, wherever he happened to be, at home, traveling, or on a military campaign, and however tired he may have been. He never missed the dawn prayer, even after a sleepless night, and when he was ill even mustered his last bit of strength to pray once again and without fail: "I saw him . . . standing to pray during his fatal illness and he only missed prayers during the three days when his mind wandered. If ever prayer time found him travelling, he would dismount and pray."[10]

Let us look beyond the panegyric discourse, but without attempting to pronounce on the question of his sincerity. It is clear that Saladin wanted to present himself as a sovereign respectful of religious duties. He liked to say his prayers in a group and had an imam in his service lead them. When the imam was absent, 'Imād al-Dīn sometimes replaced him. In addition to the five obligatory daily prayers, Saladin occasionally also said optional prayers and did not fail to invoke God every time he woke up during the night. Such devotion and fervor led Ibn Shaddād to say that his faith and trust in God were admirable.[11]

As much as possible, Saladin observed the Ramadan fast. If he happened to be prevented by the jihad or illness, at his request al-Fāḍil or Ibn Shaddād kept count of the days Saladin missed so that he could make them up, in conformity with Muslim law. Having signed the truce with the Franks a few weeks before his death, Saladin thus made up about thirty days of fasting, against the advice of his doctor, who was worried about his health. As for alms, Ibn Shaddād points out that, on the eve of his death, Saladin was not subject to them because his treasury contained only forty-odd dirhams and a single gold coin. He possessed nothing else, "no property, no house, no estate, no orchard, no village, no farm, not a single item of property of any sort."[12] That remark was undoubtedly true, but it was intended to emphasize that the sultan had sacrificed everything, including his own property, on behalf of the holy war.

And yet Saladin never completed the pilgrimage to Mecca, unlike his father, Ayyūb, and his uncle Shīrkūh, each of whom led the pilgrimage caravan departing from Damascus, one in 1157 and the other in 1160. His loyal adviser al-Fāḍil himself went twice to Mecca, in 1179 and 1180. The fact that Saladin did not perform his duty of pilgrimage is less surprising than it appears at first glance. He was far from the only ruler in that situation. Al-Fāḍil quite rightly notes that no caliph of Baghdad had been able to make his pilgrimage since Caliph Hārūn al-Rashīd (r. 786–809).[13] Although many historians have granted credence to the testimony of two fifteenth-century authors, Taqī al-Dīn al-Fāsī and al-Maqrīzī, who claim that Nūr al-Dīn performed his pilgrimage in 1161, it is very likely that he never made one either.[14] None of his contemporaries or panegyrists, however eager to describe him in his best light, makes the slightest allusion to it. In the long biography his friend Ibn 'Asākir devoted to him, the author goes on at length about Nūr al-Dīn's qualities as a devout Muslim but observes a discreet silence regarding any journey to Mecca. Conversely, he emphasizes the blessings Nūr al-Dīn showered on the residents of the holy sites of Islam and their rulers, as if seeking to minimize the oversight of the pilgrimage, to consign it to oblivion. That oversight can be explained by the fact that such a pilgrimage involved an absence of several months, which was not without risks for sovereigns, whose power was often fragile and contested.

In reality, it was only after he took power in Egypt that Saladin seems to have become truly concerned with his religious duties and to have become aware of the importance of cultivating his image as a devout sovereign, a means of asserting his authority. But because his battles—first to establish his power, then to reconquer the Frankish states—were becoming increasingly frequent, he no longer really had the possibility of absenting himself for three to four months. The length of the journey, even for those who left from Egypt—which was closer to the Hejaz—was commensurate with the difficulties encountered on the way. It took the traveler Ibn Jubayr almost three months to get from Cairo to Mecca. The most difficult part was not going up the Nile by boat to Qūs in Upper Egypt. After that, it was necessary to prepare carefully to cross the desert, to arrive at the port of 'Aydhāb, and then to face the Red Sea. The waters were infested with pirates, buffeted by unpredictable winds, and riddled with reefs. True, it took al-Fāḍil only slightly more than a month and a half to return to Cairo from Mecca during his second pilgrimage in 1180. But several times along the way, he thought he was going to die:

> We left Mecca—may God bring it glory—on the 25th day of Dhū
> al-Hijja. There were swarms of corrupt people at that time. . . . We
> arrived in Jedda on Sunday, the 27th day of Dhū al-Hijja, and took
> to sea on Tuesday the 29th. We spent Wednesday and Thursday
> night there. The wind blew us onto an island near Yemen called
> Dabādib, and one of those two nights was extremely trying. I swear
> by God, on that night, the hair on the heads of several of our com-
> panions turned white. They were overcome with despair, wishing
> to be done with it all and to shorten the time of their suffering.
> They believed they were doomed and reproached themselves, then
> used as an excuse God's decrees, against which no ruse is possible.
> We displayed patience until God—praise be to him—delivered us.
> We disembarked in a desert without potable water or camels. We
> appealed to the Beja people[15] who live on that coast, and they pro-
> vided us with emaciated camels, which they rented to us for an

exorbitant price. We mounted them and arrived in 'Aydhāb ten days later, worn out from weakness, fatigue, hunger, and thirst, since we were many and our provisions meager. Our desert crossing from 'Aydhāb to Aswān was the most difficult of all the routes we had taken and of all the distances we had traveled, since we found water only twice in eleven days. Our troubles could not have been greater and our woes as regards thirst were enormous. The difficulties are much greater in that desert than in the Syrian desert, since the route, deep-cut between two mountains, resembles a narrow and constricted path. The heat of the sun is very strong there, and between these two mountains even an imminent promise looks far away. But God granted us His kindness until our arrival in Cairo on the 17th day of Safar.[16]

In 1179, when al-Fāḍil was preparing to make his own pilgrimage, Saladin expressed his regret that he could not accompany him. Al-Fāḍil replied that the only thing that counted was the sincere intention to perform his religious duty, since God knew that the jihad and the insecurity of his territory did not allow Saladin to go.[17] In early summer 1180, after the truce was concluded with the Franks, Saladin again spoke of the pilgrimage to al-Fāḍil, who expressed his hope to the caliph of Baghdad's ambassador to finally see Saladin go on pilgrimage.[18] Having returned to Egypt on January 1, 1181, Saladin had three months available to go to Mecca, the pilgrimage being in the second half of April that year. Did he really think seriously about it? He says so in a letter to the caliph. To the governors of Yemen, al-'Ādil announced his brother's imminent departure, once the Ramadan fast was completed (January 19–February 17, 1181), and asked them to send money and provisions to the holy cities in anticipation of the sultan's arrival. Was it because of the persisting tensions with the Franks—battles resumed in Syria in May—that this plan was not realized? Yet Saladin did not leave Egypt until May to go to Damascus, where he launched new raids south of Lake Tiberias.[19] During the next ten years, the opportunity to go never again arose. His campaigns in northern Syria and in al-Jazīra, then the fighting against the Franks, absorbed him without letup until the truce with Richard the Lionheart was signed in 1192. Then the dream of pilgrimage once more became a plan, preparations for which were undertaken. But once again, fate decided otherwise: "He always intended and planned [to take the pilgrimage], especially in the year of his death. He confirmed his determination to perform it and he ordered preparations to be made. Provisions were got ready and all that remained was to set out. However, he was prevented because of lack of time and the unavailability of what was proper for such a person. He therefore put it off till the next year, but God decreed what He decreed. Everyone, high and low, knew about this."[20]

Other motives undoubtedly played a role in the cancellation of the journey. The tension between Saladin and the caliph of Baghdad was very strong at the time. In response to an embassy sent by the caliph to Damascus, Saladin's advisers recommended caution: "Write therefore to the Commander of Believers to alert him of your pilgrimage and inform him of your itinerary, so that exploits of which you would be innocent are not attributed to you, and so that everyone will know that your aim is very clear as to its realization."[21]

Again that year, in fact, the leader of the Iraqi pilgrimage was Emir Tāshtegin—the same one who was responsible in 1188 for the death of Shams al-Dīn Ibn al-Muqaddam, the leader of the Syrian pilgrimage and a close friend of Saladin's. In view of that conflict, Saladin's pilgrimage plan would not be easy to realize. Would he not be suspected of wanting to seek revenge? Al-Fādil, in any case, thought that the moment was poorly chosen. He feared that Saladin would be accused of wanting to disrupt the pilgrimage. In addition, the Franks were still occupying the coast and had not given up on Jerusalem, and the Muslims doubted that the Franks were ready to respect the treaty they had just signed: "If you set out on a journey, leaving these regions in the disorder they are in, you will be unable to tighten them once they have lost their torsion; likewise for those fortresses on the borders. Keeping them is of the utmost importance. Do not have any illusions about the armistice convention, for those men are on the lookout for an opportunity to display their might. Treachery is a habit with them; they are inspired by iniquity in full measure."[22]

To better persuade Saladin, al-Fādil pointed out that the best way to seek God's favor was to fight against injustice. That idea of a "spiritual" pilgrimage in place of the actual pilgrimage was fairly widespread in mystical circles. "There are people who circumambulate the Kaaba not with their limbs of flesh but around God, who has exempted them from the Haram [Mecca]," wrote the mystic theologian al-Hallāj in the early tenth century.[23] And in the region of Damascus, the peasants were suffering greatly from the disorder, violence, and oppression imposed on them by the holders of iqtā's. In addition, the treasury was empty. In the eyes of the head of the Egyptian administration, the most urgent tasks were to reestablish sources of revenue and defend the border cities of Islam. Saladin, not without regret, yielded to these arguments; he decided to put off his departure and to send an ambassador to the caliph of Baghdad.[24] In early 1193, he welcomed in person the pilgrims returning from Mecca to Damascus, openly displaying his sorrow that he had been unable to be among them.[25] The sincerity of his desire for pilgrimage is also perceptible in an extraordinary document found in the archives of the Damascus mosque. It is a certificate of pilgrimage attesting that a Sufi leader named 'Abd al-'Azīz al-Qushayrī completed the lesser pilgrimage ('umra) on Saladin's behalf. The document is not dated, but it must have been drawn up during Saladin's lifetime, as attested by the formula a'azza Allāh ansārahu (may God strengthen his defenders) following his name. It was relatively common at that time for a Muslim unable to make the pilgrimage to pay one of his coreligionists to do so in his place. Sometimes the pilgrimage was even made in the name of a deceased person, to attract divine favor toward him.[26]

If all the praise devoted to Saladin's piety had come solely from his panegyrists 'Imād al-Dīn and Ibn Shaddād, it might be legitimately concluded that the praise was intended for propaganda purposes alone. But that is not the case. It is also found in the writings of several other contemporary authors. The great scholar 'Abd al-Latīf al-Baghdādī, who met Saladin in Jerusalem in the last years of his reign, depicts him as a ruler who inspired respect and love, and who liked to surround himself with ulemas and to participate in their discussions.[27] Ibn Jubayr is no less laudatory when he describes the sultan's actions on behalf of pilgrims, strangers, the devout, and of pious and charitable institutions: "The memorable acts of the Sultan, his efforts for justice, and his stands in defence of Islamic lands are too numerous to count," he adds.[28] We cannot help but think that, beyond the conventional discourse on the ideal sovereign, all this praise had a basis in truth. The devout man and the astute politician were ultimately indistinguishable.

War and Hunting

Saladin spent much of his life on military campaigns. He was an excellent army chief and a true leader of men, always ready to take command of the troops. Before battles, he personally inspected the war machines. During operations, his energy seems to have been inexhaustible. By day, he could be seen leading his army, usually surrounded by his personal guard, but sometimes having at his side only one or two varlets responsible for leading his spare mounts. The first to fight, he was also the last to leave the battlefield, exhorting his men to continue the battle when discouragement loomed. With cries of "Forward! For Islam and the army of the true faith!" he galvanized even the most reluctant. In 1179, during the siege of Bayt al-Ahzān, he promised a dinar to anyone who would help put out the fire in the galleries dug under the wall.[29] It sometimes happened that he became so absorbed in the action that he forgot to eat and drink, to the great despair of his doctors, who attempted to get him at least to take the potions he had been prescribed. One day when Saladin was ill, he told 'Imād al-Dīn, who had suggested that for once the sultan let his troops do battle without him, "The army will act only if I ride with them, only if I watch and observe their actions." And 'Imād al-Dīn adds: "He spoke the truth, for he knew his men very well; in fact, led by him, they generously spilled their blood, plunged into the depths of the ocean of war, and broadened the narrow battlefield to discomfit the enemy."[30]

At night in his tent, he slept only a few hours and devoted the rest of his time to dictating letters and to praying. A few in his close circle were sometimes invited to share his meals. As a true war leader, he personally passed in review the troops sent as reinforcements, offered them a welcoming meal and gifts, and supervised them as they set up camp.[31]

When he took Jerusalem, he also spared no effort in restoring the fortifications. He sent for stonecutters from Mosul and had sharp steel picks manufactured, setting an example by personally transporting stones needed for the construction.[32] 'Abd al-Latīf al-Baghdādī's remarks are once more enlightening: "He concerned himself with the building of the rampart and the digging of the moat. He took charge of them personally and transported the stones on his shoulder. Everyone imitated him, rich and poor, robust and weak, even the secretary al-'Imād and Qādī al-Fādil. To achieve this, he was on horseback before dawn and until noon. He then returned home to eat and rest. He mounted his horse again in the afternoon and came back only in the evening. He later spent the major part of the night planning what he would do the next day."[33]

Between wars, Saladin also liked hunting, a sport highly valued by emirs and princes at the time. It had the triple advantage of offering those who practiced it a leisure activity, an equestrian exercise adapted to military activities, and training in courage. What kind of prey did they hunt at the time? All, or almost all: partridges, francolins, quail, cranes, ring doves, wild pigeons, bustards, hares, boars, gazelles, roe deer, onagers, and lions, all aptly described in the scenes of hunting written by Usāma Ibn Munqidh.[34] Saladin went hunting every time he had the chance. He found a great deal of pleasure and relaxation in the activity. ʿImād al-Dīn notes that he would return from the hunt, "his face gleaming with joy."[35] In 1178, while besieging the city of Baalbek, where Emir Ibn al-Muqaddam had rebelled, Saladin went hunting every morning. During the long siege of Acre in 1190, the Franks took advantage of one of his hunting parties to attack the Muslim camp.[36] During the rare months of rest that he granted himself during his reign, and up to the eve of his death, he hunted a great deal in the region of Damascus in the company of his close circle.

Like most of his contemporaries, Saladin particularly enjoyed falconry. ʿImād al-Dīn asked him one day if Saladin would do him the favor of giving him one of the sultan's peregrine falcons, which was reputed for its prowess. Saladin told him: "You're made for the pen and for administrative offices [dīwān], what need do you have for goshawks and falcons?" ʿImād al-Dīn jokingly replied, "Then let it be mine, and all the game it captures with my master will belong to me." Saladin agreed, and the next morning sent his secretary the seventeen birds the falcon had taken in a single hunt. That falcon remained ʿImād al-Dīn's property for five or six years, and every time Saladin took it hunting, the game was brought back to his secretary.[37]

Polo was another equestrian exercise of which Saladin was very fond, as his father had been. Nūr al-Dīn also often engaged in it, even at night by torchlight.[38] Most of the major Syrian and Iraqi cities were equipped with hippodromes, in which princes and their emirs engaged in their favorite sport. These same hippodromes were also used for parades and more military exercises. Foreign embassies sometimes employed them as places to set up their camps, and the Muslims assembled troops there before battle. Even during his military campaigns, Saladin liked to indulge in a few moments of relaxation playing polo, as he did in Harrān in 1185, before going to lay siege to Mosul.[39] Ibn Jubayr tells us that Saladin's sons also played more than one sport. They trained every evening in archery, equestrian exercises, and polo.[40]

Among His Friends and Loved Ones

Saladin also found relaxation among his friends and family. With them, he liked to listen to songs, play chess, and hear tales of the world's wonders and curiosities. His general culture allowed him to hold enjoyable conversations, during which, as Ibn Shaddād tells us, he always paid attention to his interlocutors and did not much like to speak ill of people.[41] When he wanted to bring these gatherings to an end, he simply stood up and went off to pray. Often at the end of the day, he sent for 'Imād al-Dīn, to whom he dictated letters, which his secretary then wrote up during the night, so that he could present them to the sultan in the early morning.

Saladin very much liked poetry and history. 'Imād al-Dīn portrays him in Cairo in 1177, visiting the pyramids of Giza and discussing their history by moonlight.[42] The sultan liked to hear poetry recited and wrote a little of his own from time to time. Among his favorite collections was one by Usāma Ibn Munqidh, whose son, Murhaf, had given Saladin a copy.[43] The sultan's victories were celebrated in verse, which the poets of his court came to declaim in his presence. Some sent their poems to him through his entourage, as, for example, the Egyptian poet Ibn Sanā al-Mulk, a great friend and admirer of Qāḍī al-Fāḍil. That poet's writings in honor of Saladin exalted the glorious defender of Islam, inspired by God:

I do not know for what victory you must be congratulated, O you who
  provided Islam with what it desired. . . .
You took possession of paradise, palace by palace, in conquering Syria
  fortress by fortress,
Islam spread its blessings on all creatures, but it is you who glorified it. . . .
You have a right to praise that rises higher than the heavens and to a glory
  erected above spears. . . .
You bore the ordeals of war, waged for the love of God; must not the lover
  always suffer ordeals?
You stood erect in the darkness of battle, shining like the moon, as the moon
  rose slowly in the night.
You never showed yourself in battle without looking, O Yūsūf, as handsome
  as Joseph. . . .
You possess the lands of sunrise and sunset, you dominate the horizons, the
  plains, and the steppes;
No description can attain the height of your grandeur: what word to use,
  what idea to express?
God said: Obey him. We have heard His call and have obeyed.[44]

Poetry sessions were not devoted exclusively to heaping laurels on the sultan; they could also turn toward amusement or jesting. Once, for example, 'Imād al-Dīn arranged for a poem containing Persian and Arabic words intermixed to be read aloud before the sultan, which made the audience laugh a great deal.[45] As usual, Saladin generously compensated the poet.

Not only panegyrists but also satirists sometimes let their ink flow, and they displayed surprising freedom in both tone and content. Satirical poetry (hijā') was widespread in the Middle East, from pre-Islamic times onward. Most often, it took as its target the adversary's honor, seeking above all to disconcert or humiliate him. The Prophet, himself a victim of such poetry, strongly encouraged poets to take aim at unbelievers. He said that the shots they fired did more harm than real arrows. The prevalence of smutty hijā's, which emerged in the eighth century, dropped appreciably in the following one—even as smut was introduced into prose—then enjoyed another boom in the tenth. The most widespread themes were avarice, narrow-mindedness, incompetence, humble birth, homosexuality, and any form of unbridled sexuality.[46]

Two men in Saladin's court distinguished themselves in that literary genre. Without ever attacking the sultan directly, they aimed their assaults at his closest circle. The first of these poets was al-Wahrānī. A native of Oran, he lived for a time at Saladin's court in Egypt, before moving to Damascus, where he died in 1179. He was noted for his letters, histories (maqāmāt), and accounts of dreams that violently satirized his enemies, some of them highly placed at the Ayyubid court. In particular, he attacked 'Imād al-Dīn, mocking his supposed homosexual proclivities. But that was not all—far from it. Al-Wahrānī's writings include descriptions of orgies at which people drink wine from singers' navels, while the host runs stark naked after his guests, barking like a dog. It was also al-Wahrānī who attacked Ibn Abī 'Asrūn, chief qāḍī of Damascus, whom he accused of heresy, among other things. He also castigated the avarice, incompetence, and stupidity of the chief qāḍī of Cairo, Sadr al-Dīn Ibn Durbās. He reproached that qāḍī for having named, in the localities of Egypt, Kurdish qāḍīs—donkey and cattle thieves—and he behaved very rudely toward Saladin's nephew Taqī al-Dīn 'Umar. Rather than go on jihad, al-Wahrānī told Taqī al-Dīn in substance, remain in the company of the courtesans of Damascus, Mosul, or Aleppo, and place your forgiveness in the hands of God. He went so far in his provocations that Saladin ultimately accused him of heresy. The satirist fiercely defended himself, claiming that he scrupulously respected all his duties as a believer, to which the sultan replied: "Even if I saw you walk on water, I could not see you as anything but a heretic." Through al-Wahrānī's grievances (he complained of having been dispossessed of the things Saladin had given him), the whole milieu of courtiers comes into view: they might enjoy the sultan's favors one day and then lose them the next. Never safe from exile or the seizure of their property, courtiers had to be adroit to maintain their position, to keep their possessions and, in the absence of the sultan's direct protection, to remain well integrated within his close circle.[47]

The Damascene poet Ibn 'Unayn went even further than al-Wahrānī.[48] In a poem titled *Miqrād al-a'rād* (Scissors of honor), he began by mocking the vanity of Saladin's doctors, al-Muwaffaq Ibn al-Mutrān and al-Rahbī. Ibn al-Mutrān, who hated him and urged the sultan to exile him, was one of Ibn 'Unayn's favorite targets. The poet accused him of being sexually attracted to 'Umar, a handsome young man who followed him everywhere. He could not find words harsh enough for someone "who claims that, by virtue of his wisdom, he had learned the art of medicine from Hippocrates, even though he is the most vile of those who tread this earth and the one who most merits curses and insults. . . . His existence itself is a satire of existence."[49] Qādī Ibn Abī 'Asrūn and al-Dawla'ī, preacher in the Great Mosque of Damascus, were also subjected to abuse. Al-Dawla'ī was accused of leading prayer in a state of ritual impurity, of exhausting his audience with his interminable sermons until they fled, and, even worse, of bringing bad luck to those in attendance.[50] Saladin's Egyptian companions, who had followed him to Damascus, were compared to their former black enemies: "If I were black with a head like an elephant, bulky forearms and a huge penis, then you would see to my needs, but as it is, I am white."[51] Nor was the family of the great traditionist Ibn 'Asākir spared. His nephew Tāj al-Umanā'—in charge for a time of the *dīwān* of the army—was nicknamed *kharā bi-dibs* (excrement with *dibs*) by Ibn 'Unayn, who was careful to explain that the *dibs* (a sort of syrup obtained from grape or date juice) was only an ornament. He took humiliation to the extreme by mocking his target's name: since Ibn 'Asākir literally means "Son of the Armies," the satirist suggested that any soldier could be his father.[52] But it may have been al-Fādil who had to suffer the most virulence from Ibn 'Unayn, who called him "the hunchback" and compared his head to a rat coming out of its hole. He accused al-Fādil of feigning chastity and fear of God, while thinking only of fornicating with his black male slaves: "His prostrations extend into the dark of night, only so that his black slaves will bend over him. . . . Death to the man who said that the hump on his back is a pregnancy imputable to his slaves." 'Ibn 'Unayn was merciless toward al-Fādil, even accusing him of fornicating with dogs.[53] Saladin finally lost patience with this poet, who dared write, "Our sultan is crippled, his secretary bleary-eyed, and his vizier hunchbacked."[54] He ordered the exile of Ibn 'Unayn, who was not yet thirty years old. The poet then composed these two lines: "Why have you banished an honest man who never committed a crime, who never stole? Expel the *muwazzin* [muezzin] from your country, if all are to be expelled who speak the truth."[55]

After traveling widely, from Azerbaijan to Transoxiana, Ibn 'Unayn stayed for a time at the court of Saladin's brother Tughtegin in Yemen. After Saladin's death, the poet returned to Egypt, then to Syria, where he was once again honored. He became vizier to al-Mu'azzam, the Ayyubid prince of Damascus, then to his son al-Nāsir Dā'ūd. It was there in his native city that he died in early 1232.

Little is known, unfortunately, about Saladin's private life and his relationships with women. In 1176 he married Nūr al-Dīn's widow, 'Ismat al-Dīn, in Damascus. The marriage was undoubtedly political—Saladin used his predecessor's legacy to his advantage and placed himself within his lineage—but came about with the princess's agreement and turned out to be very happy. 'Ismat al-Dīn was the daughter of Unur, the former emir of Damascus. She must have been over forty at the time of her union to Saladin (she had married Nūr al-Dīn in 1147) and produced no children with her second husband, who, it seems, was very much in love with her. A devout and generous wife known for her many alms, she founded an establishment for Sufis in Damascus (outside the ramparts, southwest of the citadel), as well as a Hanafite madrasa, to which she allotted many *waqfs*. In early 1186, while he was ill in Harrān, Saladin wrote her long letters every day. He did not know that his wife was no longer among the living: 'Ismat al-Dīn died in Damascus on January 27 that same year. At al-Fādil's request, 'Imād al-Dīn, who was at Saladin's bedside, had taken care to spare the sultan the shock of that sad news, censoring all the letters sent to him. Saladin therefore learned of his wife's death only in March. She was buried in Damascus in the mausoleum that she herself had ordered built on Mount Qāsiyūn.[56]

Saladin's two sisters also played an important role in the religious life of Damascus. After the death of her first husband, the elder one married her cousin from Homs. After completing her pilgrimage in 1187, she devoted herself entirely to works of charity during her long widowhood. She founded a *khānqāh* (institution for Sufis) and two madrasas in Damascus: one outside the walls on Mount Qāsiyūn, where she would be buried; the other inside, at her home, which was converted into a madrasa after her death in 1220.[57] Saladin's younger sister also survived her two husbands. She founded a Hanbalite madrasa outside Damascus, where she was buried after a life spanning more than eighty years.[58]

Saladin had no wives other than 'Ismat al-Dīn, but he had many concubines. Like every ruler of that time, he was anxious to assure his dynasty and quickly had to produce a large male lineage, despite a high infant mortality rate. Very little is known about his concubines, except that there were probably more than ten, and that they produced at least twenty-four children, six of whom died in infancy. Only the women who gave birth to at least one of Saladin's sons are mentioned in the sources. Two had three sons apiece, and three others produced two each. Five or six concubines had one son apiece. When a slave concubine gave birth to a son, she was immediately emancipated, in conformity with Muslim law. Saladin sometimes gave her hand in marriage to someone in his close circle, leaving her the enjoyment of her possessions and revenue.[59] He also oversaw the religious education of all these women. The sheikh who taught them the traditions of the Prophet was not allowed to see them and spoke to them from behind a curtain.[60] Concubines lived in Cairo or in Damascus, depending on the era and the individual case. In Harrān in 1186, the sultan summoned one of them to his bedside with her two sons, Tūrānshāh and Malikshāh, and had a permanent residence equipped with a bath built for them.[61] It is not known which of his concubines was his favorite, but we do know with certainty that Saladin lived surrounded by women, who were also the ones who took care of him and watched over him until his final moments.[62]

The father of many children—seventeen sons and one daughter, not counting those who died in infancy—Saladin was assured of heirs, to say the least. Whereas he and his brothers were given names drawn from Arabic, Persian, and Turkish cultures, those he gave to his sons were often inspired by the Koran: Ayyūb (Job), Ishāq (Isaac), Ya'qūb (Jacob), Mūsā (Moses), al-Khadir,[63] Dā'ūd (David), Ismā'īl (Ismail). It is unlikely that these names from the biblical tradition were chosen at random. They reflected Saladin's overt desire to use the sacred text of Islam as his point of reference. They also evoked the connections his panegyrists readily made in comparing him to Solomon, father of David, and to Joseph, son of Jacob and grandson of Job. The names of some of Saladin's other sons referred rather to the Prophet and his companions: Muhammad and

Ahmad, ʿAlī, Hasan, ʿUthmān, Marwān. Others recalled the Persian and Turkish influence on Saladin in his youth: Shādhī and Tūrānshāh, therefore, honored the memory of his grandfather and of the elder brother who had died in 1180, whereas Malikshāh, Masʿūd, and Ghāzī were common names in the genealogical trees of the Turkish dynasties.[64]

Absorbed by his many campaigns, Saladin had little time to devote to his young children, but he took great pleasure in the rare moments he spent in their company. One anecdote portrays him as a protective and affectionate father. The scene took place shortly before his death: One of his young sons, seated on his knees, had begun to cry at the sight of a Frankish messenger. Without even taking the time to hear what the Frank had to tell him, Saladin immediately ordered him to leave.[65] When he was away from his children, Saladin did not forget them: al-Fāḍil never failed to give him news of them and to sing their praises.[66] Similarly, Ibn Shaddād reports that he consented to separate from them only to wage jihad and to serve God. Tutors were responsible for the children's education,[67] but when their father was nearby in Cairo or Damascus, he personally taught them the essential principles of the Asharite doctrine, from the manual that Sheikh Quṭb al-Dīn al-Naysābūrī had written for him. Then Saladin took pleasure in hearing his children recite it by heart.[68] And whenever circumstances allowed, he traveled with part of his large family around him. In the winter of 1175–1176, he brought the young al-ʿAzīz and his mother to Damascus, and she soon gave birth to a second son. The next year, Saladin took his two sons al-Afḍal and al-ʿAzīz to Alexandria, probably with their mothers.[69]

The circumcision of the boys at about seven years of age was the occasion for a great celebration. Saladin's second son, al-ʿAzīz, his favorite according to ʿImād al-Dīn, was circumcised in 1179 along with several of his brothers and cousins, the sons of al-ʿĀdil. Seven hundred sheep were slaughtered for the occasion, and sweets were distributed in large quantities. Large swaths of silk were spread out under the hooves of Saladin's horse, and Sufi concerts accompanied the festivities until dawn. That evening, the women were also allowed to have a celebration, organized by Saladin's wife, ʿIsmat al-Dīn.[70] The sultan not only oversaw his sons' religious and military education but also monitored the people with whom they associated. For example, he once forbade al-ʿAzīz from continuing to see a musician slave woman, who Saladin thought was distracting his son from his duties.[71]

Early on, the princes were trained in the art of war. In 1191, outside the besieged city of Acre, his youngest sons, al-Ashraf Muhammad (eleven or twelve
years old at the time) and al-Mu'azzam Tūrānshāh (ten years old), and their
cousin al-Sālih Ismā'īl, the son of al-'Ādil, witnessed battles, so that they would
become accustomed to war and would train themselves in "handling the saber
and the spear."[72] Saladin's children once even asked him for permission to execute a prisoner, but Saladin refused, believing them too young to distinguish
between the death of an infidel and that of a Muslim. It was between the age of
fifteen and seventeen that his eldest sons began to take part in battles. Al-Afdal
first took up arms under the leadership of his father in Hattīn at the age of seventeen. With youthful high spirits, he cried out for joy at the first retreat of the
Franks, an enthusiasm that his father ordered him to curb so long as the battle
was not over. As for al-'Azīz, at the age of fifteen he came to join his father after
the taking of Ascalon and witnessed the capture of Jerusalem.[73] Al-Zāhir Ghāzī
also played an important role in battles against the Franks when he was only fifteen, in northern Syria in 1188. In 1191, two other sons, al-Mu'izz Ishāq (at sixteen
years old) and Najm al-Dīn Mas'ūd (seventeen years old), participated in the fighting outside the walls of Acre.[74]

Since the last years of his life were largely devoted to war against the Franks,
Saladin did not have much time to devote to his sons' political education. But
the recommendations he gave to al-Zāhir in Jerusalem in October 1192 reflect
fairly well some of the major principles that guided his reign, somewhat idealized no doubt by his approaching death and by Ibn Shaddād, who witnessed the
conversation. Saladin exhorted his son to display continually fear and respect
for God, to avoid bloodshed, to favor persuasion and negotiation, to concern
himself with the good of his subjects, and to treat his military and civil elites
well, in order to assure himself of their support.[75]

Journeys and Residences

Saladin spent a large part of his life traveling. Military operations often kept
him away from Cairo and Damascus, his chief places of residence, but he also
spent long months traveling from Egypt to Syria and from Syria to Iraq, on
lengthy roads strewn with traps. Until the reconquest of the Frankish territories of Palestine and Transjordan in 1187–1188, and the reopening of the coastal
route, it took three weeks to a month to get from Cairo to Damascus via the

Sinai Desert, Ayla, and Busra, and nearly a week to go from Damascus to Harrān in Upper Mesopotamia, by way of Aleppo and al-Bīra. The crossing of the Euphrates occurred by boat or pontoon bridge, and it sometimes took the army three days to get across the river.[76] The cost of these journeys, for the public treasury and for individuals, was very high, since mounts and provisions had to be paid for, and often desert guides as well. Al-Fādil spent two hundred dinars in fifteen days on the return journey of his pilgrimage, and 'Imād al-Dīn laid out three hundred dinars for a twenty-three-day journey between Damascus and Egypt, which is to say, approximately the annual salary of a doctor in Saladin's entourage.[77]

Under such conditions, news was often slow to arrive. Word of the death of Tūrānshāh, which occurred in Alexandria in early July 1180, reached his brother Saladin only in November, in al-Birā, northeast of Aleppo.[78] That delay was no doubt unusual, but it is certainly a sign that Saladin was relatively cut off from the governance of his states during his travels in Syria, and especially, in Mesopotamia. Mail delivery by carrier pigeon, well organized and relatively reliable, conveyed the news over distances of up to two hundred kilometers.[79] For longer distances, messengers mounted on dromedaries were entrusted with urgent messages. They could get from Aleppo to Acre in five days.[80] During his travels, however, Saladin had to count a great deal on his brother al-'Ādil and on al-Fādil to govern his states.

Saladin's mode of life was always marked by a great simplicity. When he was traveling, he lived in a tent and often shared his men's meals. As a security measure, after the Assassins' attack almost killed him in 1176, he sometimes had a tower erected inside the camp and—in town as in the countryside—never rode horseback unless he was wearing his brigandine.[81] His tent was open to anyone who made a complaint to him. Sometimes the cushions he was sitting on slipped under the feet of those pressing around him, but he did not take offense. His biographers unanimously report that he treated his guests like brothers and the complainants humanely and without affectation. Once, when he had withdrawn to get some rest,

> an old mamluke, much respected by him, approached and presented
> him with a petition on behalf of one of the warriors. Saladin said,
> "I am tired now. Keep it for a while." Taking no notice, he thrust the
> petition close to Saladin's dear face and opened it so that he could

read it. His eye fell on the name written at the head of the petition and he recognised it. "A worthy man," he said. The mamluke said, "Will the lord then endorse his petition?" to which the sultan answered, "I do not have my pen-box to hand at the moment." Saladin was sitting at the entrance to his tent, so placed that no-one could enter. The pen-box was by the back wall of the tent, which was a big one. The man who had addressed him said, "There is the pen-box at the back of the tent." This could mean nothing but "Fetch it." Then, leaning on his left arm, he stretched out his right and reached it. He endorsed the petition, and I said, "God Almighty said concerning his Prophet, 'Verily you are of a noble character' [Koran 78:4]. I can only think that our lord shares the same character with him."[82]

When Saladin arrived in a city, he often preferred his encampment to a more comfortable residence. In 1187, for example, after lifting the siege of Tyre, he returned to Acre, which had been reconquered by the Muslims, and while his son al-Afdal moved into the former tower of the Knights Templar, Saladin preferred to camp at the gates of the city. It took a violent wind and snowstorm for him to make up his mind to seek refuge in the citadel.[83] In December 1191, it was again bad weather that impelled him to break camp in Latrun and move into "the dwelling of priests" near the Holy Sepulchre in Jerusalem. This was no doubt the former residence of the Hospitallers, where his son al-Zāhir stayed in July 1192.[84]

Saladin never lived in the citadel he had undertaken to have built in Cairo, but resided in the vizier's former palace, which was restored after the pillaging that followed Shāwar's murder. That residence was situated northeast of the former caliphal palaces and was more modest than they.[85] In Damascus, he resided at the citadel but refused to live in luxury. In May 1188, the governor and treasurer Safī al-Dīn Ibn al-Qābid proposed that Saladin live in one of the palaces of the citadel that he had just renovated. At the sight of so much splendor, gilding, tapestries, and luxurious cushions, Saladin, then in the midst of jihad against the Franks, exclaimed: "What would someone expecting death do with a [splendid] dwelling? . . . In such a dwelling, thoughts of eternity would not come to our minds. . . . We did not come here to stay; yet all we desire is not to leave [this world]; but we rush about only to arrive at [the great] resting place. . . . The aim is not reached in a dwelling, especially when Faith demands its due of us [that is, holy war], and the infidels bring adversity closer to us."[86]

The governor held on to his duties as treasurer but lost his place in the sultan's council, and Saladin moved to another part of the citadel.

The sultan's austerity and simplicity also extended to his manner of dress. He preferred linen, cotton, or wool to silk. Once, when a Seljuk ambassador from Anatolia appeared before him, dressed in sumptuous garments and precious stones of all sorts, Saladin commented with a smile: "That man is traveling to have his luxury admired and to make a display of his dinars."[87] He did not like excessively luxurious or costly things. 'Imād al-Dīn himself was once reproached for using a silver-inlaid writing board. The secretary tried to justify himself, but to no avail, and from that day forward he no longer used anything but a copper writing board in Saladin's presence.[88]

Saladin's austerity was not only a matter of taste or a penchant for the hard life of warriors. It was also a question of faith. He was persuaded that luxury weakened the mind and reduced one's energy, took one away from jihad. That choice became incumbent upon him during his personal "conversion," just after taking power, when he renounced frivolous pleasures and forbidden drinks and adopted a devout and ascetic mode of life. That "conversion" is somewhat reminiscent of that of his predecessor Nūr al-Dīn, who, Ibn al-'Adīm tells us, abandoned his luxurious clothes, abolished the illegal taxes, and fought against immorality to obtain the aid and victory of God.[89] For in Islam, as in other civilizations, the image of the devout and austere prince is also that of the ideal sovereign. Plutarch had already placed the emphasis on the frugality of Alexander, who gently reprimanded his companions, "telling them he wondered that they . . . could fail to see by comparing the Persians' manner of living with their own that it was the most abject and slavish condition to be voluptuous, but the most noble and royal to undergo pain and labor?"[90] Later, in the *Book of Kings,* al-Firdawsī (d. 1020) made Alexander an exemplary figure. Aristotle had helped Alexander, through wisdom and moderation, to achieve self-restraint and contempt for the world here below.[91]

The simplicity Saladin displayed in his daily life did not prevent him from receiving distinguished guests with all the requisite pomp. In such circumstances, abundance was the mark of both his generosity and his power. His secretary did not have the words to describe the splendor of the reception in store for Prince 'Imād al-Dīn Zangī during his visit to Syria in 1188: "The tabletops sagged under delicate dishes; the walls of the tents rippled under the striped and florid fabrics. The meats were seared, flayed, dressed up, grilled, fried, flipped over and over, served and gratefully accepted: roast lamb, dairy, food of all sorts, various receptacles, trays, crockery." All accompanied by rich presents: horses, precious garments, and weapons.[92]

Although the ceremonial around Saladin was reduced to the bare essentials, certain rules were nonetheless respected. A visitor inferior in rank to him had to dismount and place his foot on the ground before the sultan: it was only when Saladin decided to honor him that he also dismounted to receive him or allowed him to remain on his horse. In 1184, for example, when he welcomed the caliph's envoys and the prince of Mosul to Damascus, Saladin joined them on the ground. Then everyone returned to the saddle.[93] Distinguished guests were received by delegations, which, each in accordance with its rank, went out a greater or lesser distance to meet the guests. Emirs and notables were those who covered the longest distance, then members of the royal family, and finally the sultan himself.[94] When Saladin wanted to honor a guest, he took him to his tent and had the guest sit down beside him. In principle, the only ones allowed to be seated in his presence were persons whom he wanted to honor. The others remained standing, arranged by rank.[95] The placement of tents in the camp also had its importance, and Saladin personally oversaw it. In 1190, for example, he had a tent erected among his own sons' tents to honor 'Alā' al-Dīn, the young Zangid prince of Mosul. He also saw to it that the Zangids' tents were set up close to one another, and he placed Emir Zayn al-Dīn of Irbil near his brother Muzaffar al-Dīn Gök-börī, an initiative less auspicious than anticipated, given the profound mistrust that divided the two brothers.[96]

19

Saladin and Suffering

Illness and Grief

As Saladin approached his fiftieth birthday, he fell gravely ill and nearly died. From that time on till the end of his days, his health remained fragile, and he often had to show great physical courage to bear the fatigue and pain. He seems to have suffered from an illness of the digestive system, if we are to believe his close friends, who several times mention violent intestinal cramps and diarrhea.[1] The first signs of illness surfaced outside Mosul in December 1185. Saladin refused to be transported on a litter and continued on his way to Harrān on horseback. There he was confined to bed, and his doctors were sent for from Syria. His condition was so desperate that he decided to dictate his last will and testament to ʿImād al-Dīn, who attended him day and night. In preparing to face God's judgment, Saladin concerned himself with doing good around him. He had money distributed to the people who flocked to his tent and who lamented at seeing him so ill. The governors of Egypt and Syria were instructed to give alms to the poor everywhere. Saladin also asked the governor of Damascus to distribute five thousand Tyrean dinars (sūrī). When ʿImād al-Dīn remarked that the governor had only Egyptian dinars (misrī), worth twice as much, Saladin replied that they would serve very well, and that God would therefore grant him a double reward. Finally, he vowed that, if God would heal him, he would devote the rest of his life to jihad.[2] In 1190, on the plain of Acre, very painful boils covered his body. Saladin faced every ordeal with great courage:

> On the plain of Acre I saw Saladin overcome by an extremely poor state of health on account of numerous boils which had appeared on his body from his waist to his knees, so that he was unable to sit down. He would simply lie on his side if he was in his tent, and he refused to have food served him because of his inability to sit. He ordered it to be distributed to the troops. Nevertheless, he had taken his station in his campaign tent close to the enemy and had disposed the troops as left wing, right wing, and centre, in battle formation. Despite all, he rode from early morning till the noonday prayer, going the rounds of the battalions, and also from late afternoon until the sunset prayer, enduring the intense pain and the violent throbbing of the boils, while I expressed my amazement at that. He would say, "When I ride, the pain goes away, until I dismount." This is divine solicitude.[3]

In the last seven years of his life, which is to say, the years of all his conquests of the Franks, Saladin knew he was ill and sensed he was near death. On the eve of the Battle of Ḥaṭṭīn, he gathered his emirs together and told them: "Now the day I was expecting has come. God has allowed our armies to unite. I am old and do not know when the end of my life will be. As for you, take advantage of this day and do battle not for my cause but for God's cause."[4] Recall as well the warning his brother al-ʿĀdil gave him: "If you die of an attack [of colic] tonight, Jerusalem will stay in the hands of the Franks."[5] In 1188, after his campaign in northern Syria, and contrary to the expectations of his entourage, he did not remain long in Damascus and departed again to seize Kerak and Kawkab, saying it was better to retake immediately the fortresses that remained in the Franks' hands, because life was short and death could take him at any moment.[6]

He had many relapses before the final ordeal that would take his life in early 1193.[7] Saladin faced all these crises with the same strength and determination, even at the risk of upsetting his entourage. His faithful adviser al-Fāḍil was one of those who continually urged the sultan to be cautious. Al-Fāḍil went so far as to exhort Saladin to consider the care of his body one of his jihads, because the Muslim community rested on him like a building on its foundations.[8] Gravitating around him were many physicians, who profited amply from his favors. The wealth of some even fostered the image of the money-grubbing doctor. When the great scholar 'Abd al-Latīf al-Baghdādī came to Syria in 1191, he received thirty dinars a month from Saladin, in addition to what the sultan's sons gave him, and thus managed to earn as much as a hundred dinars a month, which is to say, a fortune.[9] In addition, it often happened that a doctor who succeeded in curing the sultan or a member of his family would receive gifts of up to several thousand dinars.[10] In one of his letters, al-Fādil himself asked 'Imād al-Dīn to make sure that the doctors did not argue around Saladin's bed and that they truly endeavored to cure him, without any thought of enriching themselves.[11]

The citadels of Damascus and Aleppo each had a regular doctor, named by decree, who was responsible for caring for the sovereign, his family, and his court.[12] But many others were also called to his bedside. When he took power in Egypt, Saladin kept at his court the renowned doctors who had served the Fatimid caliphs. He also took Nūr al-Dīn's former doctors into his service, such as the Iraqi Muhadhdhab al-Dīn Ibn al-Naqqāsh, who was living in Damascus.[13]

These men of science, who for the most part had traveled a great deal as part of their training, were also often very cultivated men of letters. Muslims, Christians, and Jews, they came from various regions, particularly Andalusia. The famous physician and Jewish theologian Ibn Maymūn, or Maimonides, born in Cordova in 1135 (he died in Cairo in 1204), settled in Egypt after 1166, where al-Fādil granted him his protection. Al-Jilyānī too was from the region of Cordova. He was an ophthalmologist and also a poet. When he arrived in Damascus, he set up his practice in the souks to care for the population. Having been noticed and honored by Saladin, he devoted laudatory verses to the sultan and dedicated several works to him, including a book on Saladin's conquests, which has unfortunately not come down to us.[14] Like al-Jilyānī, Abū Zakariyā al-Bayāsī was Andalusian. A physician, mathematician, geometer, and musician, he accompanied Saladin on several of his campaigns before obtaining permission to reside in Damascus, where he drew a salary.[15]

Every military expedition of some distance was accompanied by at least one doctor. During the long siege of Acre, not only the fighting but also epidemics (particularly of dysentery) took many lives, including those of several emirs

close to Saladin.[16] Saladin's sons al-Afdal and al-Khadir fell ill, as did Emir Gökbörī, military governor of Damascus, and Ibn Shaddād.[17] When 'Imād al-Dīn
complained about the shortage of doctors, al-Fādil replied that there were even
fewer in Egypt and that they were also less reliable. Ibn Shaddād adds that epidemics took many more lives among the Franks than among the Muslims.
Richard the Lionheart, to cite only one case, fell gravely ill upon his arrival in
the Holy Land in 1191, and it was very likely his poor state of health that accelerated his return to the West in autumn of the following year.[18]

When Saladin was bedridden in Harrān in 1186, his two personal doctors,
Ibn al-Mutrān and al-Rabhī, were brought from Damascus to take care of him.
Ibn al-Mutrān, a Christian who had converted to Islam, was among the greatest doctors of his time. 'Imād al-Dīn, treated by him in Baalbek in 1185, had no
end of praise for him. 'Imād al-Dīn vaunted the doctor's devotion, his intelligence, and his expertise.[19] Born in Damascus into a family of doctors, Ibn al-
Mutrān trained in Iraq but also in "Christian"—probably Byzantine—territory.
He very quickly acquired a privileged place beside Saladin and as a result became very wealthy. He rarely traveled without his retinue of mamluks and,
within his luxurious house in Damascus, possessed a library of some ten thousand works. Three paid copyists were employed there full time. He himself
wrote several works, one of which, dedicated to Saladin, contained advice on
how to remain in good health.[20] To demonstrate his friendship and gratitude
for Ibn al-Mutrān, Saladin offered him the hand in marriage of one of his concubines, his wife's lady-in-waiting. Not only did he bestow a rich trousseau on
her, he also supplied the wedding banquet. That banquet took a strange turn,
however: invited by Damascene Sufis to attend their dances on the evening of
the wedding, Ibn al-Mutrān did not dare tell them he was preparing to celebrate his marriage. He accepted their invitation and moved the banquet to
their residence. Dressed for the celebration, his wife and the women of her
entourage waited for him all night.

Ibn al-Mutrān did not provide care only for Saladin and his family. He also
practiced his art in the hospital of Damascus built by Nūr al-Dīn—now a museum of medicine—where he treated the poor free of cost. He also sometimes
interceded in favor of his former coreligionists, the Christians. When he died
in 1191, he was buried on Mount Qāsiyūn near his wife's house.

Radī al-Dīn al-Rahbī (he died in 1233 at almost a hundred years old) was a
native of Iraq, where he also received his training. He had moved to Damascus

under Nūr al-Dīn's reign in 1160 and set up a stall in the souks to provide care. His talent attracted notice, and he became a doctor at the hospital; he also treated Saladin and his family at the citadel. The sultan allotted him a monthly salary of thirty dinars but did not manage to persuade al-Rahbī to follow him in his travels. Opinions about his competence varied. Some accused him of having caused Saladin's death by his blood-lettings.[21] Al-Rahbī had the peculiarity of accepting only Muslims as his students, with a few exceptions. Within the milieu of physicians, however, many Muslims, Christians, and Jews still had regular contact with one another at that time.

Saladin did not suffer only in his body. He also faced moral suffering, grief in particular, and let his emotions show on several occasions. In the Middle Ages, tears were not the exclusive preserve of women. As several historians of the Western Middle Ages have shown, they were part of the social idiom, accompanying and sometimes supplanting words.[22] Tears attested to the compassion of a sovereign and his capacity to be moved by the suffering of his people. It was therefore not unusual for a man, a warrior, even a king, to weep in public. Saladin shed tears of pain, of humiliation, of strong emotion, and of joy, tears sometimes inspired by the fear of God. He wept first and foremost for the loss of people dear to him. In 1183, outside the walls of Aleppo, when he learned that his youngest brother, Būrī, was dying at about the age of twenty, he wept. But he wanted to contain his sorrow, so as not to spoil the celebration that followed the taking of the city. His restraint was appreciated by the historian Ibn al-Athīr.[23] On November 1, 1191, upon reading the letter that announced the death of his nephew Taqī al-Dīn, of whom he was very fond, Saladin spilled abundant tears, and those in attendance wept to see him weeping, even before knowing the cause. But when Ibn Shaddād reminded him that the death was divinely decreed, Saladin humbly asked forgiveness of God and affirmed that all men belonged to Him and would return to Him. Upon the death of his son, Ismāʿīl, who had barely reached adolescence, Saladin, very afflicted, shed a tear but showed no other sign of sorrow. He did not wish to upset his entourage, who were then in the midst of an expedition against the Franks.[24] For although a sovereign was allowed to cry, it was also understood that he was to do so with moderation. In Islamic culture, self-control (hilm) is a highly prized quality:

men are therefore urged not to show their emotions too openly.[25] In another context, but for the same reasons, Jean de Joinville demonstrated his disapproval of Saint Louis's excessive manifestations of grief.[26]

Yet Saladin was easily moved to tears, and his entourage readily alluded to them only because they saw these tears as the sign of his sincere humanity, his sensitivity to human misfortune. He was seen weeping, for example, in different kinds of situations: upon receiving Nūr al-Dīn's daughter, who had come to claim the fortress of 'Azāz from him in 1176; upon hearing certain passages recited from the Koran and the Sunna; or upon welcoming the pilgrims returned from Mecca, where he himself had been unable to go.[27] When al-Mansūr, the son of Saladin's late nephew Taqī al-Dīn, came to join the sultan in his camp at Latrun, between Jerusalem and Ramla, Saladin took him in his arms, weeping, and "for a good while all present wept in sympathy."[28] In medieval Christendom, the "gift of tears" expressed the grace granted by God to be able to cry, a sign of holiness and of the divine presence in humankind;[29] by contrast, in the Muslim world, tears were part of the eschatological fear of God. To speak of Saladin's tears is thus also to associate him with a certain form of holiness. "When the revelations of the Merciful were recited to them, they fell down on their knees in tears and adoration," says a verse from the Koran (19:58) about those that God has filled with his grace. And "he who weeps for fear of God will not enter Hell," wrote al-Qushayrī, a celebrated theologian and Arab mystic of the eleventh century.[30] In Jerusalem in 1192, while Ibn Shaddād was preparing to resist the Franks, he saw tears flowing onto Saladin's gray beard as the sultan lay prostrate on his prayer rug in al-Aqsā Mosque.[31]

But Saladin's tears were not inspired solely by the fear of God, affection, or even sadness. They sometimes had the bitter taste of humiliation, anger, or despair: in 1190, for example, when the defeated Franks managed to return to their camp because the ailing Saladin was unable to pursue them; or, even worse, when Muslim prisoners were massacred outside Acre the following year.[32] In July of that year, again outside Acre, Saladin the warrior, propelled by the last glimmer of hope, "went the rounds amongst the division, himself proclaiming 'On, on for Islam!' while tears flowed from his eyes.'"[33]

Conversely, he wept for joy following the Battle of Hattīn:[34] "Heads are still bowed in prayer and the tears [of joy] have not dried up," wrote al-Fādil at the time.[35] It was also out of joy that Saladin's eyes filled with tears on the day he was reunited with Ibn Shaddād in Damascus, a few weeks before his death.[36]

Then, too, Saladin was sensitive to the tears of others. Recall his compassion for the Frankish woman who had come to implore him to return her child to her: "She was crying, the fire of her suffering blazing, her tears streaming; she was sighing sorrowfully, moaning feverishly, choking on her sobs." The sultan "had compassion for her and, with tears in his eyes," he ordered the child returned to her before the eyes of the assembly, who were also in tears.[37]

Saladin's Death

In Damascus, in the early afternoon of Wednesday, March 4, 1193, the whole crowd dissolved in tears, wailing profusely at the sight of Saladin's body enveloped in its shroud.[38] Immersed in their sorrow, the people forgot the hour of prayer. Saladin's health had been deteriorating for several weeks. He had nevertheless returned with pleasure to Damascus in early November 1192, taking advantage of the truce he had just concluded with the Franks to go hunting with his brother al-'Ādil and several of his sons. But three months later, on February 16, 1193, Ibn Shaddād, arriving in Damascus, found him tired and with no appetite. Saladin took his last excursion on horseback on February 19. In the company of his son al-Afdal and a few in his close circle, he went out that day to meet the pilgrims returning from Mecca. As the crowd pressed around Saladin, Ibn Shaddād noted with anxiety that the sultan was not wearing his brigandine, which he never removed when he was traveling. The historian took that oversight, and the fact that Saladin's fencing master could not be found, as a bad omen.

By the next day, Saladin, suffering from fever, had to take to his bed.[39] His loyal friends and advisers al-Fādil and Ibn Shaddād visited him several times a day. When Saladin was no longer well enough to receive them, they continued to come to his door to learn how he was faring. When they left the palace, the people guessed the sovereign's state of health by the expression on his advisers' faces. Surrounded by his wife and concubines, Saladin was treated by several doctors. On the fourth day of his illness, on al-Rahbī's recommendation, the decision was made to bleed him, which further weakened the sultan. By the sixth day, he was shaking uncontrollably and his mind had begun to wander. Attempts to administer laxatives and enemas did not improve matters—on the contrary. His entourage were preparing for the worst, and his eldest son, al-Afdal, began to make arrangements for his own accession to the throne and

asked the Syrian grand emirs to take a loyalty oath to him. Most agreed, sometimes setting as a condition that they would remain in possession of their lands
and would not be obliged to fight against Saladin's other sons, al-Afdal's brothers. Ibn Shaddād preserved the text of that oath: "I from this time forward devote my duty and dedicate my true mind to al-Malik al-Nāsir [Saladin] for the
duration of his life and I shall not cease to bestow my efforts to protect his dominion with my person, my wealth, my sword and my men, obeying his commands and waiting upon his good pleasure, and then subsequently to his son
al-Afdal ʿAlī. By God, I shall be subject to his allegiance and I shall protect his
dominion and his lands with my person, my wealth, my sword and my men.
I shall obey his orders and his prohibitions. In this my inner and my outer self
are one. God is my witness in what I say."[40]

On March 1, Saladin more or less lost consciousness and could hear only
intermittently the verses of the Koran that a devout imam was reciting to him.
At dawn on Wednesday, March 4, he breathed his last, in the presence of his
friend al-Fādil.[41] Al-Dawlaʿī, the preacher for the Great Mosque of Damascus,
was given the task of washing and dressing the body, while al-Afdal received
the condolences of the emirs and religious officials at the citadel. The sultan's
treasury was completely empty, so that, we are told, it was necessary to borrow money for his funeral. Saladin's body was first shown to the crowd, who
prayed for him under the guidance of Chief Qādī Muhyī al-Dīn Ibn al-Zakī.
The merchants not only closed their shops in the souks but also removed and
stored away their most valuable merchandise, since it was not unusual for the
announcement of a sovereign's death to be immediately followed by looting.

Saladin was buried that same day, in the midafternoon, inside the citadel,
under the west portico of his residence. His son al-Afdal immediately wrote to
his uncle and his absent brothers to announce the sad news. The next day, al-
Afdal continued to receive the condolences of the ulemas, who had come to
recite the Koran and to pray on the sultan's grave. During his lifetime, Saladin
had not had the time, or perhaps the desire, to have a mausoleum built for himself, but he seems to have expressed the wish to be buried on the outskirts of
Damascus, south of the Hippodrome of Pebbles, on the route for caravans and
armed expeditions, so that everyone passing by could pray for him. Al-Afdal's
entourage advised Saladin's son to have a funerary madrasa built near al-
Qadam Mosque.[42] That location, he was told, would allow his brother al-ʿAzīz
to go pray on their father's grave without having to enter Damascus. That

precaution says a great deal about the mistrust that was beginning to surface between the two brothers. But the work had hardly begun when al-'Azīz himself arrived to lay siege outside Damascus and destroyed what had just been constructed.

Al-Afdal then purchased the residence of a devout person in the heart of the city, contiguous to the north façade of the Umayyad Great Mosque. There he had a domed building (qubba) constructed, equipped with a window overlooking the mosque. The faithful could therefore see Saladin's sepulchre and pray for him. His coffin was transported there on December 15, 1195, the Day of 'Āshūra', corresponding to the tenth day of Muharram on the Muslim calendar. In Sunni tradition, this is a day of optional fasting, during which the graves of the dead are honored, a practice that continues even today in the Maghreb.[43] Saladin's coffin was carried by his former mamluks, his servants, and members of his entourage, with al-Afdal leading the procession. Having left the citadel by the eastern gate, the cortege entered the Great Mosque by the western gate, known as the Gate of the Post (Bāb al-Barīd). The coffin was then set down on the threshold to the main door of the prayer hall,[44] where Chief Qādī Muhyī al-Dīn Ibn al-Zakī uttered a prayer. It was then transported into its mausoleum, where it remains to this day. Some sources claim that Saladin was buried with his sword, a symbol of the jihad and of his battles against the Franks. Al-Fādil is even reported to have said: "He will rely on that sword to enter paradise."[45]

His mausoleum, to which many pilgrims and visitors flock even now, is a small, square, domed building. Against the east wall of the edifice once stood al-'Azīziyya madrasa, which al-'Azīz ordered built after he seized Damascus in June 1196. It is likely that he chose that place with the intention of adding his name to that of his father and of thus benefiting from the students' prayers.[46] All that remains of the madrasa today is the arch of the north īwān. The stained-glass windows set in plaster and the faience facing that can be seen inside the mausoleum date to the seventeenth century. Two cenotaphs sit side by side there. The older one, in sculpted walnut with a geometric and floral motif, dates in great part to the Ayyubid period.[47] The second cenotaph, in white marble, is much more recent, and it is this one that the German emperor William II arranged to have restored after his visit to Damascus in 1898.

It took two weeks for the news of Saladin's death to reach Baghdad. A few months later, al-Afdal sent an embassy to the caliph to obtain his investiture and recognition that al-Afdal was his father's legitimate heir. In tribute to the caliph, al-Afdal sent him Saladin's war equipment (sword, coat of mail, horse), along with many gifts and a letter, in which he gave a long panegyric of the sultan, rendered in 'Imād al-Dīn's words:

> Throughout his lifetime and until the hour of his death, my blessed father, the valiant, the just, the destroyer of idolatry, held fast on the field of zealotry, wholeheartedly expended all his efforts to perform the obligations of holy war, exhausted his wealth for acts that earned him your august favors, labored with all his strength at works of faith, which surely guided his gaze and understanding. . . . Egypt—what am I saying? the whole world—was witness to his zeal for holy war; mountains and plains were all one where his actions were concerned. Jerusalem was one of his conquests, and the kingship of this world was one of the results of his resolution. . . . It was he who subjugated the infidel princes and placed a chain around their necks; it was he who captured the fiends of idolatry and bound them with heavy bonds; who subdued the worshippers of the Cross and broke their backs; who unified the Believers, preserved them, and put their affairs in order; who closed our borders, directing our affairs with a sure hand; humiliated every enemy outside your august House; and protected it from the arms of every impudent man. . . . When Allah called him home, his justice reigned everywhere, his authority was respected. He had laid down his burden, and his works were linked to the good. . . . He left behind no unsettled business, no untrod path. . . . When he left the world here below, he was scrupulously placed under the imam's obedience; he set off for his eternal rest, taking with him the recompense for his loyalty.[48]

V

Governance

20

Guardian of the Faith

> An earthquake, larger in scale than the one felt in 1755, upended
> most of the cities of Syria and of that little state of Jerusalem; in a
> hundred places, the earth swallowed up animals and men. In ser-
> mons, the Turks were told that God was punishing the Christians;
> the Christians, that God was declaring himself against the Turks;
> and all continued to fight on the debris of Syria.
>
> Voltaire, *Essai sur les moeurs*, chap. 56, "On Saladin"

In medieval societies, natural catastrophes and military defeats were generally seen as retribution sent from God to punish men for their
sins, and victories as so many rewards for their good actions. Was the responsibility of the ruling powers alleviated as a result? No, for it was incumbent on
them to govern well, in order to attract divine favor. The first duty of a Muslim
ruler was to defend Islam. He therefore needed to be wholly in the service of
God, of God's messenger the Prophet, and of the Prophet's successor, the caliph. In the interest of his subjects, the ruler had to spread justice, peace, and
prosperity. Did Saladin conform to that model of good governance? Did he
succeed in assuming his dual task: imposing Islamic law on one hand, and, on
the other, finding a balance between his battles against the Zangids and Franks,
the pacification of his own states, and the guarantee of well-being that his subjects expected?

In the realm of religion, the works of a Sunni sovereign such as Saladin could be performed in many ways. First and foremost, he had to set an example regarding the practice of his faith. In addition, he had to foster the spread of Islamic law, attend to its application, defend religious institutions and holy places, and, finally, fight every form of heresy.

Saladin, Redresser of Wrongs

Saladin strove as much as possible to observe his duties as a believer. He also attempted, with greater or lesser success, to extend respect for Islamic law to his territory as a whole. The measures he took each time a city fell into his hands were significant in that regard. In 1171, following the death of the Fatimid caliph, he eliminated all the illegal taxes *(mukūs)* levied in the Egyptian capital. In Islam, the only canonical taxes are the *zakāt,* the alms paid by all Muslims on income above a certain level; the *kharāj,* a property tax on certain lands; and the *jizya,* a capitation imposed on non-Muslims. All other taxes, especially the many artisanal and commercial taxes levied on certain activities and on the circulation and sale of merchandise, were considered illegal and were on principle prohibited. They were often tolerated, however, because they brought in large revenues to the state. Their suppression by a sovereign therefore indicated his desire to apply religious law strictly. In doing so, he also enjoyed a boost in popularity. At the time Saladin eliminated them, these illegal taxes collected in the urban area of Cairo amounted to several hundred thousand dinars a year, a considerable sum and a patent sign of the active life of the capital.[1] The application of that measure went hand in hand with Saladin's personal "conversion"; according to his entourage, he gave up alcoholic beverages and frivolous amusements and adopted a pious and devout attitude. No doubt he was seeking thereby to mark a break from the preceding Fatimid period and to style himself the instigator of a new way, like Nūr al-Dīn, who had imposed the same rules in Syria.[2] When Saladin entered Damascus a few months after his predecessor's death, he suppressed the illegal taxes, which had just been reestablished there, and, to seal his image as a pious sovereign, went to pray in the Umayyad Great Mosque.[3] During his campaigns in al-Jazīra and northern Syria, in 1182 and 1183, he suppressed the *mukūs* in all the cities he succeeded in conquering—Aleppo in particular—and let that fact be widely known, inside and outside his territories.

Nevertheless, that image as redresser of wrongs was not disseminated by everyone. Al-Subkī, the great fourteenth-century Shafite jurist, suggests that Saladin made up his mind to abolish certain illegal practices only under pressure from the intransigent jurists. Al-Subkī thus recounts that, shortly before the Battle of Ramla against the Franks in 1177, Sheikh al-Khubūshānī, an irascible man, came to greet Saladin, asking him to suppress several noncanonical taxes. Not having obtained satisfaction, the sheikh made a prediction to the sultan that God would send him a defeat. Overcome by anger, he even went so far as to strike the sultan with his staff, so hard that Saladin lost his *qalansuwa* (a sort of skullcap worn by the sultan and members of the military). After his rout by the Franks, Saladin is said to have returned to kiss the sheikh's hand and acknowledged his error. Al-Subkī also says that, one day, al-Khubūshānī accused Saladin's nephew Taqī al-Dīn 'Umar of possessing warehouses of alcoholic beverages. Saladin is reported to have told Taqī al-Dīn: "We are powerless against that sheikh, so give him satisfaction."[4]

Other indications allow us to affirm that it was not always easy to bring the population around to greater virtue. In 1178–1179, for example, al-Fāḍil gave a very somber picture of all the reprehensible practices still common in Egypt (prostitution, usury, illicit gain) and the measures that had been taken to stop them. He also said that al-'Ādil, having summoned one of his governors to give him Saladin's instructions and to reprimand him sharply, had been met with this response: "If the reed were straight, its shadow would not be crooked. If you abstained, others would also abstain. But you are an obstacle to their being condemned, because you participate."[5]

That anecdote can of course be seen as a sign that the ruling class did not always set a good example, but it is also possible to conclude that Saladin wanted to put an end to these practices and to see that Muslim law was strictly applied, even if the results did not always live up to his hopes.

Defender of the Abbasid Caliphate and the Holy Places

The honorific title "Salāh al-Dīn," rendered in the West as "Saladin," can be translated as "uprightness of religion." Throughout his reign, Saladin claimed to be acting in the interests of Islam and its supreme leader, the Abbasid caliph. In his propaganda and in his correspondence with the caliph of Baghdad, Saladin was always presented as the author of the Fatimids' fall and hence as the chief defender of the Abbasid dynasty. Where all his predecessors had failed, Saladin had succeeded, and as a result he deserved the gratitude of the Sunni Muslims, who considered themselves the defenders of the True Way, or "orthodoxy," of Islam. Similarly, his conquest of Yemen had simply been a war against a heretic who had blasphemed by designating his father's tomb by the term "Kaaba," and who had reduced a large number of devout Muslims to slavery.

It was all the more necessary to spread these ideas since, in the Shiite circles of Egypt, Saladin was reproached for having attacked an Alid dynasty, that is, the descendants of the Prophet's family. The satirist al-Wahrānī recounts one of his dreams on that subject: Saladin's uncle Shīrkūh and father, Ayyūb, are preparing to appear before the Prophet on Resurrection Day. They come forward, each dressed in two honorific robes (khil'a), that of jihad and that of pilgrimage. Shīrkūh hopes to obtain a third khil'a from the Prophet for the conquest of Egypt, but Ayyūb, fearing that the Egyptian affair displeased the Prophet, advises him to remain silent. Shīrkūh replies that they have nothing to fear. Had not the gene-alogists demonstrated that there was no kinship tie between the Fatimids and the Prophet? And even if there were one, it would be without importance, be-cause the Fatimids had neither been killed nor betrayed, and none of their chil-dren had been imprisoned. Was it not the Fatimids, on the contrary, who had conspired to return Egypt to the infidels? In any case, says Shīrkūh, there are a sufficient number of loved ones and Companions—al-'Abbās especially—beside the Prophet who would be grateful to Shīrkūh and Ayyūb for having reestab-lished prayer in the name of the Abbasids. They would intercede in Shīrkūh's and Ayyūb's favor. Ayyūb, unconvinced by his brother's arguments, again pleads with him not to speak of Egypt and to spare him "that headache." Shīrkūh obeys, and both men approach the Prophet to introduce Saladin to him. As Saladin is kissing the Prophet's feet, the Prophet lays his hand on the sultan's head and in-vokes God on his behalf, enjoining him to care for the weak and oppressed.[6] The satirist thereby reminds the sovereign through a dream of his role as protector of ill-treated subjects, including al-Wahrānī himself in his view. His tale not only contains a veiled attack on the assaults made against the Fatimids but also points to the importance of Ayyūb's and Shīrkūh's legacy in the legitimacy granted to Saladin.

Saladin, defender of the Sunni caliphate, also styled himself the protector of the holy places of Islam. In 1181 and again in 1183, during the attacks of Regi-nald of Châtillon, Saladin proclaimed that his troops were fighting relentlessly to prevent the Franks from arriving in Medina and Mecca, while his Zangid adversaries were taking the opportunity to seize Aleppo, break their oaths, and ally themselves with the very ones Saladin was fighting, namely, the Franks and the heretical Assassins.[7] That was not mere rhetoric. Saladin took very concrete measures on behalf of the pilgrims and emirs in the holy places, though it is difficult to ignore the interplay between the political and the religious in that realm. In fact, the extension of his influence into the Hejaz was also part of his expanding domination over Yemen. In any event, from the beginning of his reign he established contact with the dynasty of the sharīfs Banū Hāshim, who ruled Mecca, making great efforts to encourage pilgrimage and to assure the supply of provisions to the holy cities. In 1174, the region of Naqada, west of Qūs, was made into a *waqf* on behalf of the servants of the Prophet's tomb. Wheat continued to arrive in the Hejaz from Upper Egypt, therefore, as it had done during the Fatimid era. In 1177 Saladin asked the sharīfs to give up the exorbitant taxes they were collecting from pilgrims, offering them in exchange wheat and *iqtā's* in Upper Egypt. That year, he himself abolished the taxes levied on pilgrims by Egyptian officials in the port of 'Aydhāb and did the same in 1181 for the city of Qūs.[8]

All these measures considerably increased his popularity, even though, if we are to believe Ibn Jubayr, they were not always strictly applied. They opened the way to a new policy, which would be followed by several of his Mamluk successors. That policy consisted of assuring revenues to the leaders of the holy cities in exchange for the suppression of taxes on the pilgrims.[9] Ibn Jubayr's account indicates as well that in 1183, Saladin's suzerainty was acknowledged in Mecca.[10] His name was pronounced at that time in the *khutba* of the Great Mosque, after the names of the Abbasid caliph of Baghdad and the emir of Mecca, eliciting the enthusiasm of those in attendance. Other sources attest that in 1186 dinars were struck in Saladin's name in the holy city.[11] Saladin also seems to have maintained good relations with the governor of Medina. In 1184, the coffins of his father and uncle were sent from Cairo to Medina to be buried in a madrasa, near the tomb of the Prophet; and three years later, Saladin most warmly welcomed the emir, who had come to pay him a visit after the victory of Hattīn. The sultan even offered to accompany the emir on his expedition of 1188 against the Franks of northern Syria.[12]

On Behalf of Sunnism

Inseparable from the defense of the Abbasid caliphate of Baghdad, the strengthening of Sunnism had begun in Syria upon the arrival of the Seljuks in the late eleventh century. A few decades later, Nūr al-Dīn gave it a new impetus by striving to maintain an equitable balance between the four legal schools of Sunnism. After him, Saladin—though he privileged the Shafite school, to which he himself belonged—endeavored to follow Nūr al-Dīn's example, setting the goals of fighting any form of heresy and especially of training a religious elite, whose support of Saladin was required to assure the success of Muslim reunification and jihad. Thus far, no general overview has been written on the religious and cultural life of Saladin's states. It is beyond the scope of this book to fill that lacuna here; let me simply insist on the measures Saladin took to strengthen Sunnism, in terms both of the major religious offices and of religious buildings and new foundations for the teaching of law and the hadith.

After taking power in Egypt in 1169, Saladin gradually and cautiously reestablished Sunni law: suppression of the Shiite call to prayer; reintroduction of the names of the first three caliphs at the Friday *khutba;* the appointment of a Shafite jurist alongside the Shiite chief qādī; the founding of several schools of Sunni law (madrasas); and finally, in 1171, the replacement of the Shiite chief qādī by a Shafite chief qādī and the definitive suppression of the Shiite *khutba* in favor of the Abbasid Sunni *khutba.* The Shafite and Malekite legal schools emerged the stronger by all these measures, and the number of Shiites fell considerably. Al-Azhar Great Mosque suspended its traditional sessions on Ismaili teachings and lost its status as the Friday mosque. The silver band that decorated its *mihrāb,* and on which the names of the Fatimid caliphs were inscribed, was removed. The mosque, converted back into a Sunni building, kept a low profile until the Mamluk period, when it was restored.[13] The Egyptian population, the majority of which had remained Sunni under the reign of the Fatimids, had little reaction to these changes, which therefore came about without violence or constraint.

In fact, even before the arrival of the Ayyubids, Sunnism had begun to raise its head, under the influence of the Maghrebi ulemas; in the wake of the Fatimids, large numbers of such ulemas had come to settle in Egypt. From the late eleventh century on, other Maghrebis had settled in Upper Egypt upon returning from their pilgrimage. Two Shafite madrasas were founded in

Alexandria in the Fatimid era, to allow Sunni personalities such as Abū l-Tāhir al-Silafī to teach there,[14] and a madrasa was established in Cairo as well. Saladin therefore had no great difficulty imposing Sunnism in Egypt, though he sometimes had to proceed cautiously. In 1173, for example, at the restoration of the Qūs mosque in Upper Egypt, a Shiite religious formula was still used at the beginning of the votive inscription out of consideration for the population of the region, which had remained more attached to Shiism than had the rest of the country.[15]

Within Sunnism, the dominant legal schools under Saladin's reign were Malekism and Shafism in Egypt, Shafism, Hanafism, and Hanbalism in Syria.[16] That legacy was bequeathed by his predecessors, and Saladin set about consolidating it. Al-Shāf'ī, the founder of Shafism, was buried in al-Fustāt, south of Cairo, and it is there that he had spent the last years of his life in the early ninth century. Hence the importance of his school in Egypt. The cult devoted to him had not waited for Saladin's arrival to develop. From the late eleventh century on, after the Seljuks' futile attempt to lay hold of his coffin and the resulting miracle, his tomb had become an oft-visited pilgrimage site. Crowds of Sunnis flocked to it, and the mosque next to the grave quickly grew too small to accommodate them.[17]

Malekism was also introduced into Egypt during the lifetime of its founder, Mālik ibn Anas (d. 795), by several of his disciples, who made Alexandria the second center—after Medina—of that legal school. Under the reign of the Fatimids, it was therefore natural for that region to welcome a large number of Maghrebi ulemas of the Malekite sect, who strengthened the influence of that school in Egypt. Although Saladin, in coming to power, entrusted the office of chief qādī to a Kurdish Shafite, Sadr al-Dīn Ibn Durbās, he remained well disposed toward Malekism. We know through Ibn Jubayr especially that the sultan established monthly subsidies on behalf of foreign Maghrebis, who liked to assemble in the old city of Cairo, inside the Ibn Tūlūn Mosque, where they often took lodgings. No other school had authority over them.[18] Saladin sometimes consulted with them on questions of law, as he did with the Shafites.[19] The Egyptian Malekites had their own leader. For a time this was Sheikh Ibn 'Awf al-Zuhrī of Alexandria, whose lessons on the hadith Saladin liked very much to follow.[20]

As for the Hanbalites and the Hanafites, they remained a minority in Egypt, though their numbers increased somewhat with the arrival of eastern ulemas.[21] That in no way prevented the Hanbalites from openly opposing the Shafites, who particularly criticized them for their anthropomorphism. The most visible Hanbalite personality was the jurisconsult, exegete, and sermonist Zayn al-Dīn Ibn Nāja, grandson on his mother's side of one of the main propagators of Hanbalism in Syria.[22] Ibn Nāja left Syria to settle in Egypt toward the end of Nūr al-Dīn's reign and played a role in foiling the conspiracy against Saladin in 1174. He then became a close friend of al-Fādil and the sultan, who often received advice from him. It was he who was given the task of pronouncing the sermon in Jerusalem on October 9, 1187, drawing tears from the crowd who had come to listen to it. In Cairo, he often found himself in the middle of the violent disputes between the Hanbalites and the Shafites, the latter under the leadership of Shihāb al-Dīn al-Tūsī and al-Khubūshānī.[23] One day, al-Khubūshānī even ordered that the remains of a poet accused of anthropomorphism be disinterred, on the grounds that he was lying too close for the sheikh's taste to al-Shāfiʿī's grave.

In 1184, a new conflict arose between Hanbalites and Asharite Shafites on a subject of speculative theology *(kalām)*, which Taqī al-Dīn, Saladin's representative in Cairo, found himself compelled to arbitrate.[24] The altercations between Ibn Najā and the Asharites continued after Saladin's death and in 1199 led to a real crisis.[25] These persistent tensions and quarrels within Sunnism, despite Saladin's efforts to gather around him jurists of various views, account for his impatience. He communicated to his close circle his disapproval of all these legal disputes, which he saw as so many crucibles of division and hatred. He even considered banning them. On that matter, ʿImād al-Dīn recounts that he once had to vouch for the respectability of the protagonists in a debate session before Saladin would agree to follow their discussions.[26]

When Saladin arrived in Syria-Palestine, Shafism and Hanafism dominated to a large degree. Hanbalism also played an important role, especially in Damascus, whereas Malekism was much less influential. Whether in Damascus, Aleppo, or Jerusalem, Saladin always opted to entrust Shafites with the major religious offices, such as the supreme judiciary or the position of preacher in the Great Mosque.[27] But he did so without alienating the Hanafites and the Hanbalites. Several members of an important Hanbalite family, the Banū Qudāma, who had lived in Damascus since the mid-twelfth century, participated in his propaganda campaign on behalf of jihad and in his military campaigns.[28] The Damascene jurist al-Nāsih 'Abd al-Rahmān, from the great Hanbalite family the Banū l-Shīrāzī, accompanied him during his expeditions of 1187 and often gave his advice freely on questions of law.[29] In Aleppo as well, the major Hanafite families, who were very influential in that city, continued to play a major role in religious and political life.[30]

Religious and Legal Foundations

The number of influential jurists and the appointments to the major religious offices give us a sense of the respective weight of the legal schools. The construction of new madrasas and the appointment of teachers of law were also part of the religious policy supported by Saladin. The sultan and his close circle had a relatively large number of madrasas built, especially in cities where they were scarce.[31] Recall that these legal-religious secondary schools, which in the eleventh century spread in Iran and then Iraq under the influence of the Seljuk Turks, appeared in Syria in the early years of the twelfth century. Designed to train a religious elite to spread Sunnism and to oppose Shiism and any form of heresy, they were associated with one or several legal schools. Their students could reside at the school and take training focused on law, the Koran, and the Arabic language. Each of these madrasas, which could accommodate about ten to forty students, was directed by a teacher named by the ruling power or by the founder. That teacher was often assisted by one or several jurisconsults. Teachers' salaries, food for the students, and building maintenance were provided by *waqfs,* mortmain properties that were in principle inalienable, whose revenues the founder earmarked for the operation of his madrasa. The number of these madrasas grew considerably in the major Syrian and Mesopotamian cities under the reign of Nūr al-Dīn, who was committed to maintaining the balance between the two main schools in Syria: the Hanafite school, to which he, like most Turks, belonged; and the Shafite school, with which a large portion of the population was associated. Saladin continued that policy of constructing madrasas, even while displaying his preference for Shafism. He set up madrasas in Egypt, where, because of the Shiite domination of the Fatimids, they were still few in number, and in Syria-Palestine—Jerusalem in particular—where the Frankish occupation had prevented them from being built until that time.

In Egypt during the Fatimid period, the mosques played the foremost role in the teaching of law and religious science: 'Amr Mosque in the old city of al-Fustāt, al-Hākim Mosque, and especially al-Azhar Mosque in the city of al-Qāhira. Alongside the House of Wisdom founded by Caliph al-Hākim (r. 996–1021), al-Azhar had become the chief center for spreading the Ismaili doctrine.[32] With the advent of Saladin, al-Azhar Mosque lost its importance. The 'Amr Mosque, which had been damaged in the great fire of al-Fustāt in 1168, was allocated new *waqfs* and was entirely restored in 1172–1173. On its marble *mihrāb*, Saladin had the name of the Abbasid caliph al-Mustadī' inscribed, along with his own.[33] By contrast, the Friday *khutba* was no longer pronounced in these two mosques but was now reserved solely for al-Hākim, the most spacious of the mosques, a shift consistent with Shafite doctrine, which recommended having only one *khutba* mosque per city, if the size of the building could accommodate the entire Muslim community gathered for Friday prayer.[34]

As for madrasas, Egypt possessed only three at Saladin's arrival: two Shafite madrasas in Alexandria, built in 1138 and 1151, and one madrasa in Cairo, constructed in 1157.[35] Saladin's ascent to power led to the founding of several others in Cairo and al-Fustāt. The most important was the one he ordered built in al-Fustāt in 1176–1177, next to al-Shāfi'ī's tomb. Was it out of respect for the imam that he chose not to give it his own name? It became known as al-Salāhiyya only later. Saladin allocated *waqfs* to it and put al-Khubūshānī in charge. With the exception of an inscription dated 1180, now in the Cairo Museum, no vestige survives of this monument, "the like of which," according to Ibn Jubayr, "has not been made in this country [Egypt], there being nothing more spacious or more finely built."[36] The objective, namely, the propagation of Sunnism and the fight against any form of heresy, was spelled out in the foundation inscription: "This madrasa was built on the authority of the sheikh, the jurisconsult, the imam . . . and the ascetic Najm al-Dīn, pillar of Islam, model for humankind, mufti of the sects [*al-firaq*], Abū l-Ba[rakāt ibn] al-Muwaffaq al-Khubūshānī—May God grant him long-lasting success—for the jurist disciples of al-Shāfi'ī—may God be well pleased with him—characterized by the unitary Asharite principles, against false doctrinal incisions and other heresies. This [was completed] in the month of Ramadan [57]5 [February 1180]."[37]

In Egypt, in fact, Saladin gave a major boost not only to Shafism but also to Asharism, a theological school to which he, like many other Shafites, subscribed.[38]

The sultan also had a new wood coffin installed in al-Shāfiʿī's mausoleum in 1178. He ordered it from a joiner from Aleppo, who probably belonged to the same family as one of the artisans whom Nūr al-Dīn had engaged to build the carved wood pulpit for al-Aqsā Mosque in Jerusalem.[39] In thus renovating that place linked to the memory of the founder of Shafism, Saladin, like his Ayyubid successors, clearly displayed his desire to place himself under al-Shāfiʿī's patronage. Even in our own time, al-Shāfiʿī's tomb is the object of great devotion, and his feast day, or *mawlid*, is celebrated every year with great pomp.

Saladin's madrasa, annexed to al-Shāfiʿī's tomb, was symbolically the most important in the Egyptian capital, but it was not the only one or even the first. In autumn 1170, while still merely a vizier, Saladin had founded two other madrasas in al-Fustāt: a Shafite madrasa called al-Nāsiriyya, built on the site of a prison (Dār al-Maʿūna) south of ʿAmr Mosque,[40] and a Malekite madrasa (al-Qamhiyya) in the same neighborhood, at the site of an old textile market (Dār al-Ghazl).[41] In al-Husayni sanctuary—where the head of ʿAlī's son al-Husayn was kept—inside the enclosure of the old Fatimid palaces, Saladin also created a place for teaching law.[42] In March 1177, in the city of al-Qāhira, near the sword market *(suyūf)*, he founded the first Hanafite madrasa (al-Suyūfiyya), converting part of the palace of the former Fatimid vizier al-Maʾmūn al-Batāʾihī.[43] In the thirteenth century, Ibn Khallikān remarks, not without reason, that Saladin's madrasas, so numerous and well supplied with *waqfs*, were not generally known under his name. He concludes that such "secret alms," that is, alms given without any publicity, were also the most meritorious.[44]

With the founding of these five new madrasas, Saladin clearly announced his program for reestablishing Sunni law in the Egyptian capital, and several members of his entourage followed his example. His brother al-ʿĀdil founded a Shafite madrasa in al-Fustāt, probably sometime after Saladin's death.[45] In 1171, his nephew Taqī al-Dīn ʿUmar had moved into a former Fatimid palace (Manāzil al-ʿIzz) overlooking the Nile, which he bought from the public treasury. A few years later, when he left Egypt for Syria, he turned that residence into a Shafite madrasa.[46] In 1174–1175, a Kurdish emir founded a new Shafite madrasa (al-Qutbiyya) in al-Qāhira.[47] Also in al-Qāhira, al-Fādil founded near his residence a madrasa that bore his name, the Fādiliyya, dedicated to the Shafite and Malekite rites. For that madrasa, completed in 1184, al-Fādil named the famous Andalusian reader Abū l-Qasim al-Shātibī[48] to teach the Koran and appointed a jurist, a native of Alexandria, to teach Malekite and Shafite law.[49] The madrasa had a magnificent library, which reportedly contained some hundred thousand volumes. It must be said that al-Fādil had recuperated a portion of the books from the former library of the Fatimid caliphs, as well as those of the very rich library of Amida. He himself spent most of his income adding to it. He never missed an opportunity to purchase rare books, such as the precious Koran in Kufic characters, attributed to Caliph 'Uthmān (r. 644–656), which he supposedly acquired for more than thirty thousand dinars. It could still be admired in his madrasa in the fifteenth century. Copyists and binders worked for him without respite. Unfortunately, most of that library was dispersed a century later, during the great famine of 1295, when starving students would sell books for a piece of bread.

The Hanbalites of Egypt also wanted to provide themselves with a madrasa. 'Izz al-Dīn 'Abd al-Hādī, a Hanbalite from Damascus whose father had accompanied Shīrkūh to Cairo, undertook to build one. He died before its completion, however, which no doubt explains why it was never finished.[50] At least nine madrasas were thus founded in the Egyptian capital under Saladin's reign, all endowed with abundant *waqfs* to assure their operation.[51] Other madrasas were constructed elsewhere in Egypt. In 1182, Saladin built one in Alexandria over the tomb of his brother al-Mu'azzam Tūrānshāh, who had died two years earlier.[52] In the principal city of Middle Egypt, Madīnat al-Fayyūm, Taqī al-Dīn also founded two secondary schools, one for Shafites and the other for Malekites.[53] In Upper Egypt, by contrast, where Shiism was more firmly implanted, it was only after Saladin's death that the first madrasas appeared.[54]

Although Saladin's personal foundations were less numerous in Syria than in Egypt—no doubt because Sunnism had already gained strength under Nūr al-Dīn—the growth of madrasas was very active, spurred on by members of his entourage.[55] The sultan had construction projects undertaken in the Umayyad Mosque in Damascus, where the Eagle Dome above the central nave was restored, the marble facing of some columns entirely redone,[56] and the Shafite *zāwiya*, located inside the mosque, allotted new *waqfs*.[57] He focused his activities as well on the north part of the building. Nūr al-Dīn, having observed that the main mosque was no longer sufficient to contain all the faithful, had added an annex in 1160 to the outside of the mosque's north wall. This annex was called al-Kallāsa, after the neighborhood where it was located, and where lime *(kils)* had previously been processed. That structure burned down during a major fire in 1174, along with the adjacent Minaret of the Fiancée. Saladin had it restored, improved the water supply system, reestablished an imam there to lead prayer, and set up a *zāwiya* for the teaching of Shafite law. Modern historians have had a tendency to believe that the building was originally a madrasa founded by Nūr al-Dīn.[58] But all the Syrian authors from the twelfth to fourteenth centuries considered it an extension of the Great Mosque and not an independent madrasa. Al-Kallāsa is always included in the description of the Umayyad Mosque, and its imam is very often mentioned, by himself or with the other imams of that mosque.[59] Ibn Jubayr, in his chapter devoted to the Umayyad Mosque, leaves not a shadow of a doubt on the subject: "On the north side of the court is a massive gateway giving on to a large mosque [*masjid*]. In the middle of this is a court with a large round marble basin into which water continuously plays from a white, octagonal, marble bowl set in the middle of the basin on the top of a tubed column up which the water rises. This place is called al-Kallasah [the Lime-Kiln], and there to-day prays our companion, the jurisprudent, ascetic, and traditionalist Abu Jaʿfar al-Fanaki of Cordova. In great numbers men come to follow him in prayers, to receive his benedictions, and to hear his fine voice."[60]

Quite quickly, sheikhs came to teach at that place, and in the thirteenth century several prestigious teachers taught there in succession. It took time, however, for the name "al-Kallāsa madrasa" to become established; that name was not commonly used until the fifteenth century.[61] In Saladin's time, the madrasa was still only an extension of the Great Mosque, and just as that mosque had a large number of teaching circles, so al-Kallāsa included a *zāwiya* where Shafite law was taught.[62] It was in the same neighborhood that al-Fādil founded a specialized establishment for teaching the Prophet's traditions.[63] Nūr al-Dīn had been the first to introduce that type of school into Syria, on the model of what was occurring in the eastern regions of Iran. Either independent or attached to another religious establishment, two such schools existed in Damascus and three in Aleppo during Saladin's lifetime.[64]

In 1174, Damascus already had about twenty madrasas, nine or ten of which had been built under Nūr al-Dīn's reign in Damascus (1154–1174).[65] Under Saladin's reign (1174–1193), which lasted approximately the same number of years, at least a dozen more madrasas were built, the majority of them Shafite and Hanafite.[66] Although most were constructed by members of his family or by emirs in his entourage, their remarkable growth attests to a religious policy desired and encouraged by Saladin.

It has always been believed that, in Damascus, Saladin did not build any new institutions of learning but simply restored or completed those that had been founded by his predecessor.[67] I have shown elsewhere, however, that he was probably the founder of a Malekite madrasa near the Nūr al-Dīn Hospital, later known under the name al-Salāhiyya.[68] It is true that the sources are rather ambiguous on the subject.[69] Ibn ʿAsākir attributes to Nūr al-Dīn the founding of a Malekite madrasa in a Damascus neighborhood called the "Golden Stone." Other sources speak of a Malekite madrasa near the Nūr al-Dīn Hospital founded by Saladin but not bearing his name. Modern historians have concluded that there was only a single Malekite madrasa, founded by Nūr al-Dīn near his hospital and undoubtedly completed by Saladin. Their view rests for the most part on the hypothesis that the Golden Stone neighborhood extended to the Nūr al-Dīn Hospital, which can still be admired today, southeast of the citadel. Yet the indications given by nearly all the medieval sources locate the Golden Stone neighborhood, known for its beautiful residences, at the northwest corner of the city, between the citadel to the west, the rampart to the north, and the Great Mosque to the east.[70] Its southern boundary is more difficult to determine precisely, but it is very unlikely that it extended to the neighborhood of the Nūr al-Dīn Hospital.

It would seem, in fact, that there were two quite distinct Malekite madrasas: one founded by Nūr al-Dīn in the Golden Stone neighborhood, and the other by Saladin in the vicinity of the Nūr al-Dīn Hospital. Since Nūr al-Dīn also founded a teaching circle for Malekites in the Great Mosque,[71] we may conclude that the Malekites possessed in Damascus three teaching sites at the end of Saladin's reign. Attributing the foundation of such a madrasa to Saladin is not without its importance, since it means he displayed toward the Malekites of Syria—whose numbers were growing as Maghrebi immigration increased—if not the same interest as in Egypt, where that community was larger and better rooted, then at least a fairly great attention.

In Aleppo, the construction of madrasas was delayed in the early twelfth century by the city's large Shiite community. Upon Saladin's arrival in 1183, there were nine (five Shafite and four Hanafite), as well as two zāwiyas in the Great Mosque (one Hanbalite and one Malekite). Saladin did not add any new madrasas in that city, where his uncle Shīrkūh and his nephew Husām al-Dīn Ibn Lājīn had already founded one apiece under Nūr al-Dīn's reign.[72] As for the Great Mosque, devastated by fire in 1169, it had just been entirely rebuilt and

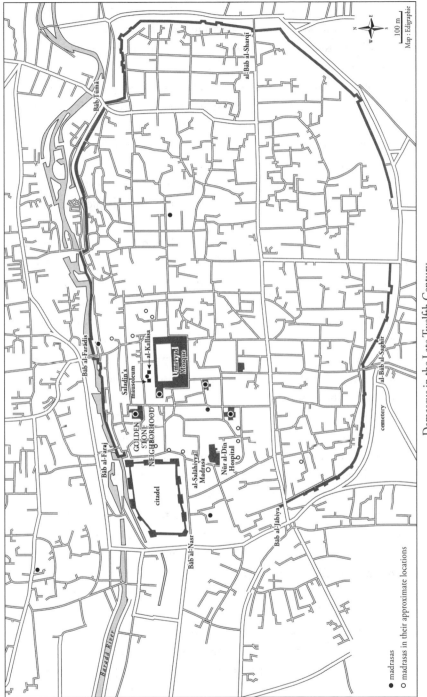

Damascus in the Late Twelfth Century

- ● madrasas
- ○ madrasas in their approximate locations

al-Bāb al-Sharqī

Bāb Tūmā

Bāb al-Farādīs

al-Kallāsa

Saladin's mausoleum

Umayyad Mosque

GOLDEN STONE NEIGHBORHOOD

Bāb al-Faraj

citadel

al-Ṣalāḥiyya Madrasa

Nūr al-Dīn Hospital

al-Bāb al-Ṣaghīr

cemetery

Bāb al-Naṣr

Bāb al-Jābiya

Barada River

100 m

Map : Edigraphie

expanded by Nūr al-Dīn, who had also endowed it with new *waqfs*. It seems to have withstood quite well the major earthquake that shook Syria in 1170, since, though its minaret swayed, Saladin did not order any major construction work to be done on it.[73]

Conversely, the sultan granted special attention to Jerusalem, where he established many *waqfs* to restore several Islamic religious monuments.[74] He began by restoring the emblematic buildings in the Noble Sanctuary (Haram al-Sharīf). Three inscriptions commemorating these restorations have been preserved, including one in situ at the Dome of the Rock.[75] Saladin personally oversaw appointments and the choice of religious staff attached to al-Aqsā Mosque (preacher, imam, muezzins) and at the Dome of the Rock (imam) and allocated generous revenues to them.

The sultan also decided to turn the Church and Convent of Saint Anne, north of the Haram al-Sharīf, into a Shafite madrasa (al-Sālahiyya). That institution, perhaps envisioned in 1187, was not completed until 1192, as indicated by its foundation inscription. Revenues from lands, gardens, springs and baths, shops, a kiln, and a mill were earmarked for its upkeep. All these mortmain properties were confiscated from Frankish religious institutions and purchased from the public treasury by Saladin, who wished to mark thereby the private dimension of his foundation. The foundation text very precisely stipulates teaching protocols. The teacher had to begin his classes each morning with verses from the Koran and a prayer for Saladin and all Muslims. The law classes were then to be followed by a *disputatio* and could be complemented with lessons in religious science. The teacher himself had to do the teaching and was not allowed to have a substitute, except under circumstances beyond his control. He was remunerated from *waqf* revenues at the rate of fifteen dinars a month, plus a few measures of wheat. Jurisconsults, placed under his leadership and authority, repeated the lessons to the students, who were obliged to live at the madrasa unless they were married. Finally, Saladin entrusted the honor of being the first teacher of that madrasa to his friend Ibn Shaddād.[76]

In Syria-Palestine as in Egypt, the Shafite school benefited the most from the foundations of Saladin and his close circle, but the other schools, especially Malekism in Egypt and Hanafism in Syria, managed to hold on to the influence they had acquired over the previous decades. That strengthening of official Sunnism did not mean the disappearance of a form of popular religiosity that appealed to all Muslims, Sunni and Shiite. The many pilgrimage sites in Cairo and in the Delta frequented by both are a good illustration.[77] Similarly, the Sunnis did not hesitate to participate in Shiite celebrations, such as Ghadīr Khumm and ʿĀshūraʾ, which the Fatimids had made official holidays.[78] When Saladin took power, he also hastened to restore, for his own benefit, the prestige of the Shiite sanctuary in Cairo, which housed the head of ʿAlī's son al-Husayn. That precious relic had been brought back from Ascalon in the mid-twelfth century, to be protected from the Frankish occupation within the surrounding wall of the caliphal palace itself. Saladin enlarged the sanctuary and endowed it with very rich presents, thus integrating it, like the nearby al-Azhar Mosque, into the Sunni faith:

> We shall begin by mentioning the monuments and blessed shrines, which for their beneficence are preserved by Great and Glorious God. Of such is the great tomb in Cairo in which is kept the head of Husayn, the son of ʿAli ibn Abi Talib, may God hold them in favour. It is in a silver casket and over it has been built a mausoleum so superb as to be beyond description and beyond the powers of the mind to comprehend. It is covered with various kinds of brocades, and surrounded by white candles that are like large columns; smaller ones are placed, for the most part, in candlesticks of pure silver and of gilt. Silver lamps are hung from it and its whole upper part is encircled with golden spheres like apples, skilfully executed to resemble a garden and holding our eyes in spell by its beauty. There too are various kinds of marble tessellated with coloured mosaics of rare and exquisite workmanship such as one cannot imagine nor come near to describing. . . . To be short, I do not believe that in all existence there is a more superb work or more exquisite and wonderful building. May God in His grace and favour sanctify the noble bones that are within it.[79]

That place continued to attract crowds and subsequently remained one of the centers of popular Egyptian Islam. As often in similar cases, Sunni historiography justified that appropriation by an extraordinary event, in this case, the invulnerability of the person who had formerly transported al-Husayn's head from Ascalon to Cairo. That devotion for the family of the Prophet is somewhat reminiscent of that surrounding the Shiite sanctuaries of Aleppo, where Sunni historiography turned to its own account the miracles that had accompanied the founding of these buildings, to explain the attention that Sunni rulers paid them. Saladin and his son al-Zāhir went there on pilgrimage and spent large sums of money for their upkeep just as, later on, the Mamluk sultan Baybars had at least one of these monuments restored.[80]

In general, the pilgrimage sites, which offered a means of expression for popular forms of devotion, attracted people of different faiths and for all sorts of reasons: because they contained cult traditions, sometimes very ancient; because they developed around figures venerated in the three monotheistic religions; or quite simply, because miracles ascribed to them were expected and hoped for by all. Those sites in Saladin's states were no exception. For example, in the early thirteenth century, the Christian pilgrim Thietmar did not neglect to note that in Saydnāya, north of Damascus, the icon of the Virgin healed Muslims as well as Christians; that in Hebron everyone meditated beside the grave of the patriarchs; and that at the Saint Catherine monastery of Sinai, "even the great sultan king of Babylon [Cairo], when he came, venerated that place with humility and entered it barefoot."[81]

Saladin and Sufism

Throughout the twelfth century, alongside Sunni institutes of learning, Syrian cities had witnessed the construction of establishments for Sufis (khānqāh or ribāt). These institutions were also part of the Sunni revival initiated by the Seljuks and their epigones. Under the influence of the Iranians who had arrived in the Seljuks' wake, Sufism in its most popular form experienced a rise in interest in Syria. In Saladin's time, there were not yet any firmly constituted brotherhoods in Syria, but the Sufis did gather together inside their establishments to devote themselves to prayer and to elevate themselves toward God through ecstasy. Music concerts and mystical dances helped them in that effort, and it was not unusual for important figures to be invited to witness them. At first, a great mistrust impelled some religious circles to oppose that form of mysticism, particularly in Aleppo, where in the early twelfth century it was believed that the Sufis' idleness and strange customs set a bad example for the residents.

Encouraged by Nūr al-Dīn, however, these establishments finally took root. Upon Saladin's arrival, there were already about ten in Damascus and nine in Aleppo.[82] It fell to Saladin to introduce them in Egypt, where some received them with the same wariness, even hostility, that the Aleppines had formerly shown. In that respect, the reaction of al-Wahrānī is significant: however much a satirist, he was reflecting the image that that form of Sufism had in certain milieus. In one of his stories, he describes Sufis crossing paths with the Prophet on Resurrection Day. The Prophet asks who they are. He is told they are members of his community, but lazy people who have abandoned their occupations and withdrawn to oratories, where they dedicate themselves to eating and drinking. In response to a question from the Prophet about their usefulness, he is told that they are not useful for anything or to anyone, and that they resemble the castor oil plant, which absorbs water in a garden and reduces the available space. The Prophet then goes on his way and refuses to grant them the slightest attention.[83] Elsewhere, al-Wahrānī makes fun of the Sufis celebrating the Feast of Sacrifice, which concludes the pilgrimage. After listening to a few lines of love poetry, they yell, howl, and stamp their feet so hard that the floor collapses beneath them. The dead are buried, even as certain Sufis, impervious to what is happening around them, continue to dance.[84]

These criticisms had no effect on Saladin, who displayed the greatest respect for mystics and ascetics who withdrew from the world. In Cairo, he founded the Khānqāh Sa'īd al-Su'adā' on behalf of foreign Sufis, in a Fatimid residence across from the old vizierial palace where he lived.[85] He appointed a sheikh and placed all the Sufis of Egypt under his authority. The sheikh's salary, the Sufis' food, and the upkeep of the building were paid for by *waqf* properties allocated to the foundation in 1173–1174. The foundation deed stipulated that any inheritance of a Sufi below twenty dinars could not be seized by the public treasury and would devolve on the Sufis of the establishment. Near the building, Saladin also had a hammam built for them. In the Mamluk era, that first *khānqāh* of Egypt was rebaptized the Duwayrat al-Sūfiyya (Small Sufi Monastery). Muslim travelers needing a place to stay could find refuge there, and the population of Cairo came every Friday to receive the blessing of the Sufis, whom they then accompanied in procession to al-Hākim Mosque. In the fifteenth century, some three hundred Sufis were still being supported there.[86] Also in Cairo, the residence of a friend of Saladin's father, who was in the habit of receiving his friends at his home on the banks of the Nile, was also turned into a residence for Sufis after his death, in accordance with his wishes.[87]

[385]

Saladin encouraged the same type of foundation in Syria-Palestine. In Jerusalem, he turned the Patriarchate across from the Holy Sepulchre into a *khānqāh* (al-Sālahiyya), to which he allotted many *waqfs* (mill, kiln, houses, lands, bath, cistern), former properties of the Latin patriarch, the Hospitallers, and the Holy Sepulchre, and he named a Shafite to be in charge of it.[88] The foundation deed stipulates that the establishment would accept Sufis of all ages and backgrounds, married or single, and that they would recite the Koran and pray for the founder and for all Muslims. The office of sheikh, that is, head of the Sufis, was hereditary, but in the absence of an heir it was supposed to fall to the best among them. In Jerusalem as elsewhere, other forms of ascetic life were also common. Some devout souls preferred to live alone, withdrawn from the world, in a little oratory, a cellar, or a cave. Saladin took various measures on their behalf. For example, he earmarked the revenues from the Mount of Olives for the support of two of them,[89] and in 1191 allowed an ascetic to move into an old Byzantine building south of the Haram al-Sharīf.[90] In the coastal cities that he managed to reconquer, Saladin similarly founded establishments for Sufis. The one in Ascalon, Duwayrat al-Khadrā' (The Green Monastery), was abandoned when the city was destroyed.[91] In Acre, the former residence of the Hospitallers was divided in two: one half was turned into an establishment for Sufis and the other into a madrasa.[92] In Damascus, finally, the house that Saladin had previously occupied after Nūr al-Dīn named him governor of the city was also turned into a *khānqāh* (al-Nāsiriyya) at an unknown date.[93]

All these actions attest to Saladin's great interest in Sufism. It is clear, however, that his actions were always those of a protector and never of an adherent, though he enjoyed attending Sufi concerts of mystic music, as in Hama in 1187.[94]

Against the Heretics

By contrast, he had great distrust for all the mystical or philosophical currents that could appear suspect in the eyes of Sunni "orthodoxy," that is, by the jurists in his entourage. He "hated the philosophers, those that denied God's attributes, the materialists and those who stubbornly rejected the Holy Law," Ibn Shaddād said of him.[95] That opinion was shared by 'Imād al-Dīn: "How often did he quash the foolishness of those who philosophized! How often did he guide people toward true knowledge by his enlightenment! Ceaselessly he defended the faith, tamed the heretics by dispersing them, let the light of the rule established by the Prophet shine bright, found the fruits of paradise to his taste, professed the Shafite rite in its principles and applications, believed in its rational and traditional elements."[96]

For the most part, the targets of these accusations were the rationalistic philosophical and theological currents. Yet the line between "orthodox" mystic currents and those that were called "heterodox," even heretical, was not always easy to draw. At times, mystics adopted odd and even extreme ascetic practices. Take, for example, the Iranian mystic Rūzbihān al-Kāzarūnī, who spent a few years of his life in Aleppo, then in Damascus, and finally in Cairo, where he died. Everywhere he went, he had the habit of shouting very loudly, even on Friday at the Great Mosque during prayer, or in the middle of a sermon. The ulemas, annoyed by his cries, dared not say anything, because miracles (karamāt) were attributed to him. Surrounded by his disciples, flutists, and singers, he walked the streets, his hair unkempt and a small ax in his hand, and lived from beggary.[97]

Those men, however eccentric they may have been, were not considered dangerous. More serious was the conduct of those who denied God's act of creation, minimized Koranic revelation and the prophetic role of Muhammad, and sometimes proclaimed themselves prophets. In 1174, for example, Saladin announced to Nūr al-Dīn that, in Alexandria, he had just arrested a heretic named Qadīd al-Qaffās, who had already done a great deal of harm in Syria and Egypt.[98] No doubt he was inclined to exaggerate the threat, to convince Nūr al-Dīn of the dangers he had to face in Egypt, which also prevented him from going to join Nūr al-Dīn in Syria. At about the same time, in Mashghará, a village in the region of Damascus, a man from the Maghreb was claiming to be a prophet, and many peasants rallied around him.[99] These men were regularly accused of seducing those considered the weakest and most credulous, that is, the peasants, the lower classes, and women.

An entirely different case was that of the great Iranian philosopher and scientist Shihāb al-Dīn Yahyā al-Suhrawardī al-Maqtūl. His 1191 execution in Aleppo illustrates Saladin's distrust of any philosophical or rationalistic mode of thought. The reasons behind the philosopher's decision to settle in Aleppo in about 1183–1184 remain obscure. He moved into the Hanafite al-Hallāwiyya madrasa, probably because all the successive teachers in that establishment, from its foundation in 1149–1150, were, like him, from Iran or Transoxiana.

He very quickly attracted notice for his intelligence, his mastery of dialectics, and his influence over Saladin's son al-Zāhir Ghāzī, then in charge of Aleppo. The "philosophy of the Illumination" *(Ishrāq)* that he advocated and sought to spread was a combination of Platonic philosophy, Persian wisdom, and Hermeticism. He proposed that a new philosophical system be constructed, founded on the harmonization of intuitive and deductive knowledge, which was supposed to lead to true knowledge, the objective of the philosophy of the Illumination.[100]

His ideas met with very strong resistance from the jurisconsults of Aleppo. He was criticized for his philosophical thinking, which was permeated with Greek and Persian influences, for his Ismaili sympathies, and for his Hermeticism. Summoned to reply to the question of whether God could send a new prophet, he responded in the affirmative, arguing on the basis of divine omnipotence. He was then accused of laying claim to prophecy, of engaging in magic and alchemy, and of rejecting holy law. The Aleppine ulemas pressured Saladin to compel his son to have al-Suhrawardī executed for heresy. At first al-Zāhir turned a deaf ear. Then a second letter from his father, threatening to pull him out of Aleppo, obliged him to obey against his will. Behind the religious arguments, to which Saladin was certainly sensitive, more political motives were likely also taking shape. Saladin's power in Aleppo was still fragile and of recent date, and he could not allow himself to alienate religious circles. In addition, there was a risk that Shiism, which was not eradicated in northern Syria, would resurface at any moment. Finally, the situation in Palestine regarding the Franks and Saladin's defeat at Acre dictated caution, and he could not take the risk of setting off a religious crisis in northern Syria. Al-Suhrawardī was therefore executed and his body put on public display for several days. Nevertheless, his philosophy enjoyed great success in Iran. In the late thirteenth century, at least five of his books could still be found in the libraries of the city of Aleppo.[101]

Among the other forms of heterodoxy that Saladin had to fight in the early part of his reign was the extremist Shiism of the Assassins of Syria. In the Middle East of that time, Shiism took various forms. The Ismaili Shiism of Egypt had lost its influence with the fall of the Fatimids. Duodecimal Shiism, dominant in northern Syria until the mid-twelfth century, had also been greatly weakened by Nūr al-Dīn's reign. Of course, the Shiites of Aleppo had recovered a bit of life under his son's reign. In particular, with the aid of the Turkish regent Gümüshtegin, they had managed to have several of their rights restored: to pray in the east part of the Umayyad Mosque; to use the Shiite call to prayer ("Come to the best work"); to evoke publicly, at markets or during funerals, the names of their twelve imams; to utter the Shiite prayer for the dead; and finally, to conduct marriage ceremonies under the authority of their imam.[102] But their religious and political influence could no longer compete with that of the Sunnis.

Did the Assassin sect represent a more serious threat in the early part of Saladin's reign? That sect of extremist Ismailis, born of a crisis of succession to the Fatimid caliphate in the late eleventh century, proclaimed that the caliphate ought to devolve on Nizār, the eldest son of Caliph al-Mustansir (1036–1094), who had been removed from power. The sect, expelled from Egypt, had first taken root in northern Iran around the fortress of Alamut, where its leader, Hasan-i Sabbāh, lived. It then spread to Syria in the early years of the twelfth century. The Assassins quickly won followers among the lower classes and peasantry of Syria, and they turned the murder of Sunni or Shiite figures who opposed the establishment of their law into a political weapon. It was in that sense that they can be called true terrorists. The name "Assassins," which was adopted by Westerners—Arab authors prefer to call them Bātinīs, Nizārīs, or Ismaili[103]—is derived from the Arabic *hashīshiyya*, a term probably employed by the local populations, not because the Assassins used hashish, as is generally believed, but because their extreme behavior suggested that of people under the drug's influence. Subsequently, it became a common noun in most European languages, used to designate a murderer who acts with premeditation.[104]

In Saladin's time, the leader of the Assassins of Syria was Rashīd al-Dīn Sinān, whom the Franks called the "Old Man of the Mountain," because the seat of his power, located in central Syria, was in the mountainous massifs of Jabal Bahrā', between the city of Hama and the coast. His ideological influence, however, was far less than what Hasan-i Sabbāh had enjoyed in Iran in his time. The power of the sect during that period in Syria rested more on the terror it inspired in the population and the services it rendered to leaders anxious to rid themselves of their rivals.

In 1164 an important religious shift had been made by the Assassins. To understand it, let us recall one of the precepts of Ismaili doctrine. Ismāʿīl, the seventh imam in the line of descent of ʿAlī, cousin and son-in-law to the Prophet, disappeared, but he will reappear one day to abrogate the law of Islam, to reveal the hidden meaning of things *(bātin),* and to establish the reign of justice by putting an end to the physical world. In the month of Ramadan 1164, the head of the Ismailis of Alamut suddenly proclaimed the end of Islamic law and declared that he had received a message from the hidden imam, making him vicar and asking him to abrogate holy law. In Syria, that abandonment of Muslim law gave rise to all sorts of rumors, which Sunni circles readily spread: "Men and women mingled in drinking parties; they practised incest," claimed the Aleppine historian Ibn al-ʿAdīm. "The women wore men's clothes, and some of them proclaimed Sinān as God."[105] In 1184, Ibn Jubayr went even further: "On [the] slopes [of the Mountains of Lebanon] are castles belonging to the heretical Ismaʿilites, a sect which swerved from Islam and vested divinity in a man. Their prophet was a devil in man's disguise called Sinan, who deceived them with falsehoods and chimera embellished for them to act upon. He bewitched them with these black arts, so that they took him as a god and worshipped him. They abased themselves before him, reaching . . . a state of [complete] obedience and subjection."[106]

The Western sources repeated these rumors and spread them in turn, as attested by the report submitted by Burchard of Strasbourg to Frederick Barbarossa in 1175, upon his return from his mission in Syria: "This breed of men live without law; they eat swine's flesh against the law of the Saracens, and make use of all women without distinction, including their mothers and sisters."[107]

Murder, idolatry, incest, the mingling and inversion of the sexes: the Assassins were accused of all the transgressions that the popular imagination generally attributes to sects suspected of heresy.

Was Saladin going to allow himself to be influenced by them? Prior to him, some leaders of Syria had been led to compromise with the Assassins, out of fear or opportunism, to obtain their support and to battle their rivals. This was especially the case of the Seljuk prince Ridwān (r. 1095–1113) in Aleppo and, to a lesser degree, of the atabeg Tughtegin (r. 1104–1128) in Damascus. Those who openly fought them often paid with their lives, such as Prince Būrī in Damascus (r. 1128–1132) and the Fatimid caliph al-Āmir (r. 1101–1130) in Cairo. The fierce anti-Shiite policy of the Zangids, Nūr al-Dīn in particular, impelled the

Assassins to fight the Zangids alongside the Franks. In 1149, for example, during the Battle of Inab, Assassins served as reinforcements for Raymond of Antioch's troops, against those of Nūr al-Dīn. In 1173 King Amalric of Jerusalem received an embassy from the Old Man of the Mountain, who had come to propose a new alliance. William of Tyre gives his version of the events:

> It is the custom of this people to choose their ruler, not by hereditary right, but by the prerogative of merit. This chief, when elected, they call the Old Man, disdaining a more dignified title. . . . For about four hundred years they have followed the law and traditions of the Saracens so strictly that by comparison all other peoples seem as prevaricators and they alone the complete observers of the law. But during our times they happened to choose as ruler over them a very eloquent man, of subtle and brilliant intelligence. Contrary to the habits of his ancestors, this man possessed the book of the Evangels and the apostolic law.
>
> The gentle and noble doctrine of Christ and His followers, when compared with that which the miserable seducer Muhammad had transmitted to his accomplices and deluded followers, caused him to despise the beliefs which he had absorbed with his mother's milk and to abominate the unclean tenets of that deceiver. He instructed his people also in the same way and made them cease observing the superstition of the prophet. He tore down the places of prayer which they had been accustomed to use, absolved them from fasting, and permitted the use of wine and pork. At length, desirous of advancing into a fuller understanding of the mysteries of God's law, he sent an envoy to the king. This man, Boaldelle [Abdallah] by name, was wise and eloquent, skilled in counsel, and fully instructed in the doctrine of his master. He bore secret propositions, the main burden and most important article of which was that if the brethren of the Temple, who held certain fortresses adjacent to the lands of the Assassins, would remit the tribute of two thousand gold pieces which was paid to them yearly by his people and would thereafter observe brotherly kindness toward them, the race of the Assassins would embrace the faith of Christ and receive baptism.[108]

On the way back, however, the ambassadors were ambushed by Knights Templar from the region of Tripoli. Amalric sent his apologies to Sinān, and that was the end of the matter. Whether the desire for conversion expressed by the Assassins was only a misinterpretation on the Franks' part of the abandonment of Islamic law, or a ruse by Sinān to eliminate the tribute paid to the Templars, the anticipated alliance never came into being. These exchanges, however, shed light on the reasons why, in the early part of his reign, Saladin many times accused the Assassins not only of heresy but also of collusion with the Franks.

It is within that context that Saladin's conflict with Nūr al-Dīn's Zangid family occurred. At the time, Gümüshtegin was acting as regent in Aleppo for the young al-Sālih, but he could not count on the support of the Syrian emirs, most of whom opposed him. He therefore sought the aid of the Assassins to consolidate his power and, especially, to get rid of Saladin. Twice Saladin was the victim of assassination attempts. The first took place in early January 1175, while he was besieging Aleppo. Thirteen assassins, armed with daggers, managed to make their way into his army's camp. One of his emirs, Khumartegin, lord of the castle of Bū Qubays, whose lands were adjacent to those of the Assassins, recognized them and sacrificed his life trying to stop them. A melee followed: all the assassins were killed as a result, but not before they killed a few soldiers and members of Saladin's close circle. Writing to his nephew Farrūkhshāh, then in charge of Damietta, Saladin recounted all these events, encouraging him to remain on his guard and to choose his collaborators with the greatest care, to avoid a similar misadventure.[109]

The precautions he took did not prevent him from being the victim of a second assassination attempt the next year. On May 22, 1176, while he was besieging 'Azāz, north of Aleppo, four assassins, disguised as soldiers in his army, managed to enter the camp. One of them flung himself on Saladin, who was observing the fighting from the tent of one of his emirs. Although protected by his helmet and brigandine, which he never took off for fear of attacks, Saladin was thrown to the ground by his assailant and was saved only through the intervention of one of Shīrkūh's old mamluks, Sayf al-Dīn Yāzkūj, who killed the assailant. Some of Saladin's other emirs rushed in and killed two of the attacker's companions; the fourth, who was trying to flee, was torn to pieces by the men of the camp. Saladin escaped with a superficial wound to the cheek, but the attack caused him a great fright, and one of his emirs died of his wounds.

Protection measures around the sultan were increased. A wood palisade was even set up around his tent, and henceforth only people he knew were allowed to approach him.[110]

It must be said that the Assassins had an impressive ability to infiltrate the close entourage of sovereigns while wearing various disguises, as this anecdote attests:

> My brother (God have mercy on him) told me that Sinān sent a messenger to Saladin (God have mercy on him) and ordered him to deliver his message only in private. Saladin had him searched, and when they found nothing dangerous on him he dismissed the assembly for him, leaving only a few people, and asked him to deliver his message. But he said: "My master ordered me not to deliver the message [except in private]." Saladin then emptied the assembly of all save two Mamluks, and then said: "Give your message." He replied: "I have been ordered only to deliver it in private." Saladin said: "These two do not leave me. If you wish, deliver your message, and if not, return." He said: "Why do you not send away these two as you sent away the others?" Saladin replied: "I regard these as my own sons, and they and I are as one." Then the messenger turned to the two Mamluks and said: "If I ordered you in the name of my master to kill this Sultan, would you do so?" They answered yes, and drew their swords, saying: "Command us as you wish." Sultan Saladin (God have mercy on him) was astounded, and the messenger left, taking them with him. And thereupon Saladin (God have mercy on him) inclined to make peace with him and enter into friendly relations with him. And God knows best.[111]

Most of the sources insinuate that Gümüshtegin was the one who ordered these assassination attempts on Saladin. The next year, in 1177, Gümüshtegin turned the Assassins' daggers against his former ally, Vizier Shihāb al-Dīn Ibn al-'Ajamī, a member of an influential family from Aleppo. Gümüshtegin did not draw any benefit from that murder, however. The young prince al-Sālih, persuaded by this close circle that Gümüshtegin was seeking to overthrow him and seize power, and was ready to sell the Franks his fortress of Hārim, east of Antioch, had Gümüshtegin arrested in late summer 1177. When

Gümüshtegin refused to return Hārim, no torture was spared him: suspended by his feet outside the walls of his fortress, he was plunged into vinegar and lime, squeezed between planks of wood, and finally strangled with a bow string. His hands and neck were broken, and his body was cast into the moat surrounding the city.[112]

It is nonetheless likely that the Assassins were not simply responding to Gümüshtegin's demands but had other reasons for attacking Saladin. No one at the time was unaware that Saladin, having entered Damascus, intended to take over all of Syria, including the territories controlled by the Assassins. Witness his raids against Sarmīn, Ma'arrat Misrīn, and the Jabal Summāq—regions where the Assassins were well implanted—beginning in spring 1175, once the cities of Homs and Hama were conquered.[113] The second assassination attempt against him, as well as the accord concluded with Aleppo on July 29, 1176, persuaded him to pursue the offensive by attacking the very base of their power: the powerful fortress of Masyāf, west of Hama, which was used as Sinān's residence. Mangonels were set up outside the wall, and the soldiers began to lay waste the surrounding lands. Then, about a week later, Saladin abruptly ordered the siege lifted.

The reasons for that abandonment have never been completely clarified. Some explain it by threats the Assassins may have made to Saladin's maternal uncle, lord of the neighboring city of Hama. That uncle may have attempted to temper the ardor of his nephew, in a context also marked by the weariness of the army and of the emirs, who were longing to return home. Others link that retreat to the Franks' offensive into Bekaa or to Tūrānshāh's withdrawal.[114] It was undoubtedly all these reasons together that impelled Saladin to lift the siege. Yet they do not account for the end of the conflict between Saladin and the Assassins. For indeed, over the following years, hostilities ended on both sides. Was there a secret accord between Sinān and Saladin to observe a truce that suited both camps? That is suggested by an Ismaili account, distorted by legend to be sure, according to which Saladin, frightened by Sinān's supernatural powers, agreed to withdraw after the prince of Hama had interceded in his favor. Sinān supposedly granted him safe conduct, and the two men then became good friends.[115]

We will undoubtedly never know whether Saladin really feared the Assassins or whether he judged that his priorities lay elsewhere, with his struggle against the Zangids and the Franks. What is certain is that Sunni historiography has preferred to hold on to the image that his entourage sought to spread, that of a sovereign violently opposed to any form of heresy. For Sibt Ibn al-Jawzī, for example, Saladin never abandoned the idea of fighting the Assassins. Saladin, he tells us, was preparing to attack them after concluding the truce with the Franks, when his death prevented him from doing so.[116]

Although they now left Saladin alone, the Assassins continued their attacks on the Aleppines and then on the Franks. In 1179–1180, after an attack by al-Sālih against a village populated by Ismailis southeast of Aleppo, Sinān sent his men to set fire to the souks of Aleppo. The fire ravaged a large portion of the markets and swallowed up considerable riches, without a single Assassin being taken.[117] On April 28, 1192, in the Frankish port of Tyre, the Assassins succeeded in killing Marquess Conrad of Montferrat, who had just been chosen king of Jerusalem but had not yet had time to be crowned. That assassination caused a great stir in the West. The chroniclers spread all sorts of stories about the Assassins, their methods, their mores, and their extreme devotion to their master, to such a degree that the Assassins even made an appearance in courtly literature: "Just as the Assassins serve their master unfailingly," says a troubadour, "so I have served Love with an unswerving loyalty."[118]

Their many assassinations and the fear they inspired made such an impression on the Western imagination that it became common to attribute to them assassinations or assassination attempts even in the heart of Europe. In the conflict between France and England, it was said sometimes that the king of France made use of their services to kill the king of England; at other times, the reverse was alleged. Rigord, author of a history of Philip Augustus, informs us that letters "from overseas" reached the king of France in Pontoise, informing him that Assassins *(Arsacides)* had been sent to kill him on the order of the king of England: "Overseas, in fact, they had already killed the marquess, the king's cousin, a man valiant in battle, who ruled the Holy Land with an admirable valor, with all his strength and all his might, before the arrival of these kings. King Philip, burning with anger upon learning the content of these letters, immediately left that castle and remained in a state of extreme distress for several days."

Also according to Rigord, Philip Augustus sent messengers to the Old Man of the Mountain to seek assurances about the veracity of that rumor: "But in the meantime, as a greater precaution, the king posted bodyguards, who always had bronze sledgehammers in hand and who watched over him by turns all night long. Upon his messengers' return, the king learned through the Old Man's letters that the rumors were false. Thanks to the report of his messengers, who had conscientiously sought out and learned the truth, the false rumor was dismissed; and his mind, freed from that false suspicion, found peace."[119]

21

Christians and Jews

Non-Muslims upon Saladin's Accession

In the twelfth century, Jews and especially Christians were still numerous in Egypt. In certain localities, the Christian population even remained in the majority: Qūs, for example, which in the eleventh century had become the economic and political capital of Upper Egypt.[1] In 1175 Burchard of Strasbourg, Frederick Barbarossa's ambassador, was surprised by the large number of churches in Alexandria and Cairo, where Muslims, Jews, and Christians freely practiced their faiths.[2] Some time later, in the early thirteenth century, the Coptic author of *The Churches and Monasteries of Egypt* counted thirty-seven churches and five monasteries for the single city of al-Fustāt and its outlying area, plus four churches and a monastery in the Fatimid city of Cairo. Christian buildings were also very numerous in the region of Giza, southwest of Cairo, on the other side of the Nile.[3] Also according to that source, in Egypt there were at least 707 churches and 181 monasteries, most of which collected large revenues from the lands granted to them by the former Fatimid caliphs.[4] Large non-Muslim communities also continued to live in Syria-Palestine, in large cities such as Damascus and Aleppo but also in the countryside, where some villages were still entirely populated by Christians.[5] Under Saladin's reign, then, the church played a not insignificant role in the economic and social life of his states.

It is very difficult to form an exact idea of the number of these non-Muslims, since the figures given by travelers and chroniclers are imprecise and vary widely from one source to another. Depending on the source, for example, in the late twelfth century Damascus counted between three thousand and ten thousand Jews, Aleppo between fifteen hundred and five thousand.⁶ The estimates for Egypt amounted to slightly more than four thousand Jews for the Egyptian capital and about half that for Alexandria.⁷ Christians were more numerous. Aleppo and the surrounding villages supposedly counted between twelve thousand and twenty-eight thousand Christians in the thirteenth century, out of a total population fluctuating between fifty and eighty thousand.⁸

Jews and Christians were subject to rules, elaborated in the seventh and eighth centuries and codified in a convention known as the "Pact of 'Umar," which granted them the status of "protected persons" *(dhimmīs)*. That status gave them the right, in exchange for a capitation, to practice their religion freely and to keep their religious institutions and buildings. The *dhimmīs* were also obliged to respect a certain number of restrictive and often discriminatory rules: not to insult Islam, not to attempt to convert a Muslim, to refrain from assisting the enemies of Islam, not to build new religious buildings or even restore any, to avoid all contact between a male *dhimmī* and a Muslim woman, to wear distinctive hairstyles and clothing, to possess neither weapons nor horses, and so on. In principle, the *dhimmīs* were also excluded from the army and public service. These rules, theoretically quite harsh, were applied very inconsistently over the course of history, depending on the power in place, the region, and the era; the atmosphere was often much more tolerant in practice than in theory. The Fatimid period in particular, with the exception of the reign of Caliph al-Hākim (996–1021), was very favorable for the *dhimmīs*, who often held important positions, especially in the administration—some were even viziers—and in medicine.

Dhimmī communities did not present a united front—far from it—and their divisions sometimes undermined their interests, giving the Muslim authorities the opportunity to play the role of arbitrator. In Egypt, the Christological quarrels of the fifth century had profoundly divided the Christians between, on one hand, the Monophysite Copts⁹—by far the most numerous—and, on the other, those who had remained faithful to the doctrine defined by the Council of Chalcedonia in 451, who for that reason were called Chalcedonians (or Melkites).¹⁰ Each community obeyed its patriarch, both of whom had left Alexandria to settle in Cairo after the founding of the Fatimid dynasty. A third Christian community was added to these in the eleventh century, that of the Armenians, also Monophysites, who came to join the Egyptian army under the viziership of Badr al-Jamālī (1073–1094), himself an Armenian. In the Egyptian capital, the Armenians were concentrated in a neighborhood called al-Husayniyya, located to the northwest, outside the walls of Cairo. Many also settled in Upper Egypt in the 1130s, under the viziership of another Armenian, known as Bahrām (1135–1137).[11]

There were many Melkites in Syria-Palestine, especially in Palestine and northern Syria, where the seat of the patriarchs of Jerusalem and Antioch was located. The installation of a Latin church in these two cities in the late eleventh century complicated the situation for the Melkites, whose patriarchs often sought refuge in Constantinople. The Chalcedonian church nevertheless kept many churches and monasteries in both Frankish and Muslim territory. The other large Christian community of Syria and Upper Mesopotamia was that of the Jacobite Syrians, who, like the Copts and Armenians, were Monophysites. They were answerable to a patriarch living in Antioch, who in Saladin's time was none other than the famous historian Michael the Syrian (patriarch from 1166 to 1199). Armenians were also present in Upper Mesopotamia, northern Syria, and Jerusalem, though in smaller numbers. As for the Maronites, followers of Monotheletism (two natures but a single will in Christ),[12] they officially embraced the view of the Church of Rome in 1182. In Saladin's time, most of them lived in the mountains of Lebanon and on the narrow coastal plain between Jubayl and Tripoli. William of Tyre estimates their number at forty thousand, calling them "a stalwart race, valiant fighters, and of great service to the Christians in the engagements which they so frequently had with the enemy."[13] They therefore seem to have leaned toward the Franks and to have played the role of intermediary. But here as elsewhere, caution is called for, since the violent opposition of part of the community to the union agreement with Rome in 1182[14] would seem to indicate that not all Maronites supported the policy of the Latins in the region. In reality, for lack of sources, their history remains extremely obscure until the end of the Middle Ages.

These many divisions among Christians—sometimes even members of a single community—greatly weakened their position vis-à-vis the Muslim authorities, which sometimes resulted in comical situations. Take the case of the Coptic priest named Ibn al-Qanbar, who, having been judged a heretic by his church hierarchy, appealed for arbitration from the sultan. He wrote al-Fādil, asking to appear before a new assembly with the patriarch presiding. Al-Fāḍil replied that a new assembly would give a ruling, but, should it sentence him to expulsion, there would be nothing more he could do but become Muslim because, he said, "you will be neither Jewish nor Christian."[15] The priest ultimately became a Melkite, which did not put an end to his disappointments, since he wasted no time in finding himself in conflict with his new superiors. That case, no doubt extreme, is nonetheless indicative of the role the Muslim authorities were sometimes led to play at the request of the Christian communities themselves.

Between Repression and Coexistence

Upon his ascent to power, Saladin was quickly faced with the question of the *dhimmīs*. During the 1160s, the Christians had seen several of their churches in al-Fustāt burned down or looted, as reprisals against the Frankish attacks and during the city's great fire of 1168. Saladin's accession to power did not initially improve matters. Very quickly, he opposed the Armenians, who constituted large contingents of cavalrymen and foot soldiers in the Fatimid army. During the revolt of the blacks in 1169, the Armenians sided with them and thus became victims of the same repression. They had to abandon a large number of their churches and monasteries, some of which were turned into mosques. In confiscating the property of the Armenian church and military, Saladin undermined the economic foundations of that community and dealt it a fatal blow.[16] The patriarch himself had to leave al-Basātīn monastery in the southern outskirts of Cairo and move to al-Zuwayla neighborhood, near the Church of Saint John the Baptist. But he did not remain long. After the definitive fall of the Fatimid caliphate dashed all hopes of the Armenians returning to their previous situation, in November 1172 he decided to go to Jerusalem, where the Armenian community, settled in that city since the fifth century, maintained good relations with the Franks. He left, taking what he could of the sacred books and liturgical vessels, and leaving an ordinary priest as his surrogate in Cairo.[17] Because the Armenians no longer had any authority to represent them, the Copts, by a decree from Saladin, obtained possession of the former al-Basātīn church, which they finished restoring in 1177. The following years were marked by a few attempts on the part of the Armenians to recover their churches. A bishop and several priests were even sent from Armenia to intercede on behalf of their community. They arrived in Cairo bearing letters from Saladin and al-ʿĀdil, recommending that Taqī al-Dīn ʿUmar treat them honorably. They managed to reclaim one of their churches, but not al-Basātīn, which remained in the hands of the Copts.

The renewed enforcement of the discriminatory measures by Shīrkūh and then by Saladin made the *dhimmīs'* situation even more difficult.[18] Not only were the *dhimmīs* compelled to respect the rules regarding distinctive clothing, but the buildings and celebrations of their faith were to remain discreet, and they were forbidden to bear arms, consume wine or pork in public, ride horses or mules, and especially, work in the administration.[19] Not all the *dhimmīs* were driven out of the administration, however, since their departure would have resulted in too great an administrative disorganization. Nevertheless, these measures prompted many to convert to Islam. A Christian source speaks of fourteen thousand conversions. Although that number may be exaggerated, it attests to the shock produced in the non-Muslim community by that new attitude of the authorities.[20] Among those who converted to hold on to their positions was al-Muhadhdhab Ibn Mammātī, secretary in the bureau of the army, and his son al-Asʿad, who succeeded him. Al-Asʿad was the author of many works, including a life of Saladin in verse and a cadastre of the inhabited places of Egypt, in which he provided very precise information about Egyptian agriculture and craft industries. He was a great friend of al-Fādil, who called him "the nightingale of the councils" because of his great eloquence and very literary style.[21]

Saladin, in reinstating the obligations bearing on the *dhimmīs,* more than likely wanted to gain the goodwill of the most radical of the ulemas who surrounded him and whose support he needed in order to govern. Among these was Qādī al-Fādil, whose influence over Saladin we have already had occasion to note. It seems to have been al-Fādil who urged the sultan to take measures to eliminate the Christians from the financial administration.[22] The Shafite jurist al-Khubūshānī, whose reputation extended far beyond the Egyptian borders,[23] was even more radical. He said he wanted to kill all the *dhimmīs* he happened to see on horseback. Once, when he ran into one of Saladin's Jewish doctors, al-Muwaffaq ibn Shūʿa, riding his horse, he threw a stone at him, hitting him full in the face and taking out an eye.[24] The leader of the Egyptian Shafites, Shihāb al-Dīn al-Tūsī, does not seem to have been any better disposed in that respect, since he extorted money and gifts from the Christians, had two churches shut down, and looted the great al-Basātīn church.[25] Despite all these pressures, a short time later Saladin allowed Christians to restore their destroyed buildings and to reclaim their positions within the administration. One Egyptian Christian source even claims that the position they came to occupy was superior to what they had had previously. Many other sources attest to the important role they continued to play in the administration in both Egypt and Syria.[26]

In fact, not all the Christians and Jews in Saladin's states saw their situation deteriorate consistently or continuously. The early years were certainly difficult, because Saladin wanted to appear, in the eyes of his entourage and in "public opinion," to be a sovereign who applied religious law strictly. That hardening of the official policy toward the *dhimmīs* gave rise to some more or less uncontrolled popular uprisings, and both the *dhimmīs'* possessions and their persons were targeted. But in such cases, Saladin always reacted forcefully, making sure that the pact of protection to which the Jews and Christians had a right by that same religious law was applied. We know, for example, that at the beginning of his reign, he recognized the protection to which the monks of the Saint Catherine Monastery of Sinai were entitled.[27] Moreover, in Aleppo in 1183, having reestablished a stricter observation of the rules imposed on the *dhimmīs*, and in the face of the outbursts that his measure provoked in the population, Saladin immediately decreed that he was reaffirming his will to protect the non-Muslim communities, out of respect for religious law:

> After we ordered that the *dhimmīs* should wear the distinctive signs
> that differentiate them in their appearance from Muslims, and that
> this should be established in accordance with the requirements of
> manifest and pure divine law, the news reached us that a band of
> irresponsible hoodlums had attacked the *dhimmīs* with despicable
> words and acts, curbing what the pact of protection [*dhimma*] had
> granted them regarding their means of subsistence and their situation. We disapproved of that, and we are obliged to prohibit such
> things from being said and done.
>
> We command what is set down in that document and judgment, namely: guard and protect those *dhimmīs;* abstain from harming and harassing them; do not cause them any wrong; do not institute wrongful proceedings against them and do not deviate from
> the straight and narrow regarding them; do not alter the justice

that is guaranteed them; do not interfere with the benefits supplied them; do not attack them in acts or words. Let them therefore not be subjected to hearing disagreeable, prejudicial, or unjust words. May they obtain the rights of the contract of protection consistent with its statutes and with justice; and may they enjoy these rights to the full in what they are granted in benevolence by them. May their blood and inviolable property be protected; may the means of subsistence distributed to them be abundant; may the activities guaranteed them be strengthened; may the interests they wish to defend be organized; and may the decrees of religious law as it is defined apply to them. . . . The emirs and other governors must execute that judgment, must guarantee these *dhimmīs* against injustice, and must protect them in every situation and, in case of incident, from any harm and loss.[28]

This decree is very significant with respect to Saladin's desire for appeasement and his wish to see non-Muslims live in peace on his territories. We learn, therefore, that the leader of the Jewish community of Egypt once sought him out to ask him for a confirmation of common practice, namely, the right of his community to judge matters of Jewish inheritance, even in cases where the legitimate heir was a minor or where no heir existed. Saladin consulted Malekite and Shafite jurists, who confirmed that the judgment truly devolved on the leader of the Jewish community, and that Muslim jurists were not to intervene, unless the two parties asked them or in the case of obvious false testimony.[29]

Saladin's clearly expressed desire to respect Muslim law does not mean that the *dhimmīs* definitively returned to peace and tranquility. More than once, they had to suffer the whims of circumstance and resign themselves to having their churches temporarily shut down following military expeditions,[30] or to being mistreated by a jurist less than well disposed toward them. In 1181–1182, after the promulgation of new decrees in Egypt intended to enforce the restrictions on non-Muslims, the population looted a few churches on the pretext that they had just been restored. The Melkites, less numerous than the Copts, were no doubt the chief victims.[31]

In al-Fustāt, however, most of the churches were ultimately restored under Saladin's reign, thanks to the gifts of wealthy members, the sale of cult objects,

and sometimes even money from simony. In one way or another, the possessions of Christians were returned and the damages repaired. In 1187, a new
church devoted to the Virgin was even dedicated near the old Church of Saint
John the Baptist, in a neighborhood south of al-Qāhira.[32] Ultimately, the Christian authors, who lament the many destructions and exactions at the beginning
of Saladin's reign, also recognize that his governance was that of a just and generous prince who ensured his subjects' well-being by eliminating the illegal
taxes and lowering prices.[33] In the commercial realm especially, the rules reinstated by Saladin ought to have doubled the customs taxes paid by the *dhimmīs*.
But, given the difficulty of enforcing that measure—as attested by the letter
from a Jew of Alexandria asking his brother, who was involved in trade in the
Indian Ocean, to entrust his merchandise to a Muslim so as to pay fewer
taxes—the idea was quickly abandoned by Saladin himself.[34]

Repercussions of the Crusades

What was the Eastern Christians' reaction upon the taking of Jerusalem by
Saladin? Did they celebrate with the Muslims as members of a community
united by history and the Arabic language? Or did they instead declare themselves in solidarity with their Crusader coreligionists? Present-day historians
do not all agree on that subject. Sometimes they point to evidence that supports the view that the Eastern Christians joined the Franks, and sometimes to
reports that argue in favor of their neutral or even welcoming attitude toward
Saladin. The reality was likely somewhere between the two, since the *dhimmīs*
never formed a monolithic bloc. Their reactions varied from one community
to another, depending on whether they were in Muslim or Christian territory,
and on the kind of relationship they maintained with one group or the other.

The Jews, who had suffered as much as the Muslims from the taking of
Jerusalem by the Franks, were subsequently able to live in peace under Latin
domination in the coastal cities, particularly Tyre and Ascalon. But since, with
a few rare exceptions, they were still banished from Jerusalem, they had some
reason to rejoice at Saladin's victory, which allowed them to return there to
live. That authorization was no doubt also intended to fill the void left by the
Franks' departure.[35] So it was that a community of Jews from Ascalon came to
settle in the holy city after Saladin destroyed their own city. The return of
these Jews to Jerusalem marked the beginning of a larger-scale immigration

movement in the thirteenth century, from Europe and the Maghreb, where there had been new outbreaks of persecution. Most of these new immigrants, however, chose to settle in Acre and the rest of the Latin kingdom rather than in Jerusalem, which was experiencing a dark period: it was destroyed a first time in 1219 by al-Mu'azzam, the Ayyubid prince of Damascus, who was afraid it would fall back into the Franks' hands; then the holy city once again came under Frankish domination in 1229, but was sacked and destroyed in 1244 by the Khwarezmians, Turkish mercenaries in the service of the Ayyubid sultan of Egypt. That eventful history hardly encouraged permanent settlers.[36]

Saladin's tolerance toward the Jews is perceptible in several Christian and Jewish sources. The prelate Bar Hebraeus, for example, recounts that during the siege of Acre, a Jewish merchant from Damascus, transporting a cargo of Egyptian sugar by boat, was arrested by the Muslims as he approached Acre. But Saladin, whom he called on for assistance, immediately had him released. Even more significant was the elaboration of a truly Jewish legend of Saladin. In Jewish circles it was recounted that in 1185, which is to say, two years before the Battle of Hattīn, a Jewish instructor saw in a dream the Muslims spilling Christian blood. That dream was immediately interpreted as the sign of the Jewish people's deliverance. Similarly, a forged letter sent to the Jews of Fez in 1187, shortly before the taking of Jerusalem, was attributed to Maimonides. It contained a declaration in which Saladin stated that he would stamp out the Franks but that, in the end, a Jewish king would rule over the holy city. Knowing that this king would seize power peacefully, Saladin expressed the hope of finding "favor in his eyes." In that legend, the sultan's capture of Jerusalem appeared as part of the divine plan, at the end of which the Jews would reclaim their land and their holy city. In about 1217, the traveler and Spanish Jewish poet al-Harizi said nothing less in his dialogue with a resident of Jerusalem:

"When did the Jews come to this city?" "Since the Ishmaelites [Muslims] captured it, the Jews settled it," he answered. "And why did they not live in it when in the hands of the uncircumcised [the Christians]?" He said: "Because they said that we killed their God and we put them to shame. Should they have found us, they would have eaten us alive." "So how did it happen that you are in this place?" He answered: "God was zealous for his name and had pity on his nation. . . . God stirred the spirit of the king of the Ishmaelites in the year four thousand nine hundred and fifty of Creation [September 14, 1189–September 3, 1190], and the spirit of wisdom and bravery rested upon him; and he and all the hosts of Egypt went up and put siege to Jerusalem and God delivered her into his hands. And he ordered that a proclamation should be made in every city, to old and young, namely: 'Speak ye on the heart of Jerusalem, whoever is from the seed of Ephraim, whether in Assyria or in Egypt, and those forsaken at the ends of the horizon, those who are willing should ingather from all the world's corners and dwell inside her boundaries.' "[37]

Joshua Prawer goes even further, asserting that the catalyst for Jewish immigration to the East in the thirteenth century lay less in the new outbreaks of persecution in the West than in the Jews' perception of Saladin's victories over the Franks. In that great confrontation between Christendom and Islam, with the possession of the Holy Land at stake, the position defended by several major Jewish personalities was that the Jews were to take possession of the Promised Land (Deut. 12) by settling there. "The living in the Land of Israel is a commandment which outweighs all other commandments," preached the great thirteenth-century scholar Nahmanides, who left Spain to settle in Jerusalem and then in Acre. On one hand, there was a resurgence of Messianic hopes, and on the other, the development of a more pragmatic approach, aimed at encouraging the Jews to settle on that land, over which the three monotheistic religions were fighting. Of that land, Nahmanides said: "Ever since we departed from it, it has not accepted a single other nation or language. They all try to settle it, but it is beyond their power."[38]

Among the Christians, the Armenians represented a special case. In Egypt, those who belonged to the Fatimid army were exterminated in great number in the early part of Saladin's reign, and their patriarch sought refuge in Jerusalem. A small Armenian community nevertheless survived in Egypt, as attested by the author of *The Churches and Monasteries of Egypt*.[39] In the Latin states, the Armenians were relatively well integrated into Frankish society, particularly in Antioch and Jerusalem. The two communities were united by many marriages, and in the late twelfth century, the formation of an Armenian kingdom of Cilicia, an ally of the Latin states, only strengthened those bonds.[40] Although, given the absence of sources, it remains difficult to know what the

Armenians living in Islamic countries thought, there is little doubt that those of them who lived outside Muslim territories had clearly chosen sides. In certain manuscript colophons, it was written that the Muslims were a "foreign people of circumcised cutthroats,"[41] and Archbishop Nerses of Tarsus, crafter of the rapprochement with the Latin church, unambiguously denounced the "arrogance" of Saladin, who had conquered the Christian princes because "they were bowed under the weight of sin." Of the kings of France and England, he said:

> From them we await salvation,
> Just as [we await] the assistance of God.
> So that the words of the prophets may be fulfilled:
> "You will deserve to rejoice."
> Amen![42]

From the seat of his power at Qal'at al-Rūm (Horomklay), a powerful fortress in the Upper Euphrates Valley locked within Islamic territory, the Armenian catholicos Gregory IV (r. 1173–1193)—the same man who wrote Saladin in 1190 to warn him against the arrival of the Third Crusade's German army—composed a long, 2,395-line plaint on the taking of Jerusalem by the Muslims:

> I come to give voice to dolorous strains,
> Plaints interspersed with tears. . . .
> I come to recount my sad fate
> And lamentable suffering. . . .
> I am the ancient Jerusalem,
> Capital of Palestine,
> Center of the Universe. . . .
> Against me marched the Scythians [Turks]
> Who punished me so severely. . . .
> [The Creator] delivered Jerusalem to a ruthless enemy
> For the sins of which we were guilty. . . .
> Jerusalem, that beautiful city,
> Capital of the Promised Land,
> The Egyptian entered it
> Like a shameless adulterer;
> He sat on the steps of the sanctuary,

and it was sullied by the abomination of the desert.[43] . . .
Golgotha was profaned,
The Temple stained,
The Holy Sepulchre shut down. . . .
[The Infidels] engaged in depravity
In the Holy of Holies,
As the law of Muhammad prescribes;
They committed acts of sodomy. . . .
They called us worshippers of a piece of wood,
Through insult and mockery;
Falling on us like wolves,
They dispatched the innocent lambs. . . .
The streets of Zion
Were stained with blood
And obstructed by their comings and goings. . . .
I suffered alone in silence,
No one coming to my aid,
Not the emperor of the Greeks,
Or my French troops,
Or those who glory in me,
Or those who found their support in me,
Or the great and powerful ruler of Germany . . .
Who came to me in droves,
Rushed inside my walls and there set to rejoicing,
Today not a single one has been found
To help me in my desperate straits. . . .
Now two years have elapsed
And still I suffer in torment.[44]

Although it is indisputable that most of the texts reflect real sorrow at the loss of Jerusalem, it is also true that they contain a more or less explicit condemnation of the Christians themselves, whose sins were considered the cause of all their misfortunes. In that respect, the sources are consistent with the medieval conception of history, a providential history whose events were solely the result of God's wise governance. These accounts often have in common a tendency to exaggerate. Muslims are accused of crimes they did not commit, such as plunging Jerusalem into a bloodbath. The objective was less to reflect reality than to rouse, and sometimes to justify one or another request for assistance from the West.

Lamentations of the same kind are found in the writings of a few Nestorian and Syrian writers from the late twelfth century, who also lived outside Muslim territories. The Jacobite patriarch of Antioch, Michael the Syrian, writes, for example: "On Saturday the fourth day of Tamouz [July], the Franks were abandoned [by God] because of our sins, and were wretchedly carved to pieces. . . . Sālah al-Dīn killed with his own hand the old Arnald [Reginald of Châtillon] and the three hundred brothers [Knights Templar and Hospitaller] and bathed in their blood. . . . How many outrages, how much abuse and contempt, the Muslims forced the persecuted Christian people to endure, in Damascus, Aleppo, Harrān, Edessa, Amida, Mardin, Mosul, and in all the rest of the empire, no words can say."[45]

The emotion caused by the loss of Jerusalem is perceptible in several colophons of Syriac manuscripts;[46] one Syriac plaint from the early years of the thirteenth century also grieves the loss of the holy city.[47] In 1247, some Nestorian Christians were still regretting that the Christian reaction to the loss of Jerusalem had not been keener: "All the churches of Christ, the monasteries, and all the faithful in the East and West should have worn hair shirts, should have sat down in sorrow and wept for Jerusalem, for what happened in our time," wrote the Nestorian catholicos Sawrīsho' V to Pope Innocent IV.[48] Particularly interesting is the testimony of the author of the *Syriac Chronicle*, who was in Jerusalem in 1187. He confirms that the Eastern Christians, once their ransom had been paid, were free to go where they liked, but he also adds that they had to sell off their possessions for a pittance or abandon them: "Words cannot describe the crimes that our eyes saw perpetrated in the city, just as no book could contain them: how the sacred vessels were sold at the city markets, in the hands of people of different races, how the churches and altars became sheds for horses and cattle and places of debauchery, of drinking and song."[49]

The Christian authors residing in Saladin's states expressed rather different feelings. In Egypt, the *History of the Patriarchs* went so far as to suggest a complicity between the Melkites of Jerusalem and the sultan. According to this book, a Christian called Joseph al-Datīt, a native of the holy city, made the acquaintance of the Ayyubid family in Damascus before the conquest of Egypt. A few years later, he moved into the former Fatimid palace of Cairo, and Saladin used him as a messenger to the Franks. The sultan charged him with urging the Melkite Christians of Jerusalem to hand over their city in exchange for money. Balian, having learned of this, proved to be better disposed toward dealing with Saladin as a result. Is that historical truth, or libel from a Coptic source hostile toward the Melkites? It is difficult to determine, though two letters sent from the Holy Land to Europe, one by the Order of the Hospitallers and the other by Genoese, repeat that rumor.[50] Of even more interest is the passage from the *History of the Patriarchs* that suggests Saladin's successes can be explained by the fact that God guided him and led him to apply the principles of the Torah and of the Gospel, unbeknownst to himself: "Sālah al-Dīn acted according to the command of these two religious laws, without knowing them, but [it was] an inspiration from God, and on account of this he died on his bed, and his end (was) praiseworthy for himself and his descendants."[51]

The prelate Bar Hebraeus deplored the fate that had befallen the Christians living in Muslim territory during Saladin's conquests. According to him, they fell prey to every sort of mockery and abuse. But he displays no particular hostility toward Saladin in his account of the events of 1187, an account inspired in great part by that of 'Imād al-Dīn. Bar Hebraeus insists rather on what he calls Raymond of Tripoli's betrayal of his own camp and Saladin's magnanimity toward the Franks.[52] As for the small community of Georgian Christians of Jerusalem, it seems to have persevered after the retaking of the city by Saladin. No doubt it endured some despoliation in 1187, but the Georgian embassy received by Saladin on September 1, 1192, had the objective, precisely, of receiving authorization to reclaim their possessions and to restore the Georgian monastery located outside the city.[53] It seems to have obtained satisfaction, since a few years later Jacques de Vitry observed that Western pilgrims hardly dared enter the holy city, whereas the Georgians could penetrate with great pomp, brandishing their flags.[54]

From all these accounts, it emerges that the reaction of non-Muslims to Saladin's conquests was not unanimous. The Armenian Christians, because of their close ties to the Latins, and because most of them resided outside Muslim territories, were without a doubt the most distressed. The Nestorians and the Syrian Jacobites from the states neighboring Saladin's also grieved the loss of

Jerusalem and the desecration of the churches. The reactions of Christians and Jews living within Saladin's states were much more cautious and mixed. It is true that the authors living in his territory could not openly side with the Franks, and we need to relativize their rather favorable views of Saladin. Nevertheless, the measures he took tended to be of a reassuring nature. In all the reconquered territories, he offered to reinstate the protected status they had had before the Frankish occupation. Most accepted that pact and kept their possessions, in exchange for the capitation.[55]

In Jerusalem, they had to pay the same ransom as the Franks but then enjoyed freedom of movement. Many remained where they were. Of course, the Jacobites had to give up their Church of Saint Mary Magdalene, northeast of the city, not far from the Saint Anne Church, but they probably recovered the old German Church of Saint Thomas in the southern part of Jerusalem. Behind that policy of relative tolerance, economic interests were being played out as well, since Saladin knew that the Christians and Jews were needed to cultivate the surrounding lands and to maintain the region's economy. That, in any case, is what his secretary suggests: "In addition to the tribute, the [Eastern] Christians who remained in Jerusalem had to pay the capitation, in order to remain wholly secure and not be harassed or expelled. Their situation was thus regulated by the jurisconsult 'Īsā. Among the Christians, four parish priests of the Church of Qumāma [the Holy Sepulchre] were also allowed to live there, enjoying total immunity and full tax exemption. Thousands of Christians remained in Jerusalem and its region. They set to work, planted vines and established plantations, and soon gathered in fruits and vegetables."[56]

The question of how Saladin treated the Eastern Christians has been raised often over the centuries, particularly in the nineteenth, when Christian communities fought—even among themselves—to have their long presence in the Holy Land acknowledged. One of their arguments was that their possessions had been recognized by the great conquerors of Jerusalem, Caliph 'Umar (r. 634–644) and Saladin in particular. It was only a small step to fabricating counterfeit documents to attest to certain rights, and some did not hesitate to take it. In 1844, for example, a Greek Orthodox archimandrite of Cyprus produced a forgery attesting to the concessions granted by Saladin to the Ethiopians of Jerusalem, whose legacy the Greeks and the Armenians had been fighting over for two centuries. But nothing allows us to conclude, on the basis of an argument e contrario, that the Eastern Christians were mistreated by Saladin or that they left his territories to seek refuge in Christian territory.[57] No Latin or Arab source mentions such a thing. It is not impossible that some Eastern Christians chose to follow the Latins in 1187, but we must refrain from drawing any overly simplistic conclusion. The reality probably lies between the representation sometimes given—of an idyllic situation in which all the Christians and Jews rejoiced at the reconquest of the holy city by the Muslims—and the overly negative view, of Christians deprived of freedom who took refuge in great number in Frankish territories.

In times of conflict, the situation of the Jews and especially of the Christians seems to have been particularly vulnerable. They could very quickly be suspected, rightly or wrongly, of aiding the Franks, and as a result could find themselves once more in the position of hostages or the object of reprisals. In 1182, for example, the Franks arrived in Dārayyā, outside the gates of Damascus, threatening to destroy its mosque. The governor of Damascus told them, through the intermediary of Eastern Christians, that it would be easy for the Muslims to restore it later but that, conversely, all the churches in Muslim territories, which he would order destroyed, could never be rebuilt. These arguments, it seems, sufficed to persuade the Franks to retreat.[58] A few years later, in September 1191, Saladin ordered the demolition of the citadel of Ramla, on the road between Jaffa and Jerusalem, to keep the Franks from seizing it, and also had the Church of Saint George in Lydda destroyed.[59] Shortly thereafter, some Eastern Christians were accused of having delivered letters to the Franks from the governor of Jerusalem, in which they noted the lack of men and provisions in that city. They were immediately executed.[60] These Christian populations could also suffer as a result of raids by the Frankish armies themselves. That is attested, for example, by the anonymous author of the *Syriac Chronicle,* who describes the Frankish expedition conducted in 1178 against Hārim, east of Antioch, and the looting to which the Christians fell victim. They were the reason, he said, that God did not give the victory to the Franks.[61]

The Role of Christians and Jews in Saladin's Entourage

Despite the renewed enforcement of the ban on *dhimmīs* serving in the administration, many of them remained in Saladin's entourage. Since the Islamic conquest, they had continued to play an essential role at every level of the administration, and Saladin could not—and probably would not—abruptly break that tradition, which would incur the risk of complete disorder. In his fiscal treatise from the late twelfth century, the Egyptian al-Makhzūmī observes that the Jews and the Christians transmitted the posts of secretary and doctor from father to son, and maintained their supremacy in that area because young Muslims were not inclined to train and work under their direction.[62] Even Saladin's father, Ayyūb, had a Christian secretary, who followed him over the course of his career, from Tikrīt to Egypt.[63] And a great deal of evidence confirms the presence of Jewish and especially Christian secretaries in the entourage of Saladin and the Ayyubid emirs. In Aleppo from 1183 to 1186, al-'Ādil employed a Christian secretary who had converted to Islam and who was himself accused of recruiting too many of his former coreligionists into the administration.[64] In 1190 'Imād al-Dīn complained of the Coptic secretaries assigned to pay the volunteers who agreed to go reinforce the garrison of Acre: "For the most part, these people were Christians from Egypt who offered to aid their coreligionists, while complicating for us what needed simplifying, muddling what we wanted to resolve."[65]

Another example of the importance of non-Muslim secretaries in Saladin's entourage, but also of the consequences resulting from the Christians' internal quarrels, is provided us by the Jacobite patriarch Michael the Syrian, who has no words harsh enough for one of his most virulent opponents:

> Then, once again, as was his habit, he reneged on his promises. He went out to find a man like himself, and plotted during the night. He made ropes, went over the convent wall, and fled to Damascus. There they composed a document in Arabic and got themselves introduced to Sālah al-Dīn, king of Egypt. He promised to give that king money if he would grant him an edict stipulating that he would be accepted as patriarch by all his states. He also libelously wrote things about me deserving of death. When his document was read before the king, he sought to know where it was from. There were a few faithful there who were scribes in the king's chancery; after they had told him his story, the king drove out the impious Bar Wahboun and did not receive him.[66]

In addition to administration, medicine was the area in which non-Muslims particularly distinguished themselves.[67] Of the dozen doctors surrounding

Saladin, Jews and Christians held a significant place. Although one of them, a Christian, converted to Islam under his reign,[68] others practiced their profession without giving up their religion. For example, the doctor who wrote a short treatise for Saladin on digestive disorders, from which the sultan chronically suffered, was Jewish. One of this doctor's colleagues and coreligionists drew a pension of twenty-four dinars a month from Saladin until the end of the doctor's life, even after he was too old to work. Saladin provided another of his Christian doctors trousseaux for his daughters valued at about thirty thousand dirhams.[69] An even greater influence on Saladin was his Jewish doctor Ibn Jumay' al-Isrā'īlī. Born and trained in Egypt, he was the author of many works, including a treatise he dedicated to the sultan on the need to reform medicine.[70] The author saw several causes for its decline: the neglect by a great number of doctors of the vast theoretical knowledge, in favor of experience alone; the lure of profit, to which some succumbed; and the lack of interest on the part of rulers in that noble discipline. He therefore advised Saladin to choose the best doctors to teach at the hospital, to select the most serious and intelligent students—allocating financial aid to the poorest of them—and to evaluate practitioners' theoretical and practical knowledge, a task for which doctors themselves ought to take responsibility, with the support of the prince and his entourage.

The most famous Jewish doctor and theologian in Saladin's entourage was without a doubt Ibn Maymūn, better known in the West by the name Maimonides, who was born in Cordova in 1135 and died in al-Fustāt in 1207. In about 1148, Maimonides and his family left Cordova to escape the Almohad persecutions. After spending several years in the Maghreb, they moved to the Egyptian capital in about 1165–1166. At first, Maimonides was supported by a profitable commerce in precious stones that his brother undertook in the Indian Ocean. But after the brother lost his life in a shipwreck, Maimonides was obliged to earn his living as a doctor. Protected by Qādī al-Fādil, he was also the doctor of Saladin's eldest son, al-Afdal, to whom he dedicated two opuscules.[71] Maimonides, though very well integrated into the sultan's court—Maimonides' brother-in-law was himself secretary to al-Afdal's mother—does not seem to have been Saladin's doctor, despite what the biographer Ibn Abī Usaybi'a says.[72] That assertion, often repeated by the tradition, is not confirmed by any other Arab source; Maimonides himself, who does not neglect to say that he treated al-Fādil and al-Afdal, never made such a claim.[73]

Maimonides was also named the leader of the Jewish community of Egypt (*ra'īs al-yahūd* in Arabic, *nagid* in Hebrew). In charge of the supreme judiciary, he was given the task of naming the rabbis and representing the Jewish community before the authorities, a position that remained in his family until the Ottoman conquest.[74] It was therefore in Egypt that he wrote a large part of his opus, often in Arabic, such as his philosophical masterpiece, *Guide for the Perplexed.* His many activities left him little time to rest, as he himself wrote to Samuel ibn Tibbon—translator of the *Guide* into Hebrew from the Arabic—in 1199, that is, a few years after Saladin's death:

> I dwell at Miṣr [Fustat] and the sultan resides at al-Qāhira [Cairo]; . . . My duties to the sultan are very heavy. I am obliged to visit him every day, early in the morning; and when he or any of his children, or any of the inmates of his harem, are indisposed, I dare not quit al-Qāhira, but must stay during the greater part of the day in the palace. It also frequently happens that one or two royal officers fall sick, and I must attend to their healing. Hence, as a rule, I repair to al-Qāhira very early in the day, and even if nothing unusual happens, I do not return to Miṣr until the afternoon. Then I am almost dying with hunger. . . . I find the antechambers filled with people, both Jews and gentiles, nobles and common people, judges and bailiffs, friends and foes—a mixed multitude who await the time of my return.
>
> I dismount from my animal, wash my hands, go forth to my patients, and entreat them to bear with me while I partake of some slight refreshment, the only meal I take in the twenty-four hours. Then I go forth to attend to my patients, and write prescriptions and directions for their various ailments. Patients go in and out until nightfall, and sometimes even, I solemnly assure you, until two hours or more in the night. I converse with and prescribe for them while lying down from sheer fatigue; and when night falls, I am so exhausted that I can scarcely speak.
>
> In consequence of this, no Israelite can have any private interview with me, except on the Sabbath. On that day the whole congregation, or at least the majority of the members, come to me after the morning service, when I instruct them as to their proceedings

during the whole week; we study together a little until noon, when they depart. Some of them return, and read with me after the afternoon service until evening prayers. In this manner I spend that day.[75]

Maimonides' renown was such that, like Saladin, he became a legend. It was claimed, for example, that Richard the Lionheart, having heard of his talents, appealed to him for medical treatment. Without a doubt, that story originated in a biographical entry devoted to the famous philosopher and doctor by a thirteenth-century Arab author:

[Ibn Maymūn] left al-Andalus for Egypt with his family and settled in the city of al-Fustāt, within the Jewish community. He openly practiced his religion and lived in the neighborhood called al-Masīsa.[76] He earned his living trading in precious stones and other businesses of the same kind; people studied the science of the ancients under his direction.[77] This occurred in the last days of the Egyptian Shiite dynasty. They wanted to use him, among other doctors, and send him to the king of the Franks in Ascalon, who had asked them for a doctor. It was he whom they chose, but he refused to participate. Then, when the Ghuzz [Turks] reigned in Egypt, and the Shiite dynasty came to an end, Qādī al-Fādil 'Abd al-Rahīm ibn 'Alī al-Baysānī took him under his wing, showed him favor, and allocated a salary to him.[78]

On the basis of this account, translated into Latin in 1760—without the passage indicating that these events unfolded at the end of the Fatimid dynasty—several nineteenth-century authors concluded that this "king of the Franks" was Richard the Lionheart, who had fallen ill during his stay in the East. In reality, if the reference to the end of the Egyptian dynasty is accurate, it can only have been Amalric (r. 1163–1174), who occupied the throne of Jerusalem during the interval between Maimonides' arrival in Egypt and the fall of the Fatimids in 1171. That probability is strengthened by the fact that Amalric did in fact send for a Christian doctor originally from Cairo.[79] This, then, is how a dual legend came into being: that Richard asked in vain to be treated by Maimonides; and that Saladin sent a doctor to the king of England.[80]

Under Saladin's reign, the *dhimmīs'* situation was not uniform, and the restrictions did not apply to his secretaries and doctors. The circumstances varied as a function of the community, the region, the evolution of conflicts with the Franks, and by social category.[81] In this area as in others, Saladin demonstrated his desire to observe religious law faithfully, but on many occasions he was also compelled to compromise in the face of reality. He therefore continued to use Christians and Jews as secretaries and doctors, while episodically recalling the observance of the rules of the *dhimma*. During his reign, although all was not peace and quiet for the *dhimmīs,* who no doubt lost some possessions and positions permanently, overall they were not prevented from maintaining their place and influence in society.

22

The State, the Prince, and the Subjects

"Bahrām used to commit tyranny, oppression, and injustice, and would not heed counsel. He had a clever vizier who summoned the people and said, 'My advice is that you leave the city for ten days'; and so they left. Bahrām awoke to find no one in the city, and stood perplexed. His vizier told him, 'You know well that a king is only a king because of his subjects; if they are no subjects, he will become miserable like this.'—'What do you advise?'— 'Change your ways.' Bahrām replied, 'I swear it, and I repent.' Then the people returned. Know therefore that kingship depends upon the populace."[1]

This Persian story, recounted in a twelfth-century Mirror for Princes, encapsulates the image people had of the good Islamic sovereign. "Treating one's subjects well is better than assembling troops," wrote al-Harawī at about the same time.[2] And in an early twelfth-century treatise, the first part of which is attributed to the great thinker al-Ghazālī, is this response of Aristotle's to Alexander, who had asked the philosopher which was superior, courage or justice: "If the king has ruled justly, he does not need courage."[3] I have already had occasion to point out the role of justice in the elaboration of the image of the ideal sovereign. According to Muslim law, that justice was exercised by qādīs named by the authorities, but the prince could intervene, especially in administrative matters or abuses of power. Saladin was often solicited by one or another man of religion, poet, or grand emir who wished to receive a post or pension, but also sometimes by ordinary people demanding the reparation of an injustice. He himself once complained to al-Fāḍil that he was being endlessly pestered by these requests. As his advisers reminded him, the favor that God granted to a prince by choosing him above others had a price, that of treating his subjects well, guaranteeing the rule of justice, preventing oppression and tyranny, and ensuring obedience to God's commandments. Saladin sometimes had difficulty compelling respect for those commandments even within his own administration. Did not the satirist al-Wahrānī complain that his money was stolen by a corrupt official? He said he had seen Saladin in a dream and that the sultan had listened to his grievance but that, urged to expedite the matter, Saladin had ordered the compensation paid in pomegranates, that is, in "funny money."[4] That barely veiled criticism of the sultan stands in contrast to the image usually conveyed by his panegyrists.

Saladin's Reforms

Assuring the subjects' well-being was possible only with a healthy and efficient administration. Saladin paid a great deal of attention to his own because the collection of taxes—in other words, the "sinews of war"—rested on it. Of all his territories, it was Egypt that provided him with the bulk of the resources necessary for constructing his many military and religious buildings and for financing his army and his military campaigns. Egypt also provided Saladin with a well-structured administrative organization, which he simply adapted to the growing needs of his army. Under the Fatimids, the administration was divided into different bureaus, or *dīwāns;* the most important were those concerned with financial affairs, the army, and the chancery.[5] Saladin retained the *dīwān* of the chancery and of the army, granting increased importance to the latter, and regrouped financial affairs into an office of the treasury called Bayt al-Māl or Dīwān al-Māl. To oversee the activities of all the bureaus, there was an "inspector of *dīwāns,*" and perhaps even already an "emir of *dīwāns,*" that is, a member of the military charged with aiding officials to collect taxes and to inspire the respect of the powerful.[6]

Saladin, who had been vizier to the last Fatimid caliph, was intelligent enough to take back into his service former Fatimid officials trained in the complex workings of the Egyptian administration. As their superior, Qādī al-Fādil took his role as head of the chancery very much to heart. In practice, he acted as a true vizier, though he never bore that title. He was responsible for managing the entire budget and for drawing up official documents. For ongoing affairs, in Saladin's absence the documents were signed by his representative in Egypt, his nephew Taqī al-Dīn or his brother al-ʿĀdil. Nevertheless, the most important documents were sent to him so that he could inscribe his *ʿalāma:* "Praise be to God, my assistance is in Him," a motto that all the Ayyubid sultans of Egypt after him also used.[7]

Al-Fādil was not the only one who served the Fatimids and then the Ayyubids, and it was often on his recommendation that other high officials from the Shiite dynasty entered Saladin's service and close circle.[8] Among the best known were members of the al-Makhzūmī and Banū Mammātī families, which produced the authors of two important administrative and fiscal treatises.[9] One of these works includes, in addition to a great deal of information on agricultural production and administrative organization, a list of Egyptian communes, based on a cadastral survey that Saladin had drawn up between 1176 and 1181. Such cadastres, which were needed to ascertain the surface area of farmlands so as to verify their legal status and estimate their fiscal yield, had existed in Egypt for centuries. Theoretically, they were to be taken every thirty years, but in reality, between the Arab conquest and the arrival of the Ottomans, the Arab sources record only six surveys of that kind. Saladin's was the fourth, and the oldest to have come down to us (in part).[10] The fact that Saladin gave the order to draw up the new cadastre, some seventy years after the one the Fatimids had done, attests to the importance of the Egyptian legacy in his policy. But also and above all, it attests to his desire to know the exact condition of the lands in that country, so as to decide how and on what basis to redistribute them to his close circle and emirs.

Other reforms of the same kind were undertaken in Egypt from the beginning of his reign. On the advice of his Egyptian administrators, he ordered an adjustment in the calendar for collecting the real estate tax called the *kharāj.* That tax, which provided the Egyptian treasury with most of its receipts, was levied proportionally on harvested crops and paid in coin or in kind, at a rate that varied depending on the nature and yield of the land under cultivation. The tax base was established in September, during the flooding of the Nile. The *"kharāj* year" followed the Coptic solar calendar, so that tax collection would occur every year in the same season, when the crops were ripe. The Hegira calendar was shorter than the Coptic calendar, resulting in an eleven-day gap every year. Approximately every thirty-three years, therefore, an adjustment of one year was made between the *kharāj* year and the Hegira year, to restore the concordance of dates and to avoid confusion. The *kharāj* year was pushed up a year—or sometimes two, when the adjustment had not been made at the proper time. When Saladin took power, the last adjustment dated from the year 501 A.H. (1107–1108). Sixty years later, in 567 (1171–1172), it was decided that a two-year adjustment would be made in the *kharāj* year, so that it would correspond to the Hegira year, and al-Fādil drew up a decree to that effect.[11]

In the fiscal domain, Saladin eliminated the noncanonical taxes *(mukūs)*, thus depriving the public treasury of a large source of revenues. These illegal taxes entailed both customs duties—not recognized by Islamic law but nevertheless applied from the Umayyad era on—and the many taxes on artisanal production, commercial transactions, and on some profitable immovable goods such as gardens, kilns, baths, and mills. Those that Saladin abolished in Cairo in 1171 had provided the state with some hundred thousand dinars per year.[12] The problem had already arisen under Nūr al-Dīn's reign in Syria. Once, Nūr al-Dīn had communicated to Shīrkūh his intention to eliminate the illegal taxes, and Shīrkūh had replied: "Master, if you do so, where will you find the money to compensate the troops, who are paid with these taxes? And you need them for raids and military expeditions."[13] That reply had not sufficed to persuade Nūr al-Dīn to give up his plan.

Saladin made up for that financial loss in part by reorganizing the collection of the *zakāt*, the legal alms levied on the possessions of Muslims (precious metals, merchandise, livestock, cereals, and fruit) beyond the tax-free threshold. The historian al-Maqrīzī says that Saladin was the first to introduce the *zakāt* in Egypt.[14] In reality, it must be understood that he was the first to organize its collection at the state level, since in theory every Muslim could himself distribute the *zakāt* to those for whom it was intended, namely, the most underprivileged, volunteers for the holy war, and travelers. The advantage of the system imposed by Saladin is that part of the money collected could thus be used by the public treasury for financing the jihad—for building up the fleet in particular—or for various charitable institutions. The traveler Ibn Jubayr notes that in Alexandria in 1183, three-eighths of the *zakāt* on precious metals went to the state, which is to say, nearly 40 percent, the rest being allocated to pious and charitable foundations.[15]

Another of Saladin's major reforms was the reorganization of the Egyptian *iqtāʿ*. "From the reign of Sultan Ṣalāh al-Dīn Yūsūf ibn Ayyūb until our own time, the lands of Egypt in its entirety were distributed as *iqtāʿs* to the sultan, his emirs, and his troops," writes al-Maqrīzī, who suggests thereby that Saladin played a decisive role in the universalization and militarization of that remunerative system.[16] The military *iqtāʿ* was widespread in the East from the tenth century on and had been present in Egypt since the Fatimid period. This *iqtāʿ* made it possible to remunerate the emirs by granting them the right to levy taxes on a land or locality in exchange for their military service, but without giving them any rights over the land itself or the people who lived there. In that essential respect, it differed from the Western fief.[17] For the duration of fighting, each emir had to equip and maintain troops with his own income. The number of troops varied as a function of the value of the *iqtāʿ*. Often *iqtāʿ* holders also obtained large-scale administrative powers over the region entrusted to them, in Syria more than in Egypt. Saladin himself held lands for the maintenance of his troops, and al-Maqrīzī's remark suggests that they too were considered *iqtāʿs*.[18]

One of Saladin's first measures in Egypt was therefore the confiscation of the lands held by the Fatimid officers and by the black and Armenian troops, which he redistributed as *iqtāʿs* to his own emirs and his close circle. His family was the first to benefit. His father, Ayyūb, was given Alexandria, Damietta, and the western region of the Delta, whereas Saladin's brother Tūrānshāh received Qūs, Aswān, and ʿAydhāb in Upper Egypt, along with a few other districts. Tūrānshāh thereby earned more than 266,000 dinars per year. His younger brother, Būrī, who had received the region of Fayyūm as an *iqtāʿ*, earned about a hundred thousand dinars annually. When Saladin entrusted the governance of Egypt to his nephew Taqī al-Dīn in 1184, he gave him al-ʿĀdil's former possessions, that is, Alexandria and Damietta, as *iqtāʿs,* as well as outright possession of various other regions, which assured him a total revenue of more than seven hundred thousand dinars.

Saladin's emirs, though they did not earn such large sums, also received major *iqtāʿs*. In Syria, beginning under Nūr al-Dīn's reign, *iqtāʿs* had gradually become hereditary. In addition, though the sovereign theoretically reserved the right to exchange or confiscate his emirs' *iqtāʿs,* in practice Saladin never abused that right,[19] which earned him the support of the great families of emirs. Upon his death, however, some of these families turned against his successors, who had to do battle more than once to impose their authority.

The large military construction projects, as well as the foundation and upkeep of the new pious establishments, were very expensive. To finance them, Saladin allocated, as *waqfs,* the old buildings rented by the state and the Fatimid emirs, usually residences and shops.[20] New measures were also taken with regard to the monetary system. Precious metals were sorely lacking in late twelfth-century Egypt. "If a golden *dīnār* were mentioned, it was as though a jealous husband's wife were talked about in his presence, and if a *dīnār* came to a man's hand it came as an earnest of paradise," writes al-Maqrīzī, describing the monetary situation of the time.[21] In the eleventh century and through the first third of the twelfth, Fatimid gold coinage had maintained a weight very close to the legal standard (4.233 grams) and an excellent alloy (more than 98 percent gold). That was part of the reason that the Crusaders, upon settling in the East, had struck a coin imitating the Fatimid dinar that the Arab authors call the *sūrī* dinar ("Sūr" was the Arabic name for Tyre). Nevertheless, the political and economic problems affecting Egypt at the end of the Fatimids' reign, the size of military expenditures, and the depletion of the gold reserves from the tombs of pharaohs and, especially, from Nubian mines, had led to a serious dinar crisis in Egypt even before Saladin's arrival.

As for the Egyptian silver coinage (the dirham), it had been devalued in the eleventh century, no doubt because silver was becoming increasingly rare and the demand for it was growing. The coins were only 30 percent silver, the rest being copper. These dirhams were commonly called "black" dirhams, or *waraq,* and usually it took between thirty-three and forty "black" dirhams to make a dinar, whereas the exchange rate for the Syrian dirham, made of an alloy of higher purity, was about ten to twelve dirhams for an Egyptian dinar. In the twelfth century, however, the minting of gold and silver in Syria had diminished appreciably, the fineness of the coinage had dropped, particularly for silver coins, and copper coins had entered general use.[22]

After Saladin took power in Egypt, he continued to issue dinars, with a weight that was probably lower than that of the Fatimid dinars, and he now had his name and that of the Abbasid caliph inscribed on them. But above all, he sought to revaluate the silver coinage, and the dirhams struck in Damascus under his reign were again of excellent purity. In 1187 he attempted to replace the Fatimid "black" dirham in Egypt, introducing a new dirham called al-nāsirī (from his title "al-Nāsir"), which was closer to the Syrian dirham. Nevertheless, good and bad coinage continued to circulate side by side, with the black dirham being used for small transactions in Egypt, the role played in Syria by copper coins.[23]

Coinage was not just the vehicle for commercial exchanges. It also had an important political and symbolic value, since on it was inscribed the legitimacy and hierarchical status of the authorities. In addition to the place and date minted, in fact, was the name of the sovereign whose power was acknowledged and that of the caliph, the supreme authority and successor to the Prophet, without whose backing no ruler could remain on the throne. The power hierarchy was also expressed in the issuance of the coinage itself. In Saladin's time and in that of his successors, the minting of gold was still reserved for Egypt. Two exceptions confirm that rule. The first was the issuance of dinars in Yemen between 1177 and 1188, a sign no doubt of the difficulty in controlling a territory relatively distant from the center of power. One of these dinars, struck in 573 A.H. (1177–1178), even bore Tūrānshāh's name instead of Saladin's, with the title "king of Yemen." What are we to think of that surprising sign of independence? At the time, Saladin's brother had already returned to Syria; he therefore cannot be suspected of personal ambition. Was it one of the governors he left behind who thought it advisable to thus proclaim his autonomy? Were these dinars genuine? Where they counterfeited later by a member of the Ayyubid family wishing to legitimate his desire for independence?[24] For the moment, nothing permits us to answer these questions. One thing is clear: from 576 (1180–1181) on, Yemenite dinars again bore Saladin's name.[25] All the Ayyubid gold coins also had the name of the Prophet on them, followed by a verse from the Koran asserting the superiority of the Muslim religion, in accordance with the practice used for the Fatimid dinars: Muhammad, Prophet of God who "sent . . . [him] with guidance and the Faith of Truth, so that He may exalt it above all religions, much as the pagans may dislike it" (Koran 61:9).

The second exception to Egypt's monopoly on the minting of gold coinage was a dinar issued by Saladin in Damascus in 1187, which must no doubt be linked to his desire to celebrate his victory over the Franks. Although the reserves of Egyptian gold remained larger than those of Syria, the fact that no other Syrian dinars were struck can be explained only by the political will to reserve the issuance of gold coins for the seat of power, that is, for Egypt.

Dirhams, by contrast, were struck in Saladin's name in all the major cities of his states. In Aleppo, beginning in 1183, a new type of dirham came into being. It bore a six-pointed star, or Solomon's seal, with the inscription appearing inside and around the image. That motif, which also existed on a few of Saladin's Mesopotamian dirhams and on the Artukid coinage of Upper Mesopotamia, was characteristic of Aleppine currency throughout the Ayyubid period. Conversely, in Damascus, Homs, and Hama, Saladin introduced a dirham whose central inscription appeared in a square, itself surrounded by subsidiary inscriptions.[26] The comparison made between Saladin and Solomon was favored by the importance granted to Jerusalem but also, no doubt, by the Koranic verses relating Solomon's battle against the kingdom of Sheba. Sheba had wandered from the straight path and had stood up to Solomon, before finally recognizing his authority (Koran 27:22–44). Did not Saladin likewise reproach the Aleppines for having joined with the enemies of Islam and for having opposed his domination, only to ultimately submit? It is not impossible—though the sources remain silent on the subject—that, for this reason, Saladin chose to have the seal of the king of Jerusalem appear on the Aleppine coinage that now bore his name.[27]

Equally unusual were the copper coins struck in Saladin's name, on which figural representations appeared. Such coins were relatively rare in the medieval Islamic world. Those from the twelfth century that have come down to us are copper coins minted in central and eastern Anatolia or in northern Mesopotamia, first on the model of Byzantine copper coins, and later in imitation of other pre-Islamic coins—Greek, Roman, Parthian, or Sassanid.[28] In Aleppo as well, a copper coin was struck in 1175–1176 with the name of al-Malik al-Ṣāliḥ and a head crowned with a diadem.[29] On copper coinage from Nisībīn, issued in 1182–1183, a bust is represented, its head topped with a Sassanid-style crown; the figure wears no beard, and the hair hangs in two sidelocks.[30] Appearing on other coins dating from 1190, with no indication of where they were struck, is a figure seated cross-legged on a low, square-backed throne and wearing a

turban, in exactly the same position as certain distinguished figures represented on Eastern miniatures from the late twelfth century. That is, the left
hand is placed on the left thigh, and the right hand, brought to the chest, holds
an object that could be a cup or globe.[31] On some of these copper coins, Saladin's name appears with that of the Abbasid caliph al-Nāsir li-Dīn Allāh or that
of a local governor. Sometimes two busts are represented, which confirms that
these figures were in no way portraits of Saladin but were merely reproducing
much older monetary models.

Saladin, then, far from obliterating the achievements of his predecessors and
starting over, knew how to use and adapt them to his needs, while imposing
the necessary political and financial reforms. In having his name and that of
the Abbasid caliph inscribed on coinage, and by introducing new numismatic
models, he asserted his power and legitimacy. The drop in receipts resulting
from the elimination of the noncanonical taxes were in part made up through
monetary reform, a new system for collecting the *zakāt,* and the takeover of
revenues from Fatimid rentals. The confiscation of lands that had belonged to
the supporters of the deposed dynasty, the establishment of a new cadastre, the
adjustment of the *kharāj* year, and the institution of the *jayshī* dinar allowed for
a better exploitation of Egyptian resources and the redistribution of lands to
Saladin's supporters. The aim of all these reforms was less to reorganize the
administration to the advantage of Egypt than to find money for the sultan's
jihad and obtain the support of his faithful.

Difficulties Balancing the Budget

These measures, however, were not sufficient to cover the considerable military expenses incurred by Saladin. Al-Fādil was well aware of this, regretting
that the Egyptian economy was so often squeezed and the public treasury ane-
mic. In 1189 he estimated the total receipts of Egypt at 4,653,019 dinars. Of that,
the share of military expenditures (for compensating the regular armies and
the emirs, Arab auxiliaries, and volunteers, and for restoring the fortifications)
amounted to about 84 percent, that is, 3,917,075 dinars. Most of the rest was
used for the operations of the administrative bureaus and for the pensions of

jurists and men of religion.³² That is an indication of the exorbitant cost of the military campaigns and the large burden borne by Egypt. In early 1184, al-Fāḍil complained to Saladin that he could no longer control the surge in extraordinary expenses. How were they to find the money to pay military leaders returning from expeditions, who had been promised increases in their incomes; the merchants who submitted letters of credit against the public treasuries; the emirs in his entourage or the royal family on whom favors had to be lavished; and especially, the soldiers in the army? How much longer, Saladin's faithful adviser wondered anxiously, could Egypt spend nearly seventeen thousand dinars a day?³³

The situation hardly improved over the years. In 1189, in reply to 'Imād al-Dīn, who complained of his difficulties in Syria, al-Fāḍil said that, had 'Imād al-Dīn been able to see the impoverished state of Egypt and its inhabitants, he would realize that the problems of Damascus were only a drop in the ocean.³⁴ The following year, al-Fāḍil also observed that communications were cut off, the markets and commerce in ruins. Egypt, he said, had lost its gold, and it was only owing to the mediocre quality of the dirhams that they too had not yet disappeared. Saladin spent the money of Egypt to conquer Syria, the money of Syria to conquer al-Jazīra, and the money of all of them to conquer the coast.³⁵ In 1191 events seemed to prove al-Fāḍil right, since not enough money could be found to continue paying the volunteers in the holy war.

It is clear that Saladin's battles against his Muslim neighbors and then against the Franks were very expensive. His policy in that area creates the impression that he was continually rushing forward. By extending himself, he hoped to increase his revenues and to receive money from his new vassals to conduct his jihad. In reality, his expenses grew constantly and his receipts fell. Various factors were involved: the elimination of the noncanonical taxes; the pillaging by his army (as in Acre in 1187); the poorly organized collection of ransoms (during the taking of Jerusalem); his family's debts, which he sometimes had to pay off (two hundred thousand dinars for his brother Tūrānshāh); and a lack of foresight—some would say excessive generosity—that impelled him to let the Franks leave with their possession or to distribute everything to his emirs and entourage. Several members of his close circle would have liked to set aside a little money for the days to come, but it was not to be. Al-'Ādil himself asserted that, after the taking of Jerusalem, he gave his brother seventy thousand dinars, which, in a single night, Saladin distributed to the devout around him. His brother had to send him another thirty thousand the next morning. Ibn Shaddād also recounts that, of the two hundred and twenty thousand dinars collected in Jerusalem, there was nothing left four weeks later; and another historian asserts that Saladin distributed three hundred thousand dinars to the ulemas, and that the emirs pocketed part of the money.[36]

In praise of his generosity, Saladin's panegyrists report many anecdotes that attest to a total absence of foresight in the area of budget management. Many around Saladin took advantage of that weakness, as 'Imād al-Dīn confides: "Of the first trip [in 1176] that I took with him to Egypt—where I arrived at the sweet and pure source of his favor—I shall relate this: the head of his *dīwān* was supposed to supply the accounts for his administration. The account was closed on seventy thousand dinars that he still owed, but the sultan did not demand them or make any mention of them. I have a notion that the sultan took no notice of them because the head of the *dīwān* had not repudiated his debt; because Saladin approved of those deeds that were performed spontaneously and sincerely, and which produced something agreeable and sweet; and because everything he spent was in the interest of liberality and holy war, and on behalf of those who made an appeal to him."[37]

The Armies and the Fleet

Saladin's victories over the Franks might suggest at first glance that he had a very powerful army. Yet it never managed to become as large as that of the Fatimids, which is reported to have numbered some forty thousand cavalrymen and more than thirty thousand black foot soldiers.[38] The Fatimid army was in great part broken up in 1169 with the elimination of the black and Armenian troops, and was replaced by another, different in size and composition.[39] At first, Saladin's army was composed primarily of the troops that Nūr al-Dīn had sent from Syria under Shīrkūh's command: two thousand cavalrymen from the regular Syrian army and five to six thousand Turkoman cavalrymen, recruited by Shīrkūh with the two hundred thousand dinars that Nūr al-Dīn had given him. Shīrkūh and the emirs who accompanied him also set out in the company of their own troops.[40] In all, then, there were some eight to nine thousand Turkish or Kurdish cavalrymen. Not all of them remained in Egypt after Saladin was appointed vizier in 1169. Several emirs who opposed his appointment returned to Syria, taking with them their men and probably some of the Turkomans.

Saladin rapidly had to make up for that loss by recruiting a personal guard of a thousand men and redistributing the Egyptian *iqtā's* to his close circle and emirs to allow them to raise troops in Egypt.

Thanks to al-Fāḍil's invaluable journal, we know that in September 1171, during a review of Saladin's troops, the cavalry counted some fourteen thousand men. If that number is accurate, it would mean that, within a few months, Saladin had almost doubled the number of cavalrymen at his disposal. That growth can be explained only if he incorporated what was left of the Fatimid army and recruited auxiliary troops composed of Arab Bedouins. Al-Fāḍil adds that, on that parade day, of the seven thousand Bedouins who were serving in the army, Saladin retained only thirteen hundred. All these cavalrymen were divided into 147 contingents *(tulb)*, composed of from seventy to two hundred men. Since about twenty other contingents were unable to present themselves that day, the army must have had in all some sixteen thousand cavalrymen, including auxiliaries. The regular cavalry must have ranged between ten and twelve thousand men.[41] They did not all possess the same strike power, however. The cavalrymen called *tawāshī*, who were heavily armed and very well paid (between seven hundred and twelve hundred dinars a year), are to be distinguished from the much more lightly armed cavalrymen *(qarāghulām)*. In 1177, during the Battle of Montgisard (defeat of Ramla), William of Tyre made the same observation: "Wishing to ascertain the actual facts, I made a careful investigation of the enemy's numbers and, from the narratives of many trustworthy people, found that twenty-six thousand light-armed cavalry, in addition to others mounted on camels and beasts of burden, had entered our territory. Of these, eight thousand belonged to those splendid soldiers called in their own language *toassin*; the other eighteen thousand were the common knights known as *caragolam*. A thousand of the most valiant knights acted as a bodyguard to Saladin. All these wore yellow silk over their breastplates, the color that Saladin himself bore."[42]

The large number of cavalrymen mentioned here, even if exaggerated, can probably be explained by the presence of Bedouins recruited for the occasion. As for the heavy cavalry in the regular army, the number advanced by William of Tyre is fairly close to that of the Arab sources. In 1181, for example, when Saladin ordered an assessment of the Egyptian *iqtā's* and of the regular troops they were able to maintain, 8,640 cavalrymen were counted, including 111 emirs, 6,976 heavy cavalrymen, and 1,553 light cavalrymen.[43] For Shīrkūh's army in

1167, William of Tyre had already estimated the number of heavily armed cavalrymen at 9,000, alongside the 3,000 light cavalrymen armed with bows and arrows, and the Bedouin troops.[44] The figures provided by the *History of the Patriarchs* are also in the range of 10,000 cavalrymen, but with a sharp drop in the number of heavy cavalrymen: at Saladin's death, his army reportedly had 4,000 *tawāshī* and 6,000 *qarāghulām*.[45] Must that be seen as the sign of a weakening of the Egyptian army toward the end of Saladin's reign? It would be unwise to make that assertion based on this evidence alone. In addition to these cavalrymen there were also the foot soldiers, whose strength is difficult to assess. Their role in Saladin's army was much less important than it had been in the Fatimid army, and the sources therefore say relatively little about them.[46]

In addition to these Egyptian soldiers, Saladin's army integrated troops from Syria as he extended his control over that region. Estimating their number, however, is more difficult than in the case of Egypt. In the first quarter of the thirteenth century, the Arab authors speak of five thousand cavalrymen for northern Syria alone. If we take into account the efforts by the Ayyubid sovereign of that region to increase the size of the army in the early thirteenth century, it is reasonable to think that, between 1183 and 1193, Saladin's army in Syria, his own troops, and those of his emirs must have amounted to at least five thousand cavalrymen and probably more.[47] Although it is true that not all of them could be mobilized in a single place and time—garrisons had to be kept in the principal cities—on several occasions Saladin also received reinforcements from Upper Mesopotamia, though there again, it is difficult to estimate the exact number, probably a few thousand. Under these conditions, how many men in all could Saladin line up to do battle against the Franks? If we had to choose just one figure, it would be that of the largest army he ever succeeded in assembling, on the eve of the Battle of Hattīn, namely, some twelve thousand career cavalrymen.[48] But that assembling of troops was the exception, and the armies led by Saladin rarely surpassed a few thousand cavalrymen.

In addition, that army remained heterogeneous in its ethnic composition, which sometimes led to conflicts among the troops. In Egypt, despite the purges of 1169, Berber and black contingents continued to serve as foot soldiers. Similarly, the Kināniyya Arabs were still a presence,[49] but on the whole the Egyptian and Syrian troops were now dominated by the Kurds and Turks. The most numerous were the Turks, whether originally free or emancipated slaves, soldiers in the regular army or seminomadic Turkomans. But the Kurds also played an important role, since they often occupied posts at the top of the chain of command. That ethnic diversity of Saladin's army is clearly underscored by the author of the *History of the Patriarchs,* when he says that in 1191, before executing the Muslim combatants taken prisoner in Acre, the Franks separated the contingents by "race" *(jins):* the Kināniyya Arabs, the blacks *(Sūdān),* the Kurds, and the Turks *(Ghuzz).*[50]

Even as he reorganized the land army, Saladin also set about rebuilding the Egyptian fleet. In that part of the Muslim world, Egypt was the only country to possess a fleet, which, in the early Fatimid period, had allowed it to fight with some success against the Byzantine and Italian fleets. In the time of Caliph al-Mu'izz (r. 953–975), that fleet is said to have counted several hundred vessels,[51] but by the end of the Fatimids' reign, it was composed of only about a hundred ships, battle galleys and transport vessels combined.[52] At that time, Egypt possessed four arsenals or naval construction sites. The ones in Alexandria and Damietta had existed since the Byzantine era;[53] in Cairo, the first arsenal, founded on Rawda Island in 673–674, had been replaced in 937 by a second one located on the banks of al-Fustāt. That one remained active until the early fourteenth century; but in the late tenth century, the Fatimids had founded a new one in al-Maqs, northwest of Cairo. There was also a workshop adjacent to the Fatimid palaces where the military equipment for the fleet was produced, and which used many Frankish prisoners. In al-Fustāt as in al-Maqs, a pavilion had been set up to allow the caliph and his vizier to witness the fleet's departure. During the great fire of al-Fustāt in 1186, the ships moored at the city's port were likely destroyed, but the Egyptian fleet as a whole was not demolished, since other vessels must have been in the ports of al-Maqs, Alexandria, or Damietta at the time.

In his first expeditions to Egypt, Saladin was able to assess the importance the fleet could have in battles against the Franks. For example, under heavy siege in Alexandria in 1167, he had to resign himself, once the truce was concluded, to negotiating the return of the Syrian wounded on Frankish ships. After he took power in 1169, he was faced with a naval attack by the Byzantines and Franks against Damietta; then, on five different occasions between 1174 and 1181, his armies prevented the Sicilians or Franks from disembarking on the Egyptian coast. During these battles, imposing fleets, possibly as many as 280 ships, were mobilized by the Christians, while the Muslims defended themselves solely on land, a sign that the Egyptian fleet was not large enough to confront the enemy. In 1174 Sicilian vessels entered the port of Alexandria without real difficulty, and the Muslims were reduced to sinking the few warships moored there to keep the Sicilians from seizing them.[54] The caliph of Baghdad himself was aware of that weakness of the Muslim army: in 1175, in the letter he sent to Saladin to give him his investiture, the caliph strongly urged him to expand the fleet to defend the strongholds on the coast.

> There is no doubt that the fleet must be developed and strengthened, since that is the weapon to which one turns to put an end to misfortune and to increase the number of slaves of both sexes. That army is the sister to Solomon's army. The latter sails on the wind's back,[55] and the former on the sea's back. May its "horses" be able to sail and be filled with zeal. . . . When they clear a path, they will be compared to a mountain enveloped by clouds; when their shape is observed, it will be said that they resemble crescent moons guided by the stars. Such "horses" require that the top price be paid, that commanders be found in great number, and that an emir with great power be placed at their head, one who will embark on the sea and follow the sea lanes, and who will not perish from ignorance but will prevail by his experience.[56]

In March 1177, having installed his power in Syria, Saladin went to inspect the ports of Damietta and Alexandria and gave the order to build and arm large numbers of ships.[57] The main obstacle to constituting a fleet in Egypt was the lack of wood, iron, and pitch, indispensable materials for building ships and for making them watertight. Like the Fatimids before him, Saladin had no recourse but to buy them from Western merchants, Italians in particular. When, in the early years of his reign, he sent his ambassador to Frederick Barbarossa, Saladin gave the ambassador the task of buying, in Europe, everything he judged necessary for the construction of the fleet.[58] And the main objective of the treaties he concluded with the Italian merchants from 1173 on was to secure supplies of these strategic raw materials.

Some time later, probably in about 1181,[59] to mark the importance he granted the fleet, Saladin created a special *dīwān* responsible for maintaining it. Among the means allocated were revenues from the region of Fayyūm,[60] from the sale of natron (a natural crystallized sodium carbonate whose exploitation could yield between eight and fifteen thousand dinars, depending on the year),[61] and the revenues confiscated from a large number of rural properties, formerly set up as *waqfs* by the Fatimid vizier, Badr al-Jamālī, on behalf of his heirs. In 1191–1192, while the siege under way in Acre was making clear the inferiority of the Muslim fleet, the revenues from the *zakāt* of al-Fustāt, namely, fifty thousand dinars a year, were added. That measure was justified by the fact that volunteers for the holy war could in theory be the beneficiaries of the *zakāt*.[62] Al-'Ādil was officially appointed to head that *dīwān,* whose management he entrusted to the man who would later become his vizier, Safī al-Dīn Ibn Shukr.

In addition to the difficulty finding money and a regular supply of wood and iron, the Egyptian fleet also ran into the problem of manpower. The Egyptians seem not to have been very good sailors in the Ayyubid period, any more than they were in the Fatimid era, no doubt because of the meager wages they were paid.[63] From the beginning of his reign, Saladin decided to compensate the crews better to boost recruitment.[64] Al-Maqrīzī has a tendency to embellish somewhat the image of sailors in the Fatimid period and under Saladin's reign, when they were called the "jihad warriors on the path of God." According to him, it was only after Saladin's death that the fleet deteriorated to the point that sailors were recruited only when an expedition was in the planning stage. In that case, they were taken at random, from anywhere, and were chained up for fear they would flee. Their reputation was so bad that the word "sailor" itself became an insult.[65] In reality, even in Saladin's time, the ship crews did not have a very good reputation. In 1187, for example, when about ten ships in Acre and a few others from the ports of Beirut and Jubayl were brought in to reinforce the siege of Tyre, 'Imād al-Dīn recounts:

> The sailors caught sight of the Franks' galleys outdistancing them so as to turn and attack and preparing to deal them a death blow. These were sailors recruited in Egypt. Their hearts were frightened by what was before their eyes, so they threw themselves into the water, fearing for their lives on the sea. They retreated straight toward land. . . . That abrupt setback, that striking lapse, demonstrated that

Saladin's delegates in Egypt had not attended properly to the fleet and had not organized the recruitment as they ought to have done. They had merely assembled an anonymous, ignorant, and unknown mob, an obviously incompetent throng, neither trained in war nor experienced. Necessarily, when they thought of fighting, they were afraid; constrained to obey, these sailors were unable to do so. One of our galleys, which seemed like a small mountain, was commanded by the lord of Jubayl with experienced and bold sailors, without cowardice or caprice; its defense continued on with weaponry; with its sail, it flew as if on wings; it outstripped the enemy and escaped. Far from being caught, its noble crew was saved, and that was their point of pride.[66]

That report clearly indicates that Egyptian sailors were not always professionals but rather men recruited for the occasion, largely inexperienced and often even undesirable. In 1168, for example, sailors joined the blacks in looting the houses of al-Fustāt after the city's fire.[67] That last-minute recruitment system was already practiced in Egypt during the previous centuries: on the eve of an expedition, a call to arms went out, and volunteers were signed up and paid for the expedition's duration.[68] To put an end to that inefficient organization, Saladin created the *dīwān* of the fleet to finance ship construction but also no doubt the training of professional sailors. Nevertheless, he did not have time to reap its benefits, and his reform was not continued by his successors.

In the Islamic countries of the Mediterranean periphery, only the Maghrebis had the reputation for being excellent sailors. There is nothing surprising about that, once we realize that the Almohad dynasty considerably strengthened its fleet, so that it could resist Christian pressures in the Mediterranean and in the Atlantic.[69] The presence of Maghrebi sailors in the Egyptian fleet is attested many times. On March 19, 1177, upon leaving the Egyptian cities of the coast, Saladin wrote a letter to his brother Tūrānshāh, telling him he had concerned himself with the fleet and its crews: "Men have been collected whom bad administration dispersed in the past, including a number of Maghribīs, whom the enemy fear."[70] The boat crews sent to the Red Sea in 1183 to counter Reginald of Châtillon's offensive, as well as those that participated in the siege of Tyre in 1187, also included Maghrebis.[71] Finally, the principal objective of the embassy Saladin sent to the Almohad caliph in 1190 was to obtain the aid of his fleet: "What is expected of that noble government, in its energy, full of vigilance and authority, and in its zeal guided by heaven, is that the Muslim West should aid the Muslims even more than the infidel West aids the infidels. It must cover the sea with its vessels, mobile mountains and cities that, black as night, navigate with their sails bright as day: they will bring hope to us, their brothers in Islam, and death to our enemies."[72]

About fifty years later, the Andalusian writer Ibn Saʿīd, who stayed for a time in the Egyptian capital, confirmed the good reputation of the Maghrebi sailors: "The poor do not have to fear being detained to serve in the navy, except the Maghrebis, for whom it is an obligation because of their knowledge of navigation. That obligation has been extended to all Maghrebis, whether or not they are versed in navigation. Upon their arrival, two cases arise: if the Maghrebi is rich, he is required to pay the tithe, and he is tormented to such a point that he ultimately flees the city; if, on the contrary, he is penniless, he is thrown into prison until the season when the fleet sets sail."[73]

Saladin's efforts were not in vain. In 1179, two years after the start of reconstruction of the fleet, al-Fāḍil was already pleased with the results obtained and noted with pride that the number of boats had doubled and now amounted to sixty galleys and twenty tarīdas,[74] constituting a fleet slightly smaller than that of the last Fatimids. Success was not long in coming. In May–June, and then in October 1179, two naval attacks conducted by the Egyptians against the Frankish coast allowed the Muslims to sink a number of enemy boats and to take booty and many prisoners.[75] In 1180 Saladin sent ships off the coast of Beirut but did not manage to seize the city. In late 1182, while he was besieging Sinjār, he learned that an Egyptian fleet had seized a Frankish ship transporting carpenters and a cargo of wood destined for Acre.[76] Similarly, in spring 1183, off the coast of Egypt, an Egyptian ship intercepted a Frankish vessel transporting weapons destined for the Latin states. The Muslims took control of the merchandise and of the men.[77] That same year, the Egyptian fleet had another victory, rapidly wiping out the ships Reginald of Châtillon had sent to the Red Sea, a success, it must be said, that was also attributable to the small number of Frankish ships mobilized.

Although the Egyptian fleet proved its efficacy in small-scale operations or pirate raids, it did not allow Saladin to reconquer the entire coast, or especially, to go up against the fleet of the Third Crusade. In 1187 Egyptian ships played no decisive role in the fall of the Frankish ports (Acre, Jaffa, Sayda, Beirut,

Jubayl, Ascalon). The ease with which the Muslims seized them lay primarily in the destruction of the Frankish army during the Battle of Hattīn and in the absence of a real fleet within the Latin states themselves. In fact, despite the presence of a few arsenals on their territory—in Tyre, Haifa, Acre, and especially, Tripoli[78]—the Franks never sought to acquire a true fleet, being content, when necessary, to requisition Western ships docked at their ports, along with their crews.[79]

In late 1187, the siege of Tyre once again demonstrated how indispensable the possession of a fleet was for taking control of the coast. The city, built on a peninsula, could not be conquered without a marine blockade. Saladin and his entourage were quite aware of that: "On this side, the infidels are left with only Tyre; if that city were not protected by the sea and accessible to ships, it would be easy to take, and its resistance would soon give out," 'Imād al-Dīn wrote a short time later.[80] The vessels brought in from the ports of Acre, Beirut, and Jubayl were quickly overpowered by the Franks. Saladin ordered the efforts to build new ships redoubled in Egypt; and on December 26, 1189, the Muslims under siege in Acre saw some fifty Egyptian galleys arriving, commanded by Emir Husām al-Dīn Lu'lu', famous for having pushed the Franks out of the Red Sea a few years earlier. Despite the season, unfavorable for sailing, the Egyptian fleet succeeded in breaking through the Franks' blockade and entered the port of Acre. But the Muslims drew no immediate military advantage, since bad weather prevented them from taking to sea again—the Franks themselves had eased up on their blockade—and the sailors were put to use maneuvering the war machines and harassing the enemy on land. With the coming of spring, did these ships return to Egypt in search of supplies, or did they remain anchored in the port of Acre? Were these the same ships that managed to resupply somewhat the residents in 1190, or were they different ones? The sources do not say.

In the following months, several other Muslim ships, sometimes disguised as Frankish merchant vessels, also succeeded in breaking through the Christian blockade.[81] But with the approach of winter, the undertaking was becoming risky. Not one of the seven ships sent by Egypt was spared by the storm that arose on December 31, 1190, while they were in sight of the port of Acre: "Everything on board was lost and a great many people perished. It was said that they numbered sixty souls. They carried vast supplies which, had they been saved, would have sufficed the inhabitants of the city for a whole year, but that was by the decree of the Mighty One, the All-Knowing. However, it brought a major setback upon the Muslims, which caused the sultan extreme anguish. . . . This was the first sign that the city was going to be taken and overcome."[82]

When good weather returned in June 1191, more ships, reportedly loaded with seven hundred men, attempted to reach Acre from Beirut. Intercepted by Richard the Lionheart's fleet, this time all of them were sunk.[83]

Throughout his reign, then, and particularly during the siege of Acre, Saladin made great efforts to strengthen the Egyptian fleet. So long as the kingdom of Jerusalem was limited to its own forces, the Egyptians could hope to have some victories with a few dozen vessels. But the Third Crusade—the first to come by sea—reached the East accompanied by a fleet so impressive that the Muslims quickly understood they could not oppose it. It must be said that, on leaving Messina, Richard the Lionheart had marshaled nearly two hundred ships, in addition to the (less numerous) Genoese ships chartered by Philip Augustus. Although not all of them arrived in the Holy Land—'Imād al-Dīn speaks of twenty-five heavily fortified English galleys—it is obvious that Saladin's fleet could not rival such naval power.[84] It was doubtless that superiority of the Crusaders' fleet that allowed the Latin states to reconquer Acre and part of the Syro-Palestinian coast.

The Role of the Arab Bedouins

Under the reign of the Fatimids, the Arab Bedouins in Syria and Egypt had been the source of major revolts, and the problem was therefore not new in Saladin's time. In fact, the urban populations and the authorities in place had rather contradictory feelings about them. On one hand, they needed their aid to find their bearings in the desert, to protect the roads, to supply the cities with meat and dairy products, and to strengthen the army; on the other, they feared their treachery and banditry. That is, they wished to make use of the Bedouins' services, and especially, to exert greater control over them; but their image of the Bedouins was very negative, as can be seen in both the Arab and Latin sources.

In the first place, the Bedouins were viewed by the settled populations as being resistant to any form of central authority. Between 1170 and 1174, after Saladin was installed in Egypt, they participated in the revolts of Upper Egypt, alongside the nostalgists for the dynasty of the Fatimids. In general, they were reproached primarily for their inconstancy and unreliability. When fighting on one side, they could very quickly go over to the other side and fight against their allies of the previous day. "As long as the result of the battle is uncertain, they look on at a distance; when it is decided, they attach themselves to the victor, pursue the conquered enemies, and enrich themselves by the spoils,"[85] says William of Tyre about them.

The Muslims criticized them for serving the Franks and betraying the cause of Islam. Harshest toward them was probably al-Fāḍil, who accused the Bedouins of Syria-Palestine of guiding the Franks in the desert, providing them with water and means of transportation, and even working for them at times as spies or hired killers. "The Bedouin are like colocynths," he wrote, "the more you give them sweet water, the bitterer are their fruit, and the more they lose their brilliant green color."[86] But like the Franks, the Muslims could not do without the Bedouins, with their military force and their skill at finding their way through the desert. In 1177 Saladin, after his defeat near Ramla, was betrayed by the Arabs guiding him and got lost in the sands. He would undoubtedly have died of exposure and thirst if al-Fāḍil had not gone in search of other Arab guides. For a long time, the Bedouins drew an advantage from that knowledge of the desert, which gave them the power to rescue their allies and destroy their enemies. In February 1799, even Napoleon Bonaparte's expedition almost paid the price, when the Arabs serving as its guides lost Jean-Baptiste Kléber's division south of Gaza.[87]

The Bedouins were also accused of making the roads and rivers unsafe. To protect caravans from their attacks and from those of the Franks on the Sinai route, Saladin had the fortresses of Sadr and Ayla built in the 1170s. Other Arabs in the Nile Delta region took advantage of the refuge offered by thickets of reeds to engage with impunity in the pillaging of boats on Lake Manzala. Sometimes conflicts between tribes caused disturbances, as in 1184, when it was necessary to send troops to put an end to the struggles tearing apart the Judhām tribe.[88]

Toward these Bedouins Saladin conducted a policy that was at once cautious and firm. In 1171 he began by greatly reducing their number in the Egyptian army.[89] Between 1171 and 1189–1190, the share of the budget devoted to them was reduced by a third.[90] These Bedouins, who served Saladin as auxiliary troops, were either paid in coin or remunerated in *iqtāʿs,* often in barren, inhospitable zones such as the Sinai Desert. Although it is difficult to identify when exactly the Bedouins began to be compensated in *iqtāʿs,* it seems to have been under Saladin's reign that the system was reintroduced, or at least, that it became widespread. Saladin, in changing the status of the lands—long controlled by the Bedouins, and which they considered their property—to a concession system (iqtā's), reasserted state control over these lands and thus reserved for himself the right to confiscate them.

But the distribution of lands was not sufficient in itself to control the tribes, and especially to prevent them from entering the Franks' service. Saladin therefore came out in favor of a much more radical policy: the deportation of the Bedouin populations living near Frankish territories. This he recommended as early as 1173 in a letter to Nūr al-Dīn:

> The reason for sending this note to our master al-Malik al-'Ādil [Nūr al-Dīn]—may God increase his power and forever extend his blessings, strengthen his aptitude for victory, elevate his rank through His assistance, make his followers victorious, and aid his auxiliaries—is as follows: his servant knows the importance our master attaches to marching against the infidels with the aim of cutting their arms off, breaking their weapons, depriving them of subsistence, and destroying their country. The best means to achieve that plan is to not allow any Arab Bedouins to remain on their territory, and to take them from the humiliation of infidelity to the glory of the faith. His servant has expended great effort and has come to believe that one of the most important methods is the expulsion of a great number of these Bedouins and the need to find a new place of residence for them, so that today, if the enemy ventures out, he will find no guide, will be reduced to powerlessness, and will no longer be able to find his way.[91]

In 1181, Bedouin tribes whom Saladin accused of providing the Franks with cereals were deported from northern Sinai and the eastern Nile Delta to the province of al-Buhayra in the western part of the Delta.[92] After 1187, the vacated lands were redistributed to other Arabs, now brought in from the regions of Syria-Palestine bordering the Frankish territories.

The aim of that strict policy toward the tribes was not to eliminate them but, on the contrary, to control them in order to make better use of them. Although their numbers in the army dropped, they continued to play an important role in it until the end of the Ayyubid period. That was especially true for the Kināni-yya, who had intervened in 1168 to aid Shīrkūh's army, besieged by the Franks in Bilbeis. A few years later, Qāḍī al-Fāḍil also turned to them to aid Saladin after the defeat of Ramla. In the state budget and also on administrative lists that assess the fiscal value of the *iqtā's,* their allotments appear very distinct from those of the "Arabs," that is, all the other auxiliary troops. They thus occupied an intermediate position within Saladin's army, between the Turks and the Kurds on one hand and the rest of the Arab troops on the other.[93]

In the Sinai and farther to the north, along the coastal route linking Egypt to Syria, Saladin also used the Arab tribes to ensure the security of the trails passing through their territories, which many merchants and pilgrims followed. Saladin thus inaugurated a policy that was later extended to the region as a whole, particularly when Baybars (1260–1277) restored the post relay system and sought to ensure its security.[94] Finally and above all, Saladin used the Bedouins to conduct lightning raids on the Franks, an area in which they excelled. In 1179 he sent them to pillage the harvested crops of the Franks of Sidon and Beirut; and after the surrender of Acre in October 1191, he dispatched some three hundred "Bedouin bandits," who infiltrated the enemy camp, stealing horses and bringing back prisoners: "As one of them was sleeping, a dagger would be held to his throat. Awakened, he would see the thief, armed with a dagger which was held at his throat, so he would keep silent and not dare to say a word. Carried off in that state away from his tent, he would be made a prisoner. Several of them did speak and had their throats cut, so those who subsequently found themselves in this predicament kept silent and chose to be taken rather than killed."[95]

Three weeks later, on Saladin's order, Bedouins once again attacked Franks who had ventured to leave their camp in search of forage and wood. Their raid led to a reprisal by the Frankish army, whom the Arabs had no trouble ambushing.[96] The Franks particularly feared these Arabs, as attested by certain Latin sources: "Also there were the Saracens who travel about in the desert, popularly called 'Bedouins': savage and darker than soot, the most redoubtable infantrymen, carrying bows and quivers and round shields. They are a very energetic and agile race. These threatened our army constantly without giving way."[97]

Saladin was the first sovereign of that region to enact an actual policy to subdue the Bedouins, which was later adapted and developed by the Mamluk sultans. Nevertheless, the control he exerted over them was never complete. On the whole, they were reluctant to accept the expansion of the *iqtā'* system and the domination of the Turkish element. At the first signs of weakness on the part of the authorities, they managed to recover a large share of autonomy.

Saladin and the Poor

Whereas in the Western Christian tradition, assistance to the poor originated almost exclusively with churchmen, then spread to laypeople and the public authorities in the twelfth and thirteenth centuries,[98] Islam from the beginning instituted alms *(zakāt)* as one of the believer's five duties. The question of whether those alms were to be paid to the authorities, who would then be responsible for redistributing them, or given directly to the beneficiaries by believers was long debated in religious circles. The response varied depending on the legal school.[99] Saladin, however, centralized the collection of the *zakāt* in Egypt. He could thus finance certain expenditures associated with assisting the poor, charity that a number of Muslim authors consider one of the sovereign's chief prerogatives. Al-Harawī does not omit to remind us: God grants the ruler the privilege of defending Islam and the Muslims, "so that he shall abolish abuses and punish the oppressor, rescue the afflicted and distribute gifts, relieve the wounded and liberate the prisoner, stand in judgment between the oppressed and the oppressor, distinguish between the ignorant and the learned, and struggle zealously to defend the integrity of Islam and the order of the world."[100] Charity, which in the Middle Ages consisted primarily of feeding and caring for the poor, supporting the widow and orphan, assisting travelers, and redeeming prisoners from the hands of the enemy, was thus among the duties of the good prince, just like piety, justice, bravery, and magnanimity. The widespread use of the system of *waqfs,* which were in principle inalienable, had also encouraged the development and maintenance of charitable institutions that survived their founders.

Saladin's generosity was great toward both rich and poor. He likely practiced charity for all sorts of reasons at once: by nature, by political calculation, or by religious conviction; he did so to be healed, to express his gratitude toward God, or to expiate his sins before breathing his last. In many circumstances, he had alms distributed to the poor, as, for example, in 1170, when his father arrived in Cairo, or in 1186 during his grave illness in Harrān. In these actions, it is not always easy to distinguish between personal charity and public charity, and in general the origin of the money distributed is not known. But apart from these occasional alms linked to episodes in Saladin's personal life, what really matters is his action at the institutional level. In Alexandria, he set in place a system of food distribution based on the *waqfs*. Twice a day, bread was handed out to foreigners without resources, usually pilgrims on their way to Mecca. Someone was appointed to carry out that task, and about two thousand loaves of bread were distributed daily. In addition, subsidies were paid monthly to provide for the needs of all those without resources who lived in makeshift dwellings in the al-Qarāfa cemetery south of Cairo.[101] It was in that same cemetery that Admiral Husām al-Dīn Lu'lu', who in 1191 had decided to retire from military life and devote himself to charitable works, regularly came to distribute food to the most impoverished. It is likely that people who were not really in need sometimes slipped in among the beneficiaries of the alms. Saladin was alerted to this but usually refused to take any notice. In 1178–1179, for example, a letter from 'Imād al-Dīn communicated the difficulties in Damascus of distinguishing the truly needy from the frauds. The sultan gave the order, however, to continue paying the eleven thousand dinars in alms without inquiring into the means of subsistence of those who benefited from them.[102]

In addition, Saladin expended a great deal of effort developing hospitals that would give the poor access to care. He was not of course breaking new ground in that realm. In the Muslim world, the old hospitals, inherited from the Sassanids, had been created under the reign of Hārūn al-Rashīd (786–809), founder of the first hospital in Baghdad. That institution, intended first and foremost to treat the destitute and to provide medical training, gradually spread to all the cities of the Middle East. In the Egyptian capital, the first hospital was founded in about 872–874 by Ahmad Ibn Tūlūn, who ruled Egypt at the time. In Syria, the first true hospitals appeared in the eleventh century.[103] Nūr al-Dīn expanded the system considerably in the twelfth century, founding a hospital in Rakka on the Euphrates, another in Aleppo, a third in Damascus, and a fourth in Hama.[104] In that area as in others, Saladin imitated his predecessor and took quite a keen interest in medicine. He encouraged the writing of several medical treatises and attempted to reform that science and rid it of its charlatans, as attested, on one hand, by the decree published in Aleppo following his conquest and, on the other, by the treatise that Ibn Jumay' dedicated to him. That Egyptian Jewish doctor specifies in his introduction that his opuscule was inspired by a conversation he had with Saladin on the deplorable state of medicine and on the means to remedy it.[105]

Saladin created two new hospitals in Egypt: one in Cairo, possibly in 1176–1177, and the other in Alexandria in 1182. In the capital, he had the former al-Fustāt Hospital restored and founded a second, much larger one, within the enclosure of the former Fatimid palaces. Ibn Jubayr gives us a beautiful description of it:

> Another of the things we saw, doing honour to the Sultan, was the *maristan* [hospital] in the city of Cairo. It is a palace, goodly for its beauty and spaciousness. This benefaction he made so that he might deserve a heavenly reward, and to acquire merit. He appointed as intendant a man of science with whom he placed a store of drugs and whom he empowered to use the potions and apply them in their various forms. In the rooms of this palace were placed beds, fully appointed, for lying patients. At the disposal of the intendant are servants whose duty it is, morning and evening, to examine the conditions of the sick, and to bring them the food and potions that befit them.
>
> Facing this establishment is another specially for women, and they also have persons to attend them. A third which adjoins them, a large place, has rooms with iron windows, and it has been taken as a place of confinement for the insane. They also have persons who daily examine their condition and give them what is fitting for them. All these matters the Sultan oversees, examining and questioning, and demanding the greatest care and attention to them.[106]

In Jerusalem, Saladin appointed Ibn Shaddād to oversee the construction of a new hospital, which he founded in the neighborhood of the Holy Sepulchre, in a church near the House of the Knights Hospitaller.[107] In Acre, finally, Saladin turned the Bishop's House into a hospital.[108] Within a few years, then, he had founded at least four hospitals in the cities he had taken over, all endowed with *waqfs* to pay for doctors and medication and for operating expenses.

In Muslim society, orphans had always occupied a privileged place among the beneficiaries of charitable works. The Koran grants special importance to the theme of protecting the orphan, no doubt linked to the fact that the Prophet himself was an orphan at birth. The good sovereign is someone who knows how to care not only for the poor but also for parentless children. In that respect as well, Saladin followed Nūr al-Dīn's example and founded several schools (*kuttāb* or *maktab*) in his states to teach the Koran, reading, and writing to poor children and orphans. Ibn Jubayr mentions one in Cairo, and another, in Jerusalem, was completed in 1198–1199, after the sultan's death. The revenues from the *waqf* allocated to the Jerusalem school made it possible to pay for the teacher's salary, the upkeep of the school, lamplight, and potable water.[109] Al-Fāḍil also founded a school of that type adjoining his madrasa in Cairo.[110] And he was not the only one in Saladin's close circle to take an interest in the poor. The sultan's sister Sitt al-Shām, during her long widowhood, devoted herself to many acts of charity. Throughout the medieval Middle East at that time, wealthy women, especially princesses, played an important role in the construction of pious establishments and in charitable works.[111] For them, actions in that area were an excellent means to intervene in the life of the commonwealth, and from that point of view, charity could be used as a real instrument of social integration.[112]

Similarly, assistance to the poor was sometimes placed in the service of political aims. Inasmuch as it was part of the representation of the ideal sovereign, it served as an argument for those seeking to legitimate their power and allowed sovereigns to rally the population behind them. In Saladin's case, it is difficult to say whether he had a natural sensitivity to the misfortunes of the poor or whether he acted out of political interest. It can be said, however, that his actions in that realm were not unusual, but conformed to the norms of his time. Hospitals already existed in Egypt and in Syria-Palestine, and food distribution is an often-recurring theme in descriptions of medieval Muslim rulers. A number of them were praised, before and after Saladin, for their charitable actions. In Egypt, Ahmad Ibn Tūlūn (r. 868–884) was described as a governor who distributed many alms; in Syria, Nūr al-Dīn was cited as an example for his charitable works; in Baghdad, Caliph al-Nāṣir (r. 1180–1225) also offered food to his population during the month of Ramadan and saw to the well-being of pilgrims returning from Mecca. The Mamluk sultans also took on the support of pilgrims and the poor and, like the Fatimid caliphs, engaged in large food distributions, especially during times of fasting.[113]

To fund the jihad, strengthen fortifications, and construct religious buildings—which cannot be assimilated to charitable works, though they are acts of piety—Saladin spent much larger sums than he did for acts of pure charity. In any event, he does not seem to have distinguished himself in the field of charity as much as his brother-in-law Gökbörī. In his city of Irbil, Gökbörī ordered the construction of residences for the sick and the blind, and for orphans, widows, and strangers; he had food and clothing distributed to the poor on a daily basis, lavished gifts on pilgrims, and dedicated large sums of money to redeeming prisoners.[114] In thirteenth-century Aleppo, establishments known as *khānqāh* were used as residences for devout women without resources or for aged eunuchs without families. Founded by Ayyubid princesses or grand emirs, these charitable establishments endowed with *waqfs* spread during the Mamluk era. They do not seem to have existed in Saladin's time.

Natural catastrophes and the misfortunes that followed from them (famine, destitution, epidemics) were relatively common at that time in the Middle East. No form of public assistance was set up in such cases to come to the aid of the population. Rescue and comfort were usually the result of individual initiatives on the part of the leaders or the residents themselves. Saladin was lucky enough to have his reign relatively spared by nature. Of course, Egypt was never safe from inadequate flooding of the Nile, which was synonymous with poor harvests, price increases, and aggravated poverty. In 1179, for example, the country suffered not only an insufficient rise of the waters but also a serious epidemic that, within a few days, claimed several thousand lives in the Cairo region. The Egyptian state, however, did not take any special measures on that occasion to come to the aid of the population. On the contrary, Egyptian officials tried to lower the amount of money paid to the poor, alleging that a number of beneficiaries were wrongly receiving it. Saladin disapproved of that measure, and three-quarters of the original amount was finally paid. But it is significant to note that no true government mobilization occurred, in striking contrast to the pomp of the celebrations held around the same time by the sultan, his brother al-ʿĀdil, and an Egyptian emir to celebrate the circumcision of their sons.[115]

During that same period, between 1176 and 1180, Syria was suffering from a major drought, which led to several years of scarcity. The situation was not judged serious enough, however, to produce a reaction on the part of the authorities. In fact, these climatic accidents seem to have been accepted as fate, and the sovereign did not judge it wise to act, except in the case of a major catastrophe. That was the situation during the earthquakes of 1201–1202, which led to a huge famine throughout the Middle East and resulted in a considerable number of deaths. At that time, Sultan al-ʿĀdil in person came to the aid of the most impoverished and provided shrouds for burying the corpses.[116]

23

Commerce and Markets

What place did Saladin grant to the economic development of his states? Did he try to place the economy in the service of his policies? Did he intervene directly to favor or develop one economic sector or another? It is rather difficult to respond to these questions, first, as Jacques Le Goff has pointed out, because "the economy," in the sense we understand that term, was not perceived as such in the Middle Ages, "either as material reality or as mental category."[1] Second, our sources remain relatively silent on what constituted the driving force of that economy, namely, agriculture. Although a few travel narratives and several administrative treatises provide information on farm produce and animals, the flooding of the Nile, the agricultural calendar, the nature of lands, and the distribution of villages, the authors' interest focuses primarily on fiscal aspects and administrative structures, and rarely on the life of the peasants and their relations with the authorities.[2]

The biographers and chroniclers say nothing about Saladin's attitude toward the rural world. The sultan's preoccupations seem to have been primarily fiscal (assuring higher receipts for the state coffers) and military (redistributing lands in the form of iqtā's to his officers and his close circle, in exchange for their military service). What we know about his intervention in that area can be summed up as follows: he maintained state control, traditionally strong in Egypt, over the organization of rural life and the collection of taxes; and he assured the security of communications to allow agricultural products to be transported to the cities. Much better known, by contrast, is the policy he conducted relating to commerce and markets.

Treaties with the Italian Cities

"Avarice belongeth to merchants and not to kings!" That line was attributed to Saladin to explain his great generosity.[3] Although the formulation attests to a certain contempt for the lure of profit, it does not come near to encapsulating the sultan's attitude toward commerce, particularly in his relations with the merchant cities of Italy. Throughout the Middle East in the second half of the twelfth century, commerce experienced a major revival, thanks in great part to the activities of Italian cities, whose ships linked Italy to Egypt, the Latin states, and the Byzantine Empire. The rise of fairs in Champagne and Flanders allowed Venetian, Genoese, and Pisan merchants to redistribute throughout Europe the products purchased in the eastern Mediterranean. In that vast trade network, Syria-Palestine and especially Egypt played the role of hubs between the East and West. Did not William of Tyre say that Alexandria was "a public mart for both worlds"?[4] As in the past, merchants in the Muslim states, including a number of Jews and Christians, continued to travel by land or sea to the Far East and the Indian Ocean, bringing back a variety of luxury products: spices, medicinal products, woods and precious stones, silks, and porcelain. These were sold to Italian merchants in the markets of Alexandria, Damietta, Acre, or Tripoli, along with other local products that Westerners needed for their textile industry, such as cotton, raw silk, flax, Egyptian alum, and dyeing products. There were various other commodities for which Egypt was renowned (sugar and glassware), not to omit the products necessary for stocking ships (salt and various foodstuffs). In exchange, the Muslims purchased metals (gold, silver, copper), cloth, and Sicilian or Spanish silks from the Italians, and especially, strategic materials such as iron, wood, and pitch, which they needed for the manufacture of weapons and the construction of the fleet.

That commerce was lucrative for everyone, which explains why neither conflicts nor the repeated prohibitions of the papacy—which did not appreciate the fact that raw materials that would be used to fight the Franks were being sold to the Muslims—managed to halt it in a lasting manner. In 1179 the eleventh general council reiterated the threat that the papacy would confiscate goods and excommunicate any person who sold the Muslims iron, weapons, wood, or ships, or who entered their service as ship's captain,[5] but to no avail. Just as sea traffic was interrupted during the winter months only to resume in the spring, so too trade resumed once the political crises had been resolved. In periods of tension, the Italian merchants and their ships could be the target of hostile popular reactions, as in June 1185 in Alexandria: "Rūmī"—which is to say, Italian—ships were looted, but those responsible were quickly arrested and punished. The Egyptian state had much too great a need for that commerce not to repress any outbursts swiftly and harshly.[6]

In that area as in others, Saladin was only continuing the policy of his Fatimid predecessors, and he struggled to maintain good relations with the cities of Venice, Pisa, and Genoa. That, among other things, is what emerges from his letter to the caliph of Baghdad in 1175:

> Among the [enemy] armies were also Venetians, Pisans, and Geno-ese. They sometimes behaved like invaders, producing a harmful effect and a maleficence that were intolerable, and sometimes like travelers, imposing their law on Islam with their imported goods and escaping strict regulation. Yet there is not a single one of them who does not come today to bring us the weapons with which they fought and conducted the holy war [jihād], not one who does not seek our favor by offering us the rare products of his labor and patrimony. I established alliances and peace accords with them all, on the conditions that we set, in keeping with our interests and against their interests.[7]

In the twelfth century, merchants from the three commercial cities of northern Italy had gradually replaced the Amalfitans, who, in the late tenth century, had been the first to do business in Egypt. The accords concluded between these cities and the Fatimid authorities allowed Italian merchants to buy and sell their products freely in the ports of the Nile Delta (Alexandria, Damietta, Tinnis) and sometimes even in the city of Cairo. Customs exemptions were generally granted to them, and they also gradually acquired the right to have at their disposal a church and a business establishment (*funduq* or *fondaco),* where they lived and conducted their business. From the first years of his reign, Saladin took care to renew these agreements, which had fallen apart during the events of 1168–1169.

He was on excellent terms with Sebastiano Ziani, doge of Venice, and it was probably in about 1172 that the Venetians obtained the right to have a *funduq* available to them in Alexandria. Their increased presence in Egypt was also the result of their having been expelled from the Byzantine Empire in 1171. That year, the Venetian merchants, who held a preponderant place in the commerce of Byzantium, were the victims of a violent popular uprising: a number of them were massacred and their Constantinople neighborhood was looted. Venetian trade therefore partly retreated to Egypt, which was already the second most important commercial destination for the city of the doge, after Constantinople and before the Latin states.[8]

The Pisans were not to be outdone in Egypt. In 1154 they had obtained a trade treaty with the Fatimid caliph, which allowed them not only to reclaim their former *funduq* in Alexandria but also to have use of a second one in al-Fustāt. Between 1154 and 1168, they also obtained the right to pray in their own church, dedicated to Saint Nicholas, in Alexandria.[9] Historians, including some major ones, have even believed that their ships were the most numerous in the port of Alexandria in the mid-twelfth century.[10] In my view, however, that claim, based on the testimony of al-Zuhrī, a mid-twelfth-century Arab geographer, can only be the result of a misreading of the text.[11] Although the author asserts that Pisa was a larger city than Genoa, that its residents were skillful builders of galleys, and that its merchants traveled as far as Syria, Egypt, the Maghreb, and al-Andalus, at no time does he say that the Pisan boats were greater in number than others in Alexandria. By no means, however, do I wish to call into doubt the importance of Pisa's trade with Egypt. In 1173 Saladin renewed the Pisans' privileges by signing a treaty with them. By its terms, their *funduq* in Alexandria—no doubt damaged during the 1168 invasion of Egypt by the Jerusalem Franks—was returned to them after being restored, and the use of their church once more granted them. The authorities also made a bath available to the Pisans once a week, and they were permitted to use their own weights and measures inside their *funduq.* They could therefore conduct certain commercial dealings among themselves and verify the weight of the merchandise they had purchased elsewhere in the country. Saladin exempted them from taxes on all the gold and silver they brought into the country and ratified a large reduction (from 19 percent to 10 percent) in the duties they paid on sales of wood, iron, and pitch. Finally, he put an end to various abuses the Pisans sometimes had to suffer (exactions from the customs service, the obligation to sell their merchandise below market price, violent measures to prevent them from departing) and granted them the right to move about freely within Egypt. They could not, however, reclaim their *funduq* in al-Fustāt.[12] After 1168, there were no longer any Latin *funduqs* in Cairo, which may indicate a desire on Saladin's part, following Frankish attempts to seize Egypt, to avoid any Latin settlements on the outskirts of the capital. Between 1176 and 1180, several other Pisan embassies to Egypt followed. Their mission was to rescue prisoners of war, but also and above all to ratify commercial privileges. They attest to the good relations existing between Pisans and Egyptians, at least during that period.[13]

Saladin also signed a treaty with Genoa in 1177, though, unfortunately, its content is not known to us.[14] The Genoese do not seem to have had a *funduq* of their own in Alexandria until sometime between 1192 and 1200. Before that, they were therefore lodged in *funduqs* set aside for Latin merchants from various places. They also seem to have shared a church with the Melkites.[15] Saladin's good relations with the Genoese are confirmed by the requests he made to them on the occasion of an embassy sent by Frederick Barbarossa between 1173 and 1182. The Muslim ambassador was given the mission of passing through Genoa and verifying with the "leader of the Genoese" that the letter previously sent by the emperor was authentic. In the event that the letter was counterfeit, the ambassador was to ask the Genoese for aid in purchasing the raw materials necessary for the construction of the fleet. He was also to negotiate the release of two prisoners, the sons of a sheikh of Alexandria.[16] The importance of the ties between Genoa and Egypt is also underscored by the fact that Ibn Jubayr took a Genoese boat to Alexandria, at a time (February 1183) when the preponderance of Italian boats in the Mediterranean, for the transport of merchandise and men, was already well established.

Of course, in 1187 commercial relations between Egypt and the Italian cities were momentarily interrupted by the major offensive Saladin launched against the Latin states. But by spring 1188, the thirty-seven Pisan, Venetian, and Genoese ships held in the port of Alexandria were permitted to leave, and normal commercial traffic resumed, even before the conclusion of the treaty between Saladin and the Franks in September 1192.[17]

Navigation on the Mediterranean occurred primarily between late February and late October, thus avoiding the winter storms, and the West–East journey lasted between three weeks and a month. It took Ibn Jubayr, for example, thirty days to get from Genoa to Alexandria. Travelers about to set off, whether merchants or pilgrims, had to equip themselves with all the necessary provisions and take precautions, since the route was long and dangerous. That is attested by Bishop Jacques de Vitry, who left Genoa for Saint-Jean-d'Acre twenty-three years after Saladin's death:

> I rented a new boat that had never been to sea. . . . I had five places set aside for me and my family, that is, a quarter of the upper forecastle, to take my meals and study my books. I would stay there during the day, unless there was a storm on the sea. In addition, I rented a cabin to sleep in during the night with my companions; I also rented another to keep my clothes in and to store food for several days. I rented a third to lodge my servants: they prepared my food for me there. And finally, I reserved another place to board my horses, which I took along on the crossing. I had them place my wine and biscuits in the bilge of the boat, as well as meats and other foodstuffs, in amounts almost sufficient to assure my subsistence for three months.[18]

Once arrived in one of the ports of the Egyptian delta (Alexandria, Damietta, or Tinnis), the Italian merchants, having faced storms and pirates, were not at the end of their troubles. They still had to submit to a series of customs inspections, a detailed list of which is provided by al-Makhzūmī.[19] An Egyptian official began by drawing up a list of passengers and merchandise, before authorizing them to disembark. The merchandise was then placed in a warehouse, where a large auction was held by the port authorities. It was during these transactions that the many taxes were collected, the total varying by the nationality of the merchant and the nature of the merchandise. Muslim travelers were not exempted, as may be seen from this well-known passage by Ibn Jubayr, who was outraged at the excess of zeal of Saladin's officials in Alexandria:

> The day of our landing, one of the first things we saw was the coming on board of the agents of the Sultan to record all that had been

brought in the ship. All the Muslims in it were brought forward one by one, and their names and descriptions, together with the names of their countries, recorded. Each was questioned as to what merchandise or money he had, that he might pay *Zakat,* without any enquiry as to what portion of it had been in their possession for a complete year and what had not. . . . The Muslims were then ordered to take their belongings, and what remained of their provisions, to the shore, where there were attendants responsible for them and for carrying to the Customs all that they had brought ashore. There they were called one by one, and the possessions of each were produced. The Customs was packed to choking. All their goods, great and small, were searched and confusedly thrown together, while hands were thrust into their waistbands in search of what might be within. The owners were then put to oath whether they had aught else not discovered. During all this, because of the confusion of hands and the excessive throng, many possessions disappeared. After this scene of abasement and shame, . . . [the pilgrims] were allowed to go.

There is no doubt that this is one of the matters concealed from the great Sultan known as Salah al-Din [Saladin]. If he heard of it, from what is related of his justice and leanings to pity, he would end it.[20]

Foreign merchants, in order to find their way through the customs maze and to learn the market prices, had no other choice but to turn to brokers, who offered them their services at a rate proportionate to the value of the merchandise. It was therefore very rare, at least in Egypt, for a merchant to freely sell his goods inside the country. During the auction, local dealers came to buy the imported products, which they then sold off to the small retailers in the souks. In Egypt, the state had a monopoly on the purchase of strategic materials (iron, wood, pitch) at a fixed price, and these goods were required to pass through a special trade bureau of sorts called a *matjar.* Once the needs of the state were met, the state then sold the surplus to individuals. The merchandise purchased by the Italians in Egypt was also subject to relatively high export duties.[21] In fact, unlike present-day economic policies, the Egyptian state did not seek to encourage exports. Its chief concern was to procure the commodities essential to its economy and military might. It also aspired to have large tax revenues, but there was a tendency to believe that any merchandise taken away by foreigners impoverished the country, especially under conditions of scarcity or inadequate supply.

In Saladin's time, Italian merchants usually made only a brief stop in Egypt, enough time to sell and buy their merchandise. When winter caught them by surprise, they sometimes stayed until the return of fair weather and less tumultuous seas. But there were not yet any true merchant colonies, as the absence of Italian notaries attests, or any permanent ecclesiastical structure in Egyptian cities. It was only in the thirteenth century that merchants began to extend their stay for several months or even years. Their numbers increased, and at that time consuls appeared, responsible for representing the interests of their community before the local authorities and for adjudicating conflicts between its members.[22]

In short, Saladin encouraged the Italian merchants to pursue their commerce in Egypt by promising them the security of their goods and persons, relative freedom of trade, a reduction in customs taxes, and the infrastructures they needed. Their activities were still supervised by the state, however. The *funduqs,* churches, and baths at their disposal did not belong to them outright and were overseen by the Egyptian authorities. They had a few private *funduqs* in Alexandria but not in Cairo. They were free to do business inside the country, which for the most part meant going to Cairo, but their movements were still closely watched.

The Red Sea Route

One region remained totally prohibited to Westerners: the Red Sea and, beyond it, the entire Indian Ocean, where only Indians and merchants from the Muslim territories or the countries of the Far East traveled. In the tenth century, with the installation of the Fatimids in Egypt, the Red Sea route had supplanted the Persian Gulf maritime route for trade between East and West. Hence the economic importance for Saladin of the conquest of Yemen: its location at the entry to the Red Sea looked to be strategic. Two ports in that region played a major role: Aden, and ʿAydhāb on the Egyptian coast. A quantity of products from India and the Far East flowed into Aden.[23] It was often there that occurred the transshipment of merchandise from the large Indian ships to lighter craft, which could more easily avoid the reefs in the Red Sea. In spite of everything, Indian merchants sometimes went to Egypt with their products.[24] The Red Sea was buffeted by violent winds and strewn with reefs, and the crossing was therefore dangerous. The ships, especially those transporting pilgrims to Mecca, were often overloaded, and shipwrecks were common. Ibn Jubayr points out that it was not rare to see castaways devoured by sharks. And the governor of Qūs, while in the East in 1184, reported that four ships with some thirteen hundred pilgrims aboard had gone down in the Red Sea.[25]

On the Egyptian side, all Muslim travelers passed through the port of 'Ayd-hāb. The city drew large revenues from rentals of the vessels necessary to cross the Red Sea and from the taxes collected on the merchandise and provisions transported by the merchants and pilgrims, though Ibn Jubayr notes a significant drop in the fees paid by the pilgrims after the measures taken by Saladin. Egyptian customs officers justified these collections as being part of the zakāt, the canonical tax levied on Muslims' wealth. For Jews and Christians, the term they used was "duties" (wājib).[26] Camels then transported the bundles of merchandise across the desert to the Nile, where barks awaited to take them to Cairo and to the ports of the Delta beyond. Aswān and especially Qūs in Upper Egypt were major stops with lively souks, where pilgrims and merchants from all parts crossed paths. But upon embarking in ships on the Nile, travelers were once again subject to the exactions of the Egyptian officials: "One of the most infamous things we saw was a group of insolent exactors, carrying in their hands long, pointed prods with handles, going aboard the ships [on the Nile] to examine what was in them. There was no bundle or sack into which they did not drive those accursed staves in case there should be in the baggage, which held nothing but provisions, some unseen goods or money."[27]

Of all the products taken from Upper Egypt to the ports of the Delta to be sold to the Italians, alum held a special place. That ore, abundant and of excellent quality in Egypt, was used as a color fixative on fabrics, and Europe's textile industry had a great need for it. Alum was not directly exploited by the state, but residents of the districts bordering the desert where it was found were obliged to supply it, and only the state could trade in it. The state used it as a means of payment, approximately two-thirds of the merchandise purchased from Western merchants being paid for in alum. That is why Saladin became particularly interested in that product and took measures to assure the security of commerce in it. In 1181 he had twenty cavalrymen stationed in Suez to guard the road by which the alum was brought "for the Franks," and sent his own brother Tughtegin to Akhmīn to oversee the transport of that precious ore.[28] Tughtegin himself bought and resold merchandise.[29] He seems to have turned to a Genoese named Ruggeronus to exchange alum for Western products. Once, the Genoese and his cargo of alum fell into the hands of Pisan pirates, and Saladin wrote to the Pisan authorities to demand his release and the restitution of the merchandise.[30] Tughtegin was far from the only one in Saladin's circle involved in commerce. His nephew Taqī al-Dīn founded two caravansaries (funduqs) in the old city of Cairo. In addition, when he decided to leave Cairo for Syria, he turned his residence, in the neighborhood of the Fatimid palaces, into a Shafite madrasa and converted the adjacent stables into funduqs.[31] Even the devout al-Fādil invested part of his money in commerce with North Africa and the Indian Ocean.[32]

Trade between Egypt and Syria

Muslim caravans laden with ordinary consumer goods, but also with precious commodities from the East, also connected Syria and Egypt by land.[33] Despite the wars, freedom of movement remained the rule, even between Frankish and Muslim territories. Ibn Jubayr, for example, could travel in both directions on a Genoese boat and, on September 13, 1184, was able to join a caravan connecting Damascus to Acre, even though Saladin was ending his campaign against Kerak and had just pillaged the region of Nablus and Jenin (September 8–10).[34]

But crossing Frankish territories entailed great disadvantages for the Muslims. The risk of attacks and pillaging was real, and the Franks collected high tolls on the caravans. Saladin turned his attention to them several times. In a letter to the caliph's vizier in 1176, the sultan said that, with his troops, he had himself escorted a caravan of merchants between Syria and Egypt, so that they would not have to pay the tolls demanded by the Franks. The next year, in a letter to his brother Tūrānshāh, he attempted to explain why it would be preferable to take a different route—was he thinking of the Red Sea?—to transport the merchandise to Egypt: "No reply has come to our letter about the need to stop the passage of the Muslim caravans . . . and it may be that this was lost because of enemy action and never arrived. The disease of the caravans is proving intractable and its cure is difficult. These merchants are risking their lives, reputations and goods and they also take the risk of strengthening the enemy.

Every time that we decide to mete out harsh punishment [for having violated the ban] to those of them who arrive here . . . the wounds that the Franks have given them are still bloody . . . and everyone pleads for them and says: 'do not add distress to distress.' "³⁵

The merchants, in the interest of greater security, sometimes took advantage of the movements of the army and traveled under its protection: in 1170, for example, when Ayyūb came to join Saladin in Egypt; in 1182, when Saladin left Egypt for Syria, escorting merchants and Syrian refugees who were returning home; or, the next year, when al-ʿĀdil went to join his brother outside the fortress of Kerak. Such journeys involved large quantities of provisions and pack animals, which slowed the army down. In such cases, it took a month to travel the distance between Cairo and Damascus on foot by the Sinai route, whereas usually it took slightly less than three weeks.³⁶

The Muslim conquests of summer 1187 radically changed the trading conditions between Egypt and Syria. Commercial traffic by the coastal route, which was much shorter than the interior Sinai route, could resume. By late August 1187, Muslim caravans taking the coastal route were no longer subject to the taxes imposed by the Franks, an event important enough to be noted by the chroniclers.³⁷ Not all the security problems were settled, however. On June 24, 1192, a caravan from Egypt en route to Jerusalem, escorted by a garrison, was attacked by the Franks. More than five hundred people and three thousand camels were captured, not counting the horses and mules. Al-Harawī, author of a treatise on governance, was advancing with the convoy and paid a high price for that attack. He managed to flee but lost all his possessions and precious notes. Richard the Lionheart promised to restore everything to him if al-Harawī went to see the king, but al-Harawī refused.³⁸

In al-Jazīra as well, the roads could be dangerous, but for reasons different from those associated with the Franks. In that region, insecurity was usually the result of the conflicts between the Turkomans and the Kurds, which sometimes arose from apparently minor incidents. In 1185, for example, Turkomans were celebrating a wedding in which Kurds wanted to participate. The Kurds were ejected, the incident escalated, and the groom was killed. That was the starting point for a conflict lasting several years and affecting not only the Turkomans and Kurds of al-Jazīra but also those of Syria, Iraq, Armenia, and Azerbaijan. The results were great insecurity, looting, and considerable bloodshed. In 1186 al-Fādil alluded to the insecurity of the thoroughfares between

Syria and al-Jazīra, which, to his great regret, prevented him from reaching the bedside of Saladin, who was ill at the time in Harrān.[39]

Although security of communications remained one of Saladin's chief concerns, the sultan also did not neglect the construction of roads and especially of bridges, particularly in Egypt, in regions that readily flooded with the periodic rise of the Nile. In 1181–1182, he ordered the governors of the region of the Delta to restore all the bridges in their provinces.[40] With the materials from the lesser pyramids of Giza, he also had a roadway constructed on the bank of the Nile west of al-Fustāt, and a bridge with forty arches opposite Giza, on the road to Alexandria, to facilitate circulation between the two banks of the river, even in times of flooding.[41] In Syria, he had a caravansary built about fifty kilometers north of Damascus, on the road to Homs. Even today, the inscription above the entry door of the building attests to that act. Called Khān al-Sultān (Sultan's Caravansary) during Ibn Jubayr's time, the site is now known by the name Khān al-ʿArūs (Bridegroom's Caravansary).[42]

The Sultan's Control over the Markets

The major cities of Egypt, Syria, and Upper Mesopotamia all had lively markets, where various commodities from the surrounding countryside or from high commerce were sold: food products, spices, raw materials necessary for the textile industry, fabric and leather, goldsmithery, pottery, hollowware, glassware, and various utensils. The prince's policies in that area were carried out by a prefect of markets (muhtasib) named directly by him. The muhtasib was, in the first place, responsible for overseeing, in the sovereign's name, the application of the Koranic obligation to enjoin what is good and prohibit what is evil, which not only conferred on the prefect a supervisory role over the markets but also gave his duties a religious and legal character. Treatises, both theoretical and practical, were often composed to remind him of the obligations attached to that position. Under Saladin's reign, a Syrian named al-Shayzarī was the author of a work of that kind, in which were listed all the rules a muhtasib was obliged to impose, with regard to the control of transactions and the repression of fraud, the maintenance of hygiene and cleanliness, the upkeep of the public thoroughfares and places of prayer, the prevention of fires, and the oversight of morality and of certain trades in the souks (those of moneychangers, hairdressers and barbers, doctors and phlebologists, and slave traders). Although the author did not compose that work at Saladin's request—he says he wrote it at the request of a *muhtasib*[43]—we know that he dedicated another to the sultan, which seems to indicate that he was part of Saladin's entourage.

In any case, once we are familiar with two other documents, there can no longer be any doubt that Saladin took an interest in the moralization and smooth operation of the markets. The first is a diploma of investiture for a *muhtasib,* drawn up by al-Fādil, no doubt at Saladin's request;[44] the second is the decree naming the *muhtasib* of Aleppo, which Saladin had 'Imād al-Dīn draw up in 1183. Its content not only informs us of the *muhtasib's* role but also gives us a picturesque glimpse of what life in the markets may have been like:

> Since we have the obligation to enjoin what is good and prohibit what is evil, to administer without fail the people's affairs in conformity with the dispositions of the Law . . . we judge it necessary to name to the position of *muhtasib* a man of noble extraction and high authority . . . a man who is strengthened by his fear of God . . . a man possessing a sincere faith that prevents him from diverging from the straight path. . . . Let him observe the people of the markets: he will treat with kindness the merchants whose probity he has observed, but will instruct those who have demonstrated total ignorance of the Law. . . . As regards intoxicating beverages, let him seek them out and spill them on the ground, and let him apply the legal punishment to anyone who has drunk of them, as soon as the guilty party has regained his sobriety. . . . Let him prohibit fraud on merchandise and coinage, usury on loans and contracts, cheating on volumes, weights, and lengths, and let him prohibit all from deviating from the customary measures allowed by religious Law. . . . Let him pursue the cheapjacks and the charlatans who practice medicine in the manner of astrologers; let him prevent [them] from treating illnesses and indispositions, from caring for the eyes and prescribing remedies blindly and in haste, from selling adulterated and unfamiliar medications, and from inventing for them uncommon names not known by the ancients. Let him drive away people who are mixed up in astrology, prestidigitation, and divination, and let him have utter scorn for the followers of the occult sciences, accustomed to behaving only in accordance with the signs they

provide. Let him protect the mosques and places of worship by preventing craftsmen from installing their booths there, public storytellers from assembling their audience there, and tradespeople and
artisans from making them into shops and lodgings. Let him condemn nudity with the greatest vigor, especially in the public baths.[45]

The duties of the *muhtasib,* and through him of the state, were thus divided
into two major categories: those relating to oversight of the markets, and those
concerning public morality and the observation of religious duties. Among his
economic functions, one of the most important was to oversee weights and
measures and to suppress fraud. He was also obliged to prevent any specula-
tion or monopolies on merchandise, so as to assure free competition. Some
people, in fact, stockpiled merchandise to resell when prices rose. In theory,
the *muhtasib* did not have the power to set prices, but he was supposed to prevent any excessive increase, particularly for basic food products such as cereals.
With the exception of strategic products such as wood, iron, and pitch, whose
prices were set by the Egyptian state, prices fluctuated as a function of many
factors, the most important being the value of the currency and the monetary mass, the relation between supply and demand, and the political situation. Low prices were usually interpreted by the residents as a sign of stability and prosperity.

In the monetary realm, Saladin gave his attention to the revaluation of the
Egyptian silver currency, a policy that did not bear fruit as he had hoped. In
terms of supply, it took only one inauspicious rise of the Nile, either a flood or
a drought, for the prices of food products to soar. Under Saladin's reign, the
general tendency was toward stability, even during the time when he took
power in Egypt, when a period of disruption might have been feared.[46] That
relative stability of prices did not prevent occasional crises, usually the result of
natural catastrophes that destroyed the harvests. In Egypt, for example, an inadequate rise of the Nile in 1179 led to a spike in prices, followed by an epidemic
that, within a few days, claimed seventeen thousand lives in the urban center
of Cairo alone.[47] Four years later, conversely, an excessive rise of the waters
flooded fields and destroyed villages. During Saladin's reign, Egypt was the
victim of several other meteorological events and epidemics[48] that had repercussions on the cost of living. In Syria as well, a drought wreaked havoc between 1176 and 1180, leading to a sharp increase in prices and to epidemics and

a serious famine, during which, as often in such situations, there were even reported cases of cannibalism.[49]

Saladin's objectives in the economic realm seem to have been to assure the supply of strategic materials and basic products to the Egyptian population and to oversee security of communications, an equitable collection of customs duties, the stability of prices, and the moralization of the markets. He did not always manage to realize these objectives, however, because of the many military conflicts, the opposition of the Arab tribes, the state's inability to control corruption among some officials, and of course, weather events.

VI

The Legend

I saw that Brutus who overthrew Tarquin,
Lucretia, Cornelia, Julia, and with these three
was Marcia. Alone, apart, was Saladin.

Dante, *Inferno*, canto 4, lines 127–129

The legend that has surrounded Saladin from the Middle Ages to our own time cannot be analyzed or understood outside the historical, literary, and political context within which it appeared and spread. From the late twelfth century on, Westerners attempted to find explanations for the sultan's many successes. In the popular imagination, Saladin took on the aspect of a scourge sent by God to punish the Christians for their impiety. A few centuries later, by contrast, Voltaire placed the sultan's image in the service of his virulent critique of Christianity. That is because, in the interval, the European representation of Saladin had ultimately erected him into the model of a fair, generous, and chivalrous ruler. In the East, the political and religious context was even more decisive in shaping the image of the conqueror of Jerusalem. In the twentieth century, the rise of nationalism, decolonization, the Arab-Israeli conflict, U.S. policy in the Middle East, the negligence on the part of a large number of Arab regimes, and the sense of humiliation felt by their populations greatly favored the emergence of Saladin as the hero embodying resistance to the West. With the loftiest virtues—courage, nobility of spirit, piety, and a sense of justice—attributed to him, he has become the model par excellence of a revalorized, ideal Arab identity. As the ideal monarch, a fearless knight beyond reproach, unifier of the three religions, hero of the great contemporary Arab causes, Saladin remains a historical figure, endlessly wavering, even today, between myth and reality.

24

Birth and Development

In the early fourteenth century, Dante's *Divine Comedy* placed the Prophet Muhammad in hell, but reserved a more enviable place, limbo, for Saladin, alongside Avicenna, Averroës, and the virtuous pagans Socrates, Plato, and Aristotle.[1] A few decades later, Petrarch's *Triumph of Fame* granted Saladin a privileged place among the men who distinguished themselves in combat.[2] That special treatment belongs to the tradition of literary epics and romances that emerged in the West in the early thirteenth century.[3]

The question arising is how a warrior, a relentless jihad fighter, who retook Jerusalem and many territories from the Franks, ultimately came to embody in the West the ideal of the Christian knight—valiant, generous, magnanimous. Before attempting to respond, let me note that Saladin was not the only Muslim leader of that time to become legend. The Western imagination enjoyed "converting" to Christianity the Islamic figures it admired. For example, one of the versions of the *Chétifs* depicts Karbūqah, the emir of Mosul who fought the Crusaders outside the walls of Antioch in 1098, renouncing his religion and adopting that of Christ. Similarly, Tughtegin, atabeg of Damascus, the Franks' chief adversary in the early twelfth century, became, under the name Huon de Tabarié (by analogy with Hugh of Tiberias), the hero of an anonymous thirteenth-century poem, the *Ordene de chevalerie (Order of Chivalry),* in which he appears as a Muslim prince converted to Christianity and fighting alongside the Franks of Jerusalem.[4] In a fifteenth-century romance in prose titled *Saladin,* that same Huon Dodequin de Tabarié, held prisoner by Saladin, is the one who dubs him a knight.[5] Without a doubt, behind these legends lay the admiration the Franks felt for the bellicosity of certain Muslim leaders. Once victory came to be interpreted as the expression of divine will, it was better to be beaten by valiant and chivalrous men motivated by common values than by infidels. In presenting adversaries as Christian knights, the Western imagination made defeat less alarming, found an explanation for the Muslims' exploits, and at the same time legitimated the admiration attributed to them, since these exploits now corresponded to the Western criteria of good and evil. That idea, that a virtuous man, a noble soul, could not be a Muslim, was not applied only to rulers and military leaders. For the same reason, several great thirteenth-century Dominicans and Franciscans attempted to show that Avicenna, the chief propagator of Aristotle's philosophy in the West, whose works were studied in the great European universities, was in reality mocking Islam.[6]

In addition, at the very end of the eleventh century, as the *Reconquista* was beginning in Spain and the Crusades were getting under way in the East, the development of an epic and romantic literature in the vernacular—in French first and foremost—favored in large part the diffusion of legends developing the theme of the battle between Christians and Muslims. The epics, poems, and romances that emerged disseminated literary themes that were for the most part chivalrous. Whether epic chansons recounting the great deeds *(gesta)* of heroes of the past, courtly love poems sung by the troubadours, or romances in verse dealing with the exploits of Alexander, King Arthur, or Charlemagne, that new literature was addressed to an audience composed in great part of knights wishing to hear the adventures of their ancestors or peers. The values diffused were those with which they were likely to identify: skill in handling weapons, largesse, courage, and respect for one's promises. What was more natural, then, than for poets and authors of romances to seek inspiration from the adventures of their contemporaries? The Crusades, with all they entailed in exploits and gallantry, extraordinary situations and exoticism, offered inexhaustible subjects for literature. Even while basing their works on the accounts of pilgrims and Crusaders returning from the East, authors could give free rein to their imaginations and transpose into their epics or romances the preoccupations and ideals of their time. It is within that context that we must attempt to understand the scope assumed in the West by the legend of Saladin.[7] That legend is characterized, first, by the early date of its appearance—it took shape in the early thirteenth century—and by a fairly great permeability between historical sources and legendary accounts. Whereas the work of William of Tyre, an eyewitness to the events, is indisputably a historical source of great value, its French continuations, as well as the *Itinerarium* and the so-called Chronicle of Ernoul, though generally considered historical texts, also integrated imaginary elements. Only a meticulous comparison of the Western and Eastern sources sometimes makes it possible to differentiate the two aspects.

The Western medieval works in which Saladin is mentioned are relatively large in number. Most belong to epic Crusader literature and are divided into what is conventionally called the two Crusade cycles.[8] The first cycle, originating in the north of France and in Flanders, developed throughout the period of the Crusades, from the early twelfth to the late thirteenth century.[9] Its principal objectives were to entertain and to offer a vernacular history of the Crusades for a relatively broad public. Depending on the place where the work was written, the exploits of one Crusader or another were highlighted and celebrated. Godefroi de Bouillon gradually came to occupy a preponderant place,[10] and, by the late thirteenth century, the history of the kingdom of Jerusalem covered Saladin's reign.[11] That first Crusade cycle, composed entirely in alexandrines arranged into laisses, acquires its unity through its literary form and its central theme, the glorification of the First Crusade. Some works are closer to the chanson de geste, others to historiography, hagiography, or the chivalrous romance. None as yet allows any real admiration for Saladin to show through. All provide an interesting viewpoint on a certain popular perception of the Crusade and on the way that Westerners represented their own past and constructed their memory.

The second Crusade cycle was composed after the fall of the Latin states—that is, after 1291—with the idea, no doubt, of encouraging a resumption of the Crusades. It appears more fictionalized than the first, and it was at that time that the geste of Saladin took shape, conveying an increasingly favorable image of him.[12] That second cycle ends with the romance *Saladin* (second half of the fifteenth century), which covers the time between his taking of power in Egypt and his death. It constitutes the last part of a trilogy titled *Jehan d'Avesnes,* composed between 1465 and 1468, whose beginning repeats a tale from the thirteenth century, *La fille du comte de Ponthieu (The Daughter of the Count of Ponthieu),* which traces the Western origins of Saladin's mother.[13]

Several other poems or romances, not part of the Crusade cycle proper but inspired by some of its episodes, also evoke Saladin: *Carmen de Saladino* (late twelfth century), the *Récits d'un ménestrel de Reims (Tales of a Minstrel from Rheims;* about 1260), the *Contes de chevaliers du temps jadis (Stories of Knights of Yore,* late thirteenth century), and *Le Pas Saladin (The Saladin Pass,* late thirteenth to early fourteenth century). In the fourteenth century, Dante (d. 1321) and Boccaccio (d. 1375) put their own stamp on that legendary tradition. The author of the *Divine Comedy* displays indulgence toward Saladin, who passes peaceful days in limbo, where noble souls who could not receive baptism reside. Similarly, in *The Banquet,* Dante mentions him with other virtuous princes and lords: "Who does not still keep a place in his heart for Alexander because of his royal acts of benevolence? Who does not keep a place for the good King of Castile, or Saladin, or the good Marquis of Monferrato, or the good Count of Toulouse, or Bertran de Born, or Galeazzo of Montefeltro? When mention is made of their gifts, certainly not only those who would willingly do the same, but those as well who would sooner die than do the same, retain in their memory a love for these men."[14]

Saladin appears in two tales of Boccaccio's *Decameron* as a benevolent, magnanimous, and generous sovereign.[15] A few centuries later, the parable of the three rings, in which Saladin plays the hero, directly inspired the German playwright Gotthold Ephraim Lessing for his play *Nathan the Wise* (1779). Once again, Saladin is vested with the same qualities: he is courteous toward women, the bearer of a humanist message, the lover of truth. Of a more historical bent, Voltaire's *Essai sur les moeurs (Essay on Morals,* 1756) retains some legendary aspects in its flattering portrait of Saladin and, in doing so, expresses Voltaire's radical critique of Christianity. This Saladin is generous, courteous, compassionate, modest, and respectful of treaties and of religions.[16] In *The Talisman* (1825), the early nineteenth-century Scottish novelist Walter Scott also shows great admiration for a courageous, intelligent Saladin, true to his word, generous, and compassionate, who battles a much more ruthless Richard the Lionheart. The author even goes so far as to wonder about that era, "in which the Christian and English monarch showed all the cruelty and violence of an Eastern sultan, and Saladin, on the other hand, displayed the deep policy and prudence of a European sovereign, whilst each contended which should excel the other in knightly qualities of bravery and generosity."[17] All the other late nine-teenth- and early twentieth-century English authors who took an interest in Saladin also had a tendency to project their own representation of the hero onto him.[18]

From the thirteenth to the nineteenth centuries, then, similar themes often fostered the legend of Saladin, reflecting both the most noteworthy aspects of the individual and the values and ideals that the West was seeking to promote.

25

Antihero or Prophet Foretold?

In contrast to that positive view, there was also in the West what could be called the "dark legend" of Saladin. It drew its inspiration primarily from the conditions surrounding his accession to power, depicting him as the very figure of imposture and illegitimacy. For example, an anonymous Latin poem, *Carmen de Saladino*, probably composed in 1187, presents him as a usurper, the bastard son of Nūr al-Dīn, who seduced his father's wife, became her lover, killed the vizier and the caliph of Cairo, poisoned Nūr al-Dīn, and thrust aside his father's legitimate son to seize the throne:

> When he should have been in the king's service,
> He was not a Joseph, should not have been a Joseph,
> In the king's bed by a crime against a woman,
> He corrupted his lady, adulterous man, a thief too bold,
> So often a foolish life pleases an easy woman.
> Once a herdsman, now he sullies the king's marriage,
> So the queen surrenders her seigneury to a servant.
> The jealous king knows nothing of that sin,
> The cheating queen recommends Saladin to the king,

To wallow more freely in adultery.
By that opportunity, Saladin rises beyond all measure,
Noradinus loves that servant more than the grandees.
In complete freedom [Saladin] comes and goes in the royal chamber,
He stays there whenever the king goes anywhere.
By general edict, Saladin becomes the first among princes,
Through such a crime becomes nearly the king's equal.[1]

A man without dynastic legitimacy who came to power by every criminal means possible: such is the poet's dark portrayal. It is amusing to observe that the reference to Joseph, so often used by the Arab authors, is now turned against Saladin. In contrast to Joseph's resistance to an attempted seduction by his master's wife (Genesis 39:7–20) is Saladin's corruption of the wife of Nūr al-Dīn. Shreds of truth, such as Saladin's modest background, the assassination of Shāwar, the caliph's death, the tension between Saladin and Nūr al-Dīn, and Saladin's subsequent marriage to his predecessor's widow, are intentionally twisted to make Saladin the anti-sovereign par excellence. His bastard origin stands opposed to the dynastic lineage, treason stands in for loyalty, violence takes precedence over the maintenance of peace.

Traces of that negative view of Saladin are found even in the Latin chronicle of the Third Crusade (*Itinerarium Peregrinorum et Gesta Regis Ricardi*), which depicts him not only as a man who came from nothing, hungry for power—as opposed to Richard the Lionheart, whose prestige was enhanced during that period of political crisis within the English monarchy—but in the guise, unexpected at the very least, of a pimp: "Saladin collected illgotten gains for himself from a levy on the girls of Damascus: they were not allowed to practise as prostitutes unless they had obtained, at a price, a licence from him for carrying on the profession of lust. . . . The pimp, who had a kingdom of brothels, an army of taverns, who studied dice and rice,[2] is suddenly raised up on high."[3]

That dark image probably originated in Saladin's duties as chief of police in Damascus in about 1165. He was a bastard for some, a pimp for others, and everything most contemptible was imputed to him, at a time when lineage and the notion of inherited authority occupied a primordial place in the West. Was it not noble blood that conferred the power to command? And that nobility was defined in the first place by parentage.[4] It is therefore Saladin's legitimacy to reign that is being called into question here, in contrast to the burgeoning legends that represented him as a model ruler, inventing a lineage for Saladin that makes him a descendant of the count of Ponthieu through his mother.[5]

William of Tyre himself was rather divided on the subject of Saladin. Although he could not conceal a certain admiration for his bellicosity and great generosity, William portrayed him as an ambitious enemy treacherously bludgeoning the caliph to death and running through all his progeny with a sword, and as a usurper devoid of all human feeling.[6] The same author also points to the sultan's humble origin and attributes his political ascent to chance rather than inheritance. William speaks of Saladin as of a tyrant, primarily because the danger the sultan represented for the Franks in William's time was real (whence his fear), but also because that portrayal corresponded to the medieval conception of history, in which tyrants are sent by God to punish the Christians for their sins. And for William, one of the explanations for the Frankish defeats lay in the fact that the sins of men—especially those of the Eastern Franks—had elicited God's wrath. God therefore punished them by sending Saladin, who now reigned without rival over a reunified Muslim territory.[7] That same idea is expressed in the papal bull *Audita tremendi* of October 29, 1187, in which Gregory VIII suggests that God gave the victory to Saladin only to punish the Christians for their dissension and sins. For the pope, however, there was no need to blacken the reputation of Saladin, who was no more and no less than an instrument of God. Peter of Blois (d. ca. 1211), by contrast, in his "Passion of Reginald," presents Saladin as a cruel Antichrist, a persecutor of Christians, and calls him the "son of perdition with the deadly and damnable name, with which, reluctantly and sorrowfully, I pollute this letter."[8]

More anecdotally, the French *Continuation* of William of Tyre attempts to explain Saladin's victories in terms of sorcery.[9] The action unfolds in the Frankish camp in Sepphoris in 1187, before the Battle of Hattīn:

> I must tell you about an incident involving the men of the host, even though it seems foolish and the Holy Church has forbidden people to believe it. When the host had left the springs of Saffuriya and had passed two leagues beyond Nazareth, some sergeants in the host found an old Saracen woman riding on a donkey. . . . They asked her where she was going at that hour, but she was unable to give them an adequate reply. So they threatened and tortured her, and she admitted that she was the slave of a Syrian of Nazareth.

Then they asked where she was going. She told them that she was
going to Saladin to collect the reward for the service she had done
him. They tortured her further to discover what this service was.
She revealed that she was a sorceress and had cast a spell on the
men of the host; for two days she had encircled them and had cast
her spells by the devil; had they stayed and not moved from the
camp she would have bound them so strongly by the devil's art that
Saladin would have taken every one of them and no one would
have escaped. She told them that things would go badly for them
and that few of them would survive.[10]

The Franks decided to burn the sorceress, but she survived the fire two
or three times. Then they beheaded her, cut her head in two, and threw her
corpse into the flames. The author adds that these events were not at all surprising for anyone who compared them to the biblical story of Balak and
Balaam (Numbers 22), in which Balak, king of Moab, offered the "sorcerer"
Balaam a large quantity of gold and silver for him to go and "cast a spell" on
the children of Israel on their way to the Promised Land. But the angel of Jeho-
vah intervened, standing in the way of the she-ass that Balaam was riding and
leading him to understand that he was not to curse the Israelites. The biblical
passage ends there, but the author of the *Continuation* of William of Tyre proceeds to another account, no doubt drawn from the *Jewish Antiquities* by the
historian Flavius Josephus (first century A.D.).[11] Unable to stamp out the Jews
with curses and sorcery, Balak resorts to a ruse: he sends them the most beautiful girls from his country, with wine to seduce them, corrupt them, and force
them to renounce their religion. The Jews succumb, and God's punishment
falls upon them. The author of the *Continuation* concludes by saying: "No one
should wonder that the land of Jerusalem was lost, for they committed so
much sin in Jerusalem that Our Lord was extremely angry. They did service to
the devil in return for which he deceived them by putting hatred between
them so that the kingdom was destroyed."[12] The moral of the story is clear:
Saladin is compared to Balak, the cunning and deceitful king who does not
hesitate to use every sort of subterfuge; but he also appears as the scourge that
God sends to the Franks to punish them for their sins, to sow discord among
them, and to take Jerusalem from them. That episode, also reported by the so-
called Chronicle of Ernoul, is illustrated in an illuminated manuscript dating

to the early fourteenth century. Appearing in the upper register of the illumination is Saladin, surrounded by his soldiers, witnessing the arrest of the sorceress by the Franks, while the lower register depicts a Christian ruler contemplating the agony of that same sorceress, condemned to be burned at the stake and about to be beheaded.[13]

In general, however, though the "dark legend" of the sultan did not totally disappear from the second Crusade cycle, the farther one moves from Saladin's time, the more positive the Western view becomes. From that perspective, Ambroise's *Estoire de la guerre sainte (History of the Holy War)*, by a poet who accompanied Richard the Lionheart on the Crusade, marks a turning point. In the early part of his work, Ambroise attributes to Saladin responsibility for the massacre of the Muslim prisoners of Acre, criticizes him for the violence of his reactions after the defeat, and describes him as a sovereign more cunning than courageous. But Saladin later appears in a better light, especially when he receives Hubert Walter, bishop of Salisbury, with courtesy and generosity.[14] Gradually, what had been treachery and perfidy is transformed into cunning and daring, and the assault of Acre takes on the appearance of prophecy. In the thirteenth century, the French continuations of William of Tyre describe the ruse thought up by Saladin to approach the caliph, and they link his taking of power in Egypt to a prophecy that the horses posted outside the caliph's palace in Cairo would be ridden by 'Alī, the Prophet's son-in-law, who would one day reappear to become master "of all Heathenry and part of Christendom; and throughout the whole world his renown would travel."[15] That version was repeated in the fifteenth century in *Saladin:*

> After all these attempts, knowing that the emir was in fact inside
> the walls, but that it was impossible to gain ascendancy over him
> except by ruse, Saladin placed a pack filled with wood on his shoul-
> ders and armed himself with a knife, which he slid down his thigh:
> that was his only weapon. Then he assembled forty knights and
> dressed them as peasants or caters, but bearing arms under their
> costumes, and to each of them he gave a donkey driver's switch.
> Before he left, he ordered his men to arm themselves and to go into
> Cairo to lend him a hand as soon as they heard the blowing of a
> horn. He had no difficulty getting someone to open the door to
> him, since the porters, who immediately recognized him, thought

it was his way of going to ask humbly for mercy from their ruler: so it was that he penetrated the city with his knights. There is no point in saying that the crowd thronged around him in the main street of Cairo, when they saw him walking on all fours like an animal, followed by his people, switches in hand: the spectacle was worth the trouble. And so great and small came running.

The news was announced to the king. He too believed that Saladin was coming to throw himself on the king's mercy and was acknowledging that he must have been a dumb beast to have attacked him. That is why the king went out to meet him, moved by pity for that man who was confessing he was an ass. But as soon as he was within Saladin's reach, the sultan stood up on his feet, cast off the pack and logs, and, having told his knights to do their duty, sounded his horn. Upon which, feeling no fear, he unsheathed his knife and struck the emir with it before the eyes of all his princes: no one dared intervene, so frightened were they by the boldness of the undertaking. . . . Upon which the princes recognized Saladin as their master and handed the palace over to him. There he found a magnificent horse that no one had as yet dared mount. It had been predicted that the one able to do so would become king of Babylon in Cairo and would acquire great renown among the Saracens. As soon as Saladin saw it, he got into the saddle, and immediately, the horse made a great show of it, whinnying, pricking up his ears, and striking his hooves. As a result, his rider was immediately honored with the title of king by the people of Cairo.[16]

Contrary to the "dark legend," which emphasizes the perfidy by which Saladin acceded to the throne, these narratives recognize a legitimacy in him, given to him by his courage (he is not afraid to kill the emir in front of all his men or to break in the horse) and especially, by prophecy. What meaning are we to give to these accounts, and where do they come from? Were such stories circulating in Egypt during Saladin's time? Why that association between 'Alī—that is, the Shiites—and Saladin? Are we to see that type of narrative, as Hannes Möhring has argued, as a claim by Saladin to be recognized as the Mahdi ("the Guided One"), the one who the Sunnis and Shiites believe will reign before the end of the world, who will inaugurate a new era, and who will restore Islam to its

original perfection?[17] I do not believe we can go so far as that. If such an identification had existed within Saladin's entourage, we would have uncovered the
traces of it in the Arab sources. But there is nothing like it. Of course, 'Imād al-
Dīn, in the introduction to his work on Saladin's conquests, after referring to
the different calendars, states that his account will begin with "a second Hegira," that of "the emigration from Islam to Jerusalem" in 1187, the date of the
conquest of the holy city by Saladin. It is also true that Saladin's return to Damascus in May 1188 is reported as follows: "The heaven of sweet delights recovered its serenity, the unbroken steeds turned docile from the success. The sultan
supported those who implored him, sated those who were thirsty, showed favor
to the upright and cut down the wicked, praised those who proved useful and
imposed the reign of justice to such a degree that it was said of him: 'He is the
Mahdi.' "[18]

But these are only rhetorical formulations and cannot be taken literally.
'Imād al-Dīn's lyrical style and love of metaphor, intended to disseminate the
image of Saladin as the model of justice and virtue, are well known. We have
already seen the numerous allusions to the Prophet, to his battles, and to his
ascent to heaven from Jerusalem in the panegyric literature regarding Saladin,
but that does not mean he was himself considered a prophet. When al-Fādil
wrote to Saladin: "Our master spent the money of Egypt to conquer Syria, the
money of Syria to conquer al-Jazīra, and the money of all to conquer the
coast. . . . if it is God's will, the money of Constantinople will be spent for
the conquest of Rome,"[19] are we to conclude that he was actually envisioning
the conquest of the Byzantine Empire and of Italy? No, of course not. Similarly,
when he tells Saladin that "God gave him two kingships as an inheritance: the
kingship here below and the kingship in the world beyond,"[20] it is divine reward, not a new era, that is at issue. On a purely political level, how could Saladin, who throughout his reign sought the support of the caliph of Baghdad,
have justified such a claim?

The origin of that story should rather be sought, it seems to me, in the many
traditions and legends circulating in Egypt, and which the population attempted
to associate, one way or another, with the events they were experiencing. We
have already mentioned, for example, the story reported by Ibn Jubayr of the
two statues of Cairo, one announcing the conquest of the Seljuks and the other,
that of the Almohads. It is not impossible that, in the Shiite circles of Cairo,
legends combining ancient traditions (Alexander breaking in Bucephalus) and

traditions attached to the family of ʿAlī were circulating. After all, did not Pseudo-Callisthenes, author of the oldest Greek version of the Romance of Alexander, live in Alexandria at the beginning of the Common Era?[21] The motif of Alexander taming the wild horse, interpreted as a prophecy of his domination of the world, was also repeated in the West and may have influenced the Latin authors. In this case, the confusion with Saladin might have come about in the Frankish circles of the Holy Land and then spread.[22] But of course, all that belongs solely to the realm of hypothesis.

26

The Valiant and Generous Knight

One of the recurrent aspects of the Saladin legend was its representation of the sultan as a knight dubbed by the Franks. That idea penetrated so deeply in the West that, as late as 1930, Charles L. Rosebault, in his book *Saladin, Prince of Chivalry* (London), devoted an entire chapter to the dubbing of Saladin by Humphrey of Toron.[1] According to some, Saladin was knighted during his captivity in the fortress of Montreal (Shawbak) by its lord, Humphrey of Toron; for others, he was dubbed by Hugues of Tiberias (sometimes assimilated to Tughtegin, atabeg of Damascus, under the name Huon Dodequin de Tabarié), himself a convert to Christianity.[2]

One of the texts best illustrating that image of Saladin as a knight is a French poem titled *Le Pas Saladin*. Probably composed in the early fourteenth century to celebrate French and English chivalry, the poem recounts Saladin's progress through a narrow mountain pass near Acre, defended by Richard the Lionheart and twelve Christian knights, a kind of *Song of Roland* in reverse, since here it is the Muslims who are defeated.[3] That story probably originated with the victory of Richard the Lionheart near Jaffa in the summer of 1192. In it Saladin is described as Muslim leaders traditionally were in chansons de geste. Associated with Mahom, Apolin, and Tervagant, three deities already present in the *Song of*

Roland, he appears arrogant but also respectful of chivalrous values. For example, he stops the fighting so as not to kill more Christian knights, having himself been dubbed by "Hues," that is, Hugues of Tiberias. Later, in the romance *Saladin,* that theme of a battle in a narrow pass was repeated, but this time in England and in another form: Saladin makes a proposal to the Christian barons that two Christian knights should fight two Muslim knights, and promises to surrender the pass if his knights are beaten. Faithful to his promise, he retreats once the battle is won by the Christians. "After his departure, the mountain pass he had been unable to conquer was called 'Saladin's pass.'"[4]

Once the qualities of Saladin the knight were recognized, he came to be represented in one-on-one battles against the other hero of that time, Richard the Lionheart. The outcome of the battle varied, depending on the context in which the work was composed. In an Anglo-Norman poem, written between 1230 and 1250 to glorify Richard the Lionheart, the battle between the two rulers occurs under rather fantastical conditions. The scene takes place outside a besieged Cairo. Inside the city, Saladin sends Richard a magnificent horse, which, however, has a formidable flaw: not only is the animal possessed by the devil, but the mare that foaled it, ridden by Saladin, has only to begin whinnying and the horse will run to her on its knees and begin to suck. Alerted by an angel, Richard releases the horse from its evil spirit and plugs its ears with wax to make it deaf to its mother's call. He therefore manages to knock Saladin off his horse and emerges victorious in the battle.[5]

The *Itinerarium* and Ambroise's *Estoire de la guerre sainte* are also very favorable toward Richard the Lionheart. In these two narratives, however, the benighted portrait of Saladin integrates his prowess and courage, thus accentuating the king of England's merit. Philip Augustus, by contrast, is described as a miserly and cowardly man, which has the effect of placing the Muslim adversary above the French.[6] In *Saladin* it is the reverse: Richard the Lionheart is brought down by the "foreign knight" Saladin. The scene takes place at a tournament unfolding in Cambrai,[7] and its outcome reflects the prevailing anti-English feeling, at a time when France's enemy was no longer the sultan but rather the king of England. Richard is in fact described as a timorous sovereign—he cries upon learning of Saladin's arrival—and as a traitor to the king of France.

Saladin was also widely represented as a knight in Western art of the thirteenth and fourteenth centuries, both in manuscript illuminations and mural paintings, as well as on tapestries and even some personal items.[8] Paintings of the famous *Pas Saladin* were done on the walls of several castles, and according to the great fourteenth-century French chronicler Jean Froissart, a theatrical production was mounted in Paris in 1389. A little while later, Marquess Thomas III of Saluzzo inserted *Le Pas Saladin* into his romance *Le chevalier errant (The Knight Errant, 1394–1395)*. One of the manuscripts of that work, dating to about 1404, contains an illumination illustrating the episode.[9] In 1252, in the context of his propaganda favoring a new Crusade, Henry III of England also had scenes from the Crusades, featuring his uncle Richard the Lionheart (a duel with Saladin in particular), represented in several of his castles.[10] Elsewhere, especially at the Chertsey Abbey in Surrey County, southeastern England, Richard was also depicted on decorated tiles, in hand-to-hand combat with Saladin.[11]

In both literature and art, Saladin was allowed to face the king of England, with arms equal to Richard's, because he was considered a noble knight. And that battle among "nobles" did not get in the way of feelings of mutual respect. On the contrary: the tradition of respect between Saladin and Richard the Lionheart long remained present in Western literature. It can also be found in *Nathan the Wise* (act 2, scene 1) and in certain nineteenth-century English novels. In her *Crusaders: An Historical Romance* (1820), Lady Louisa Sidney Stanhope attributes to Saladin the notion, already present in Ambroise's *Estoire* and in the *Itinerarium,* that if he were to lose Jerusalem, he would prefer that it be to Richard the Lionheart, whose chivalrous qualities he admired. That is also the reason why the matrimonial plans between the two families did not shock anyone and were often represented in Western literature.[12]

"The knight is obliged to keep nothing at hand. Everything that comes to him, he gives away. From his generosity he draws his strength and most of his power, or in any event, all his renown and the warm friendships surrounding him," writes Georges Duby of William Marshal.[13] Foremost among the qualities ascribed to the good knight Saladin is that of the "real" Saladin: his largesse. Even the "dark legend" makes note of it, though in a particular mode, of course, in that it attributes a criminal origin to the money distributed.[14] That is how the Minstrel of Rheims accounts for Saladin's ability to buy off Christian barons who betray their king.[15] Here, the sovereign's generosity is turned into an evil weapon. Even William of Tyre writes that giving away money was Saladin's way of winning hearts, thus implying a direct connection between the sultan's generosity and his ulterior political motives.

But in general, Saladin's generosity was considered a positive quality that earned him comparisons with great figures from the past. "Some said that even Alexander in his time would not have known how to demonstrate greater largesse," we read in *Saladin,* which goes so far as to have its hero say: "This country, like the rest of the world, belongs to me, because of good king Alexander the Great, from whom my ancestors were descended."[16] Stories reporting Saladin's generosity are legion, and it is not possible to cite them all. In *Novellino,* a collection of short stories composed in the late thirteenth century, Saladin decides one day to give two hundred marks to a man who had offered him a bouquet of roses. In drawing up the payment order, his treasurer makes a mistake, writing "three hundred." When Saladin points out his error, the treasurer attempts to correct it, but the sultan asks him to write four hundred, so that no one will be able to claim one day that his treasurer's pen was more generous than he.[17] Boccaccio's Saladin is no less lavish: in the story of the three rings, he thanks the Jew who lent him money by showering him with gifts; and in the tale of Torello, gentleman of Pavia, he is able to appreciate his guest's largesse and even rival it at the proper moment, when he sends him home covered in jewels.[18]

In addition, Saladin's magnanimity and chivalrous behavior very often inspired the literature of romance. Westerners were generally impressed by his liberation of prisoners, especially when they were distinguished figures such as the king of Jerusalem, released solely on the promise that he would no longer take up arms against the Muslims. Some narratives go so far as to say that Saladin himself sometimes paid the ransom for his prisoners.[19] According to the French *Continuation* of William of Tyre, Saladin and his brother al-'Ādil vied with each other in generosity, freeing the Franks of Jerusalem too poor to pay their ransom, a gesture that is not confirmed by any Arab source.[20] Clemency and tolerance also appear in a work written by a friend of Dante's, Busone da Gubbio. In it Saladin is shown conversing with a French guest, John of Berry. In reply to the sultan, who asks him what he thinks of his palace, John says he has never visited such a beautiful one. Pressed by his interlocutor to find something wrong with it, he responds that there is no place to spit if necessary. Saladin advises him to choose the most vile place to do it, and John spits in his face. Taking the insult as a joke, the magnanimous Saladin forgives the offense.[21]

In her novel, Lady Louisa Stanhope emphasizes how well Saladin treated his prisoner Oswald, who saved Richard the Lionheart from captivity by allowing himself to be taken in his place. That story no doubt originated in the account, fairly widespread during the Middle Ages, of Saladin's attempt to capture the king of England: Saladin sends Richard a horse that is supposed to take him back to the Muslim camp as a captive. The king puts one of his knights in the saddle; the knight falls into Saladin's hands but is treated well.[22] These legends almost always had a basis in historical fact. Exchanges of gifts were common between Richard the Lionheart and Saladin, and certain sources, such as the *Itinerarium* and the *Estoire d'Eracles,* report that al-'Ādil actually gave Richard two horses. There was also a real battle in September 1191, related by the Arab sources, during which the king of England was almost killed by a Muslim fighter and was saved only because one of his men shielded the king with his own body and died in Richard's place.[23]

In the *Récits d'un Ménestrel de Reims,* Saladin displays the same kindness. Wishing to test the charity of the Knights Hospitaller of Saint-Jean-d'Acre, he disguises himself as a poor Christian pilgrim and is welcomed by them. He finds them ready to satisfy his every demand, even consenting to have him eat the right back hoof of the charger belonging to the Grand Master of the Order. As the servants are preparing to amputate the horse's hoof, Saladin stops them and asks for mutton to eat. Once he has returned home, convinced of the good deeds of the Order, he grants them a charter allotting them a hundred bezants a year, in wartime and in peace, a promise that the knights of the Order welcome with joy, "since they knew Saladin well and knew he would never lie."[24]

The legend of the lords of Anglure also belongs to that long chivalrous tradition. With a few variants, it was diffused by several sources from the fourteenth century on.[25] Saladin is reported to have freed Lord Ogier de Saint-Chéron, better known as Saladin of Anglure, so that the lord could gather together his ransom. Having been unable to find the necessary funds, Saint-Chéron returns and places himself in Saladin's hands. The sultan, touched by his sense of honor, frees him on three conditions: that he depict the Muslim crescent on his coat of arms; that he call the firstborn sons of his lineage "Saladin"; and that he adopt "Damascus!" as his war cry.[26] Once again, it is not impossible that a real event— Ogier de Saint-Chéron's departure for the Crusade in 1190—was behind that legend, since the practice of freeing a prisoner to allow him to gather together his own ransom was fairly common. In such cases, he was required to leave behind hostages, and they were freed only upon his return. Whether true or false, that tradition was very faithfully transmitted by the Anglure family. Genealogical reconstructions attest that, from the end of the thirteenth century on, the given name "Saladin" was attributed to members of the Anglure family and that, by the fourteenth century, they had adopted the heraldic motif of the bell and crescent, considered in the West to be Saladin's emblem.[27] It is also said that, until the French Revolution, on the roof of the family's castle of Jours in Burgundy, two figurines made of lead depicted Saladin and the lord of Anglure. Even today there is a family in France that bears the name "Saladin d'Anglure."

Saladin's attitude toward women also unfailingly fed his legend, for good and for ill. The dark legend primarily accentuates his supposed cruelty toward women, his seduction of Nūr al-Dīn's wife, and his prostitution of women in Damascus. But most of the sources insist rather on his courtesy toward them and his efforts to protect their virtue. The so-called Chronicle of Ernoul recounts the story of the marriage of Humphrey IV of Toron to Isabella, King Baldwin IV's half-sister: the wedding takes place in Kerak, while Saladin is holding it under siege. Humphrey's mother has sent Saladin dishes from the banquet ("bread and wine and beef and mutton") and reminds him of when he used to take the princess in his arms, when she was merely a child and he a slave in Kerak. Saladin thanks her, and, having asked in which tower the newlyweds could be found, he orders the weapon fire turned away from it.[28] In *Saladin*, it is the wife of Reginald—his worst enemy—to whom he grants his protection as she is giving birth in Kerak. Elsewhere in the romance, he offers safe passage to the princess of Antioch and her female companions, under siege in a fortress not far from Tyre. Although he finds the princess very beautiful, Saladin declines to take her and allows her to stay in the fortress with a three-month supply of food.[29] In the same register, the pilgrim Thietmar recounts the story of Saladin and the nuns: as he is manifesting a desire to take for himself the nuns in a convent between Bethlehem and Jerusalem, they choose to mutilate themselves rather than suffer the affront. Saladin, impressed by their courage, commends them for the gesture.[30]

Even odder are the stories that depict Saladin embracing courtly love, a practice widespread in the chivalrous circles of the thirteenth century.[31] In one of the *Contes de chevaliers du temps jadis,* composed in the late thirteenth century, the sultan is shown laying siege, weapons in hand, to the castle holding his Lady, a Christian woman living in enemy territory. He then comes to understand that it is only by relaxing his hold and leaving the premises that he will prove his love to her and win her heart.[32] *Saladin* tells the story of the queen of France. In Saint-Omer, the sultan first saves the life of John of Ponthieu's sister by fighting Lambert of Berry. Shortly thereafter, before returning to Syria, he provides further evidence of his generosity, courage, and courtesy by giving a superb banquet in the course of a tournament, from which he emerges the grand winner. Saladin then appears as the true hero of a chivalrous romance. The second part of the tale relates his attempt to conquer France and England. Defeated, he returns to Jerusalem, where the queen of France finds him. Outside Damascus, the Christians do battle with Saladin, who is wounded and transported to Babylon (Cairo), where he dies after converting to Christianity.

Many other amorous conquests are attributed to him. In the *Ottimo Commento della Divina Commedia,* written by a contemporary of Dante's, Saladin falls in love with the queen of Cyprus, no doubt Isabella, who actually became queen of Cyprus only after the sultan's death. Elsewhere, in the *Récits d'un Ménestrel de Reims,* he succumbs to the advances of Eleanor of Aquitaine, which is no less anachronistic, since Eleanor traveled to the East with her husband, King Louis VII, in 1148, at a time when Saladin was only about ten. It is actually an idyll between Eleanor and Raymond of Antioch that is transposed onto that far-fetched tale. Arrested by her husband as she is preparing to set off to find Saladin, Eleanor replies straight out that King Louis is not worth "a rotten apple" and that she prefers Saladin. The king then places her under heavy guard and, once he has returned to France, repudiates her.[33] In the fifteenth century, *Saladin* replaces Eleanor with the queen of France, wife of Philip Augustus, even though that king was already a widower during the Third Crusade. In it Saladin is described not only as a valiant knight but also as a tall and handsome seducer. Despite its lack of verisimilitude, the story of the idyll between Saladin and Eleanor survived until the nineteenth century. In both cases, Eleanor and the wife of Philip Augustus, the bond between lovers is doomed, and the queen is abducted from Saladin by force.

Loyalty to his oaths, prowess, largesse, magnanimity, and courtesy: Saladin possessed all the virtues of a good knight. But he is also praised for his austerity and humility, virtues that had some basis in truth. One of the most significant stories on that subject is no doubt that of his shroud, mentioned by both Voltaire and Chateaubriand and reported many times before them in the Latin sources:

> He died three years later in Damascus, admired even by the Christians. In place of the flag raised outside his door, during his last

illness he displayed the sheet in which he was to be buried. The person holding that standard of death cried out loud: "Here is everything that Saladin, conqueror of the East, takes away from his conquests." It is said that, in his will, he left alms to be distributed equally to the Mohammedan, Jewish, and Christian poor, wishing to make clear by that provision that all men are brothers, and that to help them, one must not seek to know what they believe but rather what they suffer. Few of our Christian princes have had that magnanimity; and few of the chroniclers with which Europe is overburdened have known how to do him justice.[34]

That story was disseminated even in collections of *exempla,* models for sermons intended for Christian preachers. In Saint-Gervais in 1272–1273, for example, Henri de Provins preached the story of King Saladin, who possessed eleven kingdoms. Once the king began to meditate on the vanity of worldly display, he became a preacher. When he visited his cities, he had a shroud carried ahead of him, with someone crying out: "From all his kingdoms, Saladin will take nothing away but this winding sheet."[35] It is interesting to note that no reference is made to Saladin's religion. It is as if his virtues were now sufficient to make him a universal model. Within the repertoire of his qualities, humility also occupies its proper place. It impels him to give due consideration to his acts and on occasion to engage in self-criticism. In the first of the *Contes de chevaliers du temps jadis,* the troubadour Bertran of Born pays him a visit, in an attempt to understand the basis for his reputation as an ideal sultan. He observes Saladin's habit of holding his council every day, to make sure he had done and said nothing wrong. Hence, the storyteller seems to say, Saladin's perfection lies first and foremost in his ability to recognize his errors humbly and to correct them.[36]

27

Between Moses, Jesus, and Muhammad

The most natural way to explain why a Muslim knight was endowed with every virtue was by converting him to Christianity. But before Saladin was turned into a Christian knight, a Christian ancestry was first invented for him: he was supposedly descended on his mother's side from the count of Ponthieu. Whereas the virtues attributed to him had a more or less remote basis in reality, the legends that developed around his Christian ancestors reflected only the desire of Westerners to find an explanation for what they saw as a paradox: being virtuous without being Christian.[1] Being dubbed a knight was a first step, but it was not sufficient. A noble lineage still had to be ascribed to Saladin to legitimate his qualities as a good sovereign. And, if he were converted to Christianity, his victories over the Franks, which he could not have had without God's help, would acquire an acceptable meaning. In addition, it was more honorable to lay down one's arms before a great Christian knight than before a Muslim sultan. Finally, showing that Saladin was drawn to the West was a way to mark its superiority over the East, and to grant oneself, after the failure of the Crusades, a form of revenge after the fact.

Here again, Saladin was not the only Muslim sovereign for whom a Christian ancestry was invented. In about 1170 Nūr al-Dīn's father, Zangī, conqueror of Edessa, was portrayed by a German chronicler as the son of Ida, wife of Leopold II, margrave of Austria, a woman taken prisoner at the Battle of Heracleum in 1101.[2] Several variations of the legend claim that Saladin was related to the count of Ponthieu. One of the best known, *La fille du comte de Ponthieu*, exists in two versions: one from the thirteenth and the other from the fifteenth century.[3] It appears that the story was composed in honor of the Ponthieu family of Picardy, a region from which many Crusaders originated. Adaptations of *La fille du comte de Ponthieu* were still being done in the seventeenth and eighteenth centuries. Voltaire himself attributed a Christian mother to Saladin in *Zaïre* (act 4, scene 1). Depending on the case, the "Lady of Ponthieu" turned out to be Saladin's mother or great-grandmother. According to legend, she was captured on a boat by pirates and sent to a sultan, and it was from their union that, in the first case, Saladin was born.[4]

From there, it was only a small step to justify the appeal the Christian religion held for Saladin, and Westerners were not slow to take it. From the first half of the thirteenth century, accounts surfaced in which Saladin was portrayed as anxious to bring together the three monotheistic religions, and others in which he did not hesitate to convert to Christianity. For example, the Austrian Jans der Enikel wrote in his *Weltbuch* that Saladin, when he entrusted his soul to God, hesitated between the God of the Jews, that of the Christians, and that of the Muslims.[5] A similar idea was expressed by the Cistercian monk Aubri de Trois-Fontaines in about the mid-thirteenth century, and the *Estoires d'Outremer* depicts Saladin on his deathbed, conducting a debate between the caliph of Baghdad, the patriarch of Jerusalem, and Jewish sages. Unable to come to a decision, the sultan divides his wealth into three parts but sets aside the largest share for the Christians.[6] Another legend, that of the three rings, probably originating in the Jewish milieus of Spain in about the late eleventh century, depicts a Jew and Peter of Aragon (r. 1094–1104). Various versions of that story, especially Italian ones, substitute Saladin for Peter. The moral to be drawn was that no religion can be sure it holds the truth, because only God knows it. Boccaccio gives his version in the *Decameron*,[7] which Lessing adapted in the eighteenth century to communicate his message of tolerance and respect for other religions. In the seventeenth century, Samuel de Broë commented on Saladin's decision to hold a debate on the three religions: "Saladin had always made fun of the Koran: his mind was too sensitive and too sharp to receive such crude impressions. But though he had enough strength to reject the lie, he never had enough courage to embrace the truth."[8]

Echoes of that tradition can still be found in our own time, for example, in the fictionalized biography of Saladin by Geneviève Chauvel, who has him say on his deathbed: "There is only one God. Allah, the God of the Christians, that of the Jews, is the same God. . . . There was Abraham, Moses, Jesus, then Muhammad, and there is only one religion, that of the one and only God."[9] Without going quite so far, Ridley Scott's recent film *Kingdom of Heaven* (2005), which recounts the fictionalized adventures of Balian of Ibelin in the Holy Land between 1184 and 1187, also depicts a sultan who is good, true to his word, and tolerant toward Christianity. For example, after the taking of Jerusalem, he is shown picking up a crucifix that has fallen to the ground and placing it back on the altar.[10]

A major turning point occurred in the development of that legend when Saladin began to be depicted as a convert to Christianity. In about 1260, the Minstrel of Rheims wrote that, before dying, Saladin secretly baptized himself without the knowledge of his entourage.[11] In *Saladin,* the sultan's self-baptism also concludes the debate on the three religions.[12] There are other examples of self-baptism in Western literature, beginning with that of the Prophet himself in a work by Saint Peter Pascual (d. 1300).[13] That type of literature must undoubtedly be placed within the context of the growth of missions in the thirteenth century.[14] In 1219 Saint Francis of Assisi in person left for Damietta to join the Crusaders on the Fifth Crusade. While negotiations were unfolding, he asked to speak to Saladin's nephew Sultan al-Kāmil. The sultan received him courteously, before sending him back to his own people. No Arab source relates that event, which must have gone unnoticed in the Egyptian context of the time. But in the West, a vast legendary literature developed around that interview in the thirteenth century, disseminating the image of the saint trying to convert the sultan. Because the Saladin legend was also developing during the same period, the image of Saladin sometimes took the place of his nephew. In thirteenth-century Italy, for example, one of the *Contes des chevaliers du temps jadis* recounts that Saladin once received two Christian monks who had come to demonstrate the superiority of their religion. The "sages" in Saladin's entourage advised him to put them to death, which he declined to do, saying: "'I know these people have come to save my soul, and I know well that it would not please God if, in return, I put them to death.' Then he paid them great honors and allowed them to leave."[15]

Because of his notoriety, Saladin was placed in stories that originally had nothing to do with him. Other medieval narratives also evoke his conversion to Christianity or that of someone close to him. The *Royal Chronicle of Cologne*, composed in about 1200, reports that the object of one of Saladin's embassies to Frederick Barbarossa was to propose a marriage between Frederick's daughter and Saladin's son. On that occasion, Saladin supposedly offered to convert to Christianity and to free all the Christian prisoners.[16] By contrast, in the eighteenth and nineteenth centuries, there was no longer any need, in explaining his virtues, to demonstrate that Saladin adhered very little to Islam or that he had converted to Christianity. At the time, authors used the figure of Saladin to put forward their ideas of tolerance. Such was the case for Walter Scott (1825), who recognized many virtues in Saladin, even though he was Muslim. That way of seeing things would lead Edward Said, in his famous book *Orientalism*, to say that in establishing an exception, intended in some sense to prove the rule, the Scottish novelist was condemning Muslims as a whole.[17] That opinion has been contested by Robert Irwin, who rightly believes that we must refrain from anachronism, since Walter Scott was speaking in the voice of the twelfth-century Franks, who at that time could not conceive of Islam and Christianity as equal religions, or of the Crusaders and Muslims as two communities on the same footing.[18] In his *Histoire de France (History of France)*, Jules Michelet makes Saladin's merits redound on Islam as a whole: "That Kurd, that barbarian, the Godefroi or Saint Louis of Mohammedanism, noble soul in the service of a very meager piety, a humane and generous nature who forced intolerance on himself, taught the Christians a dangerous truth, which is that one of the circumcised could be a saint, that a Mohammedan could be born a knight through the purity of his heart and his magnanimity."[19]

Saladin was also represented as a visitor to the West, no doubt a way to appropriate him further but also to highlight his attraction for a world judged to be better. His journeys appear to be motivated by curiosity, or by the wish to spy, or by more belligerent intentions, a reverse Crusade of sorts. But on the way, Saladin also meets men who charitably help him and who later give him the opportunity (after they are taken prisoner in the East and then released by him) to show that he has a sense of honor and a chivalrous heart.[20] In some cases, his foreigner's gaze was used to criticize the abuses of Western society, the clergy, or the papacy. That theme of a journey incognito to the West by Saladin—with or without disguise—is found in several works from the fourteenth and fifteenth centuries (*Decameron, Récits d'un Ménestrel de Reims, Saladin*), but its origin may go back to a more ancient tradition that has not come down to us.[21] In *Saladin*, therefore, the sultan goes to Brindisi, then to Rome, in the company of Huon Dodequin[22] and John of Ponthieu, where he condemns the excessive veneration the pope enjoys. In reply to Huon, who explains to him the mystery of confession and the pope's power of absolution, Saladin says indignantly: "In my life I will not believe that. And by the faith I owe to all the gods that can be worshipped, if I had that pope in my power in Syria, I would have him quartered by four horses." He goes to Lombardy, then to Burgundy, before arriving in Paris, where he is struck by how uncharitably the poor are treated.[23] All that dissuades him from converting to Christianity. In about 1215, Gilles de Corbeil said in one of his poems that Saladin had come to Jerusalem under Frankish domination to learn about the Christians' mores, but that the prelate's way of life kept him from converting.[24] All these accounts attest to an overt desire to moralize to the Christians: it was probably more convenient, and more prudent, to place criticisms directed at one's coreligionists in the mouth of an infidel. In that context, Saladin truly looks like a "Persan d'avant les *Lettres*."[25]

The idealization of Saladin in the West was often supported by historical events: a gift, a gesture of courtesy, the release of Frankish prisoners, discussions between Saladin and Richard the Lionheart. These events quite obviously made an impression and elicited the admiration of Westerners, for, though there was originally a "dark legend," it quickly gave way to the golden legend. Moreover, the development of epic literature, chivalrous romances, and courtly literature in the vernacular provided the ideal conditions for the rise of that mythical view. The stories told about Saladin could only inspire authors who, beyond their desire to explain the Crusades to a popular audience, also sought to entertain them and hence to elaborate their favorite themes around the exploits of knights and courtly love. Historical anachronisms and a lack of verisimilitude were of little consequence. To consolidate the idea of Christendom's superiority over Islam, the important thing was to link the Franks' failures and the Muslims' successes to Saladin's adherence to the feudal system on which Western society was founded, and to acknowledge his aristocratic ancestry, and ultimately, his attraction and even conversion to Christianity.

Embroidering on themes in vogue in the West, such as the Crusades, military exploits, chivalry, and courtly love, most writers, from the Middle Ages to the dawn of the twentieth century, used Saladin as a pretext to express their opinions about the events of their times, in some cases to support one ruler over another in the conflict between France and England, in others to denounce the abuses of the clergy and papacy, to preach tolerance and humanism, or to criticize religions and their excesses.

28

The Myth of the Arab Hero

In the East as well, and even in his own time, Saladin was endowed with all the qualities of a virtuous and conquering ruler, an image widely elaborated and diffused by his panegyrists and by most of the chroniclers from later eras. In the thirteenth century, for example, a Syrian historian wrote: "It was reported to me that someone saw the Prophet (may God bless and hail him) in a dream, surrounded by his Companions, coming to visit the tomb of Salāh al-Dīn (may God have mercy on him) and that, having arrived at the window, they prostrated themselves."[1]

Arab posterity certainly considered Saladin the "conqueror of Jerusalem," and yet his exploits did not give rise to any truly popular medieval literature. In this he differed from the Mamluk sultan Baybars (r. 1260–1277), famous for his battles against the Franks and, by the fifteenth century, the hero of a long popular romance. Are we to seek the reason for this in the criticisms aimed at Saladin, in Baghdad or elsewhere? Or did the image of the nearly perfect sovereign, disseminated early on by his panegyrists, check the imagination of Arab storytellers? No doubt the answer to these questions must be sought in the political context of the Crusades and of the Ayyubid and Mamluk dynasties. To be sure, Saladin had retaken Jerusalem from the Franks, but his successors, most of them descendants of his brother al-ʿĀdil, did not succeed in keeping it for long. In 1229, Sultan al-Kāmil retroceded it to the Franks, who held on to it until 1244. There was no longer much sense in developing a popular romance around that theme under the Ayyubid dynasty, which, in fact, was not long in disappearing. Whereas the Ayyubids reigned for only seventy-six years in Egypt and eighty-six years in Syria, the Mamluks would impose their domination over the Middle East for two and a half centuries. The legend of Baybars therefore had all the time required to develop and to exalt the exploits of the one who was considered, and rightly so, the first great Mamluk sultan and the principal architect of the struggles against the Mongols and the Franks. It was indispensable to remind the populations of these victories, since the Mamluk dynasty's legitimacy was founded on them. It goes without saying, moreover, that a Saladin legend had little chance of developing under the reign of those who had dethroned the last representatives of his dynasty and who, in place of Kurdish power, had installed a Turkish power, which the Ottomans would prolong until the early twentieth century.

Unlike what happened in the West, the Saladin legend in the East did not benefit from any political or literary conditions favorable to its rise, until, that is, the nineteenth century. In the seventeenth century, a Turkish pasha had the interior of Saladin's mausoleum adorned with ceramic tiles and an inscription, to thank him for having delivered Jerusalem from the "stain of the infidels"; but it was not until the late nineteenth century and the birth of a Turkish and then an Arab nationalism that Saladin returned to the forefront of the scene. The reign of the Ottoman sultan Abdülhamid II (1876–1909) marked an important moment in that respect. Like Saladin, that sultan, motivated by a strong pan-Islamic desire, styled himself a reunifier of the Muslim world. It was he who, in 1878, had a first marble coffin built in Saladin's mausoleum, next to the carved wood coffin from the Ayyubid era. Twenty years later, the German emperor William II decided to restore the marble coffin. His chamberlain, Ernst Freiherr von Mirbach, provides us with a precise description not only of William's stay in Damascus but also of Saladin's mausoleum.[2] The imperial couple, received with great pomp by the municipality of Damascus on November 7, 1898, visited the city's souk the next day as well as the Umayyad Mosque, which had been destroyed shortly beforehand by a great fire but was already under reconstruction. They then went to Saladin's tomb, adjoining the Great Mosque to the north. Inside the small building, covered with a cupola, were two sarcophagi in carved and painted wood. The first was attributed to Saladin and the second to "one of his grand viziers." One of these sarcophagi, according to Mirbach, was enclosed within a second, of "rather ugly" marble. This was the one Abdülhamid had built.

At present in Saladin's mausoleum, two sarcophagi are displayed, one in carved wood and the other in decorated white marble. There is no doubt that the marble sarcophagus is the one that the Ottoman sultan ordered and that Emperor William II restored. The attribution of the carved wood sarcophagus is more difficult, since no inscription clearly attributes it to Saladin. The only inscriptions, running along the upper horizontal band, are Koranic (sura 2:255–256). Jean Sauvaget long ago pointed out that the popular tradition attributed that wood cenotaph to a "secretary" of Saladin's; but, arguing that al-Fāḍil had died in Cairo, he concluded, after a brilliant analysis of the style and richness of its carvings, that this cenotaph could only be the original one, conserved after the emperor's restoration and placed next to the new tomb. Sauvaget also noted that only two of the remaining faces of the wood cenotaph are ancient, and were themselves shortened somewhat during the last restoration, as attested by the Koranic inscription, which displays a lacuna at each of its corners. Sauvaget's attribution has been accepted by all historians to this day.[3] A few questions persist, however. Is it not surprising, in the first place, that Saladin's coffin bears neither his name nor the date of his death? The historian Ibn Khallikān himself indicates that, when it was moved to Damascus in 1281–1282, he was able to read on Saladin's coffin the date of his death (and also, no doubt, his name and titulature, since otherwise the date would have been meaningless) as well as this sentence, inspired, he was told, by Qāḍī al-Fāḍil: "Almighty God! let his soul be acceptable to thee and open to him the gates of Paradise; that being the last conquest (lit. opening) for which he hoped."[4] Of course, it may be supposed that the inscription appeared on the two lost sides of the cenotaph, but it is more likely, given its length, that it occupied the entire surface of the coffin. In addition, Sauvaget did not call attention to Mirbach's remark that there were two wood coffins in the late nineteenth century, one of which was inside the marble sarcophagus. It is clear that only a verification of the contents of the sarcophagus may allow us to shed a little light on that question. Several hypotheses remain open to this day.

On the evening of November 8, 1898, a gala dinner was held for the imperial couple, and the emperor, having listened to a young ulema shower the sultan and the emperor with praise, gave a speech in which he said he was deeply moved by the sultan's hospitality and very happy to "find himself in the place where lived one of the most chivalrous sovereigns of all time, the great sultan Saladin, a fearless knight beyond reproach, who often had to teach his enemies true chivalry."[5] He thanked the sultan and added that he hoped one day to see the 300 million Muslims living throughout the world recognize Abdülhamid as their caliph. The Turks, according to Mirbach, were very moved by the emperor's speech, since it was the first time they had heard from the mouth of such a high-placed figure words of such warmth. The next day, the emperor had flowers placed on Saladin's tomb, and it was following that visit that he decided to have it restored. Above the new coffin a silver lamp was suspended, on which were depicted side by side his monogram and that of the Ottoman sultan. A laurel wreath in gilded wood, adorned with the crown and the imperial insignia W II IR (William II Imperator Rex), the Prussian eagle, and the German iron cross was placed on the tomb. In the center, under the imperial insignia, and on a ribbon encircling the wreath, ran inscriptions evoking William II's visit to Damascus in 1898 and bearing Saladin's name.[6] In the lower part of the wreath, in larger characters, was the inscription "God loves those who do good" (Koran 2:195, 5:13). That trip by William II to the East was a diplomatic event, since it ended an isolationist period for the Ottoman Empire: each of his gestures therefore assumed great symbolic importance. On one hand, the sultan wished to stand as the leader of the Muslim world as a whole; hence William II's allusion to the caliphate and its 300 million Muslim subjects. On the other, Abdülhamid II, in opposition to the imperialism of France and England—which were accused of conducting a new "Crusade" against "the sick man of the Bosphorus"—was assured, in seeking a rapprochement with the emperor, of an important international alliance. In 1903, while the renovated tomb of Saladin was being inaugurated, the huge railroad project that Abdülhamid had conferred on the Germans, and which was supposed to connect the Black Sea to Baghdad (Baghdad-Bahn), was also getting under way. For the German emperor, that journey to Syria-Palestine was therefore the dream opportunity to claim a place in the coalition of European powers. In casting into relief the sultan's dual temporal and spiritual function, he also sought to emphasize his own position as *Summus Episcopus,* head of the Protestant church of Prussia. The religious dimension of his trip was apparent in the fact that his ultimate destination was a visit to Jerusalem and the brand-new German Lutheran

Church of the Redeemer, inaugurated a few days earlier, on October 31, 1898. That policy could only displease France and England, which believed that, with that journey, Germany was meddling in their affairs in the Middle East. When World War I broke out and Germany and the Ottoman Empire were defeated, Lawrence of Arabia therefore hastened to bring back to England, as a trophy, the laurel wreath placed on Saladin's tomb, a symbol of the Germano-Turkish alliance and the struggle of the Arab-Turkish world against any new form of "Crusade."[7]

I shall come back to the reasons behind Saladin's return to the Middle Eastern scene, but let me first note that, in reaction to French and English colonization, and especially to the creation of the state of Israel, three Arab countries—Iraq, Syria, and Egypt—embraced the legacy of that sultan, who became the symbol of resistance to the Western occupation. It is significant that, even today, forceful references to Saladin arise every time the Arab world feels humiliated or attacked by the Western countries or by the state of Israel. But why choose Saladin and not Baybars, for example, as in the medieval legend? Probably because Jerusalem rapidly became the center of all strategic interests, and Saladin's glory rested primarily on the liberation of the holy city. Neither Baybars nor Saladin was Arab. But Baybars the Turk, by virtue of his ethnicity, may have appeared too closely linked to the Ottoman dynasty, against which Arab nationalism stood opposed. The Kurdish figure of Saladin was more neutral, because no great Kurdish dynasty since the Ayyubids had taken root in the region. In addition, it was easier to "Arabize" Saladin, known for his attachment to the Arabic language and Arab culture, to religious disciplines and the defense of Islam in general, than to Arabize Baybars, the emancipated slave, warrior, and military hero. Arab historians, but also heads of state, novelists, and filmmakers, have often seized on Saladin as a personality, the model of an ideal sovereign who was able to restore Islam's pride and dignity in the face of Western Christendom.

The Saladin myth gradually acquired greater scope in the Arab countries of the twentieth century. I use the term "myth" rather than "legend" here because, unlike the Western legend, which was elaborated on the basis of a corpus of precise texts, accounts that amplified, transformed, or distorted real events in order to educate or entertain a popular public, the Saladin myth in Arab countries is closer to a political construction that freely and subjectively interprets a historical reality to adapt it to a given situation. Political myths also have "an explicative function, providing a certain number of keys for the comprehension of the present, constituting a grid through which the disconcerting chaos of facts and events seems to acquire an order. . . . Nostalgia for past golden ages generally leads to an expectation of and prophesies about their resurrection. . . . The step from denouncing evil conspiracies to calling for the Savior, the redemptive leader, is, moreover, quickly taken."[8] From this perspective, any popular orator or political leader, any state, artist, or writer, can appropriate the myth, decide to give it one form of expression or another, and use it to his or her own ends. Although the forms and vehicles of the Saladin myth have varied, the image of the individual behind it remains fixed, immutable. Tampering with it would mean destroying the myth. That image is of a charismatic, generous, and chivalrous leader, a courageous and victorious warrior, but one who respects his adversaries, the vanquisher of Western expansionism. Anyone who would call it into question or even discuss it would risk looking like an iconoclast.

The Saladin myth has given rise to many forms of expression. In the Palestinian territories, the thoroughfare crossing the Gaza Strip from north to south is called the "Saladin Highway." In Damascus, under the presidency of Hafez al-Assad, a large statue of Saladin was installed in front of the imposing citadel—a symbol of military might—reconstituted in great part during the Ayyubid era. Saladin is shown riding horseback, sword in hand, surrounded by foot soldiers, who are armed with spears and swords. According to the historian Carole Hillenbrand, who heard it from the sculptor himself, one of the figures posted on Saladin's right is a Sufi, whom the artist placed there to underscore the union of the saber and popular faith under Saladin's banner.[9] In back of the horse, dwarfed by the full height of the statue, Reginald of Châtillon and Guy of Lusignan are seated on a rock. Guy of Lusignan holds a pouch in his hand containing the money for his ransom, while Reginald is bowing his head and staring at the ground.

In Baghdad, on the right bank of the Tigris, Saddam Hussein also had a statue of the sultan installed on a raised strip of ground outside his residential complex.[10] Both presidents, of Syria and of Iraq, often used Saladin in their political propaganda. The official biographies of Saddam Hussein went so far as to change his birth date, moving it from 1939 to 1937, no doubt to make it coincide with the eight hundredth anniversary of Saladin's birth (1137). The sultan's effigy adorned stamps and banknotes; his name was introduced into the Iraqi national anthem, along with the names of the Assyrians, the Babylonians, and Hārūn al-Rashīd.[11] In the office of President Hafez al-Assad in Damascus, there was a painting depicting the Battle of Hattīn. An artist, asked to create a poster based on that painting, added above the battle scene a large portrait of al-Assad, with the words "from Hattīn to Tishrīn," an allusion to Saladin's victory on one hand, the 1973 War of October (Tishrīn) against Israel on the other. That poster was widely distributed during the referendum held in 1991, despite the fact that the slogan the artist invented underscores the contrast more than the resemblance between those two battles, since Hattīn was a great victory for Saladin and the War of October a crushing defeat for the Syrians.[12] Lisa Wedeen has noted, among the jokes circulating during President Hafez al-Assad's time, an anecdote that indicates how the popular imagination twists government propaganda. "A history teacher gives a lecture and asks his students: 'Who killed Salah al-Din?' The students become frightened and begin crying. 'We didn't do it, teacher, we swear.' The teacher is surprised and sends for the principal. The principal comes and asks, 'What is the matter?' The teacher says, 'I asked them who killed Salah al-Din and no one answered.' The students begin to cry again. The principal asks: 'Do you suspect one of them?' "[13]

In 1987, on the eight hundredth anniversary of the victory of Hattīn, three colloquia took place simultaneously—in Baghdad, Cairo, and Damascus—to celebrate the event, and many publications on Saladin appeared. The Syrian press pointed out the similarities between the past and the present, the Crusaders and the Zionists; they presented Saladin as the embodiment of the Arab nation and the Crusades as the prefiguration of the imperialist spirit.[14] In Cairo, a colloquium held by the Egyptian Afro-Asian People's Solidarity Organization took place in the presence of the grand imam of al-Azhar, the mufti of Egypt, the Coptic patriarch of Alexandria, the vice prime minister, the minister of foreign affairs, three British scholars, and many scholars from Egypt, Yemen, Libya, Lebanon, Iraq, and Sudan. The sheikh of al-Azhar insisted that the Crusades, though conducted in the name of the cross and the Messiah, were not religious wars but rather "barbaric wars of colonization." The Coptic patriarch expressed similar views, declaring that the Crusades were not directed against Muslims alone but also against the Christians of Hungary and the Byzantine Empire. The Crusaders, according to him, hid behind religious motives to conquer territories. "It is neither a question of pilgrims, nor a question of crosses, nor a question of Jerusalem. It is a question of occupation [ihtilāl]," he wrote. He also voiced vibrant praise for Saladin, a good and generous man who spared women and children and unified the Arabs.[15] The objective of all these speeches is very clearly to affirm, in an Egyptian context of proliferating assaults on the Copts in recent years, that the battle of the hero Saladin was not a battle against the Christians but that of a people (the Arabs) against a foreign invader. All the speakers therefore took care to distinguish the Westerners from the Eastern Christians, who also fought, and are still often fighting, alongside the Muslims for Arab nationalism and against the state of Israel.

It is therefore the contemporary context that is once again redrawing the lines of Saladin's image; and Saladin, whose aura is no longer contested by anyone in the Sunni world, in some sense legitimates the cause they are seeking to defend. In Baghdad, a publisher put out a children's book under the title *The Hero Saladin,* with, on its cover, a portrait of Saddam Hussein. Cavalrymen armed with swords are represented in the background. The first part of the book is a brief presentation of the life of Saladin, while the second and longer part is devoted to the new leader "Saladin II Saddam Hussein." That identification of Saddam Hussein with Saladin continued after 1987, and Iraqi propaganda gave it a place of honor during the first Gulf War in 1991. Just as Saladin resisted the Third Crusade in 1191, the propaganda claimed, Saddam Hussein would stamp out the "new Crusaders" from the West.[16] It is therefore understandable why, in that context, George W. Bush's speech calling for a new Crusade against terrorism in the wake of September 11, 2001, could only throw oil on the fire and revive fanaticism.

The figure of Saladin has been used in the Muslim world well beyond the Middle East. It is also found in the Maghreb, for example, where the Algerian theologian Abū Jara Sultāni depicts Saladin as the symbol of Muslim resistance as a whole, asserting, on the twentieth anniversary of Algerian independence, that the Algerian war represented "a second and definitive victory of Islam over the Crusade. . . . That Islamic might, which had annihilated the Crusaders by liberating Jerusalem from their infidel hands, could not be overcome by the Europeans. Their hopes were dashed even more when, in 1962, they discovered that Salāh al-Dīn and everything he symbolized had not died and that he was not an Ayyubid but a Shafite Muslim."[17] Even in Pakistan, the emblematic figure of Muhammad 'Alī Jinnah (1876–1948), the country's founder, was compared to Saladin. According to one of his biographers, the Pakistani hero, like Saladin, owed his fame to his victories; like him, Jinnah was an outsider; like him, the

Pakistani fought renowned foes; and like Saladin, he sought to reproduce the model of Muslim leadership instituted by the Prophet. The author writes that, in the popular imagination, Jinnah has been compared to Saladin more than to Gandhi, Nelson Mandela, or Charles de Gaulle, because he was first and foremost the expression of a Muslim identity.[18] In that chorus of praise, only Shiite religious communities stand out as an exception. For them, Saladin is in the first place the person who put an end to the Shiite dynasty of the Fatimids, and on certain Internet sites there are astonishingly polemical articles aimed at demonstrating that he was nothing but an ambitious and power-hungry man.[19]

Literary fiction, cinema, and more recently television have also participated in spreading the Saladin myth. The Christian writer Jurji Zaydan (Beirut, 1861–Cairo, 1914), the founder of the famous Egyptian review *Al-Hilāl* (*The Crescent*, 1892), was one of the chief inspirations for the Arab "renaissance" movement (*nahda*) of the late nineteenth century. The author of a history of Muslim civilization in five volumes (1902–1906) and of a major history of Arabic literature in four volumes (1911–1914), he was also the person who gave the historical novel its pedigree in the Arab world. His twenty-some novels enjoyed great success and still have a large readership today.[20] In the one he called *Saladin and the Assassins' Ruses* (1913),[21] his focus was neither Saladin's jihad nor his reunification of the Muslim states. The action takes place at the very beginning of Saladin's reign, when he was still in Egypt, and the plot turns on two fictional characters united by love: a sister of the Fatimid caliph named Sayyidat al-Mulk—perhaps inspired by Sitt al-Mulk, sister to the Fatimid caliph al-Hākim (r. 996–1021)—and 'Imād al-Dīn, a young soldier completely devoted to Saladin. 'Imād al-Dīn has sworn to himself to eliminate the leader of the Assassins, to prevent him from killing Saladin. Saladin appears in the background as a young man not at all predestined for power, ambitious but inexperienced. Thanks to his father's advice, he gradually transforms himself into a noble and chivalrous sovereign, gives up soliciting the hand of Sayyidat al-Mulk, and takes the young lovers under his protection.

Saladin, by contrast, is the central figure in the theatrical play written during the same period, in 1914, by the Lebanese writer Farah Antūn (1874–1922). A Christian intellectual—though secular in his thought—Antūn lived in Egypt from 1897 on. In that four-act play, titled *Sultan Saladin and the Kingdom of Jerusalem*, the action takes place between 1187 and 1189, which is to say, at the apogee of Saladin's power. It concerns neither the difficulties at the beginning of Saladin's reign nor the defeats of his last years. The author focuses exclusively on the image of the triumphant sovereign, unifier and liberator of the Arab-Muslim world. His virtues (wisdom, level-headedness, determination, loyalty) are described in absolute opposition to the vices of his Frankish adversaries (dissimulation, double-dealing, and false religious beliefs). That panegyric, as well as the speech attributed to Saladin, which is very anticolonial in tone, must be placed within the context of an Egypt occupied by the English. So long as that land holds inhabitants, they will rise up to defend it, whatever the price to be paid, and defending one's country is an absolute duty: such is the message of the play. It ends with this exchange between a Crusader messenger and Saladin:

> *The Messenger:* Keep it [his garment, which he has thrown to the ground], Sultan, along with your relics. The descendants of our grandchildren will wear a different costume to come and retake it.
>
> *Saladin:* Do you hear that warning, all of you? Beware of the slightest distraction, attend to the slightest sign of weakness. Unity, unity among all the residents of our country!

The political resonance of that text was so great that when the Ottoman Empire joined World War I alongside Germany in November 1914, the English, having established a protectorate over Egypt and censored the press and literature, banned Farah Antūn's play. The author's protests finally resulted in the play's being produced again, but not without being censored in advance.[22]

The film *Saladin* (1963) by Youssef Chahine, a famous Egyptian Christian filmmaker, also uses a certain number of these themes—not to say clichés—for political ends. The Arabness of Saladin is asserted many times: he is called "the sultan of the Arabs"; he appears as the reunifier of the Muslim world and the liberator of "Arab Jerusalem." That discourse exhorts the Arabs to reunify (the theme recurs as a leitmotif), to reject the occupation, and to recover their pride. It shows medieval barbarism as characteristic of certain Westerners (Reginald of Châtillon but not Guy of Lusignan) and wisdom on the Muslim side, a response, in some sense, to the discourse of those who currently contrast Western civilization to Islamic obscurantism. In that film, Saladin embodies (without nuance) honor, courage, perseverance, loyalty to his word, moderation, law, justice, wisdom, and piety, whereas Reginald stereotypically represents exactly the opposite: injustice and cruelty, arrogance and pridefulness, double-dealing and violence. In pointing to the presence of Christians in Saladin's army, the film also wants to convey that there was nothing religious about the conflict, even at the risk of projecting onto the Middle Ages a twentieth-century situation, that of Christian intellectuals who support a secular Arab nationalism. The message is hammered in: the Crusades were not a religious war but an economic war to fill Europe's coffers and to appropriate the "treasures of the East." Historical reality is adjusted to avoid tarnishing Saladin's image as the good, pious, and chivalrous sovereign. Reginald is portrayed as the commander of the Frankish army in Ḥaṭṭīn and the person chiefly responsible for its defeat. Even more surprising, Saladin kills him in a duel and not by executing him while Reginald is being held prisoner. Similarly, to relativize Saladin's defeat at Acre in 1191 and, as a result, his military responsibility, the Franks' victory is presented as the result of treason in the Muslim camp, that of a fictional governor called the "king of Acre and Jaffa."

With the development of new communication technologies, a rigid and almost "sacralized" image of Saladin has now spread throughout the world. One of the most recent examples is that of the Multimedia Development Corporation (MdeC) in Malaysia, which undertook to create a 3-D cartoon, with special effects, called *Saladin*. Divided into thirteen episodes, that animated film is intended for young adolescents. The Saladin it depicts is nothing but a pretext for the creation of a courageous hero, "chosen by Fate" to lead the battle against injustice and tyranny. Although this film is still inspired by Saladin's life and career, it has entered the realm of fiction and has little to do with historical reality.[23]

Conclusion

In the first pages of his book, Ibn Shaddād says that he witnessed such noble deeds and gestures on Saladin's part that no description could
do justice to them, no pen could capture them. He modestly proposes to deliver
his reader only "part of a whole," which will allow posterity to judge the rest.
Although the obstacles at present are of a different nature, we need to recognize
that every biographical reconstruction of Saladin will always have its areas of
shadow. The actions by which he distinguished himself are relatively well known,
the individual less so. Such is the fate, no doubt, of most medieval rulers. As
Jacques Le Goff says, "From the first centuries of the Middle Ages until the
twelfth century, the personalities of the protagonists of history elude us, either in
the silences that conceal their individuality, or through the absorption of that individuality into the model imposed on it."[1] But in Saladin's case, the difficulty of
grasping his true personality is amplified by the success of his legend. The question of his sincerity will forever remain controversial, since the speeches, gestures, and emotions that the medieval texts attribute to him were usually intended to show that his conduct was consistent with the notion of the ideal
sovereign prevailing at the time.

Nevertheless, over the course of these pages, a Saladin has taken shape who is not only an image: a sultan endowed with strong political instincts; an indefatigable warrior; and a man truly interested in religious life, anxious to restore Sunnism and to apply Muslim law strictly. We have seen him crowned in glory after the taking of Jerusalem, but also faced with grave setbacks, particularly toward the end of his reign. On the list of his successes, we must include his domination of a vast territory extending from the Nile to the Euphrates and from Yemen to northern Mesopotamia, as well as the reconquest of a large portion of the Latin states, Jerusalem in particular. Saladin allowed the Kurds to accede to power, but without destroying the might of the Turks, whose military role would continue to grow, especially in Egypt. He succeeded, in spite of everything, in preserving the unity of his army, thanks to his victories over the Franks and over his Muslim neighbors, as well as his firm but conciliatory attitude toward his emirs. Although the fall of the Shiite caliphate in Cairo was much more Nūr al-Dīn's accomplishment than his own, Saladin actively contributed toward strengthening Sunnism throughout his territory and thereby earned the solid support of men of religion. In the economic realm, despite the conflicts, commerce continued to develop in the Mediterranean and the Indian Ocean. Finally, Saladin's greatest success was the very positive image he managed to leave of himself, in both the East and the West.

On the negative side, there was, first, Saladin's incapacity to build a state, despite the reforms he endeavored to introduce into Egypt. He constituted an empire but did not impose any centralized state structure; used the resources of his territories to finance his wars without concerning himself about the future of those territories; and sought justice while privileging a patronage system rather than an effective administration. The emirs continued to govern as they wished in the territories entrusted to them, with the sole condition that they fulfill their military obligations. All that explains the financial difficulties at the end of Saladin's reign, the heterogeneity and demobilization of his troops; it explains as well why his empire, too closely associated with his person, did not survive his death. In conflict with the Franks, Saladin succeeded in saving his chief conquest—Jerusalem—but did not manage to eliminate the Latin states. No doubt he committed a few strategic errors (a reproach already made of him by some of his contemporaries). It would be inaccurate, however, to attribute to him sole responsibility for that failure. In addition to the unwillingness of the caliph of Baghdad and the eastern princes to come to his aid, the superiority of the Crusaders' fleet was such that he could not on his own have prevented it from controlling the seas and, as a consequence, from dominating the coast.

Undoubtedly, that is not the matter of greatest interest. The main thread of this book has been the analysis of discourse, which has allowed us to highlight the arguments that Saladin and his propaganda used to demonstrate the legitimacy of his power and to disseminate his image as the model sovereign: defender of the true way; faithful servant of the caliph of Baghdad; paragon of justice assisted by God on the battlefield, one who was magnanimous and generous toward his subjects and foes alike. All these arguments contributed toward fashioning an image of the man, an image that underwent transformations over the centuries, depending on the era, the place, and the political or ideological context. That discourse sometimes took liberties with the facts, overstated or minimized them, in the aim of conveying a message. The exaggeration of numerical figures, the choice of words and metaphors, and the disparagement of foes fired the imagination, emphasized the hero's good qualities, and transformed his weaknesses into strengths. The art of oratory—'Imād al-Dīn's in particular—played a central role.

One question remains. Did the representation of Saladin as the model of an ideal sovereign, as it was disseminated by his close circle in the twelfth and thirteenth centuries, constitute a rupture in terms of the previous and later periods, or was it continuous with them? Saladin's desire to situate himself in Nūr al-Dīn's wake and to lay claim to his political legacy has made its appearance many times: the same aspiration for Muslim unification, the same battle against Shiism, the same respect for religious law and the ulemas, the same energy to fight against the Franks. That continuity was celebrated by medieval historians, Abū Shāma in particular: "These two sovereigns appeared to me to occupy the same role among the moderns as the two 'Umars did among the ancients. In fact, the second prince in each case followed in his predecessor's footsteps on the path of justice, holy war, zeal—and what zeal!—for the greater glory of religion. Both were kings of our country and sultans of our region. God having granted us these two sovereigns as a special favor, it is our duty to apply ourselves to recalling their virtues."[2]

The allusion to the "two 'Umars," that is, 'Umar ibn al-Khattāb (r. 634–644), the second caliph after the Prophet, and 'Umar II (r. 717–720), the eighth Umayyad caliph, considered by Muslim tradition to be models of piety and justice, attests as well to a great continuity in the model of the good sovereign, from the early days of Islam to the late twelfth century.

Although Sunni historiography considered Saladin to be in continuity with Nūr al-Dīn, it saw him as constituting a complete break from the other Zangid princes and the last Fatimid caliphs, who in its view were the embodiment of heresy and collusion with the Franks. Therein may lie the chief originality of Saladin's propaganda. On one hand, he was presented as the one able to embody and realize the ideals of his predecessor; but on the other, his actions were legitimated in opposition to his Muslim foes. He was depicted in some sense as the negative image of the Fatimids and Zangids: they represented heterodoxy, disunity, and an alliance with the enemies of the Abbasid caliphate; he aspired only to orthodoxy, unification, jihad against the "infidels," and investiture by the caliph of Baghdad.

Saladin's Ayyubid successors in turn adapted the themes and persuasive power of their propaganda against the Franks to suit the political realities of their time. The division of Saladin's states, the family dissensions, and above all the advent of new external threats—the Mongols especially—played an essential role in the expansion of the army's might, particularly that of the Turkish Mamluks, who ultimately overthrew the Ayyubid dynasty and seized power in Cairo in 1250.

The representation of the ideal sovereign changed as a result. Without totally abandoning the previous themes, Mamluk propaganda introduced new ones. That is particularly true for the first great sultan of that dynasty, Baybars, who reigned from 1260 to 1277. He acceded to the throne after killing his predecessor and therefore felt the need to legitimate the power he had acquired by force. The discourse of his entourage repeated well-known themes, such as the pursuit of jihad and the defense of Islam (against the Franks and the Mongols), respect for justice and religious law, the practice of charity and generosity, the image of the sultan as benefactor of the jurists and ascetics, and the claim to exert authority over the holy cities of Islam. The same aspiration for a dynastic legitimacy is also to be found there. Saladin had been presented in his propaganda as Nūr al-Dīn's legitimate successor. Baybars was similarly described as the worthy heir to the last great Ayyubid sultan, al-Sālih Ayyūb (r. 1240–1249).[3]

But the context was different, and Baybars's personality no longer had anything to do with Saladin's. Saladin was associated with biblical figures such as

Solomon and Joseph, who symbolized justice, prudence, clemency, and uprightness. Baybars was sometimes compared to Solomon,[4] but he was primarily linked
to Alexander the Great, symbol of imperial might, and to Moses (Mūsā), a biblical
prophet considered by Islamic tradition to be a lawmaker and guide for the religious community. Upon his return from pilgrimage in 1269, Baybars paid tribute to that prophet by having a mausoleum built above Moses's presumed tomb
on the road between Jerusalem and Jericho.[5] On the foundation inscription,
Baybars was called "Iskander al-zamān" (the Alexander of his time), a title that
also appears on two other Syrian inscriptions of the period. The pairing of Alexander and Moses owed nothing to chance, since the two are linked in the Koran.
In the Cave sura (18:60–82), the narrative about Alexander is preceded by a story
no doubt inspired by a Jewish legend and by the Romance of Alexander. It is the
story of Moses and his mysterious traveling companion (named "al-Khadir" by
most Koranic commentators), a servant of God who agrees to guide Moses on his
trip, provided that Moses not ask for any explanations of the guide's behavior.
Along the way, however, al-Khadir engages in acts that are apparently criminal, and Moses, having reached the end of his patience, ultimately pleads with
him to explain himself. Al-Khadir takes his leave after enlightening Moses about
the rightness of his actions, which is simply one way to show the prophet that,
when making any judgment, he must move beyond deceptive or contingent
appearances.

As it happens, "al-Khadir" was the name of a very influential adviser to
Baybars, a sheikh known for his debauched mores and for his exactions. Baybars's interest in Moses can therefore be explained in several ways. It is not
impossible that al-Khadir, at the height of his popularity with the sultan at the
time, urged him in that direction, so that al-Khadir himself could appear to be
the new servant of God. Baybars, whose administrative and legal reforms
within his states were very significant, also wanted no doubt to link his name
to that of the great lawmaker Moses. And finally, it may not be absurd to think
that the sultan, taken from his family and enslaved while still very young, felt
some affinity with the nursling Moses, removed from his mother and rescued
from the water.

The identification between Baybars and Alexander came about even
more naturally. In the Cave sura (18:83–97), Dhū'l-Qarnayn (Two-horned man),
identified by the exegetes as Alexander the Great, builds a rampart to keep
from being overrun by a savage people, known as Ya'jūj and Ma'jūj (Gog and

Magog). In the thirteenth century, they were commonly assimilated to the Mongols, who sowed terror and destroyed everything in their path. Everyone still remembered Baybars's prowess during the victory against the Mongols at 'Ayn Jālūt in 1260. Indisputably, he appeared to be the only leader capable of repelling those terrible invaders. It was therefore natural that, for the first time in the Mamluk dynasty, he bore the title "the Alexander of his time."

The image, known in Saladin's time, of the educated sovereign versed in religious science, eager to listen to the learned, and oriented toward the devout, toward mystics and ascetics, thus yielded to that of a more belligerent sovereign, in love with justice but drawn more to military exploits than to literary or religious discussions. New representations of the providential sovereign arose at the time to justify decisions that might have appeared brutal or unjust to the population. One of the most interesting representations was spread by Ibn al-Nafīs, a well-known scholar from the second half of the thirteenth century. In a short treatise, he gives his prophetic vision of history and describes the events that will precede the end of time.[6] He includes the theme of the "last ruler" who must save the religious community, because God has sent a destructive people (the Mongols) to punish them for their sins. The author presents Baybars without naming him—al-Nafīs may have been his personal physician—as the ruler predestined by God to save the Muslims. But to achieve his objectives, the sovereign also had to show he was cruel and merciless: he had to confiscate his subjects' properties to finance the war against the infidels and, when crimes were committed, had to order exemplary punishments such as amputations and crucifixions.[7]

That image of the sovereign who saves his people by inspiring fear and displaying cruelty obviously stands in contrast to the usual panegyric literature, but it takes up themes appearing in certain apocalyptic Christian texts.[8] The portrayal of Baybars as merely the manifestation of a divine plan intended to save the Muslims clearly had the objective of legitimating the sultan's power, justifying his decisions—even the most brutal ones—and exhorting the population to accept his authority and to show patience.[9]

In the representation of Saladin as in that of Baybars, the religious factor—that is, the defense of Islam—remains central, but it is far from the only one.

Virtues such as justice, generosity, honor, and bravery are not specific to any religion and have appeared since antiquity among the qualities required of a sovereign. It was also expected that a good prince would repel invaders, maintain the cohesion of his states, administer his territories, assure order and security, reward those who support him, and know how to surround himself with wise counsel.

Although it is obvious that a number of these themes recur repeatedly, alerting the historian to be wary of clichés, it is no less clear that the discourse on the ideal or providential sovereign, far from remaining rigid, evolved as a function of the historical circumstances and of the sultans themselves. That no doubt explains the interest such a discourse elicits in anyone who attempts, on the basis of conventional or forceful panegyrics, to explain an author's aims and intentions. That is probably also the reason that the personality of a sovereign always rises to the surface in the end. Is it truly by chance that, to evoke Saladin, the figure of a wise man such as Solomon was preferred to that of a conqueror such as Alexander?

Notes

Introduction

1. Another variant is "Saladin, we're here!" The line is always quoted by historians without any reference to a source (see E. Sivan, *Mythes politiques arabes* [Paris, 1995], 31). The oldest mention I have found is in G. Puaux, *Deux années au Levant. Souvenirs de Syrie et du Liban, 1939–1940* (Paris, 1952), 29, with no reference given. [The line is often rendered in English as "Awake Saladin, we have returned." See Ahmad Faruqui, "Another Gulf War, Another al-Qaeda," *Asia Times Online,* March 20, 2003, http://www.atimes.com/atimes/Middle_East/EC20Ak06.html—trans.]

2. See C. Mayeur-Jaouen, ed., *Saints et héros du Moyen-Orient contemporain* (Paris, 2002).

3. See the Saladin historiography in the appendix to this volume.

4. See J. Le Goff, *Saint Louis* (Paris, 1996), 314.

5. Studies of the sources on Saladin's reign are numerous and very thorough. See in particular the writings of H. A. R. Gibb, P. M. Holt, D. S. Richards, Y. Lev, and L. Richter-Bernburg listed in the bibliography.

6. These excerpts have been preserved in the works of the Aleppine historian Ibn al-'Adīm (d. 1262) and of the Egyptian al-Maqrīzī (d. 1442), among others. The journal is known under several titles, the most commonly used being *al-Mutajaddidāt.* See H. Möhring, *Saladin und der Dritte Kreuzzug,* 220–221; and Y. Lev, *Saladin in Egypt,* 25. [In instances where a shortened citation is provided in the notes, the full reference appears in the bibliography.]

7. They are known either directly, in some twenty manuscripts preserved throughout the world, or through later authors (Abū Shāma and al-Qalqashandī in particular) who kept al-Fāḍil's writings as models of chancery documents. See *Encyclopaedia of Islam,* 2nd ed., "al-Ḳāḍī al Fāḍil" (C. Brocklelmann, C. Cahen); A. Helbig, *Al-Qāḍī al-Fāḍil, der Wezir Saladin's,* inaugural dissertation (Leipzig, 1908), 19–31; I.

al-Hafsī, "Correspondance officielle et privée d'al-Qāḍī al-Fāḍil," doctoral diss., Université de Paris IV–Sorbonne, 4 vols. (Paris, 1979).

8. See al-Safadi, *Al-Wāfī bi l-wafayāt*, ed. A. Fu'ād Sayyid (Wiesbaden, 1988), 18: 335–379.

9. Work titled *Kitāb al-fath al-qussī fī l-fath al-qudsī*, ed. C. Landberg, translated into French as *Conquête de la Syrie et de la Palestine par Saladin* (Paris, 1972). The title of this work (*The Eloquence of Quss [Applied] to the Conquest of Jerusalem*) is a good illustration of how titles were chosen by Arab authors, who liked to play with words and rhymes. Quss ibn Sā'ida is the name of a semilegendary figure from the pre-Islamic period known for his eloquence.

10. Of this work, titled *Al-Barq al-Shāmī*, which deals with the period 562–589/1167–1193, only volumes 3 (573–575/1177–1180) and 5 (578–580/1182–1185) have come down to us. Nevertheless, we have a summary of the book written in the early thirteenth century by al-Bundārī and titled *Sanā al-Barq al-Shāmī*, ed. F. al-Nabrāwī (Cairo, 1979).

11. Hadith are the words or deeds attributed to the Prophet and transmitted through his Companions. The summa of hadith, recorded in ninth-century collections, is the Sunna, which, alongside the Koran, is the source of Muslim law.

12. Ibn Shaddād, *Al-Nawādir al-sultāniyya wa l-mahāsin al-Yūsufiyya*, ed. J. al-Dīn al-Shayyāl (Cairo, 1964); excerpts edited and translated in *Recueils des historiens des croisades. Histoires orientaux*, vol. 3 (Paris, 1884), 1–370; translated into English by D. S. Richards as *The Rare and Excellent History of Saladin* (Aldershot, U.K., 2001).

13. Ibn al-Athīr, *Al-Ta'rīkh al-bāhir fī l-dawla al-atābakiyya*, ed. 'Abd al-Qādir Ahmad Tulaymāt (Baghdad, 1963).

14. Ibn al-Athīr, *Al-Kāmil fī l-ta'rīkh*, 13 vols. (Beirut, 1965–1967), reprint of the C. J. Tornberg edition (Leiden, 1867).

15. See Ibn al-Athīr, *Kāmil*, 11:155, trans. F. Gabrieli in *Chroniques arabes des croisades*, 205.

16. Ibn al-Athīr, *Kāmil*, 12:97, Richards trans., 2:409.

17. Only on one occasion does he seem to echo the propaganda hostile to Saladin, when he attempts to explain the cooling of relations between Saladin and the caliph of Baghdad by claiming that the sultan, one day when he was drunk, said that he was ready to reestablish the *khutba* (Friday sermon) in his territories in the name of the Fatimids. See Bar Hebraeus, *The Chronography of Gregory Abū l-Farağ the Son of Aaron*, Budge trans., 328.

18. *The History of the Churches and Monasteries of Egypt* was long attributed to an Armenian author named Abū Sālih, but in reality its main author, Abū l-Makārim (d. ca. 1190), was Coptic. See J. den Heijer, "The Composition of the History of the Churches and Monasteries of Egypt: Some Preliminary Remarks," *Acts of the Fifth International Congress of Coptic Studies, Washington, D.C., August 12–15, 1992* (Rome, 1993), 2, 1:209–219; J. den Heijer, "Coptic Historiography in the Fātimid, Ayyūbid and

Early Mamlūk Periods," *Medieval Encounters* 2, 1 (1996): 77–81; M. Martin, "Alexandrie chrétienne à la fin du XIIe siècle d'après Abû l-Makârim," in *Alexandrie médiévale* 1 (1998): 45–49.

19. A list of all these works can be found in the bibliography.

20. See R. C. Schwinges, *Kreuzzugsideologie und Toleranz. Studien zu Wilhem von Tyrus* (Stuttgart, 1977), 199–209.

21. On the complicated textual history of the French *Continuation* of William of Tyre, which was compiled in the first half of the thirteenth century, see M. R. Morgan, *The Chronicle of Ernoul and the Continuation of William of Tyre* (Oxford, 1973); P. W. Edbury, *The Conquest of Jerusalem and the Third Crusade* (Aldershot, U.K., 1996; new ed., 2002), 3–8; P. W. Edbury, "The Lyon Eracles and the Old French Continuations of William of Tyre," in *Montjoie: Studies in Crusade History in Honour of Hans Eberhard Mayer*, ed. B. Z. Kedar, J. Riley-Smith, R. Hiestand (Aldershot, 1997), 139–153.

22. The textual history of the *Itinerarium peregrinorum* has been studied in detail by H. E. Mayer (*Das Itinerarium peregrinorum. Eine zeitgenössische englische Chronik zum dritten Kreuzzug in ursprünglicher Gestalt* [Stuttgart, 1962]). Mayer has shown that most of book 1 in the W. Stubbs edition (he calls this edition "IP2") originally constituted a separate chronicle, which he calls "IP1." IP1 was probably written in Tyre by an English Knight Templar between August 1191 and September 1192. Between 1216 and 1222, Richard de Templo, canon of the priory of the Holy Trinity in London, combined IP1 and the Latin translation of a long French poem by Ambroise titled *L'Estoire de la guerre sainte* (ed. and trans. M. Ailes and M. Barber as *The History of the Holy War, Ambroise's Estoire de la Guerre Sainte*, 2 vols. [Woodbridge, 2003]). Richard thus introduced several passages from Ambroise into IP1. The end of book 1 (beginning with the events of November 19, 1190) and all the following books of the *Itinerarium peregrinorum* are taken from Ambroise's poem. The IP1 version of the *Itinerarium peregrinorum* served in turn as the basis for the Latin *Continuation* of William of Tyre (*Die lateinische Fortsetzung Wilhelms von Tyrus*, ed. M. Salloch [Leipzig, 1934]), probably composed in about 1194.

23. This chronicle (*Chronique*, ed. L. de Mas Latrie [Paris, 1871]) begins with the founding of the Latin states and ends, depending on the manuscript, in 1227 or 1231. It seems to have had as its starting point an account by a certain Ernoul, equerry to Balian of Ibelin. It is believed that that narrative did not extend past the end of 1187. The rest of the *Chronicle* is supposedly constituted of reworked versions of a text dating from the 1220s. See Edbury, *The Conquest of Jerusalem and the Third Crusade*, 4–5.

24. See J. Richard, "Les transformations de l'image de Saladin," 177–187.

1. Saladin's World

1. See P. Smoor, "'Umāra's Poetical Views," 414.

2. The 1131 attempt by an Egyptian vizier, al-Afdal Kutayfāt, to depose the Fatimid dynasty lasted little more than a year. Kutayfāt was assassinated and the Fatimid caliph reinstated. See *Encyclopaedia of Islam*, 2nd ed., "al Afḍal Kutayfāt" (S. M. Stern).

3. See C. Hillenbrand, *The Crusades*, 151–161.

2. Training Period

1. Saladin's family belonged to the Kurdish family of the Rawādiyya, one of the branches of the Hadhbāniyya tribe. On it and on Saladin's youth, about which little is known, see Ibn Wāsil, *Mufarrij*, 2:238; Ibn Khallikān, 1:255–261, 306–309; 2:523–525; 3:456–458; 7:139–218 (Saladin biography); Ibn al-Athīr, *Kāmil*, 11:341, Richards trans., 2:175–176; Ibn Shaddād, *Nawādir*, al-Shayyāl ed., 6, Richards trans., 17; Abū Shāma (based largely on Ibn Abī Tayyi'), *Rawdatayn*, 1:209–213; and V. Minorsky, "Prehistory of Saladin," 130–139.

2. See Ibn Khallikān, 1:256.

3. Shīrkūh's secretary, who predicted Saladin's glorious future, was also Christian, one of several indications of the important role played by Christians in the Muslim administration. See Abū Shāma, *Rawdatayn*, 1:211 (year 568). Ibn Khallikān (1:257) says that the victim was not a Christian but an emir guarding the door of the citadel, and that Shīrkūh killed him for having made an attempt on the honor of a woman in the harem. Ayyūb offered to turn his brother in to Bihrūz, but in the name of the friendship he had for their father, Bihrūz agreed to close his eyes, provided they leave the city. On Bihrūz's Christian *(rūmī)* background and his favorable disposition toward his former coreligionists, see Ibn Khallikān, 7:141, and Michael the Syrian, 3:325.

4. In general, the sources mention only the children who did not die in infancy.

5. Ibn Jubayr, Gaudefroy-Demombynes trans., 301, Broadhurst trans., 272.

6. See Ibn al-Athīr, *Kāmil*, 11:341–342, Richards trans., 2:175–176; N. Elisséeff, *Nūr al-Dīn*, 403; J. M. Mouton, *Damas et sa principauté sous les Saljoukides et les Bourides, 468–548/1076–1145* (Cairo, 1994), 79, 186, 199.

7. See Ibn Abī Tayyi' in Abū Shāma, *Rawdatayn*, 1:46–48; Ibn Khallikān, 7:143–144; Ibn al-Athīr, *Kāmil*, 11:342, Richards trans., 2:176; al-Maqrīzī, *Itti'āz*, 3:307.

8. See Ibn Abī Tayyi' in Abū Shāma, *Rawdatayn*, 1:58.

9. M. C. Lyons and D. E. P. Jackson, *Saladin*, 9.

10. See Ibn Abī Tayyi' in Abū Shāma, *Rawdatayn*, 1:209–213; Ibn Khallikān, 1:255–261; Ibn al-Athīr, *Kāmil*, 11:252, Richards trans., 2:110; and Ibn al-Athīr, *Al-Bāhir*, 172.

11. See Abū Shāma, *Rawdatayn*, 1:160–161; William of Tyre, Huygens ed., 871 (19.5), Babcock and Krey trans., 2:303. "A crafty and valiant commander," according to the author of the *Anonymous Syriac Chronicle* (*Anonymi auctoris chronicon*, 123).

12. See Ibn Abī Tayyi' in Abū Shāma, *Rawdatayn*, 1:173; and D. Ayalon, "From Ayyubids to Mamluks," *Revue des études islamiques* 49 (1981): 43–57. The mamluk contingents within the army customarily took the name of the master who had purchased and then emancipated them.

13. See Ibn Shaddād, *Nawādir*, al-Shayyāl ed., 44, Richards trans., 47.

14. A large mosque and a madrasa in Aleppo; two oratories, two institutions for Sufis, and a madrasa in Damascus. See Ibn Shaddād, *A'lāq* (Damascus), 151–152, 193, 196, 262, and *A'lāq* (Aleppo), 38, 103; Ibn Khallikān, 1:257.

15. See al-Bundārī, 19.

16. The jurist's name was Qutb al-Dīn Mas'ūd al-Naysābūrī. See Ibn Shaddād, *Nawādir*, al-Shayyāl ed., 7, Richards trans., 18; al-Maqrīzī, *Sulūk* 1, 1: 42; Ibn al-'Imād, *Shadharāt*, 6:432.

17. See Ibn Shaddād, *Nawādir*, al-Shayyāl ed., 34, Richards trans., 38; M. C. Lyons and D. E. P. Jackson, *Saladin*, 3.

18. Such as al-Mansūr ibn 'Umar of Hama (r. 1191–1220), al-Mu'azzam of Damascus (r. 1218–1227), and al-Amjad of Baalbek (r. 1182–1230); these men were not only politicians but also historians, jurists, men of letters, or poets.

19. See Ibn al-Athīr, *Kāmil*, 11:342, Richards trans., 2:176; Elisséeff, *Nūr al-Dīn*, 485–488.

20. The Shafite chief qādī at the time was Kamāl al-Dīn al-Shahrazūrī. See al-Bundārī, 107–108; Sibt Ibn al-Jawzī, 8:252, 327. On the different versions and dates given by the sources, see Lyons and Jackson, *Saladin*, 10 and 387n. 60. The arguments advanced by Lyons and Jackson for selecting the year 1165 seem very convincing to me. I might add that Ibn Abī Tayyi', who situates that event in 1156, is fairly often wrong about dates.

21. See Elisséeff, *Nūr al-Dīn*, 2:579–589, 602–614, 622–644; Lyons and Jackson, *Saladin*, 6–25; Y. Lev, *Saladin in Egypt*, 53–61.

22. [Verses from the Koran are from the Penguin edition, trans. N. J. Dawood (London, 1956)—trans.] See Ibn Shaddād, *Nawādir*, al-Shayyāl ed., 36, 39, Richards trans., 41, 43; Ibn al-Athīr, *Kāmil*, 11:342–343, Richards trans., 2:177.

23. See William of Tyre, Huygens ed., 901–908 (19.26–31), Babcock and Krey trans., 2:334–342.

24. See W. Heyd, *Histoire du commerce du Levant*, 1:396.

25. See 'Imād al-Dīn in al-Bundārī, 23–24. Ibn Abī Tayyi' says that Saladin received an *iqtā'* from Nūr al-Dīn in 1152, when he went to join his uncle in Aleppo (Abū Shāma, *Rawdatayn*, 1:84), but his information, which is confirmed by no other source, is less credible than that given by 'Imād al-Dīn, a direct witness to these events.

26. According to these rumors, Saladin was to marry one of Shāwar's daughters, and his sister was to marry one of Shāwar's sons. See Ibn Abī Tayyi' in Abū Shāma, *Rawdatayn*, 1:170; Lyons and Jackson, *Saladin*, 20.

27. It is the Coptic author of the *History of the Patriarchs of the Egyptian Church* (Khater and Burmester ed., vol. 3, ed., 62, trans., 104) who provides that detail. Bilbeis, northeast of Cairo, was located on the route connecting the capital to Palestine. Its fate was to be often besieged by troops wishing to conquer Egypt.

28. From four hundred thousand to two million dinars, depending on the source, considerable sums compared to the annual budget of Egypt, which was 4,635,019 dinars in 1189.

29. On Shāwar's murder, see Ibn Shaddād, *Nawādir*, al-Shayyāl ed., 39, Richards trans., 44; Ibn al-Athīr, *Kāmil*, 11:339–340, Richards trans., 2:174–175; Abū Shāma, *Rawdatayn*, 1:157, 172; al-Maqrīzī, *Itti'āz*, 3:300–302; Bar Hebraeus, 294; *Anonymi auctoris chronicon*, 125; William of Tyre, Huygens ed. (20.10), 923–924, Babcock and Krey trans., 2:357.

30. See Ibn Shaddād, *Nawādir*, al-Shayyāl ed., 36, 40, Richards trans., 41, 44.

31. Ibn al-Athīr and 'Imād al-Dīn say that Shīrkūh was even openly opposed to the act. Ibn Abī Tayyi' (quoted by Abū Shāma) and William of Tyre, conversely, present him as very much in favor of the murder.

32. N. Elisséeff, "Un document contemporain de Nūr ad-Dīn. Sa notice biographique par Ibn 'Asākir," *Bulletin d'études orientales* 25 (1972): 125–140. "Al-Asad" (the Lion) is an allusion to Asad al-Dīn Shīrkūh.

33. 'Umāra, quoted by Abū Shāma, *Rawdatayn*, 1:158. See also Lev, *Saladin in Egypt*, 13.

34. See Ibn Shaddād, *Nawādir*, al-Shayyāl ed., 40, Richards trans., 45; Abū Shāma, *Rawdatayn*, 1:160, 172.

3. Vizier in Cairo

1. On Saladin's ascent to the vizierate, see Ibn al-Athīr, *Kāmil*, 11:343–344, Richards trans., 2:176–179; Ibn Abī Tayyi' in Abū Shāma, *Rawdatayn*, 1:173–174; al-Bundārī, 42–43; al-Maqrīzī, *Itti'āz*, 3:307–309; Ibn Wāsil, *Mufarrij*, 168–170; Ibn Khallikān, 7:151–155.

2. In addition to Saladin's uncle (Shihāb al-Dīn Mahmūd al-Hārimī), the Kurdish emirs who might have had a claim to succeed Shīrkūh were Qutb al-Dīn Khusraw al-Hadhbānī and Sayf al-Dīn 'Alī al-Mashtūb al-Hakkārī. See Abū Shāma, *Rawdatayn*, 1:159; al-Maqrīzī, *Itti'āz*, 3:304. Some authors claim that Shīrkūh had designated Saladin as his successor (Sibt Ibn al-Jawzī, 8:278).

3. For example, the Turk 'Izz al-Dīn Jūrdīk, an emancipated slave of Nūr al-Dīn, and probably also the Kurd Qutb al-Dīn Khusraw, proof once again that the cleavage within the army cannot be reduced to the differences between Kurds and Turks.

Regarding Qutb al-Dīn, some sources say that he initially allowed himself to be persuaded to support Saladin, but a few months later he was heading an expedition sent by Nūr al-Dīn from Syria to Egypt. See al-Bundārī, 45.

4. See al-Maqrīzī, *Itti'āz*, 3:310, which confirms that the caliph had a high opinion of Saladin, let him enter his palace on horseback, and kept him near him for several days. Together they participated in the official religious ceremonies during the month of Ramadan or in the major religious holidays.

5. The text of the diploma is conserved in al-Qalqashandī, *Subh*, 10:91–98, reproduced in Ibn Wāsil, *Mufarrij*, 2:443–462. It displays many features in common with the one that had been conferred two months earlier on Shīrkūh. See al-Qalqashandī, *Subh*, 10:80–90.

6. There are even examples of power being entrusted to sons during their father's lifetime, as in the time of the viziers Talā'i' ibn Ruzzīk and Shāwar. See Y. Lev, *Saladin in Egypt*, 73–75; and P. Smoor, "'Umāra's Poetical Views," 411–412.

7. These honorific gifts, called *khila'* (sing. *khil'a*), were given by Muslim rulers (caliphs or sultans) to people they wanted to honor or reward. The nature and richness of the objects composing them were indicative of the rank and position of their recipient.

8. See the description of Shīrkūh's *khil'a*, also white with gold embroidery, in *History of the Patriarchs*, Khater and Burmester ed., vol. 3, ed., 63, trans., 106.

9. See Abū Shāma (*Rawdatayn*, 1:173), Ibn al-Furāt (*Ta'rīkh*, 4, 1:66), and al-Maqrīzī (*Itti'āz*, 3:304, 310–311), all three of whom reproduce the account of Ibn Abī Tayyi'.

10. Abū Shāma, *Rawdatayn*, 1:174. Abū Shāma accuses Ibn Abī Tayyi' of besmirching the image of Nūr al-Dīn, whom Ibn Abī Tayyi' reproached for having fought against the Shiites of Aleppo. The father of Ibn Abī Tayyi' was himself sent into exile at the time.

11. See Ibn Wāsil, *Mufarrij*, 1:174.

12. See Ibn al-Athīr, *Kāmil*, 11:344; Abū Shāma, *Rawdatayn*, 1:161; Ibn Wāsil, *Mufarrij*, 1:174; al-Maqrīzī, *Sulūk* 1, 1:45.

13. "Ghuzz" is the Arabic form of the name for the Oghuz Turkish people. See *Encylopaedia of Islam,* 2nd ed., "Ghuzz" (C. Cahen). For how the Arabs viewed the Turks in the Middle Ages, see U. W. Haarmann, "Ideology and History, Identity and Alterity: The Arab Image of the Turk from the 'Abbasids to Modern Egypt," *International Journal of Middle East Studies* 20 (1988): 175–196.

14. See William of Tyre, Huygens ed., 925 (20.11), Babcock and Krey trans., 2:359.

15. In Khallikān, 5:74, Slane trans., 3:235.

16. See William of Tyre, Huygens ed., 920 (20.7), Babcock and Krey trans., 2:353; *Anonymi auctoris chronicon*, 124.

17. Al-Maqrīzī notes that the Fatimid caliph had been very satisfied with the attitude of Shīrkūh, who had honored the posts held by the caliph's entourage, even though

Shīrkūh had redistributed the territories to his own companions (*Itti'āz*, 3:304). It was by distributing money that Saladin won the hearts of men, writes Ibn al-Athīr, *Kāmil*, 11:344, Richards trans., 2:178. See also Abū Shāma, *Rawdatayn*, 1:178, and al-Maqrīzī, *Itti'āz*, 3:311.

18. The eunuch's name was Mu'tamin al-Khilāfa. See Ibn al-Athīr, *Kāmil*, 11:345, Richards trans., 2:179; 'Imād al-Dīn, in Abū Shāma, *Rawdatayn*, 1:178 and in al-Bundārī, 43–44; al-Maqrīzī, *Itti'āz*, 3:311–314; al-Maqrīzī, *Khitat*, 2:2–3, Sayyid ed., 3:4–6; *History of the Patriarchs*, Khater and Burmester ed., vol. 3, ed., 66, trans., 110; M. C. Lyons and D. E. P. Jackson, *Saladin*, 33–36; Lev, *Saladin in Egypt*, 49–50.

19. See *Churches and Monasteries of Egypt*, Evetts and Butler ed., 34, trans., 92; Lyons and Jackson, *Saladin*, 22, 34.

20. The involvement of Armenian troops in that conflict is also attested by Ibn Abī Tayyi' in Abū Shāma, *Rawdatayn*, 1:196, and by the letter Saladin sent to the caliph in 1175.

21. The presence of these blacks within the palace or in Saladin's army is attested in the accounts of the revolts that unfolded in the following years and in the statements of certain sources, who mention black soldiers in the garrison of Acre in 1191. See Lev, *Saladin in Egypt*, 148.

22. See Abū Shāma, *Rawdatayn*, 1:241–244, trans. *Recueils des historiens des croisades. Histoires orientaux* (hereafter cited as *RHC Or.*), 4:170–180.

23. See Ibn al-Athīr, *Kāmil*, 11:351–352, Richards trans., 2:183.

24. Navigation was generally suspended in early December and did not resume until spring. See al-Qalqashandī, *Subh*, 2:385. On that expedition, see Ibn al-Athīr, *Kāmil*, 11:351–352, Richards trans., 2:183–184; Ibn Shaddād, *Nawādir*, al-Shayyāl ed., 41–43, Richards trans., 45–46, Abū Shāma, *Rawdatayn*, 1:180–181; Ibn Wāsil, *Mufarrij*, 1:179–184, who follows, but without citing him, 'Imād al-Dīn, also cited by Abū Shāma; al-Maqrīzī, *Itti'āz*, 2:315–316; William of Tyre, Huygens ed., 927–933 (20.14–16), Babcock and Krey trans., 2:362–368; N. Elisséeff, *Nūr al-Dīn*, 2:645–650; A. S. Ehrenkreutz, "Saladin in Naval History," 104; Lyons and Jackson, *Saladin*, 36–38.

25. See Abū Shāma, *Rawdatayn*, 1:241–243, trans. *RHC Or.*, 4:170–180, reproduced in Ibn Wāsil, *Mufarrij*, 2:486–493.

26. Not all the sources agree on the circumstances surrounding Ayyūb's departure. Ibn Abī Tayyi' says that Nūr al-Dīn sent Ayyūb to Cairo to urge his son to put an end to the Fatimid caliphate. Others claim that it was Saladin who asked Nūr al-Dīn for authorization to have his father come. 'Imād al-Dīn, finally, reports that it was Ayyūb who asked for Nūr al-Dīn's permission to go join his sons in Egypt. These differences are of little import, the essential thing being that Nūr al-Dīn did not oppose that departure in any way. See Ibn al-Athīr, *Kāmil*, 11:353, Richards trans., 2:184; Ibn Shaddād, *Nawādir*, al-Shayyāl ed., 44, Richards trans., 47; Ibn Wāsil,

Mufarrij, 1:185–186; Abū Shāma, *Rawdatayn*, 1:183–184; Ibn Khallikān, 1:257–258; Lyons and Jackson, *Saladin*, 38.

27. The Pearl Palace, or Qasr al-Lu'lu'a. See al-Maqrīzī, *Khitat*, 1:469, Sayyid ed., 2:532.

28. On these expeditions, see William of Tyre, Huygens ed., 936–939 (20.19–20), Babcock and Krey trans., 2:371–375; Abū Shāma, *Rawdatayn*, 1:191; al-Bundārī, 57; Lyons and Jackson, *Saladin*, 42–44.

29. See J. M. Mouton, "Autour des inscriptions," 71–77; J. M. Mouton and S. S. 'Abd al-Malik, "Forteresse de l'île de Graye," 75–90; J. M. Mouton et al., "Route de Saladin," 41–70; Mouton, *Le Sinaï médiéval*, 82–86.

30. At the time, Nūr al-Dīn was busy settling the succession of his brother Qutb al-Dīn in Mosul by installing his two nephews, the younger, Sayf al-Dīn, in Mosul, and the elder, 'Imād al-Dīn Zangī, in Sinjār. See Lyons and Jackson, *Saladin*, 40.

31. That is how he presents himself in his letter sent to the caliph in 1175 (Abū Shāma, *Rawdatayn*, 1:241–243, trans. *RHC Or.*, 4:170–180, reproduced in Ibn Wāsil, *Mufarrij*, 2:486–493). For most Muslims, "Station of Abraham" (Maqām Ibrāhīm) is an expression designating the stone in the sanctuary of Mecca that bears the imprint of Abraham's feet (see Koran 2:125).

4. The End of the Fatimids

1. See Abū Shāma, *Rawdatayn*, 1:183. On the fall of the last Fatimid caliph and the distribution of his possessions, see Abū Shāma, *Rawdatayn*, 1:193–200; al-Bundārī, 58; al-Maqrīzī, *Itti'āz*, 3:316–322; Ibn al-Athīr, *Kāmil*, 11:368–371, Richards trans., 2:196–198; Ibn Wāsil, *Mufarrij*, 1:178–179, 200–221; al-Maqrīzī, *Khitat*, 1:384, 496–498, Sayyid ed., 2:285–286, 608–612.

2. See Abū Shāma, *Rawdatayn*, 1:191–192; al-Maqrīzī, *Itti'āz*, 3:322; and al-Maqrīzī, *Khitat*, 2:366, Sayyid ed., 4, 2:461.

3. Their leader was an Iranian Shafite, Najm al-Dīn al-Khubūshānī, who was strongly opposed to Fatimid power.

4. See Abū Shāma, *Rawdatayn*, 1:193ff.; Ibn al-Athīr, *Kāmil*, 11:368–371, Richards trans., 2:196–198; M. C. Lyons and D. E. P. Jackson, *Saladin*, 45–46; Y. Lev, *Saladin in Egypt*, 83.

5. 'Imād al-Dīn claims it was a Syrian preacher, Muhammad al-Ba'labakkī, who pronounced the first *khutba* in the name of the Abbasids; Ibn al-Athīr claims it was an Iranian; and others say it was an Andalusian Koran reader. These rival claims are a sign of the importance of that event, whose merit everyone wanted to appropriate.

6. The last two legends are recorded primarily in the Christian sources. See *History of the Patriarchs*, Khater and Burmester ed., vol. 3, ed., 66, trans., 111; *Anonymi auctoris chronicon*, 130. Ibn Abī Tayyi' also reports it in Abū Shāma, *Rawdatayn*, 1:196.

7. See H. A. R. Gibb, "The Armies of Saladin," 76.

8. Abū Shāma, *Rawdatayn*, 1:197–198.

9. See *The Churches and Monasteries of Egypt*, Evetts and Butler ed., 3ff., trans., 3ff. See also M. Canard, "Notes sur les Arméniens en Égypte à l'époque fatimide," *Annales de l'Institut d'études orientales de la faculté des lettres d'Alger* 13 (1995): 143–157, repr. *Miscellanea Orientalia* (London, 1973).

10. See Nāsir-i-Khusraw, *Book of Travels*, trans. W. M. Thackston (New York, 1986), 57.

11. See William of Tyre, Huygens ed., 887–888 (19.18), Babcock and Krey trans., 2:319–320; and *Croisades et pèlerinages*, 666–667.

12. A gate and a few friezes were reused in constructing the hospital and mausoleum of the Mamluk sultan Qalā'ūn (r. 1279–1290) and were thus fortunately preserved. See A. Fu'ād Sayyid, "Le grand palais fatimide au Caire," in *L'Égypte fatimide, son art et son histoire*, ed. M. Barrucand (Paris, 1999), 117–125; and other reproductions of these friezes in *Trésors fatimides du Caire*, catalog for the exhibition held at the Institut du monde arabe, April 28–August 30, 1998 (Paris, 1998), 88–95. In the same book, see also Viktoria Meinecke-Berg's article "Le trésor des califes," 96–142, and the many illustrations that accompany it.

13. See al-Maqrīzī, *Khitat*, 1:427, 435, Sayyid ed., 2:409–410, 429; al-Bundārī, 29; Lyons and Jackson, *Saladin*, 49.

14. The most complete description we have of that library is found in al-Maqrīzī, *Khitat*, 1:408–409, Sayyid ed., 355–359, translated into French by R. G. Khoury as "Une description fantastique des fonds de la Bibliothèque royale Ḥizānat al-kutub au Caire, sous le règne du calife fatimide al-'Azīz bi-llāh (975–997)," in *Proceedings of the Ninth Congress of the Union européenne des arabisants et islamisants, Amsterdam, September 1978*, ed. R. Peeters (Leiden, 1981), 123–140. On the dispersal of the library, see also Abū Shāma, *Rawdatayn*, 1:200; al-Bundārī, 116; Lyons and Jackson, *Saladin*, 118.

15. See this example and others in Y. Eche, *Les bibliothèques arabes publiques et semi-publiques en Mésopotamie, en Syrie et en Égypte au Moyen Âge* (Damascus, 1967), 130, 132, 146–148.

16. See Bar Hebraeus, Budge trans., 315.

17. See al-Maqrīzī, *Khitat*, 1:364, 384, 496–498, Sayyid ed., 2:286, 608–612.

5. Nūr al-Dīn's Lieutenant in Egypt

1. See M. C. Lyons and D. E. P. Jackson, *Saladin*, 67–68; Y. Lev, *Saladin in Egypt*, 49–50, 86–94; M. Chamberlain, "The Crusader Era and the Ayyūbid Dynasty," in *The Cambridge History of Egypt*, vol. 1: *Islamic Egypt, 640–1517* (Cambridge, U.K., 1998), 211–241, esp. 216.

2. *Encyclopaedia of Islam*, 2nd ed. (hereafter cited as *EI* 2), "Ṣa'īd" (J. C. Garcin).

3. In the second half of the eleventh century, the black troops in conflict with the Turkish contingents had retreated to the region of Aswān and had joined the great

tribal revolts of the time. Not until the drastic actions taken by the Fatimid vizier Badr al-Jamālī in 1077 would order finally be reestablished.

4. The name of the emir who repressed the 1170 revolt was Raslān ibn Daghmash. See Abū Shāma, *Rawdatayn*, 1:184, 191; al-Maqrīzī, *Itti'āz*, 3:317, 321; J. C. Garcin, *Qūṣ*, 125–126.

5. See *The Churches and Monasteries of Egypt*, Evetts and Butler ed., 266–267; J. Cuoq, *Islamisation de la Nubie chrétienne: VIIe–XVIe siècle* (Paris, 1986), 65–67.

6. Ibn Jubayr (Gaudefroy-Demombynes trans., 81–82, Broadhurst trans., 66) cannot find words harsh or contemptuous enough to describe the black tribes called Beja, who lived in Upper Egypt and Nubia, between the Nile and the Red Sea: "This race from the Sudan is more astray from the (right) path, and have less reason, than the animals. They have no religion save the formal words professing the unity of God, which they utter to display that they are Muslims. But behind that are corrupt beliefs and practices that cannot be condoned and are unlawful." Nubia is today divided between Egypt and Sudan. The border that separates Egypt proper from Nubia is located at the first cataract of the Nile, near Aswān. See *EI* 2, "Nūba" (S. Hillelson et al.) and "Bedja" (P. M. Holt).

7. See Ibn al-Athīr, *Kāmil*, 11:386–387, Richards trans., 2:209–210; Garcin, *Qūṣ*, 47–49, 127; Lyons and Jackson, *Saladin*, 60–61.

8. The emir was named Kanz al-Dawla and had been appointed governor of Aswān by Saladin. Aided by a certain number of Arab Bedouins, blacks, and Fatimid nostalgists, he attacked the district of Qūṣ, while a parallel uprising, purely Arab in that case, took place in Tawd, south of Luxor on the eastern bank of the Nile.

9. See al-Maqrīzī, *Sulūk*, 1, 1:79–80; Ibn Shaddād, *Nawādir*, ed., 47–48, Richards trans., 49, Abū Shāma, *Rawdatayn*, 1:235; Garcin, *Qūṣ*, 129–130.

10. See al-Maqrīzī, *Khitat*, 1:233, Sayyid ed., 1:633; Garcin, *Qūṣ*, 130.

11. Some say it was the Hanbalite Zayn al-Dīn Ibn Najā who alerted Saladin, while others claim it was Ibn Masāl, former governor of Alexandria. See Abū Shāma, *Rawdatayn*, 1:219–224; Ibn al-Athīr, *Kāmil*, 11:398–401, Richards trans., 2:218–221; al-Maqrīzī, *Sulūk* 1, 1:53; A. S. Ehrenkreutz, *Saladin*, 112–115; Lyons and Jackson, *Saladin*, 67–68; Lev, *Saladin in Egypt*, 86–94.

12. Including the leader of the Ismaili missionaries, Ibn' Abd al-Qawī, and Chief Qāḍī Diyā' al-Dīn Ibn Kāmil, two very influential figures within the former Fatimid state. See al-Maqrīzī, *Muqaffā*, 8:740–756; Ibn Khallikān, 3:431–436; H. Derenbourg, *'Oumâra du Yémen, sa vie et son oeuvre*, vol. 2 (French part) (Paris, 1904), 349ff.

13. See P. Smoor, "'Umāra's Poetical Views," 424–426.

14. Quoted in P. Sanders, *Rituals, Politics and the City in Fatimid Cairo* (New York, 1994), 137.

15. See Lyons and Jackson, *Saladin*, 67–68.

16. See Ibn al-Athīr, *Kāmil*, 12:24, Richards trans., 2:357; Ibn Wāsil, *Mufarrij*, 2:276; Lyons and Jackson, *Saladin*, 292.

17. See Abū Shāma, *Rawdatayn*, 2:178.

18. In the fortress of Salkhad, on the southern slope of the Jebel Druze. See al-Maqrīzī, *Sulūk* 1, 1:110–111; Ehrenkreutz, *Saladin*, 223. The revolt noted by Ibn al-Dawādārī (7:109) for 1191 is no doubt the same as the one reported by the other sources for 1188.

19. See Ibn al-Athīr, *Kāmil*, 11:396–398, Richards trans., 2:217–218; Abū Shāma, *Rawdatayn*, 1:216–217; al-Maqrīzī, *Sulūk*, 1, 1:52–53; N. Elisséeff, *Nūr al-Dīn*, 2:684–686; Lyons and Jackson, *Saladin*, 65–66; Garcin, *Qūṣ*, 131–133; G. R. Smith, *The Ayyūbids and Early Rasūlids in the Yemen*, 2 vols. (London, 1978), 2:31–49.

20. A tyrannical prince of Zabīd, a Kharijite named 'Abd al-Nabī ibn Mahdī.

21. See Ibn Shaddād, *Nawādir*, ed., 47, Richards trans., 49; Ibn al-Athīr, *Kāmil*, 11:371–373, Richards trans., 2:199–200; Abū Shāma, *Rawdatayn*, 1:203–204 (year 567); Elisséeff, *Nūr al-Dīn*, 2:670–674; Lyons and Jackson, *Saladin*, 68–69.

22. See Ibn al-Athīr, *Kāmil*, 11:373, Richards trans., 2:199–200.

23. On these events, see Elisséeff, *Nūr al-Dīn*, 2:674–675 and 678–680; Lyons and Jackson, *Saladin*, 62–64.

24. Nūr al-Dīn then gave the zebra and the elephant to the caliph of Baghdad. See Abū Shāma, *Rawdatayn*, 2:154–156; al-Bundārī, 64–65; Lyons and Jackson, *Saladin*, 61–62.

25. See al-Bundārī, 65–66; Abū Shāma, *Rawdatayn*, 1:206.

26. On that expedition, see also Ibn Shaddād, *Nawādir*, ed., 45, Richards trans., 48; al-Maqrīzī, *Sulūk*, 1, 1:50; Lyons and Jackson, *Saladin*, 63.

27. Curiously, Ibn al-Athīr (*Kāmil*, 11:392–394, Richards trans., 2:213–214) is the only one to give a rather different version of these events. According to him, Saladin and Nūr al-Dīn had agreed to meet in the region of Kerak. Saladin arrived first, in May–June 1173; learning of Nūr al-Dīn's imminent arrival, he feared he would be dismissed and decided to return to Egypt, arguing that his father was ill and that threats against his authority were looming. Nūr al-Dīn was very unhappy, though he did not let it show. As Lyons and Jackson have already pointed out (*Saladin*, 63), this version, which reproduces in its main lines the events of late 1171, is not credible: in July 1173, Nūr al-Dīn was still busy fighting the Seljuks of Anatolia in the region of the Taurus Mountains. It is possible that here Ibn al-Athīr was once again echoing Zangid propaganda from the beginning of Saladin's reign, which, to show the illegitimacy of how Saladin had taken power, emphasized the tensions between the two men at the end of Nūr al-Dīn's reign. That argument carries weight once we know how insistently Saladin laid claim to Nūr al-Dīn's legacy after the latter's death. H. Möhring ("Heiliger Krieg," 434–435) believes that, unbeknownst to Nūr al-Dīn, an agreement bound Saladin to Amalric of Jerusalem at the time, which would explain Saladin's rapid withdrawal. Möhring bases himself on the letter of condolence Saladin sent to the king's son Baldwin IV following Amalric's

death, in which he expatiated on the friendship that bound him to Amalric (al-Qalqashandī, *Subh*, 7:115–116; repr. in Ibn Wāsil, *Mufarrij*, 3:320–321). I do not share that point of view, since no allusion is made in that letter to a real alliance between the two men.

28. See Abū Shāma, *Rawdatayn*, 1:219 (with a detailed list of the gifts, based on Ibn Abī Tayyi'); al-Bundārī, 68.

29. Ibn Shaddād, *Nawādir*, ed., 47, Richards trans., 49; Ibn al-Athīr, *Kāmil*, 11:402, Richards trans., 2:221.

30. See Lyons and Jackson, *Saladin*, 69.

31. See Abū Shāma, *Rawdatayn*, 1:228.

6. Usurper or Legitimate Sultan?

1. Nisībīn, Harrān, Edessa, Sarūj, Rakka, and the region of Khabur. His elder brother, 'Imād al-Dīn, was already lord of Sinjār. See M. C. Lyons and D. E. P. Jackson, *Saladin*, 72.

2. See Lyons and Jackson, *Saladin*, 78–79; Ibn al-'Adīm, *Zubda*, 3:14, 17–18.

3. See Abū Shāma, *Rawdatayn*, 1:234; al-Bundārī, 76; Lyons and Jackson, *Saladin*, 79.

4. See al-Bundārī, 32–34; Abū Shāma, *Rawdatayn*, 1:230–231; Ibn Wāsil, *Mufarrij*, 2:480–481; Ibn al-Athīr, *Kāmil*, 11:405–406, Richards trans., 2:224; Ibn al-'Adīm, *Zubda*, 3:13.

5. One of the two was Nūr al-Dīn's foster brother, and 'Imād al-Dīn considered both of them his friends (al-Bundārī, 76).

6. See Abū Shāma, *Rawdatayn*, 1:241–243, trans. *Recueils des historiens des croisades. Histoires orientaux* (hereafter cited as *RHC Or.*), 4:170–180.

7. See Lyons and Jackson, *Saladin*, 81; Ibn Wāsil, *Mufarrij*, 2:20.

8. Abū Shāma, *Rawdatayn*, 1:237.

9. Al-Bundārī, 82; see also Sibt Ibn al-Jawzī, 8:328.

10. Michael the Syrian, 3:365 (literally: "a dog barking at his master").

11. See William of Tyre, Huygens ed., 968 (21.6), 971–972 (21.8), Babcock and Krey trans., 2:405, 408.

12. See Ibn al-Athīr, *Kāmil*, 11:418, Richards trans., 2:233–234.

13. See al-Bundārī, 84; Lyons and Jackson, *Saladin*, 89; William of Tyre, Huygens ed., 951–952 (20.28), 967–969 (21.6), 971–973 (21.8), Babcock and Krey trans., 2:390, 405, 409.

14. See William of Tyre, Huygens ed., 972–973 (21.8), Babcock and Krey trans., 2:410.

15. See al-Bundārī, 86–88; Ibn al-Athīr, *Kāmil*, 11:421–422, Richards trans., 2:235–236; Ibn Abī Tayyi' in Abū Shāma, *Rawdatayn*, 1:249–250; Ibn al-'Adīm, *Zubda*, 3:23.

16. The name of the emir in question was Fakhr al-Dīn Ibn al-Za'farānī. See Lyons and Jackson, *Saladin*, 98–99.

17. See Lyons and Jackson, *Saladin*, 100–101, based on al-Bundārī, 91, and Abū Shāma, *Rawdatayn*, 1:253.

18. See C. Cahen, *Syrie du Nord*, 405; A. S. Ehrenkreutz, *Saladin*, 144.

19. See Ibn al-Athīr, *Kāmil*, 11:427, Richards trans., 2:241; *Anonymi auctoris chronicon*, 135; al-Bundārī, 94.

20. See Ibn al-ʿAdīm, *Zubda*, 3:30–31; Abū Shāma, *Rawdatayn*, 1:261.

21. Al-Sālih's mother was undoubtedly a concubine. Known as "the Lady" (al-Sitt), she lived near her son in Aleppo and survived him, since it was she who had him buried in her mausoleum at the foot of the citadel.

22. Nūr al-Dīn himself had married ʿIsmat al-Dīn in 1147 to seal his alliance with her father, the emir of Damascus, and in 1150 he married the daughter of the Seljuk sultan of Anatolia for similar reasons. See N. Elisséeff, *Nūr al-Dīn*, 2:403, 455.

23. See Ibn Shaddād, *Nawādir*, ed., 52, Richards trans., 54; al-Bundārī, 105, 114.

24. Raʿbān, present-day Altintaşkale on the Nahr ʿArabān, the western tributary of the Upper Euphrates.

25. The Artukids belonged to a small dynasty of Turkish governors installed north of Upper Mesopotamia by the Seljuks in the early twelfth century. See *Encyclopaedia of Islam*, 2nd ed. (hereafter *EI 2*), "Artuḳids" (C. Cahen). Emir Nūr al-Dīn Muhammad had married the daughter of Qilij Arslān, who accused him of abandoning her for several singers. When the Seljuks demanded the return of the lands granted as a dowry, Nūr al-Dīn appealed to Saladin, who put pressure on Qilij Arslān to negotiate. See Cahen, *Syrie du Nord*, 420–421; Lyons and Jackson, *Saladin*, 134–138, 149.

26. See Lyons and Jackson, *Saladin*, 150–151.

27. See Ibn Shaddād, *Aʿlāq* (Aleppo), 93; J. Sauvaget, *Les perles choisies d'Ibn ach-Chihna*. *Matériaux pour servir à l'histoire d'Alep* (Beirut, 1933), 99; Ibn al-ʿAdīm, *Bughya*, 4:1822–1826 (a biography of the young ruler).

28. See Lyons and Jackson, *Saladin*, 159; al-Mansūr, *Midmār*, 61; Ibn al-Athīr, *Kāmil*, 11:473, Richards trans., 2:278; al-Bundārī, 185; Abū Shāma, *Rawdatayn*, 2:21, 24.

29. See Lyons and Jackson, *Saladin*, 158–161.

30. See Lyons and Jackson, *Saladin*, 176; Ibn al-Athīr (*Kāmil*, 11:484, Richards trans., 2:284) says he handed over Edessa to Emir Gökböri, lord of Harrān, who had encouraged him to invade Upper Mesopotamia; also in Abū Shāma, *Rawdatayn*, 2:30, 32.

31. See Lyons and Jackson, *Saladin*, 191.

32. See Ibn Abī Tayyiʾ in Abū Shāma, *Rawdatayn*, 2:39.

33. A detailed list of the gifts based on Ibn Abī Tayyiʾ can be found in Abū Shāma, *Rawdatayn*, 2:45.

34. Ibn Wāsil, *Mufarrij*, 2:117; see also Lyons and Jackson, *Saladin*, 199.

35. Quoted in J. Prawer, *Histoire du royaume latin de Jérusalem*, 1:619.

36. See Lyons and Jackson, *Saladin*, 214–216.

37. See Ibn al-Athīr, *Kāmil*, 11:514, Richards trans., 2:306.

38. At the time, the term "Turkoman" designated Turks who had come from Syria in the late eleventh century in the wake of the Seljuks, and who had maintained a seminomadic mode of life. They usually lived off raids and rapines on the borders of Muslim territories, off sheep raising, and off the funds they received from the Muslim rulers when they lent a hand in their battles.

39. The embassy included his future adviser and biographer Ibn Shaddād.

40. 'Izz al-Dīn abandoned his rights over Jazīrat ibn 'Umar and Irbil, which had recognized Saladin's authority, and gave up the region of Shahrazūr, east of the Tigris; Tikrīt, between Mosul and Baghdad; and al-Hadītha and 'Ana, two cities west of Tikrīt on the Euphrates. In exchange, Saladin recognized his claim to the territories between Nisībīn and the Tigris, which he took from Sanjarshāh, lord of Jazīrat Ibn 'Umar. On Saladin's full campaign in al-Jazīra, see Lyons and Jackson, *Saladin*, 233–241; Ibn Shaddād, *Nawādir*, ed., 68–71, Richards trans., 66–68; Abū Shāma, *Rawda-tayn*, 2:64ff.; Ibn al-Athīr, *Kāmil*, 11:511–518, Richards trans., 2:304–309.

41. See Ibn al-'Adīm, *Bughya*, 6:2842–2845 (based on al-Fādil).

42. Quoted in Lyons and Jackson, *Saladin*, 190. The governor's name was Sārim al-Dīn Khutlubā.

43. See al-Maqrīzī, *Sulūk*, 1, 1:78. Tughtegin probably arrived in Yemen in 1182.

44. See Abū Shāma, *Rawdatayn*, 2:26; al-Bundārī, 192.

45. See P. Balog, *Coinage*, 284. On Tughtegin and his son, see Ibn Khallikān, 2:523–525.

46. Was this an homage to the founder of the Zaydite dynasty of Yemen, al-Hādī ilā l-Haqq (897–911)? See *EI* 2, "Zaydiyya" (W. Madelung).

47. See Ibn Khallikān, 2:524.

48. Qūs in particular. See J. C. Garcin, *Qūṣ*, 132.

49. See J. M. Mouton, "La conquête de la Cyrénaïque," 59–69. In addition to the sources indicated in that article, see the fairly detailed account in al-Mansūr, *Mid-mār*, 34–38, 53, 67–72, 164, 202, 229.

50. See J. Thiry, "L'Égypte et le déclin de l'Afrique du Nord (XIe–XIIe siècles)," in *Egypt and Syria in the Fatimid, Ayyubid and Mamluk Eras*, vol. 2, ed. U. Vermeulen and D. De Smet (Louvain, 1998), 237–248; D. Valérian, *Bougie, port maghrébin à la fin du Moyen Âge* (Paris, 2000), 188–196.

51. See al-Idrīsī, *Description de l'Afrique et de l'Espagne*, ed. and trans. R. Dozy and M. J. De Goeje (Leiden, 1866), 124, 142, 157–158; Benjamin of Tudela, in *Corpus of Early Arabic Sources for West African History*, ed. N. Levtzion and J. F. P. Hopkins (Cambridge, U.K., 1981; 2nd ed., Princeton, 2000), 135–136; al-Mansūr, *Midmār*, 164.

52. See al-Maqrīzī, *Sulūk*, 1, 1:48.

53. Ibn al-Athīr (*Kāmil*, 11:389, 467, Richards trans., 2:211, 273) places the taking of Gafsa in the month of Shawwal 572/April 1177, but the city was retaken by the Almohads in early 576/1180.

54. Taqī al-Dīn's other emir was named Ibrāhīm ibn Qarātakīn. The exact chronology of the conquests is difficult to establish, since it varies from one source to another, and a number of places were retaken, sometimes by the Almohads and sometimes by the Egyptian troops. See al-Tijānī, *Rihla*, ed. H. H. ʿAbd al-Wahhāb (Tunis, 1958), repr. in F. Sezgin, *Islamic Geography* (Frankfurt am Main, 1994), 185:103ff., 111ff., trans. into French by A. Rousseau as "Voyage du scheikh et-Tidjani dans la régence de Tunis pendant les années 706, 707 et 708 de l'Hégire (1306–1309)," *Journal Asiatique* 20 (1852): 57–208, esp. 152–163.

55. Emir Shujāʿ al-Dīn was sent with reinforcements in about 1182. Having received from Qarāqūsh several fortresses and about forty demesnes, which he squeezed for taxes, he was not long in entering into conflict with Qarāqūsh. Toward the end of 1186, another of Taqī al-Dīn's emirs, Zayn al-Dīn Yūzabā, also allowed himself to be tempted into launching a foray into North Africa, despite his master's order to come join him in Syria. His troops, combined with those of Qarāqūsh and of the Banū Ghāniya, devastated a large part of Ifriqiya. It is al-Mansūr (*Midmār*, 34–38, 67–72, 164, 202) who gives the most details about Shujāʿ al-Dīn's arrival and the rivalries between emirs.

56. Abū Shāma, *Rawdatayn*, 2:171, trans. *RHC Or.*, 4:495–496; see also M. Gaudefroy-Demombynes, "Une lettre de Saladin au calife almohade," *Mélanges R. Basset* 2 (1925): 279–304, esp. 298. On the looting by the Turkish armies in Ifriqiya, see Ibn al-Athīr, *Kāmil*, 11:520, Richards trans., 2:310–311, and Thiry, "L'Égypte et le déclin de l'Afrique du Nord," 245.

57. See Abū Shāma, *Rawdatayn*, 2:70.

7. The Caliph's Backing

1. The letter Saladin sent to the caliph in 1175 is reproduced in full in Abū Shāma, *Rawdatayn*, 1:241–243, trans. *Recueils des historiens des croisades. Histoires orientaux*, 4:170–180 (hereafter cited as *RHC Or.*); see also Ibn Wāsil, *Mufarrij*, 2:486–493.

2. See M. C. Lyons and D. E. P. Jackson, *Saladin*, 171.

3. See Lyons and Jackson, *Saladin*, 192, based on the letters from Qādī al-Fādil.

4. Abū Shāma, *Rawdatayn*, 2:49.

5. Abū Shāma, *Rawdatayn*, 2:48.

6. Abū Shāma, *Rawdatayn*, 1:241–243, trans. *RHC Or.*, 4:170–180; see also Ibn Wāsil, *Mufarrij*, 2:486–493.

7. See Abū Shāma, *Rawdatayn*, 2:31ff., trans. *RHC Or.*, 4:225–229; Lyons and Jackson, 193, 227.

8. See al-Qalqashandī, *Subh*, 10:135–144; Lyons and Jackson, *Saladin*, 98; A. S. Ehrenkreutz, *Saladin*, 138; E. Sivan, *L'Islam et la croisade*, 100.

9. That notion coincides with the idea of the "soul's battle against the vices" that developed in the Western Christian world. See N. Bériou, *L'avènement des maîtres de la parole. La prédication à Paris au XIIIe siècle*, 2 vols. (Paris, 1998), 567.

10. An oft-cited hadith, but one that is probably apocryphal.

11. See Lyons and Jackson, *Saladin*, 112–113, 129, 132–133.

12. See A. Hartmann, *An Nāsir li-Dīn Allāh*, 86–90; E. Sivan, "Saladin et le calife al-Nāṣir," 126–145.

13. See Abū Shāma, *Rawdatayn*, 2:19.

14. See al-Mansūr, *Midmār*, 83, 119, 124; Bar Hebraeus, Budge trans., 328.

15. Al-Khazrajī, *Ta'rīkh dawlat al-Akrād wa l-Atrāk*, Istanbul ms., Suleymaniye, Hekimoğlu Ali Paşa, 695, fol. 20b.

16. See 'Imād al-Dīn, *Fath*, Massé trans., 86–91.

17. See 'Imād al-Dīn, *Fath*, Massé trans., 395; Abū Shāma, *Rawdatayn*, 2:205, 211, trans. *RHC Or.*, 5:83, 91.

18. See 'Imād al-Dīn, *Fath*, Massé trans., 157–158; al-Maqrīsī, *Sulūk*, I, 1:101–102.

19. Shahrazūr is the province located east of the Tigris, northeast of Tikrīt, in the western part of Kurdistan.

20. Abū Shāma, *Rawdatayn*, 2:176, trans. *RHC Or.*, 4:506.

21. See al-Qalqashandī, *Subh*, 7:126–134 (reproduced in Ibn Wāsil, *Mufarrij*, 3:357–360); Lyons and Jackson, *Saladin*, 324.

22. See 'Imād al-Dīn, *Fath*, Massé trans., 342–344, 348–349; Lyons and Jackson, *Saladin*, 339, 341–342.

23. See Ibn Shaddād, *Nawādir*, ed., 199, Richards trans., 191; and Abū Shāma, *Rawdatayn*, 2:193.

24. See Ibn Shaddād, *Nawādir*, ed., 238, Richards trans., 234.

25. See 'Imād al-Dīn, *Fath*, Massé trans., 425–429; and Abū Shāma, *Rawdatayn*, 2:225, trans. *RHC Or.*, 5:103, based on Ibn al-Qādisī (d. 1234), an author well informed about the events in Iraq and Mecca.

8. Conception of Power

1. See M. C. Lyons and D. E. P. Jackson, *Saladin*, 52, based on Ibn Mammātī, 77–78; and al-Qalqashandī, *Subh*, 3:281.

2. Acre in 1179, Tripoli in 1180, and Beirut in 1182.

3. See Lyons and Jackson, *Saladin*, 212.

4. Abū Shāma, *Rawdatayn*, 2:177.

5. See A. M. Eddé, *Principauté ayyoubide d'Alep*, 258, 328.

6. From October 1176 to October 1177, from December 1177 to February 1178, and from January 1181 to March 1182.

7. See R. S. Humphreys, *From Saladin to the Mongols*, 74.

8. Abū Shāma, *Rawdatayn*, 1:243, trans. *Recueils des historiens des croisades. Histoires orientaux*, 4:179.

9. See Ibn Shaddād, *Nawādir*, al-Shayyāl ed., 241, Richards trans., 237.

10. Al-Bundārī, 278.

11. Abū Shāma, *Rawdatayn*, 2:58–59; al-Bundārī, 246–249; Sibṭ Ibn al-Jawzī, 8:380–381.

12. The Koranic expression "by the Fig, and by the Olive" (95:1) supposedly refers to Syria.

13. That remark relies on a play on words: *haram* (pyramid) and *ḥaram* (sacred esplanade).

14. *Ḥubb al-waṭan min al-īmān.* See Ibn Shaddād, *Aʿlāq* (Aleppo), 3; al-Suyūṭī, *al-Durar al-muntathira fī l-aḥādīth al-mustahira*, ed. M. al-Arnaʾūt and M. Qahwajī (Kuwait, 1989), letter h.

15. For example, in the notion of *amor soli naturalis* (love of the native soil) propounded by Humbert of Romans, a Dominican from the thirteenth century.

16. See *Encyclopaedia of Islam*, 2nd ed., "Waṭan" (U. Haarmann).

17. A. S. Ehrenkreutz, *Saladin*, 187. That motif of the city compared to a prostitute is reminiscent of certain Muslim traditions that characterized Constantinople in that way (see D. Cook, *Studies in Muslim Apocalyptic* [Princeton, 2002], 60).

18. The quality of apricots whose kernel *(lawz)* is sweet.

19. Ibn Khallikān, ed., 1:308, Slane trans., 1:286.

20. See Lyons and Jackson, *Saladin*, 150–151, based on Abū Shāma, *Rawdatayn*, 2:17.

21. See Lyons and Jackson, *Saladin*, 181–182.

22. See al-Harawī, *Tadhkira*, Sourdel-Thomine trans., 223.

23. ʿImād al-Dīn, *Fath*, Massé trans., 187–189; see also Ibn Shaddād, *Nawādir*, al-Shayyāl ed., 114, Richards trans., 105–106.

24. Many examples of councils held by Saladin can be found in ʿImād al-Dīn, *Fath*, Massé trans., 170, 345–346, 389–391; Ibn al-Athīr, *Kāmil*, 11:532, 549, 556, Richards trans., 2:320, 332, 337; Ibn Shaddād, *Nawādir*, al-Shayyāl ed., 171, Richards trans., 161.

25. Abū Shama, *Rawdatayn*, 2:47 (line 1), based on Ibn Abī Tayyiʾ. This line is very similar to one Saladin supposedly uttered concerning the Franks, which suggests he was applying the same policy toward his Muslim and his Christian adversaries.

9. Founding a Dynasty

1. See D. Aigle, "Les transformations d'un mythe d'origine. L'exemple de Gengis Khan et de Tamerlan," in *Figures mythiques des mondes musulmans*, ed. D. Aigle, issue of *Revue des mondes musulmans et de la Méditerranée* 89–90 (July 2000): 151–168, esp. 162.

2. See Ibn Khallikān, 2:524–525, 7:140; Abū Shāma, *Rawdatayn*, 1:210.

3. Ibn Khaldūn, *Al-Muqaddima*, Monteil trans., 1:276, Rosenthal trans., 1:284 [translation modified—trans.]. See also *Encyclopaedia of Islam*, 2nd ed. (hereafter cited as *EI 2*), "ʿAṣabiyya" (F. Gabrieli).

4. See R. S. Humphreys, *From Saladin to the Mongols*, 66–75.

5. Ibn Wāsil, *Mufarrij*, 1:174.

6. Rabīʿa died in the last days of 1245 or early in 1246 at more than eighty years old, according to Ibn Khallikān, 4:120. She must therefore have been between five and ten years old in 1170.

7. Sitt al-Shām's husband was named Zayn al-Dīn Ibn Lājīn and their son was Husām al-Dīn Ibn Lājīn. The sources sometimes have a tendency to confuse their given names (ʿUmar in one case, Muhammad in the other). See al-Bundārī, 48.

8. See Abū Shāma, *Rawdatayn*, 2:88, 147, 195, trans. *Recueils des historiens des croisades. Histoires orientaux* (hereafter cited as *RHC Or.*), 4:302, 425; ʿImād al-Dīn, *Fath*, Massé trans., 361.

9. See M. C. Lyons and D. E. P. Jackson, *Saladin*, 38–39.

10. See the biographies of these Ayyubid princes in Ibn Khallikān, 1:255–261 (Ayyūb), 290–292 (Tāj al-Mulūk Būrī), 306–309 (Tūrānshāh), 2:452–453 (Shāhanshāh and his son Farrukhshāh), 456–458 (Taqī al-Dīn ʿUmar), 523–525 (Tughtegin and his son al-Muʿizz Ismāʿīl), 5:74–79 (al-ʿĀdil). See also al-Maqrīzī, *Muqaffā*, 2:378–381 (Ayyūb).

11. Bārīn, Kafartāb, and a few villages in the region of Maʿarrat al-Nuʿmān.

12. On Tūrānshāh, see Lyons and Jackson, *Saladin*, 102, 109–110, 126, 130–131, 136–137, 151; al-Wahrānī, *Manāmāt*, 187–188; al-Bundārī, 162; Ibn al-Athīr, *Kāmil*, 11:444, 451, 469, Richards trans., 2:254, 260, 274; Abū Shāma, *Rawdatayn*, 1:184, 193, 259–260; Ibn Wāsil, *Mufarrij*, 2:48; Ibn Khallikān, 1:307; H. A. R. Gibb, "The Armies of Saladin," 75.

13. See al-Bundārī, 233; Ibn Jubayr, Gaudefroy-Demombynes trans., 54–55, Broadhurst trans., 43.

14. The four sons were Ghāzī, Khadir, Masʿūd, and Yaʿqūb. The marriage of al-Zāhir Ghāzī was ratified in late 1186. See al-Maqrīzī, *Sulūk*, 1, 1:76.

15. A French knight who had taken refuge in Damascus—no doubt the John Gale who appears in the Latin sources—had led Taqī al-Dīn's son to believe that the king of Jerusalem would grant his wish if the son accompanied the knight into Frankish territories. See Abū Shāma, *Rawdatayn*, 1:273, trans. *RHC Or.*, 4:185; al-Bundārī, 130–131; J. Richard, "The Adventure of John Gale," 191–192.

16. Alexandria and Damietta were given to Taqī al-Dīn as *iqtāʿs*, but he was given outright possession of al-Buhayra and Samannud in the Delta, in the region of al-Wāhāt (that is, the great oases located in the Western Desert of Egypt, west of the Nile), Fayyūm, Fuwwa, and two other localities (al-Muzāhamatayn and Hawf Ramsīs).

17. See al-Mansūr, *Midmār*, 155; al-Maqrīzī, *Sulūk* 1, 1:82.

18. See Ibn Wāsil, *Mufarrij*, 2:143; *The Churches and Monasteries of Egypt*, Evetts and Butler ed., 9, trans., 204.

19. Among Nāsir al-Dīn's other possessions were Zalūbiyya, a fortress of lesser importance north of Rahba, and perhaps also Salamiyya, east of the Orontes, between Homs and Hama. Salamiyya is cited by ʿImād al-Dīn in the diploma by which Saladin

granted Nāsir al-Dīn's possessions to the latter's son Shīrkūh after Nāsir al-Dīn's death in 1186 (al-Bundārī, 277). The city also appears, however, on the list of Taqī al-Dīn's possessions (along with Hama) in 1191 (Ibn Wāsil, *Mufarrij*, 2:340, and Ibn Shaddād, *Nawādir*, ed., 208, Richards trans., 201). Perhaps it changed hands between those two dates.

20. See Ibn al-Athīr, *Kāmil*, 11:485, Richards trans., 2:285.

21. See Ibn al-Athīr, *Kāmil*, 11:518, Richards trans., 2:309; al-Khazrajī, folio 12b; Sibt Ibn al-Jawzī, 8:86, 388; al-Bundārī, 277; Lyons and Jackson, *Saladin*, 238.

22. See al-Maqrīzī, *Sulūk*, 1, 1:85.

23. The story is first reported in Ibn al-Athīr, *Kāmil*, 11:525, Richards trans., 2:314, repeated by Ibn al-ʿAdīm, *Zubda*, 3:85 (who rightly corrects "al-ʿAzīz is in Egypt" to "al-Afdal is in Egypt"), and Ibn Wāsil, *Mufarrij*, 2:183.

24. On the reorganization of 1186, see also al-Bundārī, 278–281; Lyons and Jackson, *Saladin*, 244–246; Humphreys, *From Saladin to the Mongols*, 58–60.

25. That is, Hama, Salamiyya, Maʿarrat al-Nuʿmān, Apamea, Kafartāb, Manbij, and Qalʿat Najm.

26. Namely, Kerak, Shawbak, al-Salt opposite Jericho, and the agricultural district of al-Balqāʾ.

27. Balātunus.

28. Harrān, Samosata, Edessa, and al-Muwazzar. On Gökbörī, see Ibn Khallikān, 4:113–121; *EI* 2, "Begteginids" (C. Cahen).

29. On Taqī al-Dīn, see the chronicle written by his son al-Mansūr (d. 1220), *Midmār al-haqāʾiq wa sirr al-khalāʾiq* (Cairo, 1968); *EI* 2, "al-Mansūr" (A. Hartmann); Lyons and Jackson, *Saladin* (index).

30. He kept Hama, Salamiyya, Maʿarrat al-Nuʿmān, Apamea, Kafartāb, Manbij, and Qalʿat Najm. See Ibn Shaddād, *Nawādir*, ed., 207–208, Richards trans., 199–201; Lyons and Jackson, *Saladin*, 347–348; Humphreys, *From Saladin to the Mongols*, 65.

10. The Support of the Elites

1. See al-Subkī, 6:41–42, 397–398; Ibn Khallikān, 3:435.

2. See al-Bundārī, 205; al-Mansūr, *Midmār*, 108–109.

3. See al-Maqrīzī, *Sulūk*, 1, 1:63; al-Bundārī, 686–687; Y. Frenkel, "Political and Social Aspects," 16.

4. Ibn al-Athīr, *Kāmil*, 12:25, Richards trans., 2:357–358.

5. Abū Shāma (*Rawdatayn*, 2:7) kept a record of the letters Saladin and al-Fādil exchanged on that occasion.

6. Al-Fādil, *Dīwān al-Qādī al-Fādil*, ed. A. Badawī and I. al-Ibyārī (Cairo, 1961).

7. That was the belief, in any case, of the Coptic author of the *History of the Patriarchs of the Egyptian Church* (Khater and Burmester ed., vol. 3, ed., 64, trans., 107).

8. See Ibn 'Unayn, *Dīwān*, 182, 184, 189–190.

9. Al-Fādil, *Dīwān*, 341.

10. 'Imād al-Dīn, *Fath*, Massé trans., 280; see also al-Bundārī, 84–85.

11. See Abū Shāma, *Rawdatayn*, 1:210; D. S. Richards, "'Imād al-Dīn al-Isfahānī Administrator, Litterateur and Historian," in *Crusaders and Muslims in Twelfth Century Syria*, ed. M. Shatzmiller (Leiden, 1993), 133–146.

12. 'Imād al-Dīn, *Fath*, Massé trans., 10 (see also 327).

13. See M. C. Lyons and D. E. P. Jackson, *Saladin*, 122, 294, 305.

14. Ibn Abī Usaybi'a, 687, and *Recueils des historiens des croisades. Histoires orientaux*, 3:435–436 (hereafter cited as *RHC Or.*); see also al-Maqrīzī, *Khitat*, 2:367, Sayyid ed., 4, 2:463–465; Lyons and Jackson, *Saladin*, 56.

15. Quoted in al-Bundārī, 128.

16. See 'Imād al-Dīn, *Fath*, Massé trans., 365; Abū Shāma, *Rawdatayn*, 2:195; Sibt Ibn al-Jawzī, 8:413; Ibn Shaddād, *A'lāq* (Damascus), 144.

17. Not to be confused with Sharaf al-Dīn Qarāqūsh al-Armanī, the mamluk of Saladin's nephew Taqī al-Dīn 'Umar, who was given the task of conquering Tripolitana. See Ibn Khallikān, 4:91–92; 'Imād al-Dīn, *Fath*, Massé trans., 108, 278, 401; Ibn Shaddād, *Nawādir* (index: "Bahā' al-Dīn Qarāqūsh"); *Répertoire chronologique d'épigraphie arabe*, vol. 9, nos. 123–124; *Encyclopaedia of Islam*, 2nd ed., "Karākūsh" (M. Sobernheim).

18. 'Imād al-Dīn, *Fath*, Massé trans., 108.

19. Ten to thirty thousand dinars, according to Ibn Khallikān and Bar Hebraeus (340). Ibn Shaddād (*Nawādir*, al-Shayyāl ed., 240, Richards trans., 236) puts forward the figure of eighty thousand (dinars?).

20. See al Maqrīzī, *Sulūk*, I, 1:146.

21. See Ibn Mammātī, *Kitāb al-fāshūsh fī ahkām Qarāqūsh*, ed. and trans. with two other satires of the same kind by P. Casanova as "Karakoûch," *Mémoires publiés par les membres de la mission archéologique française du Caire* 6 (1892): 415–491, esp. 468–491.

22. See Ibn al-Athīr, *Kāmil*, 11:456, Richards trans., 2:265; no doubt this is the same as the "Ivelinus" mentioned by William of Tyre in 1177 (Huygens ed., 988–989 [21.20 (21)], Babcock and Krey trans., 2:428) as being at the head of Saladin's army, whom William calls a converted Armenian, a valorous warrior ready for every adventure.

23. See Ibn al-Athīr, *Kāmil*, 11:486, Richards trans., 2:286; Lyons and Jackson, *Saladin*, 233. His brother Sayf al-Dīn Mahmūd was sent by Saladin to besiege Kawkab in December 1187. But he was caught sleeping and killed by the Franks ('Imād al-Dīn, *Fath*, Massé trans., 82).

24. See 'Imād al-Dīn, *Fath*, Massé trans., 63, 246, 375, 399; Ibn Shaddād, *Nawādir*, al-Shayyāl ed., 206, 239–240, Richards trans., 199, 236–237 (the population of Nablus does not seem to have had a high opinion of his administration); Abū Shāma,

Rawdatayn, 2:209; Sibt Ibn al-Jawzī, 8:420; Ibn al-Furāt, *Ta'rīkh,* 4:2, 98; Lyons and Jackson, *Saladin,* 277, 323, 360. Then there was Sārim al-Dīn Qāymāz, one of Ayyūb's former Turkish mamluks. He faithfully served Saladin, who entrusted to him the governorship of Tiberias, then the siege of the fortress of Kawkab. He also commanded several attacks against the Frankish army during the siege of Acre and the battles that followed ('Imād al-Dīn, *Fath,* Massé trans., index); Ibn Shaddād, *Nawādir,* al-Shayyāl ed., 189, Richards trans., 181; Lyons and Jackson, *Saladin* (index).

25. See Ibn Khallikān, 3:497, Slane trans., 2:430–431.

26. See al-Maqrīzī, *Itti'āz,* 3:318; Abū Shāma, *Rawdatayn,* 1:273; Ibn Abi Usaybi'a, 588; C. Cahen, "Indigènes et croisés. Quelques mots à propos d'un médecin d'Amaury et de Saladin," *Syria* 15 (1934): 351–360, repr. in C. Cahen, *Turcobyzantina et Oriens christianus* (London, 1974); Lyons and Jackson, *Saladin,* 232, 276.

27. See al-Bundārī, 72, 108; Abū Shāma, *Rawdatayn,* 1:262–263; Ibn Wāsil, *Mufarrij,* 2:49–50; Lyons and Jackson, *Saladin,* 10, 84.

28. This was Jamāl al-Dīn Ibn al-Harastānī, a very respected Shafite personality and the future chief qādī of Damascus. See Abū Shāma, *Rawdatayn,* 2:2 (lines 12ff.); 'Imād al-Dīn, *Fath,* Massé trans., 59; al-Mansūr, *Midmār,* 83–84; Ibn Khallikān, 3:54; Lyons and Jackson, *Saladin,* 146, 227; L. Pouzet, *Damas au VIIe/XIIIe siècle,* 127–128.

29. Muhyī al-Dīn Ibn al-Zakī, who was already chief qādī of Aleppo, presided over the supreme judiciary in Damascus from 1192 to 1202. See al-Bundārī, 113; Ibn Khallikān, 4:229–237; Ibn al-'Imād, *Shadharāt,* 4:337; H. Laoust, *Les schismes dans l'Islam* (Paris, 1965), 228–229; Pouzet, *Damas au VIIe/XIIIe siècle,* 121; A. M. Eddé, *Principauté ayyoubide d'Alep,* 30–51.

30. The position of chief qādī was conferred on Ibn al-Zakī, who continued to reside in Damascus and named one of his cousins, Zayn al-Dīn Ibn al-Bāniyāsī, as surrogate (Abū Shāma, *Rawdatayn,* 2:47, trans. *RHC Or.,* 4:238; Ibn al-'Adīm, *Zubda,* 3:72, 132; Ibn Wāsil, *Mufarrij,* 3:133), while the position of preacher was entrusted to Sa'īd Ibn Hāshim, a member of a large Aleppine family that produced at least six preachers in the twelfth and thirteenth centuries. Another very influential Shafite family, the Banū l-'Ajamī, was also treated with a great deal of respect. Saladin entrusted to members of that family the directorship of the *waqfs* for the Great Mosque and ratified their control of the oldest Shafite madrasa of Aleppo, known as the glass-workers' madrasa.

31. Al-Hallāwiyya madrasa, founded by Nūr al-Dīn. See Eddé, *Principauté ayyoubide d'Alep,* 372–373.

32. Among the eastern ulemas who had moved to Egypt in Saladin's wake was, for example, Qādī Sadr al-Dīn Ibn Durbās, a Kurd from the Mosul region (al-Dhahabī, *Siyar,* 21:474). The two other Shafite leaders, al-Khubūshānī and Shihāb al-Dīn al-Tūsī, were from Iran. The former, born in a locality in the Nishapur region, moved to Egypt in 1169–1170, and the latter, from Tūs, east of Iran, had passed

through Baghdad and Mecca before settling in Cairo in 1183–1184 (Abū Shāma, *Tarājim*, 18–19; Ibn Khallikān, 4:224; Ibn al-'Imād, *Shadharāt*, 6:534–535). Similarly, Majd al-Dīn Muhammad al-Khutanī, whom Saladin named instructor in the Suyū-fiyya madrasa, was a Hanafite jurist from Transoxiana, who, having traveled a great deal between Samarkand, Damascus, and Mecca, ultimately settled in Egypt under Saladin's reign. Saladin had great respect for him, and it was even said that it was in response to his demands that he eliminated the illegal taxes (Ibn Abī l-Wafā' al-Qurashī, 2:125–126; al-Maqrīzī, *Muqaffā*, 7:91–92; Y. Frenkel, "Political and Social Aspects," 11).

33. See Lyons and Jackson, *Saladin*, 41.
34. See Abū Shāma, *Rawdatayn*, 2:5, quoted in Lyons and Jackson, *Saladin*, 68.
35. See Sibt Ibn al-Jawzī, 8:474; al-Maqrīzī, *Khitat*, 2:85–86, Sayyid ed., 3:283–285; Y. Lev, *Charity, Endowments and Charitable Institutions*, 33.
36. See 'Imād al-Dīn, *Fath*, Massé trans., 77, 84, 316, 368, 395; Ibn Shaddād, *Nawādir*, al-Shayyāl ed., 240, Richards trans., 237; Ibn Kathīr, *Bidāya*, 8:520–521; Lyons and Jackson, *Saladin*, 356; R. S. Humphreys, *From Saladin to the Mongols*, 78–79, 100–101.
37. Shayzar, Bu Qubays, and, in 1188, Bikisrā'īl and probably Jabala.
38. See 'Imād al-Dīn, *Fath*, Massé trans., 350; Abū Shāma, *Rawdatayn*, 2:46, trans. *RHC Or.*, 4:237, 358; Lyons and Jackson, *Saladin*, 343; Eddé, *Principauté ayyoubide d'Alep*, 41, 265.
39. See Ibn Shaddād, *Nawādir*, al-Shayyāl ed., 178, Richards trans., 169; 'Imād al-Dīn, *Fath*, Massé trans., 332, 345, 350; Lyons and Jackson, *Saladin*, 164; Eddé, *Principauté ayyoubide d'Alep*, 42, 267.
40. He received the fortresses of Tall Bāshir, Tall Khālid, and Burj al-Rasās; see Ibn Shaddād, *Nawādir*, al-Shayyāl ed., 227, 232, Richards trans., 223, 238; 'Imād al-Dīn, *Fath*, Massé trans., 75–76; Lyons and Jackson, *Saladin*, 359–360; Eddé, *Principauté ayyoubide d'Alep*, 164.
41. See al-Bundārī, 254; Ibn Khallikān, 4:113–121; Lyons and Jackson, *Saladin*, 174, 224–226.
42. Quoted in Lyons and Jackson, *Saladin*, 224.
43. See 'Imād al-Dīn, *Fath*, Massé trans., 121, 261; al-Bundārī, 255; Ibn al-Athīr, *Kāmil*, 11:511, Richards trans., 2:304; Ibn Khallikān, 4:114; Lyons and Jackson, *Saladin*, 256, 300.
44. Bārīn, Kafartāb, and villages in the region of Ma'arrat al-Nu'mān.
45. See Ibn al-'Imād, *Shadharāt*, 6:454; Lyons and Jackson, *Saladin*, 132–133, 284.
46. Ibn Shaddād, *Nawādir*, al-Shayyāl ed., 207–209, Richards trans., 200–202.

11. The Elaboration of an Image

1. See A. Borrut, "Entre tradition et histoire: Genèse et diffusion de l'image de 'Umar II," in *Regards croisés sur le Moyen Âge arabe. Mélanges à la mémoire de Louis Pouzet s.j. (1928–2002),* ed. A. M. Eddé and E. Gannagé (Beirut, 2005), 329–378, esp. 336–339.

2. Ibn al-Athīr, *Kāmil,* 1:7, trans. A. M. Eddé and F. Micheau, in *L'Orient au temps des croisades,* 302.

3. See 'Imād al-Dīn, *Fath,* Massé trans., 402, 407, 409, 422, 426, 434; Abū Shāma, *Rawdatayn,* 2:215–216, trans. *Recueils des historiens des croisades. Histoires orientaux,* 5:98–101 (hereafter cited as *RHC Or.*).

4. See Ibn Abī Tayyi', in Abū Shāma, *Rawdatayn,* 2:85.

5. See the example of the Egyptian saint al-Badawī, heir to Moses, Jesus, and Muhammad, in C. Mayeur-Jaouen, *Al-Sayyid al-Badawī. Un grand saint de l'islam égytien* (Cairo, 1994), 519–524.

6. See *Répertoire chronologique d'épigraphie arabe,* 9, no. 3423 (hereafter cited as *RCEA*).

7. See *Encyclopaedia of Islam,* 2nd ed. (hereafter cited as *EI* 2), "Naṣīhat al-mulūk" (C. E. Bosworth).

8. These included a brief "Essay Relating to the Ruses of War," likely dedicated by its Persian author, al-Harāwī, to Saladin or to his son al-Zāhir Ghāzī. It occupies an intermediate place in Arabic literature of that time, between the Mirror for Princes and the treatise on military strategy. See J. Sourdel-Thomine, "Les conseils du šayḫ al-Harawī à un prince ayyubide," *Bulletin d'études orientales* 17 (1961–1962): 205–266.

9. See *The Sea of Precious Virtues (Baḥr al-Fawā'id): A Medieval Islamic Mirror for Princes.*

10. See *Ghazālī's Book of Counsel for Kings,* trans. F. R. C. Bagley (Oxford, 1964), 6–30, 45, 59; *The Sea of Precious Virtues,* 82–83.

11. See Ibn Shaddād, *Nawādir,* al-Shayyāl ed., 6–34, Richards trans., 17–38.

12. He held his sessions on Mondays and Thursdays, in keeping with an ancient Palestinian custom adopted by Islamic culture and also followed by the Jews. These days were traditionally market days. The peasants brought in their products and took the opportunity to settle legal matters while in town (S. D. F. Goitein, *A Mediterranean Society,* 2:342–343); Ibn Shaddād, *Nawādir,* al-Shayyāl ed., 13–16, Richards trans., 22–25; 'Imād al-Dīn, *Fath,* Massé trans., 112; Ibn Wāsil, *Mufarrij,* 2:36.

13. See E. Geoffroy, *Jihad et contemplation: Vie et enseignement d'un soufi au temps des croisades* (Paris, 1997), 26; and P. M. Holt, "The Sultan as Ideal Ruler," 127. See also Abū Shāma, *Rawdatayn,* 1:4 (lines 1–2), trans. *RHC Or.,* 4:9–10.

14. Abū Shāma, *Rawdatayn,* 1:14–15, trans. *RHC Or.,* 4:31–35; Ibn Shaddād, *Nawādir,* al-Shayyāl ed., 13–16, Richards trans., 22–25.

15. See *Ghazālī's Book of Counsel for Kings,* Bagley trans., 102.

16. Ibn Jubayr, Gaudefroy-Demombynes trans., 347–348, Broadhurst trans., 311 [translation modified—trans.].

17. See Plutarch, "Alexander," 39.1, in *Plutarch's Lives of Illustrious Men*, trans. J. Dryden, J. Langhorne, and W. Langhorne (Philadelphia, n.d. [1932]), 829.

18. Ibn Shaddād, *Nawādir*, al-Shayyāl ed., 17, Richards trans., 25.

19. See William of Tyre, Huygens ed., 968 (21.6), Babcock and Krey trans., 2:405; Lyons and Jackson, *Saladin*, 83.

20. Ibn Shaddād, *Nawādir*, al-Shayyāl ed., 17–18, Richards trans., 25–26; 'Imād al-Dīn, *Fath*, Massé trans., 409, 429; Ibn Abī Usaybi'a, 652; Ibn Jubayr, Gaudefroy-Demombynes trans., 43–44, Broadhurst trans., 32.

21. See Abū Shāma, *Rawdatayn*, 2:217.

22. See Bar Hebraeus, Budge trans., 342.

23. More than thirty inscriptions in Saladin's name have been identified. See G. Wiet, "Les inscriptions de Saladin," *Syria* 3 (1922): 307–328; *RCEA*, 9, nos. 3297, 3334, 3335, 3343, 3344, 3359, 3367, 3368, 3374, 3380, 3386–3394, 3399, 3402, 3420–3423, 3438, 3445, 3449, 3450, 3453, and 3471; J. M. Mouton, "Autour des inscriptions de la forteresse de Ṣadr," 29–57; J. M. Mouton, "Addendum," *Annales islamologiques* 30 (1996): 71–77; J. M. Mouton and S. S. 'Abd al-Malik, "La forteresse de l'île de Graye," 75–90. See also Saladin's titulature in D. Sourdel and J. Sourdel-Thomine, *Certificats de pèlerinage*, 141. For coins, see P. Balog, *Coinage*, 58–103.

24. Or, in Arabic, in the same order: *Sultān al-Islām wa l-muslimīn, al-mu'ayyad, al-mansūr, al-mujāhid, al-murābit, jāmi' kalimat al-īmān, qāmi' 'abadat al-sulbān, khalīl amīr al-mu'minīn, muhyī dawlat amīr al-mu'minīn, sāhib al-'izz wa l-tamkīn wa l-nasr al-mubīn, munqidh al-Bayt al-muqaddas min aydī al-mushrikīn, khādim al-Haramayn al-sharīfayn.* See Wiet, "Les inscriptions de Saladin," 307–328; Ibn Shaddād, *Nawādir*, al-Shayyāl ed., 3, Richards trans., 13.

25. See *Ghazālī's Book of Counsel for Kings*, Bagley trans., 45.

26. 'Imād al-Dīn, *Fath*, Massé trans., 140.

27. Al-Qalqashandī, *Subh*, 10:137–138.

28. The gold and silver coins minted by Saladin in Cairo and Alexandria between the years 567 and 569 A.H. (1171–1174 C.E.) do not bear his name but rather the names of Nūr al-Dīn and Caliph al-Mustadī' (P. Balog, *Coinage*, 35–60). In Damascus in 570/1174–1175, Saladin had copper coins struck in his name and in the name of al-Sālih Ismā'īl (P. Balog, 60–61). The minting of gold coinage was reserved for Egypt (Cairo, Misr, Alexandria) between 570 and 575/1174 and 1179, with, arranged in two circles, the words "Muhammad, messenger of God 'who has sent forth His apostle with guidance and the true Faith to make it triumphant over all religions, though the idolaters abhor it' [Koran 9:33 and 61:9]. May God bless him and his family."

29. See Abū Shāma, *Rawdatayn*, 1:130 (line 13); William of Tyre, Huygens ed., 870 (19.5), 890 (19.20), Babcock and Krey trans., 2:302, 323.

30. See N. Elisséeff, "La titulature de Nūr al-Dīn d'après ses inscriptions," *Bulletin d'études orientales* 14 (1952–1954): 155–196. The title "sultan of Islam and of the

Muslims," already borne by Nūr al-Dīn, appears in Saladin's titulature in 1180 (see *RCEA*, 9, no. 3359). The title "sultan of the armies" was also part of the Fatimid titulature granted to Shīrkūh (Ibn Wāsil, *Mufarrij*, 2:443).

31. The complete inscription is: "Our master the sultan [*mawlāna al-sultān*], the king [*al-malik*], the assisted [*al-mu'ayyad*], the rescued [of God] [*al-mansūr*], the warrior in the holy war [*al-mujāhid*], Abū l-Muzaffar Yūsuf, associate [*qasīm*] of the emir of believers."

32. In addition, the title "associate [*qasīm*] of the emir of believers," which suggests that its holder shared the caliph's power and authority, was borne by Seljuk sultans but never by Ayyubid rulers, who were merely the "friends [*khalīl*] of the emir of believers."

33. See *RCEA*, 9, nos. 3386–3394; Wiet, "Les inscriptions de Saladin," 319–328; E. Baer, *Metalwork in Medieval Islamic Art* (New York, 1983), 211.

34. That title, however, was inscribed on Ayyubid coins only after the caliph had officially bestowed it, in 1245, on the last Ayyubid ruler, al-Sālih Ayyūb (r. 1240–1249). See A. M. Eddé, *Principauté ayyoubide d'Alep*, 197.

35. See al-Subkī, *Tabaqāt*, 5:315.

36. See, for example, the titulature of the Artukids of Mayyāfāriqīn (*RCEA*, 9, no. 3351) or of Diyārbakīr (*RCEA*, 9, no. 3383). Even in the eleventh century, Mahmūd ibn Nasr received from the caliph a much lengthier titulature: *al-amīr al-ajall, husām al-dawla al-'abbāsiyya, za'īm juyūshihā al-shāmiyya, tāj al-mulūk, nāsir al-dīn, sharaf al-umma, dhu l-hasabayn, khalīsat al-mu'minīn*. See T. Bianquis, *Damas et la Syrie sous la domination fatimide (359–468/969–1076)*, 2 vols. (Damascus, 1986–1989), 591.

37. See *EI* 2, "Ḳiṣaṣ al-anbiyā'" (T. Nagel).

38. See Van Reeth, "La barque de l'Imām aš-Šāfiʿī," 256–264.

39. See al-Muqaddasī, *Ahsan at-taqāsīm fī ma'rifat al-aqālīm (The Best Distribution for Knowledge of the Provinces)*, partial translation in A. Miquel (Damascus, 1963), 146n. 7, 165n. 90, 177n. 132; al-Harāwī, *Kitāb al-ishārāt*, Sourdel-Thomine ed., ed., 10, 21, 25, 27, 32, trans., 24, 53, 64, 66, 75; A. Borrut, "La Syrie de Salomon: L'appropriation du mythe salomonien dans les sources arabes," *Pallas* 63 (2003): 107–120.

40. See *EI* 2, "Sulaymān b. Dāwūd" (J. Walker-[P. Fenton]).

41. See P. Balog, *Coinage*, 89–92, 99.

42. Koran 27:22–44.

43. See J. M. Mouton, *Le Sinaï médiéval*, 85–86.

44. See al-Qalqashandī, *Subh*, 6:511.

45. Words attributed to Saladin by 'Imād al-Dīn in Abū Shāma, *Rawdatayn* 2:93–94, trans. *RHC Or.*, 4:324. See also 'Imād al-Dīn, *Fath*, Massé trans., 58.

46. Later, in the fourteenth century, the historian Ibn Khaldūn would make the Umayyads Solomon's direct heirs to highlight their art of governance. See A. Borrut, "Entre mémoire et pouvoir: L'espace syrien sous les derniers Omeyyades et les

premiers Abbassides (v. 72–193/692–809)," doctoral diss., Université de Paris I (Paris, 2007), 195.

47. See H. Möhring," Zwischen Joseph-Legende und Mahdi-Erwartung," 177–225.

48. See al-Harawī, *Kitāb al-isharāt*, Sourdel-Thomine ed., ed., 24, trans., 61.

49. See Ibn Shaddād, *Nawādir*, al-Shayyāl ed., 44, Richards trans., 47.

50. Bar Hebraeus, Budge trans., 300.

51. Quoted in Möhring, "Zwischen Joseph-Legende und Mahdi-Erwartung," 187. In Koran 12:31, the women who gather around Potiphar's wife are so amazed by Joseph's beauty that they forget they are holding knives and cut their hands. See also the lines of the Yemenite poet 'Umāra comparing Saladin to Joseph the Truthful *(al-Siddīq)* at a time when the poet was still hoping to gain the sultan's favor (H. Derenbourg, *Oumara du Yémen, sa vie et son oeuvre* [Paris, 1904], 380–381).

52. Abū Shāma, *Rawdatayn*, 2:215, trans. *RHC Or.,* 5:97.

53. Koran 12:6, 22, 24, 38, 90.

54. Abū Shāma, *Rawdatayn*, 2:86–87, trans. *RHC Or.,* 4:297; see also M. C. Lyons and D. E. P. Jackson, *Saladin*, 267.

55. See Ibn al-Athīr, *Kāmil*, 11:539–540, Richards trans., 2:325.

56. See Lyons and Jackson, *Saladin*, 275.

57. See Abū Shāma, *Rawdatayn*, 2:115.

58. 'Imād al-Dīn, *Fath*, Massé trans., 61–62.

59. See Ibn Shaddād, *Nawādir*, al-Shayyāl ed., 7, Richards trans., 25.

60. 'Imād al-Dīn in Abū Shāma, *Rawdatayn*, 2:138.

61. Ibn al-Athīr, *Al-Bāhir*, 167, 173.

62. See Ibn Khallikān, 3:435; Yāqūt, *Udabā'*, 19:316.

63. See Abu Shama, *Rawdatayn*, 1:257 (lines 32ff.); Lyons and Jackson, *Saladin*, 106.

64. See al-Bundārī, 156; Lyons and Jackson, *Saladin*, 132.

65. Lyons and Jackson, *Saladin*, 228.

66. Ibn al-Athīr, *Kāmil*, 11:430, Richards trans., 2:243; Abū Shāma, *Rawdatayn*, 1:258; al-Bundārī, 101.

67. See Ibn al-Athīr, *Kāmil*, 11:543, 555–556, Richards trans., 2:328, 337–338.

68. See Sibt Ibn al-Jawzī, 8:398.

69. See 'Imād al-Dīn, *Fath*, Massé trans., 333–335.

70. 'Imād al-Dīn, *Fath*, Massé trans., 346.

71. 'Imād al-Dīn, *Fath*, Massé trans., 385.

72. See 'Imād al-Dīn, *Fath*, Massé trans., 139; Abū Shāma, *Rawdatayn*, 2:128, trans. *RHC Or.,* 4:361–362.

73. See Ibn Shaddād, *Nawādir*, al-Shayyāl ed., 168, Richards trans., 159; Lyons and Jackson, *Saladin*, 346.

74. See Ibn al-Athīr, *Kāmil*, 12:71, Richards trans., 2:391; 'Imād al-Dīn, *Fath*, Massé trans., 346.

75. See Ibn Shaddād, *Nawādir*, al-Shayyāl ed., 224–229, Richards trans., 220–225; Ibn al-Athīr, *Kāmil*, 12:85, Richards trans., 2:401; Lyons and Jackson, *Saladin*, 356–358.

12. Image and Propaganda

1. Jerusalem, that is. Abū Shāma, *Rawdatayn*, 1:243, trans. *Recueils des historiens des croisades. Historiens orientaux*, 4:180 (hereafter cited as *RHC Or.*).

2. With titles such as "subjugator of the slaves of the cross," "servant of the temple sanctified by God, its guardian against the infidel rebels," and, after the retaking of Jerusalem, "rescuer of Jerusalem from the hands of the infidels." See *Répertoire chronologique d'épigraphie arabe*, nos. 3559, 3464 (hereafter cited as *RCEA*); G. Wiet, "Inscriptions de Saladin," 315; E. Sivan, *L'Islam et la croisade*, 106–108.

3. Thus implying that the condition set by the caliph, namely, that the governance of Aleppo be left to al-Sālih, Nūr al-Dīn's son, was null and void once al-Sālih was dead. See M. C. Lyons and D. E. P. Jackson, *Saladin*, 162–163.

4. See Lyons and Jackson, *Saladin*, 192; Abū Shāma, *Rawdatayn*, 2:49.

5. See P. M. Holt, "The Presentation of Qalāwūn by Shāfiʿ ibn ʿAlī," in *The Islamic World from Classical to Modern Times*, ed. C. E. Bosworth et al. (Princeton, 1989), 141–150.

6. Abū Shāma, *Rawdatayn*, 2:49, quoted in Sivan, *L'Islam et la croisade*, 104.

7. Ibn al-Athīr, *Kāmil*, 11:532, Richards trans., 2:320, quoted in Sivan, *L'Islam et la croisade*, 105.

8. Ibn Shaddād, *Nawādir*, al-Shayyāl ed., 21, Richards trans., 28; see also F. Gabrieli, *Chroniques arabes des croisades*, 128; C. Hillenbrand, *The Crusades*, 183–186.

9. Quoted in Sivan, *L'Islam et la croisade*, 109.

10. See Ibn Shaddād, *Nawādir*, al-Shayyāl ed., 21–22, Richards trans., 28–29.

11. Abū Shāma, *Rawdatayn*, ed. and trans. *RHC Or.*, 4:363.

12. See Abū Shāma, *Rawdatayn*, ed. and trans. *RHC Or.*, 4:390.

13. See al-Bundārī, 132 (after the defeat of Ramla). That same idea dominates the autobiography of Usāma Ibn Munqidh: whether in success or failure, the will of God is always expressed.

14. ʿImād al-Dīn, *Fath*, Massé trans., 59.

15. ʿImād al-Dīn, *Fath*, Massé trans., 7, 9.

16. Ibn Shaddād, *Nawādir*, al-Shayyāl ed., 167, Richards trans., 157.

17. See Ibn Shaddād, *Nawādir*, al-Shayyāl ed., 8, Richards trans., 19.

18. This theme of the import of Friday for the outcome of a battle was not specific to Saladin. See C. Hillenbrand, *Turkish Myth and Muslim Symbol: The Battle of Manzikert* (Edinburgh, 2007), 121–122.

19. Ibn Shaddād, *Nawādir*, al-Shayyāl ed., 92, Richards trans., 85–86; see also ed., 82, trans., 77. In reality, the date of the Prophet's ascent has been the object of a great

deal of controversy, and it is the night of the 16th day of Rajab (rather than the 26th) that is generally accepted. See Abū Shāma, *Rawdatayn*, 2:93; *Encyclopaedia of Islam*, 2nd ed. (hereafter cited as *EI* 2), "Miʿrādj" (J. E. Bencheikh).

20. See Ibn Shaddād, *Nawādir*, al-Shayyāl ed., 171, Richards trans., 162.

21. P. Lory, *Le rêve et ses interprétations en Islam* (Paris, 2003), 7.

22. See *EI* 2, "Ruʾyā" (T. Fahd and H. Daiber).

23. See A. Guillaume, *Prophecy and Divination among the Hebrews and Other Semites* (London, 1938).

24. In the Sunni Muslim tradition, Jesus will return to earth at the end of time to kill Dajjāl, the Antichrist, a figure endowed with miraculous powers who will appear on earth to impose the reign of injustice. Jesus will then go to Jerusalem to pray in accordance with the Muslim ritual, will kill the pigs, break the crosses, destroy the churches and synagogues, and kill the Christians who do not want to believe in him. He will stay for forty days, during which time he will impose the reign of justice. Then he will die, to be followed by the Mahdi. See *EI* 2, "ʿĪsā" (G. C. Anawati) and "Dadjdjāl" (A. Abel).

25. Abū Shāma, *Rawdatayn*, 2:85, trans. revised based on *RHC Or.*, 4:292.

26. Quoted in Abū Shāma, *Rawdatayn*, 2:104, trans. *RHC Or.*, 4:337.

27. The doctor's name was Abū Sulaymān Dāʾūd. The year 1270 was when Ibn Abī Usaybiʿa died: he said that the family still enjoyed that privilege in his time (588); H. Möhring, "Zwischen Joseph-Legende und Mahdi-Erwartung," 194.

28. [Translation modified. In French translations of the Koran, *al-Rūm* is generally translated as "Romains" ("Romans"); in the Dawood translation, it is translated as "Greeks" (i.e., Byzantines).—trans.]

29. Muhyī al-Dīn Ibn al-Zakī and Majd al-Dīn Ibn Jahbal. See Abū Shāma, *Rawdatayn*, 2:45, 113.

30. See ʿImād al-Dīn in Abū Shāma, *Rawdatayn*, 2:72; and al-Bundārī, 283. Other predictions of Saladin's victories are found in Abū Shāma, *Rawdatayn*, 2:177, line 13 (in a dream, al-Fāḍil sees the defeat of the German Crusade outside the fortress of Kawkab and announces it to Saladin); Ibn al-ʿAdīm, *Bughya*, 8:3599 (the ascetic Rabīʿ al-Mārdīnī predicts the taking of Jerusalem to a pilgrim on his way to Mecca, a year before it occurred); al-Bundārī, 226 (ʿImād al-Dīn composes verses to ask Saladin for a female slave taken prisoner in 1176–1177, and ends with his hope that he will soon be able to lay claim to women prisoners from Jerusalem).

31. See L. Pouzet, *Damas au VIIe/XIIIe siècle*, 372–377.

32. *Itinerarium*, Mayer ed. (IP1), 263, Nicholson trans., 37.

33. ʿImād al-Dīn, *Fath*, Massé trans., 178 and 290. ʿImād al-Dīn also tells the story of Philip Augustus's ash-gray falcon, which escaped from the king after his arrival in Acre in 1191 and landed on the city's rampart. It was then given to Saladin.

34. See al-Qalqashandī, *Subh*, 10:143.

35. 'Imād al-Dīn, *Fath*, Massé trans., 6; see also Abū Shāma, *Rawdatayn*, 2:89, trans. *RHC Or.*, 4:304.

36. See Abū Shāma, *Rawdatayn*, 1:4 (line 1), trans. *RHC Or.*, 4:9–10.

37. See Mujīr al-Dīn, *al-Uns al-jalīl*, 1:341.

38. Abū Shāma, *Rawdatayn*, 2:65; al-Bundārī, 269. In the fourteenth century, the great writer al-Subkī (*Tabaqāt*, 5:315) also claimed that only four Muslim leaders were worthy of being compared to the Umayyad caliph 'Umar ibn 'Abd al-'Azīz for their virtues and good governance: the Ghaznavid sultan Mahmūd ibn Sebüktegin; the Seljuk vizier Nizām al-Mulk; Nūr al-Dīn; and Saladin, conqueror of Jerusalem.

39. See Sivan, *L'Islam et la croisade*, 116–119; Hillenbrand, *The Crusades*, 188–195.

40. Quoted in Abū Shāma, *Rawdatayn*, 1:269; Sivan, *L'Islam et la croisade*, 115.

41. See the examples of letters and sermons in 'Imād al-Dīn, *Fath*, Massé trans., 53–54, 59–61, 92–101; Yāqūt, *Udabā'*, 19:20; al-Qalqashandī, *Subh*, 6:496–504, 7:282–289; Abū Shāma, *Rawdatayn*, 2:96ff.

42. See Abū Shāma, *Rawdatayn*, 2:112. That *minbar* remained in al-Aqsā Mosque until 1969, at which time it was destroyed by a fanatical Australian. But photographs of it were preserved, on the basis of which an exact copy was made in Jordan. It was installed in al-Aqsā Mosque in January 2007. See Hillenbrand, *The Crusades*, 151–160.

43. 'Imād al-Dīn, *Fath*, Massé trans., 48, 60, 98, 367; see also Ibn Wāsil, *Mufarrij*, 3:337.

44. See H. Busse, "Jerusalem and Mecca, the Temple and the Kaaba: An Account of Their Interrelation in Islamic Times," in *The Holy Land in History and Thought*, ed. M. Sharon (Leiden, 1988), 236–246.

45. See al-Harawī, *Kitāb al-ishārāt*, Sourdel-Thomine ed., ed., 27, trans., 67; Ibn Shaddād, *A'lāq* (Damascus), 287.

46. See al-Qalqashandī, *Subh*, 10:142–143.

47. These three titles attributed to Jerusalem figured in the *khutba* pronounced in Jerusalem in 1187. See Abū Shāma, *Rawdatayn*, 2:110; Ibn Shaddād, *A'lāq* (Lebanon, Palestine, Jordan), 211–220; Ibn Khallikān, 4:232, Slane trans., 2:637.

48. See the chapters that Muslim geographers have devoted to Jerusalem since the tenth century: Ibn al-Faqīh al-Hamadhānī, *Mukhtasar kitāb al-buldān*, ed. M. J. De Goeje, 2nd ed. (Leiden, 1967), 93–102; al-Muqaddasī, *Ahsan al-taqāsīm fī ma'rifat al-aqālīm*, partial trans. by A. Miquel (Damascus, 1963), 186–197. See also the works vaunting "the merits" of Jerusalem (*Fadā'il al-Quds*) from the beginning of the eleventh century on (Hillenbrand, *The Crusades*, 162–165); A. Elad, *Medieval Jerusalem and Islamic Worship, Holy Places, Ceremonies, Pilgrimage* (Leiden, 1995), 6–22; A. Neuwirth, "The Spiritual Meaning of Jerusalem in Islam," in *City of the Great King: Jerusalem from David to the Present*, ed. Nitza Rosovsky (Cambridge, Mass., 1996), 93–116; and A. Neuwirth, "The Significance of Jerusalem in Islam," in *Militia Sancti Sepulcri: Idea e istituzioni*, ed. K. Elm and C. D. Fonseca (Vatican City, 1998), 141–159.

49. See Sivan, *L'Islam et la croisade*, 118–119.

50. 'Imād al-Dīn, *Fath*, Massé trans., 50, 60.

51. The Muslims called the Christians "associationists" or "polytheists" because the Muslims did not understand the doctrine of the Trinity, a single God in three persons.

52. See A. J. Wensinck et al., *Concordance et indices de la tradition musulmane*, 8 vols. (Leiden, 1936–1969), 4:33; Hillenbrand, *The Crusades*, 284.

53. 'Imād al-Dīn, *Fath*, Massé trans., 55.

54. "Bayt al-Maqdis" is also the Arabic name for Jerusalem. Frederick II saw that inscription while visiting the city (Sibt Ibn al-Jawzī, 8:656).

55. See Sivan, *L'Islam et la croisade*, 113; Hillenbrand, *The Crusades*, 317.

56. Ibn Jubayr, Gaudefroy-Demombynes trans., 355, Broadhurst trans., 318.

57. Quoted in J. Tolan, "Affreux vacarme: Sons de cloches et voix de muezzins dans la polémique interconfessionnelle en péninsule Ibérique," in *Guerre, pouvoirs et idéologies dans l'Espagne chrétienne aux alentours de l'an mil*, ed. T. Deswarte and P. Sénac (Turnhout, 2005), 51–64, esp. 63.

58. Ibn Shaddād, *Nawādir*, al-Shayyāl ed., 217, Richards trans., 210.

59. See Lyons and Jackson, *Saladin*, 342.

60. Abū Shāma, *Rawdatayn*, 2:204 (verses from Ibn al-Mujāwir and Ibn al-Sāʿātī).

61. That is what he is called by many thirteenth- and fourteenth-century authors. See Ibn Shaddād, *Aʿlāq* (Damascus), 253; Ibn Kathīr, *Bidāya*, 13:139, 145, 171, 173; al-Nuʿaymī, *Dāris*, 1:331; al-ʿAynī, *ʿIqd al-Jumān*, vol. 2 (665–688/1266–1289), ed. M. M. Amīn (Cairo, 1988), 122.

62. See Sivan, *L'Islam et la croisade*, 119–120.

63. See al-Tarsūsī, *Tabsirat*, Bodleian ms., Hunt. 264, fol. 192a–197b. For the West, see A. Vauchez, *La sainteté en Occident aux derniers siècles du Moyen Âge d'après les procès de canonisation et les documents hagiographiques* (Rome, 1988), 14.

64. Ibn Shaddād, *Nawādir*, al-Shayyāl ed., 112, Richards trans., 104.

65. 'Imād al-Dīn, *Fath*, Massé trans., 177.

66. See A. Morabia, *Le Gihad dans l'islam médiéval*, 168.

67. See A. J. Wensinck, *The Oriental Doctrine of the Martyrs* (Amsterdam, 1921), 152.

68. See Morabia, *Le Gihad dans l'islam médiéval*, 254–255; *EI* 2, "Shahīd" (E. Kohlberg).

69. 'Imād al-Dīn, *Fath*, Massé trans., 180.

70. Ibn Shaddād, *Nawādir*, al-Shayyāl ed., 23, Richards trans., 29; Gabrieli, *Chroniques arabes des croisades*, 130.

71. Quoted in Lyons and Jackson, *Saladin*, 304.

72. Quoted in Morabia, *Le Gihad dans l'islam médiéval*, 309.

73. See Abū Shāma, *Rawdatayn*, 2:177.

74. See Lyons and Jackson, *Saladin*, 194.

75. See *Itinerarium*, Mayer ed. (IP1), 285, Nicholson trans., 53.

76. Ibn Shaddād, *Nawādir*, al-Shayyāl ed., 22, Richards trans., 29.

77. Möhring, "Zwischen Joseph-Legende und Mahdi-Erwartung," 205.

78. Louis-Antoine Fauvelet de Bourrienne, *Mémoires du secrétaire intime du premier consul*, ed. D. Rey and J. Grindler (Paris, 2004), 150, quoted in Lyons and Jackson, *Saladin*, 372 [except for the words "that will take its place in posterity"—trans.]; see also M. C. Lyons, "The Crusading Stratum in the Arabic Hero Cycles," in *Crusaders and Muslims in Twelfth Century Syria*, ed. M. Shatzmiller (Leiden, 1993), 147–161, esp. 158–160.

79. See F. de Polignac, "Cosmocrator: L'Islam et la légende antique du souverain universel," in *The Problematics of Power, Eastern and Western Representations of Alexander the Great*, ed. M. Bridges and J. C. Bürgel (Bern, 1996), 149–164.

80. See H. Laurens, *L'expédition d'Égypte 1798–1801* (Paris, 1989), 40; and J. Derogy and H. Carmel, *Bonaparte en Terre sainte* (Paris, 1992), 15, 20, 24.

81. See *EI* 2, "(al-)Ḳusṭanṭīniyya" (J. H. Mordtmann).

82. See D. Cook, *Studies in Muslim Apocalyptic* (Princeton, 2002), 59–66.

83. See M. Canard, "Les expéditions des Arabes contre Constantinople dans l'histoire et dans la légende," *Journal Asiaique* 208 (1926): 61–121.

13. Strategic Interests

1. Al-Bundārī, 77; see also Abū Shāma, *Rawdatayn*, 1:234, trans. *Recueils des historiens des croisades. Historiens orientaux*, 4:164–167 (hereafter cited as *RHC Or.*); William of Tyre, Huygens ed., 963 (21.3), Babcock and Krey trans., 2:399; Ibn Wāsil, *Mufarrij*, 2:16; al-Maqrīzī, *Sulūk*, 1, 1:55–56; M. C. Lyons and D. E. P. Jackson, *Saladin*, 76; F. Chalandon, *Histoire de la domination normande en Italie et en Sicile*, 2 vols. (Paris, 1907; repr. 1960), 392–398; H. Wieruszowski, "The Norman Kingdom of Sicily and the Crusades," in *A History of the Crusade*, vol. 2: *The Later Crusades, 1189–1131*, ed. R. L. Wolff and H. W. Hazard, 2nd. ed. (Madison, Wisc., 1969), 3–42.

2. See A. S. Ehrenkreutz, "Saladin in Naval History," 104–105; Y. Lev, *Saladin*, 165. Subsequently, however, their offensives were directed more against the Byzantine Empire than against Egypt.

3. See al-Maqrīzī, *Sulūk*, 1, 1:72; A. S. Ehrenkreutz, *Saladin*, 172; J. Prawer, *Histoire du royaume latin de Jérusalem*, 1:611.

4. See al-Maqrīzī, *Sulūk*, 1, 1:88; Ehrenkreutz, *Saladin*, 186.

5. See Abū Shāma, *Rawdatayn*, 191–192, 269; al-Maqrīzī, *Itti'āz*, 3:320–321; A. Raymond, *Le Caire*, 89–97; Lev, *Saladin*, 164.

6. A total of 29,300 cubits, according to the ancient sources (see Raymond, *Le Caire*, 96). Al-Maqrīzī (*Itti'āz*, 3:296) says that three of the gates built by Shāwar survived until about the mid-thirteenth century, which would seem to indicate that the Ayyubid plans followed at least partly what the Fatimid vizier had intended. See N. D. MacKenzie, *Ayyubid Cairo: A Topographical Study* (Cairo, 1992), 51–78; N. Rab-

bat, *The Citadel of Cairo: A New Interpretation of Royal Mamluk Architecture* (Leiden, 1995), 10–11.

7. See N. Elisséeff, *Nūr al-Dīn*, 3:705–720.

8. See al-Bundārī, 119; Abū Shāma, *Rawdatayn*, 1:268; 2:2; Ibn al-Athīr, *Kāmil*, 11:436; Ibn Wāsil, *Mufarrij*, 2:52–53; al-Maqrīzī, *Sulūk*, 1, 1:111; *Répertoire chronologique d'épigraphie arabe*, 9, no. 3380 (hereafter cited as *RCEA*); Raymond, *Le Caire*, 86–97. In 1998, following the embankment work conducted for the construction of al-Azhar Park by the Aga Khan Trust for Culture Service for Egypt, a large part of the east wall of Cairo was unearthed. Restored beginning in 1999, that portion of wall, as well as the interior space alongside it, was the object of archaeological excavations by a Franco-Egyptian team. See S. Pradines, B. Michaudel, J. Monchamp, "La muraille ayyoubide du Caire: Les fouilles archéologiques de Bāb al-Barqiyya et Bab al-Maḥrūq," *Annales islamologiques* 36 (2002): 287–337; and S. Pradines, "Les murailles du Caire: Des califes fatimides aux sultans mamelouks," *Archéologia* 418 (2005): 60–73.

9. See Rabbat, *The Citadel of Cairo*, 12–17, 50–73; P. Casanova, "Histoire et description de la Citadelle du Caire," *Mémoires publiés par les membres de la Mission archéologique française au Caire* 6 (1894): 509–781 (hereafter cited as *MMAF*); K. A. C. Creswell, *Muslim Architecture of Egypt* (New York, 1978), 2:1–40.

10. The legendary aspect of that type of narrative is confirmed by the fact that it is found during different eras and in different Islamic countries, in the account, for example, of the founding of the 'Adūdī Hospital in Baghdad in the tenth century, or in that of the hospital of Aleppo by Nūr al-Dīn in the twelfth. See Elisséeff, *Nūr al-Dīn*, 3:840; *Encyclopaedia of Islam*, 2nd ed., "Bīmāristān" (D. M. Dunlop).

11. Fifty thousand, according to al-Maqrīzī, *Khitat*, 1:87, 2:203–204, Sayyid ed., 1:234, 3:644ff., an exaggerated figure no doubt, but one that indicates the large number of prisoners who were used for that task; see also Gibb, "The Armies of Saladin," 77.

12. The reuse of ancient Egyptian materials in the construction of the fortifications is attested by the discovery of several stones bearing hieroglyphics in the masonry of the towers and curtains of Saladin's wall, east of Cairo and north of the citadel. See Pradines, "Les murailles du Caire," 60–73, esp. 66.

13. See Ibn Jubayr, Gaudefroy-Demombynes trans., 55, 63–64; 'Abd al-Latīf, de Sacy trans., 171–172.

14. In *The Citadel of Cairo*, Rabbat proposes extending the boundaries of that first citadel farther to the south so as to include the well whose construction Saladin ordered.

15. Bent-axis entry gates were not unknown in Middle Eastern Islamic countries, but until the late twelfth century they were much less widespread than gates with a straight axis entry. It was only with Saladin's reign that they became common. See B. Michaudel, "Fortifications ayyoubides et mameloukes," 504–509.

16. See al-Maqrīzī, *Sulūk*, I, 1:72–73; Lyons and Jackson, *Saladin*, 113, 163; Ehrenkreutz, *Saladin*, 168.

17. See al-Maqrīzī, *Sulūk*, I, 1:72.

18. *Croisades et pèlerinages*, 951–952.

19. See J. M. Mouton et al., "La route de Saladin," 41–70; J. M. Mouton, "Saladin et les bédouins du Sinaï," 197–206; J. M. Mouton, *Le Sinaï médiéval*, 82–88; J. M. Mouton and S. 'Abd al-Malik, "La forteresse de l'île de Graye," 75–90; D. Pringle, "The Castles of Ayla (al-'Aqaba) in the Crusader, Ayyubid and Mamluk Periods," in *Egypt and Syria in the Fatimid Ayyubid and Mamluk Eras*, ed. U. Vermeulen and J. Van Steenbergen (Louvain, 2005), 333–353.

20. See Lyons and Jackson, *Saladin*, 129, 211; al-Bundārī, 139; Abū Shāma, *Rawdatayn*, 2:48; Mouton, *Le Sinaï médiéval*, 87.

21. See Ibn al-Athīr, *Kāmil*, 11:470, Richards trans., 2:276; Lyons and Jackson, *Saladin*, 157; Prawer, *Histoire du royaume latin de Jérusalem*, 1:597.

22. See C. Hillenbrand, "The Imprisonment of Reynald of Châtillon," in *Texts, Documents and Artefacts: Islamic Studies in Honour of D. S. Richards*, ed. C. F. Robinson (Leiden, 2003), 79–102, esp. 99–100.

23. See Ibn Jubayr, Gaudefroy-Demombynes trans., 66; Ibn al-Athīr, *Kāmil*, 11:490–491, trans. *RHC Or.*, 1:658–659; Abū Shāma, *Rawdatayn*, 2:35–36; al-Maqrīzī, *Sulūk*, I, 1:78–79; al-Maqrīzī, *Khitat*, 2:86, Sayyid ed., 3:284; Prawer, *Histoire du royaume latin de Jérusalem*, 1:613; Lyons and Jackson, *Saladin*, 186; G. La Viere Leiser, "The Crusader Raid in the Red Sea in 578/1182–83," *Journal of the American Research Center in Egypt* 14 (1977): 87–100; H. E. Mayer, *Die Kreuzfahrerherrschaft Montréal (Sōbak). Jordanien im 12 Jahrhundert* (Wiesbaden, 1990), 254–256; A. Mallet, "A Trip Down the Red Sea with Reynald of Châtillon," *Journal of the Royal Asiatic Society* 18 (2008): 141–153.

24. See D. Cook, *Studies in Muslim Apocalyptic* (Princeton, 2002), 78, 261.

25. See Lyons and Jackson, *Saladin*, 186–187.

26. See Ibn Jubayr, Gaudefroy-Demombynes trans., 65–66; al-Maqrīzī, *Sulūk*, I, 1:79; Prawer, *Histoire du royaume latin de Jérusalem*, 1:615 (the Latin sources are largely silent on this subject).

27. *Croisades et pèlerinages*, 951.

28. For the details, see Lyons and Jackson, *Saladin*, 109ff.

29. Called the Battle of Montgisard by the Franks, the defeat of Ramla by the Muslims.

30. See William of Tyre, Huygens ed., 988–992 (21.20–22), Babcock and Krey trans., 2:428–432; Lyons and Jackson, *Saladin*, 121–125. During these events, Saladin lost one of his great-nephews (Taqī al-Dīn 'Umar's son); Taqī al-Dīn's other son, Shāhanshāh, fell into Frankish hands and was held captive for seven years. Among the many prisoners was the jurist Diyā al-Dīn 'Īsā and his brother, who were freed a few

years later, in 1179, in exchange for sixty or seventy thousand dinars and the release of several Christian prisoners (Abū Shāma, *Rawdatayn*, 1:273; al-Bundārī, 131).

31. Gümüshtegin, the commander of the army, was accused of ordering the murder of Vizier al-ʿAdl by members of the Assassin sect. Arrested on September 5, 1177, he was tortured outside the walls of Hārim to compel the garrison to surrender, but in vain (Lyons and Jackson, *Saladin*, 126).

32. William of Tyre, Huygens ed., 994 (21.24), Babcock and Krey trans., 2:434–435, and French trans. in *Croisades et pèlerinages*, 701.

33. Saladin arrived in Damascus on April 15, 1178. See Lyons and Jackson, *Saladin*, 126–129.

34. Jacob's Ford (Jisr Banāt Yaʿqūb in Arabic); according to the Arab authors, Bayt al-Ahzān (The House of Grief) was so called because Jacob, the father of Joseph, had lamented being separated from his son at that place. See G. Le Strange, *Palestine*, 412.

35. See Lyons and Jackson, *Saladin*, 133; Prawer, *Histoire du royaume latin de Jérusalem*, 1:555ff.; Ibn Abī Tayyiʾ in Abū Shāma, *Rawdatayn*, 2:8.

36. William of Tyre, Huygens ed., 1002 (21.28), Babcock and Krey trans., 2:443, French trans. in *Croisades et pèlerinages*, 704; see also al-Mansūr, *Midmār*, 16–17; Abū Shāma, *Rawdatayn*, 2:10; al-Bundārī, 164–166; Lyons and Jackson, *Saladin*, 136–141; Prawer, *Histoire du royaume latin de Jérusalem*, 1:558–560. ʿImād al-Dīn, however, says that his body was claimed by the Franks and exchanged for a Muslim prisoner.

37. Abū Shāma, *Rawdatayn*, 2:11–13ff., trans. *RHC Or.*, 4:203–209; al-Bundārī, 168–172; al-Mansūr, *Midmār*, 29; Lyons and Jackson, *Saladin*, 142–143.

38. See Prawer, *Histoire du royaume latin de Jérusalem*, 1:600, 605; Lyons and Jackson, *Saladin*, 167, 170.

39. William of Tyre, Huygens ed., 1043 (22.24 [23]), Babcock and Krey trans., 2:486, French trans. in *Croisades et pèlerinages*, 715–716; see Prawer, *Histoire du royaume latin de Jérusalem*, 1:617.

40. See Lyons and Jackson, *Saladin*, 178; Prawer, *Histoire du royaume latin de Jérusalem*, 1:609.

41. Ibn Wāsil, *Mufarrij*, 2:118; see Ehrenkreutz, *Saladin*, 177.

42. Quoted in Prawer, *Histoire du royaume latin de Jérusalem*, 1:619.

43. See Mayer, *Die Kreuzfahrerherrschaft Montréal*, 239.

44. See Ibn al-Athīr, *Kāmil*, 11:502, Richard trans., 2:297–298; William of Tyre, Huygens ed., 1059–1060 (22.31), Babcock and Krey trans., 2:503–504; Lyons and Jackson, *Saladin*, 10.

45. See Ibn Shaddād, *Nawādir*, al-Shayyāl ed., 66, Richards trans., 65.

46. See Lyons and Jackson, *Saladin*, 219.

47. See Prawer, *Histoire du royaume latin de Jérusalem*, 1:633. The date long accepted by historians as that of Baldwin IV's death, namely April 15, has been called into question

by T. Vogtherr, "Die Regierungsdaten der lateinischen Könige von Jerusalem," *Zeitschrift des deutschen Palästina Vereins* 110 (1994): 66ff. In any event, he died before May 16, 1185, at which time a charter was promulgated by Baldwin V with no mention of Baldwin IV.

14. The Victorious Campaigns

1. See P. W. Edbury, "Propaganda and Faction in the Kingdom of Jerusalem: The Background to Hattin," in *Crusaders and Muslims in Twelfth Century Syria,* ed. M. Shatzmiller (Leiden, 1993), 173–189; Edbury has called into question the real existence of a "party of old families" opposed to a "party of the court." It is still convenient, however, to designate them as such in speaking of the divisions tearing apart the kingdom of Jerusalem at the time.

2. See Abū Shāma, *Rawdatayn,* 2:74–75; M. C. Lyons and D. E. P. Jackson, *Saladin,* 247–248.

3. See *History of the Patriarchs,* vol. 3, ed., 71, Khater and Burmester trans., 120.

4. In his biography, Ibn Shaddād does not mention the breaking of the truce, saying simply that Saladin, having decided to attack Kerak, assembled his troops from Egypt and Syria.

5. See C. M. Brand, "The Byzantines and Saladin," 169–170.

6. Troops from Mardin, Mosul, Sinjār, Nisībīn, Amida, and Irbil arrived from the east. See 'Imād al-Dīn in Abū Shāma, *Rawdatayn,* 2:76, trans. *Recueils des historiens des croisades. Historiens orientaux,* 4:263 (hereafter cited as *RHC Or.*); Ibn al-Athīr, *Kāmil,* 11:531, Richards trans., 2:319.

7. See H. E. Mayer, *The Crusades,* 134 (about eighteen thousand, including twelve hundred heavy cavalry and four thousand light cavalry); J. Richard, *Histoire des croisades,* 217 (twelve hundred to two thousand knights and twenty thousand other fighters); Lyons and Jackson, *Saladin,* 253 (twelve hundred knights and fifteen to eighteen thousand foot soldiers; the number "twelve thousand" can only be a typographical error).

8. Ibn al-Athīr, *Kāmil,* 11:533, Richards trans., 2:321, trans. F. Gabrieli in *Chroniques arabes des croisades,* 148–149 (slightly modified). The anonymous author of *De expugnatione Terrae Sanctae per Saladinum,* a witness to the events, confirms that position of Raymond III. See Stevenson ed., 221, Brundage trans., 155–156.

9. 'Imād al-Dīn, *Fath,* Massé trans., 24.

10. See Lyons and Jackson, *Saladin,* 258.

11. See Mayer, *The Crusades,* 135.

12. The literature is plentiful on the battle of Hattīn and its consequences. See in particular Mayer, *The Crusades,* 126–135; J. Prawer, *Histoire du royaume latin de Jérusalem,* 1:641–680; Richard, *Histoire des croisades,* 216–218; Lyons and Jackson, *Saladin,*

255–266; B. Z. Kedar, "The Battle of Ḥaṭṭīn Revisited," 190–212; P. Cole, "Christian Perceptions of the Battle of Ḥaṭṭīn (583–1187)," *al-Masâq, Studia Arabo-Islamica Mediterranean* 6 (1993): 9–39.

13. Ibn al-Athīr, *Kāmil*, 11:536, Richards trans., 2:323.

14. See A. Morabia, *Le Gihad dans l'islam médiéval*, 233.

15. Ibn Shaddād, *Nawādir*, al-Shayyāl ed., 79, Richards trans., 75.

16. See al-Bundārī, 298.

17. See Abū Shāma, *Rawdatayn*, 2:82, trans. *RHC Or.*, 4:288–289.

18. Rigord, *Gesta Philippi Augusti*, ed. and trans. E. Carpentier, G. Pon, and Y. Chauvin as *Histoire de Philippe Auguste* (Paris, 2006), 243 (chap. 61).

19. ʿImād al-Dīn, *Fath*, Massé trans., 29.

20. According to Ibn al-Qādisī in Abū Shāma, *Rawdatayn*, 2:225, trans. *RHC Or.*, 5:103.

21. See ʿImād al-Dīn, *Fath*, Massé trans., 28; Ibn al-Athīr, *Kāmil*, 11:538, Richards trans., 2:324.

22. Some remains are still visible today. See Thietmar in *Croisades et pèlerinages*, 933; Kedar, "The Battle of Ḥaṭṭīn Revisited," 207; Zvi Gal, "Saladin's Dome of Victory at the Horns of Ḥaṭṭīn," in *The Horns of Ḥaṭṭīn*, ed. B. Z. Kedar, 213–215; G. Le Strange, *Palestine*, 451.

23. See Baybars al-Mansūrī, *Zubdat al-fikra fī taʾrīkh al-hijra*, ed. D. S. Richards (Beirut, 1998), 71; P. Thorau, *The Lion of Egypt: Sultan Baybars I and the Near East in the Thirteenth Century* (Harlow, U.K., 1992), 77.

24. See Lyons and Jackson, *Saladin*, 260; Kedar, "The Battle of Ḥaṭṭīn Revisited," 197.

25. On all these events, see Lyons and Jackson, *Saladin*, 267–272.

26. Ibn Jubayr, Gaudefroy-Demombynes trans., 355, Broadhurst trans., 318.

27. The *mihrāb* is the niche in the wall of a mosque that indicates the direction of prayer.

28. See Ibn Shaddād, *Nawādir*, al-Shayyāl ed., 33–34, 79, Richards trans., 38 and 75; *RHC Or.*, 4:296–300; Ibn al-Athīr, *Kāmil*, 11:539, Richards trans., 2:324–325.

29. See Abū Shāma, *Rawdatayn*, 2:87, trans. *RHC Or.*, 4:301–302; al-Bundārī, 302–303.

30. Ibn al-Athīr, *Kāmil*, 11:541, Richards trans., 2:326.

31. ʿImād al-Dīn, *Fath*, Massé trans., 42.

32. See Ibn Shaddād, *Nawādir*, al-Shayyāl ed., 80, Richards trans., 76; ʿImād al-Dīn in Abū Shāma, *Rawdatayn*, 2:91, trans. *RHC Or.*, 4:312; Lyons and Jackson, *Saladin*, 270.

33. Al-Bundārī, 307; partly quoted in Lyons and Jackson, *Saladin*, 271.

34. *La Continuation de Guillaume de Tyr*, Morgan ed., 61, Edbury trans., 52–53; ʿImād al-Dīn in Abū Shāma, *Rawdatayn*, 2:90, trans. *RHC Or.*, 4:310. The date of Conrad's arrival at Acre remains uncertain (see the state of the question in H. E. Mayer, *Kanzlei der lateinischen Könige von Jerusalem*, 2 vols. (Hanover, Germany, 1996), 2:879 (RRH no. 659). Since his arrival in Tyre seems at the last minute to have prevented the city from falling into Saladin's hands, it is very likely that it occurred during

Saladin's return south after the taking of Beirut (see Lyons and Jackson, *Saladin*, 271). Ibn al-Athīr (*Kāmil*, 11:544, Richards trans., 2:329) also confirms this, implying that refugees from Beirut were there when Conrad reached Tyre, which would argue in favor of an arrival in early August.

35. See al-Bundārī, 306.

36. On the taking of Jerusalem, see Lyons and Jackson, *Saladin*, 267–277; Prawer, *Histoire du royaume latin de Jérusalem*, 1:669–680. The main sources are: Abū Shāma, *Rawdatayn*, 2:92ff., trans. *RHC Or.*, 4:317–341; Ibn Shaddād, *Nawādir*, al-Shayyāl ed., 81–82, Richards trans., 77–78; 'Imād al-Dīn, *Fath*, Massé trans., 44–63; al-Bundārī, 309–317; Ibn al-Athīr, *Kāmil*, 11:552, Richards trans., 2:334–335; *La Continuation de Guillaume de Tyr*, Morgan ed., 63–73, Edbury trans., 55–65; *De expugnatione Terrae Sanctae per Saladinum*, Stevenson ed., 241–251, Brundage trans., 159–163.

37. 'Imād al-Dīn in Abū Shāma, *Rawdatayn*, 2:95, trans. *RHC Or.*, 4:328.

38. See *Anonymi auctoris chronicon*, Abouna trans., 149.

39. See *La Continuation de Guillaume de Tyr*, Morgan ed., 71, Edbury trans., 62–63.

40. Michael the Syrian, 3:404.

41. 'Imād al-Dīn in Abū Shāma, *Rawdatayn*, 2:95, trans. *RHC Or.*, 4:330; al-Bundārī, 311–312.

42. 'Imād al-Dīn, *Fath*, Massé trans., 49.

43. See *Anonymi auctoris chronicon*, Abouna trans., 149; *La Continuation de Guillaume de Tyr*, Morgan ed., 74, Edbury trans., 65–66; R. Grousset, *Histoire des croisades*, 2:818–819; Richard, *Histoire des croisades*, 220–221.

44. See al-Harawī, *Kitāb al-ishārāt*, Khater and Burmester ed., ed., 25–26, trans., 64.

45. From the fourth century on, pilgrims were shown the footprint of Jesus in the basilica of the Ascension. See *Encyclopaedia of Islam*, 2nd ed., "Mi'rādj," 100b (B. Schrieke–J. Horovitz).

46. See Ibn Kathīr (*Bidāya*, 12:327), who says that Saladin was at first favorable to the destruction of the Holy Sepulchre; Bar Hebraeus, 327.

47. Ten dinars, according to the *Anonymi auctoris chronicon*, Abouna trans., 150.

48. See R. Röhricht, *Geschichte des Königreichs Jerusalem*, 463 (based on a letter sent by the Grand Master of the Knights Templar in 1188 to King Henry II of England); and H. Vincent and L. F. M. Abel, *Jérusalem: Recherches de topographie, d'archéologie et d'histoire*, 2: *Jérusalem nouvelle*, 4 parts in 2 vols. (Paris, 1914–1926), 2:648; D. S. Richards, "Saladin's Hospital," 72–74.

49. Called Zāwiya al-Dargah (of the Palace). See Ibn Shaddād, *Nawādir*, al-Shayyāl ed., 221, Richards trans., 216; Mujīr al-Dīn, *al-Uns al-jalīl*, ed., 2:47, Sauvaire trans., 165; Richards, "Saladin's Hospital," 72–74; J. Pahlitzsch, "The Transformation of Latin Religious Institutions into Islamic Endowments," 53. Ibn al-Athīr's indication (*Kāmil*, 11:553, Richards trans., 2:335) that a church of the Hospitallers was turned into a Shafite madrasa by Saladin is not confirmed by any other source. Perhaps he

confused Saladin's hospital with his madrasa, founded in the Saint Anne Convent. See J. Prawer, *Crusader Institutions* (Oxford, 1980), 301–303, for a map of that district.

50. See 'Imād al-Dīn, *Fath,* Massé trans., 58.

51. See A. Palmer, "The History of the Syrian Orthodox in Jerusalem," *Oriens Christianus* 75 (1991): 16–43, esp. 30, which says that they probably kept Saint Thomas, the old German church south of the city. See the location of the churches of Jerusalem in J. Riley-Smith, *Atlas des croisades,* French trans. by C. Cantoni (Paris, 1996), 44–45.

52. See 'Imād al-Dīn, *Fath,* Massé trans., 58. Vincent and Abel (*Jérusalem nouvelle,* 2:463) say it was left to the local Christians, but without indicating their source. On the Christians, see also 'Imād al-Dīn in Abū Shāma, *Rawdatayn,* 2:115, trans. *RHC Or.,* 4:340; Bar Hebraeus, 325.

53. Al-Maymūniyya madrasa, founded by Emir Fāris al-Dīn Maymūn. See Mujīr al-Dīn, *al-Uns al-jalīl,* ed., 2:48, Sauvaire trans., 166–167, 185; A. Palmer, "The History of the Syrian Orthodox in Jerusalem, part 2: Queen Melisende and the Jacobite Estates," *Oriens Christianus* 76 (1992): 74–94, esp. 90–94.

54. 'Imād al-Dīn, *Fath,* Massé trans., 52.

55. Among the other Koranic verses cited: "Praise be to God, Lord of the Universe, / The Compassionate, the Merciful, Sovereign of the Day of Judgement!" (1:2–4), followed by "Praise be to God who has created the heavens and the earth and ordained darkness and light" (6:1); "Say: 'Praise be to God who has never begotten a son'" (17:111); "Praise be to God who sent the Book down to his Servant!" (17:1 [translation modified—trans.]).

56. 'Imād al-Dīn, *Fath,* Massé trans., 53–54; and Abū Shāma, *Rawdatayn,* 2:110ff.

57. 'Imād al-Dīn, in Abū Shāma, *Rawdatayn,* 2:95, trans. *RHC Or.,* 328.

58. See Abū Shāma, *Rawdatayn, RHC Or.,* 4:309, 353, 356, 358; Prawer, *Histoire du royaume latin de Jérusalem,* 1:666.

59. See 'Imād al-Dīn, *Fath,* Massé trans., 63–79; Lyons and Jackson, *Saladin,* 279–283.

60. See 'Imād al-Dīn, *Fath,* Massé trans., 71.

61. See Ibn al-Athīr, *Kāmil,* 11:556, Richards trans., 2:337.

62. Ibn al-Athīr, *Kāmil,* 11:555, Richards trans., 2:337; see also F. Gabrieli, *Chroniques arabes des croisades,* 205.

63. The emir was Qutb al-Dīn Suqmān. See 'Imād al-Dīn, *Fath,* Massé trans., 111.

64. See 'Imād al-Dīn, *Fath,* Massé trans., 112–145; Ibn Shaddād, *Nawādir,* al-Shayyāl ed., 87–94, Richards trans., 82–87; Ibn al-Athīr, *Kāmil,* 12:7–20, Richards trans., 2:344–354; Abū Shāma, *Rawdatayn,* 2:124ff., trans. *RHC Or.,* 4:351–381; Lyons and Jackson, *Saladin,* 286–291; Richard, *Histoire des croisades,* 223; C. Cahen, *Syrie du Nord,* 428–430; R. B. C. Huygens, "La campagne de Saladin en Syrie du Nord (1188)," 273–283.

65. Yahmūr (Chastel Rouge), 'Arqā, 'Urayma. See 'Imād al-Dīn, *Fath,* Massé trans., 122.

66. See Bar Hebraeus, Budge trans., 328.

67. Sixty, according to 'Imād al-Dīn, *Fath,* Massé trans., 125; fifty, according to the *Itinerarium,* with five hundred knights (Mayer ed. [IPI], 271, Nicholson trans., 43–44).

68. Between Tartūs and Jabala therefore: Mariqiyya (Maraclea), whose lord had been taken prisoner in Hattīn; Bāniyās; and Balda. See 'Imād al-Dīn, *Fath,* Massé trans., 97, 125, 126 (read "Bānīyās" for "Buluniyās"); Abū Shāma, *Rawdatayn,* 2:127, trans. *RHC Or.,* 4:357.

69. 'Imād al-Dīn, quoted by Abū Shāma, *Rawdatayn,* 2:128, trans. *RHC Or.,* 4:362.

70. The most important were Sahyūn, located on a rock spur thirty kilometers northeast of Latakia (July 29); Balātunus, about twenty-seven kilometers east-southeast of Latakia (August 1); and the twin fortress of Shughr-Bakās (August 12), near the crossing of the Orontes on the road between Latakia and Aleppo. Sarmāniyya, about ten kilometers to the south, surrendered to al-Zāhir on August 19.

71. See Ibn al-Athīr, *Kāmil,* 12:14–17, Richards trans., 2:349–352.

72. Baghrās was destroyed on an order from Saladin in 1191, then reoccupied by the Armenians; along the way, Saladin no doubt also took the citadels of Darkūsh and Kafardubbīn. On these fortresses, see A. M. Eddé, *Principauté ayyoubide d'Alep,* 41, 53, and 56.

73. 'Imād al-Dīn, *Fath,* Massé trans., 134 and 143.

74. See Ibn Shaddād, *Nawādir,* al-Shayyāl ed., 94, Richards trans., 87; *Itinerarium,* Mayer ed. (IPI), 270, Nicholson trans., 43. That clause can be understood from the Frankish viewpoint but seems more surprising from the Muslim perspective. It attests, in any case, to the only hope remaining for the Franks and to the exhaustion of the Muslims, who opted to pretend to believe in that promise rather than continue a fight that might still prove long and difficult.

75. 'Imād al-Dīn, *Fath,* Massé trans., 145.

76. Sābiq al-Dīn Ibn al-Dāya and 'Alam al-Dīn Ibn Jandar in particular.

77. Sābiq al-Dīn 'Uthmān Ibn al-Dāya, already lord of Shayzar, received Bikisrā'īl as well as Jabala, but he had to give up Jabala some months later to Saladin's nephew Taqī al-Dīn; Darbsāk and Baghrās were entrusted to 'Alam al-Dīn Sulaymān Ibn Jandar, lord of 'Azāz; Mangüverish Ibn Khumartegin received the large fortress of Sahyūn, and 'Izz al-Dīn Ibrāhīm, son of Emir Ibn al-Muqaddam, received the fortress of Burzayh. The twin fortress of Shughr-Bakās was given to Ghars al-Dīn Qilij; Taqī al-Dīn received Latakia and Balātunus, which he added to his possessions in Hama. See Ibn Shaddād, *Nawādir,* al-Shayyāl ed., 94, Richards trans., 88; 'Imād al-Dīn, *Fath,* Massé trans., 35, 135; Lyons and Jackson, *Saladin,* 291; Eddé, *Principauté ayyoubide d'Alep,* 41–42.

78. See 'Imād al-Dīn, *Fath,* Massé trans., 148–154; Ibn Shaddād, *Nawādir,* al-Shayyāl ed., 95–96, Richards trans., 88–90; Ibn al-Athīr, *Kāmil,* 12:20–23, Richards trans., 2:354–356; Lyons and Jackson, *Saladin,* 291–294.

79. Were they afraid that the Hospitallers would return to seize it? It was Sārim al-Dīn Qāymāz who finally accepted it.

80. 'Imād al-Dīn, *Fath,* Massé trans., 153.

81. Visits to the holy sites during the pilgrimage to Mecca are made collectively between the eighth and twelfth days of the month of Dhū l-Hijja on the Hegira calendar.

82. In Syria-Palestine on the ninth day of Dhū l-Hijja, the day of the pause or halt *(wuqūf)* of pilgrims outside Jabal al-Rahma (a small rocky eminence of the Arafat Valley about twenty-five kilometers from Mecca), the same worship rites as in Arafat were commonly performed in the Great Mosques at the end of afternoon prayer *('asr)* (see Ibn Jubayr, Gaudefroy-Demombynes trans., 339). That custom must have been fairly ancient: according to Sibt Ibn al-Jawzī, it went back to the reign of 'Abd al-Malik, who in 692 is said to have barred the Syrians from completing the pilgrimage to Mecca, where Ibn al-Zubayr had revolted. He then had the Dome of the Rock and al-Aqsā Mosque built "to divert their attention from the *ḥajj.* They used to stand by the Rock and circumambulate it as they used to circumambulate the Ka'ba, and slaughter beasts on the day of the feast [i.e., 'Id al-Aḍhā]." A. Elad, *Medieval Jerusalem and Islamic Worship, Holy Places, Ceremonies, Pilgrimage* (Leiden, 1995), 53 (English trans. of the passage from Sibt Ibn al-Jawzī), 61–62. Saladin did not give that custom special importance until 1189, in Jerusalem.

83. In particular, the Krac des Chevaliers, Sāfītā (Chastel Blanc), the citadel of Tartūs, 'Arqa, and 'Akkār (Gibelacar). See 'Imād al-Dīn (one of his letters to Baghdad) in Abū Shāma, *Rawdatayn, RHC Or.,* 4:392.

15. The Third Crusade

1. On the Western context of the Third Crusade, see H. E. Mayer, *The Crusades,* 137–140; J. Richard, *Histoire des croisades,* 228–231; J. Prawer, *Histoire du royaume latin de Jérusalem,* 2:9–33.

2. See al-Maqrīzī, *Sulūk,* 1, 1:72; C. Cahen, *Syrie du Nord,* 422.

3. That rapprochement is not explicitly mentioned by the Greek sources but is attested in a Byzantine letter preserved by a German chronicler, Magnus of Reichersberg. In "Domestic Opposition to Byzantium's Alliance with Saladin: Niketas Choniates and His Epiphany Oration of 1190" *(Byzantine and Modern Greek Studies* 30 [2006]: 49–68), D. G. Angelov has also shown that Nicetas Choniates (1155/7–1217), who could not have been unaware of the embassies exchanged between the two sovereigns, implicitly alluded to them—without mentioning Saladin—in a panegyric speech addressed to Emperor Isaac on January 6, 1190. In it, he urged the emperor to go liberate Palestine and Jerusalem in order to reestablish Byzantine authority there. See also G. Ostrogorsky, *Histoire de l'État byzantin* (Paris, 1983), 423n. 1;

Prawer, *Histoire du royaume latin de Jérusalem*, 2:37; Cahen, *Syrie du Nord*, 424–425; C. M. Brand, "The Byzantines and Saladin," 167ff.; H. Möhring, *Saladin und der Dritte Kreuzzug*, 171–177; M. C. Lyons and D. E. P. Jackson, *Saladin*, 222; Mayer, *The Crusades*, 126, 302n. 65; Richard, *Histoire des croisades*, 209; R. J. Lilie, *Byzantium and the Crusader States*, *1096–1204*, trans. J. C. Morris and J. E. Ridings (Oxford, 1993), 230–241.

4. See Brand, "The Byzantines and Saladin," 169–171. The rumor spread in the West that among the gifts sent to the emperor was a large quantity of poisoned cereals, flour, and wine, to be distributed to the Franks upon their arrival.

5. See Brand, "The Byzantines and Saladin," 172, 181. In an anonymous letter recorded in the chronicle of Magnus of Reichersberg, Issac Angelus agreed to restore the Muslim faith of Constantinople. A *minbar* was sent by Saladin, but it fell into the hands of the Genoese, who brought it to Tyre and used it to demonstrate the evil intentions of Byzantium (Möhring [*Saladin und der Dritte Kreuzzug*, 175–176] does not believe this version). According to Ibn Shaddād (*Nawādir*, al-Shayyāl ed., 132, Richards trans., 121), everything went well and the reopening of the mosque was a great day; Ostrogorsky, *Histoire de l'État byzantin*, 429–430; Abū Shāma, *Rawdatayn*, 2:177–178, trans. *Recueils des historiens des croisades. Historiens orientaux*, 4:508–509 (hereafter cited as *RHC Or.*); Sibt Ibn al-Jawzī, 8:404.

6. See Ibn Shaddād, *Nawādir*, al-Shayyāl ed., 132–133, Richards trans., 121–122.

7. See *Itinerarium*, Mayer ed. (IP1), 292ff., Nicholson trans., 57–58.

8. See Abū Shāma, *Rawdatayn*, 2:178, trans. *RHC Or.*, 4:509–510; Möhring, *Saladin und der Dritte Kreuzzug*, 186–188.

9. Even if the Seljuk sultan did consider marrying his son Qutb al-Dīn to Saladin's daughter, that union never took place. See Ibn al-Athīr, *Kāmil*, 12:89, Richards trans., 2:403; C. Cahen, *La Turquie pré-ottomane* (Istanbul, 1988), 58; Möhring, *Saladin und der Dritte Kreuzzug*, 191; 'Imād al-Dīn (in Abū Shāma, *Rawdatayn*, *RHC Or.*, 4:346–347) does speak of a marriage, but it is between al-'Ādil's daughter and Qutb al-Dīn Suqmān ibn Muhammad ibn Qarā Arslān, lord of Amida.

10. See Abū Shāma, *Rawdatayn*, 2:154, trans. *RHC Or.*, 4:452 (translation slightly modified).

11. Quoted in Lyons and Jackson, *Saladin*, 324.

12. This was Mu'izz al-Dīn Qaysarshāh, lord of Malatyā.

13. See 'Imād al-Dīn, *Fath*, Massé trans., 347, 354; Ibn al-Athīr, *Kāmil*, 12:76, Richards trans., 2:395.

14. This was Qutb al-Dīn Malikshāh. See Ibn Shaddād, *Nawādir*, al-Shayyāl ed., 220, Richards trans., 214.

15. On the exchanges of embassies between Frederick Barbarossa and Saladin, see Mayer, *The Crusades*, 140; and Möhring, *Saladin und der Dritte Kreuzzug*, 93–137.

16. Preserved in three manuscripts and in Arnold of Lübeck's *Chronicle of the Slavs,* ed. and trans. into Italian by Sabino De Sandoli as *Itinera Hierosolymitana crucesignato-rum (sec. XII–XIII),* vol. 2: *Tempore Regum Francorum (1100–1187)* (Jerusalem, 1980), 393–411. See J. Tolan, "Veneratio Sarracenorum: Dévotion commune entre musulmans et chrétiens selon Burchard de Strasbourg, ambassadeur de Frédéric Barberousse auprès de Saladin (v. 1175)," in *Chrétiens et musulmans en Méditerrannée médiévale (VIIIe–XIIIe siècles): Contacts et échanges,* ed. N. Prouteau and P. Sénac (Poitiers, 2003), 185–195.

17. This embassy is attested in a letter that Qāḍī al-Fāḍil sent to the ambassador in question, whose name was al-Qāḍī al-Sadīd Abū Tāhir Ismāʿīl ibn ʿAbd al-ʿAzīz, son of the qāḍī of Acre (*al-Durr al-naẓīma min tarassul ʿAbd al-Raḥīm,* Badawi ed., 37–42, 44ff.). He is called Butair Esmair in the Latin translation that has come down to us of Saladin's letter to the emperor. The date of that embassy remains very uncertain. R. Röhricht dates it to 1180–1182 ("Zur Geschichte der Kreuzzüge," *Neues Archiv* 11 [1886]; 571–579, esp. 575ff.). Upon analyzing the content of the two letters and the titulature conferred on Saladin, Möhring dates it instead to 1173 (Möhring, *Saladin und der Dritte Kreuzzug,* 129–130). It is true that, in the Latin translation, Saladin appears primarily as lord of Egypt (al-Fustāt, Cairo, Alexandria), and Damascus is not mentioned. He is, however, called "protector of the Emir of Believers," a title indicating the acknowledgment of his power by the caliph, which he could not have had before Nūr al-Dīn's death (1174). Since that letter was written in Egypt, it must have been drafted between October 1176 and February 1178 or between January 1181 and March 1182, the periods during which Saladin was staying in Cairo. It was in 1177 that Saladin received a Genoese messenger, Rubeo della Volta, who had come to conclude an accord with him (see D. Jacoby, "Les Italiens en Égypte" [2000], 358), and it was also in that year that he undertook to rebuild the Egyptian fleet. The letter from al-Fāḍil to the ambassador in fact mentions the fleet being rebuilt. That embassy cannot in any case have occurred later than 1183, since Saladin left Egypt at that time, never to return.

18. No doubt the expedition of 1169.

19. Möhring thinks that these negotiations were conducted against Byzantium (Möhring, "Heiliger Krieg und politische Pragmatik," 427).

20. See *Itinerarium,* Mayer ed. (IP1), 280–288, Nicholson trans., 49–54.

21. See Möhring, *Saladin und der Dritte Kreuzzug,* 93–98; Mayer, *The Crusades,* 140.

22. In 1169 and 1174.

23. It is therefore possible to translate "servitor [or "salvator"] domini excelsi" as "the servant avid [for the mercy] of Almighty God" (*al-faqīr illā llāh taʿālā*); "adunator veridici verbi" as "the one who unites the word and the faith" (*jāmiʿkalimat al-īmān*); "comptor vexilli veritatis" as "standard-bearer of justice and beneficence"

(rāfi' 'alam al-'adl wa l-ihsān); "corrector orbis et legis" as "uprightness of this world and of religion" *(salāh al-dunya wa l-dīn);* "soldanus Sarracenorum et Paganorum" as "sultan of Islam and of the Muslims" *(sultan al-islām wa l-muslimīn);* "servitor duarum sanctarum domorum et sancte domus Ierusalem" as "servant of the two noble sanctuaries and of Jerusalem" *(khādim al-Haramayn al-sharīfayn wa hādha l-Bayt al-Muqaddas);* "Patris victorum Joseph filii Job" as "Abū l-Muzaffar Yūsūf ibn Ayyūb"; "suscitator progeniei Mirmuraeni" as "reinvigorator of the dynasty of the Emir of Believers" *(muhyī dawlat amīr al-mu'minīn).* See also the titulature at the top of the *waqf* deed for his *khānqāh* in Jerusalem (J. Pahlitzsch, "The Transformation of Latin Religious Institutions," 60).

24. See Möhring, *Saladin und der Dritte Kreuzzug,* 98–125. Among the arguments advanced: Saladin's titles ought to have appeared at the beginning and not the end of the letter; the form of the *tasliyya* (invocation to God on behalf of the Prophet) is incorrect; the title "protector of the two sanctuaries" granted to Saladin does not appear in the other sources in our possession before 1191; and Saladin is mentioned as lord of Edessa, or lord of India, and not as lord of Aleppo. Although all these observations are pertinent, the letters and documents that have come down to us show that though there were norms, they were not always rigorously followed; also, certain variants could have been introduced by the translators of these documents.

25. See Prawer, *Histoire du royaume latin de Jérusalem,* 2:35; Möhring, *Saladin und der Dritte Kreuzzug,* 90; Cahen, *La Turquie préottomane,* 57.

26. See Mayer, *The Crusades,* 142; M. L. Favreau, *Studien zur Frühgeschichte des Deutschen Ordens* (Stuttgart, 1974).

27. See Prawer, *Histoire du royaume latin de Jérusalem,* 2:43–68; Lyons and Jackson, *Saladin,* 295–330; S. Painter, "The Third Crusade: Richard the Lionhearted and Philip Augustus," in *A History of the Crusades,* ed. K. M. Setton, 2:45–85; Mayer, *The Crusades,* 142–146; Richard, *Histoire des croisades,* 235–239.

28. 'Imād al-Dīn, *Fath,* Massé trans., 184.

29. See Ibn Shaddād, *Nawādir,* al-Shayyāl ed., 113, Richards trans., 104.

30. See Abū Shāma, *Rawdatayn,* 2:152, trans. *RHC Or.,* 4:442.

31. See 'Imād al-Dīn, *Fath,* Massé trans., 362–365.

32. See Ibn Shaddād, *Nawādir,* al-Shayyāl ed., 117–118, Richards trans., 108.

33. The Syrians in the first place, with Saladin's young cousin Shīrkūh of Homs, and Emirs Sābiq al-Dīn 'Uthmān and Ibn al-Muqaddam, sons of 'Izz al-Dīn, as well as a certain number of Arab or Turkoman Bedouins. Then, between May and June, troops arrived from Aleppo, Upper Mesopotamia, Harrān, Sinjār, Jazirat Ibn 'Umar, and from Irbil and Mosul, commanded, respectively, by Saladin's son al-Zāhir, 'Imād al-Dīn Mahmūd of Dara, Muzaffar al-Dīn Gökböri, Zangī, Sanjarshāh, Zayn al-Dīn Yūsuf, and 'Izz al-Dīn's son 'Alā' al-Dīn. One of 'Alā' al-Dīn's emirs, known as al-Rabīb Abū l-Ma'ālī As'ad al-Mawsilī, who accompanied the expedition, wrote

a travel narrative *(rihla)* on that occasion. A few excerpts from that narrative, which has unfortunately been lost, are preserved in Ibn al-'Adīm's biographical dictionary *(Bughya,* 4:1577–1580).

34. The seat of the leader of the Armenian church was at the time Qal'at al-Rūm (Rūm Kal'esi), on the right bank of the Euphrates, now in eastern Turkey. Since the mid-twelfth century, it had been locked within Muslim territory. The content of the letter from Gregory IV has come down to us through Ibn Shaddād, *Nawādir,* al-Shayyāl ed., 124–126, Richards trans., 114–116.

35. Namely, Nasir al-Dīn of Manbij, 'Izz al-Dīn Ibn al-Muqaddam of Shayzar, and Bah-rāmshāh of Baalbek.

36. See Ibn Shaddād, *Nawādir,* al-Shayyāl ed., 127–128, Richards trans., 117.

37. In early October, they were also joined by Frederick of Swabia and the survivors of the German Crusade. Ibn Shaddād speaks of five thousand cavalrymen and foot soldiers *(Nawādir,* al-Shayyāl ed., 154, Richards trans., 143), 'Imād al-Dīn of about fifteen thousand ('Imād al-Dīn, *Fath,* Massé trans., 251); Lyons and Jackson, *Saladin,* 316. Frederick of Swabia would die outside Acre in January 1191.

38. Abū Shāma, *Rawdatayn,* 2:176, trans. *RHC Or.,* 4:507.

39. See Abū Shāma, *Rawdatayn,* 2:165–171, 176–178.

40. Al-Zāhir left behind a contingent in northern Syria to secure the defense of the territory; it repelled an attack of troops from Antioch ('Imād al-Dīn, *Fath,* Massé trans., 258).

41. Abū Shāma, *Rawdatayn,* 2:174.

42. See D. Cook, *Studies in Muslim Apocalyptic* (Princeton, 2002), 82.

43. See Ibn Jubayr, Gaudefroy-Demombynes trans., 90–91.

44. Al-Zuhrī, "Kitāb al-Dja'rāfiyya. Mappemonde du calife al-Ma'mūn reproduite et commentée par Fazārī (IIIe/IXe s.) rééditée et commentée par Zuhrī (VIe/XIIe)," ed. M. Hadj-Sadok, *Bulletin d'études orientales* 21 (1968): 7–312, esp. 230. The other historians were Ibn Hayyān, Ibn al-Athīr, Ibn 'Idhārī, al-Himyārī, and Ibn Khaldūn, according to P. Sénac, *Les Carolingiens et al-Andalus (VIIIe–IXe siècles)* (Paris, 2002), 13.

45. See C. Picard, *La mer et les musulmans d'Occident au Moyen Âge VIIIe–XIIIe* (Paris, 1997), 75–96. The superiority of the Almohad fleet over the eastern fleet is under-scored by Ibn Khaldūn *(Al-Muqaddima,* Rosenthal trans., 2:43–45).

46. See Abū Shāma, *Rawdatayn,* 2:170, trans. *RHC Or.,* 4:491–496. The ambassador was Emir 'Abd al-Rahmān Ibn Munqidh.

47. The one that was probably written in 1189 is known to us through the great Egyp-tian encyclopedist al-Qalqashandī *(Subh,* 6:526–530). The other, composed a year later and entrusted to the ambassador Ibn Munqidh, has been preserved in Abū Shāma's chronicle *(Rawdatayn,* 2:171–173, trans. *RHC Or.,* 4:497–506). The differ-ences between the two versions led M. Gaudefroy-Demombynes ("Une lettre de Saladin au calife almohade," 286) to say that there may have been two letters.

48. Al-Qalqashandī, *Subh*, 6:527; and M. Gaudefroy-Demombynes, "Une lettre de Sala-din au calife almohade," 281. On the different versions of that embassy, see Möhring, *Saladin und der Dritte Kreuzzug*, 192–209.

49. In Arabic: *al-faqīr illā llāh taʿālā Yūsūf Ibn Ayyūb.*

50. The *ʿalāma* was a formula consisting of praises to God used as a signature. The *ʿalāma* of the Ayyubids of Egypt was most often "Praise be to God, my assistance is in Him." See S. M. Stern, "Two Ayyubid Decrees from Sinaï," in *Documents from Islamic Chanceries*, ed. S. M. Stern (Oxford, 1965), repr. in S. M. Stern, *Coins and Documents from the Medieval Middle East* (London, 1986), chap. 9; S. Heidemann, C. Müller, and Y. Rāġib, "Un décret d'al-Malik al-ʿĀdil 571/1176 relatif aux moines du mont Sinaï," 92. The letter from al-Fādil to Saladin is reproduced in Abū Shāma, *Rawdatayn*, 2:174–176.

51. Möhring (*Saladin und der Dritte Kreuzzug*, 196) calls into doubt the sincerity of al-Fādil's arguments on behalf of the Abbasid caliphate, which he had scarcely de-fended when he was in the service of the Fatimids. Although it is certain, as Möhring says, that al-Fādil abided by Saladin's propaganda in support of the caliph of Baghdad, there is no reason to doubt his sincerity, given his hostility toward the Almohads. In addition, in his many letters to Saladin, he was accustomed to reveal-ing his deepest thoughts, even when he was not in agreement with his master.

52. The letter to the Almohad is also preserved in the work of the Muslim Ibn Mahmūd al-Shayzarī (d. 1229), *Jamharat al-islām dhāt al-nathr wa l-nizām*, facsimile ed. of the Leiden Or. ms. 287, F. Sezgin (Frankfurt, 1986), fol. 249a–251b. See A. Helbig, *Al-Qādī al-Fādil, der Wezir Saladin's*, Inaugural-Dissertation (Berlin, 1909), 72. This ver-sion also mentions the death of Frederick Barbarossa, but it appears closer to the instructions given to the ambassador. Contrary to the other sources, however, in it the ambassador's name is Murhaf. Möhring (*Saladin und der Dritte Kreuzzug*, 198–199) thinks that this letter is probably a forgery and notes that the author does not seem to know that the Almohad caliph was in Seville at the time.

53. Ibn Khaldūn (*Al-Muqaddima*, Rosenthal trans., 2:44–45) says that the Umayyad caliph received the ambassador with many honors, but, annoyed at not being called the Emir of Believers, the caliph did not respond to his request. According to Ibn ʿIdhārī, a Maghrebi historian who died in the early fourteenth century (*Al-Bayān al-mughrib fī akhbār mulūk al-Andalus wa l-Maghrib, Qism al-muwahhidīn*, ed. M. I. al-Kattānī et al. [Beirut, 1985], 209), the Almohad learned of the arrival of Ibn Munqidh in Ifriqiya in August 1190, when the Almohad was in Seville. Given the time it would have taken his governor of Ifriqiya to send him the news, Ibn Munqidh must have arrived, in that case, in the first part of June 1190 at the earliest. But these dates do not correspond to the content of the letter re-produced by Abū Shāma, which mentions the death of Barbarossa (June 10, 1190), the attack of the army in northern Syria against his son, and the imminent

arrival of that son in Acre (early October). See Möhring, *Saladin und der Dritte Kreuzzug*, 199–200.

54. See Abū Shāma, *Rawdatayn*, 2:188 (lines 35ff.).

55. The territories he exchanged for Irbil included Harrān, Edessa, al-Muwazzar, and Samosata. See Ibn Shaddād, *Nawādir*, al-Shayyāl ed., 145, Richards trans., 133; 'Imād al-Dīn, *Fath*, Massé trans., 261 ('Imād al-Dīn adds that Saladin gave him Shahrazūr as well, a region on which the caliph also had designs); Lyons and Jackson, *Saladin*, 319.

56. Quoted in Lyons and Jackson, *Saladin*, 320 [translation slightly modified—trans.].

57. See Ibn al-Athīr, *Kāmil*, 12:61–62, Richards trans., 2:384–385; Lyons and Jackson, *Saladin*, 322. An accord negotiated by one of Saladin's messengers finally took effect, under pressure from the emirs of Sinjār and Irbil.

58. See Mayer, *The Crusades*, 144.

59. See 'Imād al-Dīn, *Fath*, Massé trans., 304; William of Tyre, Huygens ed., 981 (21.14), Babcock and Krey trans., 419; Lyons and Jackson, *Saladin*, 327; it is not impossible that 'Imād al-Dīn confused Isabella's supposed pregnancy with the child of Conrad's she was carrying when, a year and half later, she married Henry of Champagne, though he does report both pregnancies in his book. See 'Imād al-Dīn, *Fath*, Massé trans., 377.

60. See Ibn Shaddād, *Nawādir*, al-Shayyāl ed., 153, Richards trans., 141–142.

61. See 'Imād al-Dīn, *Fath*, Massé trans., 258; Ibn Shaddād, *Nawādir*, al-Shayyāl ed., 154, 155, 157, Richards trans., 142, 144, 146; Prawer, *Histoire du royaume latin de Jérusalem*, 2:62; Lyons and Jackson, *Saladin*, 323.

62. See Ibn Shaddād, *Nawādir*, al-Shayyāl ed., 152–153, Richards trans., 140–141; 'Imād al-Dīn, *Fath*, Massé trans., 273–275; Abū Shāma, *Rawdatayn*, 2:181, trans. *RHC Or.*, 4:518.

63. On that part of the siege of Acre, see 'Imād al-Dīn, *Fath*, Massé trans., 289–329; Ibn Shaddād, *Nawādir*, al-Shayyāl ed., 156ff., Richards trans., 145ff.; Abū Shāma, *Rawdatayn*, 2:183ff., trans. *RHC Or.*, 5:6ff.; Lyons and Jackson, *Saladin*, 326–330.

64. 'Imād al-Dīn, *Fath*, Massé trans., 289–290. See also Ibn Shaddād, *Nawādir*, al-Shayyāl ed., 156–157, Richards trans., 145.

65. The Lusignan family were from Poitou, which is to say, they were vassals of the king of England.

66. 'Imād al-Dīn, *Fath*, Massé trans., 297; the author of the *Itinerarium* (Stubbs ed. [IP2], 196, Nicholson trans., 189) says that Richard's army in Cyprus counted forty ships so powerfully armed that they were worth sixty. In addition to the warships, Richard's fleet probably had a great number of other vessels as well: Roger of Howden (*Chronica*, 3:46) estimates there were 106, the author of the *Itinerarium*, 108 (Stubbs ed. [IP2], 147, Nicholson trans., 149).

67. Recalled by the king of France, he returned shortly thereafter to Acre and actively participated in negotiations leading to the capitulation of the Muslims. During the

long siege of Acre, between September 1189 and July 12, 1191, he made several visits of varying length to Tyre.

68. Led by Sābiq al-Dīn of Shayzar, Asad al-Dīn of Homs, and Badr al-Dīn Dildirim of Tall Bāshir.

69. See Ibn Shaddād, *Nawādir,* al-Shayyāl ed., 170–171, Richards trans., 161.

70. ʿImād al-Dīn, *Fath,* Massé trans., 318–326.

71. See Ibn al-Athīr, *Kāmil,* 12:67–68, Richards trans., 2:388–389; ʿImād al-Dīn, *Fath,* Massé trans., 329; Ibn Shaddād, *Nawādir,* al-Shayyāl ed., 173–175, Richards trans., 163–165; Sibt Ibn al-Jawzī, 8:408; *Itinerarium,* Stubbs ed. (IP2), 243, Nicholson trans., 231; *La Continuation de Guillaume de Tyr,* Morgan ed., 129, Edbury trans., 108 (the figure of sixteen thousand prisoners is obviously out of all proportion); Roger of Howden, *Chronica,* 3:131; Lyons and Jackson, *Saladin,* 332–333.

72. See *Historia de Expeditione Friderici Imperatoris, der sogenannte Ansbert,* in *Quellen zur Geschichte der Kreuzzuges Kaiser Friedrichs,* ed. A. Chroust (Berlin, 1928), 99. Rigord (*Gesta Philippi Augusti,* ed. and trans. into French as *Histoire de Philippe Auguste* by E. Carpentier, G. Pon, Y. Chauvin [Paris, 2006], 307–309 [chap. 89]) is not inclined to defend the king of England and also insists on his greed. See J. Gillingham, *Richard I* (New Haven, 1999), 170.

73. According to Roger of Howden, *Chronica,* 3:87. See Mayer, *The Crusades,* 146.

74. ʿImād al-Dīn, *Fath,* Massé trans., 320. Given that the figure is cited in one of his letters announcing the fall of Acre, it might be thought that it was exaggerated to "console" the Muslims about their defeat.

75. Sivan, *L'Islam et la croisade,* 121.

76. See Abū Shāma, *Rawdatayn,* 2:177.

77. See al-Nābulusī, *Kitāb lamaʿ al-qawānīn al-mudiyya fī dawāwīn al-Diyār al-Misriyya,* ed. C. Cahen and C. Becker, *Bulletin d'études orientales* 16 (1960): 1–78 and 118–134, esp. 12.

78. Ibn Shaddād, *Nawādir,* al-Shayyāl ed., 186, Richards trans., 178. See also ʿImād al-Dīn, *Fath,* Massé trans., 346–347; and Ibn al-Athīr, *Kāmil,* 12:71, Richards trans., 2:391.

79. See Mujīr al-Dīn, *Al-Uns al-jalīl,* Sauvaire trans., 16.

80. Ibn Battūta, *Voyages,* trans. C. Defremery and B. R. Sanguinetti (repr. Paris, 1982), 1:164; see also Mujīr al-Dīn, *al-Uns al-jalīl,* 1:380, 2:74, Sauvaire trans., 214.

81. See Ibn Shaddād, *Nawādir,* al-Shayyāl ed., 179ff., Richards trans., 181ff.

82. See Lyons and Jackson, *Saladin,* 342–344.

83. See Ibn Shaddād, *Nawādir,* al-Shayyāl ed., 194, Richards trans., 186.

84. The *Itinerarium* does not speak of these marriage plans, and the French *Continuation* of William of Tyre (Morgan ed., 150, Edbury trans., 120) takes care to say that Richard would have considered that marriage only if al-ʿĀdil agreed to become Christian, a plan that, in the author's view, led Saladin to fear he would lose his power.

85. See *Itinerarium*, Stubbs ed. (IP2), 296, Nicholson trans., 272.

86. See Lyons and Jackson, *Saladin*, 346, based on al-Maqrīzī, *Sulūk*, 1, 1:111.

87. See Lyons and Jackson, *Saladin*, 347, based on Ibn Shaddād, *Nawādir*, al-Shayyāl ed., 205, Richards trans., 197–198.

88. Ibn Shaddād, *Nawādir*, al-Shayyāl ed., 207, Richards trans., 200.

89. See the different interpretations of that assassination in Ibn Shaddād, *Nawādir*, al-Shayyāl ed., 208, Richards trans., 200–201; Ibn al-Athīr, *Kāmil*, 12:78–79, Richards trans., 2:396–397; Ambroise, *L'Estoire de la guerre sainte*, 8725–8855, Ailes and Barber trans., 2:150–151; *Itinerarium*, Stubbs ed. (IP2), 341–342, 444–445, Nicholson trans., 307–308 and 384–385; 'Imād al-Dīn, *Fath*, Massé trans., 376–377; Lyons and Jackson, *Saladin*, 348; B. Lewis, *The Assassins*, 117–118.

90. See S. Guyard, "Un grand maître des Assassins au temps de Saladin," *Journal Asiatique*, 7th series, 9 (1877): 324–489, esp. 463–466, and an excerpt in F. Gabrieli, *Chroniques arabes des croisades*, 267.

91. See Richard, *Histoire des croisades*, 241.

92. Some five hundred prisoners, according to Ibn Shaddād, *Nawādir*, al-Shayyāl ed., 214, Richards trans., 208; Lyons and Jackson, *Saladin*, 351.

93. See Ibn Shaddād, *Nawādir*, al-Shayyāl ed., 217, Richards trans., 210.

94. See Ibn Shaddād, *Nawādir*, al-Shayyāl ed., 222–226, Richards trans., 217–221; 'Imād al-Dīn, *Fath*, Massé trans., 384–385; Lyons and Jackson, *Saladin*, 357.

95. See 'Imad al-Dīn, *Fath*, Massé trans., 391.

96. See Ibn Shaddād, *Nawādir*, al-Shayyāl ed., 234, Richards trans., 231.

97. See Ibn Shaddād, *Nawādir*, al-Shayyāl ed., 235, Richards trans., 232.

98. See Ibn Shaddād, *Nawādir*, al-Shayyāl ed., 240, Richards trans., 237; 'Imād al-Dīn, *Fath*, Massé trans., 399–400.

16. The Rules of War

1. See 'Imād al-Dīn, *Fath*, Massé trans., 145, 390; Abū Shāma, *Rawdatayn*, 2:6, trans. *Recueils des historiens des croisades. Historiens orientaux*, 4:195 (hereafter cited as *RHC Or.*).

2. Which could be extended. See *Encyclopaedia of Islam*, 2nd ed. (hereafter cited as *EI 2*), "Ṣulh" (M. Khadduri).

3. See M. C. Lyons and D. E. P. Jackson, *Saladin*, 145.

4. See Lyons and Jackson, *Saladin*, 221–222.

5. 'Imād al-Dīn, *Fath*, Massé trans., 393.

6. See Lyons and Jackson, *Saladin*, 147.

7. See Abū Shāma, *Rawdatayn*, 2:11, trans. *RHC Or.*, 4:205.

8. See Ibn Shaddād, *Nawādir*, al-Shayyāl ed., 132, Richards trans., 121.

9. See *Itinerarium*, Mayer ed. (IP1), 280–288, Nicholson trans., 49–54, esp. 53–54.

10. Ibn Shaddād, *Nawādir*, al-Shayyāl ed., 163, Richards trans., 153 (see also ed., 201, trans., 193); Lyons and Jackson, *Saladin*, 344.

11. Ibn Shaddād, *Nawādir*, al-Shayyāl ed., 182, Richards trans., 173.

12. On the interpreters, see Ibn Shaddād, *Nawādir*, al-Shayyāl ed., 178, 182, Richards trans., 168-169, 173; 'Imād al-Dīn, *Fath*, Massé trans., 340.

13. Abū Shāma, *Rawdatayn*, 2:185, trans. *RHC Or.*, 5:15, based on a letter from al-Fādil.

14. See Ibn Shaddād, *Nawādir*, al-Shayyāl ed., 206-207, Richards trans., 199-200.

15. See Lyons and Jackson, *Saladin*, 224, 252, 348. In July 1191, Reginald of Sidon, who was conducting the negotiations, asked to speak to Najīb al-Dīn al-'Adl, a trusted man of Saladin's who had already served as intermediary ('Imād al-Dīn, *Fath*, Massé trans., 317); Abū Shāma, *Rawdatayn*, *RHC Or.*, 5:23). Al-'Adl was also in charge of the negotiations in April 1192 between Saladin and Conrad. And it was he who was negotiating at the time of the final accord (Ibn Shaddād, *Nawādir*, al-Shayyāl ed., 208, 233-234, Richards trans., 200, 229-231).

16. See Ibn Shaddād, *Nawādir*, al-Shayyāl ed., 133, Richards trans., 122.

17. See Ibn Shaddād, *Nawādir*, al-Shayyāl ed., 165, Richards trans., 155; 'Imād al-Dīn, *Fath*, Massé trans., 309.

18. 'Imād al-Dīn, *Fath*, Massé trans., 310.

19. See G. Le Strange, *Palestine*, 419.

20. See Lyons and Jackson, *Saladin*, 329, based on al-Maqrīzī, *Sulūk*, 1, 1:94.

21. See Ibn Shaddād, *Nawādir*, al-Shayyāl ed., 220, 231, Richards trans., 215, 227.

22. See al-Harawī, *Tadhkira*, Sourdel-Thomine trans., 228.

23. See Abū Shāma, *Rawdatayn*, 1:220-221, reproduced in Ibn Wāsil, *Mufarrij*, 2:476.

24. See Abū Shāma, *Rawdatayn*, 2:131, trans. *RHC Or.*, 4:374.

25. See J. Prawer, *Histoire du royaume latin de Jérusalem*, 2:67.

26. See al-Fādil's letter on that subject in Lyons and Jackson, *Saladin*, 156-157; *La Continuation de Guillaume de Tyr*, Morgan ed., 149, Edbury trans., 118 ("Some bedouins made contact with the king and received a safe conduct from him. They swore that they would serve him loyally"); *Itinerarium*, Stubbs ed. (IP2), 385-386, Nicholson trans., 339.

27. See Ibn Shaddād, *Nawādir*, al-Shayyāl ed., 217, Richards trans., 211-212.

28. See Ibn Shaddād, *Nawādir*, al-Shayyāl ed., 191, 220, 236, Richards trans., 183, 214, 233.

29. Ibn Shaddād, *Nawādir*, al-Shayyāl ed., 234, Richards trans., 230-231 (Lyons and Jackson, *Saladin*, 360).

30. See William of Tyre, Huygens ed., 1026 (22.15 [14]), Babcock and Krey trans., 2:468.

31. See William of Tyre, Huygens ed., 1028 (22.16 [15]), Babcock and Krey trans., 2:470; 'Imād al-Dīn, in Abū Shāma, *Rawdatayn*, trans. *RHC Or.*, 4:277 (at least until 1187).

32. See 'Imād al-Dīn, *Fath*, Massé trans., 144.

33. See William of Tyre, Huygens ed., 907 (19.31), Babcock and Krey trans., 2:341.

34. See Abū Shāma, *Rawdatayn*, 1:168-169.

35. See Lyons and Jackson, *Saladin*, 361; Ibn Shaddād, *Nawādir*, al-Shayyāl ed., 236, Richards trans., 232; ʿImād al-Dīn, *Fath*, Massé trans., 394.

36. Jean de Joinville, quoted in L. Le Goff, *Saint Louis* (Paris, 1996), 199.

37. ʿImād al-Dīn, *Fath*, Massé trans., 178; Ibn Shaddād, *Nawādir*, al-Shayyāl ed., 108–109, Richards trans., 101. The tale is repeated in Bar Hebraeus, Budge trans., 331.

38. See ʿImād al-Dīn, *Fath*, Massé trans., 286; Ibn Shaddād, *Nawādir*, al-Shayyāl ed., 206, Richards trans., 198.

39. For example, Saladin's battle against the Zangids in 1175, or the Battle of Ramla in 1177, when the Muslims were much more numerous than the Franks.

40. See Ibn al-Athīr, *Kāmil*, 11:428, Richards trans., 2:241–242.

41. Ibn Shaddād, *Nawādir*, al-Shayyāl ed., 109, 111, 129, Richards trans., 101, 103, 118.

42. See I. Guyot-Bachy, "Cris et trompettes. Les échos de la guerre chez les historiens et les chroniqueurs," in *Haro! Noël! Oyé! Pratiques du cri au Moyen Âge*, ed. D. Lett and N. Offenstadt (Paris, 2003), 103–115; M. Hinds, "The Banners and Battle Cries of the Arabs at Ṣiffīn (657 A.D.)," *al-Abhāth* 24 (1971): 3–42.

43. Ibn Shaddād, *Nawādir*, al-Shayyāl ed., 183, Richards trans., 175; see also ed., 148–149, trans., 137.

44. See Abū Shāma, *Rawdatayn*, trans. *RHC Or.*, 4:271–272; Ibn Shaddād, *Nawādir*, al-Shayyāl ed., 150, Richards trans., 138.

45. See A. M. Eddé, *Principauté ayyoubide d'Alep*, 309.

46. Scc Abū Shāma, *Rawdatayn*, 2:225 (line 16), trans. *RHC Or.*, 5:103.

47. Usāma, Miquel trans., 153, Hitti trans., 69–70.

48. See D. Nicolle, *Early Medieval Islamic Arms and Armour*, special issue of *Gladius* (1976): 123–125.

49. Al-Tarsūsi, *Tabsirat*, 127, 129.

50. Al-Tarsusi, *Tabsirat*, 137. A representation of a shield and a sword from Saladin's time can be found above the entry door of the fortress of Sadr in Sinai. See J. M. Mouton, *Saladin*, 60 and 64.

51. See Ibn Abī Tayyi' in Abū Shāma, *Rawdatayn*, 1:58.

52. See Ibn Shaddād, *Nawādir*, al-Shayyāl ed., 109, Richards trans., 101.

53. See William of Tyre, Huygens ed., 991 (21.22), Babcock and Krey trans., 2:431, French trans. in *Croisades et pèlerinages*, 700. Saladin's yellow standards are cited many times: in 1179, after the victory of Bayt al-Ahzān (Ibn Wāsil, *Mufarrij*, 2:84; and al-Mansūr, *Midmār*, 31); in 1183, when they were raised above the citadel of Aleppo (Abū Shāma, *Rawdatayn*, 2:44); and in 1187, during the taking of Tiberias (ʿImād al-Dīn, *Fath*, Massé trans., 22) or on the walls of Sidon (Abū Shāma, *Rawdatayn*, 2:90, trans. *RHC Or.*, 4:308). ʿImād al-Dīn, in a burst of lyricism, compares the color of Damascus apricots to the yellow of his standards (ʿImād al-Dīn, *Fath*, Massé trans., 119). See *Itinerarium*, Stubbs ed. (IP2), 273, Nicholson trans., 255 (Saladin's emirs bore yellow banners equipped with a colored pennon).

54. See Ibn Khallikān, 7:206, Slane trans., 4:547.

55. See Ibn Abī Usaybi'a, 652; 'Imād al-Dīn, *Fath,* Massé trans., 22. Guy of Lusignan's tent on the day of the Battle of Hattīn was also red (Abū Shāma, *Rawdatayn,* 2:87, trans. *RHC Or.,* 4:298).

56. *Asfar* (yellow) can also designate a tawny or russet color. See A. Morabia, "Recherches sur quelques noms de couleur en arabe classique," *Studia Islamica* 21 (1964): 61–99, esp. 84.

57. See K. Athamina, "The Black Banners and the Socio-Political Significance of Flags and Slogans in Medieval Islam," *Arabica* 36 (1989): 307–327.

58. Even in the ancient Roman world, blue, the color of the barbarians, was devalued. No one dressed in blue, and it was disturbing to have blue eyes. On the symbolism of these different colors, see *EI* 2, "Lawn" (A. Morabia); M. Pastoureau, *Les couleurs de notre temps* (Paris, 2003), 18, 32–37, 111, 156; and M. Pastoureau, *Figures et couleurs. Étude sur la symbolique et la sensibilité médiévales* (Paris, 1986), 15–34.

59. "They shall dwell in the gardens of Eden, where rivers will roll at their feet. Reclining there upon soft couches, they shall be decked with bracelets of gold, and arrayed in garments of fine green silk and rich brocade" (Koran 18:31); see also Koran 55:76 and 76:21.

60. According to Athamina, "Black Banners," 311 and 325, it has not been demonstrated that green was the symbol of the Alids or that it was the color of the Umayyads, as many are inclined to think.

61. Not counting black and white. See Morabia, "Recherches sur quelques noms de couleur en arabe classique," 71.

62. See A. J. Wensinck et al., *Concordance et indices de la tradition musulmane,* 8 vols. (Leiden, 1936–1969), 2:322 and 6:155–156.

63. Among those who had yellow and sometimes yellow and red banners: al-Ashtar Mālik ibn al-Hārith; and members of the Azd, Hudhayl, and Thaqīf Arab tribes. See Hinds, "The Banners and Battle Cries of the Arabs," 3–42.

64. See M. Fierro, "Al-Asfar," *Studia Islamica* 77 (1993): 169–181, esp. 177; Athamina, "Black Banners," 323. By contrast, some sources say that, during the Battle of Siffīn in 657, the Iraqis supporting 'Alī, as a distinctive sign *('alāma),* kept their heads or shoulders covered with a white cloth, whereas the Umayyad Syrians wore yellow cloths: see Hinds, "The Banners and Battle Cries of the Arabs," 9.

65. Among the Shiites, the belief in the return of the Mahdi took on particular intensity, in that some descendants of the Prophet's son-in-law (various ones, depending on the Shiite sect) were identified as the Mahdi but could not fulfill the hopes placed in them during their lifetimes. The Shiites therefore believe in the occultation of these Mahdis and await their return. See *EI* 2, "al-Mahdī" (W. Madelung).

66. See *EI* 2, " 'Isā" (G. C. Anawati) and "Dadjdjāl" (A. Abel).

67. See Ibn Khaldūn, *Al-Muqaddima,* Rosenthal trans., 2:194.

68. See al-Masʿūdī, *Le livre de l'avertissement et de la révision*, trans. B. Carra de Vaux (Paris, 1897), 434; W. Madelung, "The Sufyānī between Tradition and History," *Studia Islamica* 63 (1986): 5–48, esp. 13–23; *EI* 2, suppl., "Sufyānī" (W. Madelung); H. Möhring, "Zwischen Joseph-Legende und Madhi-Erwartung," 205–206; see also D. Cook, *Studies in Muslim Apocalyptic* (Princeton, 2002), 82–83, 122–136, 174–175.

69. See P. Sanders, *Ritual, Politics and the City in Fatimid Cairo* (New York, 1994), 96.

70. See *EI* 2, "Rank" (N. Rabbat). In the West itself, the use of coats of arms did not become widespread until about the mid-twelfth century. See M. Pastoureau, *Typologie des sources du Moyen Âge occidental*, vol. 20: *Les armoiries* (Turnhout, 1976), 24–29; and M. Pastoureau, *Traité d'héraldique* (Paris, 2003), 37–58.

71. See Jean de Joinville, *Vie de Saint Louis*, ed. J. Monfrin (Paris, 1997), chap. 282, p. 140.

72. See Ibn Abī Usaybiʿa, 588.

73. See L. A. Mayer, *Saracenic Heraldry* (Oxford, 1933), 195; N. Rabbat, "The Meaning of the Sultan: A Clue from the Double-Headed Eagle Figure," in *L'exercice du pouvoir à l'âge des sultanats*, proceedings of the Institut Français d'Archéologie Orientale-American Research Center in Egypt (IFAO-ARCE), March 24–26, 2006 (forthcoming).

74. See Mouton, *Saladin*, 33, 39.

75. See M. Pastoureau, "Introduction à l'héraldique imaginaire (XIIe–XVIe siècle)," *Revue française d'héraldique et de sigillographie* 48 (1978): 19–25; and M. Pastoureau, "Figures et couleurs péjoratives en héraldique médiévale," in *Figures et couleurs*, 193–207, esp. 195–196, 200–204; F. Caroff, "L'adversaire, l'autre, l'oriental," 284ff.

76. Coats of arms "of gold fretted with gules and strewn with silver bells" (see Caroff, "L'adversaire, l'autre, l'oriental," 292–295). It is certain that the family's coat of arms, at least as of the fourteenth century, combined the motifs of the bell and the crescent. According to legend, one of its members, Ogier de Saint-Chéron, known as "Saladin of Anglure," received them during the Third Crusade from Saladin himself.

77. The crescent, a Sassanid legacy, appears on Islamic currency as of the late seventh century and on many other supports (mosaics, metals, ceramics, leather, manuscripts). Its use as an emblem of Islam became widespread only belatedly (late eighteenth century), but a study of its emblematic value in both texts and iconography remains to be done. See *EI* 2, "Hilāl" (R. Ettinghausen).

78. See Caroff, "L'adversaire, l'autre, l'oriental," 300–331.

79. *Saladin*, trans. M. de Combardieu du Grès in *Croisades et pèlerinages*, 431.

80. Ibn Shaddād, *Nawādir*, al-Shayyāl ed., 149, Richards trans., 137. The *Itinerarium* (Stubbs ed. [IP2], 249, Nicholson trans., 237) also says that the king of England's banner was hoisted high, "like a ship's mast," on boards mounted on four wheels. It was fiercely protected, since its fall could lead to a rapid rout of the troops.

81. See Fulcher of Chartres, *Historia Hiersolymitana*, ed. H. Hagenmeyer (Heidelberg, 1913), 326, 413, 498.

82. See Ibn Shaddād, *Nawādir*, al-Shayyāl ed., 113, 131, Richards trans., 104, 120.

83. ʿImād al-Dīn, *Fath*, Massé trans., 238.

84. See Caroff, "L'adversaire, l'autre, l'oriental," 136–142.

85. See Usāma, Miquel trans., 323.

86. The same was true in the West. See C. Gauvard, *Violence et ordre public au Moyen Âge* (Paris, 2005).

87. See *Répertoire chronologique d'épigraphie arabe*, no. 3335 (hereafter cited as *RCEA*); N. Elisséeff, *La description de Damas d'Ibn ʿAsākir* (Damascus, 1959), 300n. 4; D. Sack, *Damaskus*, 2/16; B. Michaudel, "Fortifications ayyoubides et mameloukes," 1:155; L. Korn, *Ayyubidische Architektur in Ägypten und Syrien. Bautätigkeit im Kontext von Politik und Gesellschaft 564–658/1169–1260*, 2 vols. (Heidelberg, 2004). In Aleppo, the fortifications had already been restored by Nūr al-Dīn. After Saladin's death, his son al-Zāhir undertook major construction on them.

88. ʿImād al-Dīn, *Fath*, Massé trans., 357, 371; Ibn Abī Usaybiʿa, 688.

89. That extension is attested by the texts and confirmed by archaeological excavations; see Ibn al-Athīr, *Kāmil*, 12:87, Richards trans., 2:402; E. Stern, ed., *New Encyclopedia of Archaeological Excavations in the Holy Land* (Jerusalem, 1993), 2:789; Lyons and Jackson, *Saladin*, 346–347.

90. See Lyons and Jackson, *Saladin*, 362.

91. See Michaudel, "Fortifications ayyoubides et mameloukes," 1:172–189, 195–214, 221–234.

92. See al-Harawī, *Tadhkira*, Sourdel-Thomine trans., 228.

93. See Ibn al-Athīr, *Kāmil*, 11:486, Richards trans., 2:286.

94. See ʿAbd al-Lātif al-Baghdādī, quoted in al-Maqrīzī, *Sulūk* 1, 1:94, trans. *RHC Or.*, 3:438–439; Lyons and Jackson, *Saladin*, 329.

95. See Ibn Shaddād, *Nawādir*, al-Shayyāl ed., 129, Richards trans., 118.

96. ʿImād al-Dīn, *Fath*, Massé trans., 202–203; Gabrieli, *Chroniques arabes des croisades*, 231–232.

97. See William of Tyre, Huygens ed., 994 (21.24), Babcock and Krey trans., 2:434; Lyons and Jackson, *Saladin*, 128.

98. ʿImād al-Dīn, *Fath*, Massé trans., 45–46.

99. Ibn Shaddād, *Nawādir*, al-Shayyāl ed., 120, Richards trans., 110; see also ed., 162, trans., 151; ʿImād al-Dīn, *Fath*, Massé trans., 299–300; Ibn al-Athīr, *Kāmil*, 12:45, Richards trans., 2:372; Prawer, *Histoire du royaume latin de Jérusalem*, 2:54. An example of one use of these towers *(dabbābāt)* by Saladin's armies is in ʿImād al-Dīn, *Fath*, Massé trans., 68; Ibn al-Athīr, *Kāmil*, 11:554, Richards trans., 2:336.

100. ʿImād al-Dīn, *Fath*, Massé trans., 253–254; see also Lyons and Jackson, *Saladin*, 317.

101. See Ibn al-Athīr, *Kāmil*, 12:65, Richards trans., 2:387.

102. See Ibn al-Athīr, *Kāmil*, 11:506, Richards trans., 2:300; Abū Shāma, *Rawdatayn*, 2:56, trans. *RHC Or.*, 4:254; al-Bundārī, 242; Lyons and Jackson, *Saladin*, 217.

103. See Ibn Shaddād, *Nawādir,* al-Shayyāl ed., 160, Richards trans., 149–150. See also 'Imād al-Dīn, *Fath,* Massé trans., 297.

104. 'Imād al-Dīn, *Fath,* Massé trans., 256; Ibn Shaddād, *Nawādir,* al-Shayyāl ed., 140–142, Richards trans., 129–131.

105. According to Ibn Shaddād, a quintal *(qintār)* was the equivalent of one hundred *ratls,* a Syrian *ratl* being about two kilos in Syria during that time. See *EI* 2, "Makāyil" (E. Ashtor).

106. See the many descriptions in 'Imād al-Dīn, *Fath,* Massé trans. (index: *sape*); and the description of the sapping that demolished the castle of Bayt al-Ahzān in 1179, in Abū Shāma, *Rawdatayn,* 2:11, trans. *RHC Or.,* 4:204.

107. See Abū Shāma, *Rawdatayn,* 2:148, trans. *RHC Or.,* 4:431; 'Imād al-Dīn, *Fath,* Massé trans., 204.

108. See 'Imād al-Dīn, *Fath,* Massé trans., 217–218; Lyons and Jackson, *Saladin,* 313.

109. See William of Tyre, Huygens ed., 1032 (22.17 [16]), 1039 (22.21 [20]), Babcock and Krey trans., 2:475, 482; Lyons and Jackson, *Saladin,* 229.

110. A. Morabia, *Le Gihad dans l'islam médiéval,* 232–236; G. Cipollone, *Cristianità-Islam,* 191–203.

111. See al-Harawī, *Tadhkira,* Sourdel-Thomine trans., 219.

112. See Y. Lev, "Charity and Social Practice: Egypt and Syria from the Ninth to the Twelfth Century," *Jerusalem Studies in Arabic and Islam* 24 (2000): 472–507, esp. 477.

113. See Abū Shāma, *Rawdatayn,* 1:170; Ibn al-Athīr, *Kāmil,* 12:159, Richards trans., 3:53; al-Safadī, *Al-Wāfī bī l-wafayāt* 18, ed. A. F. Sayyid (Wiesbaden, 1962), 345; S. Hassan Abd al-Wahab, "Captives Waqf in Syria and Egypt (491–589 H. 1097–1193 A.D.)," in *La liberazione dei "captivi" tra cristianità e Islam. Oltre le crociata e il Jihād: Tolleranza e servizio umanitario,* ed. G. Cipollone (Vatican City, 2000), 559–567, esp. 563.

114. Ibn Jubayr, Gaudefroy Demombynes trans., 360, Broadhurst trans., 322.

115. See Lev, "Charity," 495–496; and Lev, "Treatment of Prisoners of War," 25–26; Y. Friedman, "The 'Great Precept' of Ransom: The Jewish Perspective," in Cipollone, ed., *La liberazione dei "captivi" tra cristianità e Islam,* 161–171.

116. Y. Friedman, "The Ransom of the Captives in the Latin Kingdom of Jerusalem," in *Autour de la première croisade,* ed. M. Balard (1996), 177–189, esp. 178.

117. See P. Contamine, *La guerre au Moyen Âge* (Paris, 1980), 427.

118. J. Richard, "Les prisonniers et leur rachat au cours des croisades," in *Fondations et oeuvres charitables au Moyen Âge,* ed. J. Dufour and H. Pratelle (Paris, 1999), 63 and 73.

119. The Order of the Trinitarians was founded by John of Matha in the last decade of the twelfth century. See G. Cipollone, *Cristianità-Islam, Cattività e liberazione in nome di Dio. Il tempo di Innocenzo III dopo "il 1187"* (Rome, 1992); and Cipollone, ed., *La liberazione dei "captivi" tra cristianità e Islam;* J. W. Brodman, *Ransoming Captives in Crusader Spain: The Order of Merced on the Christian-Islamic Frontier* (Philadelphia, 1986), 103–116.

120. See al-Bundārī, 166; Abū Shāma, *Rawdatayn*, 2:8, trans. *RHC Or.*, 4:199. See also Ibn Shaddād, *Nawādir*, al-Shayyāl ed., 113, Richards trans., 104 (after a battle outside Acre, Saladin's secretaries tallied up the losses).

121. See al-Bundārī, 170, Abū Shāma, *Rawdatayn*, 2:11, trans. *RHC Or.*, 4:205; al-Mansūr, *Midmār*, 29; Lyons and Jackson, *Saladin*, 142.

122. See Abū Shāma, *Rawdatayn*, 2:89, trans. *RHC Or.*, 4:307.

123. In Islamic countries of the Middle Ages, the average price of a slave was for a long time about twenty dinars, that is, roughly five to six times that of a donkey; but the price of first-rate slaves started at sixty dinars and could reach several thousand (see Y. Rāġib, "Les marchés aux esclaves en terre d'Islam," in *Mercati e mercanti nell'alto Medioevo: L'area euroasiatica a l'area mediterranea* [Spoleto, 1993], 758).

124. See al-Bundārī, 166.

125. See al-Bundārī, 194. See also Ibn al-Athīr, *Kāmil*, 11:482, Richards trans., 2:283; William of Tyre, Huygens ed., 1026 (22.15 [14]), Babcock and Krey trans., 2:467; Lyons and Jackson, *Saladin*, 165. On the carrying capacity of ships, see C. Picard, *L'Océan Atlantique musulman de la conquête arabe à l'époque almohade* (Paris, 1997), 320 (450 passengers on average in the Almohad period); Ibn Jubayr (Gaudefroy-Demombynes trans., 364) speaks of more than 2,000 passengers for the Genoese ships. In 1233, Marseilles concluded a contract with the Knights Templar and the Knights Hospitaller limiting the number of pilgrim vessels allowed to leave Marseilles. Each ship was to contain no more than 1,500 pilgrims (see J. Delaville Le Roulx, *Cartulaire général des Hospitaliers de Saint Jean*, vol. 2 [Paris, 1897], 462, no. 2067). See also B. Keder, "The Passenger List of a Crusader Ship, 1250: Towards the History of the Popular Element on the Seventh Crusade," *Studi Medievali* 13, 1 (1972): 267–279, esp. 269.

126. In May 1182, the entire Latin community of Constantinople was exterminated by a popular uprising. On the boarded and searched ship, see Abū Shāma, *Rawdatayn*, 2:32. William of Tyre (Huygens ed., 1025 [22.14 (13)], Babcock and Krey trans., 2:467) does not speak of that capture but says that a shipload of refugees arrived in Syria.

127. See Abū Shāma, *Rawdatayn*, 2:37, 47; Ibn al-Athīr, *Kāmil*, 11:495, Richards trans., 2:292–293; al-Mansūr, *Midmār*, 150.

128. See 'Imād al-Dīn, *Fath*, Massé trans., 258, 286, 292, 399; Ibn Shaddād, *Nawādir*, al-Shayyāl ed., 155, 158, 196, Richards trans., 144, 147, 188.

129. See Lyons and Jackson, *Saladin*, 219.

130. See *La Continuation de Guillaume de Tyr*, Morgan ed., 192, Edbury trans., 108; *Itinerarium*, Stubbs ed. (IP2), 243, Nicholson trans., 231; Ibn Shaddād, *Nawādir*, al-Shayyāl ed., 173, Richards trans., 164; 'Imād al-Dīn, *Fath*, Massé trans., 328–329.

131. See Ibn Shaddād, *Nawādir*, al-Shayyāl ed., 174–175, Richards trans., 165.

132. See J. Gillingham, *Richard I* (New Haven, 1999), 170; P. Contamine, "Un contrôle étatique croissant. Les usages de la guerre du XIVe au XVIIIe siècle: Rançons et butin," in *Guerre et concurrence entre les États européens du XIVe au XVIIIe siècle*, ed.

P. Contamine (Paris, 1998), 199–236, esp. 204–205. In the same way, Napoleon Bonaparte ordered the execution of some 2,500 prisoners who had surrendered in Jaffa in March 1799, even though they had done so with the understanding that their lives would be spared. See L. A. F. Bourrienne, *Mémoires du secrétaire intime du premier consul,* ed. D. Rey, J. Grindler (Paris, 2004), 141–144; H. Laurens, *L'expédition d'Égypte 1798–1801* (Paris, 1989), 187–188.

133. See Ibn Jubayr, Gaudefroy-Demombynes trans., 55, Broadhurst trans., 43; see also 'Abd al-Lātif, de Sacy trans., 171–172; al-Maqrīzī, *Khitat,* 2:203–205, Sayyid ed., 3:644–654.

134. See Richard, "Les prisonniers et leur rachat," 63–73.

135. See *La Continuation de Guillaume de Tyr,* Morgan ed., 62, Edbury trans., 53–54. There is a similar account in *Itinerarium,* Mayer ed. (IP1), 266, Nicholson trans., 40; see Y. Friedman, *Encounter between Enemies,* 89; G. Ligato, *La croce in catene,* 531–534.

136. See 'Imād al-Dīn, *Fath,* Massé trans., 159–162.

137. See *La Continuation de Guillaume de Tyr,* Morgan ed., 8off., Edbury trans., 72; *Estoire de Eracles,* in *Recueils des historiens des croisades. Historiens occidentaux,* 2:188 (hereafter cited as *RHC Occ.*).

138. See Peter Tudebode, *Historia de Hierosolymitano itinere,* Hill and Hill ed., ed., 79–80, trans., 58; J. Tolan, *Les Sarrasins* (Paris, 2003), 168.

139. See Abū Shāma, *Rawdatayn,* 2:8; Ibn al-Athīr, *Kāmil,* 11:456, Richards trans., 2:264; Bar Hebraeus, Budge trans., 305; William of Tyre, Huygens ed., 952 (20.28), 972 (21.8), Babcock and Krey trans., 2:390, 409; Friedman, *Encounter between Enemies,* 82, 84; and Friedman, "The Ransom of the Captives in the Latin Kingdom of Jerusalem," 177–189, esp. 184.

140. See Abū Shāma, *Rawdatayn,* 2:225, trans. *RHC Or.,* 5:103 and 70n. 41.

141. See Abū Shāma, *Rawdatayn,* 2:273ff.; al-Bundārī, 130–131.

142. See R. Röhricht, "Zur Geschichte der Kreuzzüge," *Neues Archiv* 11 (1886): 571–579, esp. 573; and R. Röhricht, "Zur Correspondenz der Päpste mit den Sultanen und Mongolenchanen des Morgenlandes im Zeitalter der Kreuzzüge," *Theologische Studien und Kritiken* 64 (1891): 357–369; H. Möhring, "Zwei aiyūbidische Briefe," 197–216; Ligato, *La croce in catene,* 571–574.

143. See 'Imād al-Dīn, *Fath,* Massé trans., 158; al-Maqrīzī, *Sulūk,* 1, 1:101–102; *EI 2,* "Naṣāra" (M. Fiey); Ligato, *La croce in catene,* 530.

144. See G. Ligato, "Saladino e i prigionieri di guerra," 649–654.

145. See *La Continuation de Guillaume de Tyr,* Morgan ed., 65, Edbury trans., 57 (Saladin agrees to rescue from captivity the sons of Baldwin of Ibelin and Raymond of Jubayl); ed., 71–72, trans., 62–63 (Saladin protects the Christians of Jerusalem from exactions and releases a great number of the poor without requiring a ransom); ed., 72, trans., 64 (his chivalrous spirit toward noblewomen); Bar Hebraeus, Budge

trans., 326–327; H. J. Nicholson, "Women on the Third Crusade," *Journal of Medieval History* 23 (1997): 335–349.

146. See al-Harawī, *Tadhkira*, Sourdel-Thomine trans., 231. See also the image of Alexander as it appears in Ibn al-Athīr's chronicle, *Kāmil*, 1:282–291, 12:360, Richards trans., 3:203: a powerful and wise sovereign who conquers the world without bloodshed.

147. See F. de Polignac, "L'image d'Alexandre dans la littérature arabe," *Arabica* 29 (1982): 296–306; and F. de Polignac, "Un 'Nouvel Alexandre' mamelouk, al-Malik al-Ashraf Khalīl et le regain eschatalogique du XIIIe siècle," in Aigle, ed., *Figures mythiques des mondes musulmans,* 73–87; D. Aigle, "Les inscriptions de Baybars dans le Bilād al-Shām. Une expression de la légitimité du pouvoir," *Studia Islamica* 97 (2003): 57–85; M. Bridges and J. C. Bürgel, eds., *The Problematics of Power: Eastern and Western Representations of Alexander the Great* (Bern, 1996). In one of his letters, Qāḍī al-Fāḍil compares Saladin's army to that of Heraclius and his resolve to that of Alexander (C. P. Melville and M. C. Lyons, "Saladin's Ḥaṭṭīn Letter," in *The Horns of Ḥaṭṭīn,* ed. B. Z. Kedar [London, 1992], 210).

148. 'Imād al-Dīn, *Fath,* Massé trans., 49.

149. Ibn Shaddād, *Nawādir,* al-Shayyāl ed., 79, Richards trans., 75.

150. 'Imād al-Dīn, *Fath,* Massé trans., 269; Abū Shāma, *Rawdatayn,* 2:180, trans. *RHC Or.,* 4:517.

151. Quoted in Lyons and Jackson, *Saladin,* 272.

152. Ibn Shaddād, *Nawādir,* al-Shayyāl ed., 156, Richards trans., 145 ("ten months" in the translation, but "months" in the al-Shayyāl edition); 'Imād al-Dīn, *Fath,* Massé trans., 288.

153. Ibn Shaddād, *Nawādir,* al-Shayyāl ed., 158–159, Richards trans., 148; see also ed., 32–33, trans., 37; 'Imād al-Dīn, *Fath,* Massé trans., 294–295.

154. See *Itinerarium,* Mayer ed. (IP1), 261, Nicholson trans., 35.

155. See *La Continuation de Guillaume de Tyr,* Morgan ed., 81, Edbury trans., 72.

156. See *Chronique d'Ernoul et de Bernard le trésorier,* 57 (trans. in P. W. Edbury, *The Conquest of Jerusalem and the Third Crusade,* 151–152). It is very difficult to distinguish between reality and legend in that narrative, as indicated by the episode in which Baldwin is literally covered with gold by the Byzantine emperor.

157. 'Imād al-Dīn, *Fath,* Massé trans., 31; Lyons and Jackson, *Saladin,* 265; Lev, "Treatment of Prisoners of War," 11–27; P. V. Claverie, "Le statut des templiers capturés en Orient durant les croisades," in G. Cipollone, ed., *La liberazione dei "captivi" tra cristianità e Islam,* 501–511, esp. 502–503.

158. *La Continuation de Guillaume de Tyr,* Morgan ed., 55–56, Edbury trans., 48. That detail, however, is not confirmed by any Arab source. When Michael the Syrian says, regarding the execution of the prisoners, that Saladin "bathed in their blood" (3.404), it is only a metaphor.

159. See Cipollone, *Cristianità-Islam*, 204–215.

160. See al-Bundārī, 170; Abū Shāma, *Rawdatayn*, 2:11, trans. *RHC Or.*, 4:205; Lyons and Jackson, *Saladin*, 142.

161. See Ibn Jubayr, Gaudefroy-Demombynes trans., 65–66; al-Maqrīzī, *Sulūk*, 1, 1:79; Prawer, *Histoire du royaume latin de Jérusalem*, 1:615 (the Latin sources say little about the subject); and Lyons and Jackson, *Saladin*, 186–187.

162. Ibn Shaddād, *Nawādir*, al-Shayyāl ed., 33, Richards trans., 37.

163. Ibn al-Athīr, *Kāmil*, 12:69, Richards trans., 2:390; see also Ibn Shaddād, *Nawādir*, al-Shayyāl ed., 177–179, Richards trans., 168–170.

164. Ibn Shaddād, *Nawādir*, al-Shayyāl ed., 163–164, Richards trans., 153; see also 'Imād al-Dīn, *Fath*, Massé trans., 303.

165. See C. Gauvard, *Violence et ordre public au Moyen Âge* (Paris, 2005).

166. See *EI* 2 "Diya" (E. Tyan); "Ḳiṣāṣ" (J. Schacht); "Tha'r" (F. H. Steward).

167. See Richard, "The Adventure of John Gale," 190.

168. See J. Richard, "An Account of the Battle of Hattîn Referring to Frankish Merce-naries in Oriental Moslem States," *Speculum* 27 (1952): 168–177; and J. Richard, "Les mercenaires francs dans les armées musulmanes au temps des croisades," in *Regards croisés sur le Moyen Âge arabe, Mélanges à la mémoire de Louis Pouzet s.j. (1928–2002)*, ed. A. M. Eddé and E. Gannagé (Beirut, 2006), 227–237.

169. See Richard, "Les mercenaires francs," 230–232. The conversion to Islam of beauti-ful Frankish slave women became a literary motif, as can be seen in a tale from the *Thousand and One Nights* (V. Chauvin, *Bibliographie des ouvrages arabes ou relatifs aux Arabes publiés dans l'Europe chrétienne de 1810 à 1885*, 12 vols. [Liège, 1892–1922], vol. 5, no. 140). See Y. Friedman, "Women in Captivity and Their Ransom during the Cru-sader Period," in *Cross Cultural Convergences in the Crusader Period: Essays Presented to Arieh Graboïs on His Sixty-fifth Birthday*, ed. M. Goodich, S. Menache, and S. Schein (New York, 1995), 75–87, esp. 85–87.

170. *La Continuation de Guillaume de Tyr*, Morgan ed., 58, Edbury trans., 50; and Richard, "The Adventure of John Gale," 189–195.

171. La Roche-Guillaume might be the present-day site of Tchivlan Kalé (Hajar Shugh-lān), about thirty kilometers north of Antioch. See P. Deschamps, *Les châteaux des croisés en Terre sainte*, vol. 3: *La défense du comté de Tripoli et de la principauté d'Antioche* (Paris, 1973), 127–133, 364.

172. See al-Bundārī, 130–131; Abū Shāma, *Rawdatayn*, 1:273 (line 11) and trans. *RHC Or.* 4:185 (correcting the translation, since it is clear that the *musta'min* in this case is a Frank protected by the Muslims and not the reverse).

173. 'Imād al-Dīn, *Fath*, Massé trans., 290–291.

174. See Abū Shāma, *Rawdatayn*, trans. *RHC Or.*, 4:360–363.

175. See 'Imād al-Dīn, *Fath*, Massé trans., 262–263; Abū Shāma, *Rawdatayn*, *RHC Or.*, 4:490.

176. See Ibn Shaddād, *Nawādir*, al-Shayyāl ed., 154, Richards trans., 142–143.

177. See ʿImād al-Dīn, *Fath*, Massé trans., 304; Abū Shāma, *Rawdatayn*, trans. *RHC Or.*, 5:14. See also Ibn Shaddād, *Nawādir*, al-Shayyāl ed., 197, 200, Richards trans., 189, 193; Lyons and Jackson, *Saladin*, 343.

178. See J. Richard, "Les Turcoples au service des royaumes de Jérusalem en Chypre: Musulmans convertis ou chrétiens orientaux?" *Revue des études islamiques* 56 (1989): 259–270; and J. Richard, *Histoire des croisades*, 114.

179. See Lyons and Jackson, *Saladin*, 349, based on Ibn Shaddād, *Nawādir*, al-Shayyāl ed., 210, Richards trans., 203.

180. See Ibn al-Athīr, *Kāmil*, 12:32–33, Richards trans., 2:364.

181. See Lyons and Jackson, *Saladin*, 350.

182. See ʿImād al-Dīn, *Fath*, Massé trans., 144.

183. *Itinerarium*, Stubbs ed. (IP2) 230, Nicholson trans., 218.

184. See Abū Shāma, *Rawadatyn*, 2:167 (line 34).

17. The Gaze of the Other

1. See Usāma, Miquel trans., 299, 303–304.

2. See Usāma, Miquel trans., 353, 355; C. Hillenbrand, *The Crusades*, 267–271; P. M. Cobb, *Usama ibn Munqidh: Warrior Poet of the Age of Crusades* (Oxford, 2005).

3. Usāma, Miquel trans., 291, Hitti trans., 161.

4. *The Sea of Precious Virtues* (Baḥr al-Fawāʾid): *A Medieval Islamic Mirror for Princes*, 231–232.

5. See Ibn al-Athīr, *Kāmil*, 12:33, Richards trans., 2:364, trans. F. Gabrieli, *Chroniques arabes des croisades*, 210.

6. See al-Harawī, *Kitāb al-ishārāt*, Sourdel-Thomine ed., ed., 28, trans., 68–69.

7. Allusion to the Koran 20:63–67.

8. Abū Shāma, *Rawdatayn*, 2:93; see also Hillenbrand, *The Crusades*, 319.

9. Ibn Shaddād, *Nawādir*, al-Shayyāl ed., 194, Richards trans., 186; see also Abū Shāma, *Rawdatayn*, 2:193, trans. *Recueils des historiens des croisades. Historiens orientaux*, 5:47 (hereafter cited as *RHC Or.*).

10. See ʿImād al-Dīn, *Fath*, Massé trans., 394.

11. Al-Qalqashandī, *Subh*, 8:285, 6:500, repr. in Ibn Wāsil, *Mufarrij*, 3:239.

12. It was finally sent to Baghdad in 1193 through Saladin's son al-Afdal. See ʿImād al-Dīn, *Fath*, Massé trans., 331. On the True Cross in the Frankish armies, see A. V. Murray, " 'Mighty against the Enemies of Christ': The Relic of the True Cross in the Armies of the Kingdom of Jerusalem," in *The Crusades and Their Sources: Essays Presented to Bernard Hamilton*, ed. J. France and W. G. Zajac (Aldershot, 1998), 217–238.

13. Abū Shāma, *Rawdatayn*, 2:162 (lines 6–7); E. Sivan, *L'Islam et la croisade*, 115.

14. Abū Shāma, *Rawdatayn*, 2:149 (lines 9–10).

15. Quoted in Sivan, *L'Islam et la croisade,* 114–115.

16. 'Imād al-Dīn, *Fath,* Massé trans., 185.

17. Ibn al-Athīr, *Kāmil,* 12:32, Richards trans., 2:363, trans. Gabrieli, *Chroniques arabes des croisades,* 209.

18. Ibn Shaddād, *Nawādir,* al-Shayyāl ed., 136–137, Richards trans., 125.

19. See Ibn Shaddād, *Nawādir,* al-Shayyāl ed., 194, Richards trans., 186; *Itinerarium,* Stubbs ed. (IP2), 295, Nicholson trans., 272. See B. Kedar, "Croisade et *Jihâd* vus par l'ennemi, une étude des perceptions mutuelles des motivations," in *Autour de la première croisade,* ed. M. Balard (Paris, 1996), 345–355, esp. 350–355.

20. See N. Daniel, *Islam and the West: The Making of an Image* (Edinburgh, 1960), 39–45, 309–313; J. Tolan, *Les Sarrasins* (Paris, 2003), 180–186.

21. Ibn al-Athīr, *Kāmil,* 12:48, Richards trans., 2:374.

22. See 'Imād al-Dīn, *Fath,* Massé trans., 18–19.

23. 'Imād al-Dīn, *Fath,* Massé trans., 30.

24. See 'Imād al-Dīn, *Fath,* Massé trans., 13, 23, 24–26, 33, 41, 66, 142, 150, 174, 179, 293; Abū Shāma, *Rawdatayn,* trans. *RHC Or.,* 4:322, 378, 385, 387; al-Bundārī, 66; Usāma, Miquel trans., 223.

25. See 'Imād al-Dīn, *Fath,* Massé trans., 25, 26, 28, 94, 150, 179, 293.

26. See 'Imād al-Dīn, *Fath,* Massé trans., 225–226.

27. See Abū Shāma, *Rawdatayn,* 2:83 (line 12), trans. *RHC Or.,* 4:290.

28. See 'Imād al-Dīn, *Fath,* Massé trans., 93.

29. See 'Imād al-Dīn, *Fath,* Massé trans., 41, 50, 60–61, 64, 72–73, 94–95, 97; Sivan, *L'Islam et la croisade,* 111.

30. Al-Qalqashandī, *Subh,* 6:496–504 and 8:282–289; Ibn Wāsil, *Mufarrij,* 3:336–343.

31. See Tolan, *Les Sarrasins,* 183–192.

32. The Islamic creed is: "There is no god but God and Muhammad is His Prophet."

33. 'Imād al-Dīn, *Fath,* Massé trans., 8.

34. Ibn Shaddād, *Nawādir,* al-Shayyāl ed., 242, Richards trans., 239.

35. Usāma, Miquel trans., 299, Hitti trans., 165–166.

36. Hillenbrand, *The Crusades,* 272.

37. See N. Elisséeff, *La description de Damas d'Ibn 'Asākir* (Damascus, 1959), 277–285. For the thirteenth century, see Ibn Shaddād, *A'lāq* (Damascus, 1956), 291–302, and Ibn Shaddād, *A'lāq* (Damascus, 1953), 130–138.

38. See al-Mas'ūdī in Le Strange, *Palestine,* 202–203.

39. 'Imād al-Dīn, *Fath,* Massé trans., 377.

40. Usāma, Miquel trans., 299, Hitti trans., 164–165.

41. See 'Imād al-Dīn, *Fath,* Massé trans., 202–203.

42. See Jacques de Vitry, *Historia Hierosolimitana,* ed. Jacques Bongars, in *Gesta Dei per Francos* (Hanau, 1611), 1:1088, trans. M. G. Grossel as *Histoire orientale de Jacques de Vitry* (Paris, 2005), 204–205; J. Richard, "Le statut de la femme dans l'Orient latin,"

in *La femme*, pt. 2 (Brussels, 1962), 377–388; repr. in J. Richard, *Orient et Occident au Moyen Âge: Contacts et relations* (London, 1976), chap. 12.

43. 'Imād al-Dīn, in Abū Shāma, *Rawdatayn*, 2:149, 162 (line 2), trans. *RHC Or.*, 4:434, 479. See also 'Imād al-Dīn, *Fath*, Massé trans., 312; Ibn Shaddād, *Nawādir*, al-Shayyāl ed., 130, Richards trans., 119; Ibn al-Athīr, *Kāmil*, 12:32, Richards trans., 2:364.

44. See A. M. Eddé, "Images de femmes en Syrie à l'époque ayyoubide," in *Au cloître et dans le monde. Femmes, hommes et sociétés (IXe–XVe siècle)*, ed. P. Henriet and A. M. Legras (Paris, 2000), 65–77, esp. 66.

45. In J. Rikabi, *La poésie profane sous les Ayyûbides*, 76.

46. See Gabrieli, *Chroniques arabes des croisades*, 165; al-Bundārī, 298.

47. Quoted in Gabrieli, *Chroniques arabes des croisades*, 321, based on Ibn Wāsil, *Mufarrij*, ms. BnF Arabic, 1702, fol. 369a–b (the quotation is not reproduced in the 'U. 'A. Tadmurī edition).

48. Ibn al-Athīr, *Kāmil*, 12:68, Richards trans., 2:389; 'Imād al-Dīn, *Fath*, Massé trans., 329.

49. Ibn al-Athīr, *Kāmil*, 11:335, Richards trans., 2:172.

50. Abū Shāma, *Rawdatayn*, 1:234, trans. *RHC Or.*, 4:163.

51. Al-Qalqashandī, *Subh*, 7:115–116, repr. in Ibn Wāsil, *Mufarrij*, 3:320–321. H. Möhring ("Heiliger Krieg und politische Pragmatik," 433–439) sees these words as the offer of an alliance that would have allowed Saladin to resist Nūr al-Dīn. In my view, however, nothing in the sources allows us to confirm such an interpretation.

52. See Abū Shāma, *Rawdatayn*, 1:275, trans. *RHC Or.*, 4:192.

53. Quoted in M. C. Lyons and D. E. P. Jackson, *Saladin*, 197.

54. See Ibn al-Athīr, *Kāmil*, 11:526, Richards trans., 2:315; Abū Shāma, *Rawdatayn*, 2:74, trans. *RHC Or.*, 4:258; al-Bundārī, 289.

55. See 'Imād al-Dīn, *Fath*, Massé trans., 17.

56. Fulcher of Chartres, *Historia Hierosolymitana*, ed. H. Hagenmeyer (Heidelberg, 1913), 748; *Recueils des historiens des croisades. Historiens occidentaux*, 3:468 (hereafter cited as *RHC Occ.*).

57. Usāma, Miquel trans., 303, Hitti trans., 169; Cobb, *Usama ibn Munqidh*, 104.

58. Ibn Shaddād, *Nawādir*, al-Shayyāl ed., 97–98, Richards trans., 90–91; Abū Shāma, *Rawdatayn*, 2:139 (lines 23ff.), trans. *RHC Or.*, 4:396–397.

59. See *La Continuation de Guillaume de Tyr*, Morgan ed., 81, Edbury trans., 73; information repeated in R. Grousset, *Histoire des croisades*, 2:834.

60. See Abū Shāma, *Rawdatayn*, 2:140, trans. *RHC Or.*, 4:400.

61. See Lyons and Jackson, *Saladin*, 343–344.

62. See Ibn Shaddād, *Nawādir*, al-Shayyāl ed., 182, Richards trans., 173.

63. At present Châtillon-Coligny in the French department of Loiret.

64. 'Imād al-Dīn, in Abū Shāma, *Rawdatayn*, 2:75, trans. *RHC Or.*, 4:258–259; al-Bundārī, 289; Ibn al-Athīr, *Kāmil*, 11:527, Richards trans., 2:316.

65. Ibn Shaddād, *Nawādir*, al-Shayyāl ed., 53, Richards trans., 54; H. E. Mayer, *The Crusades*, 129; J. Richard, "The Adventure of John Gale," 193.

66. ʿImād al-Dīn, *Fath*, Massé trans., 27. The Western view of Reginald was different, of course. He was criticized by some—no one took the trouble to pay his ransom when he was kept prisoner for sixteen years in Aleppo, and his cruelty toward the patriarch of Antioch (he covered his head with honey, then exposed him to the sun and flies) did not improve his reputation—but was praised by others. Peter of Blois, one of the main Crusader preachers, wrote the "Passion of Reginald" in 1187–1188 (ed. R. B. C. Huygens, *Petri Blesensis tractatus duo* [2002], 31–73), in which he glorifies that knight and makes him out to be a martyr.

67. Abū Shāma, *Rawdatayn*, 2:90, trans. *RHC Or.*, 4:310.

68. See Ibn al-Athīr, *Kāmil*, 12:79, 86, Richards trans., 2:397, 402; Gabrieli, *Chroniques arabes des croisades*, 267.

69. See Ibn Shaddād, *Nawādir*, al-Shayyāl ed., 161, Richards trans., 150; Ibn al-Athīr, *Kāmil*, 12:65, Richards trans., 2:387.

70. See J. Gillingham, *Richard I* (New Haven, 1999), 15ff.

71. See Ibn al-Athīr, *Kāmil*, 12:73, Richards trans., 2:392.

72. Ibn Shaddād, *Nawādir*, al-Shayyāl ed., 227, Richards trans., 223.

73. See Abū Shāma, *Rawdatayn*, 2:203 (line 34), trans. *RHC Or.*, 5:79.

74. See *La Continuation de Guillaume de Tyr*, Morgan ed., 151, Edbury trans., 119–120.

75. Usāma, Miquel trans., 291, Hitti trans., 161.

18. Between Image and Reality

1. An expression used by P. Briant regarding Darius.

2. In a letter to his brother Tūrānshāh in 1177, he composed a few lines of poetry (Ibn al-Athīr, *Kāmil*, 11:443, Richards trans., 2:254; Ibn Wāsil, *Mufarrij*, 2:62). In 1185 al-Fādil assured al-Afdal that Saladin had recovered from his illness (in fact, he had not) and that al-Fādil had received a letter written in the sultan's own hand (M. C. Lyons and D. E. P. Jackson, *Saladin*, 235). Ibn Khallikān (3:54) read a letter written in Saladin's hand that the sultan had sent to Qādī al-Fādil. See also Abū Shāma, *Rawdatayn*, 2:7.

3. Ibn Shaddād, *Nawādir*, al-Shayyāl ed., 7, Richards trans., 18; F. Gabrieli, *Chroniques arabes des croisades*, 116.

4. See Ibn al-ʿImād, *Shadharāt*, 7:289.

5. See Ibn Shaddād, *Nawādir*, al-Shayyāl ed., 9, Richards trans., 20; other examples of the hadith sessions Saladin liked to attend are in al-Bundārī, 121; Abū Shāma, *Rawdatayn*, 1:269, 2:21.

6. See Lyons and Jackson, *Saladin*, 163; al-Bundārī, 188; Abū Shāma, *Rawdatayn*, 2:24.

7. The ascetic in question, Abū Zakariyyā' al-Maghribī, lived in seclusion in the village of Dayr Naqīra, east of Ma'arrat al-Nu'mān. See 'Imād al-Dīn, *Fath*, Massé trans., 146; Ibn Shaddād, *Nawādir*, al-Shayyāl ed., 94, Richards trans., 88.

8. See 'Imād al-Dīn, *Fath*, Massé trans., 430; see also Ibn Abi Usaybi'a, 688.

9. See Lyons and Jackson, *Saladin*, 246; Abū Shāma, *Rawdatayn*, 2:65.

10. See Ibn Shaddād, *Nawādir*, al-Shayyāl ed., 8, Richards trans., 18; Gabrieli, *Chroniques arabes des croisades*, 117.

11. See Ibn Shaddād, *Nawādir*, al-Shayyāl ed., 7–8, 11–12, 177, 217, Richards trans., 18, 21, 167, 211; 'Imād al-Dīn, *Fath*, Massé trans., 433.

12. Ibn Shaddād, *Nawādir*, al-Shayyāl ed., 8, Richards trans., 19; Abū Shāma, *Rawdatayn*, 1:269; Ibn Wāsil, *Mufarrij*, 2:56; Gabrieli, *Chroniques arabes des croisades*, 117.

13. See Abū Shāma, *Rawdatayn*, 2:178 (lines 24–25).

14. See N. Elisséeff, *Nūr al-Dīn*, 3:558–559; N. Elisséeff, "Monuments de Nūr al-Dīn," *Bulletin d'études orientales* 13 (1949–1951): 5–43, esp. 34; H. Möhring, "Mekkawallfahrten orientalischer und afrikanischer Herrscher im Mittelalter," *Oriens* 34 (1994): 314–329, esp. 318, where the author rightly places in doubt the reality of Nūr al-Dīn's pilgrimage.

15. Nomadic tribes of Upper Egypt and Sudan.

16. Abū Shāma, *Rawdatayn*, 2:14.

17. See Abū Shāma, *Rawdatayn*, 2:3.

18. See Lyons and Jackson, *Saladin*, 147.

19. See Abū Shāma, *Rawdatayn*, 2:19; Lyons and Jackson, *Saladin*, 156.

20. Ibn Shaddād, *Nawādir*, al-Shayyāl ed., 8, Richards trans., 19; see also ed., 235, 237, trans., 231, 233; Gabrieli, *Chroniques arabes des croisades*, 117–118.

21. 'Imād al-Dīn, *Fath*, Massé trans., 395.

22. 'Imād al-Dīn, *Fath*, Massé trans., 395; Abū Shāma, *Rawdatayn*, trans. *Recueils des historiens des croisades. Historiens orientaux*, 5:83, 91 (hereafter cited as *RHC Or.*), based on Muhammad Ibn al-Qādisī.

23. Quoted in L. Pouzet, *Damas au VIIe/XIIIe siècle*, 350n. 55.

24. See Lyons and Jackson, *Saladin*, 361–362.

25. See 'Imād al-Dīn, *Fath*, Massé trans., 408.

26. See D. Sourdel and J. Sourdel-Thomine, *Certificats de pèlerinage d'époque ayyoubide. Contribution à l'histoire de l'idéologie de l'islam au temps des croisades* (Paris, 2006), 141–144.

27. See Ibn Abi Usaybi'a, 688, trans. *RHC Or.*, 3:437.

28. See Ibn Jubayr, Gaudefroy-Demombynes trans., 44, Broadhurst trans., 35.

29. See Ibn Shaddād, *Nawādir*, al-Shayyāl ed., 109, 129, 166, Richards trans., 101, 118, 157; al-Mansūr, *Midmār*, 28.

30. 'Imād al-Dīn, *Fath*, Massé trans., 190–191.

31. See Ibn Shaddād, *Nawādir,* Richards trans., 20, 26–27, 99, 101, 110, 118, 149, 157, 158, 171, 175; Ibn Wāsil, *Mufarrij,* 2:44; Abū Shāma, *Rawdatayn,* trans. *RHC Or.,* 4:295, 371, 425; ʿImād al-Dīn, *Fath,* Massé trans., 68, 374; al-Bundārī, 153, 222.

32. See ʿImād al-Dīn, *Fath,* Massé trans., 357, 371–372.

33. Ibn Abī Usaybiʿa, 688, trans. *RHC Or.,* 3:438.

34. See Usāma, Miquel trans., 385–429.

35. ʿImād al-Dīn, *Fath,* Massé trans., 408; Ibn Shaddād, *Nawādir,* al-Shayyāl ed., 241, Richards trans., 238.

36. See Ibn Shaddād, *Nawādir,* al-Shayyāl ed., 116, Richards trans., 107; see also Ibn Wāsil, *Mufarrij,* 2:57; Abū Shāma, *Rawdatayn,* 2:151, trans. *RHC Or.,* 4:440; Lyons and Jackson, *Saladin,* 132, 310.

37. ʿImād al-Dīn, in Abū Shāma, *Rawdatayn* 2:73; al-Bundārī, 286.

38. See Abū Shāma, *Rawdatayn,* 1:100, 209–210; al-Bundārī, 23; al-Maqrīzī, *Sulūk,* 1, 1:71–72.

39. See al-Bundārī, 255.

40. See Ibn Jubayr, Gaudefroy-Demombynes trans., 336.

41. See Ibn Shaddād, *Nawādir,* al-Shayyāl ed., 34, Richards trans., 38; Abū Shāma, *Rawdatayn,* 1:270.

42. See al-Bundārī, 115; Lyons and Jackson, *Saladin,* 118.

43. See al-Bundārī, 111; Abū Shāma, *Rawdatayn,* 1:264.

44. In J. Rikabi, *La poésie profane sous les Ayyûbides,* 75–76.

45. See al-Bundārī, 270.

46. See *Encyclopaedia of Islam,* 2nd ed. (hereafter cited as *EI 2*), "Hidjāʾ" (C. Pellat, A. Bausini, F. İz, A. Ahmad).

47. See al-Wahrānī, *Manāmāt,* 53–55, 81, 84, 103–106, 108–111; Lyons and Jackson, *Saladin,* 118–119.

48. On this poet, see Ibn Khallikān, 5:14–19; Sibt Ibn al-Jawzī, 8:411–412; Rikabi, *La poésie profane sous les Ayyûbides,* 78–81 (a biography of Ibn ʿUnayn); Lyons and Jackson, *Saladin,* 119.

49. Ibn ʿUnayn, *Dīwān,* 179, 180, 193.

50. See Ibn ʿUnayn, *Dīwān,* 182, 183, 188, 191–192.

51. Ibn ʿUnayn, *Dīwān,* 236, quoted in Lyons and Jackson, *Saladin,* 119.

52. See Ibn ʿUnayn, *Dīwān,* 200.

53. Ibn ʿUnayn, *Dīwān,* 182, 184, 189–190.

54. Ibn ʿUnayn, *Dīwān,* 210; Sibt Ibn al-Jawzī, 8:411.

55. Ibn Khallikān, 5:14, Slane trans., 3:177.

56. See al-Bundārī, 113, 272; Abū Shāma, *Rawdatayn,* 2:66; Sibt Ibn al-Jawzī, 8:385; Ibn Wāsil, *Mufarrij,* 2:51; Ibn Shaddād, *Aʿlāq* (Damascus, 1956), 192, 205; A. S. Ehrenkreutz, *Saladin,* 153; Lyons and Jackson, *Saladin,* 236; R. S. Humphreys, "Women as Patrons of Religious Architecture," 42–43.

57. After the death of her first husband, Lājīn, Sitt al-Shām Zumurrud Khātūn married her cousin Nāsir al-Dīn ibn Shīrkūh. She was buried beside her half-brother Tūrānshāh, her second husband, and her son, Husām al-Dīn ʿUmar. See Sibt Ibn al-Jawzī, 8:389; Ibn Khallikān, 1:307; Humphreys, "Women as Patrons of Religious Architecture," 47.

58. Rabīʿa Khātūn had married Saʿd al-Dīn Ibn Unur, then Muzaffar al-Dīn Gökbörī. See al-Nuʿaymī, Dāris, 2:80; Humphreys, "Women as Patrons of Religious Architecture," 46.

59. See Ibn Abi Usaybiʿa, 653; al-Bundārī, 200.

60. See A. M. Eddé, "Images de femmes en Syrie à l'époque ayyoubide," in Au cloître et dans le monde. Femmes, hommes et sociétés (IXe–XVe siècle). Mélanges en l'honneur de Paulette L'Hermite-Leclercq, ed. P. Henriet and A. M. Legras (Paris, 2000), 65–77, esp. 68.

61. See al-Bundārī, 271.

62. See Ibn Shaddād, Nawādir, al-Shayyāl ed., 246, Richards trans., 243.

63. Al-Khadir is a popular and legendary figure associated with Mūsā (Moses) in sura 18:59–81.

64. On Saladin's children, see Abū Shāma, Rawdatayn, 1:276–277; Ibn Wāsil, Mufarrij, 2:423; Ibn Shaddād, Nawādir, al-Shayyāl ed., 26–27, Richards trans., 31–32; Sibt Ibn al-Jawzī, 8:434; al-Bundārī, 141.

65. See Ibn Shaddād, Nawādir, al-Shayyāl ed., 242, Richards trans., 239.

66. See Abū Shāma, Rawdatayn, 2:3, 167.

67. See Abū Shāma, Rawdatayn, 1:267. In 1176–1177, his children's tutor was a certain al-Nāsih, who had a house on the Nile and belonged to the literary circle frequented by ʿImād al-Dīn. Al-ʿAzīz also had a teacher called Najm al-Dīn Yūsuf ibn al-Husayn Ibn al-Mujāwir al-Dimashqī (d. between 1203 and 1205). See Ibn Khallikān, 7:342.

68. See Ibn Shaddād, Nawādir, al-Shayyāl ed., 7, Richards trans., 18; al-Maqrīzī, Khitat, 2:358, Sayyid ed., 4, 1:440.

69. See al-Maqrīzī, Sulūk, 1, 1:63.

70. See Abū Shāma, Rawdatayn, 2:14; al-Bundārī, 172; al-Wahrānī, Manāmāt, 187, 192.

71. See Ibn Khallikān, 3:161.

72. ʿImād al-Dīn, Fath, Massé trans., 287; Ibn Shaddād, Nawādir, al-Shayyāl ed., 155–156, Richards trans., 144–145.

73. See Abū Shāma, Rawdatayn, 2:92, trans. RHC Or., 4:316.

74. See ʿImād al-Dīn, Fath, Massé trans., 306.

75. See Ibn Shaddād, Nawādir, al-Shayyāl ed., 238, Richards trans., 235.

76. In 1185, for example, when Saladin went from Damascus to Mosul (al-Bundārī, 253).

77. See Lyons and Jackson, Saladin, 310.

78. See Lyons and Jackson, Saladin, 152.

79. See Y. Ragheb, *Les messagers volants en terre d'Islam* (Paris, 2002), 18–19.

80. See Ibn Shaddād, *Nawādir*, al-Shayyāl ed., 131, Richards trans., 120.

81. See Ibn Shaddād, *Nawādir*, al-Shayyāl ed., 242–243, Richards trans., 240.

82. Ibn Shaddād, *Nawādir*, al-Shayyāl ed., 28–29, Richards trans., 33; Gabrieli, *Chroniques arabes des croisades*, 134–135; 'Imād al-Dīn, *Fath*, Massé trans., 430.

83. See 'Imād al-Dīn, *Fath*, Massé trans., 83; Lyons and Jackson, *Saladin*, 283; see also Abū Shāma, *Rawdatayn*, trans. *RHC Or.*, 4:300; 'Imād al-Dīn, *Fath*, Massé trans., 116–117.

84. See Ibn Shaddād, *Nawādir*, al-Shayyāl ed., 221, Richards trans., 216; 'Imād al-Dīn, *Fath*, Massé trans., 355, 371; Lyons and Jackson, *Saladin*, 346.

85. See al-Maqrīzī, *Itti'āz*, 3:302; and al-Maqrīzī, *Khitat*, 1:438–439, Sayyid ed., 2:439.

86. 'Imād al-Dīn, *Fath*, Massé trans., 114–115. In 1186, when he came back to Damascus, Saladin moved into the citadel, where he was reunited with his family (al-Bundārī, 278).

87. Abū Shāma, *Rawdatayn*, 2:124, trans. *RHC Or.*, 4:347.

88. See 'Imād al-Dīn, *Fath*, Massé trans., 433.

89. See Ibn al-'Adīm, *Zubda*, 2:315; Ibn Shaddād, *Nawādir*, al-Shayyāl ed., 40, Richards trans., 45.

90. See Plutarch, "Alexander," 40.1, in *Plutarch's Lives of Illustrious Men*, trans. J. Dryden, J. Langhorne, and W. Langhorne (Philadelphia, n.d. [1932]), 830; see also 22.7 (815–817).

91. See *EI* 2, "Iskandar Nāma" (A. Abel).

92. 'Imād al-Dīn, *Fath*, Massé trans., 117–119.

93. See al-Mansūr, *Midmār*, 162.

94. See 'Imād al-Dīn, *Fath*, Massé trans., 213, 221.

95. See 'Imād al-Dīn, *Fath*, Massé trans., 117–118.

96. See Ibn Shaddād, *Nawādir*, al-Shayyāl ed., 122–123, Richards trans., 112–113.

19. Saladin and Suffering

1. See Ibn al-Athīr, *Kāmil*, 12:40, Richards trans., 2:369; M. C. Lyons and D. E. P. Jackson, *Saladin*, 271.

2. See al-Bundārī, 271; Abū Shāma, *Rawdatayn*, 2:65; Lyons and Jackson, *Saladin*, 241.

3. Ibn Shaddād, *Nawādir*, al-Shayyāl ed., 24, Richards trans., 29–30; F. Gabrieli, *Chroniques arabes des croisades*, 130–131.

4. According to Muhammad Ibn al-Qādisī, quoted by Abū Shāma, *Rawdatayn*, 2:82, trans. *Recueils des historiens des croisades. Historiens orientaux*, 4:286 (hereafter cited as *RHC Or.*).

5. Quoted in Lyons and Jackson, *Saladin*, 271.

6. See Ibn al-Athīr, *Kāmil*, 12:20.

7. See Ibn Shaddād, *Nawādir*, al-Shayyāl ed., 25, 103, 114–115, 188, 211, Richards trans., 30, 96, 106, 179, 204; ʿImād al-Dīn, *Fath*, Massé trans., 190.

8. See Abū Shāma, *Rawdatayn*, 2:168 (lines 33–34), 169 (line 28).

9. See Ibn Abī Usaybiʿa, 688.

10. A physician received seven thousand dinars for healing al-ʿĀdil in 1213–1214. See Ibn Abī Usaybiʿa, 730.

11. See Lyons and Jackson, *Saladin*, 237.

12. See A. M. Eddé, *Principauté ayyoubide d'Alep*, 476.

13. See Ibn Abī Usaybiʿa, 635–636; S. Jadon, "The Physicians of Syria during the Reign of Salāh al-Dīn," 323–340.

14. See al-Maqqarī, *Nafh al-tīb min ghusn al-Andalus al-ratīb*, ed. I. ʿAbbās, 8 vols. (Beirut, 1968), 2:636–637; Ibn Abī Usaybiʿa, 630–635; L. Pouzet, "Maghrébins à Damas au VIIe/XIIIe siècle," *Bulletin d'études orientales* 28 (1975): 167–199, esp. 168n. 3.

15. See Ibn Abī Usaybiʿa, 637.

16. Among the dead: Husām al-Dīn Sunqur al-Khilātī in September 1189; Diyāʾ al-Dīn ʿĪsā al-Hakkārī in December 1189; Zayn al-Dīn Yūsuf of Irbil in October 1190 (Ibn Shaddād, *Nawādir*, al-Shayyāl ed., 105, 116, 144, Richards trans., 98, 107, 133; ʿImād al-Dīn, *Fath*, Massé trans., 260–261).

17. See Ibn Shaddād, *Nawādir*, al-Shayyāl ed., 126–127, 167, Richards trans., 116, 157.

18. See Ibn Shaddād, *Nawādir*, al-Shayyāl ed., 166, 236, Richards trans., 155, 233; ʿImād al-Dīn, *Fath*, Massé trans., 307, 394; Lyons and Jackson, *Saladin*, 323.

19. See ʿImād al-Dīn, *Fath*, 365–366. See also Ibn Abī Usaybiʿa, 651–659; Sibt Ibn al-Jawzī, 8:411–412; Bar Hebraeus, Budge trans., 329.

20. Its title was *al-Maqāla al-Nāsiriyya fī hafz al-umūr al-sihhiyya*. Ibn Abī Usaybiʿa (659) saw a first version of that book, which bore the title *al-Maqalā al-Najmiyya*. He thought that Ibn al-Mutrān had begun it for Najm al-Dīn Ayyūb but that, upon the latter's death, the author dedicated it to Saladin.

21. See Sibt Ibn al-Jawzī, 8:430; Ibn Abi Usaybiʿa, 672–675; A. M. Eddé, "Les médecins dans la société syrienne du VIIe/XIIIe siècle," *Annales islamologiques* 29 (1995): 91–109, esp. 95.

22. See N. Offenstadt, "Les femmes et la paix à la fin du Moyen Âge: Genre, discours, rites," in *Le règlement des conflits au Moyen Âge, XXIe Congrès de la S.H.M.E.S. (Angers, juin 2000)* (Paris, 2001), 317–333, esp. 328.

23. Ibn al-Athīr, *Kāmil*, 11:498, Richards trans., 2:295; Abū Shāma, *Rawdatayn*, 2:42.

24. See Ibn Shaddād, *Nawādir*, al-Shayyāl ed., 26, 27, 197–198, Richards trans., 31, 32, 190.

25. See P. M. Cobb, *Usama ibn Munqidh*, 85.

26. See J. Le Goff, *Saint Louis* (Paris, 1996), 491; M. Zink, "Joinville ne pleure pas mais il rêve," *Poétique* 33 (1978): 28–45.

27. See Ibn Shaddād, *Nawādir*, al-Shayyāl ed., 9–10, Richards trans., 20; Gabrieli, *Chroniques arabes des croisades*, 118; Abū Shāma, *Rawdatayn*, 1:261; ʿImād al-Dīn, *Fath*, Massé trans., 408.

28. Ibn Shaddād, *Nawādir*, al-Shayyāl ed., 231, Richards trans., 227.

29. See P. Nagy-Zombory, "Les larmes aussi ont une histoire," *L'Histoire* 218 (1998): 68–71; and P. Nagy Zombory, *Le don des larmes* (Paris, 2000).

30. Quoted in N. Amri, *Les saints en islam, les messagers de l'espérance* (Paris, 2008), 91–98.

31. See Ibn Shaddād, *Nawādir*, al-Shayyāl ed., 12, 217, Richards trans., 22, 211.

32. See Ibn Shaddād, *Nawādir*, al-Shayyāl ed., 150, Richards trans., 138; Sibt Ibn al-Jawzī, 8:408; Lyons and Jackson, *Saladin*, 322.

33. Ibn Shaddād, *Nawādir*, al-Shayyāl ed., 166, Richards trans., 157.

34. See Ibn al-Athīr, *Kāmil*, 11:536, Richards trans., 2:323.

35. Abū Shāma, *Rawdatayn*, 2:83, trans. *RHC Or.*, 4:289.

36. See Ibn Shaddād, *Nawādir*, al-Shayyāl ed., 242, Richards trans., 239.

37. 'Imād al-Dīn, *Fath*, Massé trans., 294–295; Ibn Shaddād, *Nawādir*, al-Shayyāl ed., 159, Richards trans., 148.

38. See Ibn Shaddād, *Nawādir*, al-Shayyāl ed., 247, Richards trans., 244. See also Sibt Ibn al-Jawzī, 8:430; 'Imād al-Dīn, *Fath*, Massé trans., 408–409.

39. See Ibn Kathīr (*Bidāya*, 8:504), who attributes his death to a biliary fever. It is clear that Saladin, who had long suffered from chronic intestinal distress, died of an illness of the digestive system.

40. Ibn Shaddād, *Nawādir*, al-Shayyāl ed., 245, Richards trans., 242–243, in *RHC Or.*, 3:366.

41. He died in a small room of the Dār al-Qasaba, the same room where his great-nephew al-Kāmil would die in 1238 (Ibn Kathīr, *Bidāya*, 9:30).

42. The Mosque of the Prophet's Footprint (*Qadam*), in a populated area south of Damascus. See Ibn 'Asākir, *Ta'rīkh Dimashq*, Elisséeff trans., 173.

43. See *Encyclopaedia of Islam*, 2nd ed., "'Āshūrā'" (P. Marçais).

44. Bāb al-Nasr (Eagle Gate). The Damascenes used the term *Nasr* to designate the large cupola atop the principal nave of the mosque. Popular tradition claimed that the name was attributed to it because the cupola, the axial nave, and the transversal nave, taken together, rose skyward like an eagle in flight (Ibn Jubayr, Gaudefroy-Demombynes trans., 305). That was an interpretation of a term whose origin had been lost by the twelfth century. K. A. C. Creswell has convincingly argued that it probably came originally from the Greek word *aetos* (eagle), which was used as a technical term to designate the highest point of a building. That term, undoubtedly used during the construction of the mosque in the eighth century by Greek-speaking artisans, was translated literally into Arabic as eagle *(nasr)*. See K. A. C. Creswell, *Early Muslim Architecture*, 2nd ed. (Oxford, 1969), I, 1: 169.

45. Abū Shāma, *Rawdatayn*, 2:214, trans. *RHC Or.*, 5:95–96, based on 'Imād al-Dīn, *'Utbā al-zamān*; Ibn Kathīr, *Bidāya*, 8:505.

46. On al-'Azīziyya madrasa, see Abū Shāma, *Rawdatayn*, 2:231; Ibn Shaddād (*A'lāq* [Damascus, 1956], 239) says it was founded by al-Afdal and completed by al-'Azīz.

Nevertheless, Abū Shāma's account, based on 'Imād al-Dīn, a witness to the events, attributes its founding to al-'Azīz, which is more credible. Perhaps al-Afdal planned to build a madrasa at that place and the plan was later realized by al-'Azīz. See A. Moaz, "Note sur le mausolée de Saladin," 183–189.

47. One of the long sides and one of the short sides are original, as are the four uprights at the corners, and the inscription, which was shortened somewhat during one of its restorations. See J. Sauvaget, "Le cénotaphe de Saladin," 168–175.

48. 'Imād al-Dīn, *Fath*, Massé trans., 427.

20. Guardian of the Faith

1. See al-Maqrīzī, *Khitat*, 1:104, Sayyid ed., 1:279; M. C. Lyons and D. E. P. Jackson, *Saladin*, 50.

2. See Ibn Shaddād, *Nawādir*, al-Shayyāl ed., 40, Richards trans., 45; Ibn al-'Adīm, *Zubda*, 2:315; *The Sea of Precious Virtues*, xi.

3. See Abū Shāma, *Rawdatayn*, 1:237, based on Ibn Abī Tayyi'.

4. Al-Subkī, *Tabaqāt*, 7:16–17, repr. in al-Maqrīzī, *Muqaffā*, 7:227.

5. Al-Bundārī, 152–153.

6. Al-Wahrānī, *Manamāt*, 49–50.

7. See al-Bundārī, 187–188; al-Mansūr, *Midmār*, 62–65; Lyons and Jackson, *Saladin*, 162.

8. See Y. Lev, *Saladin in Egypt*, 133–134.

9. See Y. Lev, *Charity, Endowments and Charitable Institutions*, 79.

10. See Ibn Jubayr, Gaudefroy-Demombynes trans., 115.

11. See Abū Shāma, *Rawdatayn*, 2:74 (lines 13–14), based on Ibn al-Qādisī (twelfth century); see also the letter sent to the emir of Mecca in al-Qalqashandī, *Subh*, 7:109–110; and Ibn Wāsil, *Mufarrij*, 3:377–378. Emir Mukthir ibn 'Isā, who ruled Mecca in 1183, found no favor in Ibn Jubayr's eyes (Gaudefroy-Demombynes trans., 91); *Encyclopaedia of Islam*, 2nd ed., (hereafter cited as *EI* 2), "Makka," 147b (A. J. Wensinck-C. E. Bosworth); E. Sivan, *L'Islam et la croisade*, 99; J. C. Garcin, *Qūs*, 105, 134, 138.

12. The emir of Medina at the time was 'Izz al-Dīn al-Qāsim ibn al-Muhannā al-Husaynī. See 'Imād al-Dīn, *Fath*, Massé trans., 32; Ibn al-Athīr, *Kāmil*, 12:20; Ibn Wāsil, *Mufarrij*, 1:230–231.

13. See al-Maqrīzī, *Itti'āz*, 3:319–320; and al-Maqrīzī, *Khitat*, 2:275, Sayyid ed., 4, 1:100; *EI* 2, "al-Azhar" (J. Jomier).

14. See al-Maqrīzī, *Muqaffā*, 1:708; G. Leiser, "Hanbalism in Egypt before the Mamlûks," 161.

15. The governor was named Mubārak Ibn Munqidh. See Garcin, *Qūs*, 125–127, 130; and *Répertoire chronologique d'épigraphie arabe*, 9, no. 3298 (hereafter cited as *RCEA*).

16. See W. Madelung, "The Spread of Māturīdism and the Turks," in *Actas do IV congresso de estudos Árabes e Islâmicos* (Coimbra, 1968; Leiden, 1971), 109–168.

17. See J. Van Reeth, "La barque de l'Imām aš-Šāfiʿī," 250.

18. See Ibn Jubayr, Gaudefroy-Demombynes trans., 56.

19. See al-Subkī, *Tabaqāt*, 6:41–42.

20. See al-Maqrīzī, *Muqaffā*, 2:183; al-Subkī, *Tabaqāt*, 7:339.

21. See al-Maqrīzī, *Khitat*, 2:343, Sayyid ed., 4, 1:396.

22. Abū l-Faraj al-Shīrāzī (d. 1093). See Ibn al-ʿImād, *Shadharāt*, 6:554; Ibn Rajab, *Kitāb al-dhayl*, 1:436–440; ʿImād al-Dīn, *Fath*, Massé trans., 54; al-Bundārī, 246; Abū Shāma, *Tarājim*, 34; Ibn Kathīr, *Bidāya*, 8:539; Sibt Ibn al-Jawzī, 8:414; H. Laoust, *Les schismes dans l'Islam* (Paris, 1965), 229; and H. Laoust, "Le hanbalisme sous le califat de Bagdad (241–656/856–1258)," *Revue des études islamiques* 27 (1959): 67–128, esp. 126; Lyons and Jackson, *Saladin*, 67–68; Leiser, "Hanbalism in Egypt before the Mamlûks," 155–181.

23. Al-Khabūshānī (Yāqūt, *Muʿjam al-buldān*, 2:344) or al-Khubūshānī (Ibn Khallikān, 4:239–240); al-Maqrīzī, *Muqaffā*, 7:225–229; Leiser, "Hanbalism in Egypt before the Mamlûks," 166. On al-Tūsī, see Ibn Khallikān, 4:224; Ibn al-ʿImād, *Shadharāt*, 6:534–535.

24. See al-Maqrīzī, *Sulūk*, 1, 1:88.

25. See Ibn Kathīr, *Bidāya*, 8:524.

26. See Abū Shāma, *Rawdatayn*, 2:74, 179; al-Bundārī, 287; Lyons and Jackson, *Saladin*, 246.

27. Kamāl al-Dīn Ibn al-Sharazūrī (d. 1176) would remain chief qāḍī in Damascus, and in 1183 Muhyī al-Dīn Ibn al-Zakī was named chief qāḍī in Aleppo. The position of Aleppine preacher devolved on the family of the Banū Hāshim (A. M. Eddé, *Principauté ayyoubide d'Alep*, 350, 360). In Jerusalem, Ibn Shaddād was named chief qāḍī, and the position of preacher at al-Aqṣā Mosque, from the late thirteenth to the early sixteenth century, remained in the hands of another important Shafite family, that of the Banū Jamāʿa. See K. Salibi, "The Banū Jamāʿa: A Dynasty of Shafiʿite Jurists in the Mamluk Period," *Studia Islamica* 9 (1958): 97–109; H. Halm, "The Reestablishment of Sunnī fiqh in Jerusalem under Ayyūbid rule," 111.

28. See Sivan, *L'Islam et la croisade*, 103; Ibn Kathīr, *Bidāya*, 13:59.

29. See Ibn al-ʿImād, *Shadharāt* 7:289; Ibn Rajab, *Kitāb al-dhayl*, 2:193–201.

30. See Eddé, *Principauté ayyoubide d'Alep*, 350–377.

31. See C. Cahen, "Réflexions sur le *waqf* ancien," *Studia Islamica* 14 (1961): 37–56, repr. in *Les peuples musulmans dans l'histoire musulmane* (Damascus, 1977), 287–306; Y. Frenkel, "Political and Social Aspects," 1–20.

32. See al-Maqrīzī, *Khitat*, 2:273ff. and 363, Sayyid ed., 4, 1:90ff. and 4, 2:452.

33. See *RCEA*, 9, no. 3297; the ʿAmr Mosque reportedly had thirty Egyptian dinars per day for its upkeep and the salary of the intendants, imams, Koran readers, and guards. See Ibn Jubayr, Gaudefroy-Demombynes trans., 54.

34. See al-Maqrīzī, *Khitat*, 2:275–276, Sayyid ed., 4, 1:102–103; Lev, *Saladin in Egypt*, 136; *EI* 2, "Masdjid" (J. Pedersen).

35. See L. Korn, " 'Die Bauten Saladins,' " 214n. 13 (correct "552/1151" to "552/1157");
    H. Halm, *Die Ausbreitung der šāfiʿitischen Rechtsschule von den Anfängen bis zum 8./14.*
    Jahrhundert (Wiesbaden, 1974), 240.

36. Ibn Jubayr, Gaudefroy-Demombynes trans., 51, Broadhurst trans., 40. In the fif-
    teenth century, al-Maqrīzī (*Khitat*, 2:343, Sayyid ed., 4, 1:397) called it "al-Nāsiriyya,"
    but in the twelfth and thirteenth centuries, Ibn Jubayr (Gaudefroy-Demombynes
    trans., 51, Broadhurst trans., 40), Ibn al-Athīr (*Kāmil*, 11:440, Richards trans., 2:252),
    and Abū Shāma (*Rawdatayn*, 1:268) said simply that it was built near the tomb of
    Imam al-Shāfiʿī.

37. In G. Wiet, "Les inscriptions du mausolée de Shāfiʿī," *Bulletin de l'institut d'Égypte*,
    15, 2 (1933): 167–185; *RCEA*, 9, nos. 3331–3333, 3339; J. Van Reeth, "La barque de l'Imām
    aš-Šāfiʿī," 249.

38. Qutb al-Dīn al-Naysābūrī, whose teachings Saladin had followed in his youth in
    Syria, was very likely the source of his adherence to that theological school. Later,
    in Cairo, the teacher and preacher Tāj al-Dīn Muhammad al-Barmakī dedicated
    a book to him setting out the major principles of Asharism. See al-Subkī, *Tabaqāt*,
    7:23–25; al-Maqrīzī, *Khitat*, 2:273, 343, 358, Sayyid ed., 4, 1:90, 396, 440; Leiser, "Han-
    balism in Egypt before the Mamlûks," 167; Madelung, "The Spread of Māturīdism
    and the Turks," 158–159 and n. 132. A manuscript of al-Barmakī's work, titled *Hadāʾiq*
    al-fusūl wa-jawāhir al-usūl, was held in Cairo (C. Brockelmann, *Geschichte der Ara-*
    bischen Literatur, 2 vols. [Weimar, 1898–1902; 2nd ed. Leiden, 1943–1949; 3 supple-
    ments, Leiden, 1937–1942], suppl. 2, 977).

39. ʿUbayd ibn Maʿālī for al-Shāfiʿī's coffin and Salmān ibn Maʿālī for the pulpit. See
    Wiet, "Les inscriptions du mausolée de Shāfiʿī," 172–179; M. Van Berchem, *Matéri-*
    aux pour un corpus inscriptionum arabicarum, Deuxième partie, Syrie du Sud, II, Jerusa-
    lem "Haram" (Cairo, 1927), 393–400; L. A. Mayer, *Islamic Woodcarvers and Their Works*
    (Geneva, 1958), 63, 65; J. Van Reeth, "La barque de l'Imām aš-Šāfiʿī," 249–250. The
    mausoleum that even today holds al-Shāfiʿī's tomb was later rebuilt (in 1211) by Sala-
    din's nephew al-Kāmil. See K. A. C. Creswell, *Muslim Architecture of Egypt*, 2:64ff.,
    figs. 30–31, pl. 22–26.

40. The jurist Ahmad ibn al-Muzaffar al-Dimashqī, known by the name Ibn Zayn al-
    Najjār (d. 1194–1195), taught there, and that madrasa later took his name (no doubt to
    distinguish it from Saladin's other madrasa). It was later named al-Sharīfiyya ma-
    drasa, because Sharīf Muhammad ibn al-Husayn al-Urmawī, qādī of the army
    (d. 1252–1253), taught there beginning in 1232–1233; see Abū Shāma, *Rawdatayn*, 1:191;
    al-Bundārī, 57; Ibn al-Athīr, *Kāmil*, 11:366, Richards trans., 2:194; al-Maqrīzī, *Khitat*,
    2:363, Sayyid ed., 454–455; al-Maqrīzī, *Muqaffā*, 1:664, 5:597–598; Lev, *Saladin in Egypt*,
    124; S. Denoix, *Décrire Le Caire (Fustāt-Misr), d'après Ibn Duqmāq et Maqrīzī* (Cairo,
    1992), 125.

41. It was called al-Qamhiyya (wheat madrasa), because the four teachers who taught there received wheat, which was sent to them from a village in Fayyūm; Lev, *Saladin in Egypt*, 125; see al-Maqrīzī, *Khitat*, 2:364, Sayyid ed., 4, 2:455–456; Denoix, *Décrire Le Caire (Fustāt-Misr)*, 127.

42. See al-Maqrīzī, *Khitat*, 1:427, Sayyid ed., 2:410; Ibn Khallikān, 7:206.

43. Vizier from 1121 to 1125. See al-Maqrīzī, *Khitat*, 2:365, Sayyid ed., 4, 2:460–461. Al-Maqrīzī saw the foundation deed with Saladin's signature (*al-hamdu li llāh wa bihi tawfīqī*). He also gives the names of the witnesses who signed it. Saladin appointed Majd al-Dīn Muhammad al-Khutanī (d. 1180) to teach there, with a salary of eleven dinars a month (that is, one-fifth that of a teacher at the new Shafite madrasa). On Majd al-Dīn Muhammad al-Khutanī, see Ibn Abī l-Wafā', *al-Jawāhir al-mudiyya* (Cairo, 1993), 3:348–349, no. 1521. After him, teaching was assigned to Abū Muhammad 'Abd Allāh al-Harīrī (d. 1181), an Iraqi whom Saladin used several times as an ambassador. See Madelung, "The Spread of Māturīdism and the Turks," 162 and n. 138.

44. Ibn Khallikān, 7:207. Several hadith affirmed the same thing. See *EI* 2, "Sadaka" (T. H. Weir-[A. Zysow]).

45. In fact, the only teacher mentioned by al-Maqrīzī is the grandson of Ibn Shās, a jurist who died in 1219. See al-Maqrīzī, *Khitat*, 2:365, Sayyid ed., 4, 2:458–459.

46. See al-Maqrīzī, *Itti'āz*, 3:320, and *Khitat*, 1:485; 2:364–356; Sayyid ed., 2:576, and 4, 2:456–458; al-Bundārī, 58; Abū Shāma, *Rawdatayn*, 1:191; Lev, *Saladin in Egypt*, 125; Denoix, *Décrire Le Caire (Fustāt-Misr)*, 126 (among its *waqfs* were a hammam and the cowshed of the former residence that was turned into a *funduq*). The faqīh Bahā' al-Dīn 'Alī (d. 1188) taught there. See Ibn Shaddād, quoted by Ibn Khallikān, 7:88.

47. Its founder was Qutb al-Dīn Khusraw al-Hadhbānī. See al-Maqrīzī, *Khitat*, 2:365, Sayyid ed., 4, 2:459–460.

48. A Shafite, even though he was Andalusian. Upon his death, he was buried in al-Fādil's mausoleum in al-Qarāfa cemetery; see Ibn Khallikān, 3:162; Ibn Kathīr, *Bidāya*, 13:10; Ibn al-'Imād, *Shadharāt*, 6:494–495; *EI* 2, "al-Shātibī" (A. Neuwirth).

49. Abū l-Qāsim 'Abd al-Rahmān al-Iskandarānī. See al-Maqrīzī, *Khitat*, 2:366–367, Sayyid ed., 4, 2:462–465.

50. His father was 'Abd al-Wahhāb al-Shīrāzī; see Ibn Rajab, *Kitāb al-dhayl*, 1:370; Leiser, "Hanbalism in Egypt before the Mamlûks," 167.

51. In addition to the nine madrasas already mentioned, there was that of Ibn al-Arsūfī (in 1174–1175), a shopkeeper from Ascalon (al-Maqrīzī, *Khitat*, 2:364, Sayyid ed., 4, 2:456). L. Korn ("'Die Bauten Saladins,'" table 1, p. 226) counts more, because he includes two other madrasas, one built by an emir of Shīrkūh's and then of Saladin's, Sayf al-Dīn Ayāzkūj al-Asadī in 1195–1196, and the other by his wife (al-'Cshūriyya) at an undetermined date (before 1198, the year before the death of the

Jewish doctor Ibn Jumay', from whom she bought the house where she founded her madrasa). See al-Maqrīzī, *Khitat*, 2:367–368, Sayyid ed., 4, 2:465, 468; G. Leiser, "Notes on the Madrasa in Medieval Islamic Society," *Muslim World* 76 (1986): 16–23, esp. 18–19; I. M. Lapidus, "Ayyūbid Religious Policy and the Development of the Schools of Law in Cairo," *Colloque international sur l'histoire du Caire (27 mars–5 avril 1969)* (Gräfenhainichen, Germany, n.d.), 279–286.

52. See al-Maqrīzī, *Sulūk*, 1, 1:76.

53. See al-Maqrīzī, *Khitat*, 2:365, Sayyid ed., 4, 2:458.

54. Late twelfth century in Aswān and 1210 in Qūs. See Garcin, *Qūṣ*, 16, 173.

55. See M. Barrucand, "Damaskus und Saladin," in Wieczorek et al., eds., *Saladin und die Kreuzfahrer*, 261–263; Korn, "'Die Bauten Saladins,'" 217–222; A. M. Eddé, "Saladin's Religious Foundations in Damascus," 62–76.

56. As attested by two inscriptions that bear his name. See *RCEA*, 9, nos. 3343, 3344.

57. *Zāwiya* literally means "recess" or "angle." In the twelfth-century Middle East, the term usually designated a corner or a room in a religious building set aside for legal and religious teaching (as was the case here), or sometimes an ascetic's place of residence. Known as the *zāwiya* of Sheikh Nasr al-Maqdisī (d. 1097), it was located under the north portico of the Great Mosque. Saladin allocated to it the revenues of a village in Hauran and appointed the jurist Qutb al-Dīn al-Naysābūrī to oversee the *waqf* (for the teacher's salary). See Abū Shāma, *Rawdatayn*, 1:263; Ibn Shaddād, *A'lāq* (Damascus, 1956), 246; N. Elisséeff, *Nūr al-Dīn*, 3:919.

58. See in particular G. Le Strange, *Palestine*, 247; K. A. C. Creswell, "The Origin of the Cruciform Plan of Cairene Madrasas," *Bulletin de l'institut français d'archéologie orientale* (1922) 21:1–54, esp. 27; Elisséeff, *Nūr al-Dīn*, 924–925; D. Sack, *Damaskus*, no. 1/18; Korn, "'Die Bauten Saladins,'" 218; L. Korn, "The Structure of Architectural Patronage," 79; K. Wulzinger and C. Watzinger, *Damaskus*, vol. 2: *Die islamische Stadt* (Berlin, 1924), 63. These are the only ones who speak of "al-Kallāsa Mosque," but they do not go into detail; L. Korn, *Ayyubidische Architektur* (2004), 2:106, no. 8.

59. See Ibn Shaddād, *A'lāq* (Damascus, 1956), 76–77, 84–85, 248; Ibn Shaddād, *Nawādir*, al-Shayyāl ed., 246, Richards trans., 243; Ibn Khallikān, 4:450; Ibn Kathīr, *Bidāya*, 9:386; al-Safadī, *A'yān al-'asr wa a'wān al-nasr*, 6 vols. (Beirut, 1997–1998), 5:546; Ibn Battūta, *Tuhfat al-nuzzār fī gharā'ib al-amsār wa 'ajā'ib al-asfār*, ed. and trans. C. Défrémery and B. R. Sanguinetti, 4 vols. (Paris, 1853–1859; repr. in 2 vols., with introduction and notes by S. Yerasimos [Paris, 1982]), 1:222; Ibn al-'Adīm, *Bughya*, 10:4442, 4504, 4629. See also L. Pouzet, *Damas au VIIe/XIIIe siècle*, 45n. 121, 98.

60. Ibn Jubayr, Gaudefroy-Demombynes trans., 308, Broadhurst trans., 278.

61. In the time of al-Nu'aymī (d. 1521), it was considered a madrasa, but, regarding the origin of the edifice, al-Nuwayrī faithfully reproduces Ibn Shaddād's account (*Al'āq* [Damascus, 1956], 76), which says that al-Kallāsa "was established as an annex [zi-

yāda] when the Great Mosque became too small to contain the people." Renowned teachers such as Kamāl al-Dīn Abū Muhammad Ibn al-Harastānī (d. 1226–1227), Shams al-Dīn ibn 'Abd al-Kāfī al-Siqillī al-Dimashqī (d. 1251–1252), and Bahā' al-Dīn Ibn al-Zakī (d. 1287) taught there in the thirteenth century (see al-Nu'aymī, Dāris, 1:167, 189, 222, 447–451).

62. Ibn Shaddād, A'lāq (Damascus, 1956), 248 ("al-Salāhiyya zāwiya in al-Kallāsa") and 84–85: the author lists twenty-two teaching circles in the Great Mosque (called, depending on the case, halqa, mī'ād, zāwiya, or madrasa), including that of al-Kallāsa, not to mention, he says, 128 circles for teaching the Koran. See also Ibn Jubayr, Gaudefroy-Demombynes trans., 313; al-Nu'aymī, Dāris, 1:333.

63. Dār al-hadīth, located between al-'Azīziyya madrasa and the Great Mosque. See al-Nu'aymī, Dāris, 1:89–96; Ibn Kathīr, Bidāya, 8:505; map of this neighborhood in Wulzinger and Watzinger, Damaskus. Die islamische Stadt (Berlin, 1924), reproduced in A. Moaz, "Note sur le mausolée de Saladin à Damas," pl. 1.

64. See Elisséeff, Nūr al-Dīn, 3:762–764; Eddé, Principauté ayyoubide d'Alep, 401–402 and fig. 51.

65. See Elisséeff, Nūr al-Dīn, 3:919–930.

66. See Ibn Shaddād, A'lāq (Damascus, 1956), 199–264 (with references to al-Nu'aymī's book in the notes); Korn, " 'Die Bauten Saladins,' " 227. The exact number is difficult to determine because, when the date of construction is not mentioned, the founder's name does not always indicate whether the foundation took place before or after Saladin's death.

67. Restoration of al-Kallāsa, north of the Geat Mosque, and endowment of waqfs to the madrasa (the 'Imādiyya/Salāhiyya) that had just been built by Nūr al-Dīn's son. See Ibn Shaddād, A'lāq (Damascus, 1956), 237.

68. See Eddé, "Saladin's Religious Foundations in Damascus," 67–74.

69. See Ibn 'Asākir, Ta'rīkh Dimashq, Munajjid ed., 2:77, Elisséeff trans. in Description de Damas, 137: a mosque "in the Nūriyya madrasa that Nūr al-Dīn constituted as a waqf for the Malekites at the Golden Stone." Al-Dhahabī, Ta'rīkh al-islām wa wafayāt al-mashāhīr wa l-a'lām, ed. 'U. Tadmurī (Beirut, 1995), 151; Ibn Shaddād, A'lāq (Damascus, 1956), 245, 253–254, does not give any name for that madrasa. The name al-Salāhiyya was added by the editor based on al-Nu'aymī, Dāris, 2:10). Ibn Khallikān, 7:207, trans. Recueils des historiens des croisades. Historiens orientaux, 3:429 (hereafter cited as RHC Or.). See Ibn Battūta, Tuhfat al-nuzzār fī gharā'ib al-amsār wa 'ajā'ib al-asfār, 1:228; al-Nu'aymī, Dāris, 1:331 and 2:3, 10. N. Elisséeff, "Les monuments de Nūr al-Dīn," Bulletin d'études orientales 13 (1949–1951): 5–43, esp. 28; N. Elisséeff, Nūr al-Dīn, 928; L. Pouzet, "Maghrébins à Damas au VIIe/XIIIe siècle," Bulletin d'études orientales 28 (1975): 167–199, esp. 168 and 189; Korn, " 'Die Bauten Saladins,' " 218; and L. Korn, Ayyubidische Architektur (2004), 112, no. 29.

70. See Ibn ʿAsākir, *Taʾrīkh Dimashq*, Munajjid ed., 2:364, Elisséeff trans. in *Description de Damas*, 238–239; Ibn Kathīr, *Bidāya*, 5:759; Al-Safadī, *al-Wāfī bi l-wafayāt*, vol. 16, ed. W. al-Qādī (Wiesbaden, 1982), 7; al-Nuʿaymī, *Dāris*, 1:398.

71. Described at length by Ibn Jubayr, Gaudefroy-Demombynes trans., 332, 314.

72. The three Hanafite madrasas founded by former emirs of Nūr al-Dīn in the last decade of the twelfth century probably date from the beginning of al-Zāhir's reign (1193–1216). See Eddé, *Principauté ayyoubide d'Alep*, 646–650.

73. See Ibn Shaddād, *Aʿlāq* (Damascus, 1953), 35.

74. See Frenkel, "Political and Social Aspects," 1–20; J. Pahlitzsch, "The Transformation of Latin Religious Institutions into Islamic Endowments by Saladin in Jerusalem," 47–69; Korn, "The Structure of Architectural Patronage in Ayyubid Jerusalem," 47–69 and 71–89; Halm, "The Re-establishment of Sunnī fiqh in Jerusalem under Ayyūbid Rule," 111–116.

75. An inscription dated 585/1189–1190 in situ inside the Dome of the Rock (Le Strange, *Palestine*, 134), another on the Qubbat Yūsuf on the esplanade; a third commemorated the restoration of al-Aqsā Mosque and its *mihrāb*. See *RCEA*, 9, nos. 3423 and 3447.

76. See ʿImād al-Dīn, *Fath*, Massé trans., 58; K. J. al-ʿAsalī, *Maʿāhid al-ʿilm fī Bayt al-Maqdis* (Amman, 1981), 61–79. The foundation inscription can be found in *RCEA*, 9, no. 3453. See also Frenkel, "Political and Social Aspects," 8; and Pahlitzsch, "The Transformation of Latin Religious Institutions into Islamic Endowments by Saladin in Jerusalem," 53–59. The madrasa was converted back into a church in the nineteenth century.

77. See al-Harawī, *Kitāb al-ishārāt*, Sourdel-Thomine ed., ed., 35–39, 46–47, trans., 80–93, 108–110.

78. See D. De Smet, "La translation du Raʾs al-Ḥusayn au Caire fatimide," in *Egypt and Syria in the Fatimid, Ayyubid and Mamluk Eras*, ed. U. Vermeulen and D. De Smet, vol. 2 (Louvain, 1998), 41n. 61.

79. Ibn Jubayr, Gaudefroy-Demombynes trans., 47–48, Broadhurst trans., 36–37.

80. See Eddé, *Principauté ayyoubide d'Alep*, 449–450.

81. Thietmar, in *Croisades et pèlerinages*, 939, 945, 952.

82. See Elisséeff, *Nūr al-Dīn*, 3:764–771; Eddé, *Principauté ayyoubide d'Alep*, 426–429 and fig. 52.

83. See al-Wahrānī, *Manāmāt*, 48.

84. See al-Wahrānī, *Manāmāt*, 106–107.

85. That *khānqāh* bore the name of a teacher at the grand palace from the time of Caliph al-Mustansir (r. 1036–1094).

86. The monument, transformed during the Mamluk era, still exists. The residents' cells were arranged around a central court with four iwans, the east one serving as

a prayer hall. See al-Maqrīzī, *Khitat*, 2:415–416, Sayyid ed., 4, 2:727–732; *EI* 2, "Sa'īd al-Su'adā'" (S. Denoix).

87. See al-Bundārī, 121.

88. Ghānim ibn 'Alī ibn Ibrāhīm Ibn 'Asākir (d. 1235); see Mujīr al-Dīn, *al-Uns al-jalīl*, 2:47, 146, Sauvaire trans., 77, 166; Ibn al-'Imād, *Shadharāt*, 7:270–271; 'Imād al-Dīn, *Fath*, Massé trans., 396; D. P. Little, "Jerusalem under the Ayyūbids and Mamlūks," 180; Pahlitzsch, "The Transformation of Latin Religious Institutions into Islamic Endowments by Saladin in Jerusalem," 49–52 and 60–68, with the publication and translation of the *waqf* deed that has come down to us through its sixteenth-century corroboration (see K. J. al-'Asalī, *Wathā'iq maqdisiyya ta'rīkhiyya*, 2 vols. [Amman, 1983–1985], 1:81–104).

89. Two Kurds from the al-Hakkārī family, Walī al-Dīn Abū l-'Abbās Ahmad ibn Abī Bakr ibn 'Abd Allāh and his son Abū l-Hasan 'Alī. But the *waqf* was not signed until 584/1198. See Mujīr al-Dīn, *al-Uns al-jalīl*, 2:61.

90. The present-day al-Khataniyya *zāwiya*. The ascetic was named Jalāl al-Dīn Muhammad al-Shāshī. See Mujīr al-Dīn, *al-Uns al-jalīl*, 2:34, 144, Sauvaire trans., 140–141; K. J. 'Asalī, *Ma'āhid al-'ilm fī Bayt al-Maqdis* (Amman, 1981), 100–103.

91. See Ibn al-'Adīm, *Bughya*, 5:2285 (Ascalon); A. M. Eddé, "Religious Circles in Jerusalem in the Ayyubid Period," in *Ayyubid Jerusalem: The Holy City in Context, 1187–1250*, ed. R. Hillenbrand (Edinburgh, 2009), 195–201.

92. The Bishop's Palace was turned into a hospital. See al-Bundārī, 324; and Ibn Kathīr, *Bidāya*, 8:478 (correct the editing mistake to read: *waqafa dār al-isbitāriyya nisfayn*).

93. Ibn Shaddād, *A'lāq* (Damascus, 1956), 193. Moreover, Saladin warmly welcomed the Sufi 'Alī ibn 'Abd Allāh Abī l-Faraj, son of a former vizier of Baghdad who had been assassinated by the Ismailis under the caliphate of al-Mustadī' (1171–1180). 'Alī himself had founded an establishment for Sufis inside the caliphal palace in Baghdad before moving to Damascus, where he died in 1187 (Sibt Ibn al-Jawzī, 8:391).

94. See Ibn Taghribirdī, *al-Nujūm al-zāhira*, 16 vols. (Cairo, 1963–1972), 6:42.

95. Ibn Shaddād, *Nawādir*, al-Shayyāl ed., 10, Richards trans., 20.

96. 'Imād al-Dīn, *Fath*, Massé trans., 434.

97. See Ibn al-'Adīm, *Bughya*, 8:3719–3722; Eddé, *Principauté ayyoubide d'Alep*, 423.

98. Letter composed by al-Fādil and reproduced in Abū Shāma, *Rawdatayn*, 1:221, lines 33ff.; Ibn Wāsil, *Mufarrij*, 2:476.

99. According to the Shiite historian Ibn Abī Tayyi', in Abū Shāma, *Rawdatayn*, 1:251–252.

100. H. Ziai contests the theosophical term often used in reference to the doctrine of al-Suhrawardī. See H. Ziai, *Knowledge and Illumination: A Study of Suhrawardī's Hikmat al-ishrāq* (Atlanta, 1990); H. Ziai, "The Source and Nature of Authority: A Study of Suhrawardī's Illuminationist Political Doctrine," in *The Political Aspects of*

Islamic Philosophy, ed. C. Butterworth (Cambridge, Mass., 1992), 304–344; and *EI* 2, "al-Suhrawardī" (H. Ziai). See also C. D'Ancona, *Storia della filosofia nell'islam medievale*, 2 vols. (Turin, 2005), 2:637–645. The philosopher al-Suhrawardī must not be confused with his namesake, the great Sufi of Sunni Islam who died in 1234.

101. See Eddé, *Principauté ayyoubide d'Alep*, 424.

102. Sharīf Abū l-Makārim Hamza Ibn Zuhra. See Ibn Abī Tayyi' in Abū Shāma, *Rawdatayn*, 1:238.

103. "Nizārīs," after Nizār, eldest son of the Fatimid caliph al-Mustansir (1036–1094), whose side they had taken in 1094; "Bātinīs" from *bātin*, an allusion to the "internal" meaning of the sacred texts, which is hidden behind the literal or "external" (*zāhir*) meaning; "Ismaili" because they originally belonged to the same branch as the Fatimids, who were awaiting the return of Ismāʿīl, the seventh, hidden, imam in ʿAlī's line of descent.

104. See B. Lewis, *The Assassins*, 10–12.

105. B. Lewis, "Kamāl al-Dīn's Biography of Rašīd al-Dīn Sinān," ed. and trans. *Arabica* 13 (1966): 225–267, esp. 241.

106. Ibn Jubayr, Gaudefroy-Demombynes trans., 294, Broadhurst trans., 264.

107. Quoted in Lewis, *The Assassins*, 2.

108. William of Tyre, Huygens ed., 953–954 (20.29), trans. *Croisades et pèlerinages*, 686–687, Babcock and Krey trans., 2:391–392.

109. See al-Bundārī, 83; Lyons and Jackson, *Saladin*, 87–88; Lewis, *The Assassins*, 113.

110. See Abū Shāma, *Rawdatayn*, 1:258, based on ʿImād al-Dīn (see also al-Bundārī, 100–101).

111. Lewis, "Kamāl al-Dīn's Biography of Rašīd al-Dīn Sinān," 236 and 266; Lewis, *The Assassins*, 116–117.

112. Ibn al-ʿAdīm, *Zubda*, 3:32–33; Abū Shāma, *Rawdatayn*, 1:275.

113. Sibt Ibn al-Jawzī, 8:329; A. S. Ehrenkreutz, *Saladin*, 141; Lewis, *The Assassins*, 114.

114. See Ibn al-Athīr, *Kāmil*, 11:436, Richards trans., 2:249; al-Bundārī, 106; Abū Shāma, *Rawdatayn*, 1:261; Lyons and Jackson, *Saladin*, 108–109.

115. See Lewis, *The Assassins*, 115; S. Guyard, "Un grand maître des Assassins au temps de Saladin," *Journal Asiatique*, 7th series, 9 (1877): 324–489 (a hagiographical and late Ismaili biography of Sinān).

116. See Sibt Ibn al-Jawzī, 8:419.

117. See Ibn al-ʿAdīm, *Zubda*, 3:28–29; Lewis, *The Assassins*, 117.

118. Quoted in Lewis, *The Assassins*, 5.

119. Rigord, *Histoire de Philippe Auguste*, ed. E. Carpentier, G. Pon, and Y. Chauvin (Paris, 2006), 313–315 (chap. 93).

21. Christians and Jews

1. See J. C. Garcin, *Qūṣ*, 120–123.
2. See Burchard of Strasbourg, 399, 401, 405, 407.
3. Some fifty churches and the same number of monasteries.
4. Not counting a large part of Lower Egypt. See *The Churches and Monasteries of Egypt*, Evetts and Butler ed., trans., 347–352; Y. Lev, *Saladin in Egypt*, 187–188.
5. See A. M. Eddé, "Chrétiens d'Alep et de Syrie du Nord à l'époque des croisades: Crises et mutations," in *Mémorial Monseigneur Joseph Nasrallah*, ed. P. Canivet and J. P. Rey-Coquais (Damascus, 2006), 153–180. The Western pilgrim Thietmar noted in 1217 that Bethlehem was populated solely by Christians (*Croisades et pèlerinages*, 944).
6. Depending on whether one follows Benjamin of Tudela or Pethahiah of Regensburg. The numbers also vary depending on the manuscript of Benjamin of Tudela's work that is consulted. See J. M. Mouton, *Damas et sa principauté sous les Saljoukides et les Bourides, 468–548/1076–1154* (Cairo, 1994), 348; A. M. Eddé, *Principauté ayyoubide d'Alep*, 461.
7. According to the documents of the genizah of al-Fustāt. By contrast, Benjamin of Tudela gives the figure of seven thousand Jews for the capital of al-Fustāt-Cairo. See S. D. F. Goitein, *A Mediterranean Society*, 2:139–140; N. A. Stillman, "The Non-Muslim Communities: The Jewish Community," in *The Cambridge History of Egypt*, vol. 1: *Islamic Egypt, 640–1517*, ed. C. F. Petry (Cambridge, 1998), 202. In Bilbeis as well, there was a small Jewish community composed of Maghrebis who had decided to stop on their pilgrimage route to the Holy Land, and of Jews from Ascalon who had fled Frankish domination in 1153 (see J. Prawer, *History of the Jews*, 71).
8. See Eddé, *Principauté ayyoubide d'Alep*, 461.
9. Monophysism (from the Greek: "a single nature" of Christ) insisted on Christ's divine nature.
10. From *malik*, "king" or "emperor" in Arabic, because these Christians had remained faithful to the doctrine followed by the Byzantine emperor. The Egyptian Jewish community also experienced internal tensions, as indicated by certain documents of the genizah of Cairo (Goitein, *A Mediterranean Society*, 2:105, 406).
11. See M. Canard, "Notes sur les Arméniens en Égypte à l'époque fatimide," *Annales de l'institut d'études orientales de la faculté des lettres d'Alger* 13 (1955): 143–157, repr. in M. Canard, *Miscellanea Orientalia* (London, 1973); Lev, *Saladin in Egypt*, 185–186.
12. A doctrine that Emperor Heraclius had in vain tried to impose in the seventh century to unify Chalcedonian and Monophysite Christians.
13. William of Tyre, Huygens ed., 108 (22.9[8]), French trans. in *Croisades et pèlerinages*, 710, Babcock and Krey trans., 2:459.
14. See J. Prawer, "Minorities," 3.

15. *The Churches and Monasteries of Egypt*, Evetts and Butler ed., ed., 15, trans., 27.

16. See *The Churches and Monasteries of Egypt*, Evetts and Butler ed., ed., 77, 85, 113, trans., 183, 198, 250; Y. Frenkel, "Political and Social Aspects," 9.

17. See *The Churches and Monasteries of Egypt*, Evetts and Butler ed., ed., 3–9, trans., 3–13; Prawer, "Minorities," 84–85; G. Dédéyan, *Les Arméniens entre Grecs, musulmans et croisés: Étude sur les pouvoirs arméniens dans le Proche-Orient méditerranéen (1068–1150)*, 2 vols. (Lisbon, 2003), 2:863.

18. See the details of these measures in al-Maqrīzī, *Sulūk*, 1, 1:47; *History of the Patriarchs*, vol. 3, 2, ed., 63–64, 97–98, trans., 106–107, 164–166; *Anonymi auctoris chronicon*, Abouna trans., 125–126; Eddé, *Principauté ayyoubide d'Alep*, 464–465.

19. Similar measures were taken in 1182–1183 by the Abbasid caliph of Baghdad. See al-Mansūr, *Midmār*, 73.

20. See *Anonymi auctoris chronicon*, Abouna trans., 125–126.

21. His administrative treatise is titled *Kitāb Qawānīn al-dawāwīn (Book on the Rules of the Diwāns)*. See *Encyclopaedia of Islam*, 2nd ed. (hereafter cited as *EI 2*), "Ibn Mammātī" (A. S. Atiya). Other cases of conversion are noted under Saladin's reign or influence, such as that of the famous doctor al-Muwaffaq ibn al-Mutrān (al-Maqrīzī, *Muqaffā*, 2:98; Bar Hebraeus, Budge trans., 329) and of the former priest of the Frankish territories Abū Muhammad ʿAbd al-Rahmān al-Nāsirī, known as al-Fāris, a professor in Damascus and a specialist in ancient texts (Ibn al-ʿAdīm, *Bughya*, 7:3398).

22. See *History of the Patriarchs*, Khater and Burmester ed., vol. 3, 2, ed., 64, trans., 107.

23. Ibn Jubayr (Gaudefroy-Demombynes trans., 51), who paid him a visit, had heard of him in Spain.

24. See Ibn Abī Usaybiʿa, 581.

25. See *The Churches and Monasteries of Egypt*, Evetts and Butler ed., ed., 8–9, trans., 12. Others claim that Muhyī al-Dīn Ibn al-Zakī, chief qādī of Damascus, who accused the Christians of misappropriation of funds and of every sort of vice, had a deciding influence on the sultan (see the treatise against the Christians by al-Asnawī [d. 1370], edited and translated by M. Perlmann in "Asnawi's Tract against Christian Officials," in *Ignace Goldziher Memorial Volume*, part 2 [Jerusalem, 1958], 172–208, esp. 192–194 and 18–20 of the Arabic text). That remains to be verified, since Ibn al-Zakī did not assume his duties as chief qādī until 1192.

26. See *History of the Patriarchs*, Khater and Burmester ed., vol. 3, 2, ed., 64, 97, trans., 107, 165. Even an author as ill disposed toward the Christians as Ibn al-Wāsitī (d. 1312) points out, in his treatise on religious polemics, that most of the secretaries in Egypt under Saladin's reign were Christian, which according to him had deleterious effects on the administration. See Ibn al-Wāsitī, *Radd ʿalā ahl al-dhimma wa man tabiʿahum*, ed. and trans. R. Gottheil as "An Answer to the Dhimmis," *Journal of the American Oriental Society* 41 (1921): 383–457, esp. 402 and trans., 438–439.

27. As attested by a decree promulgated in 1176 by al-'Ādil, Saladin's representative in Egypt at the time. In the first lines of the document, the order is given to respect and protect the monks, to prevent any harm from being done them, and to "obey the lofty decrees of our master al-Malik al-Nāsir Salāh al-Dīn." This indicates that measures had already been taken by Saladin. See S. Heidemann, C. Müller, and Y. Rāġib, "Un décret d'al-Malik al-'Ādil 571/1176 relatif aux moines du mont Sinaï," 81–107.

28. A. M. Eddé and F. Micheau, *L'Orient au temps des croisades*, 344–345; Eddé, *Principauté ayyoubide d'Alep*, 464–465; H. A. Hein, "Beiträge zur ayyubidischen Diplomatik," 183–185.

29. See Subkī, 6:41–42.

30. Taqī al-Dīn's military expedition into Nubia in 1172 resulted in many Christian deaths. The Church of Ibrīm was looted, then burned down, and the bishop was imprisoned and tortured. *The Churches and Monasteries of Egypt*, Evetts and Butler ed., ed., 122, trans., 267.

31. Of the five churches they possessed in the neighborhood of al-Hamrā' in al-Fustāt, only one remained theirs after the destruction by the Turks and Kurds (*The Churches and Monasteries of Egypt*, Evetts and Bulter ed., ed., 37, trans., 96–97). On the measures of 1181–1182, see al-Maqrīzī, *Sulūk*, 1, 1:77; Lyons and Jackson, *Saladin*, 163; Lev, *Saladin in Egypt*, 189.

32. See *The Churches and Monasteries of Egypt*, Evetts and Butler ed., ed., 34, trans., 92, and many examples of churches destroyed, then rebuilt, ed., 33, 35, 37, 40, 47–49, 53, 57, trans., 90–91, 94–97, 106, 119, 123–125, 132, 137–138.

33. See *History of the Patriarchs*, Khater and Burmester ed., 3, 2, ed., 61, trans., 102; *Anonymi auctoris chronicon*, Abouna trans., 126.

34. See Goitein, *A Mediterranean Society*, 1:38, 61–62, 345.

35. See J. Prawer, *Histoire du royaume latin de Jérusalem*, 1:522–535 and 2:397–418; Goitein, *A Mediterranean Society*, 2:137. Even in the twelfth century, Emir Zangī, Nūr al-Dīn's father, had brought in several hundred Jewish families to replace the Armenians, who were allies of the Franks in Edessa (N. Elisséeff, *Nūr al-Dīn*, 2:383).

36. See Prawer, *History of the Jews*, 69–71, 85–86, 149ff.

37. Prawer, *History of the Jews*, 67–68.

38. Prawer, *History of the Jews*, 158; see also 154–157.

39. He was probably writing in the early years of the thirteenth century. Armenians continued to live in Upper Egypt and, under Saladin's reign, still had a church (al-Zuhrī), located between al-Fustāt and Cairo. They later reclaimed a second one. See *The Churches and Monasteries of Egypt*, Evetts and Butler ed., ed., 7–9, trans., 8–13 (see also trans., 1–2, 162–163, 255); Lev, *Saladin in Egypt*, 192–193.

40. See C. Mutafian, *Le royaume arménien de Cilicie, XIIe–XIVe siècle* (Paris, 1993), 27–41.

41. Excerpt from a colophon composed by a monk writing in the early twelfth century, on Mount Cassius, near Antioch, under Frankish domination. See G. Dédéyan,

"Les colophons des manuscripts arméniens comme sources pour l'histoire des croisades," in *The Crusades and Their Sources: Essays Presented to B. Hamilton,* ed. J. France and W. G. Zajac (Aldershot, 1998), 89–110. A colophon consists of the last lines of a manuscript or text, in which the scribe often reveals his name, the date, and the place where his copy was made.

42. Dédéyan, "Les colophons des manuscrits arméniens," 106, 108.

43. Allusion to the Antichrist, who is to come out of the desert.

44. *Recueil des Historiens des Croisades. Documents arméniens,* vol. 1 (Paris, 1869), 272–283.

45. See Michael the Syrian, 3:404.

46. See J. M. Fiey, *Chrétiens syriaques sous les Abbassides, surtout à Bagdad (749–1258)* (Louvain, 1980), 258.

47. Attributed without certainty to George Warda, a Nestorian from the region of Irbil in Upper Mesopotamia, who was writing in the first half of the thirteenth century (see D. Bundy, "Interpreter of the Acts of God and Humans: George Warda, Historian and Theologian of the Thirteenth Century," *Harp,* 6, 1 [April 1993]: 7–20; and T. Nöldeke ed., "Zwei syrische Lieder auf die Einnahme Jerusalems durch Saladin," *Zeitschrift der Deutschen Morgenländische Gesellschaft* 27 [1873]: 489–510).

48. In S. Giamil, *Genuinae relationes inter Sedem Apostalicam et Assyriorum Orientalium seu Chaldaeorum Ecclesiam* (Rome, 1902), 2.

49. *Anonymi auctoris chronicon,* Abouna trans., 150.

50. See *History of the Patriarchs,* Khater and Burmester ed., vol. 3, 2, ed., 78, trans., 132; Prawer, *Histoire du royaume latin de Jérusalem,* 1:670–671.

51. *History of the Patriarchs,* Khater and Burmester ed., vol. 3, 2, ed., 82, trans., 139; F. Micheau, "Croisades et croisés vus par les historiens arabes chrétiens d'Égypte," in *Itinéraires d'Orient. Hommages à Claude Cahen, Res Orientales* 6 (1994): 169–185, esp. 180.

52. With the exception of the military orders. See Bar Hebraeus, Budge trans., 324–327.

53. See Ibn Shaddād, *Nawādir,* al-Shayyāl ed., 237, Richards trans., 230.

54. See Prawer, "Minorities," 88, based on Jacques de Vitry, *Historia,* 1:1095, Grossel trans., 229–230.

55. See Abū Shāma, *Rawdatayn,* 2:88, trans. *Recueils des historiens des croisades. Historiens orientaux,* 4:302 (hereafter cited as *RHC Or.*).

56. Abū Shāma, *Rawdatayn,* 2:115, trans. *RHC Or.,* 4:340, based on 'Imād al-Dīn (translation slightly modified).

57. E. Van Donzel, "Were the Ethiopians in Jerusalem at the Time of Saladin's Conquest in 1187?" in *East and West in the Crusader States: Context-Contacts-Confrontations,* vol. 2, ed. K. Ciggaar and H. Teule (Louvain, 1999), 125–130, esp. 128. Van Donzel wrongly attributes to E. Cerulli an interpretation of Jacques de Vitry's words tending in that direction. Jacques de Vitry merely says in his letters that in 1217 he met

Eastern Christians in Acre, but he does not say anywhere that they had been driven out of Jerusalem by Saladin. See Jacques de Vitry, *Historia*, 1:1091–1092, Grossel trans., 207–214; and Jacques de Vitry, *Lettres de la cinquième croisade*, Huygens ed., 563, Duchet-Suchaux trans., 47–49. E. Cerulli, *Etiopi in Palestina: Storia della comunità Etiopica di Gerusalemme*, 2 vols. (Rome, 1943–1947), 1:31–35. See also J. Richard, *Histoire des Croisades*, 221–222, who thinks that some of the Christians followed the Latins, and that to replace them, Saladin appealed to the descendants of the former Muslim residents and to the Jews.

58. See Ibn al-Athīr, *Kāmil*, 11:484, Richards trans., 2:285; Ibn Wāsil, *Mufarrij*, 2:118.

59. See Lyons and Jackson, *Saladin*, 341.

60. See Ibn Shaddād, *Nawādir*, al-Shayyāl ed., 189, Richards trans., 181.

61. See *Anonymi auctoris chronicon*, Abouna trans., 142.

62. See Lyons and Jackson, *Saladin*, 56, based on al-Makhzūmī, ms. British Museum, 103 (missing from the C. Cahen and Y. Rāġib edition [Cairo, 1986]). Lamentations about the role of the Christians—particularly the Copts—in the administration, a role that was judged too large, are also found until the end of the Ayyubid period. See Qāḍī ʿUthmān al-Nābulusī's opuscule *Kitāb tajrīd sayf al-himma li-stikhrāj mā fī dhimmat al-dhimma*, ed. C. Cahen in "Histoires coptes d'un cadi médiéval," *Bulletin de l'institut français d'archéologie orientale* 59 (1960): 133–150.

63. See Abū Shāma, *Rawdatayn*, 1:211, based on Ibn Abī Tayyiʾ.

64. See Lyons and Jackson, *Saladin*, 211; Eddé, *Principauté ayyoubide d'Alep*, 465.

65. ʿImād al-Dīn, *Fath*, Massé trans., 275; see also Lyons and Jackson, *Saladin*, 323.

66. Michael the Syrian, 3:386.

67. See S. Jadon, "The Physicians of Syria during the Reign of Ṣalāḥ al-Dīn (570–589/1174–1193)," *Journal of the History of Medicine and Allied Sciences* 25 (1970): 323–340.

68. Ibn al-Mutrān, one of the doctors closest to him.

69. On these Jewish and Christian doctors, named ʿAfīf Ibn Sukkara, Abū l-Bayān Ibn al-Mudawwar, and Abū l-Faraj al-Nasrānī, see Ibn Abī Usaybiʿa, 580, 638, 661.

70. Titled *Maqāla al-Salāhiyya fī ihyāʾ al-sināʿat al-tibbiya*, ed. and trans. H. Fähndrich as *Treatise to Ṣalāḥ ad-Dīn on the Revival of the Art of Medicine*, *Abhandlungen für die Kunde des Morgenlandes* 46, 3 (1983).

71. The two opuscules are titled *Fī tadbīr al-sihha (On the Regulation of Health)* and *Maqāla fī bayān al-aʿrād (Treatise on the Explanation of Symptoms)*. He also composed a short treatise on poisons that he dedicated to his protector al-Fāḍil *(al-Risāla al-Fāḍiliyya)* and an epistle on sexual intercourse *(fī l-jimāʿ)*, which he dedicated to Saladin's nephew Taqī al-Dīn ʿUmar. See J. Drory, "The Early Decades of Ayyūbid Rule," in *Perspectives on Maimonides: Philosophical and Historical Studies*, ed. J. L. Kraemer (Oxford, 1986), 295–302, esp. 302n. 43.

72. See Ibn Abī Usaybiʿa, 582: the sultan "held him in high esteem and was treated by him, as was his son al-Afdal."

73. See B. Lewis, *Islam in History* (New York, 1973), 166–176, esp. 175–176.

74. See Stillman, "The Non-Muslim Communities," 204–205.

75. *Encyclopaedia Judaica*, 11, col. 754–781, esp. col. 757; see also Ibn Abī Usaybi'a, 582; *EI* 2, "Ibn Maymūn" (G. Vajda); S. Harvey, "Maimonides in the Sultan's Palace," in Kraemer, *Perspectives on Maimonides*, 47–75.

76. Or al-Massāsa, according to al-Maqrīzī, *Khitat*, 2:471, Sayyid ed., 4, 2:939, a neighborhood later called Darb al-Karma.

77. That is what the Arabs called the sciences inherited from the Greeks (philosophy, medicine, astronomy, geography).

78. Ibn al-Qiftī, *Ta'rīkh al-hukamā'*, ed. J. Lippert (1903), 318–319; see also B. Lewis, "Maïmonides, Lionheart and Saladin," *Eretz-Israël* 7 (1963): 70–75; and Lewis, *Islam in History*, 166–176.

79. His name was Abū Sulaymān Dā'ūd Ibn Abī Fāna, and some time later he played an important role in the liberation of Emir Diyā' al-Dīn al-Hakkārī, who was taken prisoner by the Franks in 1177 and subsequently fell gravely ill. Abū Sulaymān guaranteed his person, had him released from his chains, and cared for him at his own home. See Ibn Abī Usaybi'a, 588; C. Cahen, "Indigènes et croisés, un médecin d'Amaury," *Syria* 15 (1934): 351–360.

80. See Ibn Shaddād (*Nawādir*, al-Shayyāl ed., 231, Richards trans., 227), who says simply that the ailing king of England asked Saladin for fruit and ices.

81. Al-Makhzūmī explains in his fiscal treatise that the capitation paid by the *dhimmīs* was four dinars for the rich, two dinars for the middle class, and one dinar for the poor, who according to him were the most numerous. See C. Cahen, "Contribution à l'étude des impôts," 248.

22. The State, the Prince, and the Subjects

1. *The Sea of Precious Virtues* (Bahr al-Fawā'id): *A Medieval Islamic Mirror for Princes*, trans. J. S. Meisami (Salt Lake City, 1991), 83.

2. Al-Harawī, *Tadhkira*, Sourdel-Thomine trans., 219.

3. Al-Ghazālī, *Nasīhat al-mulūk*, translated into English by F. R. C. Bagley as *Ghāzalī's Book of Counsel for Kings* (London, 1964), 75; see also C. Hillenbrand, "A Little-Known Mirror for Princes of al-Ghazālī," in *Words, Texts, and Concepts: Cruising the Mediterranean Sea*, ed. R. Arnzen and J. Thielmann (Louvain, 2004), 593–601, esp. 597 and 600.

4. Al-Wahrānī, *Manāmāt*, 82.

5. *Dīwān al-nazar, dīwān al-majlis, dīwān al-tahqīq* for financial affairs, *dīwān al-jaysh* for the army, and *dīwān al-inshā'* for the chancery. See H. Rabie, *The Financial System of Egypt*, 38–41, 144–161; and A. Fu'ād Sayyid's introduction to his edition of Ibn al-Tuwayr, *Nuzhat al-Muqlatayn fī akhbār al-dawlatayn* (Beirut, 1992), 53–67.

6. The inspector of *dīwāns* was called *nāzir al-dawāwīn*, and the emir of *dīwāns*, *mush-idd al-dawāwīn*. See Rabie, *The Financial System of Egypt*, 149–153.

7. In Arabic: *al-hamdu li-llāh wa bihi tawfīqī*. See Abū Shāma, *Rawdatayn*, 1:263; *History of the Patriarchs*, Khater and Burmester ed., vol. 3, ed., 64, trans., 107; A. M. Eddé, *Principauté ayyoubide d'Alep*, 320.

8. For example, al-Athīr ibn Bunān (d. 1199), a former head of the financial *dīwān*, who served Saladin and then his brother Tughtegin in Yemen (al-Maqrīzī, *Muqaffā*, 7:154–157); Qādī 'Alam al-Dīn Ismā'īl al-Suwaytī (d. 1213–1214), head of the *dīwān* of the army under Saladin and his successors (al-Maqrīzī, *Muqaffā*, 7:116–117); and Fakhr al-Dawla al-Aswānī (d. 1185–1186), a former Fatimid propagandist who later worked in Saladin's chancery (al-Maqrīzī, *Sulūk*, 1, 1:90, Broadhurst trans., 80; and al-Maqrīzī, *Muqaffā*, 1:269). Y. Lev, *Saladin in Egypt*, 76–79.

9. Abū l-Hasan 'Alī al-Makhzūmī, the author of the first of these treatises (*Kitāb al-minhāj fī 'ilm kharāj Misr*, ed. C. Cahen and Y. Rāġib [Cairo, 1986]), had been inspector of the fisc under the Fatimids (*Encyclopaedia of Islam*, 2nd ed. [hereafter cited as *EI 2*], "al-Makhzūmī" [C. Cahen]); one of his sons, known as al-Qādī al-Ashraf, was named by Saladin to head the bureau responsible for *waqfs* (Ibn al-'Adīm, *Bughya*, 6:2947–2952; al-Maqrīzī, *Muqaffā*, 3:665–666), while another, called al-Murtadā 'Abd al-Rahmān, was employed at the chancery from the beginning of Saladin's reign (al-Nābulusī, *Luma' al-qawānīn*, Cahen and Becker ed., 11 and n. 7; 'Imād al-Dīn, *Fath*, Massé trans., 281). In the Banū Mammātī family, Abū l-Ma-līh Zakariyyā' was the first to work in the Fatimid administration (Ibn al-'Adīm, *Bughya*, 4:1561–1565; *EI 2*, "Ibn Mammātī" [A. S. Atiya]). His son al-Muhadhdhab succeeded him as secretary in the bureau of the armies and made the transition from the Fatimid to the Ayyubid regimes. To keep his position, however, he had to convert to Islam when Shīrkūh and Saladin began to enforce the restrictions concerning the *dhimmīs*. We are beholden to his son al-As'ad, who succeeded him as head of the bureau of the armies and occupied the post of inspector of *dīwāns*, for a second administrative treatise (*Kitāb Qawānīn al-dawāwīn*, ed. A. S. Atiya [Cairo, 1943]), composed for Saladin's son al-'Azīz (r. 1193–1198). It is in that book, only part of which has come down to us, that the cadastral survey drawn up by Saladin can be found.

10. See *EI 2*, "Rawk" (H. Halm).

11. That decree has come down to us through the great fourteenth-century encyclopedist al-Qalqashandī (*Subh*, 13:71–74, repr. in Ibn Wāsil, *Mufarrij*, 3:373); al-Maqrīzī, *Khitat*, 1:281–282, Sayyid ed., 1:762–763; Rabie, *The Financial System of Egypt*, 133–134.

12. Al-Maqrīzī recorded a list of them. See al-Maqrīzī, *Khitat*, 1:104, Sayyid ed., 1:279–280.

13. Abū Shāma, *Rawdatayn*, 1:15.

14. See al-Maqrīzī, *Sulūk*, 1, 1:44–45, Broadhurst trans., 38; and al-Maqrīzī, *Khitat*, 1:108, Sayyid ed., 1:291; Rabie, *The Financial System of Egypt*, 96; M. C. Lyons and D. E. P. Jackson, *Saladin*, 50–51; Lev, *Saladin in Egypt*, 133–134. For details on the collection of that tax, see C. Cahen, "L'évolution de l'*iqṭāʿ* du IXe au XIIIe siècle. Contribution à une histoire comparée des sociétés médiévales," *Annales: Économies, sociétés, civilisations* (1953): 25–52, repr. in C. Cahen, *Les peuples musulmans dans l'histoire médiévale* (Damascus, 1977), 231–269, esp. 252–256.

15. See Ibn Jubayr, Gaudefroy-Demombynes trans., 43; Lyons and Jackson, *Saladin*, 51.

16. See al-Maqrīzī, *Khitat*, 1:97, Sayyid ed., 1:261; see also al-Maqrīzī, *Sulūk* 1, 1:73, Broadhurst trans., 65 (the lands of Fayyūm devolved to Saladin).

17. *Iqṭāʿ* revenues were calculated on the basis of an estimate of their fiscal value (*'ibra*), in a unit of account introduced by Saladin and called the *jayshī* (military) dinar, which combined payment in cash and payment in kind in the form of crops. Hence a *jayshī* dinar was the equivalent of 0.25 gold dinars and a measure (*irdabb*) of grain, which meant that an *iqṭāʿ* valued at a hundred *jayshī* dinars was supposed to yield an annual revenue of twenty-five gold dinars and one hundred *irdabbs* of grain. It is very difficult, however, to establish a rate of exchange between the *jayshī* dinar and the gold dinar because the value of the *jayshī* dinar varied depending on the origin or position of the emir holding the *iqṭāʿ*: the *jayshī* dinar of a Turkish or Kurdish emir, for example, was worth eight times that of an Arab auxiliary. See Ibn Mammātī, 369 and n. 9; Rabie, *The Financial System of Egypt*, 8.

18. See Rabie, *The Financial System of Egypt*, 26ff.; Cahen, "L'évolution de l'*iqṭāʿ*," 259–264; Lev, *Saladin in Egypt*, 115–116, 158–160.

19. There was the very well-known case of Emir Ibn al-Muqaddam, from whom Saladin took away Baalbek in 1179 to give to his own brother Tūrānshāh. After attempting to resist, Ibn al-Muqaddam gave in and received in exchange the territories of Bārīn, Kafartāb, and the villages around Maʿarrat al-Nuʿmān. See Lyons and Jackson, *Saladin*, 130–133.

20. See Ibn Mammātī, 341; al-Maqrīzī, *Sulūk*, 1, 1:76, Broadhurst trans., 67; Cahen, "L'évolution de l'*iqṭāʿ*," 256–257; Y. Frenkel, "Political and Social Aspects," 9.

21. Al-Maqrīzī, *Sulūk*, 1, 1:46, Broadhurst trans., 39; Rabie, *The Financial System of Egypt*, 162ff.; E. Ashtor, *Prix et salaires*, 119–123.

22. See J. M. Mouton, *Damas et sa principauté sous les Saljoukides et les Bourides, 468–548/1076–1154* (Cairo, 1994), 225–229; C. Cahen, *Orient et Occident au temps des croisades*, 140–141, 194–195.

23. See A. S. Ehrenkreutz, "The Crisis of the Dīnār in the Egypt of Saladin," 178–184; M. L. Bates and D. M. Metcalf, "Crusader Coinage with Arabic Inscriptions," 421–482; P. Balog, *Coinage*, 35–40; C. Cahen, "Monetary Circulation in Egypt," in *Islamic Middle East (700–1900): Studies in Economic and Social History*, ed. A. L. Udovich (Princeton, 1981), 315–333; and S. D. Goitein, "The Exchange Rate of Gold and Sil-

ver Money in Fatimid and Ayyubid Times: A Preliminary Study of the Relevant Geniza Material," *Journal of the Economic and Social History of the Orient* 8 (1965): 1–46. In Egypt, tokens made of hard opaque glass and bearing the name of the Abbasid caliph were also used as small change (see *L'Orient de Saladin*, 44; and A. Wieczorek et al., eds., *Saladin und die Kreuzfahrer*, 455).

24. We know that al-Malik al-Muʿizz Ismāʿīl (d. 1202), Tughtegin's son and Saladin's nephew, even attempted to proclaim himself caliph in Yemen with the title al-Hādī (Ibn Khallikān, 2:524).

25. See Balog, *Coinage*, 77 (Damascus), 89–92 (Aleppo), 283–284 (Aden); *L'Orient de Saladin*, 36–37.

26. See Balog, *Coinage*, 78–79; *L'Orient de Saladin*, 43.

27. See Eddé, *Principauté ayyoubide d'Alep*, 206–209.

28. The oldest of them (early twelfth century) bear Byzantine inscriptions. See Bates and Metcalf, "Crusader Coinage with Arabic Inscriptions," 438; E. J. Whelan, "A Contribution to Dānishmendid History: The Figured Copper Coins," *Museum Notes* (The American Numismatic Society) 25 (1980): 133–166; and *The Public Figure: Political Iconography in Medieval Mesopotamia* (London, 2006), 311–315.

29. See G. Hennequin, *Catalogue des monnaies musulmanes de la Bibliothèque nationale, Asie pré-mongole: Les Salǧūqs et leurs successeurs* (Paris, 1985), 308 and pl. 15.

30. See Balog, *Coinage*, 101.

31. Or vice versa. See Balog, *Coinage*, 103; Hennequin, *Catalogue des monnaies musulmanes de la Bibliothèque nationale, Asie pré-mongole*, 381–387, 406–407, 462–463, 467–470, pl. 19, 20, 25, 26; Wieczorek et al., eds., *Saladin und die Kreuzfahrer*, 321; J. M. Mouton, *Saladin*, 40–41.

32. See al-Maqrīzī, *Khitat*, 1:86–87, Sayyid ed., 1:233; al-Nābulusī, *Lumaʿ al-qawānīn*, Cahen ed., 12; H. A. R. Gibb, "The Armies of Saladin," 310.

33. See al-Maqrīzī, *Khitat*, 1:86–87 and 100, Sayyid ed., 1:233–235, 270; al-Bundārī, 286–287 (Saladin bought precious fabrics from a merchant in Damascus and asked ʿImād al-Dīn to give him a letter of credit drawn on the Egyptian treasury); Lyons and Jackson, *Saladin*, 212.

34. See Lyons and Jackson, *Saladin*, 293.

35. See Lyons and Jackson, *Saladin*, 318.

36. See al-Bundārī, 317; Ibn Shaddād, *Nawādir*, al-Shayyāl ed., 82, Richards trans., 78; Sibt Ibn al-Jawzī, 8:397; Lyons and Jackson, *Saladin*, 277.

37. ʿImād al-Dīn, *Fath*, Massé trans., 431.

38. Al-Maqrīzī, *Khitat*, 1:86 (more than thirty thousand blacks), 94 (thirty-six thousand foot soldiers), Sayyid ed., 1:231, 254.

39. See Gibb, "The Armies of Saladin," 304–320; Lev, *Saladin in Egypt*, 141–160.

40. Shīrkūh had some five hundred emancipated Turkish slaves (mamluks), called Asadiyya, with him in Egypt. See Abū Shāma, *Rawdatayn*, 1:173.

41. See al-Maqrīzī, *Khitat*, 1:86 (8,640 cavalrymen), 94 (2,000 cavalrymen), Sayyid ed., 1:233–234, 254.

42. William of Tyre, Huygens ed., 991 (21.22[23]), trans. *Croisades et pèlerinages*, 700, Babcock and Krey trans., 2:430–431 [translation slightly modified—trans.].

43. See al-Maqrīzī, *Khitat*, 1:86–87, Sayyid ed., 1:233–234.

44. See William of Tyre, Huygens ed., 898 (19.25); Lev, *Saladin in Egypt*, 145.

45. See *History of the Patriarchs*, Khater and Burmester ed., vol. 3, ed., 96, trans., 163.

46. See Y. Lev, "Infantry in Muslim Armies during the Crusades," in *Logistics of Warfare in the Age of the Crusades*, ed. J. H. Pryor (Aldershot, 2006), 185–207.

47. See Gibb, "The Armies of Saladin," 311–315 (whose estimates for Syria seem low to me); Eddé, *Principauté ayyoubide d'Alep*, 234–238.

48. See Abū Shāma, *Rawdatayn*, 2:76, trans. *Recueils des historiens des croisades. Historiens orientaux*, 4:263 (hereafter cited as *RHC Or.*); Ibn al-Athīr, *Kāmil*, 11:531, Richards trans., 2:319.

49. On the role of the Kināniyya in the Egyptian army, see Y. Lev, *State and Society in Fatimid Egypt* (Leiden, 1991), 103n. 34 and 126–127.

50. See *History of the Patriarchs*, Khater and Burmester ed., vol. 3, ed., 91, trans., 155; the presence of the blacks is also attested in *Itinerarium*, Stubbs ed. (IP2), 262, Nicholson trans., 246. See Lev, *Saladin in Egypt*, 148.

51. More than six hundred according to Ibn al-Tuwayr, 96; al-Maqrīzī, *Khitat*, 2:193, Sayyid ed., 3:611–612.

52. See Lev, *Saladin in Egypt*, 160.

53. Called *dār al-sinā'a* or *sinā'at al-inshā'*, depending on the case. See C. Picard, "Les arsenaux musulmans de la Méditerranée et de l'océan Atlantique (VIIe–XVe siècle)," in D. Coulon et al., *Chemins d'outre-mer. Études d'histoire sur la Méditerranée médiévale offertes à Michel Balard* (Paris, 2004), 691–710.

54. See Abū Shāma, *Rawdatayn*, 1:234, trans. *RHC Or.*, 4:165; A. S. Ehrenkreuz, "Saladin in Naval History," 104.

55. Allusion to a verse from the Koran, 21:81: "To Solomon We subjected the raging wind."

56. Al-Qalqashandī, *Subh*, 10:143.

57. See Ibn Abī Tayyi', in Abū Shāma, *Rawdatayn*, 1:269.

58. See al-Fādil, *al-Durr al-nazīma min tarassul 'Abd al-Rahīm*, Badawī ed., 44ff., according to al-Hafsī, *Correspondance officielle et privée d'al-Qāḍī al-Fāḍil*, 1167ff.; Lyons and Jackson, *Saladin*, 114.

59. That is the date given by al-Maqrīzī, *Sulūk*, 1, 1:73, 107–108, Broadhurst trans., 65, 95; and al-Maqrīzī, *Khitat*, 2:194, Sayyid ed., 3:614; Lev, *Saladin in Egypt*, 168; Rabie, *The Financial System of Egypt*, 86; Ibn Abī Tayyi', reported by Abū Shāma (*Rawdatayn*, 1:269), situates that reorganization in 1177, but he is less reliable for Egyptian chronology than al-Maqrīzī's sources.

60. Revenues from Fayyūm could amount to one hundred thousand dinars a year, and the sources tell us they were collected by Saladin's brother al-Būrī (d. 1183), then by his nephew Taqī al-Dīn 'Umar after 1184. No doubt only a portion of the revenues of Fayyūm were allotted to the *dīwān* of the fleet.

61. Over the centuries, natron was put to many uses in Egypt, ranging from mummification and ritual purification to fumigation, the production of faience, and especially, medicine. See *EI* 2, "Naṭrūn" (A. Dietrich).

62. See Y. Lev, *Charity, Endowments and Charitable Institutions*, 7.

63. See Lev, *State and Society in Fatimid Egypt*, 121.

64. See al-Maqrīzī, *Sulūk*, 1, 1:45, Broadhurst trans., 39.

65. Al-Maqrīzī, *Khitat*, 2:194, Sayyid ed., 3:615.

66. 'Imād al-Dīn, *Fath*, Massé trans., 71; see also Lyons and Jackson, *Saladin*, 114.

67. See Lyons and Jackson, *Saladin*, 22.

68. See Ibn al-Tuwayr, 96.

69. See C. Picard, *L'Océan Atlantique musulman de la conquête arabe à l'époque almohade* (Paris, 1997), 123–126.

70. Quoted in Lyons and Jackson, *Saladin*, 114.

71. See Ibn Jubayr, Gaudefroy-Demombynes trans., 66; Abū Shāma, *Rawdatayn*, 2:119, trans. *RHC Or.*, 4:342.

72. Excerpt from the letter composed in Saladin's name by Qāḍī al-Fāḍil and sent to the Almohad caliph (Abū Shāma, *Rawdatayn*, trans. *RHC Or.*, 4:503).

73. Reported by al-Maqrīzī, *Khitat*, 1:368, Sayyid ed., 2:231, translated in Blachère, "L'agglomération du Caire vue par quatre voyageurs arabes du Moyen Âge," *Analecta* (1975): 549–574, esp. 572.

74. More specifically, *tarīdas* were designed to transport troops, matériel, and horses. See Abū Shāma, *Rawdatayn*, trans. *RHC Or.*, 4:203, 209–211; Ehrenkreutz, "Saladin in Naval History," 106.

75. See Abū Shāma, *Rawdatayn*, 2:9, 14; al-Wahrānī, *Manāmāt*, 187; J. Prawer, *Histoire du royaume latin de Jérusalem*, 1:561–562; Ehrenkreutz, "Saladin in Naval History," 106.

76. See al-Bundārī, 208.

77. See Ibn al-Athīr, *Kāmil*, 11:495, Richards trans., 2:292–293; Abū Shāma, *Rawdatayn*, 2:47–48.

78. See M. Balard, *Croisades et Orient latin, XIe–XIVe siècle* (Paris, 2001), 193.

79. See William of Tyre, Huygens ed., 792 (Ascalon in 1153) and 1034 (Beirut in 1182). See M. L. Favreau-Lilie, *Die Italiener im Hl. Land vom ersten Kreuzzug bis zum Tode Heinrichs von Champagne (1098–1197)* (Amsterdam, 1989), 20–35.

80. 'Imād al-Dīn, in Abū Shāma, *Rawdatayn*, trans. *RHC Or.*, 4:388.

81. See Lyons and Jackson, *Saladin*, 313, 316.

82. Ibn Shaddād, *Nawādir*, al-Shayyāl ed., 153, Richards trans., 142; Lyons and Jackson, *Saladin*, 322.

83. See Lyons and Jackson, *Saladin*, 327.

84. See ʿImād al-Dīn, *Fath*, Massé trans., 297; the number of ships chartered by the Crusaders varies from one source to another but is rarely smaller than about a hundred. See R. W. Unger, "The Northern Crusaders: The Logistic of English and Other Northern Crusade Fleets," in Pryor, *Logistics of Warfare in the Age of the Crusade*, 251–273, esp. 257–259.

85. William of Tyre, Huygens ed. (21.23 [24]), 993, Babcock and Krey trans., 2:433.

86. Partly quoted in Lyons and Jackson, *Saladin*, 62. See also Lyons and Jackson, *Saladin*, 156–157; Gibb, "The Armies of Saladin," 317n. 71; J. M. Mouton, "Saladin et les bédouins du Sinaï," 198.

87. See Alexandre Berthier, *Relation des campagnes du général Bonaparte en Égypte et en Syrie* (Paris, year VIII [1799–1800]), 56–57; H. Laurens et al., *L'expédition d'Égypte* (Paris, 1989), 186.

88. See al-Maqrīzī, *Sulūk*, 1, 1:74, 87, Broadhurst trans., 63, 77.

89. See al-Maqrīzī, *Sulūk*, 1, 1:47, Broadhurst trans., 41; and al-Maqrīzī, *Khitat*, 1:86, Sayyid ed., 1:233.

90. It dropped from 1 million dinars a year to 659,308 dinars; 234,296 dinars for Arab Bedouins generally and 425,012 dinars for Kināniyya Arabs. See al-Maqrīzī, *Khitat*, 1:87, Sayyid ed., 1:234; Gibb, "The Armies of Saladin," 310.

91. Abū Shāma, *Rawdatayn*, 1:206, repr. in Ibn Wāsil, *Mufarrij*, 1:225 and 2:75.

92. The Banū Judhām and a portion of the Banū Thaʿlaba in the first case, the Banū Thaʿlaba and the Banū Jarm in the second. See al-Maqrīzī, *Sulūk*, 1, 1:71, Broadhurst trans., 63; Gibb, "The Armies of Saladin," 317; Mouton, "Saladin et les bédouins du Sinaï," 200–206.

93. See Ibn Mammātī, 369, translation and commentary in C. Cahen, "L'administration financière de l'armée fatimide d'après al-Makhzūmī," *Journal of the Economic and Social History of the Orient* 15 (1972): 163–182, esp. 178–179; al-Maqrīzī, *Khitat*, 1:87, Sayyid ed., 1:234; Gibb, "The Armies of Saladin," 307–308.

94. See J. C. Garcin, *Qūs*, 367; J. M. Mouton, "Bédouins entre Syrie et Égypte," 299.

95. Ibn Shaddād, *Nawādir*, al-Shayyāl ed., 193, Richards trans., 184.

96. See Ibn Shaddād, *Nawādir*, al-Shayyāl ed., 200, Richards trans., 192.

97. *Itinerarium*, Stubbs ed. (IP2), 262, Nicholson trans., 246.

98. See D. Le Blévec, "Fondations et oeuvres charitables au Moyen Âge," in *Fondations et oeuvres charitables au Moyen Âge*, ed. J. Dufour and H. Platelle (Paris, 1999), 7–22; and D. Le Blévec, *La part du pauvre. L'assistance dans les pays du Bas-Rhône du XIIe au milieu du XXe siècle*, 2 vols. (Rome, 2000).

99. See Lev, *Charity, Endowments and Charitable Institutions*, 4–8.

100. Al-Harawī, *Tadhkira*, Sourdel-Thomine trans., 219.

101. See Ibn Jubayr, Gaudefroy-Demombynes trans., 43, 53.

102. See Lev, *Charity, Endowments and Charitable Institutions*, 17 (based on Abū Shāma, *Rawdatayn*, 2:5) and 33. For Alexandria, see Ibn Jubayr, Gaudefroy-Demombynes trans., 43–44.

103. An Arab tradition reported by al-Maqrīzī (*Khitat*, 2:405, Sayyid ed., 4, 2:691) attributes the founding of the first hospitals to the Umayyad caliph al-Walīd Ibn ʿAbd al-Malik (r. 705–715), but there is nothing allowing us to verify it. See Yāqūt, *Muʿjam al-buldān*, 2:283; A. Issa Bey, *Histoire des bimaristans (hôpitaux) à l'époque islamique* (Cairo, 1928), 95; *EI* 2, "Bīmāristān" (D. M. Dunlop).

104. The hospital of Hama is attested under the name Bīmāristān al-Nūrī in al-Sakhāwī, *al-Daw' al-lāmiʿ*, 12 parts in 4 vols. (Cairo, 1353–1355 AH/1934–1936), 11:40, and mentioned without attribution by Ibn Jubayr, Gaudefroy-Demombynes trans., 296.

105. See Ibn Jumayʿ, ed. and trans. H. Fähndrich, *Treatise to Salāh ad-Dīn on the Revival of the Art of Medicine* (Wiesbaden, 1983).

106. Ibn Jubayr, Gaudefroy-Demombynes trans., 55–56, Babcock and Krey trans., 44; see also, on the hospital of Alexandria, Gaudefroy-Demombynes trans., 42. Ibn Khallikān (4:240), Ibn al-Athīr (*Kāmil*, 11:441, Richards trans., 2:252), and Abū Shāma (*Rawdatayn*, 1:268) situate the founding of that hospital in 1176–1177; al-Maqrīzī (*Khitat*, 1:407, Sayyid ed., 2:350, based on al-Fādil; and *Sulūk*, 1, 1:76, Broadhurst trans., 67) gives the date of March 1182. Ibn Abī Usaybiʿa (736) does not specify the date. See also Issa Bey, *Histoire des bimaristans (hôpitaux) à l'époque islamique*, 36–39; Lyons and Jackson, *Saladin*, 164.

107. See ʿImād al-Dīn, *Fath*, Massé trans., 396; Ibn Shaddād, *Nawādir*, al-Shayyāl ed., 239, Richards trans., 236; D. S. Richards ("Saladin's Hospital in Jerusalem," 70–83) thinks that it could be Saint Mary Major, located south of the Holy Sepulchre, a church and hospice belonging to Benedictine nuns. In the mid-eleventh century, the Persian traveler Nāsir-i-Khusraw mentioned the existence of a hospital in the eastern part of Jerusalem (*Nāṣer-e Khosraw's Book of Travels*, trans. W. M. Thackston [New York, 1986], 23).

108. See al-Bundārī, 324; and Ibn Kathīr, *Bidāya*, 8:478.

109. See Ibn Jubayr, Gaudefroy-Demombynes trans., 57; *Répertoire chronologique d'épigraphie arabe*, 9, no. 3514 (hereafter cited as *RCEA*); Eddé, *Principauté ayyoubide d'Alep*, 395; Ibn Jubayr also describes a school of that type in Damascus, which provided for the support of orphans, but he does not say who founded it (Ibn Jubayr, Gaudefroy-Demombynes trans., 314). It is also known that the same type of school had existed in Damascus at least since the early eleventh century (see al-Nuʿaymī, *Dūr al-Qur'ān fī Dimashq*, ed. S. al-Dīn al-Munajjid [Damascus, 1946], 11).

110. See al-Maqrīzī, *Khitat*, 2:366, Sayyid ed., 4, 2:463.

111. See Abū Shāma, *Rawdatayn*, 2:66; Sibt Ibn al-Jawzī, 8:389; Ibn Khallikān, 1:307; R. S. Humphreys, "Women as Patrons of Religious Architecture in Ayyubid Damascus," *Muqarnas* 11 (1994): 35–54.

112. See Lev, *Charity, Endowments and Charitable Institutions*, 31–32, 39.

113. See Lev, *Charity, Endowments and Charitable Institutions*, 39–49, 130–134.

114. See Ibn Khallikān, 4:113–121.

115. Seventeen thousand died in the Egyptian capital, according to al-Maqrīzī, *Sulūk*, I, 1:70, Broadhurst trans., 62; Lyons and Jackson, *Saladin*, 143.

116. See Ibn al-Athīr, *Kāmil*, II:451, Richards trans., 2:261; Lyons and Jackson, *Saladin*, 113, 126, 146; Lev, *Charity, Endowments and Charitable Institutions*, 134–135.

23. Commerce and Markets

1. J. Le Goff, *Saint Louis* (Paris, 1996), 658.

2. See C. Cahen, "Contribution à l'étude des impôts," 244–278; 'Abd al-Latīf al-Baghdādī enumerates the plants and animals (and especially, the breeding of chickens) that he saw in Egypt: *Kitāb al-Ifāda wa l-i'tibār*, Sacy trans., 31–107, Zand et al. trans., 31–107.

3. Bar Hebraeus, Budge trans., 342.

4. William of Tyre, Huygens ed., 903 (19.27), Babcock and Krey trans., 2:336.

5. See W. Heyd, *Histoire du commerce du Levant au Moyen Âge*, 386.

6. See al-Maqrīzī, *Sulūk*, I, 1:90, Broadhurst trans., 79.

7. Abū Shāma, *Rawdatayn*, 1:243, trans. *Recueils des historiens des croisades. Historiens orientaux*, 4:178 (hereafter cited as *RHC Or.*).

8. See C. Cahen, *Orient et Occident*, 131; D. Jacoby, "Les Italiens en Égypte," 79.

9. They seem to have shared that church with the Melkites. See M. Martin, "Alexandrie chrétienne à la fin du XIIe siècle d'après Abû l-Makârîm," in *Alexandrie médiévale I (Études alexandrines 3)*, ed. C. Décobert (Cairo, 1998), 45–49.

10. See Cahen, *Orient et Occident*, 125; Jacoby, "Les Italiens en Égypte," 77.

11. See M. Hadj-Sadok, ed., "Kitāb al-Dja'rāfiyya, Mappemonde du calife al-Ma'mūn reproduite par Fazārī (IIIe/IXe s.) rééditée et commentée par Zuhrī (VIe/XIIe s.)," *Bulletin d'études orientales* 21 (1968): 9–312, esp. 92–93, 229.

12. See M. Amari, *I diplomi arabi*, 257–261; Heyd, *Histoire du commerce du Levant au Moyen Âge*, 397; Jacoby, "Les Italiens en Égypte," 78.

13. Three letters from Saladin or from his brother al-'Ādil in reply to these embassies have been preserved in Latin or Italian translation in the Florentine archives. They bear, respectively, the dates of Rajab 572 [January 3–February 1, 1177], the 16th day of Ramadan, 574 [Feburary 25, 1179], and Shawwal 575 [February 29–March 28, 1180]. See Amari, *I diplomi arabi*, 264, 265–266, 267; Heyd, *Histoire du commerce du Levant au Moyen Âge*, 397–398.

14. See Jacoby, "Les Italiens en Égypte," 79.

15. See Martin, "Alexandrie chrétienne à la fin du XIIe siècle d'après Abû l-Makârîm," 45–49.

16. See al-Fādil, *Al-Durr al-nazīma min tarassul 'Abd al-Rahīm*, Badawī ed., 44ff., based on al-Hafsī, "Correspondance officielle et privée d'al-Qadī al-Fādil," 1078; M. C. Lyons and D. E. P. Jackson, *Saladin*, 114.

17. See Heyd, *Histoire du commerce du Levant au Moyen Âge*, 399; Jacoby, "Les Italiens en Égypte," 80 (a commercial contract involving trade with Egypt was concluded in Genoa in February of that year).

18. Jacques de Vitry, *Lettres de la cinquième croisade*, 33–35.

19. See C. Cahen, "Douanes et commerce," 217–314.

20. Ibn Jubayr, Gaudefroy-Demombynes trans., 39, Broadhurst trans., 31–32.

21. Usually between 10 and 30 percent, depending on the nature of the merchandise.

22. See Jacoby, "Les Italiens en Égypte," 82–87.

23. See al-Idrīsī, *Opus Geographicum*, fasc. 1, Cerulli et al. ed., 54–55.

24. See Ibn Jubayr, Gaudefroy-Demombynes trans., 73; Thietmar, Deluz trans. in *Croisades et pèlerinages*, 951.

25. See Ibn Jubayr, Gaudefroy-Demombynes trans., 80; al-Maqrīzī, *Sulūk*, 1, 1:87, Broadhurst trans., 77.

26. See Ibn Mammātī, 327; Cahen, "Douanes et commerce," 222.

27. Ibn Jubayr, Gaudefroy-Demombynes trans., 71, Broadhurst trans., 56.

28. See H. Rabie, *The Financial System of Egypt*, 84, based on al-Maqrīzī, *Sulūk*, 1, 1:72, Broadhurst trans., 64; C. Cahen, "L'alun avant Phocée. Un chapitre d'histoire économique islamo-chrétienne au temps des croisades," *Revue d'histoire économique et sociale* 41 (1963): 433–447.

29. See Ibn al-Athīr, *Kāmil*, 12:130, Richards trans., 3:31.

30. See Amari, *I diplomi arabi*, 262; Heyd, *Histoire du commerce du Levant au Moyen Âge*, 399.

31. See al-Maqrīzī, *Khitat*, 2:364, Sayyid ed., 4, 2:457; S. Denoix, *Décrire Le Caire (Fustāt-Misr) d'après Ibn Duqmāq et Maqrīzī* (Cairo, 1992), 126.

32. See Lyons and Jackson, *Saladin*, 55, based on al-Maqrīzī, *Khitat*, 2:367, Sayyid ed., 4, 2:465.

33. See al-Maqrīzī, *Khitat*, 2:93, Sayyid ed., 3:309.

34. With a few exceptions, the documents found in the genizah of Cairo only rarely refer to political obstacles to commerce, as in the story of the three poor strangers who were denounced as "enemies of the king" and thrown into prison. See S. D. F. Goitein, *A Mediterranean Society*, 1:59.

35. Quoted in Lyons and Jackson, *Saladin*, 115; see also Lyons and Jackson, *Saladin*, 113.

36. See Lyons and Jackson, *Saladin*, 165, 209.

37. For example, al-Maqrīzī, *Sulūk*, 1, 1:99, Broadhurst trans., 87.

38. See al-Harawī, *Kitāb al-ishārāt*, Sourdel-Thomine ed., ed., 30, trans., 72; Ibn Shaddād, *Nawādir*, al-Shayyāl ed., 214, Richards trans., 208.

39. That conflict had repercussions beyond the Muslim territories. The Turkomans, victorious over the Kurds, in 1185–1186 devastated the Christian and Muslim territories from the borders of Georgia to Cappadocia, and Qilij Arslān, Seljuk sultan of Anatolia, was unable to stop them. During the winter of 1186–1187, they passed through and pillaged northern Cilicia, where they were fought off by Leon of

Armenia. The Turkomans also attacked the region of Antioch and Latakia and spread into the Lower Orontes and southern Amanus, but were defeated by Bohemond of Antioch. In Anatolia, they remained the true rulers of the state until Qilij Arslān's death in 1192. See Ibn al-Athīr, *Kāmil*, 11:519, Richards trans., 2:310; Cahen, *Syrie du Nord*, 426; Lyons and Jackson, *Saladin*, 234, 237.

40. See al-Maqrīzī, *Sulūk*, 1, 1:75, Broadhurst trans., 66.

41. See Ibn Jubayr, Gaudefroy-Demombynes trans., 57. ʿAbd Latīf (*Kitāb al-Ifāda wa l-iʿtibār*, Zand et al. trans., 109) notes that, in 1200–1201, the bridge was destroyed as a result of negligence on the part of the person in charge of it. Wishing to make a dam of sorts so that the waters of the Nile would rise in the region of Giza, he came up with the idea of plugging up the arches, an action that, because of the pressure from the river, had the effect of destroying them.

42. *Répertoire chronologique d'épigraphie arabe*, 9, no. 3368 (hereafter cited as *RCEA*). See the enthusiastic description of Ibn Jubayr, who stopped there in 1184 (Gaudefroy-Demombynes trans., 299–300). Other caravansaries were built in the second half of the twelfth century on the road connecting Damascus to Homs, Hama, and Aleppo, though it is not always possible, on the basis of their ruins, to distinguish between those that were built under Nūr al-Dīn's reign and those constructed under Saladin's reign. See J. Sauvaget, "Caravansérails syriens du Moyen Âge," *Ars Islamica* 6 (1939): 48–55, esp. 50–52 for Khān al-ʿArūs.

43. See al-Shayzarī, *Nihāyat al-rutba fī talab al-hisba*, 3.

44. See al-Qalqashandī, *Subh*, 10:460–462.

45. Excerpt published in A. M. Eddé and F. Micheau, *L'Orient au temps des croisades*, 185–189. For ʿImād al-Dīn's complete diploma, see ʿImād al-Dīn, *al-Barq*, 5:135–136; H. A. Hein, "Beiträge zur ayyubidischen Diplomatik," doctoral diss., Freiburg im Brisgau, 1968, 142–148, no. 29; C. Pellat, "Un traité de *hisba* signé: Saladin," 593–598.

46. The figures given by the sources are not always in agreement, but they do allow us to give some price ranges: one dinar bought between three and ten *irdabbs* of wheat, eight to twenty *irdabbs* of barley, beans, or lentils (at the time, an Egyptian *irdabb* was equal to about seventy kilograms). It took between 1.5 and 3 dinars to buy a *qintār* of white cane sugar, a renowned product of Egypt, and 1.75 to 4 dinars to buy a *qintār* of honey (one *qintār* equaled a hundred *ratl*, and the *ratl* for weighing honey and sugar in Egypt equaled about 964 grams). For comparison, the wage of an imam in a mosque in Alexandria was about five dinars a month, while a teacher at a madrasa could earn between eleven and forty dinars a month, depending on the prestige of the establishment and the authority of the teacher. See Ibn Jubayr, Gaudefroy-Demombynes trans., 44; al-Maqrīzī, *Khitat*, 2:365, 400, Sayyid ed., 4, 2:460, 631. See also E. Ashtor, *Prix et salaires*, 228–229.

47. See al-Maqrīzī, *Sulūk*, 1, 1:70, Broadhurst trans., 62; Lyons and Jackson, *Saladin*, 143.

48. See al-Maqrīzī, *Sulūk*, 1, 1:86, 88, 91, 108, 111, Broadhurst trans., 77–78, 79, 95, 98.

49. See Ibn al-Athīr, *Kāmil*, 11:451–452, Richards trans., 2:261 (the Arabic word *mayta* means both "corpse" and "carrion").

24. Birth and Development

1. See Dante Alighieri, *Inferno*, trans. M. Palma (New York, 2002), 36–45 (canto 4).
2. See E. H. Wilkins, "On Petrarch's Rewriting the *Triumph of Fame*," *Speculum* 39 (1964): 440–443.
3. See J. Tolan, "Mirror of Chivalry: Salah al-Dîn in the Medieval European Imagination," *Images of the Other: Europe and the Muslim World before 1700, Cairo Papers on Social Science* 19 (1996): 7–38, repr. in J. Tolan, *Sons of Ishmael: Muslims through European Eyes in the Middle Ages* (Gainesville, Fla., 2008), 79–100.
4. See J. Richard, "Huon de Tabarié. La naissance d'une figure épique," in *La chanson de geste et le mythe carolingien. Mélanges R. Louis* (Saint-Père-sous-Vézelay, 1982), 1073–1078.
5. See *Saladin* (chap. 10), trans. Combarieu du Grès in *Croisades et pèlerinages*, 450–453.
6. See J. Tolan, "Saracen Philosophers Secretly Deride Islam," *Medieval Encounters* 8 (2002): 184–206.
7. See R. Irwin, "Saladin and the Third Crusade: A Case Study in Historiography and the Historical Novel," 139–152.
8. See M. Jubb, *The Legend of Saladin*, 170–194.
9. The central trilogy of the first cycle, including the *Chanson d'Antioche* (ca. 1100), the *Chanson (Conquête) de Jérusalem* (ca. 1135), and *Les Chétifs* (ca. 1149), was composed in the first half of the twelfth century but has come down to us only in a reworked version from the late twelfth century (ca. 1180–1190).
10. As in *La naissance du chevalier au cygne; Le chevalier au cygne; La fin d'Elias, Les Enfances Godefroi;* and *Le retour de Cornumaran.*
11. With works such as *La Chrétienté Corboran; La prise d'Acre; La mort Godefroi;* and *La chanson des rois Baudouin.*
12. Continuations of the *Chanson de Jérusalem* were thus written in verse in about the mid-fourteenth century: *Le chevalier au cygne et Godefroid de Bouillon; Baudouin de Sebourc;* and *Le bâtard de Bouillon.*
13. See *Saladin*, intro. and trans. M. de Combarieu du Grès in *Croisades et pèlerinages*, 417–496.
14. Dante Alighieri, *Il convivio*, 4.11.14, trans. R. Lansing (1998), n.p. <http://dante.ilt.columbia.edu/books/convivi/convivio4.html#11>.
15. See Boccaccio, *Decameron*, book 1.3 and 10.9 (the parable of the three rings and of Torello, gentleman of Pavia).
16. See Voltaire, *Essai sur les moeurs*, chap. 56.
17. W. Scott, *The Talisman* (London, 1894), x.

18. For example, G. A. Henty and Rider Haggard. See Irwin, "Saladin and the Third Crusade," 143–144; Jubb, *The Legend of Saladin*, 203–205.

25. Antihero or Prophet Foretold?

1. G. Paris, "La légende de Saladin," 285; G. Paris, "Un poème latin contemporain sur Saladin," *Revue de l'Orient latin* 1 (1893): 433–444; M. Jubb, *The Legend of Saladin*, 5–9; L. Pouzet, "al Sulṭān Ṣalāḥ al-Dīn al-Ayyūbī fī l-turāth al-faransī," 291–292. Many thanks to my colleague and friend Dominique Poirel for his translation of these lines.

2. *Aleis* and *alliis*, literally, dice and garlic, associated with taverns and the lower classes.

3. *Itinerarium*, Mayer ed. (IP1), 252, Nicholson trans., 27–28.

4. See D. Barthélemy, *L'ordre seigneurial XIe–XII siècle* (Paris, 1990), 129.

5. See *Le cycle de la fille du comte de Ponthieu*, trans. D. Quéruel in *Splendeurs de la cour de Bourgogne*, ed. Daniel Régnier-Bohler (Paris, 1995), 371–479.

6. William of Tyre, Huygens ed., 925, 967–968, 1037 (20.11, 21.6, 22.20), Babcock and Krey trans., 2:358–359, 405, 480; J. Richard, "Les transformations de l'image de Saladin," 181.

7. See William of Tyre, Huygens ed., 969 (21.7), Babcock and Krey trans., 2:406; Jubb, *The Legend of Saladin*, 22, 25; H. Möhring, "Heiliger Krieg," 461–462.

8. *Petri Blesensis tractatus duo*, ed. R. B. C. Huygens (Turnhout, 2002), 46 ("Ille filius perditionis Saladinus, cuius funesto et dampnato nomine invitus et dolens hanc epistolam contamino"), 84 ("Ille filius perditionis, cuius nomino presentem nolo epistolam funestare"). See J. Tolan, "Mirror of Chivalry," 11–22; Jubb, *The Legend of Saladin*, 90.

9. Sorcery in the service of the armies is also mentioned during the First Crusade in the French translation of William of Tyre (*Recueil des historiens des croisades. Historiens occidentaux*, vol. 1 [Paris, 1884], 347): "two old enchantresses" and "three maidens" were supposedly given the task of casting spells on the war machines of the Crusaders during the siege of Jerusalem.

10. *La Continuation de Guillaume de Tyr*, Morgan ed., 47, Edbury trans., 40.

11. See Flavius Josephus, *Jewish Antiquities*, 4.6.

12. *La Continuation de Guillaume de Tyr*, Morgan ed., 49, Edbury trans., 42.

13. See *Chronique d'Ernoul et de Bernard le trésorier*, ed. L. de Mas-Latrie (Paris, 1871), 163–166; F. Caroff, "L'adversaire, l'autre, l'oriental," 118 and fig. 65 (Baltimore ms., Walters Art Gallery, ms. W 142, fol. 244b).

14. See Ambroise, *L'Estoire de la guerre sainte*, lines 12067–12158, Ailes and Barber trans., 2:190–191; Tolan, "Mirror of Chivalry," 18–22; Jubb, *The Legend of Saladin*, 151–153.

15. *Chronique d'Ernoul et de Bernard le trésorier*, ed. M. L. de Mas-Latrie (Paris, 1871), 37–44; see also *Estoires d'Outremer et de la naissance de Salehadin*, Jubb ed., 99–101;

Jubb, *The Legend of Saladin*, 15–16; P. R. Grillo, "The Saladin Material in the Continuations of the First Crusade Cycle," in *Aspects de l'épopée romane: Mentalités, idéologies, intertextualités* (Groningen, 1995), 159–166.

16. *Roman de Saladin* (book 1), trans. M. de Combarieu du Grès, *Croisades et pèlerinages*, 423–424; see also Jubb, *The Legend of Saladin*, 13.

17. See H. Möhring, "Zwischen Joseph-Legende und Mahdi-Erwartung," 177–225, esp. 196–197.

18. 'Imād al-Dīn, *Fath*, Massé trans., 113.

19. Abū Shāma, *Rawdatayn*, 2:177.

20. See Abū Shāma, *Rawdatayn*, 2:82–83.

21. See A. Abel, *Le Roman d'Alexandre, légendaire médiéval* (Brussels, 1955), 11ff.

22. See Plutarch, "Alexander," 6.1–8, in *Plutarch's Lives of Illustrious Men*, trans. J. Dryden, J. Langhorne, and W. Langhorne (Philadelphia, n.d. [1932]), 804–805; F. C. Tubach, *Index Exemplorum: A Handbook of Medieval Religious Tales* (Helsinki, 1969; 2nd ed. 1981), no. 96.

26. The Valiant and Generous Knight

1. See M. Jubb, *The Legend of Saladin*, 14, 26–31, 68–85.

2. See *Saladin* (chap. 10), trans. Combarieu du Grès in *Croisades et pèlerinages*, 448–453; *Itinerarium*, Mayer ed. (IPI), 251, Nicholson trans., 27; *Chronique d'Ernoul*, Mas-Latrie ed., 36; Jubb, *The Legend of Saladin*, 27, 67–85; J. Richard, "Les transformations de l'image de Saladin," 183.

3. See Jubb, *The Legend of Saladin*, 134–139.

4. *Saladin* (chaps. 22–24), trans. Combarieu du Grès in *Croisades et pèlerinages*, 478–481.

5. See G. Paris, "La légende de Saladin," 491; Jubb, *The Legend of Saladin*, 144.

6. See Jubb, *The Legend of Saladin*, 151–153.

7. See *Saladin*, chap. 16, trans. Combarieu du Grès in *Croisades et pèlerinages*, 463.

8. See Paris, "La légende de Saladin," 491–496; R. S. Loomis, "*Richard Coeur de Lion* and the *Pas Saladin* in Medieval Art," *PMLA* 30 (1915): 509–528; and R. S. Loomis, "The *Pas Saladin* in Art and Heraldry," in *Studies in Art and Literature for Belle da Costa Greene*, ed. D. Milner (Princeton, 1954), 83–91.

9. See F. Caroff, "L'adversaire, l'autre, l'oriental," 286–287 and fig. 148 (manuscript at the Bibliothèque nationale de France, ms. fr. 12559, fol. 127).

10. See J. Tolan, "Mirror of Chivalry," 22–23.

11. See Jubb, *The Legend of Saladin*, 136–137, 145–148; R. S. Loomis, "Illustrations of Medieval Romance on Tiles from Chertsey Abbey," *University of Illinois Studies in Language and Literature* 2, 2 (May 1916): 5–96, esp. 82–86; C. Tyerman, *England and the Crusades 1095–1588* (Chicago, 1988), 117.

12. As in Walter Scott's *Talisman* (London, 1894). See Jubb, *The Legend of Saladin*, 200.

13. G. Duby, *Guillaume le Maréchal* (Paris, 1984), 108.

14. See Jubb, *The Legend of Saladin*, 33–34.

15. See *Récits d'un ménestrel de Reims*, Wailly ed., chap. 6, sections 33–35, Grossel trans., 48.

16. *Saladin*, chaps. 15 and 22, trans. Combarieu du Grès in *Croisades et pèlerinages*, 460, 478.

17. See *Novellino, suivi de Contes de chevaliers du temps jadis*, 85; Jubb, *The Legend of Saladin*, 37–38.

18. See Boccaccio, *Decameron*, books 1.3 and 10.9.

19. See Jubb, *The Legend of Saladin*, 38.

20. See *La Continuation de Guillaume de Tyr*, Morgan ed., 71ff., Edbury trans., 62–63.

21. See Jubb, *The Legend of Saladin*, 79.

22. See *Chronique d'Ernoul*, Mas-Latrie ed., 281–282; *Estoires d'Outremer et de la naissance de Salehadin*, Jubb ed., 229–230; *Saladin*, chap. 20, trans. Combarieu du Grès in *Croisades et pèlerinages*, 474; Jubb, *The Legend of Saladin*, 141–145 and 200–201.

23. The episode is reported both by the Arab sources (Ibn Shaddād, *Nawādir*, al-Shayyāl ed., 190, Richards trans., 181) and by the Latin sources (Ambroise, *L'Estoire de la guerre sainte*, lines 7068–7134; Ailes and Barber trans., 128; *Itinerarium*, Stubbs ed. [IP2], 286–287, 440; Nicholson trans., 266, 380: in the Latin version, the king's rescuer is not killed but exchanged for ten Turkish prisoners). See J. Gillingham, *Richard I* (New Haven, 1999), 180 and n. 24.

24. *Récits d'un ménestrel de Reims*, Wailly ed., chap. 21, sections 199–308, Grossel trans., 149–152; see also Tolan, "Mirror of Chivalry," 28; A. Saunier, "Saladin et l'Hôpital de Saint-Jean d'Acre dans le récit du Ménestrel de Reims," 423–433.

25. See Jubb, *The Legend of Saladin*, 39–40; L. Jolivet, *Notice historique sur Anglure* (Châlons-sur-Marne, 1910), 21–25.

26. See J. Longnon, *Les compagnons de Villehardouin. Recherches sur les croisés de la quatrième croisade* (Geneva, 1978), 23; and J. Longnon, *Le Saint Voyage de Jhérusalem du seigneur d'Anglure* (Paris, 1978), xxx–xxxii.

27. As attested by a seal dating to 1368 and several collections of coats of arms. See Caroff, "L'adversaire, l'autre, l'oriental," 294.

28. See *Chronique d'Ernoul*, Mas-Latrie ed., 103.

29. See *Saladin*, chaps. 2, 10, trans. Combarieu du Grès in *Croisades et pèlerinages*, 426, 447–448.

30. See "Le pèlerinage de Maître Thietmar," trans. Deluz in *Croisades et pèlerinages*, 945–946.

31. See Jubb, *The Legend of Saladin*, 125–130.

32. See *Novellino, suivi de Contes de chevaliers du temps jadis*, 297–299.

33. See *Récits d'un ménestrel de Reims*, Wailly ed., chap. 2, sections 7–10, Grossel trans., 31–32.

34. See Voltaire, *Essai sur les moeurs*, chap. 56, "De Saladin." See also Chateaubriand, *Itinéraire de Paris à Jérusalem*, part 4, "Voyage de Jérusalem." This story is also found in the chronicle of Aubri de Trois-Fontaines and that of Guillaume de Nangis, as well as in Jacques de Vitry's writings and in the *Récits d'un ménestrel de Reims*. See Jubb, *The Legend of Saladin*, 43.

35. See N. Bériou, *L'avènement des maîtres de la parole. La prédication à Paris au XIIIe siècle*, 2 vols. (Paris, 1998), 1:358.

36. See *Novellino, suivi de Contes de chevaliers du temps jadis*, 295–297 (*Conto del Saladino*).

27. Between Moses, Jesus, and Muhammad

1. See M. Jubb, *The Legend of Saladin*, 53–111.

2. See *Historia Welforum Weingartensis*, ed. L. Weiland, *Monumenta Germaniae Historica, Scriptores*, vol. 21 (Hanover, 1869), 457–472; Jubb, *The Legend of Saladin*, 54. Some Western authors similarly claim that the mother of Saladin's nephew al-Kāmil was a Christian slave from Europe. See R. Röhricht, *Geschichte des Königreichs Jerusalem*, 358–359n. 2.

3. See *La fille du comte de Ponthieu et Jehan d'Avesnes*, in *Splendeurs de la cour de Bourgogne*, 373–464.

4. See Jubb, *The Legend of Saladin*, 55ff., 63.

5. See Jubb, *The Legend of Saladin*, 92.

6. See *Estoires d'Outremer et de la naissance de Salehadin*, Jubb ed., 235.

7. See Boccaccio, *Decameron*, book 1.3.

8. Samuel de Broë, *Histoire de la conqueste du royaume de Jérusalem sur les Chrestiens par Saladin, traduite d'un ancien manuscrit* (Paris, 1679); and Jubb, *The Legend of Saladin*, 98.

9. G. Chauvel, *Saladin*, 364.

10. Walter Scott's influence on that screenplay is apparent even in the early part of the film, during the aborted battle between Balian and a Muslim cavalryman. Balian takes the soldier for a mere varlet, though he is in Saladin's close circle. That meeting in the desert and the friendship that eventually unites the two men are nothing other than an adaptation of the first pages of *The Talisman*, where the Scottish knight Sir Kenneth encounters an emir, who is Saladin in disguise.

11. See *Récits d'un ménestrel de Reims*, Wailly ed., chap. 21, section 212, Grossel trans., 153–154.

12. See *Saladin*, chap. 31, trans. Combarieu du Grès in *Croisades et pèlerinages*, 495.

13. See Jubb, *The Legend of Saladin*, 100; J. Tolan, "Barrières de haine et de mépris: La polémique anti-islamique de Pedro Pascual," in *Identidad y representación de la frontera*

en la España medieval (siglos XI–XIV), ed. C. de Ayala, P. Josserand, and P. Buresi (Madrid, 2001), 253–266.

14. In the mid-thirteenth century, for example, the English chronicler Matthew Paris wrote, under the year 1169, that the Seljuk sultan of Anatolia converted to Christianity after being invited to that country in a letter from Pope Alexander III. See Matthew Paris, *Chronica maiora,* ed. H. R. Luard, 7 vols. (London, 1872–1883), 2:250–260; H. Möhring, *Saladin und der Dritte Kreuzzug,* 128.

15. *Novellino, suivi de Contes de chevaliers du temps jadis,* 303; see also J. Tolan, *Le saint chez le sultan* (Paris, 2007), 92.

16. See Möhring, *Saladin und der Dritte Kreuzzug,* 127.

17. E. Said, *Orientalism* (New York, 1978), 101.

18. See R. Irwin, "Saladin and the Third Crusade: A Case Study in Historiography and the Historical Novel," 142–143.

19. J. Michelet, *Oeuvres complètes* (Paris, 1895–1898), 330.

20. See Jubb, *The Legend of Saladin,* 119, based on Busone da Gubbio (1311); Boccaccio, *Decameron,* book 10.9.

21. See Jubb, *The Legend of Saladin,* 113–124.

22. A reference to Tughtegin, atabeg of Damascus in the early twelfth century, who according to legend converted to Christianity.

23. *Saladin,* chap. 11, trans. Combarieu du Grès in *Croisades et pèlerinages,* 454–455; Jubb, *The Legend of Saladin,* 103–109.

24. See Paris, "La légende de Saladin," 294; Richard, "Les transformations de l'image de Saladin dans les sources occidentales," 185.

25. [Both "Persian *avant la lettre*" and "Persian before [Montesquieu's] *Lettres persanes*"—trans.] This is Micheline de Combarieu du Grès's expression in *Croisades et pèlerinages,* 418.

28. The Myth of the Arab Hero

1. Abū Shāma, *Rawdatayn,* 2:215, trans. *Recueils des historiens des croisades. Historiens orientaux,* 5:97 (hereafter cited as *RHC Or.*).

2. See Ernst Freiherr von Mirbach, *Die Reise des Kaisers und der Kaiserin nach Palästina. Drei Vorträge* (Berlin, 1899), 96–103.

3. See J. Sauvaget, "Le cénotaphe de Saladin," 168–175; E. Herzfeld, "Damascus: Studies in Architecture—III," *Ars Islamica* 11–12 (1946): 1–71, esp. 47–48; A. Moaz, "Note sur le mausolée de Saladin à Damas," 183–189; A. Wieczorek, M. Fansa, and H. Meller, eds., *Saladin und die Kreuzfahrer,* 462.

4. Ibn Khallikān, 7:206, Slane trans., 4:547.

5. *Die Reden Kaiser Wilhelms II in den Jahren 1896–1900,* speeches collected and edited by J. Penzler, vol. 2 (Leipzig, n. d. [1904]), 126ff.

6. See Wieczorek, Fansa, and Meller, *Saladin und die Kreuzfahrer*, 459–465; J. Wilson, *T. E. Lawrence, London National Portrait Gallery*, catalog of the T. E. Lawrence exhibit, London, December 1988–March 1989 (London, 1988), 115.

7. Now held at the Imperial War Museum in London.

8. R. Girardet, *Mythes et mythologies politiques* (Paris, 1986), 13–15.

9. See C. Hillenbrand, *The Crusades*, 6–7, 596–599. Without the clarification provided by the sculptor ʿAbd Allah al-Sayed, it would be difficult to distinguish the warrior from the Sufi.

10. Reported by P. Perotto in *Est Républicain*, February 7, 2004.

11. See O. Bengio, *Saddam's Word: Political Discourse in Iraq* (New York, 1998), 82–83. The Iraqi national anthem has changed since the fall of Saddam Hussein, but the words of the former anthem can be found on several Internet sites. See for example <http://en.wikipedia.org/wiki/Ardh_Alforatain>.

12. See L. Wedeen, *Ambiguities of Domination: Politics, Rhetoric, and Symbols in Contemporary Syria* (Chicago, 1999), 3. See also the painting depicting two parallel battles, that of Hattīn and, no doubt, a battle from the Iran-Iraq war (1980–1988), beneath smiling portraits of Saladin and Saddam Hussein, in Hillenbrand, *The Crusades*, 595.

13. Wedeen, *Ambiguities of Domination*, 126.

14. E. Sivan, *Mythes politiques arabes*, trans. from the Hebrew by N. Weill (Paris, 1995), 63–64.

15. See *800 ʿām, Ḥiṭṭīn, Ṣalāḥ al-Dīn wa l-ʿamal al-ʿarabī al-muwaḥḥad (Eight Hundred Years: Hattīn, Saladin, and Unified Arab Action)*, proceedings of the colloquium held by the Afro-Asian People's Solidarity Organization *(al-Lijna al-Miṣriyya li tadāmun al-shuʿūb al-Ifrīqiyya al-Asyawiyya)* and the London Centre of Arab Studies (Cairo, 1989), 18–19, 28, 30–31.

16. Bengio, *Saddam's Word*, 82–83.

17. A. Rouadjia, *Les frères et la mosquée: Enquête sur le mouvement islamiste en Algérie* (Paris, 1990), 147–149 (the text says "Hanafite Muslim," but I cannot say whether this is an error on the part of the theologian or of the book's author); see also P. Partner, "Holy War, Crusade and Jihād: An Attempt to Define Some Problems," in *Autour de la première croisade*, ed. M. Balard (Paris, 1996), 342.

18. See A. S. Akbar, *Jinnah, Pakistan and Islamic Identity: The Search for Saladin* (London, 1997), xvii–xviii, 86ff.

19. See <http://www.14masom.com/hkaek-mn-tareek/11.htm>.

20. See Z. Ben Lagha, "Le personnage historique dans l'oeuvre romanesque de Gurgî Zaydân: Entre figure exemplaire et personnage de roman," doctoral diss., Institut national des langues et civilisations orientales (INALCO), under the directorship of L. W. Deheuvels, December 2006.

21. See Jurji Zaydan, *Saladin et les Assassins*, trans. Jean-Marie Lesage (Paris, 2003).

22. See L. W. Deheuvels, "Le Saladin de Faraḥ Anṭūn," 189–203.
23. See <http://www.saladin.tv/main.php>.

Conclusion

1. L. Le Goff, *Saint Louis* (Paris, 1996), 521.
2. Abū Shāma, *Recueils des historiens des croisades. Historiens orientaux,* 4:9–10.
3. See Ibn 'Abd al-Zāhir, *Al-Rawd al-zāhir fī sīrat al-Malik al-Zāhir,* ed. 'A. al-Khuwaytir (Riyadh, 1976), 47ff.; Ibn Shaddād, *Al-Rawdat al-zāhira fī sīrat al-Zāhira,* ed. A. Hutait (Wiesbaden, 1983), 271–319; P. M. Holt, "The Virtuous Ruler in the Thirteenth-Century Mamluk Royal Biographies," *Nottingham Medieval Studies* 24 (1980): 31–34; P. M. Holt, "The Sultan as Ideal Ruler: Ayyūbid and Mamlūk Prototypes," in *Suleyman the Magnificent and His Age: The Ottoman Empire in the Early Modern World,* ed. Metin Kunt and C. Woodhead (London, 1995), 129–136.
4. See Ibn 'Abd al-Zāhir, *Al-Rawd al-zāhir,* 272.
5. The complex built by Baybars on the site currently known as Nabī Mūsā became an important Muslim pilgrimage destination from that time on. See *Répertoire chronologique d'épigraphie arabe,* 12, nos. 4556, 4557, 4612; Y. Frenkel, "Baybars and the Sacred Geography of Bilād al-Shām: A Chapter in the Islamization of Syria's Landscape," *Jerusalem Studies in Arabic and Islam* 25 (2001): 153–170; D. Aigle, "Les inscriptions de Baybars dans le Bilād al-Šām. Une expression de la légitimité du pouvoir," *Studia Islamica* 97 (2003): 57–85.
6. *Al-Risāla al-Kāmiliyya fī sīrat al-nabawiyya (Treatise Relating to Kāmil on the Biography of the Prophet),* ed. and trans. M. Meyerhof and J. Schacht as *The Theologus Autodidactus of Ibn al-Nafīs* (Oxford, 1968); R. Kruk, "History and Apocalypse: Ibn Nafīs' Justification of Mamlūk Rule," *Der Islam* 72 (1995): 324–337.
7. See *The Theologus Audodidactus of Ibn al-Nafīs,* Meyerhof and Schacht ed., 45–46, trans., 68–69; D. Aigle, "Legitimizing a Low-Born, Regicide Monarch: The Case of the Mamluk Sultan Baybars and the Ilkhans in the Thirteenth Century," in *Governing through Representation in Ancient Inner Asia* (Bellingham, Wash., forthcoming).
8. A. Abel, "Changements politiques et littérature eschatologique dans le monde musulman," *Studia Islamica* 2 (1954): 23–43.
9. Several historians describe the cruel executions that occurred during his reign. He had come to power after participating in the murder of two of his former masters, al-Sālih Ayyūb in 1249, then Qutuz in 1260. The Damascenes in particular keenly opposed him in 1268, when he attempted to confiscate the gardens surrounding the city by arguing that they had been occupied by the Mongols before being reconquered by the Mamluk state. Hanafite law, which recognized the central power's ownership of wealth that had gone over to the non-Muslim enemy, allowed

him to do so. A compromise was finally arrived at, by the terms of which the population still had to pay an annual special tax, which was abrogated only after the sultan's death. See J. Sublet, "Le séquestre sur les jardins de la Ghouta (Damas 666/1267)," *Studia Islamica* (1976): 81–86; L. Pouzet, *Damas au VIIe/XIIIe siècle*, 272–278, 370.

Saladin Historiography

For a long time, the early advent of the Saladin legend and the idealized image it disseminated of the sultan influenced the historical studies on him. The biography by one of his close advisers, Bahā' al-Dīn Ibn Shaddād, edited and translated into Latin for the first time in 1732 by the Dutch Orientalist Albert Schultens, would mark Western historians' views of Saladin in a lasting manner. In 1758 Louis-François Marin published the first real biography of Saladin, using Arabic, Syriac,[1] and Latin sources, a remarkable achievement for the time. The sultan, in keeping with his legend, was depicted as a just, pious, and beneficent sovereign. At the same time, however, the historian strove to reestablish a certain historical truth, rejecting Saladin's supposed Christian ancestry and the idea of a free-thinking monarch and *philosophe,* as Lessing and Voltaire still saw him at that time: "Those who claim he died a philosopher are wrong; he lived and died a pious man. It seems to some writers of our time that no man can be truly great without the philosophy that consists of confessing no religion."[2]

In his great history of the Crusades, published in 1812–1822, the historian Joseph-François Michaud reaffirms the strong Islamic dimension to Saladin's actions, while acknowledging his human and political qualities:

> Possessing less boldness and bravery than Richard, Saladin had a
> graver character, and especially, one more suited to conducting a

---

1. Such as Ibn Shaddād, Ibn al-Athīr, Bar Hebraeus, and Abū l-Fidā.

2. L. F. C. Marin, *Histoire de Saladin,* 2:399. Marin does not give an opinion on the question of Saladin's knighting but cautiously adds, after reporting the legend (2:401): "I do not claim to guarantee that deed attested by our ancient writers."

religious war. He followed through on his plans to a greater degree; and, better in control of himself, he was better able to command others. He was not born for a throne, and his crime was to
ascend to it; but it must be said that once he sat on it, he proved
worthy of it. We know that, in seizing Nūr al-Dīn's empire, he was
obeying his penchant less than his good fortune and destiny. Once
he was the master, he had only two passions left, that of reigning
and that of assuring the triumph of the Koran. Whenever a kingdom or the glory of the Prophet was not in question, when neither
his ambitions nor his beliefs were thwarted, the son of Ayyūb displayed only moderation.[3]

It was not until 1898 and the Scottish Orientalist Stanley Lane-Poole that
the Western public really discovered the historical figure of Saladin. The large-
scale effort to edit and translate the Arabic texts on the Crusades, undertaken
in the second half of the nineteenth century, allowed Lane-Poole to have access
to the chief sources on Saladin. Saladin is portrayed at the beginning of his career as a self-effacing young man without great political ambitions. But then
his qualities as a chivalrous sovereign, which compelled the Crusaders to admire him, reveal themselves. That work appeared in a series entitled National
Heroes, with no indication as to which "nation" was at issue. As Margaret Jubb
rightly notes, Lane-Poole, a great admirer of Walter Scott, seems to have been
won over by the qualities of the perfect "gentleman" Saladin, who appears in
his writings as a hero more Scottish than Eastern. Lane-Poole's work, written
in a clear and enjoyable style, was a great success, to such a degree that it continues to be reprinted to this day.[4]

Studies have multiplied since the late nineteenth century, and countless
portraits of Saladin have been drawn, either in general histories of the Crusades or in studies devoted more specifically to him. I shall note only the most
significant here. The description of Saladin by the historian René Grousset,
member of the Académie Française, in his famous *Histoire des croisades et du*

---

3. J. F. Michaud, *Histoire des croisades*, 3 vols. (Paris, 1812–1822), 2:526.

4. See R. Irwin, "Saladin and the Third Crusade," 144ff.; and M. Jubb, *The Legend of Saladin*, 213.
The most recent edition of S. Lane-Poole's book, *Saladin and the Fall of the Kingdom of Jerusalem*, dates to
2002. It is preceded by an introduction by D. Nicolle, a specialist in military art during the age of the
Crusades.

royaume franc de Jérusalem (*History of the Crusades and of the Frankish Kingdom of Jerusalem, 1934–1936*) merits a moment's pause:

> After so many Arab and Turkish dynasties, the advent of Saladin therefore marked that of a new race. With him the Kurdish, that is, the Indo-European, element seized hegemony over the Muslim world. That significant event has not been adequately taken into account, for the mantle of Islamic internationalism habitually dissimulates ethnic and social differences, which, however, explain history as a whole. Yet behind that apparent uniformity, what is more distinctive than the decadent shrewdness of the Arab caliphal dynasties (the Abbasids in Baghdad and the Fatimids in Cairo); the belligerent coarseness of the first generation of Turkish adventurers such as Zangī; and the spontaneity, the intellectual and moral richness of the Kurdish dynasty of the Ayyubids? From the beginning, the Ayyubids proved to be superior to their environment. The freshness of new blood, the vigor of that mountain-dwelling race of Kurds who had not been touched by Abbasid decadence, brought to Islam of the Later Empire a store of energy and, as it were, a youthful vitality, without the savagery of the Turkish element. That advent of an Indo-European dynasty, as the mythologists of ethnicity would say, or, as we will say more simply, of a family of highlanders, would reform the face of Syro-Egyptian Islam.

These few lines, written at a time when racial anthropology was thriving (its objective being to classify and hierarchize the "races"),[5] appear today, disturbingly, to have fallen under the sway of ideologies whose perils the author likely did not perceive in full. Without totally embracing the ideology of the superiority of the Indo-European "race," represented here by the Kurds, Grousset nevertheless grants a preponderant place to Saladin's "Kurdishness," which, according to him, accounts for the sultan's humane qualities and political successes. "Saladin, the Kurdish hero," is particularly admired because he stands in contrast to the "decadence" of the Arabs and the "savagery" of the Turks, and because he diverges from the tradition of the Oriental despot, generally portrayed in nineteenth- and

5. See C. Reynaud-Paligot, *Races, racisme et antiracisme dans les années 1930* (Paris, 2007).

early twentieth-century historiography as a double-dealing and bloodthirsty tyrant.[6]

Along the same lines as Grousset, but in a more moderate manner, Albert Champdor also elevates Saladin to the rank of a hero whose "new blood, a Kurdish blood, would regenerate Islam." "The soul of an Islam that had remained young, healthy, and dynamic," Saladin is described as a capable sovereign, clement and generous, a valiant warrior who was able to take advantage of a less ardent Christendom to conduct holy war.[7]

In the 1950s, the writings of Hamilton A. R. Gibb, a major British Orientalist and, like Stanley Lane-Poole, an admirer of Walter Scott, would both modify our knowledge of Saladin and reinforce his image as a virtuous, courageous, humble, generous, and guileless sultan: "He was no simpleton, but for all that an utterly simple and transparently honest man. He baffled his enemies, internal and external, because they expected to find him animated by the same motives as they were, and playing the political game as they played it. Guileless himself, he never expected and seldom understood guile in others—a weakness of which his own family and others sometimes took advantage, but only (as a general rule) to come up at the end against his single-minded devotion, which nobody and nothing could bend, to the service of his ideals."[8]

That view not only belonged to the tradition of a historiography favorable to Saladin; it was also, as Edward Said has shown very well, consistent with the rest of Gibb's writings, one of whose objectives was to incite Westerners to take an interest in the East by showing them all the benefit they could draw in terms of understanding and leading the world in the twentieth century.[9]

A few decades later, Andrew S. Ehrenkreutz took a diametrically opposed position, striving to show that Saladin's actions were motivated only by his ambition and thirst for power. Here are his concluding lines: "Most of Saladin's significant historical accomplishments should be attributed to his military and governmental experience, to his ruthless persecution and execution of political opponents and dissenters, to his vindictive belligerence and calcu-

6. See R. Grousset, *Histoire des croisades*, 2:535–536. These passages are reproduced verbatim, without commentary from the editor, in the new edition from Librairie Jules Tallandier (Paris, 1981), 5:121.

7. See A. Champdor, *Saladin, le plus pur héro de l'islam*, 46, 342–343.

8. H. A. R. Gibb, "The Achievement of Saladin," 53.

9. See E. Said, *Orientalism* (New York, 1978).

lated opportunism, and to his readiness to compromise religious ideals to political expediency."[10]

No doubt that book had the merit of calling into question what was until then an overly civilized image of the man. But in thus condemning Saladin and conducting the debate at a level more moral than historical, Ehrenkreutz in no way introduced a new problematic. Good or bad, disinterested or opportunistic, magnanimous or cruel, sincere or calculating: so long as historians remained attached to that psychological approach to Saladin and sought at all cost to plumb his intentions, to fathom his most personal aspirations, every one of his words or gestures could be interpreted positively by some, negatively by others.

The first to have freed themselves from that reductive view were the historians Malcolm C. Lyons and David E. P. Jackson, authors of the best biography of Saladin to date. They strove to retrace, as faithfully as possible and without value judgments—and to place within their original context—the notable events of his reign, his actions promoting the unification of the Muslim world and the pursuit of jihad against the Franks. One of the major contributions of their biography was its systematic exploitation of the many official documents from Saladin's chancery and the large body of correspondence by his secretaries 'Imād al-Dīn al-Isfahānī and al-Fādil, which had been little studied before then. Their excellent book has provided us with a very detailed study of Saladin's reign, though the approach remained deliberately chronological and focused primarily on military and diplomatic aspects.

Other published studies have dealt with key periods during that reign. Among the most notable are Hannes Möhring's extensive research on Saladin and the Third Crusade and on the sultan's image, and the innovative studies by Yacov Lev on Saladin's governance of Egypt. In addition to these book-length studies, there are many articles, of which only a selection is provided in the bibliography to this book. In that vast historical production, it is striking to observe how small a place is occupied by French historiography.[11] In France, no

---

10. A. S. Ehrenkreutz, *Saladin*, 238.

11. Many other books on Saladin have been published, especially in English; these overviews, of varying quality, add nothing new, however. In France, G. Chauvel's *Saladin rassembleur de l'Islam* (Paris, 1991) is a fictionalized "autobiography." By contrast, J. M. Mouton's little book, *Saladin le sultan chevalier* (Paris, 2001), is a very good summation of Saladin's reign and contains several original documents.

doubt, the age of the Crusades was long studied from a primarily Western point of view, sometimes under the influence of a colonial ideology, though the main Arabic sources were known from the eighteenth century on. Claude Cahen (1909–1991), however, strongly influenced by the Annales school of history, was one of the first to take an interest in the economic and social history of the medieval Muslim world. This was also someone who clearly changed the direction of the French historiography of the Crusades, by discovering and publishing many previously neglected Arabic sources. In his wake, new studies appeared in the second half of the twentieth century on various aspects of economic, social, cultural, and urban history. But biography, applied to the great political figures of medieval Islam, was a genre long since abandoned, even though, during the same period, excellent biographies of philosophers, theologians, jurists, and mystics came to enrich our knowledge of the history of Muslim thought. Only the book that Nikita Elisséeff devoted to Nūr al-Dīn (r. 1146–1174) may stand as an exception.[12] It, however, is much more the history of a reign than the biography of a ruler.

The Arab historiography on Saladin raises a different set of problems. From the beginning, it had some difficulty separating the past from the present, history from current events; and historical and scientific method too often gave way to political and ideological reactions. The attention focused on that sovereign accompanied the rise of studies devoted to the Crusades in the late nineteenth century.[13] Parallels were systematically drawn between that historical era and the contemporary period. Just as, in the West, the first studies of the Crusades were often marked by colonial ideology, in the East the hostile position of Western countries toward the Ottoman Empire, as well as French and English colonization, and finally, the creation of the state of Israel were all experienced as an assault on Islamic countries, which had the effect of reviving the memory of the

12. See N. Elisséeff, *Nūr al-Dīn.*

13. The first biography of Saladin written in modern times in the Muslim world was by a Turk, Namik Kemal (1844–1888), published in 1872 in response to Joseph F. Michaud's *Histoire des croisades* (Paris, 1812–1822), which had just been translated into Turkish. It was published in the same volume as biographies of two great sovereigns and heroes of Ottoman history, Mehmed II the Conqueror and Selim I the Grim. See C. Hillenbrand, *The Crusades,* 593; W. Ende, "Wer ist ein Glaubensheld, wer ist ein Ketzer?" *Die Welts des Islams* 23 (1984): 70–94, esp. 79–81.

Crusades. Emphasis was placed at the time on the similarities between these two periods of history: the same Muslim divisions, which fostered the Western undertaking; the same abandonment of Palestine by the neighboring Muslim states; the same economic draw of the region; the same occupation and colonization of the country by non-Muslims. Since the age of the Crusades had ended to the advantage of the Muslims, that look backward was also intended to improve the morale of the population, to restore their hope and confidence, to prove to them that their humiliating situation would one day come to an end, and to make them forget the negligence of the regimes in place.

Within that tumultuous context, Arab historians succumbed to the temptation to seek from the past examples for the present. The figure of Saladin appeared as the savior, the model for the ideal sovereign, someone who was able to restore the pride and dignity of Muslims vis-à-vis the Franks. It hardly mattered that he was Kurdish and not Arab. Historians highlighted his linguistic and cultural "Arabness" and his defense of Islam, and made him a hero of the Arab-Muslim cause.[14] Three countries vied for the privilege of having had him on their soil: Egypt, Syria, and Iraq. And it is significant that, in 1987, three colloquia took place simultaneously in Cairo, Damascus, and Baghdad to celebrate with great pomp the anniversary of the Battle of Hattīn. The Nasserian period in Egypt (1952–1970) witnessed the flourishing of biographies of Saladin, since his role as a leader was reminiscent of that of Gamal Abdel Nasser. There was even a penchant for pointing out their shared name, "al-Nāsir."[15] Historians at the time had a tendency to situate the birth of the Egyptian nation at the start of Saladin's reign, because of the break he introduced in the history of that country. Since the advent of the Muslim occupation, Egypt had been ruled only by more or less autonomous governors of the Sunni caliphate of Damascus and then of Baghdad, before being the seat of the Shiite caliphate of the Fatimids. Honor therefore devolved on Saladin, both for having established an independent dynastic power and for having restored Sunni orthodoxy.

During the last few decades and throughout the Middle East, the image of Saladin has also fostered both political discourses and literary and cinematic

14. See *Salāh al-Dīn al-Ayyūbī*, *Dirāsāt Islāmiyya* 5 (1994–1995): 15. In the words of the president of the Institut des hautes études islamiques (Institute of Higher Islamic Studies), Hishām Nashshāba: "Saladin was Kurdish, as you know, but his Kurdishness did not prevent him from being an Arab and Muslim hero."

15. Nasser's name in Arabic is Gamāl 'Abd al-Nāsir, and Saladin bore the title "al-Malik al-Nāsir."

fictions. To mention only historical studies (which deserve more thorough research than the overview I give here), the many publications that have appeared—first, in the Nasserian era; then in 1987, on the occasion of the anniversary of the Battle of Hattīn; and finally, in 1993, for the eight hundredth anniversary of Saladin's death—are indicative of the representation of him still current in intellectual Arab circles. Through the analysis of Saladin and his reign, it is contemporary events, in this case the Israeli-Palestinian conflict, that repeatedly surface. Efforts are made to draw lessons from history, to understand by what means Saladin was victorious in his jihad, in order to incite Arabs of today to follow his example. The emphasis is placed in particular on the need to reconstitute Muslim unity, which alone allowed Saladin to reconquer Jerusalem. The medieval sources are usually reproduced uncritically, with no inquiry into the meaning that ought to be given to such evidence and with no distinction between the sultan and the image of him conveyed through propaganda. When the sources diverge, most historians credit one or the other, generally choosing the version most favorable to the sultan. It comes as no great surprise, therefore, that the result is altogether consistent with the portrait of the exemplary sovereign preoccupied with justice and the religious ideal, as his panegyrists have described Saladin since the twelfth century.

To cite only a few examples, for Qadrī Qalʿajī, whose biography of Saladin has been reprinted at least four times since 1956, Saladin is a man of peace, not a man of war, and only circumstances forced him to fight. He always faced conflicts with magnanimity and clemency, served as an example to others, and sustained the Arabs by his virtues and generosity much more than by his use of armed force.[16] Walīd Nuwayhid inquires a bit more deeply into the origins of the Crusades and their impact in Europe. He is not afraid to consider the different interpretations that have been provided of Saladin's personality and politics. Nevertheless, the limited number of sources he cites and, in many cases, his outdated bibliography do not allow him to move beyond fairly general considerations.[17] For Nuʿmān al-Tayyib Sulaymān, present-day Israelis are the Crusaders of the past, whom he presents from the first page as the "enemies of

---

16. See Q. Qalʿajī, *Salāh al-Dīn al-Ayyūbī* (Beirut, 1992), 366, 368.

17. See W. Nuwayhid, *Salāh al-Dīn al-Ayyūbī, Suqūt al-Quds wa tahrīruhā (qirāʾa muʿāsira)* (Beirut, 1997). See also Sawsan Muhammad Nasrā, *Al-Qādī al-Fādil wa Salāh al-Dīn wa l-wahda al-islāmiyya* (Cairo, 1990), which provides a fairly clear exposition of the events, but without great originality.

religion and of the Arabs."[18] At a much more polemical level, 'Arafāt Hijāzī says that he is awaiting a "new Saladin," who will return hope to the Arabs and liberate Jerusalem. The author sees little difference between the Crusades of the past and the present-day conflict in the Middle East. With little historical rigor, he assimilates the Crusaders to Western Jews of today.[19] Similarly, 'Abd al-Qādir Nūrī, dedicating his book to Almighty God, implores him to come to the aid of Palestine today, as he once did by sending Saladin.[20]

In all these works, we cannot fail to be struck by the almost total absence of the vast recent Western bibliography on the Crusades in general and on Saladin in particular, the result no doubt of the chasm, all too great, that still separates Western and Arab academic circles.[21] Nevertheless, within that disappointing historiographical panorama, Muhammad Mu'nis 'Awad's recent *Salāh al-Dīn al-Ayyūbī bayn al-ta'rīkh wa l-ustūra* opens new vistas.[22] The author strives to adopt a more scientific approach, particularly by placing Saladin within his historical context. An entire chapter is also devoted to his Western legend, and though a few fundamental works do not appear in his bibliography,[23] it is almost exhaustive in Arab studies and more updated in the Western field than that of any of his predecessors. We can therefore hope that, in the years to come, Arab historiography will turn toward a more "objective" view of Saladin's history, toward the analysis of the discourse of which he was the object, and toward studies of the representation that Arab authors from the twelfth century to our own time have sought to give of him.

18. See Nu'mān al-Tayyib Sulaymān, *Manhaj Salāh al-Dīn al-Ayyūbī fī l-hukm wa l-qiyāda* (Cairo, 1991).

19. See 'Arafāt Hijāzī, *Salah al-Dīn, dhikrā murūr 800 'ām 'ala fath al-Quds* (Amman, 1987), 10.

20. See 'Abd al-Qādir Nūrī, *Siyāsat Salāh al-Dīn al-Ayyūbī fī bilād Misr wa l-Shām wa l-Jazīra 570–589/1174–1193* (Baghdad, 1976).

21. The Western bibliography cited in works on Saladin written in Arabic generally ends in the mid-twentieth century. H. A. R. Gibb is cited most often, and A. Champdor's biography can also be found there. On the Crusades, it is R. Grousset's history that most often appears.

22. Muhammad Mu'nis 'Awad, *Salāh al-Dīn al-Ayyūbī bayn al-ta'rīkh wa l-ustūra* (Cairo, 2008).

23. Particularly those of M. C. Lyons and D. E. P. Jackson and M. Jubb.

Bibliography

The bibliography on Saladin and his time is so vast that it is hardly possible to give an exhaustive list here. The titles selected are those that have been of direct use in the elaboration of this book. [When an English-language edition or translation of a source is provided, passages quoted in the body of the text are from that edition. If no English-language source is provided, the passage is my translation from the French.—trans.]

The Sources

Arabic and Syriac Sources

ʿAbd al-Laṭīf al-Baghdādī. *Kitāb al-Ifāda wa l-iʿtibār fī l-umūr al-mushāhada wa l-ḥawādith al-muʿāyana.* Translated into French by S. de Sacy as *Relation de l'Égypte.* Paris, 1810. Facsimile edition of the autograph manuscript at the Bodleian Library. Translated into English by K. H. Zand, J. A. Videan, and I. E. Videan as *The Eastern Key.* London, 1965.

Abū Shāma. *Kitāb al-rawḍatayn fī akhbār al-dawlatayn.* 2 vols. Bulaq, 1871–1875. Excerpts edited and translated by A. C. Barbier de Meynard in *Recueils des historiens des croisades. Historiens orientaux (RHC Or.),* vols. 4 and 5. Paris, 1848–1906.

———. *Tarājim rijāl al-qarnayn al-sādis wa l-sābiʿ.* Edited by al-Kawtharī. Cairo, 1947.

Amari, M. *I diplomi arabi del R. archivio fiorentino.* Florence, 1863.

Anonymi auctoris chronicon ad A.C. 1234 pertinens. Part. 2. Translated by A. Abouna. Vol. 354 of *Corpus scriptorum christianorum orientalium,* part 154: *Scriptores Syri.* Louvain, 1974.

Bar Hebraeus. *The Chronography of Gregory Abū l-Faraǧ the Son of Aaron.* Edited and translated by E. A. W. Budge. 2 vols. London, 1932.

Bundārī, al-. *Sanā al-Barq al-shāmī*. Edited by F. al-Nabrāwī. Cairo, 1979.

The Churches and Monasteries of Egypt and Some Neighbouring Countries, Attributed to Abū Ṣālih, the Armenian. Edited and translated by B. T. A. Evetts and A. J. Butler. Oxford, 1895. *Abu al-Makarem: History of the Churches and Monasteries in Lower Egypt in the Thirteenth Century*. Edited by Bishop Samuel. Cairo, 1992.

Dhahabī, al-. *Siyar aʻlām al-nubalāʼ*. Edited by S. al-Arnaʼūṭ et al. 25 vols. Beirut, 1981–1988.

Fāḍil, al-. *Dīwān al-Qāḍī al-Fāḍil*. Edited by A. Badawī and I. al-Ibyārī. Cairo, 1961.

———. *Al-Durr al-naẓīma min tarassul ʻAbd al-Raḥīm*. Edited by A. Badawī. Cairo, n.d.

Gabrieli, F. *Chroniques arabes des croisades*. Translated into French from the Italian by V. Pâques. Paris, 1977.

Ḥafṣī, I. al-. "Correspondance officielle et privée d'al-Qāḍī al-Fāḍil." Doctoral diss., Université de Paris IV-Sorbonne. 4 vols. Paris, 1979. More than eight hundred letters assembled from twenty-one manuscripts and various printed works.

Harawī, al-. *Kitāb al-ishārāt ilā maʻrifat al-ziyārāt*. Edited and translated by J. Sourdel-Thomine as *Guides des lieux de pèlerinage*. 2 vols. Damascus, 1953–1957.

———. *Al-Tadhkira al-Harawiyya fī l-ḥiyal al-ḥarbiyya*. Edited and translated by J. Sourdel-Thomine as "Les conseils du šayḫ al-Harawī à un prince ayyūbide," *Bulletin d'études orientales* 17 (1961–1962): 205–266.

History of the Patriarchs of the Egyptian Church. Edited and translated by A. Khater and O. H. E.-K. H. S. Burmester. 4 vols. Cairo, 1970–1974.

Ibn Abī Uṣaybiʻa. *ʻUyūn al-anbāʼ fī ṭabaqāt al-aṭibbāʼ*. Edited by N. Riḍā. Beirut, 1965.

Ibn Abī l-Wafāʼ al-Qurashī. *Al-Jawāhir al-muḍiyya fī ṭabaqāt al-Ḥanafiyya*. 2 parts in one volume. Hyderabad, 1913.

Ibn al-ʻAdīm. *Bughyat al-ṭalab fī taʼrīkh Ḥalab*. Edited by S. Zakkār. 11 vols. Damascus, 1988.

———. *Zubdat al-ḥalab min taʼrīkh Ḥalab*. Edited by S. Dahan. 3 vols. Damascus, 1951–1968.

Ibn ʻAsākir. *Taʼrīkh Dimashq*. Edited by Ṣ. al-D. Munajjid. 2 vols. Damascus, 1951–1954. Also edited by ʻU al-ʻAmrawī. Beirut, 1995–2000, 80 vols. Partial translation in N. Elisséeff, *La description de Damas d'Ibn ʻAsākir*. Damascus, 1959.

Ibn al-Athīr. *Al-Kāmil fī l-taʼrīkh*. 13 vols. Beirut, 1965–1967. Reprint of the C. J. Tornberg edition. Leiden, 1867. Translated into English by D. S. Richards as *The Chronicle of Ibn al-Athīr for the Crusading Period from al-Kāmil fī-l-taʼrīkh*. 3 vols. Aldershot, U.K., 2006–2008.

———. *Al-Taʼrīkh al-bāhir fī l-dawla al-atābakiyya*. Edited by ʻAbd al-Qādir Aḥmad Ṭulaymāt. Baghdad, 1963.

Ibn al-Dawādārī. *Kanz al-durar wa jāmiʻ al-ghurar*. Vol. 7. Edited by S. ʻĀshūr. Cairo, 1972.

Ibn al-Furāt. *Taʼrīkh al-duwal wa l-mulūk*. Edited by Ḥ. al-Shammāʻ. Vol. 4, pt. 1 (years 563–586). Busra, 1967. Vol. 4, pt. 2 (years 587–599). Busra, 1969.

Ibn al-ʿImād. *Shadharāt al-dhahab fī akhbār man dhahab.* Edited by ʿA. al-Q. al-Arnaʾūṭ and M. al-Arnaʾūṭ. 10 vols. Damascus, 1986–1995.

Ibn Jubayr. *Riḥla.* Edited by W. Wright and revised by M. J. De Goeje in *E. J. W. Gibb Memorial Series,* vol. 5. Leiden, 1907. Translated into French by M. Gaudefroy-Demombynes as *Voyages.* 4 vols. Paris, 1949–1965. Translated into English by R. J. C. Broadhurst as *The Travels of Ibn Jubayr, Being the Chronicle of a Mediaeval Spanish Moor.* London, 1952.

Ibn Jumayʿ. *Al-Maqāla al-Ṣalāḥiyya fī iḥyāʾ al-ṣināʿa al-ṭibbiyya.* Edited and translated into English by H. Fähndrich as *Treatise to Ṣalāḥ ad-Dīn on the Revival of the Art of Medicine, Abhandlungen für die Kunde des Morgenlandes 46,* 3 (1983).

Ibn Kathīr. *Al-Bidāya wa l-nihāya.* Edited by Ṣ. al-ʿAṭṭār et al. 11 vols. Beirut, 1998–2001.

Ibn Khaldūn. *Al-Muqaddima.* Translated into French by V. Monteil as *Discours sur l'histoire universelle.* 3 vols. Beirut, 1967–1968. Translated into English by F. Rosenthal as *The Muqaddimah: An Introduction to History.* 3 vols. New York, 1958.

Ibn Khallikān. *Kitāb wafāyat al-aʿyan wa anbāʾ abnāʾ al-zamān.* Edited by I. ʿAbbās. 8 vols. Beirut, 1968–1972. Translated into English by M. G. de Slane as *Ibn Khallikan's Biographical Dictionary.* 4 vols. Paris and London, 1843–1871.

Ibn Mammātī. *Kitāb qawānīn al-dawāwīn.* Edited by A. S. Atiya. Cairo, 1943.

Ibn Rajab. *Kitāb al-dhayl ʿalā ṭabaqāt al-ḥanābila.* Edited by M. H. al-Fiqqī. 2 vols. Cairo, 1952.

Ibn Shaddād Bahāʾ al-Dīn. *Al-Nawādir al-sulṭāniyya wa l-maḥāsin al-Yūsufiyya.* Edited by J. al-Dīn al-Shayyāl. Cairo, 1964. Excerpts edited and translated into French in *Recueils des historiens des croisades. Historiens orientaux (RHC Or.).* Vol. 3. Paris, 1884, 1–370. Translated into English by D. S. Richards as *The Rare and Excellent History of Saladin.* Aldershot, 2001.

Ibn Shaddād ʿIzz al-Dīn. *Al-Aʿlāq al-khaṭīra fī dhikr umarāʾ al-Shām wa l-Jazīra.* Edited by D. Sourdel. Damascus, 1953 (description of Aleppo). Edited by S. al-Dahhān. Damascus, 1956 (description of Damascus) and 1963 (description of Lebanon-Palestine-Jordan).

Ibn al-Ṭuwayr. *Nuzhat al-muqlatayn fī akhbār al-dawlatayn.* Edited by A. F. Sayyid. Beirut, 1992.

Ibn ʿUnayn. *Dīwān.* Edited by Khalīl Mardam Bey. Damascus, 1946.

Ibn Wāṣil. *Mufarrij al-kurūb fī akhbār Banī Ayyūb.* Edited by J. al-D. al-Shayyāl (vols. 1–3), Ḥ. Rabīʿ and S. ʿĀshūr (vols. 4 and 5), and ʿU. ʿA. Tadmurī (vol. 6). 6 vols. Cairo, 1953–2004.

Idrīsī, al-. *Kitāb nuzhat al-mushtāq fī-khtirāq al-āfāq.* Edited by E. Cerulli, F. Gabrieli, G. Levi Della Vida et al. as *Opus Geographicum.* 9 fascicles. Naples, 1970–1984. Edited and partial French translation by R. Dozy and M. J. De Goeje in *Description de l'Afrique et de l'Espagne.* Leiden, 1866.

'Imād al-Dīn al-Iṣfahānī. *Al-Barq al-shāmī*. Vol. 5 (years 578–580/1182–1185). Edited by F. Ḥusayn. Amman, 1987.

———. *Kitāb al-fatḥ al-qussī fī l-fatḥ al-qudsī*. Edited by C. Landberg. Leiden, 1888. Translated into French by H. Massé as *Conquête de la Syrie et de la Palestine par Saladin*. Paris, 1972.

Khazrajī, al-. *Ta'rīkh dawlat al-Akrād wa l-Atrāk*. Istanbul ms., Suleymaniye, Hekimoğlu Ali Paša, 695.

Makhzūmī, al-. *Kitāb al-minhāj fī 'ilm kharāj Miṣr*. Edited by C. Cahen and Y. Rağib. Cairo, 1986.

Manṣūr ibn Shāhanshāh, al-. *Miḍmār al-ḥaqā'iq wa sirr al-khalā'iq*. Edited by Ḥasan Ḥabashī (years 575–582/1180–1186). Cairo, 1968.

Maqrīzī, al-. *Itti'āz al-ḥunafā'*. Edited by M. Ahmad. Cairo, 1973.

———. *Kitāb al-muqaffā al-kabīr*. Edited by M. al-Ya'lāwī. 8 vols. Beirut, 1991.

———. *Kitāb al-mawā'iz wa l-i'tibār bi dhikr al-khiṭaṭ wa l-athār*. Bulaq, 1880. Edited by A. Fu'ād Sayyid. 5 parts in 6 vols. London, 2002–2004.

———. *Kitāb al-sulūk li ma'rifat duwal al-mulūk*. Vol. 1, parts 1 and 2. Edited by M. Ziyāda. Cairo, 1956. English translation of the Ayyubid period (567–648/1171–1250) by R. J. C. Broadhurst as *A History of the Ayyūbid Sultans of Egypt*. Boston, 1980.

Michael the Syrian. *Chronique syriaque*. Edited and translated by J. B. Chabot. 4 vols. Paris, 1899–1914.

Mujīr al-Dīn. *Al-Uns al-jalīl bi-ta'rīkh al-Quds wa l-Khalīl*. 2 vols. Najaf, 1968. Partial French translation in H. Sauvaire, *Histoire de Jérusalem et d'Hébron depuis Abraham jusqu'à la fin du XVe siècle de J.-C. Fragments de la chronique de Moudjir-ed-dyn traduits sur le texte arabe*. Paris, 1876.

Mundhirī, al-. *Al Takmila li-wafayāt al-naqala*. Edited by B. 'A. Ma'rūf. 4 vols. Beirut, 1981.

Nābulusī, al-. *Kitāb luma' al-qawānīn al-muḍiyya fī dawāwīn al-Diyār al-Miṣriyya*. Edited by C. Cahen and C. Becker. *Bulletin d'études orientales* 16 (1960): 1–78 and 118–134.

Nu'aymī, al-. *Al-Dāris fī ta'rīkh al-madāris*. Edited by J. al-Ḥasanī. 2 vols. Damascus, 1948–1951.

Qalqashandī, al-. *Ṣubḥ al-a'shā fī ṣinā'at al-inshā'*. Edited by M. 'Abd al-Rasūl Ibrāhīm. 2nd ed. 14 vols. Cairo, 1963.

Recueils des historiens des croisades. Historiens orientaux (RHC Or.). 5 vols. Paris, 1872–1906.

Sauvaire, H. "La description de Damas." Translated by al-'Ilmawī, author of a summary of al-Nu'aymī. *Journal asiatique*, 9th series, 3 (1894): 251–318, 385–501; 4 (1894): 242–331, 460–503; 5 (1895): 269–315, 377–411; 6 (1895): 221–313, 409–484; 7 (1896): 185–285, 369–459.

The Sea of Precious Virtues (Bahr al-Fawā'id): A Medieval Islamic Mirror for Princes. Translated by J. S. Meisami. Salt Lake City, 1991.

Shayzarī, al-. *Kitāb nihāyat al-rutba fī ṭalab al-ḥisba.* Edited by al-Bāz al-'Arīnī. Cairo, 1948. Translated into French by W. Behrnauer as "Mémoire sur les institutions de police chez les Arabes, les Persans et les Turcs." *Journal asiatique,* 5th series, 16 (1860): 347–392; 17 (1861): 5–76.

Sibṭ Ibn al-Jawzī. *Mir'āt al-zamān.* Vol. 8 (part 1 of 2, for years 495–654/1101–1256). Hyderabad, 1951–1952.

Subkī, al-. *Ṭabaqāt al-shāfi'iyya al-kubrā.* Edited by M. al-Ṭanāḥī and A. al-Ḥilū. 10 vols. Cairo, 1964–1976.

Ṭarsūsī, al-. *Tabṣirat arbāb al-albāb.* Bodleian ms., Hunt. 264. Edited with partial French translation by C. Cahen as "Un traité d'armurerie composé par Saladin." *Bulletin d'études orientales* 12 (1947–1948): 103–163.

'Umāra. *Al-Nukta al-'aṣriyya fī akhbār al-wuzarā' al-Miṣriyya.* Edited by H. Derenbourg in *Oumara du Yémen, sa vie et son oeuvre.* Paris, 1897–1904.

Usāma Ibn Munqidh. *Kitāb al-i'tibār.* Translated into French by A. Miquel as *Des enseignements de la vie. Souvenirs d'un gentilhomme syrien du temps des croisades.* Paris, 1983. Translated into English by P. K. Hitti as *An Arab-Syrian Gentleman and Warrior in the Period of the Crusades, Memoirs of Usāmah Ibn Munqidh.* 3rd ed. Princeton, 1987.

Wahrānī, al-. *Manāmāt al-Wahrānī wa maqāmātuhu wa rasā'iluh.* Edited by I. Sha'lān and M. Naghash. Cairo, 1968.

Yāqūt. *Mu'jam al-buldān.* 5 vols. Beirut, 1955–1957.

———. *Mu'jam al-udabā'.* Edited by D. S. Margoliouth. 20 parts in 10 vols. 3rd ed. Cairo, 1980.

Sources in Western Languages

Ambroise. *L'Estoire de la guerre sainte.* Edited and translated by G. Paris. Paris, 1897. Edited and translated into English by M. Ailes and M. Barber as *The History of the Holy War, Ambroise's Estoire de la Guerre Sainte.* 2 vols. Woodbridge, U.K., 2003.

Burchard of Strasbourg. Edited with an Italian translation by S. de Sandoli in *Itinera Hierosolymitana crucesignatorum (saec. XII–XIII). Studium Biblicum Franciscanum.* Collectio Maior, no. 24, vol. 2. Jerusalem, 1980, 393–411.

Chronique d'Ernoul et de Bernard le trésorier. Edited by L. de Mas Latrie. Paris, 1871.

La Continuation de Guillaume de Tyr (1184–1197). Edited by M. R. Morgan. Paris, 1982. Translated into English by P. W. Edbury as *The Conquest of Jerusalem and the Third Crusade.* Aldershot, 1996.

Croisades et pèlerinages, récits, chroniques et voyages en Terre sainte, XIIe–XVIe siècle. Edited by D. Régnier-Bohler. Paris, 1997.

L'Estoire de Eracles empereur et la conqueste de la terre d'Outremers. In *Recueils des historiens des croisades. Historiens occidentaux (RHC Occ.),* 2:483–639. See also *La Continuation de Guillaume de Tyr.*

Estoires d'Outremer et de la naissance de Salehadin. Edited by M. Jubb. London, 1990.

De expugnatione Terrae Sanctae per Saladinum, libellus. Edited by J. Stevenson as an appendix to Ralph Coggeshall, ed., *Chronicon Anglicanum* (London, 1875), 209–262. Excerpts translated into English by J. A. Brundage in *The Crusades: A Documentary Survey.* Milwaukee, 1962, 153–163.

La fille du comte de Ponthieu and *Jehan d'Avesnes.* In *Splendeurs de la cour de Bourgogne,* edited by Danielle Régnier-Bohler. Paris, 1995, 373–464.

Itinerarium peregrinorum et gesta regis Ricardi auctore, ut videtur, Ricardo canonico Sanctae Trinitatis Londoniensis. Edited by W. Stubbs as *Chronicles and Memorials of the Reign of Richard I.* Vol. 1. London, 1864; *Das Itinerarium peregrinorum. Eine zeitgenössische englische Chronik zum dritten Kreuzzug in ursprünglicher Gestalt.* Edited by H. E. Mayer. Stuttgart, 1962. Translated into English by H. J. Nicholson as *Chronicle of the Third Crusade: A Translation of the Itinerarium Peregrinorum et Gesta Regis Ricardi.* Aldershot, 1997.

Jacques, de Vitry. *Historia Hiersolimitana.* Edited by J. Bongars as *Gesta Dei per Francos.* Vol. 1 (1095). Hanau, 1661. Translated into French by M. G. Grossel as *Histoire orientale de Jacques de Vitry.* Paris, 2005.

———. *Lettres de la cinquième croisade.* Edited by R. B. C. Huygens and translated by G. Duchet-Suchaux. Brepols, 1998.

Novellino, suivi de Contes de chevaliers du temps jadis. Introduction, translation, and notes by G. Genot and P. Larivaille. Paris, 1988.

Peter Tudebode. *Historia de Hierosolymitano itinere.* Edited by J. H. Hill and L. L. Hill. Paris, 1977. Translated into English by J. H. Hill and L. L. Hill. Philadelphia, 1974.

Récits d'un ménestrel de Reims. Edited by Natalis de Wailly. Paris, 1876. Translated into modern French by M. G. Grossel. Valenciennes, 2002.

Recueils des historiens des croisades. Historiens occidentaux (RHC Occ.). 5 vols. Paris, 1844–1895.

Roger of Howden. *Chronica,* edited by W. Stubbs. 4 vols. London, 1868–1871.

Saladin. Suite et fin du deuxième cycle de la croisade. Edited by L. S. Crist. Geneva, 1972. Partial translation by M. de Combarieu du Grès in *Croisades et pèlerinages. Récits, chroniques et voyages en Terre sainte, XIIe–XVIe siècle,* edited by D. Régnier-Bohler. Paris, 1997, 417–496.

Thietmar. "Le pèlerinage de Maître Thietmar." Translated by C. Deluz in *Croisades et pèlerinages. Récits, chroniques et voyages en Terre sainte, XIIe–XVIe siècle,* edited by D. Régnier-Bohler. Paris, 1997, 928–958.

William of Tyre. *Chronique*, edited by R. B. C. Huygens. 2 vols. Turnhout, 1986. Translated into English by E. A. Babcock and A. C. Krey as *A History of Deeds Done beyond the Sea*. 2 vols. New York, 1941; repr. 1976.

General and Reference Works

Ashtor, E. *Histoire des prix et salaires dans l'Orient médiéval*. Paris, 1969.

Brockelmann, C. *Geschichte der Arabischen Literatur*. 2 vols. Weimar, 1898–1902; 2nd. ed., Leiden 1943–1949; 3 supplements, Leiden, 1937–1942.

The Cambridge History of Egypt. Vol. 1: *Islamic Egypt, 640–1517*. Edited by C. F. Petry. Cambridge, U.K., 1998.

Encyclopaedia Judaica. Edited by C. Roth and G. Wigoder. 17 vols. Jerusalem, 1971–1972.

Encyclopaedia of Islam. 2nd ed. (EI 2). Edited by H. A. R. Gibb et al. 12 vols. Leiden, 1960–2009.

Goitein, S. D. F. *A Mediterranean Society: The Jewish Communities of the Arab World as Portrayed in the Documents of the Cairo Geniza*. 6 vols. Berkeley, 1967–1993.

Heyd, W. *Geschichte des Levantehandels im Mittelalter*. 2 vols. Stuttgart, 1879. Translated into French as *Histoire du commerce du Levant au Moyen Âge*. 2 vols. Leipzig, 1885–1886; anastatic reprint, Amsterdam, 1983.

Répertoire chronologique d'épigraphie arabe (RCEA). Edited by E. Combe, J. Sauvaget, G. Wiet et al. 17 vols. Cairo, 1931–1982.

Riley-Smith, J. *The Atlas of the Crusades*. New York, 1990.

Works on Saladin and His Time

800 *'ām, Ḥiṭṭīn Ṣalāḥ al-Dīn wa l-'amal al-'arabī al-muwwaḥḥid*. Proceedings of the colloquium held by al-Lajna al-Miṣriyya li taḍāmun al-shu'ūb al-ifrīqiyya al-āsiyawiyya (Egyptian Committee for Afro-Asian Solidarity) and the Centre for Arabic Studies in London. Cairo, 1989.

Ailes, M. J. "The Admirable Enemy? Saladin and Saphadin in Ambroise's Estoire de la Guerre Sainte." In *Knighthoods of Christ: Essays on the History of the Crusades and the Knights Templar, Presented to Malcolm Barber*, edited by N. Housley. Aldershot, 2007, 51–64.

Ashtor, E. "Saladin and the Jews." *Hebrew Union College Annual* 27 (1956): 310–313.

'Awad, M. M. *Salāḥ al-Dīn al-Ayyūbī bayn al-ta'rīkh wa l-ustūra*. Cairo, 2008.

Balog, P. *The Coinage of the Ayyubids*. London, 1980.

Bates, M. L., and D. M. Metcalf. "Crusader Coinage with Arabic Inscriptions." In *A History of the Crusades*, K. M. Setton, general editor. Vol. 6: *The Impact of the Crusades on Europe*, edited by H. W. Hazard and N. Zacour. Madison, 1989, 421–482.

Brand, C. M. "The Byzantines and Saladin, 1185–1192: Opponents of the Third Crusade." *Speculum* 37 (1962): 167–181.

Cahen, C. "Contribution à l'étude des impôts dans l'Égypte médiévale." *Journal of the Economic and Social History of the Orient* 5, 3 (1962): 244–278.

———. "Douanes et commerce dans les ports méditerranéens de l'Égypte médiévale d'après le Minhādj d'al-Makhzūmī." *Journal of the Economic and Social History of the Orient* 7 (1964): 217–314. Reprinted in C. Cahen, *Makhzūmiyyāt. Études sur l'histoire économique et financière de l'Égypte médiévale.* Leiden, 1977, 57–154.

———. "Indigènes et croisés. Quelques mots à propos d'un médecin d'Amaury et de Saladin." *Syria* 15 (1934): 351–360.

———. *Orient et Occident au temps des croisades.* Paris, 1983.

———. *La Syrie du Nord à l'époque des croisades et la principauté franque d'Antioche.* Paris, 1940.

Champdor, A. *Saladin, le plus pur héros de l'islam.* Paris, 1956.

Cipollone, G. *Cristianità-Islam. Cattività e liberazione in nome di Dio. Il tempo di Innocenzo III dopo "il 1187."* Rome, 1992.

———, ed. *La liberazione dei "captivi" tra Cristianità e Islam. Oltre la crociata e il Gihad: Tolleranza e servizio umanitario.* Vatican City, 2000.

Cobb, P. M. *Usama ibn Munqidh: Warrior Poet of the Age of Crusades.* Oxford, 2005.

Creswell, K. A. C. *The Muslim Architecture of Egypt.* Vol. 2: *Ayyubids and Early Bahrite Mamluks, 1171–1326.* Oxford, 1960.

Eddé, A. M. *La principauté ayyoubide d'Alep (579/1183–658/1260).* Stuttgart, 1999.

———. "Saladin's Religious Foundations in Damascus: Some New Hypotheses." In *Living Islamic History: Studies in Honour of Professor Carole Hillenbrand,* edited by Y. Suleiman. Edinburgh, 2008, 62–76.

Eddé, A. M., and F. Micheau. *L'Orient au temps des croisades.* Paris, 2002.

Ehrenkreutz, A. S. "The Crisis of the Dīnār in the Egypt of Saladin." *Journal of the American Oriental Society* 76 (1956): 178–184.

———. "The Place of Saladin in the Naval History of the Mediterranean Sea in the Middle Ages." *Journal of the American Oriental Society* 75 (1955): 100–116.

———. *Saladin.* New York, 1972.

Elisséeff, N. *Nūr al-Dīn, un grand prince musulman de Syrie au temps des croisades.* 3 vols. Damascus, 1967.

Frenkel, Y. "Political and Social Aspects of Islamic Religious Endowments (awqāf): Saladin in Cairo (1169–1173) and Jerusalem (1187–1193)." *Bulletin of the School of Oriental and African Studies* 62 (1999): 1–20.

Friedman, Y. *Encounter between Enemies: Captivity and Ransom in the Latin Kingdom of Jerusalem.* Leiden, 2002.

Garcin, J. C. *Un centre musulman de la Haute-Égypte médiévale: Qūṣ.* Cairo, 1976.

Gaudefroy-Demombynes, M. "Une lettre de Saladin au calife almohade." In *Mélanges René Basset. Études nord-africaines et orientales.* 2 vols. Paris, 1923–1925, 2:279–304.

Gibb, H. A. R. "The Achievement of Saladin." *Bulletin of the John Rylands Library* 35 (1952): 44–60.

———. "The Arabic Sources for the Life of Saladin." *Speculum* 25 (1950): 58–72.

———. "The Armies of Saladin." *Cahiers d'histoire égyptienne,* series 3, fasc. 4 (1951): 304–320; repr. in H. A. R. Gibb, *Studies on the Civilization of Islam,* edited by S. J. Shaw and W. R. Polk. London, 1962, 74–90.

———. "Al-Barq al-Shāmī: The History of Saladin by the Kātib 'Imād al-Dīn al-Iṣfahānī." *Wiener Zeitschrift für die Kunde des Morgenlandes* 52 (1953–1955): 93–115; repr. in H. A. R. Gibb, *Saladin: Studies in Islamic History,* edited by Q. Ibish. Beirut, 1974, 76–103.

Grousset, R. *Histoire des croisades.* 3 vols. Paris, 1934–1936.

Halm, H. "The Re-establishment of Sunnī fiqh in Jerusalem under Ayyūbid Rule." In *The Third International Conference on Bilād al-Shām: Palestine (April 19–24, 1980).* Vol. 1: *Jerusalem.* Amman, 1983.

Hartmann, A. *An-Nāṣir li-Dīn Allāh (1180–1225). Politik, Religion, Kultur in der späten 'Abbāsidenzeit.* Berlin, 1975.

Heidemann, S., C. Müller, and Y. Rāġib. "Un décret d'al-Malik al-'Ādil 571/1176 relatif aux moines du mont Sinaï." *Annales islamologiques* 31 (1997): 81–107.

Hein, H. A. "Beiträge zur ayyubidischen Diplomatik." Doctoral diss., Freiburg im Breisgau, 1968.

Hillenbrand, C. *The Crusades: Islamic Perspectives.* Edinburgh, 1999.

Holt, P. M. "Saladin and His Admirers: A Biographical Reassessment." *Bulletin of the School of Oriental and African Studies* 46 (1983): 235–239.

———. "The Sultan as Ideal Ruler: Ayyubid and Mamluk Prototypes." In *Süleyman the Magnificent and His Age: The Ottoman Empire in the Early Modern World,* edited by M. Kunt and C. Woodhead. London, 1995, 122–137.

Humphreys, R. S. *From Saladin to the Mongols: The Ayyubids of Damascus, 1193–1260.* New York, 1977.

———. "Women as Patrons of Religious Architecture in Ayyubid Damascus." *Muqarnas* 11 (1994): 35–54.

Huygens, R. B. C. "La campagne de Saladin en Syrie du Nord (1188)." In *Colloque Apamée de Syrie. Bilan de recherches archéologiques 1969–1971.* Brussels, 1974, 273–283.

Jacoby, D. "Les Italiens en Égypte aux XIIe et XIIIe siècles: Du comptoir à la colonie?" In *Coloniser au Moyen Âge,* edited by M. Balard and A. Ducellier. Paris, 1995, 76–89 and 102–107. Repr. in F. Micheau, ed., *Les relations des pays d'Islam avec le monde latin, du milieu du Xe siècle au milieu du XIIIe siècle.* Paris, 2000, 348–382.

Jadon, S. "The Physicians of Syria during the Reign of Ṣalāḥ al-Dīn (570–589/1174–1193)." *Journal of the History of Medicine and Allied Sciences* 25 (1970): 323–340.

James, B. *Saladin et les Kurdes. Perception d'un groupe au temps des Croisades*. Paris, 2006.

Jubb, M. "Saladin vu par Guillaume de Tyr et par l'Eracles: Changement de perspectives." In *Autour de la première croisade*, edited by M. Balard. Paris, 1996, 443–451.

Kedar, B. Z. "The Battle of Ḥaṭṭīn Revisited." In *The Horns of Ḥaṭṭīn*, edited by B. Z. Kedar. London, 1992, 190–207.

———. "Croisade et Jihâd vus par l'ennemi, une étude des perceptions mutuelles des motivations." In *Autour de la première croisade*, edited by M. Balard. Paris, 1996, 345–355.

———, ed. *The Horns of Ḥaṭṭīn*. London, 1992.

Korn, L. *Ayyubidische Architektur in Ägypten und Syrien. Bautätigkeit im Kontext von Politik und Gesellschaft 564–658/1169–1260*. 2 vols. Heidelberg, 2004.

———. "'Die Bauten Saladins': Kairo, Damaskus und Jerusalem in der Baupolitik des an-Nāṣir Ṣalāḥ ad-Dīn Yūsuf Ibn Ayyūb." In *Egypt and Syria in the Fatimid, Ayyubid and Mamluk Eras*, edited by U. Vermeulen and D. De Smet. Vol. 2. Louvain, 1998, 209–235.

———. "The Structure of Architectural Patronage in Ayyubid Jerusalem." In *Governing the Holy City: The Intersection of Social Groups in Jerusalem between the Fatimid and the Ottoman Period*, edited by L. Korn and J. Pahlitzsch. Wiesbaden, 2004, 71–89.

Lane-Poole, S. *Saladin and the Fall of the Kingdom of Jerusalem*. London, 1906. Repr. with a new introduction by D. C. Nicolle. London, 2002.

Leiser, G. "Ḥanbalism in Egypt before the Mamlûks." *Studia Islamica* 54 (1981): 155–181.

Le Strange, G. *Palestine under the Moslems: A Description of Syria and the Holy Land*. London, 1890; repr. Beirut, 1965.

Lev, Y. *Charity, Endowments and Charitable Institutions in Medieval Islam*. Gainesville, Fla., 2005.

———. "Charity and Social Practice in Egypt and Syria from the Ninth to the Twelfth Century." *Jerusalem Studies in Arabic and Islam* 24 (2000): 472–507.

———. *Saladin in Egypt*. Leiden, 1999.

———. "Treatment of Prisoners of War during the Fatimid-Ayyubid Wars with the Crusaders." In *Tolerance and Intolerance: Social Conflict in the Age of the Crusades*, edited by M. Gervers and J. M. Powell. Syracuse, N.Y., 2001, 11–27.

Lewis, B. *The Assassins: A Radical Sect in Islam*. New York: Basic Books, 1968.

———. "Maïmonides, Lionheart and Saladin." *Eretz-Israël* 7 (1963): 70–75. Repr. under the title "The Sultan, the King and the Jewish Doctor" in B. Lewis, *Islam in History: Ideas, Men and Events in the Middle East*. London, 1973, 166–176.

———. "Saladin and the Assassins." *Bulletin of the School of Oriental and African Studies* 15 (1953): 239–245.

Ligato, G. *La croce in catene. Prigionieri e ostaggi cristiani nelle guerre di Saladino (1169–1193)*. Spoleto, 2005.

———. "Saladino e i prigionieri di guerra." In *La liberazione dei "captivi" tra Cristianiatà e Islam. Oltre la crociata e il Ǧihād: Tolleranza e servizio umanitario,* edited by G. Cipollone. Vatican City, 2000, 649–654.

Little, D. P. "Jerusalem under the Ayyūbids and Mamlūks, 1187–1516 A.D." In *Jerusalem in History,* edited by K. J. Asali. London, 1989.

Lyons, M. C., and D. E. P. Jackson. *Saladin: The Politics of Holy War.* Cambridge, U.K., 1982.

MacKenzie, N. D. *Ayyubid Cairo: A Topographical Study.* Cairo, 1992.

Marin, L. F. C. *Histoire de Saladin, sulthan d'Égypte et de Syrie.* Paris, 1758.

Mayer, H. E. *The Crusades.* 2nd revised and expanded ed. Oxford, 1988.

Melville, C. P., and M. C. Lyons. "Saladin's Ḥaṭṭīn Letter." In *The Horns of Ḥaṭṭīn,* edited by B. Z. Kedar. London, 1992, 208–212.

Michaudel, B. "Les fortifications ayyoubides et mameloukes en Syrie côtière de la fin du XIIe siècle au début du XIVe siècle." Doctoral diss., Université de Paris IV–Sorbonne. Paris, 2005.

Minorsky, V. "Prehistory of Saladin." In *V. Minorsky, Studies in Caucasian History.* Cambridge, 1953, 107–168.

Moaz, A. "Note sur le mausolée de Saladin à Damas: Son fondateur et les circonstances de sa fondation." *Bulletin d'études orientales* 39–40 (1987–1988): 183–189.

Möhring, H. "Heiliger Krieg und politische Pragmatik: Salahadinus Tyrannus." *Deutsches Archiv für Erforschung des Mittelalters* 39 (1983): 417–466.

———. "Mekkawallfahrten orientalischer und afrikanischer Herrscher im Mittelalter." *Oriens* 34 (1994): 314–329.

———. *Saladin und der Dritte Kreuzzug.* Wiesbaden, 1980.

———. "Zwei aiyūbidische Briefe an Alexander III. und Lucius III. bei Radulf de Diceto zum Kriegsgefangenenproblem." *Archiv für Diplomatik* 46 (2000): 197–216.

———. "Zwischen Joseph-Legende und Mahdi-Erwartung: Erfolge und Ziele Sultan Saladins im Spiegel zeitgenössicher Dichtung und Weissagung." In *War and Society in the Eastern Mediterranean, 7th–15th Centuries,* edited by Y. Lev. Leiden, 1997, 177–225.

Morabia, A. *Le Gihad dans l'islam médiéval.* Paris, 1993.

Mouton, J. M. "Autour des inscriptions de la forteresse de Ṣadr (Qal'at al-Ǧindī) au Sinaï." *Annales islamologiques* 28 (1994): 71–77.

———. "Les bédouins entre Syrie et Égypte au temps des croisades." In *Orient et Occident du IXe au XVe siècle,* edited by G. Jehel. Paris, 2000, 293–300.

———. "La conquête de la Cyrénaïque et de la Tripolitaine par Qarāqūsh: Initiative individuelle ou entreprise d'État?" In *Aux rivages des Syrtes: La Libye, espace et développement de l'Antiquité à nos jours,* edited by C. Chanson-Jabeur, D. Gallet, A. Laronde, and C. Lochon. Paris, 2000, 59–69.

———. "Saladin et les bédouins du Sinaï." In *Le Sinaï de la conquête arabe à nos jours,* edited by J. M. Mouton. Cairo, 2001, 197–206.

———. *Saladin, le sultan chevalier*. Paris, 2001.

———. *Le Sinaï médiéval. Un espace stratégique de l'islam*. Paris, 2000.

Mouton, J. M., and S. Ṣ. ʿAbd al-Malik. "La forteresse de l'île de Graye (Qalʿat Ayla) à l'époque de Saladin, étude épigraphique et historique." *Annales islamologiques* 29 (1995): 75–90.

Mouton, J. M., S. Ṣ. ʿAbd al-Malik, O. Jaubert, and C. Piaton. "La route de Saladin (ṭarīq Ṣadr wa Ayla) au Sinaï." *Annales islamologiques* 30 (1996): 41–70.

Naṣrâ, S. M. *Al-Qāḍī al-Fāḍil wa Ṣalāḥ al-Dīn wa l-waḥda al-islāmiyya*. Cairo, 1990.

Nuwayhiḍ, W. *Ṣalāḥ al-Dīn al-Ayyūbī, Suqūt al-Quds wa taḥrīruhā (qirāʾa muʿāṣira)*. Beirut, 1997.

L'Orient de Saladin, l'art des Ayyoubides. Exposition présentée à l'Institut du monde arabe, Paris, du 23 octobre 2001 au 10 mars 2002. Paris, 2001.

Pahlitzsch, J. "The Transformation of Latin Religious Institutions into Islamic Endowments by Saladin in Jerusalem." In *Governing the Holy City: The Interaction of Social Groups in Jerusalem between the Fatimid and the Ottoman Period*, edited by J. Pahlitzsch and L. Korn. Wiesbaden, 2004, 47–69.

Pellat, C. "Un traité de ḥisba signé: Saladin." In *Studi in onore di Francesco Gabrieli*, edited by R. Traini. Vol. 2. Rome, 1984, 593–598.

Pouzet, L. *Damas au VIIe/XIIIe siècle. Vie et structures religieuses dans une métropole islamique*. Beirut, 1988.

Prawer, J. *Histoire du royaume latin de Jérusalem*. Translated from the Hebrew by G. Nahon. Revised and expanded by the author. 2nd. ed. 2 vols. Paris, 1975.

———. *The History of the Jews in the Latin Kingdom of Jerusalem*. Oxford, 1988.

———. "Social Classes in the Crusaders States: The 'Minorities.'" In *History of the Crusades*, general editor, M. Setton. Vol. 5: *The Impact of the Crusaders on the Near East*, edited by H. W. Hazard and N. P. Zacour. Madison, 1985, 59–116.

Qalʿajī, Q. *Ṣalāḥ al-Dīn al-Ayyūbī*. Beirut, 1956.

Rabie, H. *The Financial System of Egypt, 564–741/1169–1341*. London, 1972.

Raymond, A. *Le Caire*. Paris, 1993.

Richard, J. "The Adventure of John Gale, Knight of Tyre." In *The Experience of Crusading*, edited by P. W. Edbury and J. Phillips. 2 vols. Cambridge, 2003, vol. 2: *Defining the Crusader Kingdom*, 189–195.

———. *Histoire des croisades*. Paris, 1996.

———. "Les prisonniers et leur rachat au cours des croisades." In *Fondations et oeuvres charitables au Moyen Âge*, edited by J. Dufour and H. Platelle. Paris, 1999, 63–73.

Richards, D. S. "A Consideration of Two Sources for the Life of Saladin." *Journal of Semitic Studies* 25 (1980): 46–65.

———. "The Early History of Saladin." *Islamic Quarterly* 17 (1973): 140–159.

————. "Saladin's Hospital in Jerusalem: Its Foundation and Some Later Archival Material." In *The Frankish Wars and Their Influence on Palestine*, edited by K. Athamina and R. Heacock. Birzeit, 1994, 70–83.

Richter-Bernburg, L. *Der syrische Blitz. Saladins Sekretär zwischen Selbstdarstellung und Geschichtsschreibung*. Stuttgart, 1998.

Rikabi, J. *La poésie profane sous les Ayyûbides et ses principaux représentants*. Paris, 1949.

Röhricht, R. *Geschichte des Königreichs Jerusalem (1100–1291)*. Innsbruck, 1898; repr. Amsterdam, 1966.

Sack, D. *Damaskus: Entwicklung und Struktur einer orientalisch-islamischen Stadt*. Mainz, 1989. Translated into Arabic by Q. Ṭuwayr. Damascus, 2005.

Ṣalāḥ al-Dīn al-Ayyūbī bi-munāsabat murūr 800 sana ʿalā wafātihi (*Ṣalāḥ al-Dīn the Ayyubid: The Eight Hundreth Anniversity of His Death*). Special issue of *Dirāsāt Islāmiyya* 5 (1994–1995). Proceedings of the colloquium held in Beirut in 1993 by the Institut des hautes études islamiques.

Sauvaget, J. "Le cénotaphe de Saladin." *Revue des arts asiatiques* (1930): 168–175.

Setton, K. M., general editor. *A History of the Crusades*. Vol. 1: *The First Hundred Years*, edited by M. W. Baldwin. 2nd ed. Madison, 1969. Vol. 2: *The Later Crusades, 1198–1311*, edited by R. L. Wolff and H. W. Hazard. 2nd ed. Madison, 1969. Vol. 5: *The Impact of the Crusades on the Near East*, edited by H. W. Hazard and N. P. Zacour. Madison, 1985. Vol. 6: *The Impact of the Crusades on Europe*, edited by H. W. Hazard and N. P. Zacour. Madison, 1989.

Sivan, E. *L'Islam et la croisade: Idéologie et propagande dans les réactions musulmanes aux croisades*. Paris, 1968.

————. "Note sur la situation des chrétiens à l'époque ayyoubide." *Revue d'histoire des religions* 172 (1967): 117–130.

————. "Saladin et le calife al-Nāṣir." In *Studies in History*, edited by David Asheri and Israel Shatzman. Jerusalem, 1972, 126–145.

Smith, G. R. *The Ayyūbids and Early Rasūlids in the Yemen (567–694/1173–1295)*. 2 vols. London, 1974–1978.

Smoor, P. " 'Umāra's Poetical Views of Shāwar, Dirghām, Shīrkūh and Ṣalāḥ al-Dīn as Viziers of the Fatimid Caliphs." In *Culture and Memory in Medieval Islam: Essays in Honour of Wilferd Madelung*, edited by F. Daftary and J. W. Meri. London, 2003, 410–432.

Sourdel, D., and J. Sourdel-Thomine. *Certificats de pèlerinage d'époque ayyoubide. Contribution à l'histoire de l'idéologie de l'islam au temps des croisades*. Paris, 2006.

Van Reeth, J. "La barque de l'Imām aš-Shāfiʿī." In *Egypt and Syria in the Fatimid, Ayyubid and Mamluk Eras*, edited by U. Vermeulen and D. De Smet. Vol. 2. Louvain, 1998, 249–264.

Wieczorek, A., M. Fansa, and H. Meller, eds. *Saladin und die Kreuzfahrer*. Mainz, 2005.

Wiet, G. "Les inscriptions de Saladin." *Syria* 3 (1922): 307–328.

Winter, M. "Saladin's Religious Personality, Policy, and Image." In *Perspectives on Maimonides: Philosophical and Historical Studies,* edited by J. L. Kraemer. Oxford, 1986, 309–322.

A Fictional Autobiography of Saladin

Chauvel, G. *Saladin rassembleur de l'Islam.* Paris, 1991.

Studies on the Saladin Legend

Caroff, F. "L'adversaire, l'autre, l'oriental. L'iconographie du monde musulman dans le contexte des croisades." Doctoral diss., Université de Paris I, 2002.

Deheuvels, L. W. "Le Saladin de Faraḥ Anṭūn, du mythe littéraire au mythe politique." In *Figures mythiques de l'Orient musulman,* edited by D. Aigle, *Revue du monde musulman et de la Méditerranée* 89–90 (2000): 189–203.

Grillo, P. R. "The Saladin Material in the Continuations of the First Crusade Cycle." In *Aspects de l'épopée romane: Mentalités, idéologies, intertextualités,* edited by H. van Dijk and W. Noomen. Groningen, 1995, 159–166. Proceedings of the thirteenth congress of the Société Rencesvals, Groningen, August 22–27, 1994.

Hillenbrand, C. "The Evolution of the Saladin Legend in the West." In *Regards croisés sur le Moyen Âge arabe. Mélanges à la mémoire de Louis Pouzet, s.j. (1928–2002),* edited by A. M. Eddé and E. Gannagé. Beirut, 2005, 497–510.

Irwin, R. "Saladin and the Third Crusade: A Case Study in Historiography and the Historical Novel." In *Companion to Historiography,* edited by M. Bentley. London, 1997, 139–152.

Jubb, M. *The Legend of Saladin in Western Literature and Historiography.* Lewiston, N.Y., 2000.

Paris, G. "La légende de Saladin." *Journal des Savants* 215 (1893): 284–299, 354–365, 428–438, 486–498.

Pouzet, L. "Al-Sulṭān Ṣalāḥ al-Dīn al-Ayyūbī fī l-turāth al-faransī min al-ʿuṣūr al-wusṭā ḥattā l-yawm" ("Saladin's French Legacy from the Middle Ages to the Present"). *Dirāsāt Islāmiyya* (1994–1995): 285–306.

Quéruel, D. "Le 'vaillant Turc et courtois Salhadin': Un Oriental à la cour de Bourgogne." In *Images et signes de l'Orient dans l'Occident médiéval.* Aix-en-Provence, 1982, 299–311.

Richard, J. "La Chanson de Syracon et la légende de Saladin." *Journal asiatique* (1949): 155–158.

———. "Les transformations de l'image de Saladin dans les sources occidentales." In *Figures mythiques de l'Orient musulman,* edited by D. Aigle, *Revue du monde musulman et de la Méditerranée* 89–90 (2000): 177–187.

Saunier, A. "Saladin et l'Hôpital de Saint-Jean d'Acre dans le récit du Ménestrel de Reims, ou le regard d'un Oriental sur une institution occidentale." *Tous azimuts, mélanges offerts à M. G. Jehel, Histoire médiévale et archéologie* 13 (2002): 423–433.

Tolan, J. "Mirror of Chivalry: Salāh al-Dīn in the Medieval European Imagination." In *Images of the Other: Europe and the Muslim World before 1700,* edited by David R. Blanks. Cairo, 1996, 7–38.

Acknowledgments

This book came into being as the result of a meeting I was fortunate enough to have with Hélène Fiamma, series director at Flammarion. Without her enthusiasm, her encouragement, and her patience, this project would likely never have come to fruition. Her attentive reading, her advice, and her corrections greatly aided me in making the results of my lengthy research accessible to the largest number of readers. I would like to express my profound gratitude to her here.

I would also like to acknowledge all the friends and colleagues who gave me the benefit of their suggestions and erudition. Hans E. Mayer provided me with countless bibliographical references. He also read and corrected the chapter on the Franks. John Tolan very kindly agreed to read the chapter on the Saladin legend. Hikmet Nahra helped me to make sense of certain Arabic texts, composed in rhymed prose or in verse, which were difficult to decipher. My thanks especially to Carole Hillenbrand, who did me the honor and great favor of reviewing the entire text. Her remarks and encouragement were very valuable to me.

And finally, I owe a great debt of gratitude to my sister, Dominique Eddé, whose writing talent contributed toward making many pages of this book more agreeable to read.

Needless to say, I alone am responsible for any errors that might remain.

Index

The endnotes have not been indexed, and names that recur often (e.g., Saladin, Syria, Egypt, Palestine, Franks) have also been omitted. The alphabetization disregards "-al," and, when it occurs in the middle of the name, "ibn."